Quick Reference Guide

(continued)

Skill Builders

Looking Out/Looking In

FROM THE WADSWORTH SERIES IN COMMUNICATION STUDIES

Twelfth Edition

Looking Out/Looking In

Ronald B. Adler
Santa Barbara City College

Russell F. Proctor, II
Northern Kentucky University

Australia • Canada • Mexico • Singapore • Spain • United Kingdom • United States

THOMSON

WADSWORTH

Looking Out/Looking In, Twelfth Edition
Ronald B. Adler, Russell F. Proctor II

Publisher: Lyn Uhl
Acquisitions Editor: Jaime Perkins
Senior Development Editor: Greer Lleuad
Assistant Editor: John Gahbauer
Editorial Assistant: Kimberly Gengler
Technology Project Manager: Lucinda Bingham
Marketing Manager: Erin Mitchell
Marketing Assistant: Kassie Tossiello
Marketing Communications Manager: Jessica Perry
Project Manager, Editorial Production: Catherine
    Morris
Creative Director: Rob Hugel
Art Director: Maria Epes

Print Buyer: Judy Inouye
Permissions Editor: Sarah D'Stair
Production Service: Lachina Publishing Services
Text Designer: Janet Alleyn
Photo Researcher: Sandra Lord
Illustrator: Lachina Publishing Services
Cover Designer: Janet Alleyn
Cover Image: Stephanie Dalton Cowan. © Thomson
Cover Printer: Phoenix Color Corp
Compositor: Lachina Publishing Services
Printer: R.R. Donnelley/Willard

Thomson Higher Education
10 Davis Drive
Belmont, CA 94002-3098
USA

Library of Congress Control Number:
ISBN 0-495-09580-X

For more information about our products,
contact us at:
Thomson Learning Academic Resource Center
1-800-423-0563
For permission to use material from this text or
product, submit a request online at
http://www.thomsonrights.com.
Any additional questions about permissions can
be submitted by e-mail to
thomsonrights@thomson.com.

Brief Contents

Contents

Chapter Four

Emotions: Thinking, Feeling, and Communicating   120

Part II   Looking Out

Chapter Five

Language: Barrier and Bridge   156

Chapter Six

Nonverbal Communication: Messages beyond Words   194

You can understand the goal and approach of *Looking Out/Looking In* by trying a simple experiment. Jot down the name of every college course you have taken, or at least the ones you can remember. (If this is your first college course, substitute your classes from high school.) Next, consider how much each of those courses has made a significant difference in what you know, how you think, and the way you act.

If you're like most people, your sorted list will contain three categories: courses that made little or no difference, ones that had a modest effect, and those—probably a handful—that have had a major impact on your life.

We have dedicated several years of our professional lives toward making *Looking Out/Looking In* a book that will help make your first academic look at interpersonal communication one of those life-changing educational experiences. Along with learning how people, in general, communicate in important relationships, this book (as its title suggests) will help you understand how *you* communicate with others and how you can do an even better job.

What's Familiar

This twelfth edition of *Looking Out/Looking In* takes the same approach that has served almost 2 million readers of past editions. Most noticeable is its user-friendly voice, which links scholarship to everyday life. Virtually every page-spread contains an attention-grabbing assortment of materials that support the text: quotations, poetry, music lyrics, newspaper articles, cartoons, and art. A prominent treatment of ethical issues helps readers explore how to communicate in a principled manner. An extensive package of ancillary resources (described in detail in the following pages) aims at helping students learn and instructors teach efficiently and effectively.

This edition of *Looking Out/Looking In* continues to emphasize the transactional nature of interpersonal relationships. It presents communication not as a collection of techniques we use *on* others, but as a process we engage in *with* them. Readers also learn that even the most competent communication doesn't always seek to create warm, fuzzy relationships, that even less personal interaction usually has the best chance of success when handled in a constructive, respectful manner.

As in the past, this edition continues to integrate the discussion of similarities and differences involving gender and culture from beginning to end rather than isolating them in separate chapters. It also retains a non-ideological approach to these topics, citing research that shows how other variables are often at least as important in shaping interaction. As in recent editions, a series of "Looking at Diversity" profiles provide first-person accounts of how culture, physical factors, and technology influence interaction. (You can read about profiles new to this edition on the next page.) Long-time users will also find the same class-tested organizational structure that has proved its value. The basic focus of the chapters has remained constant, and Chapters 2 through 11 can be covered in whatever order works best for individual situations.

New to This Edition

While retaining the features that have served users well in the past, this new edition has been improved in several ways.

New chapter expands material on relational dynamics   Long-time users will notice that the previous chapter on relational dynamics (Chapter 8) has been broken into two chapters (Chapters 8 and 9), making the material more manageable for both instructors and students. (A sample syllabus is available in the *Looking Out/Looking In* Instructor's Resource Manual to help ease the transition to this new chapter lineup.) The two-chapter treatment also includes new material on repairing damaged relationships—including a section on forgiveness—and expanded discussions of intimacy, self-disclosure, and other dynamics of relational communication.

Expanded coverage of culture and gender   To reflect the diverse nature of contemporary society, this edition offers expanded coverage of culture and gender issues throughout the book, both within the main body of the text as well as in each chapter's features, cartoons, and art. A new section of Chapter 1 discusses the skills and attitudes necessary for competence in intercultural encounters; Chapter 3 introduces an expanded discussion of stereotyping and ethnocentrism; Chapter 4 addresses the influence of both gender and culture on emotional expression; Chapter 5 contains updated information on gender and language use; Chapter 7 introduces new research on gender and listening; and Chapter 9 examines how gender and culture shape expressions of intimacy in close relationships.

Updated and expanded discussion of technology in interpersonal relationships   This edition continues to reflect the fact that more and more interpersonal communication occurs via e-mail, instant messages, text messaging, and other forms of electronic media. For example, Chapter 2 discusses identity management on social networking sites; Chapter 4 addresses emotionally abusive messages on the Internet; Chapter 5 discusses the evolution of communicative rules in instant messaging; and Chapter 9 describes how socially isolated teens build close relationships on the Internet. In addition, Chapter 4 features a new section on communication channels, with a focus on computer-mediated communication and emotion expression, and Chapter 9 includes a new section on intimacy in computer-mediated communication.

Additional self-assessment opportunities for students   To streamline student's study time and support classroom learning, this edition offers a new self-assessment opportunity: the ThomsonNOW™ online study system. This system helps students identify concepts they don't fully understand, then creates a personalized study plan that allows them to put their study time to the best use. For more information about ThomsonNOW, see page xiv–xv.

New ABC News video activities   Throughout the book, readers are directed to ABC News stories that show how concepts from the text operate in a variety of everyday life settings. Stories include how using sign language with babies can help them develop their language skills and help families build stronger relationships, how social and personal rules for language have developed in an online environment, and how adolescent girls deal with aggression among their peers. Each ABC clip described in the book is featured on the *Looking Out/Looking In* Online Textbook Resources described on pages xiv–xv.

New "Looking at Diversity" profiles   Throughout the book, new sidebars provide first-person accounts by communicators from a wide range of backgrounds. In Chapter 3, an honor roll student who is also on public assistance describes how she is stereotyped both on and off campus. In Chapter 5, a trainer in India explains how she teaches new customer-service telephone representatives the cultural rules of communicating with American customers. In Chapter 10, a gang member describes how he helps teens turn away from violence.

New discussions of feature films and TV programs   As in the past, this edition shows how art imitates communicative life by describing feature films—

and now also television programs—that illustrate concepts from the text. New films discussed in this edition include *Akeelah and the Bee* (self-concept), *Crash* (stereotyping), *The Upside of Anger* (debilitative emotions), and *Transamerica* (self-disclosure). Television series include *The Office* (communication competence), *Seinfeld* (nonverbal communication), *Friends* (transactional relationships), and *30 Days* (empathy). Descriptions of these and many other films and TV programs can be accessed via the *Looking Out/Looking In* Film in Communication Database described on page xiv.

Other changes Beyond specific changes like these, this edition contains new material that keeps the book current. For example, Chapter 1 has a new discussion of intercultural communication competence. Chapter 3 includes a new section on how psychological disorders affect perception and a new discussion of face-saving through perception-checking. Chapter 7 features a new section, "Listening Defined," which includes distinctions between mindless and mindful listening. Chapter 11 includes a completely revamped discussion of conflict styles.

Pedagogical Aids

Looking Out/Looking In features a variety of in-text pedagogical devices to help students learn concepts and develop skills most effectively.

Activities Activities throughout the book help readers take a closer look at important concepts. They are labeled by type: "Invitations to Insight" help readers understand how theory and research applies to their own lives. "Skill Builders" help them improve their communication skills. "Ethical Challenges" highlight some challenges communicators face as they pursue their own goals.

Communication Transcripts These transcripts describe how the skills and concepts from the text sound when used in everyday life. Dramatized versions of many of these transcripts are featured on the *Looking Out/Looking In* Online Textbook Resources described below.

"Looking at Diversity" profiles Throughout the book, sidebars provide first-person accounts by communicators from a wide range of back-

grounds. In Chapter 1, a woman describes how effective communication varies in two strikingly different environments: her home neighborhood of South-Central Los Angeles and her school in the suburban San Fernando Valley. In Chapter 2, a Korean-born adoptee describes how she manages her identity in the U.S. In Chapter 4, a Native American man reflects on the differences between the ways Zuñi and Anglo cultures deal with emotional expression. In Chapter 6, an African-American man describes the nonverbal communication he employs to put strangers at ease. In Chapter 7, a man with a hearing disability discusses his approach to communication. In Chapter 8, a young man who stutters discusses how the Internet helps him start and build relationships. In Chapter 10, a Moroccan man describes the challenges of being an Arab living in the U.S. after the September 11 terrorist attacks.

End-of-chapter media resources The *Looking Out/Looking In* Media Resources section appears at the end of each chapter and highlights media resources that add rich descriptions of the principles introduced in the text. Included in this section is information about how students can access the digital resources that accompany this edition as well as InfoTrac® College Edition exercises, prompts to the Film in Communication Database, and a visual prompt to the *Looking Out/Looking In* Online Textbook Resources.

Teaching and Learning Resources

Along with the text itself, *Looking Out/Looking In* is accompanied by an extensive array of materials that will make teaching and learning more efficient and effective.

■ Available with each student text is the *Looking Out/Looking In* **Online Textbook Resources,** which provide your students with one-stop access to all the integrated technology resources that accompany the book. These resources include chapter-by-chapter resources at the *Looking Out/Looking In* Premium Book Companion Website, *Looking Out/Looking In* Communication Scenarios, InfoTrac College Edition, ABC News video clips and activities, and the ThomsonNOW online study system. All of these resources are referenced in the text and highlighted with an icon. Integrated throughout the chapters and expanded upon at the ends of chapters in the Media Resources section, these references direct students to numerous digital activities and reinforce and enrich the concepts presented. See the inside back cover of this book for instructions on how to access the *Looking Out/Looking In* Online Textbook Resources. **Note to faculty:** If you want your students to have access to the Online Textbook Resources, please be sure to order this option for your course. If you do not order this option, your students will not have access to this online content.

■ If you order the Online Textbook Resources packaged with the text, your student will have access to the *Looking Out/Looking In* **Premium Book Companion Website,** which provides numerous student and instructor resources. For students, chapter-by-chapter resources include learning objectives, online activities, a digital glossary, a list of recommended readings, and review quizzes. In addition, all of the **web links** included in the book, which prompt students to explore chapter concepts online, are maintained for each chapter at the website. **InfoTrac College Edition exercises** guide students in using InfoTrac College Edition to complete engaging and practical exercises that expand chapter content, guarantee currency of presentation, and help students use InfoTrac College Edition in a directed way. And accessible via this website is the **Film in Communication Database,** which allows students and faculty to search for feature films that illustrate communication concepts by key term. For instructors, the website includes test questions, lecture notes, a revised set of Microsoft PowerPoint slides, and links to many other Internet resources. **Note to faculty:** If you want your students to have access to the premium book companion website, please be sure to order this option for your course. If you do not order this option, your students will not have access to this online content.

■ *Looking Out/Looking In* **Communication Scenarios,** based on the Communication Transcripts features described earlier, allow students to view videos of communication encounters. These video scenarios make concepts previously presented in the abstract come alive. Students maximize their learning experience by reading, watching, listening to, critiquing, and analyzing these model communication encounters. **Note to faculty:** If you want your students to have access to the Communication Scenarios, please be sure to order the Online Textbook Resources for your course.

■ If you order the Online Textbook Resources packaged with the text, your students will have access to **InfoTrac College Edition,** a virtual library of more than 18 million reliable, full-length articles from 5,000 academic and popular periodicals that students can retrieve almost instantly. They will also have **InfoMarks®**—stable URLs that can be linked to articles, journals, and searches to save valuable time when doing research—and to the **InfoWrite** online resource center, where students can access grammar help, critical-thinking guidelines, guides to writing research papers, and much more.

■ When you adopt this text packaged with the Online Textbook Resources, your students will also have access to **vMentor™,** live one-on-one tutoring. vMentor gives your students access to virtual office hours—one-on-one online tutoring help from a subject-area expert, at no additional cost with the text. In vMentor's virtual classroom, students interact with the tutor and other students using two-way audio, an interactive whiteboard for illustrating the problem, and instant messaging. To ask a question, students simply click to raise a "hand." *For proprietary college and university adopters only. For additional information, please contact your Thomson Wadsworth sales representative.*

■ If you order the Online Textbook Resources packaged with the text, your students will also have access to the **ThomsonNOW online study system.** Using chapter-by-chapter diagnostic pretests that identify concepts students don't fully understand, this system creates a personalized study plan for each chapter. Each plan directs your students to specific resources designed to improve their understanding, including pages from the text in e-book format. Chapter post-tests give them an opportunity to measure how much they've learned and let them know if they are ready for graded quizzes and exams.

- The **Student Activity Manual and Study Guide** has been revised by Jeanne Elmhorst, Central New Mexico Community College. It contains a wealth of resources to help students understand and master concepts and skills introduced in the text.

- A comprehensive **Instructor's Resource Manual,** revised by Heidi Murphy, Central New Mexico Community College, provides tips and tools for both new and experienced instructors. The manual also contains hard copy of over 1,200 class-tested exam questions, indexed by page number and level of understanding.

- The **Multimedia Manager/Instructor's Resource CD-ROM** contains an electronic version of the Instructor's Resource Manual, ExamView Computerized Testing, and predesigned Microsoft PowerPoint presentations. The PowerPoint presentations contain text and images, and can be used as is or customized to suit your course needs.

- **Communication Scenarios for Critique and Analysis Videos** include the video scenarios included in the *Looking Out/Looking In* Online Textbook Resources as well as additional scenarios covering interviewing and group work. *Contact your Thomson Wadsworth sales representative for details.*

- **Communication in Film III: Teaching Communication Courses Using Feature Films** by Russell F. Proctor, II, Northern Kentucky University, expands on the film tips in each chapter of *Looking Out/Looking In*. This guide provides detailed suggestions for using both new and classic films to illustrate communication principles introduced in the text.

- **Media Guide for Interpersonal Communication** by Charles G. Apple, University of Michigan-Flint. This guide provides a faculty with media resource listings focused on general interpersonal communication topics. Each listing provides compelling examples of how interpersonal communication concepts are illustrated in

particular films, books, plays, websites, or journal articles. Discussion questions are provided.

- **InfoTrac College Edition Student Activities Workbook for Interpersonal Communication** features extensive group and individual activities that focus on specific topics and make use of InfoTrac College Edition. This workbook also includes faculty and student guidelines that describe how to maximize the use of InfoTrac College Edition.

- **The Teaching Assistant's Guide to the Basic Course** by Katherine G. Hendrix, University of Memphis. Based on leading communication teacher training programs, the guide covers general teaching and course management topics as well as specific strategies for communication instruction, such as providing effective feedback on performance, managing sensitive class discussions, and conducting mock interviews.

- **A Guide to the Basic Course for ESL Students** by Esther Yook, Mary Washington College. Available bundled with the text, this guide assists the nonnative speaker. Features FAQs, helpful URLs, and strategies for accent management and overcoming speech apprehension.

- **The Art and Strategy of Service Learning** by Rick Isaacson and Jeff Saperstein. This handbook can be bundled with the text and is an invaluable resource for students in the basic course that integrates or is planning to integrate a service learning component. The handbook provides guidelines for connecting service learning work with classroom concepts and advice for working effectively with agencies and organizations. The handbook also provides model forms and reports and a directory of online resources.

- **ThomsonNOW on WebCT and Blackboard**. Now you and your students can access ThomsonNOW's powerful and fully integrated online teaching and learning system through your familiar WebCT or Blackboard interface, giving you all the course management and communication tools you know, paired with the flexibility and control of ThomsonNOW.

Acknowledgments

This edition of *Looking Out/Looking In* owes its success to the contributions of many people. The best place to begin is with our families, who tolerated our absences and distraction over the year that we worked on this book. We also thank our students, who over the years have helped us understand how to present material in ways that make sense and make a difference.

We are grateful for the ideas of colleagues whose reviews helped shape this new edition: Susan B. Barnes, Rochester Institute of Technology; Ronald L. Biddle, Clovis Community College; Alice Denise Danford, Delaware Community College; Mary Haslerud Opp, University of North Dakota; Jacqueline M. Martinez, Arizona State University; Randall R. Mueller, Gateway Technical College; Carla S. Ross, Meredith College; Deborah Stieneker, Arapahoe Community College; and Nancy J. Willets, Cape Cod Community College.

We continue to appreciate the input of colleagues whose reviews of earlier editions have shaped the book you are holding: Hilary R. Altman, Merritt College; Charles Apple, University of Michigan, Flint; Marion Boyer, Kalamazoo Valley Community College; Edward Brewer, Murray State University; Jeanne Dunphy, Los Angeles Community College; Karen C. Evans, Ohio University; Gwin Faulconer-Lippert, Oklahoma City Community College; Keith T. Hardeman, Westminster College; Victoria Leonard, College of the Canyons; Ralph Long, Collin County Community College; Barbara Mayo, South Texas Community College; Diane Monahan, Keene State College; Glenn Morris, McNeese State University; John T. Morrison, Rollins College; John Olson, Everett Community College; Lisa M. Orick, Albuquerque Technical Vocational Institute; James Pauff, Tarleton State University; Bruce Punches, Kalamazoo Valley Community College; Narissra Punyanunt, Texas Tech University; Dee Quatraro, Bakersfield College; Susan Richardson, Prince George's Community College; Janet Smart, Jacksonville State University; Candice Taffolla-Schreiber, Southwestern College; Tasha Van Horn, Citrus College; and Julie Zink, University of Southern Maine.

Our thanks also go to the team of publishing professionals who have played a role in this edition from start to finish: Holly J. Allen, Lianne Ames, Barbara Armentrout, Annie Beck, Lucinda Bingham, Matt Fornadel, John Gahbauer, Mandy Hetrick, Nancy Knight, Carol Kurila, Greer Lleuad, Laura Localio, Sandra Lord, Erin Mitchell, Catherine Morris, Jaime Perkins, Jessica Perry, Kimberly Russell, Carol Siedell, and Lyn Uhl.

We hope you share our appreciation for the handsome appearance of the book you are reading now. We are grateful for the design talents of Janet Alleyn, as well as for the keen eye of Sherri Adler, who selected the art.

About the Authors

Since this is a book about interpersonal communication, it seems appropriate for us to introduce ourselves to you, the reader. The "we" you'll be reading throughout this book isn't just an editorial device: It refers to two real people—Ron Adler and Russ Proctor.

 Ron Adler lives in Santa Barbara, California, with his wife, Sherri. Their oldest daughter, Robin (who had just been born when the first edition of this book was published), now has two children of her own. Rebecca, their other daughter, is an accomplished designer and a fundraiser for worthy nonprofit organizations, and their son, Daniel, is a college student studying Chinese and international political economy.

Ron spends most of his professional time writing about communication. In addition to helping create *Looking Out/Looking In*, he has contributed to six other books about topics including business communication, public speaking, small group communication, assertiveness, and social skills. Besides writing and teaching, Ron helps professional and business people improve their communication on the job. Cycling and hiking help keep Ron physically and emotionally healthy.

 Russ Proctor is a professor at Northern Kentucky University, where his sons, R. P. and Randy, are both students. Russ's wife, Pam, is an educator too, training teachers, students, and businesses to use energy more efficiently.

Russ met Ron Adler at a communication conference in 1990, where they quickly discovered a shared interest in using feature films as a teaching tool. Russ and Ron have written and spoken extensively on this topic over the years, and they have also co-authored several textbooks and articles. When he's not teaching, writing, or presenting, Russ's hobbies include sports (especially baseball), classic rock music (especially Steely Dan), and cooking (especially for family and friends on his birthday each year).

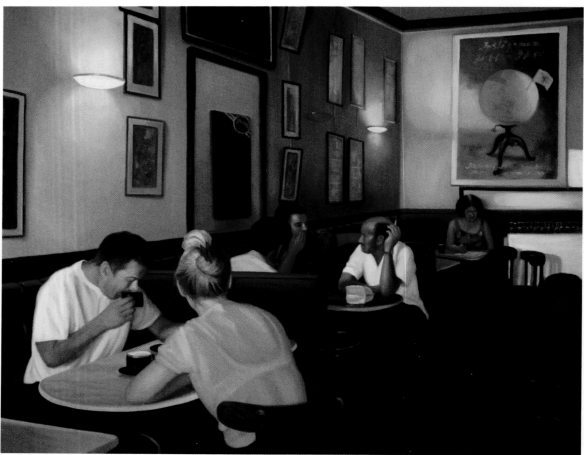

A First Look at Interpersonal Communication

1

The Silencing

As his name was called, James J. Pelosi, the 452nd West Point cadet of the class of '73, drew in his breath and went to the podium—steeling himself for one last moment of humiliation. The slender, bespectacled young man accepted his diploma, then turned to face the rows of starched white hats and—so he expected—a chorus of boos. Instead, there was only silence. But when he returned to his classmates, the newly fledged lieutenant was treated to something new—a round of handshakes. "It was just as if I were a person again," he said. Thus ended one of the strangest and most brutal episodes in the long history of the corps.

A year earlier, the Long Island cadet was hauled up before the West Point Honor Committee and charged with cheating on an engineering exam. In spite of conflicting testimony given at his trial and his own determined plea of innocence, the third-year cadet, one of the most respected in his company and himself a candidate for the Honor Committee, was convicted. Pelosi's case was thrown out by the Academy superintendent after his military lawyer proved there had been undue influence over the proceeding by the Honor Committee adviser, but that wasn't the end of it. The Academy honor code reserves a special fate for those thought by the majority to be guilty even when there is insufficient evidence to convict. It is called "silencing."

© Bettye Lane/Photo Researchers

Pelosi's fellow cadets voted to support the Honor Committee sentence. And so for most of his third and all of his fourth year at West Point, Pelosi was ostracized. He was transferred by the Academy to what one friend called a "straight-strict" company—"one of the toughest in the corps." He ate alone each day at a table for ten; he lived by himself in a room meant for two or three; he endured insult and occasional brickbats tossed in his direction; he saw his mail mutilated and his locker vandalized. And hardly anyone, even a close friend who wept when he heard the silencing decision, would talk to him in public. Under those conditions, most cadets resign. But even though he lost 26 pounds, Pelosi hung tough. "When you're right," he said later, "you have to prove yourself. . . . I told myself I didn't care."

And in the end, James Pelosi survived—one of only a handful of Academy cadets in history to graduate after silencing. Now that he is out, Lieutenant Pelosi is almost dispassionate in his criticism of the Academy and his fellow cadets. About as far as he will go is to say that "Silencing should be abolished. It says cadets are above the law. This attitude of superiority bothers me." As for his own state of mind during the ordeal he told *Newsweek*'s Deborah Beers, "I've taken a psychology course and I know what isolation does to animals. No one at the Academy asks how it affects a person. Doesn't that seem strange?"

Newsweek

Perhaps you played this game as a child. The group of children chooses a victim—either as punishment for committing a real or imagined offense or just for "fun." Then for a period of time, that victim is given the silent treatment. No one speaks to him or her, and no one responds to anything the victim says or does.

If you were the subject of this silent treatment, you probably experienced a range of emotions. At first you might have felt—or at least acted—indifferent. But after a while the strain of being treated as a nonperson probably began to grow. If the game went on long enough, it's likely you found yourself either retreating into a state of depression or lashing out with hostility—partly to show your anger and partly to get a response from the others.

Adults, as well as children, have used the silent treatment in virtually every society throughout history as a powerful tool to express displeasure and for social control.[1] We all know intuitively that communication—the company of others—is one of the most basic human needs and that lack of contact is among the cruelest punishments a person can suffer.

Besides being emotionally painful, being deprived of companionship is so serious that it can affect life itself. Fredrick II, emperor of Germany from 1196 to 1250, may have been the first person to prove the point systematically. A medieval historian described one of his significant, if inhumane, experiments:

> He bade foster mothers and nurses to suckle the children, to bathe and wash them, but in no way to prattle with them, for he wanted to learn whether they would speak the Hebrew language, which was the oldest, or Greek, or Latin, or Arabic, or perhaps the language of their parents, of whom they had been born. But he labored in vain because all the children died. For they could not live without the petting and joyful faces and loving words of their foster mothers.[2]

Fortunately, contemporary researchers have found less barbaric ways to illustrate the importance of communication. In one study of isolation, subjects were paid to remain alone in a locked room. Of the five subjects, one lasted for eight days. Three held out for two days, one commenting, "Never again." The fifth subject lasted only two hours.[3]

The need for contact and companionship is just as strong outside the laboratory, as individuals who have led solitary lives by choice or necessity have discovered. W. Carl Jackson, an adventurer who sailed across the Atlantic Ocean alone in fifty-one days, summarized the feelings common to most loners:

> I found the loneliness of the second month almost excruciating. I always thought of myself as self-sufficient, but I found life without people had no meaning. I had a definite need for somebody to talk to, someone real, alive, and breathing.[4]

Why We Communicate

You might object to stories like this, claiming that solitude would be a welcome relief from the irritations of everyday life. It's true that all of us need solitude, often more than we get. On the other hand, each of us has a point beyond which we do not want to be alone. Beyond this point solitude changes from a pleasurable to a painful condition. In other words, we all need relationships. We all need to communicate.

Physical Needs

Communication is so important that its presence or absence affects physical health. In extreme cases communication can even become a matter of life or death. When he was a Navy pilot, U.S. Senator John McCain was shot down over North Vietnam and held as a prisoner of war for six years, often in solitary confinement. He describes how POWs set up clandestine codes in which they sent messages by tapping on walls to laboriously spell out words. McCain describes the importance of keeping contact and the risks that inmates would take to maintain contact with one another:

> The punishment for communicating could be severe, and a few POWs, having been caught and beaten for their efforts, had their spirits broken as their bodies were battered. Terrified of a return trip to the punishment room, they would lie still in their cells when their comrades tried to tap them up on the wall. Very few would remain uncommunicative for long. To suffer all this alone was less tolerable than torture. Withdrawing in silence from the fellowship of other Americans . . . was to us the approach of death.[5]

> We must love one
> another or die.
>
> W. H. Auden

The link between communication and physical well-being isn't restricted to prisoners. Medical researchers have identified a wide range of health threats that can result from a lack of close relationships. For instance:

- A lack of social relationships jeopardizes coronary health to a degree that rivals cigarette smoking, high blood pressure, blood lipids, obesity, and lack of physical activity.[6]
- Socially isolated people are four times more susceptible to the common cold than those who have active social networks.[7]
- Social isolates are two to three times more likely to die prematurely than are those with strong social ties. The type of relationship doesn't seem to matter: Marriage, friendship, religious ties, and community ties all seem to increase longevity.[8]
- Divorced men (before age 70) die from heart disease, cancer, and strokes at double the rate of married men. Three times as many die from hypertension; five times as many commit suicide; seven times as many die from cirrhosis of the liver; and ten times as many die from tuberculosis.[9]
- The rate of all types of cancer is as much as five times higher for divorced men and women, compared to their married counterparts.[10]
- The likelihood of death increases when a close relative dies. In one Welsh village, citizens who had lost a close relative died within one year at a rate more than five times greater than the rate of those who had not lost a relative.[11]
- People who are defensive suffer from higher blood pressure compared to those more willing to acknowledge their possible limitations.[12]

Research like this demonstrates the importance of having satisfying personal relationships. Not everyone needs the same amount of contact, and the quality of communication is almost certainly as important as the quantity. The important point is that personal communication is essential for our well-being.

Identity Needs

Communication does more than enable us to survive. It is the way—indeed, the *only* way—we learn who we are. As Chapter 2 explains, our sense of identity comes from the way we interact with other people. Are we smart or stupid, attractive or ugly, skillful or inept? The answers to these questions don't come from looking in the mirror. We decide who we are based on how others react to us.

Deprived of communication with others, we would have no sense of ourselves. In his book *Bridges Not Walls*, John Stewart dramatically illustrates this fact by citing the case of the famous "Wild Boy of Aveyron," who spent his early childhood without any apparent human contact. The boy was discovered in January 1800 digging for vegetables in a French village garden. He showed no behaviors that one would expect in a social human. The boy could not speak but rather uttered only weird cries. More significant than this lack of social skills was his lack of any identity as a human being. As author Roger Shattuck put it, "The boy had no human sense of being in the world. He had no sense of himself as a person related to other persons."[13] Only with the influence of a loving "mother" did the boy begin to behave—and, we can imagine, think of himself—as a human.

Like the boy of Aveyron, each of us enters the world with little or no sense of identity. We gain an idea of who we are from the way others define us. As Chapter 2 explains, the messages we receive in early childhood are the strongest, but the influence of others continues throughout life.

Social Needs

Besides helping to define who we are, communication provides a vital link with others. Researchers and theorists have identified a whole range of social needs that we satisfy by communicating. These include pleasure, affection, companionship, escape, relaxation, and control.[14]

Needs like these arise in virtually every relationship—with friends, fellow workers, family members, lovers, spouses, and even strangers. And communication

© Carmen Cartiness Johnson

Two are better than one, because they have a good reward for their labor. For if they fall, one will lift up his companion. But woe to him who is alone when he falls, for he has no one to help him up.

Ecclesiastes 4:9, 10

is the primary way we satisfy our social needs. In fact, some social scientists have argued that communication is the principal way by which relationships are created.[15] For example, a study of 1,800 southern Californians showed that "good old-fashioned chats" with neighbors are the surest way to build a sense of community.[16]

Research suggests a strong link between effective interpersonal communication and happiness. In one study of over 200 college students, the happiest 10 percent described themselves as having a rich social life. (The very happy people were no different from their classmates in any other measurable way such as amount of sleep, exercise, TV watching, religious activity, or alcohol consumption.)[17] In another study, women reported that "socializing" contributed more to a satisfying life than virtually any other activity, including relaxing, shopping, eating, exercise, TV, or prayer.[18]

A variety of evidence suggests that many people aren't very successful at managing their interpersonal relationships. For example, one study revealed that one-quarter of the more than 4,000 adults surveyed knew more about their dogs than they did about their neighbors' backgrounds.[19] Americans believe that communication problems "very frequently" cause a marriage or a relationship to end—more than money, relatives or in-laws, sex, previous relationships, or children.[20]

Who can enjoy alone?

John Milton, *Paradise Lost*

Because relationships with others are so vital, some theorists have gone as far as to argue that communication is the primary goal of human existence. Anthropologist Walter Goldschmidt terms the drive for meeting social needs the "human career."[21] If you pause now and make a mental list of your own relationships, you'll probably see that, no matter how successful your relationships at home, with friends, at school, and at work, there is plenty of room for improvement in your everyday life. The information that follows will help you improve the way you communicate with the people who matter most to you.

Practical Goals

Besides satisfying social needs and shaping our identity, communication is the most widely used approach to satisfying what communication scholars call **instrumental goals**: getting others to behave in ways we want. Some instrumental goals are quite basic: Communication is the tool that lets you tell the hair stylist to take just a little off the sides, lets you negotiate household duties, and lets you convince the plumber that the broken pipe needs attention *now*!

Invitation to Insight

The Human Need to Communicate

ThomsonNOW˙ View the ABC News clip "Babies and Sign Language." You can find this clip through your ThomsonNOW for *Looking Out/Looking In*. (See the pages near the inside front and back covers of this book for more about your ThomsonNOW.)

This story describes how babies as young as six months old can learn basic sign language. It shows that the imperative to communicate begins early in life, and how even very young children can satisfy their needs by expressing themselves and understanding others.

Other instrumental goals are more important. Career success is the prime example. Communication skills—the ability to speak and listen effectively—are the top factors in helping college graduates find jobs in an increasingly competitive workplace, ranking higher than technical competence, work experience, and specific degree earned.[22] Good communication on the job is just as important. Economist James Flanigan explains: "Communication skills will fetch premium pay. The person who talks on the phone to mutual fund investors will have to be even more knowledgeable, efficient, and personable than the bank teller of old. Competition for such jobs won't be based on pay alone but on skills."[23] This means that good personal skills aren't just a social nicety: They can mean the difference between success and failure on the job.

Psychologist Abraham Maslow suggested that the physical, identity, social, and practical needs we have been discussing fall into five hierarchical categories, each of which must be satisfied before we concern ourselves with the less fundamental needs.[24] The most basic of these needs are *physical:* sufficient air, water, food, and rest, and the ability to reproduce as a species. The second of Maslow's needs is *safety:* protection from threats to our well-being. Beyond physical and safety needs are the *social needs* we have mentioned already. Beyond these, Maslow suggests, each of us has *self-esteem* needs: the desire to believe that we are worthwhile, valuable people. The final category of needs described by Maslow is *self-actualization:* the desire to develop our potential to the maximum, to become the best person we can be. As you read on, think about the ways in which communication is often necessary to satisfy each level of need.

The Process of Communication

We have been talking about *communication* as though the meaning of this word were perfectly clear. Before going further we need to explain systematically what happens when people exchange messages with one another. Doing so will introduce you to a common working vocabulary and, at the same time, preview some of the topics that are covered in later chapters.

A Linear View

In the early days of studying communication as a social science, researchers created models to illustrate the communication process. Their first attempts resulted in a **linear communication model**, which depicts communication as something a sender "does to" a receiver. According to the linear model in Figure 1.1,

A **sender** (the person creating the message)
encodes (puts thoughts into symbols, usually words) a

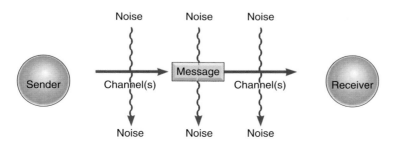

FIGURE 1.1
Linear Communication Model

message (the information being transmitted), sending it through a
channel (the medium through which the message passes) to a
receiver (the person attending to the message) who
decodes (makes sense of the message), while contending with
noise (distractions that disrupt transmission).

Notice how the appearance and vocabulary in Figure 1.1 represent how radio and television broadcasting operate. This isn't a coincidence: The scientists who created it were primarily interested in electronic media. The widespread use of this model has affected the way we think and talk about communication. There is a linear, machinelike quality to familiar phrases such as "We're having a communication breakdown" and "I don't think my message is getting through."

These familiar phrases (and the thinking they represent) obscure some important differences between mechanical and human communication. Does interpersonal communication really "break down," or are people still exchanging information even when they're not talking to each other? Is it possible to "get a message through" to someone loudly and clearly, but still not get the desired reaction? Here are some other questions to consider about the shortcomings of the linear model:

- When you're having a conversation with a friend, is there only one sender and one receiver, or do both of you send and receive messages simultaneously?
- Do you purposely encode every message you send, or are there behaviors you engage in unconsciously that still communicate messages to others?
- Does communication take place in a vacuum, or is a message's meaning affected by larger factors such as culture, environment, and relational history?

These and other questions have led scholars to create models that better represent interpersonal communication. We will look at one of these models now.

A Transactional View

A **transactional communication model** (Figure 1.2) updates and expands the linear model to better capture communication as a uniquely human process. Some concepts and terms from the linear model are retained in the transactional model, while others are enhanced, added, or eliminated.

The transactional model uses the word *communicator* instead of *sender* and *receiver*. This term reflects the fact that people send and receive messages simultaneously and not in a unidirectional or back-and-forth manner, as suggested by the

FIGURE 1.2
Transactional Communication Model

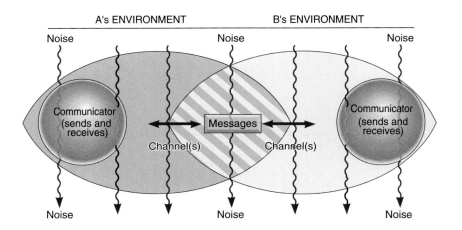

linear model. Consider, for example, what might happen when you and a house-mate negotiate how to handle household chores. As soon as you begin to hear (receive) the words sent by your housemate, "I want to talk about cleaning the kitchen . . . ," you grimace and clench your jaw (sending a nonverbal message of your own while receiving the verbal one). This reaction leads your housemate to interrupt herself defensively, sending a new message: "Now wait a minute. . . ."

A transactional model also shows that communicators often occupy different **environments**—fields of experience that affect how they understand others' behavior. In communication terminology, *environment* refers not only to a phys-ical location but also to the personal experiences and cultural background that participants bring to a conversation.

Consider just some of the factors that might contribute to different environments:

■ Person A might belong to one ethnic group and person B to another.
■ A might be rich and B poor.
■ A might be rushed and B have nowhere to go.
■ A might have lived a long, eventful life and B might be young and inexperienced.
■ A might be passionately concerned with the subject and B indifferent to it.

Notice how the model in Figure 1.2 shows that the environments of individu-als A and B overlap. This area represents the background that the communicators have in common. As the shared environment becomes smaller, communication becomes more difficult. Consider a few examples in which different perspectives can make understanding difficult:

■ Bosses who have trouble understanding the perspective of their employees will be less effective managers, and workers who do not appreciate the challenges of being a boss are more likely to be uncooperative (and probably less suitable for advancement).
■ Parents who have trouble recalling their youth are likely to clash with their children, who have never known and may not appreciate the responsibility that comes with parenting.
■ Members of a dominant culture who have never experienced how it feels to be "different" may not appreciate the concerns of people from minority co-cultures, whose own perspectives make it hard to understand the cultural blindness of the majority.

Communication channels retain a significant role in the transactional model, as they did in the linear model. Although it's tempting to see channels simply as neutral conduits for delivering a message, a closer look reveals the important role they play. For instance, should you say "I love you" in person? Over the phone? By renting space on a billboard? By sending flowers and a card? With a singing telegram? Via e-mail? In a voice mail? Each channel has its differences, and each affects the meaning of the message.

The transactional model also retains the concept of noise but with a broader focus. In the linear model, the focus is on noise in the channel—what is known as *external noise*. For instance, loud music or too much cigarette smoke in a crowded room might make it hard for you to pay attention to another person. The transactional model shows that noise also resides *within* communicators. This includes *physiological noise*, which involves biological factors that interfere with accurate reception: illness, fatigue, hearing loss, and so on. Communicators can also encounter *psychological noise*: forces within that interfere with the ability

Like paths and alleys overgrown with hardy, rank-growing weeds, the words we use are overgrown with our individual, private, provincial associations, which tend to choke the meaning.

Stefan Themerson

© Zits Partnership. Reprinted by special permission of King Features Syndicate.

to understand a message accurately. For instance, a student might become so upset upon learning that she failed a test that she would be unable (perhaps *unwilling* is a better word) to understand clearly where she went wrong. Psychological noise is such an important communication problem that we have devoted much of Chapter 10 to investigating its most common form, defensiveness.

For all the insights they offer, models can't capture some important features of interpersonal communication. A model is a "snapshot," while communication more closely resembles a "motion picture." In real life it's difficult to isolate a single discrete "act" of communication from the events that precede and follow it.[25] Consider the "Zits" cartoon on this page. If you read only the final frame, it appears that Jeremy is the victim of his mother's nagging. If you then read the first three frames, you might conclude that if Jeremy were more responsive to his mother, she might not need to be so persistent. And if you watched the two of them interact over the days and weeks preceding the incident in this cartoon, you would have a larger (but still incomplete) picture of the relational history that contributed to this event. In other words, the communication pattern that Jeremy and his mother have created together contributes to the quality of their relationship.

This leads to another important point: Transactional communication isn't something that we do *to* others; rather, it is an activity that we do *with* them. In this sense, person-to-person communication is rather like dancing—at least the kind of dancing we do with partners. Like dancing, communication depends on the involvement of a partner. And like good dancing, successful communication doesn't depend only on the person who takes the lead. A great dancer who forgets to consider and adapt to the skill level of his or her partner can make both people look bad. In communication and dancing, even having two talented partners doesn't guarantee success. When two skilled dancers perform without coordinating their movements, the results feel bad to the dancers and look foolish to an audience. Finally, relational communication—like dancing—is a unique creation that arises out of the way in which the partners interact. The way you dance probably varies from one partner to another. Likewise, the way you communicate almost certainly varies from one partner to another.

The transactional nature of communication shows up dramatically in relationships between parents and their children. We normally think of "good parenting" as a skill that some people possess and others lack. We judge the ability of a mother and father in terms of how well their children turn out. In fact, research suggests that the quality of interaction between parents and children is a two-way affair—that children influence parents just as much as the reverse.[26] For example, children who engage in what social scientists call "problematic behavior" evoke more high-control responses from their parents than do cooperative children. By contrast, youngsters with mild temperaments are less likely to provoke coercive reactions by their parents than are more-aggressive children. Parents with low self-esteem tend to send more messages that weaken the self-esteem of their children, who in turn

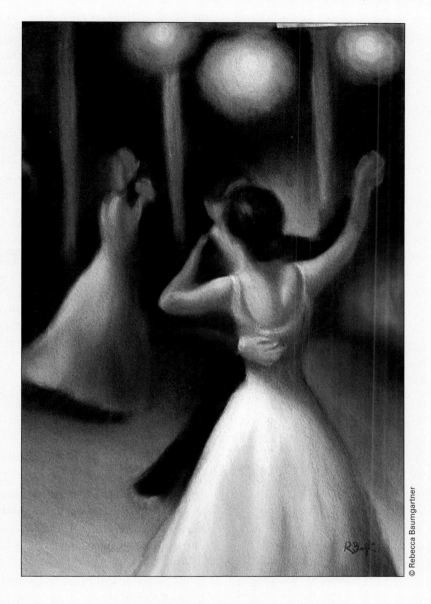

© Rebecca Baumgartner

Let it be a dance we do.
May I have this dance
    with you?
Through the good times
And the bad times, too,
Let it be a dance.

Learn to follow, learn to
    lead,
Feel the rhythm, fill the
    need.
To reap the harvest, plant
    the seed.
And let it be a dance.

Morning star comes out at
    night,
Without the dark there is
    no light.
If nothing's wrong, then
    nothing's right.
Let it be a dance.

Ric Masten

are likely to act in ways that make the parents feel even worse about themselves. Thus, a mutually reinforcing cycle arises in which parents and children shape one another's feelings and behavior. In cases like this it's at least difficult and probably impossible to identify who is the "sender" and who is the "receiver" of messages. It's more accurate to acknowledge that parents and children—just like husbands and wives, bosses and employees, teachers and students, or any other people in relationships—act in ways that mutually influence one another.

Now we can summarize the definition of *communication* that we have been developing. **Communication** is a transactional process involving participants who occupy different but overlapping environments and create relationships through the exchange of messages, many of which are affected by external, physiological, and psychological noise. Whether or not you memorize this definition is a matter for you and your instructor to decide. In any case, notice how it reflects a more sophisticated view of the process than you might have had before reading this far.

Invitation to Insight

Comparing and Contrasting Communication Models

ThomsonNOW Visit the Pragmatic Communication Model website. You can find the link to this site through your ThomsonNOW for *Looking Out/Looking In*. Read the explanation and then, in your own words, summarize the similarities and differences between the Pragmatic Model at this site and the Transactional Model in your textbook. What does each have in common? What does one model explain better than the other? Which one do you prefer and why?

Communication Principles and Misconceptions

Before we look at the qualities that distinguish interpersonal communication, it's important to define what communication is and what it isn't and to discuss what it can and can't accomplish.

Communication Principles

It's possible to draw several important conclusions about communication from what you have already learned in this chapter.

Communication Can Be Intentional or Unintentional Some communication is clearly intentional: You probably plan your words carefully before asking the boss for a raise or offering constructive criticism. Some scholars argue that only intentional messages like these qualify as communication. Others argue that even unintentional behavior is communicative. Suppose, for instance, that a friend overhears you muttering complaints to yourself. Even though you didn't intend for her to hear your remarks, they certainly did carry a message. In addition to these slips of the tongue, we unintentionally send many nonverbal messages. You might not be aware of your sour expression, impatient shifting, or sigh of boredom, but others view them nonetheless. Scholars have debated without reaching consensus about whether unintentional behavior should be considered communication, and it's unlikely that they will ever settle this issue.[27]

In *Looking Out/Looking In* we will look at the communicative value of both intentional and unintentional behavior.

"We can pause, Stu—we can even try fast-forwarding—but we can never rewind."

Communication Is Irreversible   We sometimes wish that we could back up in time, erasing words or acts and replacing them with better alternatives. Unfortunately, such reversal is impossible. Sometimes, further explanation can clear up another's confusion, or an apology can mollify another's hurt feelings, but other times no amount of explanation can erase the impression you have created. It is no more possible to "unreceive" a message than to "unsqueeze" a tube of toothpaste. Words said and deeds done are irretrievable.

It's Impossible Not to Communicate   Because both intentional and unintentional behaviors send a message, many theorists agree that it is impossible not to communicate. Whatever you do—whether you speak or remain silent, confront or avoid, act emotional or keep a poker face—you provide information to others about your thoughts and feelings. In this sense we are like transmitters that can't be shut off.

Of course, the people who decode your message may not interpret it accurately. They might take your kidding seriously or underestimate your feelings, for example. The message that you intend to convey may not even resemble the one that others infer from your actions. Thus, when we talk about "a communication breakdown" or "miscommunication," we rarely mean that communication has ended. Instead, we mean that it is inaccurate, ineffective, or unsatisfying.[28]

This explains why the best way to boost understanding is to discuss your intentions and your interpretations of the other person's behavior until you have negotiated a shared meaning. The perception-checking skills described in Chapter 3, the tips on clear language offered in Chapter 5, and the listening skills introduced in Chapter 7 will give you tools to boost the odds that the meanings of messages you send and receive are understandable to both you and others.

Communication Is Unrepeatable   Because communication is an ongoing process, it is impossible to repeat the same event. The friendly smile that worked so well when meeting a stranger last week might not succeed with the person you meet

"C'mon, let's get outta here," I said. "You give me a royal pain in the ass, if you want to know the truth."
Boy, did she hit the ceiling when I said that. I know I shouldn't have said it, and I probably wouldn't've ordinarily, but she was depressing the hell out of me. Usually I never say crude things like that to girls. Boy, did she hit the ceiling. I apologized like a madman, but she wouldn't accept my apology.

J. D. Salinger,
Catcher in the Rye

tomorrow: It might feel stale and artificial to you the second time around, or it might be wrong for the new person or occasion. Even with the same person, it's impossible to re-create an event. Why? Because neither you nor the other person is the same person. You've both lived longer. Your feelings about each other may have changed. You need not constantly invent new ways to act around familiar people, but you should realize that the "same" words and behavior are different each time they are spoken or performed.

Communication Has a Content and a Relational Dimension   Practically all exchanges operate on two levels. The **content dimension** involves the information being explicitly discussed: "Turn left at the next corner." "You can buy that for less online." "You're standing on my foot." In addition to this sort of obvious content, all messages also have a **relational dimension** that expresses how you feel about the other person: whether you like or dislike the other person, feel in control or subordinate, feel comfortable or anxious, and so on.[29] For instance, consider how many different relational messages you could communicate by simply saying, "I'm busy tonight, but maybe some other time" in different ways.

Sometimes the content dimension of a message is all that matters. For example, you probably don't care much about how the customer service rep feels about you as long as you get a technician scheduled to fix your car. At other times, though, the relational dimension of a message is more important than the content under discussion. This explains why arguments can develop over apparently trivial subjects like whose turn it is to wash the dishes or how to spend the weekend. In cases like this, what's really being tested is the nature of the relationship. Who's in control? How important are we to each other? Chapter 8 will explore these key relational issues in detail.

Communication Misconceptions

It's just as important to know what communication is *not* as to know what it is.[30] Avoiding the following misconceptions can save you a great deal of personal trouble.

More Communication Is Not Always Better   Whereas not communicating enough can cause problems, there are also situations when *too much* communication is a mistake. Sometimes excessive communication is simply unproductive, as when two people "talk a problem to death," going over the same ground again and again without making progress. There are other times when talking too much actually aggravates a problem. We've all had the experience of "talking ourselves into a hole"—making a bad situation worse by pursuing it too far. As one communication book puts it, "More and more negative communication merely leads to more and more negative results."[31]

Meanings Are Not in Words   The biggest mistake we can make is to assume that *saying* something is the same thing as *communicating* it. As Chapter 3 explains, the words that make perfect sense to you can be interpreted in entirely different ways by others. Chapter 5 describes the most common types of verbal misunderstandings and suggests ways to minimize them. Chapter 7 introduces listening skills that help ensure that the way you receive messages matches the ideas that a speaker is trying to convey.

Successful Communication Doesn't Always Involve Shared Understanding   Mutual understanding is sometimes a measure of successful communication, but there are times when success comes from *not* completely understanding one another. For example, we are often deliberately vague in order to spare another's feelings. Imagine how you might reply when a friend asks, "What do you think about my new tattoo?" You might tactfully say, "Wow—that's really unusual," instead of honestly and clearly answering, "I think it's grotesque." In cases like this we sacrifice clarity for the sake of kindness and to maintain our relationships.

Some research suggests that satisfying relationships depend in part on flawed understanding. As the cartoon on this page suggests, couples who

"My wife understands me."

think their partners understand them are more satisfied with each other than those who *actually* understand what the other says and means.[32] In other words, more-satisfying relationships can sometimes come from less-than-perfect understanding. Chapter 9 describes in detail the way we sometimes sacrifice clarity for the sake of maintaining relationships.

No Single Person or Event Causes Another's Reaction   Although communicative skill can often make the difference between satisfying and unsatisfying outcomes, it's a mistake to suggest that any single thing we say or do causes an outcome. Many factors play a role in how others will react to your communication in a single situation. Suppose, for example, that you lose your temper and say something to a friend that you regret as soon as the words escape your lips. Your friend's reaction will depend on a whole host of events besides your unjustified remark: her frame of mind at the moment (uptight or mellow), elements of her personality (judgmental or forgiving), your relational history (supportive or hostile), and her knowledge of any factors in your life that might have contributed to your unjustified remark. Because communication is a transactional, ongoing, collaborative process, it's usually a mistake to think that any event occurs in a vacuum.

Communication Will Not Solve All Problems   Sometimes even the best-planned, best-timed communication won't solve a problem. Imagine, for example, that you ask an instructor to explain why you received a poor grade on a project that you believe deserved top marks. The instructor clearly outlines the reasons why you received the poor grade and sticks to that position after listening thoughtfully to your protests. Has communication solved the problem? Hardly.

Sometimes clear communication is even the *cause* of problems. Suppose, for example, that a friend asks you for an honest opinion of the $200 outfit he has just bought. Your clear and sincere answer, "I think it makes you look fat," might do more harm than good. Deciding when and how to self-disclose isn't always easy. See Chapter 9 for suggestions.

I don't care who's wrong or right.
I don't really wanna fight no more.
Too much talking, babe.
Let's sleep on it tonight.
I don't really wanna fight no more.
This is time for letting go.

Recorded by Tina Turner

The Nature of Interpersonal Communication

Now that you have a better understanding of the overall process of human communication, it's time to look at what makes some types uniquely interpersonal.

Two Views of Interpersonal Communication

Scholars have characterized **interpersonal communication** in a number of ways.[33] The most obvious definition focuses on the number of people involved. A **quantitative** definition of interpersonal communication includes any interaction between two people, usually face to face. Social scientists call two people interacting a **dyad**, and they often use the adjective *dyadic* to describe this type of communication. So, in a quantitative sense, the terms *dyadic communication* and *interpersonal communication* can be used interchangeably. Using a quantitative definition, a salesclerk and customer or a police officer ticketing a speeding driver would be examples of interpersonal acts, whereas a teacher and class or a performer and audience would not.

You might object to the quantitative definition of interpersonal communication. For example, consider a routine transaction between a salesclerk and customer or the rushed exchange when you ask a stranger on the street for directions. Communication of this sort hardly seems interpersonal—or personal in any sense of the word. In fact, after transactions like this we commonly remark, "I might as well have been talking to a machine."

The impersonal nature of some two-person exchanges and the personal nature of others have led some scholars to argue that *quality*, not quantity, is what distinguishes interpersonal communication.[34] Using a **qualitative** definition, interpersonal communication occurs when people treat one another as unique individuals, regardless of the context in which the interaction occurs or the number of people involved. When quality of interaction is the criterion, the opposite of interpersonal communication is **impersonal communication**, not group, public, or mass communication.

Several features distinguish qualitatively interpersonal communication from less-personal communication.[35] The first feature is *uniqueness*. Communication in impersonal exchanges is determined by social *rules* (laugh politely at others' jokes, don't dominate a conversation, and so on) and by social *roles* (the customer is always right, be especially polite to senior citizens). Qualitatively interpersonal relationships are characterized by the development of unique rules and roles. For example, in one relationship you might exchange good-natured insults, whereas in another you are careful never to offend your partner. Likewise, you might handle conflicts with one friend or family member by expressing disagreements as soon as they arise, whereas the unwritten rule in another relationship is to withhold resentments until they build up and then clear the air periodically. One communication scholar coined the term *relational culture* to describe people in close relationships who create their own unique ways of interacting.[36]

A second feature of qualitatively interpersonal relationships is *irreplaceability*. Because interpersonal relationships are unique, they can't be replaced. This explains why we usually feel so sad when a close friendship or love affair cools down. We know that no matter how many other relationships fill our lives, none of them will ever be quite like the one that just ended.

© Images.com/Corbis

I marvel

At the large quantity

Of communication

Between the two of us

Otherwise

I can only

get discouraged

By its bleak

Quality.

Vlado Uzunangelov

Interdependence is a third feature of qualitatively interpersonal relationships. At the most basic level the fate of the partners is connected. You might be able to brush off the anger, affection, excitement, or depression of someone you're not involved with personally, but in an interpersonal relationship the other's life affects you. Sometimes interdependence is a pleasure, and at other times it is a burden. In either case, it is a fact of life in qualitatively interpersonal relationships. Interdependence goes beyond the level of joined fates. In interpersonal relationships, our very identity depends on the nature of our interaction with others. As psychologist Kenneth Gergen puts it: "One cannot be 'attractive' without others who are attracted, a 'leader' without others willing to follow, or a 'loving person' without others to affirm with appreciation."[37]

A fourth feature of interpersonal relationships is often (though not always) the amount of *disclosure* of personal information. In impersonal relationships we don't reveal much about ourselves, but in interpersonal relationships we feel more comfortable sharing our thoughts and feelings. This doesn't mean that all interpersonal relationships are warm and caring, or that all self-disclosure is positive. It's possible to reveal negative, personal information: "I'm really mad at you. . . ."

A fifth feature of interpersonal communication is *intrinsic rewards.* In impersonal communication we seek payoffs that have little to do with the people involved. You listen to professors in class or talk to potential buyers of your used car in order to reach goals that have little to do with developing personal relationships. By contrast, you spend time in qualitatively interpersonal relationships with friends, lovers, and others because you find the time personally rewarding. It often doesn't matter *what* you talk about: The relationship itself is what's important.

Because relationships that are unique, irreplaceable, interdependent, disclosing, and intrinsically rewarding are rare, qualitatively interpersonal communication is relatively scarce. We chat pleasantly with shopkeepers or fellow passengers on the bus or plane; we discuss the weather or current events with most classmates and neighbors; we deal with co-workers and teachers in a polite way; but considering the number of people with whom we communicate, personal relationships are by far in the minority.

The rarity of personal relationships isn't necessarily unfortunate. Most of us don't have the time or energy to create personal relationships with everyone we encounter. In fact, the scarcity of qualitatively interpersonal communication contributes to its value. Like precious jewels and one-of-a-kind artwork, interpersonal relationships are special because of their scarcity.

Technology and Interpersonal Communication

Face-to-face conversation isn't the only way people can create and maintain personal relationships. Along with the telephone and old-fashioned correspondence, **computer-mediated communication (CMC)** provides another way to interact. Instant messaging, e-mailing, blogging, and online chat are some of the many ways that acquaintances—and strangers—can communicate through CMC.

A growing body of research reveals that CMC isn't the threat to relationships that some critics once feared. Most Internet users—both adults and children—report the time they spend online has no influence on the amount of time they spend with their family or friends. Over three-quarters of these people say they never feel ignored by another household member spending time online.[38] In fact, the majority of Internet users said that IMing, e-mail, websites, and chat rooms had a "modestly positive impact" on their ability to communicate with family members and make new friends. Over half of the people surveyed state that the number of their personal relationships has grown since they started to use the Internet.[39]

More recent studies are similarly positive about the role that CMC plays in people's relationships and decision making.[40] They show that mediated communication enriches social networks. This is especially true among teens and younger adults who have grown up using the Internet, but findings prove true across generations. For example,

- Internet users have more social networks than non-users.
- CMC is a source of "glocalization," connecting people to distant friends and relatives as well as to those who live nearby.
- CMC encourages offline interaction with close friends by keeping relationships alive and active.
- Text-only format of e-mail and instant messages can bring people closer by minimizing the perception of differences due to gender, social class, ethnicity, and age.

It's important to note that CMC isn't a replacement for face-to-face communication. One study of college students who frequently use instant messaging concluded that "nothing appears to compare to face-to-face communication in terms of satisfying individuals' communication, information, and social needs."[41] Rather than diminishing other forms of communication, CMC actually promotes and reinforces them. Furthermore, there is an interactive relationship between CMC, phone contact, and in-person communication. In other words, if you regularly communicate with friends and family over the computer, it is likely that you will also call them and try to see them more often.[42]

To know all your neighbors on the global level does not mean that you will automatically love them all; it does not, in and of itself, introduce a reign of peace and brotherhood. But to be potentially in touch with everybody at least makes fighting more uncomfortable. It becomes easier to argue instead.

Isaac Asimov, "The Fourth Revolution"

It's a Small World

© Richard Cook/Images.com

She was 7,000 miles away from our apartment in China, ensconced in the suburbs of New York City attending to her ill father. I was in a place where the phone system barely worked and the idea of public Internet access was laughable—Kabul, the war-wasted capital of Afghanistan.

Nonetheless, there it was, uploaded through the ether from Long Island on a January morning, bounced off an orbiting satellite, beamed back down to an antenna on the second-floor balcony of an Afghan house. My wife's missive reached me in an instant, offering the romantic interrogative of a high-velocity world.

"You there?" Melissa asked, beeping as her pixilated box appeared.

And there she was, luminous as ever in her usual online outfit—10-point Times New Roman, with her name draped in brilliant royal blue.

Instant messaging (or IMing for short) is becoming to the dawn of the 21st century what the telephone was to the beginning of the 20th—a

normal way of communicating in real time across previously uncrossable distances, making faster, if not better, typists of us all.

How different it is, and how little we realize it. Could human beings really have once existed in a world where we had to communicate by paper, where ink-smeared messages took weeks, even months to cross oceans and inform recipients that someone far away loved them?

Today, that old absence that once made the heart grow fonder is assuaged by the new-message notification. Souls that once ached across impassable divides wondering and waiting can now connect in seconds—via satellite.

It may not be the most personal way of relating. But for us, separated by the miles and by general craziness, it has made being apart a bit less miserable.

It's not just her, either. More than email or even the telephone, it connects me to my confidantes—from

New York City to Pittsburgh, Arkansas to Egypt to suburban Virginia and the North Carolina mountains. One friend in New York starts work precisely at 8 A.M. I hear the "door" of AOL Instant Messenger open, and she immediately chimes in: "Hello there."

In 1979, when I was 11 and living in Beijing the first time, we made one overseas telephone call all year—to my sister on her birthday. And we had to go through three operators to do it.

Today, my 78-year-old mother—born before the era of the dial tone—is an avid IM user. She pops in from sub-urban Pittsburgh while I'm at work, *"just saying hi"* from 13 time zones away. *"Is everything OK?"* I ask her each day, worried about my parents' health. She responds: *"Dad and I are fine. It's quiet here."*

Our instantaneous mini-universes hold pitfalls: You can't hear tone, so the danger of misinterpretation always looms. A breezy joke dispatched on one side can arrive as snippiness on the other end. And, of course, all the :)s and ;)s in the universe can't approximate an in-person smile, an actual hug.

"It's a blessing," my wife wrote me in August (from New York to Beijing), "but it's also become a substitute that's so much like something real that people can almost skip the real getting together. I wonder what effect it'll have down the road. On our generation and the one after."

A fascinating question. What's the next step in the story of human communication? I guess I'll have to ask our new baby.

We're having one next summer, it seems. In our frenzied, information-saturated marriage, clearly we've managed to transcend typing at least once.

Ted Anthony

Invitation to Insight

How Networked Are You?

The studies cited in this section suggest that CMC—computer-mediated communication—can and does enhance interpersonal relationships and networking. See if you agree or disagree by answering the questions below.

Can you identify a relationship that . . .

1. . . . has been enhanced by regular CMC interactions, such as IMing, e-mailing, or blogging?

2. . . . was created through CMC, perhaps in chat rooms, IMing/e-mailing, listservs, or online dating services?

3. . . . would suffer or perhaps end if computers weren't available?

What do your answers tell you about the impact of CMC on interpersonal relationships? Can you think of times when CMC has hurt or hindered relationships?

There are several reasons why CMC can increase both the quantity and quality of interpersonal communication. For one thing, CMC makes communication easier.[43] Busy schedules and long distances can make quality time in face-to-face contact difficult or impossible. The challenge of finding time is especially tough for people who are separated by long distances and multiple time zones. In relationships like this, the *asynchronous* nature of e-mail provides a way to share information that otherwise would be impossible. Communicators can create their own message and respond to one another without having to connect in real time. Instant messaging is another way to keep in touch: Discovering that a friend or relative is online and starting an electronic conversation is "like walking down the street and sometimes running into a friend," says Laura Balsam, a New York computer consultant.[44]

Even when face-to-face communication is convenient, some people find it easier to share personal information via CMC. Sociolinguist Deborah Tannen describes how e-mail transformed the quality of two relationships:

> E-mail deepened my friendship with Ralph. Though his office was next to mine, we rarely had extended conversations because he is shy. Face to face he mumbled so, I could barely tell he was speaking. But when we both got on e-mail, I started receiving long, self-revealing messages; we poured our hearts out to each other. A friend discovered that e-mail opened up that kind of communication with her father. He would never talk much on the phone (as her mother would), but they have become close since they both got on line.[45]

Experiences like these help explain why Steve Jobs, the co-founder of Apple Computer, suggested that personal computers be renamed "*inter*personal computers."[46]

Personal and Impersonal Communication: A Matter of Balance

Now that you understand the differences between qualitatively interpersonal and impersonal communication, we need to ask some important questions. Is interpersonal communication better than impersonal communication? Is more interpersonal communication the goal?

Most relationships aren't *either* interpersonal *or* impersonal. Rather, they fall somewhere on a continuum between these two extremes. Your own experience probably reveals that there is often a personal element in even the most impersonal situations. You might appreciate the unique sense of humor of a grocery checker or connect on a personal level with the person cutting your hair. And even the most tyrannical, demanding, by-the-book boss might show an occasional flash of humanity.

Just as there's a personal element in many impersonal settings, there is also an impersonal element in our relationships with the people we care most about. There are occasions when we don't want to be personal: when we're distracted, tired, busy, or just not interested. In fact, interpersonal communication is rather like rich food—it's fine in moderation, but too much can make you uncomfortable.

The personal-impersonal mixture of communicating in a relationship can change over time. The communication between young lovers who talk only about their feelings may change as their relationship develops, so that several years later their communication has become more routine and ritualized, and the percentage of time they spend on personal, relational issues drops and the conversation about less intimate topics increases. Chapter 8 discusses how communication changes as relationships pass through various stages and also describes the role of self-disclosure in keeping those relationships strong. As you read this information, you will see even more clearly that, although interpersonal communication can make life worth living, it isn't possible or desirable all the time.

It's clear that there is a place in our lives for both impersonal and interpersonal communication. Each type has its uses. The real challenge, then, is to find the right balance between the two types.

What Makes an Effective Communicator?

It's easy to recognize good communicators and even easier to spot poor ones. But what are the characteristics that distinguish effective communicators from their less successful counterparts? Answering this question has been one of the leading challenges for communication scholars.[47] Although all the answers aren't yet in, research has identified a great deal of important information about communication competence.

Invitation to Insight

How Personal Are Your Relationships?

Use the characteristics of qualitatively interpersonal communication described on pages 18–20 to think about your own relationships.

1. Make a list of several people who are close to you—family members, people you live with, friends, co-workers, and so on.

2. Use the scales that follow to rate each relationship. To distinguish the relationships from one another, use a different color of ink for each one.

3. Consider comparing your results with those of classmates or friends.

After completing the exercise, ask yourself the important question: How satisfied are you with the answers you have found?

Uniqueness

| 1 | 2 | 3 | 4 | 5 |
Standardized, habitual _____ Unique

Replaceability

| 1 | 2 | 3 | 4 | 5 |
Replaceable _____ Irreplaceable

Dependence

| 1 | 2 | 3 | 4 | 5 |
Independent _____ Interdependent

Disclosure

| 1 | 2 | 3 | 4 | 5 |
Low disclosure _____ High disclosure

Intrinsic rewards

| 1 | 2 | 3 | 4 | 5 |
Unrewarding _____ Rewarding

Communication Competence Defined

Defining **communication competence** isn't as easy as it might seem. Although scholars are still struggling to agree on a precise definition, most would agree that effective communication involves achieving one's goals in a manner that, ideally, maintains or enhances the relationship in which it occurs.[48] A closer look at this definition helps us talk about several important characteristics of communication competence.

There Is No "Ideal" Way to Communicate   Your own experience shows that a variety of communication styles can be effective. Some very successful communicators are serious, whereas others use humor; some are gregarious, whereas

Ethical Challenge

Martin Buber's *I and Thou*

Martin Buber is arguably the most influential advocate of qualitatively interpersonal communication as defined on pages 18–20. His book *Ich und Du* (*I and Thou*) is a worldwide classic, selling millions of copies since its publication in 1922.

Buber states that "I-It" and "I-Thou" represent two ways in which humans can relate to one another. "I-It" relationships are stable, predictable, detached. In an "I-It" mode we deal with people because they can do things for us: pump gas, laugh at our jokes, buy products we are selling, provide information or amusement. "I-It" is also the approach of science, which attempts to understand what makes people tick in order to explain, predict, and control their behavior. Buber would have regarded advertisers as operating in an "I-It" mode, crafting messages that lead people to buy their products or services. "I-It" relationships exist in personal relationships as well as impersonal ones: On an everyday basis parents and children, bosses and employees, service providers and customers—even lovers—deal with one another as objects ("I wish she would leave me alone"; "Can you pick me up after work?"; "How can I get him/her to love me?").

In profound contrast to "I-It" relationships, Buber described an "I-Thou" way of interacting. "I-Thou" relationships are utterly unique. Because no two teachers or students, parents or children, husbands or wives, bosses or employees are alike, we encounter each person as an individual and not as a member of some

category. An "I-Thou" posture goes further: Not only are people different from one another, but also they themselves change from moment to moment. An "I-Thou" relationship arises out of how we are now, not how we might have been yesterday or even a moment ago. In an "I-Thou" relationship, persuasion and control are out of the question: We certainly may explain our point of view, but ultimately we respect the fact that others are free to act.

Buber acknowledges that it is impossible to create and sustain pure "I-Thou" relationships. But without this qualitatively interpersonal level of contact, our lives are impoverished. To paraphrase Buber, without "I-It" we cannot exist; but if we live only with "I-It," we are not fully human.

Think of your most important relationships:

1. To what degree can they be described as "I-Thou" or "I-It"?
2. How satisfied are you with this level of relating?
3. What obligation do you have to treat others in an "I-Thou" manner?

Based on your answers to these questions, how might you change your style of communication?

An English translation of Martin Buber's *I and Thou* was published in 1970 by Scribner's. For useful descriptions of its central themes, see John Stewart, "A Philosopher's Approach," in J. Stewart, ed., *Bridges Not Walls*, 9th ed. (New York: McGraw-Hill, 2006); and H. J. Paton's chapter "Martin Buber," in *The Modern Predicament* (London: Allen & Unwin, 1955).

others are quieter; and some are more straightforward, whereas others hint diplomatically. Just as there are many kinds of beautiful music or art, there are many kinds of competent communication. It certainly is possible to learn new, effective ways of communicating from observing models, but it would be a mistake to try to copy others in a way that doesn't reflect your own style or values.

As you'll read throughout this book, what qualifies as competent behavior in one culture might be completely inept, or even offensive, in another.[49] On an obvious level, customs like belching after a meal or appearing nude in public that might be appropriate in some parts of the world would be considered outrageous in others. But there are more subtle differences in competent communication. For example, qualities like self-disclosing and speaking clearly that are valued in the United States are likely to be considered overly aggressive and insensitive in many Asian cultures, where subtlety and indirectness are considered important.[50] Even within a single society, members of various co-cultures may have different notions of appropriate behavior. One study revealed that ideas of how good friends should communicate varied from one ethnic group to another.[51] As a group, Latinos valued relational support most highly, whereas African Americans valued respect and acceptance. Asian Americans prized a caring, positive exchange of ideas, and Anglo Americans prized friends who recognized their needs as individuals. Findings like these mean that there can be no sure-fire list of rules or tips that will guarantee your success as a communicator. They also mean that competent communicators are able to adapt their style to suit the individual and cultural preferences of others.[52] See pages 34–36 for specific tips about communicating most effectively with people from different backgrounds.

© Images.com/Corbis

Competence Is Situational   Even within a culture or relationship, the specific communication that is competent in one setting might be a colossal blunder in another. The joking insults you routinely trade with one friend might offend a sensitive family member, and last Saturday night's romantic approach would most likely be out of place at work on Monday morning.

Because competent behavior varies so much from one situation and person to another, it's a mistake to think that communication competence is a trait that a person either has or does not have. It's more accurate to talk about *degrees* or *areas* of competence.[53] You might deal quite skillfully with peers, for example, but feel clumsy interacting with people much older or younger, wealthier or poorer, more or less attractive than yourself. In fact, your competence with one person may vary from situation to situation. This means that it's an overgeneralization to say in a moment of distress, "I'm a terrible communicator!" when it's more accurate to say, "I didn't handle this situation very well, even though I'm better in others."

> You did the best that you knew how. Now that you know better, you'll do better.
>
> Maya Angelou

Competence Is Relational   Because communication is transactional—something we do with others rather than to others—behavior that is competent in one relationship isn't necessarily competent in others. One important measure of competence is whether the people with whom you are communicating view your approach as effective.[54] For example, researchers have uncovered a variety of ways by which people deal with jealousy in their relationships.[55] The ways include keeping closer tabs on the partner, acting indifferent, decreasing affection, talking the matter over, and acting angry. The researchers concluded that approaches that work in some relationships would be harmful to others. Findings like these demonstrate that competence arises out of developing ways of interacting that work for you and for the other people involved.[56]

Competence Can Be Learned   To some degree, biology is destiny when it comes to communication style.[57] Studies of identical and fraternal twins suggest that traits including sociability, anger, and relaxation seem to be partially a function of our genetic makeup. Chapter 2 will have more to say about the role of neurobiology in communication traits.

Fortunately, biology isn't the only factor that shapes how we communicate. Communication competence is, to a great degree, a set of skills that anyone can learn. Skills training has been found to help communicators in a variety of ways, ranging from overcoming speech anxiety[58] to becoming more perceptive in detecting deception.[59] Research also shows that college students typically become more competent communicators over the course of their undergraduate studies.[60] In other words, your level of competence can improve through education and training—which means that reading this book and taking this course can help you become a more competent communicator.

Characteristics of Competent Communicators

Despite the fact that competent communication varies from one situation to another, scholars have identified several common denominators that characterize effective communication in most contexts.

A Wide Range of Behaviors   Effective communicators are able to choose their actions from a wide range of behaviors.[61] To understand the importance of having a large communication repertoire, imagine that someone you know repeatedly tells jokes—perhaps racist or sexist ones—that you find offensive. You could respond to these jokes in a number of ways:

- You could decide to say nothing, figuring that the risks of bringing the subject up would be greater than the benefits.
- You could ask a third party to say something to the joke teller about the offensiveness of the jokes.
- You could hint at your discomfort, hoping your friend would get the point.
- You could joke about your friend's insensitivity, counting on humor to soften the blow of your criticism.
- You could express your discomfort in a straightforward way, asking your friend to stop telling the offensive jokes, at least around you.
- You could even demand that your friend stop.

With this choice of responses at your disposal (and you can probably think of others as well), you could pick the one that has the best chance of success. But if you were able to use only one or two of these responses when raising a delicate issue—always keeping quiet or always hinting, for example—your chances of success would be much smaller. Indeed, many poor communicators are easy to spot by their limited range of responses. Some are chronic jokers. Others are always belligerent. Still others are quiet in almost every situation. Like a piano player who knows only one tune or a chef who can prepare only a few dishes, these people are forced to rely on a small range of responses again and again, whether or not they are successful.

Ability to Choose the Most Appropriate Behavior   Simply possessing a large range of communication skills is no guarantee of success. It's also necessary to know which of these skills will work best in a particular situation. This ability to choose the best approach is essential because a response that works well in one setting would flop miserably in another one.

Although it's impossible to say precisely how to act in every situation, there are at least three factors to consider when you are deciding which response to choose. The first factor is the communication *context*. The time and place will almost always influence how you act. Asking your boss for a raise or your lover for a kiss might produce good results if the time is right, but the identical request might backfire if your timing is poor. Likewise, the joke that would be ideal at a bachelor party would probably be inappropriate at a funeral.

Your *goal* will also shape the approach you take. Inviting a new neighbor over for a cup of coffee or dinner could be just the right approach if you want to encourage a friendship; but if you want to maintain your privacy, it might be wiser to be polite but cool. Likewise, your goal will determine your approach in situations in which you want to help another person. As you will learn in Chapter 7, there are times when offering advice is just what is needed. But when you want to help others develop the ability to solve problems on their own, it's better to withhold your own ideas and function as a sounding board to let them consider alternatives and choose their solutions.

Finally, your *knowledge of the other person* should shape the approach you take. If you're dealing with someone who is very sensitive or insecure, your response might be supportive and cautious. With an old and trusted friend you might be blunt. The social niche of the other party can also influence how you communicate. For instance, you would probably act differently toward an 80-year-old person than you would toward a teenager. Likewise, there are times when it's appropriate to treat a man differently than a woman, even in this age of gender equity.

Skill at Performing Behaviors   After you have chosen the most appropriate way to communicate, it's still necessary to perform the required skills effectively. There is a big difference between knowing *about* a skill and being able to put it into practice. Simply being aware of alternatives isn't much help unless you can skillfully put these alternatives to work.

Just reading about communication skills in the following chapters won't guarantee that you can start using them flawlessly. As with any other skills—playing a musical instrument or learning a sport, for example—the road to competence in communication is not a short one. As you learn and practice the communication skills in the following pages, you can expect to pass through several stages,[62] shown in Figure 1.3.

Daria Muse: Competent Communication in Suburbia and the Inner City

In this profile Daria Muse describes how effective communication varies in two strikingly different environments: her home neighborhood of South-Central Los Angeles and her school in the suburban San Fernando Valley. This account demonstrates some of the elements of communication competence introduced in Chapter 1: a wide range of behaviors, the ability to choose the best behavior for a given situation, and skill at performing that behavior.

During my elementary and middle-school years, I was a well-behaved, friendly student at school and a tough, hard-nosed "bad girl" in my neighborhood. This contrast in behavior was a survival tool, for I lived in a part of South-Central Los Angeles where "goody-goodies" aren't tolerated, and I attended school in Northridge, where trouble-makers aren't tolerated.

Beckford Ave. Elementary School was in the heart of middle-class suburbia, and I, coming from what has been described as the "urban jungle," was bused there every day for six years.

In a roundabout way, I was told from the first day of school that if I wanted to continue my privileged attendance in the hallowed classrooms of Beckford, I would have to conform and adapt to their standards. I guess I began to believe all that they said because slowly I began to conform.

Instead of wearing the tight jeans and T-shirt that were the style in South-Central at the time, I wore schoolgirl dresses like those of my female classmates. I even changed my language. When asking a question, instead of saying, "Boy! Gimme those scissors before I knock you up you head!" in school, I asked, "Excuse me, would you please hand me the scissors?" When giving a compliment in school I'd say, "You look very nice today," instead of "Girl, who do you think you are, dressin' so fine, Miss Thang."

This conformation of my appearance and speech won me the acceptance of my proper classmates at Beckford Elementary School, but after getting out of the school bus and stepping onto the sidewalks of South-Central, my appearance quit being an asset and became a dangerous liability.

One day, when I got off the school bus, a group of tough girls who looked as though they were part of a gang approached me, looked at my pink and white lace dress, and accused me of trying to "look white." They surrounded me and demanded a response that would prove to them that I was still loyal to my black heritage. I screamed, "Lay off me, girl, or I'll bust you in the eyes so bad that you'll need a telescope just to see!" The girls walked away without causing any more trouble.

From then on, two personalities emerged. I began living a double life. At school I was prim and proper in appearance and in speech, but during the drive on the school bus from Northridge to South-Central, my other personality emerged. Once I got off the bus I put a black jacket over my dress, I hardened my face, and roughened my speech to show everyone who looked my way that I was not a girl to be messed with. I led this double life throughout my six years of elementary school.

Now that I am older and can look back at that time objectively, I don't regret displaying contrasting behavior in the two different environments. It was for my survival. Daria, the hard-nosed bad girl, survived in the urban jungle and Daria, the well-behaved student, survived in the suburbs.

As a teen-ager in high school I still display different personalities: I act one way in school, which is different from the way I act with my parents, which is different from the way I act with my friends, which is different from the way I act in religious services. But don't we all? We all put on character masks for our different roles in life. All people are guilty of acting differently at work than at play and differently with co-workers than with the boss. There's nothing wrong with having different personalities to fit different situations; the trick is knowing the real you from the characters.

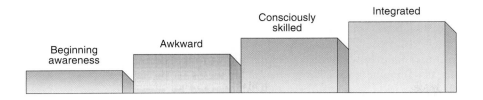

FIGURE 1.3
Stages in Learning
Communication Skills

Beginning Awareness   The first step in learning any new skill is a beginning awareness. This is the point at which you first learn that there is a new and better way of behaving. If you play tennis, for example, awareness might grow when you learn about a new way of serving that can improve your power and accuracy. In the area of communication, *Looking Out/Looking In* should bring this sort of awareness to you.

Awkwardness   Just as you were awkward when you first tried to ride a bicycle or drive a car, your initial attempts at communicating in new ways may also be awkward. This doesn't mean that there's anything wrong with these ways, but rather that you need more experience with them. After all, if it's reasonable to expect difficulty learning other skills, you ought to expect the same fumbling with the concepts in this book. As Ringo Starr put it when talking about music, "Got to pay your dues if you wanna sing the blues . . . you know it don't come easy."

Skillfulness   If you are willing to keep working at overcoming the awkwardness of your initial attempts, you will arrive at the third learning stage, which is skillfulness. At this stage you'll be able to handle yourself well, although you will still need to think about what you're doing. As in learning a new language, this is the time when you're able to speak grammatically and use the correct words, even though you still need to work hard to express yourself well. As an interpersonal communicator, you can expect the stage of skillfulness to be marked by a great deal of thinking and planning and also by good results.

Integration   Finally, after a period of time in the skillful stage, you'll find yourself at the final stage—integration. This occurs when you're able to perform well without thinking about it. The behavior becomes automatic, a part of you. Integrated speakers of a foreign language converse without translating mentally from their native tongue. Integrated cyclists ride skillfully and comfortably, almost as if the bike were an extension of each cyclist's own body. And integrated communicators express themselves in skillful ways, not because they are acting self-consciously, but rather because that is who they have become.

It's important to keep these stages in mind as you try out the ideas in this book. Prepare yourself for the inevitable awkwardness, knowing that if you're willing to keep practicing the new skills you will become more and more comfortable and successful with them. Realize that the effort is worth it because after you have learned new methods of communicating, you'll be rewarded with more-satisfying relationships.[63]

Cognitive Complexity   Social scientists use the term **cognitive complexity** to describe the ability to construct a variety of frameworks for viewing an issue. Researchers have found that cognitive complexity increases the chances of having

> You have to be willing to look bad in order to get good.
>
> Jack Canfield

satisfying communication among married couples,[64] helping others who are feeling distressed,[65] being persuasive,[66] and achieving career advancement,[67] to name a few contexts.

To understand how cognitive complexity can increase competence, consider an example. Imagine that a longtime friend seems to be angry with you. One possible explanation is that your friend is offended by something you've done. Another possibility is that something has happened in another part of your friend's life that is upsetting. Or perhaps nothing at all is wrong, and you're just being overly sensitive. Considering the issue from several angles might prevent you from overreacting or misunderstanding the situation, increasing the odds of finding a way to resolve the problem constructively. The sections on perception checking in Chapter 3, listening in Chapter 7, and preventing defensiveness in Chapter 10 provide specific tools for developing your cognitive complexity.

Empathy   Seeing a situation from multiple points of view is important, but there's another step that goes beyond understanding different perspectives. *Empathy* involves feeling and experiencing another person's situation, almost as they do. This ability is so important that some researchers have labeled empathy the most important aspect of communication competence.[68] Chapters 3 and 7 introduce you to a set of skills that can boost your ability to empathize. For now, it's enough to note that getting a feel for how others view the world is a useful and important way to become a more effective communicator.

Self-Monitoring   Whereas increased cognitive complexity and empathy help you understand others better, self-monitoring is one way to understand *yourself* better. Psychologists use the term **self-monitoring** to describe the process of paying close attention to one's behavior and using these observations to shape the way one behaves. Self-monitors are able to separate a part of their consciousness and observe their behavior from a detached viewpoint, making observations such as:

> "I'm making a fool out of myself."
> "I'd better speak up now."
> "This approach is working well. I'll keep it up."

Although too much self-monitoring can be problematic (see Chapter 2), people who are aware of their behavior and the impression it makes are more skillful communicators than people who are low self-monitors.[69] For example, they are more accurate in judging others' emotional states, better at remembering information about others, less shy, and more assertive. By contrast, low self-monitors aren't able even to recognize their incompetence. One study revealed that poor communicators were blissfully ignorant of their shortcomings and more likely to overestimate their skill than were better communicators.[70] For example, experimental subjects who scored in the lowest quartile on joke-telling skills were more likely than their funnier counterparts to grossly overestimate their sense of humor.

Whereas low self-monitors may blunder through life, succeeding or failing without understanding why, high self-monitors have the detachment to ask themselves the question "How am I doing?" and to change their behavior if the answer isn't positive.

Commitment   One feature that distinguishes effective communication—at least in qualitatively interpersonal relationships—is commitment. In other words, people who seem to care about relationships communicate better than those who don't.[71] This care shows up in at least two ways. The first is *commitment to the other person*. Concern for the other person is revealed in a variety of ways: a desire to spend time with him or her instead of rushing, a willingness to listen carefully instead of doing all the talking, the use of language that makes sense to the other person, and openness to change after hearing the other person's ideas. Effective communicators also care about *the message*. They appear sincere, seem to know what they are talking about, and demonstrate through words and deeds that they care about what they say.

How do you measure up as a competent communicator? Competence isn't a trait that people either have or do not have. Rather, it's a state that we achieve more or less frequently. A realistic goal, then, is not to become perfect but rather to boost the percentage of time when you communicate in ways outlined in this section.

Skill Builder

Check Your Competence

Other people are often the best judges of your competence as a communicator. They can also offer useful information about how to improve your communication. Find out for yourself by following these steps:

1. Choose a person with whom you have an important relationship.

2. In cooperation with this person, identify several contexts in which you communicate. For example, you might choose different situations such as "handling conflicts," "lending support to friends," or "expressing feelings."

3. For each situation, have your friend rate your competence by answering the following questions:

   a. Do you have a wide repertoire of response styles in this situation, or do you always respond in the same way?

   b. Are you able to choose the most effective way of behaving for the situation at hand?

   c. Are you skillful at performing behaviors? (Note that knowing how you *want* to behave isn't the same as being *able* to behave.)

   d. Do you communicate in a way that leaves others satisfied?

4. After reviewing your partner's answers, identify the situations in which your communication is most competent.

5. Choose a situation in which you would like to communicate more competently, and with the help of your partner:

   a. Determine whether your repertoire of behaviors needs to be expanded.

   b. Identify the ways in which you need to communicate more skillfully.

   c. Develop ways to monitor your behavior in the key situation to get feedback on your effectiveness.

© Images.com/Corbis

Competence in Intercultural Communication

Throughout history, most people lived and died within a few miles of where they were born. They rarely had much to do with people from different backgrounds. Today is a different story. To use a familiar metaphor, we live in a "global village," our lives intertwined with people from very different personal histories and communication styles.

Relatively cheap transportation has reduced the barrier of distance, making international travel easier for more people than ever before, and cell phones and the Internet have made it possible to meet and keep in touch with people from almost anywhere on earth.

Immigration and birth patterns have changed the ethnic makeup of the United States and other Western countries. For example, the population of Miami is two-thirds Hispanic; the same percentage of Washington, D.C. residents are African-American, and one-third of San Franciscans are Asian Americans.[72] According to the U.S. Census Bureau, the nation's Hispanic and Asian populations will triple over the next half-century, and non-Hispanic whites will represent about one-half of the total population by 2050.[73]

As our world becomes more multicultural, the likelihood of working with people from different parts of the world is greater than ever. Over 10,000 foreign companies and their subsidiaries operate in the United States.[74] Eight of the 10 leading chemical companies, 9 of the 10 leading banks, and all of the leading construction companies are based outside the U.S.[75] At the same time the North American economy becomes more global and more Americans are working abroad. Over eight million were working overseas in 2003,[76] many for the 3,000 U.S. firms with global operations and others for over 36,000 foreign companies in more than 180 countries.[77]

National and ethnic differences aren't the only dimensions of culture. Within a society co-cultures have different communication practices. Consider just a few co-cultures:

> age (e.g., teen, senior citizen)
> race/ethnicity (e.g., Asian American, Puerto Rican)
> occupation (fashion model, long-distance trucker)
> sexual orientation (lesbian, gay male)
> physical disability (e.g., wheelchair user, deaf)
> religion (e.g., Evangelical Christian, Muslim)
> activity (e.g., biker, gamer)

Some scholars have even characterized men and women as belonging to different co-cultures, claiming that each gender's style of communication is distinct. We'll have more to say about that topic throughout this book.

Communicating successfully with people from different cultural backgrounds calls for the same elements of competence outlined in the pages you have just read. But beyond these basic qualities, communication researchers have identified several other especially important ingredients of successful intercultural communication.[78]

Most obviously, it helps to know the rules of a specific culture. For example, the kind of self-deprecating humor that Americans are likely to find amusing is likely to fall flat among Arabs from the Middle East.[79] But beyond knowing the specific rules of an individual culture, there are also attitudes and skills called "culture-general" that help communicators build relationships with people from other backgrounds.[80]

To illustrate the ingredients of culture-general communication competence, imagine you've just been hired to work in a Japanese-owned company in the United States that has manufacturing operations in Mexico and customers around the world. In your new job, you are surrounded by co-workers, supervisors, and clients who come from cultures and co-cultures that are different from your own. You are also required to make occasional trips abroad. How will you handle the communication demands of this position? Ideally, you'll possess the following attributes.

Motivation   The desire to communicate successfully with strangers is an important start. For example, people high in willingness to communicate with people from other cultures report a greater number of friends from different backgrounds than those who are less willing to reach out.[81] Having the proper motivation is important in all communication, but particularly so in intercultural interactions because they can be quite challenging.

In your multinational company, you'll need motivation to reach out to people whose communication style is different from yours. For example, during visits to China you might first be pleased, and then exhausted to discover that parties and banquets, typically with much alcohol, are part of the business scene. Even if you are a seasoned partygoer, you may need to draw on a deep well of motivation to spend yet another evening of jovially toasting strangers when you would rather be recovering from jet lag and hard work.

Tolerance for Ambiguity   Communicating with people from different backgrounds can be confusing. A tolerance for ambiguity makes it possible to accept, and even embrace, the often equivocal and sometimes downright incomprehensible messages that characterize intercultural communication.

If you happen to work with colleagues raised in traditional Native American co-cultures, you may find them much quieter and less outgoing than you are used to. Your first reaction might be to chalk up this reticence to a lack of friendliness. However, it may just be a reflection of a co-culture in which reticence is valued more than extroversion, and silence more than loquacity. In cross-cultural situations like this, ambiguity is a fact of life, and a challenge.

Open-Mindedness   It's one thing to tolerate ambiguity; it's another thing to become open-minded about cultural differences. There is a natural tendency to view others' communication choices as "wrong" when they don't match our cultural upbringing. In some parts of the world, you may find that women are not regarded with the same attitude of equality that is common in the West. Likewise, in other cultures, you may be aghast at the casual tolerance of poverty beyond anything at home, or with practices of bribery that don't jibe with homegrown notions of what is ethical. In situations like these, principled communicators aren't likely to compromise deeply held beliefs about what is right.

At the same time, competence requires an attitude that recognizes that people who behave differently are most likely following rules that have governed their whole lives. Chapter 3 will offer more guidance on the challenges of viewing the world from others' perspectives.

Knowledge and Skill   The rules and customs that work with one group might be quite different from those that succeed with another. For example, when traveling in Latin America, you are likely find that meetings there usually don't begin or end at their scheduled time, and that it takes the participants quite awhile to "get down to business." Rather than viewing your hosts as irresponsible and unproductive, you'll want to recognize that the meaning of time is not the same in all cultures. Likewise, the gestures others make, the distance they stand from you, and the eye contact they maintain have ambiguous meanings that you'll need to learn and follow.

At your new job, you'll want to engage in *mindfulness*—awareness of your own behavior and that of others.[82] Communicators who lack this quality blunder through intercultural encounters *mindlessly*, oblivious of how their own behavior may confuse or offend others, and how behavior that they consider weird may be simply different. When you're in a mindful state, you can use three strategies for moving toward a more mindful, competent style of intercultural communication.[83] *Passive observation* involves noticing what behaviors members of a different culture use and using these insights to communicate in ways that are most effective. *Active strategies* include reading, watching films, asking experts and members of the other culture how to behave, as well as taking academic courses related to intercultural communication and diversity.[84] The third strategy, *self-disclosure*, involves volunteering personal information to people from the other culture with whom you want to communicate.

One type of self-disclosure is to confess your cultural ignorance: "This is very new to me. What's the right thing to do in this situation?" This approach is the riskiest of the three described here, since some cultures may not value candor and self-disclosure as much as others. Nevertheless, most people are pleased when strangers attempt to learn the practices of their culture, and they are usually more than willing to offer information and assistance.

Summary

Communication is essential on many levels. Besides satisfying practical needs, effective communication can enhance physical health and emotional well-being. As children, we learn about our identity via the messages sent by others, and as adults our self-concept is shaped and refined through social interaction. Communication also satisfies social needs: involvement with others, control over the environment, and giving and receiving affection.

The process of communication is not a linear one that people "do" to one another. Rather, communication is a transactional process in which participants create a relationship by simultaneously sending and receiving messages, many of which are distorted by various types of noise.

Interpersonal communication can be defined quantitatively by the number of people involved or qualitatively by the nature of interaction between them. In a qualitative sense, interpersonal relationships are unique, irreplaceable, interdependent, and intrinsically rewarding. Qualitatively interpersonal communication can occur in computer-mediated contexts as well as in traditional ones. Qualitatively interpersonal communication is relatively infrequent, even in the strongest relationships. Both personal and impersonal communications are useful, and most relationships have both personal and impersonal elements.

All communication, whether personal or impersonal, content or relational, follows the same basic principles. Messages can be intentional or unintentional. It is impossible not to communicate. Communication is irreversible and unrepeatable. Messages have both a content and a relational dimension. Some common misconceptions should be avoided when thinking about communication: Meanings are not in words, but rather in people. More communication does not always make matters better. Communication will not solve all problems. Finally, communication—at least effective communication—is not a natural ability.

Communication competence is the ability to get what you are seeking from others in a manner that maintains the relationship on terms that are acceptable to all parties. Competence doesn't mean behaving the same way in all settings and with all people; rather, competence varies from one situation to another. The most competent communicators have a wide repertoire of behaviors, and they are able to choose the best behavior for a given situation and perform it skillfully. They are able to understand others' points of view and respond with empathy. They also monitor their own behavior and are committed to communicating successfully. In intercultural communication, competence involves having the right motivation, a tolerance for ambiguity, open-mindedness, and the knowledge and skill to communicate effectively.

Key Terms

channel (10)
co-culture (34)
cognitive complexity (31)
communication (14)
communication
    competence (25)
computer-mediated
    communication (CMC) (21)
content dimension (16)
decode (10)

dyad (18)
encode (9)
environment (11)
impersonal communication (18)
instrumental goals (8)
interpersonal communication
    (quantitative and
    qualitative) (18)
linear communication
    model (9)

message (10)
noise (external, physiological,
    psychological) (10)
receiver (10)
relational dimension (16)
self-monitoring (32)
sender (9)
transactional communication
    model (10)

Media Resources

ThomsonNOW For quick access to the online resources that accompany this chapter, access your ThomsonNOW for *Looking Out/Looking In* at www.thomson.edu.com. (See the pages near the inside front and back covers of this book for more about how to access and use these resources.)

The ThomsonNOW online study system helps you identify concepts you don't fully understand, allowing you to put your study time to the best use. Using chapter-by-chapter diagnostic pre-tests, the system creates a **personalized study plan** for each chapter. Each plan directs you to specific resources designed to improve your understanding, including pages from the text in ebook format. Chapter post-tests give you an opportunity to measure how much you've learned and let you know if you are ready for graded quizzes and exams.

ThomsonNOW for *Looking Out/Looking In* also includes the **ABC News video clip** described on page 8; **vocabulary activities** to help you master key terms; self-study **review quizzes** to test your comprehension of the material in this chapter and prepare for exams; **online exercises**, including the Skill Builder and Invitation to Insight activities in the book; **web links** you can use to further explore topics in this chapter; access to a **feature film database** where you can locate information about movies that illustrate communication principles; and access to the

InfoTrac® College Edition searchable database of over 10 million articles from both scholarly journals and the popular press.

Films and Television

ThomsonNOW In addition to the films suggested here, use the link to the ThomsonNOW for *Looking Out/Looking In* to link to the **Film in Communication Database**, where you can locate movie clips that illustrate various aspects of interpersonal communication.

The Importance of Interpersonal Communication

About Schmidt (2002) Rated R
Warren Schmidt (Jack Nicholson) is starving for human interaction. He recently retired from his job, his wife has died unexpectedly, and now he is all alone. He has no close friends or family; his life has become an exercise in quiet desperation.

Warren isn't good at building and maintaining relationships, so he reaches out for human contact in a relatively safe way: by writing lengthy letters to a Tanzanian orphan whom he "met" through a TV ad for a children's charity. Over time, he makes (clumsy) attempts to strike up conversations with in-laws and strangers, and ultimately he tries to restore his strained relationship with his daughter. What Warren learns is that even if interpersonal communication is scary, difficult, and risky, it beats the alternative of loneliness and isolation.

Transactional Communication

Friends (TV series) Rated TV-14
This long-running television series chronicles the interconnected lives of six twenty-something (and later thirty-something) New Yorkers. Over ten seasons, dedicated viewers followed the many changes in the relationships of this group. Knowledge of their complex relational history helps viewers understand and appreciate each episode. This series illustrates the principle that communication is a transactional process. For example, the other characters' affection for Joey and Phoebe leads them to regard their simpleminded statements with affection; Rachel's former relationship with Ross influences their friendship; and everyone's knowledge of Monica's need for order and cleanliness allows them to not take her neurotic comments personally.

Communication Competence

The Office (TV series) Rated TV-14
This TV mock documentary portrays the world of the cubicle jockeys at Dunder Mifflin Paper Supply Company in Scranton, Pennsylvania. Most of the action centers on the exploits of regional manager Michael Scott (Steve Carrell). Michael believes he is funny, a fountain of business wisdom, and revered by his staff. In truth, his misguided sense of humor and bumbling management style make him an object of ridicule. From a communication perspective, Michael is a paragon of poor self-monitoring and incompetent communication.

World's Fastest Indian (2006) Rated PG-13.
New Zealander Burt Munro (Anthony Hopkins) has always dreamed of riding his 1920 Indian motorcycle during Speed Week at Utah's Bonneville Salt Flats. In his 60s, and against all the odds, Burt sets out to live his dream. Along the way, he meets a diverse array of characters including a motorcycle gang, a transvestite hotel clerk, a Latino car salesman, a Native American who lives in the desert, and a U.S. Air Force officer on leave from dropping napalm in Vietnam. In all these encounters, Burt exhibits the kind of intercultural competence described in this chapter. He is extremely open-minded, and he seems quite comfortable with ambiguities that are unlike anything he encountered in his provincial New Zealand hometown. As a consequence, Burt leads a rich and rewarding life, turning potential adversaries into friends. Based on a true story.

Chapter 1 ~ A First Look at Interpersonal Communication

Introduction | Critique | Notes

ALEX THEG
USED BABY SIGN LANGUAGE

TIME   01:04 / 03:44

THOMSON
WADSWORTH

1.   Chapter 1 (pp. 5–9) described how communication satisfies a variety of needs: physical, identity, social, and practical. Identify at least one need from each of these categories that pre-verbal babies could satisfy by using sign language. Discuss how the ability to satisfy these needs could improve the quality of relationship between babies and their caregivers.

Looking Out, Looking In, 12e | Adler and Proctor | Copyright 2008 Thomson Wadsworth

Chapter 1 | Chapter 2 | Chapter 3 | Chapter 4 | Chapter 5 | Chapter 6 | Chapter 7 | Chapter 8
Chapter 9 | Chapter 10 | Chapter 11

Communication and Identity: Creating and Presenting the Self

2

Who are you? Take a moment now to answer this question. You'll need the following list as you read the rest of this chapter, so be sure to complete it now. Try to include all the characteristics that describe you:

> Your moods or feelings (for example, happy, angry, excited)
> Your appearance (for example, attractive, short)
> Your social traits (for example, friendly, shy)
> Talents you have or do not have (for example, musical, nonathletic)
> Your intellectual capacity (for example, smart, slow learner)
> Your strong beliefs (for example, religious, environmentalist)
> Your social roles (for example, parent, girlfriend)
> Your physical condition (for example, healthy, overweight)

Now take a look at what you've written. How did you define yourself? As a student? A man or woman? By your age? Your religion? Your occupation? There are many ways of identifying yourself. List as many ways as you can. You'll probably see that the words you've chosen represent a profile of what you view as your most important characteristics. In other words, if you were required to describe the "real you," this list ought to be a good summary.

Communication and the Self-Concept

What you've done in developing this list is to give a partial description of your **self-concept**: the relatively stable set of perceptions you hold of yourself. If a special mirror existed that reflected not only your physical features but also other aspects of yourself—emotional states, talents, likes, dislikes, values, roles, and so on—the reflection you'd see would be your self-concept.

You probably recognize that the self-concept list you recorded earlier is only a partial one. To make the description complete, you'd have to keep adding items until your list ran into hundreds of words.

Take a moment now to demonstrate the many parts of your self-concept by simply responding to the question "Who am I?" over and over again. Add these responses to the list you started earlier.

Of course, not every item on your self-concept list is equally important. For example, the most significant part of one person's self-concept might consist of social roles, and for another person it might be physical appearance, health, friendships, accomplishments, or skills.

You can discover how much you value each part of your self-concept by rank-ordering the items on your list. Try it now: Place a "1" next to the most fundamental item about you, a "2" next to the second-most fundamental item, and continue in this manner until you've completed your list.

This self-concept you've just described is extremely important. To see just how important it is, try the following exercise.

Invitation to Insight

Take Away

1. Look over the list of words you've just used to describe yourself. If you haven't already done so, pick the ten words that describe the most fundamental aspects of who you are. Be sure that you've organized these words so that the most fundamental one is in first place and the one that is least central to your identity is number 10, arranging the words or phrases in between in their proper order.

2. Now find a comfortable spot where you can think without being interrupted. You can complete this exercise in a group with the leader giving instructions, or you can do it alone by reading the directions yourself when necessary.

3. Close your eyes and get a mental picture of yourself. Besides visualizing your appearance, you should also include in your image your less-observable features: your disposition, your hopes, your concerns, including all the items you described in step 1.

4. Keep this picture in mind, but now imagine what would happen if the tenth item on your list disappeared from your makeup. How would you be different? Does the idea of giving up that item leave you feeling better or worse? How hard was it to let go of that item?

5. Now, without taking back the item you just abandoned, give up the ninth item on your list, and see what difference this makes to you. After pausing to experience your thoughts and feelings, give up each succeeding item on your list one by one.

6. After you've abandoned the number-one feature of who you are, take a few minutes to add back the parts of yourself that you abandoned, and then read on.

For most people this exercise dramatically illustrates just how fundamental the concept of self is. Even when the item being abandoned is an unpleasant one, it's often hard to give it up. And when asked to let go of their most central feelings or thoughts, most people balk. "I wouldn't be *me* without that," they

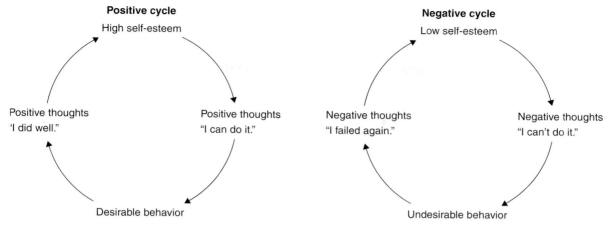

FIGURE 2.1
The Relationship between Self-Esteem and Communication Behavior

insist. Of course, this proves our point: The concept of self is perhaps our most fundamental possession. Knowing who we are is essential because without a self-concept it would be impossible to relate to the world.

Self-esteem is the part of the self-concept that involves evaluations of self-worth. A hypothetical communicator's self-concept might include being quiet, argumentative, or serious. His or her self-esteem would be determined by how he or she felt about these qualities: "I'm glad that I am quiet," or "I am embarrassed about being so quiet," for example.

Figure 2.1 on this page pictures the relationship between self-esteem and communication behavior. People who feel good about themselves have positive expectations about how they will communicate. These expectations increase the chance that communication will be successful, and successes contribute to positive self-evaluations, which reinforce self-esteem. Of course, the same principle can work in a negative way with communicators who have low self-esteem.

Invitation to Insight

Your Self-Esteem

ThomsonNOW Take a self-guided tour of your self-esteem provided by the National Association of Self-Esteem. As you explore, consider how past and present messages (ego-busters and ego-boosters) have shaped your current level of self-esteem. Additionally, speculate about how your current level of self-esteem affects your own communication style and interpersonal relationships. You can find the link to this site through your ThomsonNOW for *Looking Out/Looking In*. The test will take about 10 to 15 minutes.

Biological and Social Roots of the Self

How did you become the kind of communicator you are? Were you born that way? Are you a product of your environment? As you'll now see, the correct answer to both of these questions is "yes."

Biology and the Self Take another look at the "Who am I?" list you developed at the beginning of this chapter. You will almost certainly find some terms that describe your **personality**—characteristic ways that you think and behave across a variety of situations. Your personality tends to be stable throughout your life, and often it grows more pronounced over time.[1] Research suggests that personality is, to a large degree, part of our genetic makeup.[2] For example, people who were judged shy as children still show a distinctive reaction in their brains as adults when they encounter new situations.[3]

In fact, biology accounts for as much as half of some communication-related personality traits, including extroversion,[4] shyness,[5] assertiveness,[6] verbal aggression,[7] and overall willingness to communicate.[8] In other words, to some degree, we come "programmed" to communicate in characteristic ways. You can get a rough measure of your personality by taking the online test described in the Invitation to Insight, "Your Personality Profile" on page 45.

Social scientists have grouped personality traits into five primary categories, which are outlined in Table 2.1.[9] These trait categories seem to be universal, and they are recognized in cultures as diverse as German and Chinese.[10] Take a look at that table now and identify the terms that best describe your personality. Although labels like "neurotic" and "antagonistic" can be hard to acknowledge, the descriptors underneath them may be more typical of you than the words under their "stable" and "agreeable" counterparts. You will notice that several dimensions of these personality types relate to communication. How does your communication reflect your personality?

Personality and self-concept come together most clearly on the neurotic–stable spectrum. As Table 2.1 shows, a communicator with neurotic tendencies is likely to be self-critical and insecure, whereas someone with a more stable personality is likely to feel more self-satisfied and calm about the way he or she communicates. Although most personality traits have both positive and negative characteristics, it's hard to think of *any* benefits of being neurotic. Fortunately, there are ways to challenge and overcome neurotic thinking. Chapter 4 will describe them in detail.

Before you become distressed about being stuck with a personality that makes communication difficult, keep two important points in mind. First, realize

Table 2.1	The "Big Five" Personality Traits		
Extroverted	**Introverted**	**Agreeable**	**Antagonistic**
Sociable	Reserved	Courteous	Rude
Fun-loving	Sober	Selfless	Selfish
Talkative	Quiet	Trusting	Suspicious
Spontaneous	Self-controlled	Cooperative	Uncooperative
Open	**Not Open**	**Neurotic**	**Stable**
Imaginative	Unimaginative	Worried	Calm
Independent	Conforming	Vulnerable	Hardy
Curious	Incurious	Self-pitying	Self-satisfied
Broad interests	Narrow interests	Impatient	Patient
Conscientious	**Undirected**		
Careful	Careless		
Reliable	Undependable		
Persevering	Lax		
Ambitious	Aimless		

that these traits are a matter of degree, not an either-or matter. It's an over-simplification to think of yourself as shy *or* sociable, argumentative *or* agreeable, self-controlled *or* spontaneous. It's more accurate to realize that almost every-one's personality fits at some point on a spectrum for each trait. You may be somewhat shy, a little argumentative, or moderately self-controlled.

Second, while you may have a disposition toward traits like shyness or aggressiveness, you can do a great deal to control how you actually communicate. Even shy people can learn how to reach out to others, and those with aggressive tendencies can learn to communicate in more-sociable ways. Throughout this book you will learn about communication skills that, with practice, you can build into your repertoire.

Finally, realize that although your personality may shape the way you communicate to a degree, your self-concept determines how you *feel about* the way you relate to others. Consider how different self-concepts can lead to very different ways of thinking about your communication:

Quiet	"I'm a coward for not speaking up."
	"I enjoy listening more than talking."
Argumentative	"I'm pushy, and that's obnoxious."
	"I stand up for my beliefs."
Self-controlled	"I'm too cautious."
	"I think carefully before I say or do things."

As you will soon read, our self-concept and self-esteem are shaped to a great extent by both the messages we receive from others and the way we think about ourselves.

Your Personality Profile

ThomsonNOW™ You can get an idea of your personality and how it affects your communication by taking a self-test online. You can find the link to this site through your ThomsonNOW for *Looking Out/Looking In*. The test will take approximately 20 minutes.

Socialization and the Self-Concept   How important are others in shaping our self-concept? Imagine growing up on a deserted island, with no one to talk to or share activities. How would you know how smart you are—or aren't? How would you gauge your attractiveness? How would you decide if you're short or tall, kind or mean, skinny or fat? Even if you could view your reflection in a mirror, you still wouldn't know how to evaluate your appearance without appraisals from others or people with whom to compare yourself. In fact, the messages we receive from the people in our lives play the most important role in shaping how we regard ourselves. To gain an appreciation for this role, try the following exercise.

"Now look what you've done!"

Invitation to Insight

"Ego Boosters" and "Ego Busters"

1. Either by yourself or with a partner, recall someone you know or once knew who was an "ego booster"—who helped enhance your self-esteem by acting in a way that made you feel accepted, competent, worthwhile, important, appreciated, or loved. This person needn't have played a crucial role in your life as long as the role was positive. Often your self-concept is shaped by many tiny nudges as well as by a few giant events. A family member with whom you've spent most of your life can be an "ego booster," but so can the stranger on the street who spontaneously offers an unexpected compliment.

2. Now recall an "ego buster" from your life—someone who acted in a large or small way to reduce your self-esteem. As with ego-booster messages, ego-buster messages aren't always intentional. The acquaintance who forgets your name after you've been introduced or the friend who yawns while you're describing an important problem can diminish your feelings of self-worth.

3. Now that you've thought about how others shape your self-concept, recall a time when you were an ego booster to someone else—when you intentionally or unintentionally boosted another's self-esteem. Don't merely settle for an instance in which you were nice: Look for a time when your actions left another person feeling valued, loved, needed, and so on. You may have to ask the help of others to answer this question.

4. Finally, recall a recent instance in which you were an ego buster for someone else. What did you do to diminish another's self-esteem? Were you aware of the effect of your behavior at the time? Your answer might show that some events we intend as boosters have the effect of busters. For example, you might joke with a friend in what you mean as a friendly gesture, only to discover that your remarks are received as criticism.

After completing the exercise (you *did* complete it, didn't you?), you should begin to see that your self-concept is shaped by those around you. This process of shaping occurs in two ways: reflected appraisal and social comparison.

> We are not only our brother's keeper; in countless large and small ways, we are our brother's maker.
>
> Bonaro Overstreet

As early as 1912, sociologist Charles Cooley used the metaphor of a mirror to identify the process of **reflected appraisal**: the fact that each of us develops a self-concept that reflects the way we believe others see us.[11] In other words, we are likely to feel less valuable, lovable, and capable to the degree that others have communicated ego-busting signals; and we will probably feel good about ourselves to the degree that others affirm our value. The principle of reflected appraisal will become clear when you realize that the self-concept you described in the list at the beginning of this chapter is a product of the positive and negative messages you have received throughout your life.

To illustrate this point further, let's start at the beginning. Children aren't born with any sense of identity: They learn to judge themselves only through the way others treat them. As children learn to speak and understand language, verbal messages contribute to a developing self-concept. Every day a child is bombarded with scores of messages about him- or herself. Some of these are positive: "You're so cute!" "I love you." "What a big girl." Other messages are negative:

Watch me perform!

© SuperStock

I walk a tightrope of
  unique design.
I teeter, falter, recover
  and bow.
You applaud.

I run forward, backward,
  hesitate and bow.
You applaud.
If you don't applaud I'll
  fall.

Cheer me! Hurray me!
Or you push me
Down.

Lenni Shender Goldstein

"What's the matter with you? Can't you do anything right?" "You're a bad boy."
"Leave me alone. You're driving me crazy!" Evaluations like these are the mirror
by which we know ourselves; and because children are trusting souls who have
no other way of viewing themselves, they accept at face value both the positive
and negative evaluations of the apparently all-knowing and all-powerful adults
around them.

These same principles in the formation of the self-concept continue in later
life, especially when messages come from what sociologists term **significant
others**—people whose opinions we especially value. (See the story "Cipher in the

In order to get at any
truth about myself, I
must have contact
with another person.
The other is indispen-
sable to my own exis-
tence, as well as to
my knowledge about
myself.

Jean-Paul Sartre

It is thus with most of us; we are what other people say we are. We know ourselves chiefly by hearsay.

Eric Hoffer

Snow" on pages 49–50 for an example.) A look at the ego boosters and ego busters you described in the previous exercise will show that the evaluations of a few especially important people can be powerful. Family members are the most obvious type of significant other.[12] Others, though, can also be significant others: a special friend, a teacher, or perhaps an acquaintance whose opinion you value can leave an imprint on how you view yourself. To see the importance of significant others, ask yourself how you arrived at your opinion of yourself as a student, as a person attractive to others, as a competent worker, and you'll see that these self-evaluations were probably influenced by the way others regarded you.

The impact of significant others remains strong during adolescence. Inclusion in (or exclusion from) peer groups is a crucial factor in self-concept development for teenagers.[13] The good news is that parents who are understanding of their children's self-concepts during the adolescent years typically have better communication with their teens and can help them create a strong self-concept.[14]

The influence of significant others becomes less powerful as people grow older. After most people approach the age of 30, their self-concepts don't change radically, at least without a conscious effort.[15] By contrast, the self-concept of younger people is still flexible. For example, the self-esteem of about two-thirds of the males in one study (ages 14 to 23) increased.[16] The same study revealed that about 57 percent of females in the same age group grew to feel *less* good about themselves.

So far we have looked at the way by which others' messages shape our self-concept. In addition to these messages, each of us forms our self-image by the process of **social comparison**: evaluating ourselves in terms of how we compare with others.

Two types of social comparison need highlighting. In the first, we decide whether we are *superior* or *inferior* by comparing ourselves to others. Are we attractive or ugly? A success or failure? Intelligent or stupid? It depends on those against whom we measure ourselves.[17] For instance, research shows that young women who regularly compare themselves with ultra-thin media models develop negative appraisals of their own bodies, in some cases leading to eating disorders.[18] In one study, young women's perceptions of their bodies changed for the worse after watching just thirty minutes of televised images of the "ideal" female

ZITS   *BY JERRY SCOTT AND JIM BORGMAN*

Cipher in the Snow

It started with tragedy on a biting cold February morning. I was driving behind the Milford Corners bus as I did most snowy mornings on my way to school. It veered and stopped short at the hotel, which it had no business doing, and I was annoyed as I had to come to an unexpected stop. A boy lurched out of the bus, reeled, stumbled, and collapsed on the snow bank at the curb. The bus driver and I reached him at the same moment. His thin, hollow face was white even against the snow.

"He's dead," the driver whispered.

It didn't register for a minute. I glanced quickly at the scared young faces staring down at us from the school bus. "A doctor! Quick! I'll phone from the hotel. . . ."

"No use, I tell you he's dead." The driver looked down at the boy's still form. "He never even said he felt bad," he muttered. "Just tapped me on the shoulder and said, real quiet, 'I'm sorry. I have to get off at the hotel.' That's all. Polite and apologizing like."

At school, the giggling, shuffling morning noise quieted as the news went down the halls. I passed a huddle of girls. "Who was it? Who dropped dead on the way to school?" I heard one of them half-whisper.

"Don't know his name; some kid from Milford Corners" was the reply.

It was like that in the faculty room and the principal's office. "I'd appreciate your going out to tell the parents," the principal told me. "They haven't a phone and, anyway, somebody from school should go there in person. I'll cover your classes."

"Why me?" I asked. "Wouldn't it be better if you did it?"

© Comstock Images/Picture Quest

"I didn't know the boy," the principal admitted levelly. "And, in last year's sophomore personalities column I note that you were listed as his favorite teacher."

I drove through the snow and cold down the bad canyon road to the Evans place and thought about the boy, Cliff Evans. His favorite teacher! I thought. He hasn't spoken two words to me in two years! I could see him in my mind's eye all right, sitting back there in the last seat in my afternoon literature class. He came in the room by himself and left by himself. "Cliff Evans," I muttered to myself, "a boy

Continued

who never talked." I thought a minute. "A boy who never smiled. I never saw him smile once."

The big ranch kitchen was clean and warm. I blurted out my news somehow. Mrs. Evans reached blindly toward a chair. "He never said anything about bein' ailing."

His stepfather snorted. "He ain't said nothin' about anything since I moved in here."

Mrs. Evans pushed a pan to the back of the stove and began to untie her apron. "Now hold on," her husband snapped. "I got to have breakfast before I go to town. Nothin' we can do now anyway. If Cliff hadn't been so dumb, he'd have told us he didn't feel good."

After school I sat in the office and stared blankly at the records spread out before me. I was to close the file and write the obituary for the school paper. The almost bare sheets mocked the effort. Cliff Evans, white, never legally adopted by stepfather, five young half-brothers and sisters. These meager strands of information and the list of D grades were all the records had to offer.

Cliff Evans had silently come in the school door in the mornings and gone out the school door in the evenings, and that was all. He had never belonged to a club. He had never played on a team. He had never held an office. As far as I could tell he had never done one happy, noisy kid thing. He had never been anybody at all.

How do you go about making a boy into a zero? The grade-school records showed me. The first and second grade teachers' annotations read "sweet, shy child," "timid but eager." Then the third grade note had opened the attack. Some teacher had written in a good, firm hand, "Cliff

won't talk. Uncooperative. Slow learner." The other academic sheep had followed with "dull"; "slow-witted"; "low I.Q." They became correct. The boy's I.Q. score in the ninth grade was listed as 83. But his I.Q. in the third grade had been 106. The score didn't go under 100 until the seventh grade. Even shy, timid, sweet children have resilience. It takes time to break them.

I stomped to the typewriter and wrote a savage report pointing out what education had done to Cliff Evans. I slapped a copy on the principal's desk and another in the sad, dog-eared file. I banged the typewriter and slammed the file and crashed the door shut, but I didn't feel much better. A little boy kept walking after me, a little boy with a peaked, pale face; a skinny body in faded jeans; and big eyes that had looked and searched for a long time and then had become veiled.

I could guess how many times he'd been chosen last to play sides in a game, how many whispered child conversations had excluded him, how many times he hadn't been asked. I could see and hear the faces and voices that said over and over, "You're a nothing, Cliff Evans."

A child is a believing creature. Cliff undoubtedly believed them. Suddenly it seemed clear to me: When finally there was nothing left at all for Cliff Evans, he collapsed on a snowbank and went away. The doctor might list "heart failure" as the cause of death, but that wouldn't change my mind.

We couldn't find ten students in the school who had known Cliff well enough to attend the funeral as his friends. So the student body officers and a committee from the junior class went as a group to the church,

being politely sad. I attended the services with them, and sat through it with a lump of cold lead in my chest and a big resolve growing through me.

I've never forgotten Cliff Evans nor that resolve. He has been my challenge year after year, class after class. I look for veiled eyes or bodies scrouged into a seat in an alien world. "Look, kids," I say silently, "I may not do anything else for you this year, but not one of you is going to come out of here a nobody. I'll work or fight to the bitter end doing battle with society and the school board, but I won't have one of you coming out of here thinking himself a zero."

Most of the time—not always, but most of the time—I've succeeded.

Jean Mizer

form.[19] Men, too, who compare themselves to media-idealized male physiques, evaluate their bodies negatively.[20] You'll probably never be as beautiful as a Hollywood star, as agile as a professional athlete, or as wealthy as a millionaire. When you consider the matter logically, these facts don't mean you're worthless. Nonetheless, many people judge themselves against unreasonable standards and suffer accordingly.[21] These distorted self-images can lead to serious behavioral disorders such as depression, anorexia nervosa, and bulimia. You'll read more about how to avoid placing perfectionistic demands on yourself in Chapter 4.

In addition to feelings of superiority and inferiority, social comparison provides a way to decide if we are the *same as* or *different from* others. A child who is interested in ballet and who lives in a setting where such preferences are regarded as weird will start to accept this label if there is no support from others. Likewise, adults who want to improve the quality of their relationships but are surrounded by friends and family who don't recognize or acknowledge the importance of these matters may think of themselves as oddballs. Thus, it's easy to recognize that the **reference groups** against which we compare ourselves play an important role in shaping our view of ourselves.

You might argue that not every part of one's self-concept is shaped by others, insisting that there are certain objective facts that are recognizable by self-observation. After all, nobody needs to tell a person that he is taller than others, speaks with an accent, has acne, and so on. These facts are obvious. Though it's true that some features of the self are immediately apparent, the *significance* we attach to them—the rank we assign them in the hierarchy of our list and the interpretation we give them—depends greatly on the opinions of others. After all, many of your features are readily observable, yet you don't find them important at all because nobody has regarded them as significant.

We once heard a woman in her 80s describing her youth. "When I was a girl," she declared, "we didn't worry about weight. Some people were skinny and others were plump, and we pretty much accepted the bodies God gave us." In those days it was unlikely that weight would have found its way onto the self-concept list you constructed because it wasn't considered significant. Compare this attitude with what you find today: It's seldom that you pick up a popular magazine or visit a bookstore without reading about the latest diet fads, and television ads are filled with scenes of slender, happy people. As a result you'll rarely find a person who doesn't complain about the need to "lose a few pounds." Obviously, the reason for such concern comes from the attention paid to fitness. We generally see slimness as desirable because others tell us it is. In a society where obesity is the ideal, a person who regards herself as extremely heavy would be a beauty. In the same way, the fact that one is single or married, solitary or sociable, aggressive or passive takes on meaning depending on the interpretation that society attaches to those traits.

By now you might be thinking, "It's not my fault that I've always been shy or insecure. Because I developed a picture of myself as a result of the way others have treated me, I can't help being what I am." Though it's true that to a certain extent you are a product of your environment, to believe that you are forever doomed to a poor self-concept would be a big mistake. Having held a poor self-image in the past is no reason for continuing to do so in the future. You *can* change your attitudes and behaviors, as you'll soon read.

Characteristics of the Self-Concept

Now that you have a better idea of how your self-concept has developed, we can take a closer look at some of its characteristics.

Once riding in old Baltimore,
Heart-filled, head-filled with glee,
I saw a Baltimorean
Keep looking straight at me.

Now I was eight and very small,
And he was no whit bigger,
And so I smiled, but he poked out
His tongue and called me, "Nigger."

I saw the whole of Baltimore
From May until December:
Of all the things that happened there
That's all that I remember.

Countee Cullen, "Incident"

Self-love, My liege, is
not so vile a sin as
self-neglecting.

Shakespeare. *King Henry V*

The Self-Concept Is Subjective   Although we tend to believe that our self-concept is accurate, in truth it may well be distorted. Some people view themselves more favorably than objective facts would merit. For example, researchers have found that there is no relationship between the way college students rate their ability as interpersonal communicators, public speakers, or listeners and their true effectiveness. In all cases, the self-reported communication skill is higher than actual performance. Similarly, online daters often have a "foggy mirror"—that is, they see themselves more positively than others do.[22] This leads to inflated self-descriptions that don't always match what an objective third party might say about them.

Not all distortion of the self-concept is positive. Many people view themselves more harshly than the objective facts warrant. We have all experienced a temporary case of the "uglies," convinced that we look much worse than others assure us we really look. Research confirms what common sense suggests: People are more critical of themselves when they are experiencing these negative moods than when they are feeling more positive.[23] Although we all suffer occasional bouts of self-doubt that affect our communication, some people suffer from long-term or even permanent states of excessive self-doubt and criticism.[24] It's easy to understand how this chronic condition can influence the way they approach and respond to others.

Distorted self-evaluations like these can occur for several reasons. One reason is *obsolete information*. The effects of past failures in school or social relations can linger long after they have occurred, even though such events don't predict failure in the future. Likewise, your past successes don't guarantee future success. Perhaps your jokes used to be well received or your work was superior, but now the facts have changed.

Distorted feedback also can create a self-image that is worse or better than the facts warrant. Overly critical parents are one of the most common causes of a negative self-image. In other cases the remarks of cruel friends, uncaring teachers, excessively demanding employers, or even memorable strangers can have a lasting effect. Other distorted messages are unrealistically positive. A boss may think of herself as an excellent manager because her assistants shower her with false praise in order to keep their jobs or gain promotions. Likewise, a child's inflated ego may be based on the praise of doting parents.

Along with obsolete information and distorted feedback, another cause for a strongly negative self-concept is the emphasis on *perfection*, which is common in our society. From the time most of us learn to understand language we are exposed to models who appear to be perfect. Children's stories and advertisements imply that the way to be a hero, the way to be liked and admired, is to show no flaws. Unfortunately, many parents perpetuate the myth of perfection by refusing to admit that they are ever mistaken or unfair. Children, of course, accept this perfectionist façade for a long time, not being in any position to dispute the wisdom of such powerful beings. And from the behavior of the adults around them comes a clear message: "A well-adjusted, successful person has no faults." Given this naive belief that everyone else is perfect and the knowledge that one isn't, it's easy to see how one's self-concept would suffer.

Don't misunderstand: It's not wrong to aim at perfection as an *ideal.* We're suggesting only that achieving this state of perfection is usually not possible, and to expect that you should do so is a sure ticket to an inaccurate and unnecessarily low self-esteem.

A final reason why people often sell themselves short is connected to *social expectations.* Curiously, the perfectionist society to which we belong rewards those people who downplay the strengths we demand that they possess (or pretend to possess). We term these people "modest" and find their behavior agreeable. On the other hand, we consider those who honestly appreciate their strengths to be "braggarts" or "egotists," confusing them with the people who boast about accomplishments they do not possess.[25] This convention leads most of us to talk freely about our shortcomings while downplaying our accomplishments. It's all right to proclaim that you're miserable if you have failed to do well on a project; but it's considered boastful to express your pride at a job well done.

After a while we begin to believe the types of statements we repeatedly make. The disparaging remarks are viewed as modesty and become part of our self-concept, and the strengths and accomplishments go unmentioned and are thus forgotten. And in the end we see ourselves as much worse than we are.

Self-esteem may be based on inaccurate thinking, but it still has a powerful effect on the way we relate to others. Table 2.2 summarizes some important differences between communicators with high and low self-esteem. Differences like these make sense when you realize that people who dislike themselves are likely to believe that others won't like them either. Realistically or not, they imagine that others are constantly viewing them critically, and they accept these imagined or real criticisms as more proof that they are indeed unlikable people. Sometimes this low self-esteem is manifested in hostility toward others because the communicator takes the approach that the only way to look good is to put others down.

One way to avoid falling into the trap of becoming overly critical is to recognize your strengths. The following exercise will give you a chance to suspend the ordinary rules of modesty and appreciate yourself publicly for a change.

The Self-Concept Resists Change   Despite the fact that we all change, there is a tendency to cling to an existing self-concept, even when evidence shows that it is obsolete. This tendency to seek and attend to information that conforms to an existing self-concept has been labeled **cognitive conservatism**.

This tendency toward cognitive conservatism leads us to seek out people who support our self-concept. For example, both college students and married couples with high self-esteem seek out partners who view them favorably, whereas those with negative self-esteem are more inclined to interact with people who view them unfavorably.[26] It appears that we are less concerned with learning the "truth" about ourselves than with reinforcing a familiar self-concept.

It's understandable why we're reluctant to revise a previously favorable self-concept. A student who did well in earlier years but now has failed to study might be unwilling to admit that the label "good scholar" no longer applies. Likewise, a previously industrious worker might resent a supervisor's mentioning increased absences and low productivity. These people aren't *lying* when they insist that they're doing well in spite of the facts to the contrary; they honestly believe that the old truths still hold precisely because their self-concepts are so resistant to change.

Curiously, the tendency to cling to an outmoded self-perception also holds when the new self-perception would be more favorable than the old one. We

I am not what I think I am. I am not what you think I am. I am what I think you think I am.

Aaron Bleiberg
and Harry Leubling

Table 2.2	**Differences between Communicators with High and Low Self-Esteem**

People with High Self-Esteem

1. Likely to think well of others.
2. Expect to be accepted by others.
3. Evaluate their own performance more favorably than people with low self-esteem.
4. Perform well when being watched: not afraid of others' reactions.
5. Work harder for people who demand high standards of performance.
6. Inclined to feel comfortable with others they view as superior in some way.
7. Able to defend themselves against negative comments of others.

People with Low Self-Esteem

1. Likely to disapprove of others.
2. Expect to be rejected by others.
3. Evaluate their own performance less favorably than people with high self-esteem.
4. Perform poorly when being watched: sensitive to possible negative reaction.
5. Work harder for undemanding, less-critical people.
6. Feel threatened by people they view as superior in some way.
7. Have difficulty defending themselves against others' negative comments; more easily influenced.

Summarized by Don E. Hamachek. *Encounters with the Self*, 2nd ed. (New York: Holt, Rinehart, and Winston, 1982), pp. 3–5.

recall a former student whom almost anyone would have regarded as beautiful, with physical features attractive enough to appear in any glamour magazine. In spite of her appearance, in a class exercise this woman characterized herself as "ordinary" and "unattractive." When questioned by her classmates, she described how as a child her teeth were extremely crooked and how she had worn braces for several years in her teens to correct this problem. During this time she was often kidded by her friends, who never let her forget her "metal mouth," as she put it. Even though the braces had been off for two years, our student reported that she still saw herself as ugly and brushed aside our compliments by insisting that we were just saying these things to be nice—she knew how she *really* looked.

Examples like this show one problem that occurs when we resist changing an inaccurate self-concept. Our student denied herself a much happier life by clinging to an obsolete picture of herself. In the same way, some communicators insist that they are less talented or less worthy of friendship than others would suggest, thus creating their own miserable world when it needn't exist. These unfortunate souls probably resist changing because they aren't willing to go through the disorientation that comes from redefining themselves, correctly anticipating that it *is* an effort to think of oneself in a new way. Whatever their reasons, it's sad to see people in such an unnecessary state.

A second problem arising from the persistence of an inaccurate self-concept is self-delusion and lack of growth. If you hold an unrealistically favorable picture of yourself, you won't see the real need for change that may exist. Instead of

It has become something of a cliché to observe that if we do not love ourselves, we cannot love anyone else. This is true enough, but it is only part of the picture. If we do not love ourselves, it is almost impossible to believe fully that we are loved by someone else. It is almost impossible to accept love. It is almost impossible to receive love. No matter what our partner does to show that he or she cares, we do not experience the devotion as convincing because we do not feel lovable to ourselves.

Nathaniel Branden, *The Psychology of Romantic Love*

Invitation to Insight

Recognizing Your Strengths

1. This exercise can be done either alone or with a group. If you are with others, sit in a circle so that everyone can see one another.

2. Each person should share three personal strengths or accomplishments. These needn't feature areas in which you are an expert, and they don't have to be concerned with momentous feats. On the contrary, it's perfectly acceptable to talk about some part of yourself that leaves you feeling pleased or proud. For instance, you might say that, instead of procrastinating, you completed a school assignment before the last minute, that you spoke up to a friend even though you were afraid of disapproval, or that you bake a fantastic chocolate cake.

3. If you're at a loss for items, ask yourself:

   a. What are some ways in which you've grown in the past year? How are you more skillful, wiser, or a better person than you previously were?

   b. Why do certain friends or family members care about you? What features do you possess that make them appreciate you?

4. After you've finished, consider the experience. Did you have a hard time thinking of things to share? Would it have been easier to list the things that are *wrong* with you? If so, is this because you are truly a wretched person, or is it because you are in the habit of stressing your defects and ignoring your strengths? Consider the impact of such a habit on your self-concept, and ask yourself whether it wouldn't be wiser to strike a better balance distinguishing between your strengths and weaknesses.

learning new talents, working to change a relationship, or improving your physical condition, you'll stay with the familiar and comfortable delusion that everything is all right. As time goes by, this delusion becomes more and more difficult to maintain, leading to a third type of problem: defensiveness.

To understand this problem, you need to remember that communicators who are presented with information that contradicts their self-perception have two choices: They can either accept the new data and change their perception accordingly, or they can keep their original perception and in some way refute the new information. Because most communicators are reluctant to downgrade a favorable image of themselves, their tendency is to opt for refutation, either by discounting the information and rationalizing it away or by counterattacking the person who transmitted it. The problem of defensiveness is so great that we will examine it in Chapter 10.

Culture, Gender, and Identity

We have already seen how experiences in the family, especially during childhood, shape our sense of who we are. Along with the messages we receive at home, many other forces shape our identity, and thus our communication, including age, physical ability/disability, sexual orientation, and socioeconomic status. Along with these forces, culture and gender are powerful forces in shaping how we view ourselves and others and how we communicate. We will examine each of these forces now.

Culture   Although we seldom recognize the fact, our sense of self is shaped, often in subtle ways, by the culture in which we have been reared.[27] Most Western cultures are highly individualistic, whereas traditional other cultures—most Asian ones, for example—are much more collective. When asked to identify themselves, individualistic people in the United States, Canada, Australia, and Europe would probably respond by giving their first name, surname, street, town, and country. Many Asians do it the other way around.[28] If you ask Hindus for their identity, they will give you their caste and village as well as their name. The Sanskrit formula for identifying one's self begins with lineage and goes on to state family, house, and ends with one's personal name.[29] When members of different cultures were asked to create an "I am" list similar to the one you completed earlier in this chapter, those from collectivist cultures made far more group references than those from individualistic cultures.[30]

These conventions for naming aren't just cultural curiosities: They reflect a very different way of viewing one's self and of what kinds of relationships are important. In collective cultures a person gains identity by belonging to a group. This means that the perceived degree of interdependence among members of the society and its subgroups is high. Feelings of pride and self-worth are likely to be shaped not only by what the individual does but also by behavior of other members of the community. This linkage to others explains the traditional Asian denial of self-importance—a strong contrast to the self-promotion that is common in individualistic western cultures.[31] In Chinese written language, for example, the pronoun *I* looks very similar to the word for selfish.[32] Table 2.3 summarizes some differences between individualistic cultures and more collective ones.

This sort of cultural difference isn't just a matter of interest to anthropologists. It shows up in the level of comfort or anxiety that people feel when communicating. In collective societies, there is a higher degree of communication apprehension. For example, as a group, residents of China, South Korea, and Japan exhibit a significantly higher degree of anxiety about speaking out than do members of individualistic cultures such as the United States and Australia.[33] It's important to realize that different levels of communication apprehension don't mean that shyness is a "problem" in some cultures. In fact, just the opposite is true: In these societies reticence is valued. When the goal is to *avoid* being the nail that sticks out, it's logical to feel nervous when you make yourself appear different by calling attention to yourself. A self-concept that includes "assertive" might make a westerner feel proud, but in much of Asia it would more likely be cause for shame.

The difference between individualism and collectivism shows up in everyday interaction. Communication researcher Stella Ting-Toomey has developed a theory that explains cultural differences in important norms, such as honesty and directness.[34] She suggests that in individualistic western cultures where there is a strong "I" orientation, the norm of speaking directly is honored; whereas in collectivistic cultures, where the main desire is to build connections between the self and others, indirect approaches that maintain harmony are considered more desirable. "I gotta be me" could be the motto of a westerner, but "If I hurt you, I hurt myself" is closer to the Asian way of thinking.

In Japan, in fact, everything had been made level and uniform—even humanity. By one official count, 90 percent of the population regarded themselves as middle-class; in schools, it was not the outcasts who beat up the conformists, but vice versa. Every Japanese individual seemed to have the same goal as every other—to become like every other Japanese individual. The word for "different," I was told, was the same as the word for "wrong." And again and again in Japan, in contexts varying from the baseball stadium to the watercolor canvas, I heard the same unswerving, even maxim: "The nail that sticks out must be hammered down."

Pico Iyer,
Video Night in Katmandu

Table 2.3	**The Self in Individualistic and Collectivistic Cultures**

Individualistic Cultures

- Self is separate, unique individual; should be independent, self-sufficient
- Individual should take care of him-/herself and immediate family
- Many flexible group memberships; friends based on shared interests and activities
- Reward for individual achievement and initiative; individual decisions encouraged; individual credit and blame assigned
- High value on autonomy, change, youth, individual security, equality

Collectivistic Cultures

- People belong to extended families or in-groups; "we" or group orientation
- Person should take care of extended family before self
- Emphasis on belonging to a very few permanent in-groups that have a strong influence over the person
- Reward for contribution to group goals and well-being; cooperation with in-group members; group decisions valued; credit and blame shared
- High value on duty, order, tradition, age, group security, status, and hierarchy

Adapted by Sandra Sudweeks from material in H. C. Triandis, "Cross-Cultural Studies of Individualism and Collectivism," in J. Berman, ed., *Nebraska Symposium on Motivation* 37 (Lincoln: University of Nebraska Press, 1990), pp. 41–133.

You don't need to travel overseas to appreciate the influence of culture on the self. Within societies, co-cultural identity plays an important role in how we see ourselves and others. For example, ethnicity can have a powerful effect on how people think of themselves and how they communicate. Recall how you described yourself in the "Who Am I?" list you created when you began this chapter. If you are a member of a nondominant ethnic group, it's likely that you included your ethnicity in the most important parts of who you are. There's no surprise here: If society keeps reminding you that your ethnicity is important, then you begin to think of yourself in those terms. If you are part of the dominant majority, you probably aren't as conscious of your ethnicity. Nonetheless, it plays an important part in your self-concept. Being part of the majority increases the chances that you have a sense of belonging to the society in which you live and of entitlement to being treated fairly. These are feelings that members of less privileged ethnic groups often don't have.

Sex and Gender   One way to appreciate the tremendous importance of gender on your sense of self is to imagine how your identity would be different if you had been born as a member of the opposite sex. Would you express your emotions in the same way? Deal with conflict? Relate to friends and strangers? The answer is almost certainly a resounding "no."

From the earliest months of life, being male or female shapes the way others communicate with us, and thus how they shape our sense of self. Think about the first questions most people ask when a child is born. One of them is almost always "Is it a boy or a girl?" As the "Cathy" cartoon on the next page shows, after most people know what the baby "is," they often behave accordingly.[35] They use different pronouns and often choose gender-related nicknames. With boys, comments often focus on size, strength, and activity; comments about girls more often address beauty, sweetness, and facial responsiveness. It's not surprising that these messages shape a child's sense of identity and how he or she will communicate. The implicit message is that some ways of behaving are masculine and others feminine. Little girls, for example, are more likely to be reinforced for acting "sweet" than are little boys. The same principle operates in adulthood: A man who stands up for his beliefs might get approval for being "tough" or "persistent," whereas a woman who behaves in the same way could be described by critics as a "nag" or "bitch."[36] It's not hard to see how the gender roles and labels like these can have a profound effect on how men and women view themselves and on how they communicate.

Self-esteem is also influenced by gender. In a society that values competitiveness more in men than in women, it isn't surprising that the self-esteem of adolescent young men is closely related to having abilities that are superior in some way to those of their peers, whereas teenage women's self-worth is tied more closely to the success of their social relationships and verbal skills.[37]

Don't resign yourself to being a prisoner of expectations about your gender. Research demonstrates that our sense of self is shaped strongly by the people with whom we interact and by the contexts in which we communicate.[38] For example, a nonaggressive young man who might feel unwelcome and inept in a macho environment might gain new self-esteem by finding others who appreciate his style of communicating. A woman whose self-esteem is stifled by the limited expectations of bosses and co-workers can look for more hospitable places to work. Children usually can't choose the reference groups that shape their identities, but adults can.

The Self-Fulfilling Prophecy and Communication

The self-concept is such a powerful force on the personality that it not only determines how you see yourself in the present but also can actually influence your future behavior and that of others. Such occurrences come about through a phenomenon called the self-fulfilling prophecy.

A **self-fulfilling prophecy** occurs when a person's expectations of an event, and his or her subsequent behavior based on those expectations, make the event more likely to occur than would otherwise have been true. A self-fulfilling prophecy involves four stages:

1. Holding an expectation (for yourself or for others)
2. Behaving in accordance with that expectation
3. The expectation coming to pass
4. Reinforcing the original expectation

You can see how this process operates by considering an example. Imagine you're scheduled to interview for a job you really want. You are nervous about how you'll do, and not at all sure you are really qualified for the position. You share your concerns with a professor who knows you well and a friend who works for the company. Both assure you that you're perfect for the job and that the firm would be lucky to have you as an employee. Based on these comments, you come to the interview feeling good about yourself. As a result, you speak with authority and sell yourself with confidence. The employers are clearly impressed, and you receive the job offer. Your conclusion: "My friend and professor were right: I'm the kind of person an employer would want!"

This example illustrates the four stages of a self-fulfilling prophecy. Thanks to the assurances of your professor and friend, your expectations about the interview were upbeat (Stage 1). Because of your optimistic attitude, you communicated confidently in the interview (Stage 2). Your confident behavior—along with your other qualifications—led to a job offer (Stage 3). Finally, the positive results reinforced your positive self-assessment, and you'll probably approach future interviews with greater assurance (Stage 4).

Expectations shape communication in powerful ways, but they don't explain or affect all subsequent behavior. There are certainly times when the expectation of an event's outcome won't bring it about. Your hope of drawing an ace in a card game won't in any way affect the chance of that card turning up in an already shuffled deck, and your belief that good weather is coming won't stop the rain from falling. In the same way, believing that you'll do well in a job interview when you're clearly not qualified for the job is unrealistic. Similarly, there will probably be people you don't like and occasions you won't enjoy, no matter what your attitude. To connect the self-fulfilling prophecy with the "power of positive thinking" is an oversimplification.

Keeping these qualifications in mind, you will find it important to recognize the tremendous influence that self-fulfilling prophecies play in our lives. To a great extent we become what we believe. In this sense, we and those around us constantly create and re-create our self-concepts.

Types of Self-Fulfilling Prophecies   There are two types of self-fulfilling prophecies. *Self-imposed prophecies* occur when your own expectations influence your behavior. In sports you've probably "psyched" yourself into playing either better or worse than usual, so that the only explanation for your unusual performance was your attitude. Similarly, you've probably faced an audience at one time or another with a fearful attitude and forgotten your remarks, not because you were unprepared, but because you said to yourself, "I know I'll blow it."

Research has demonstrated the power of self-imposed prophecies. In one study, communicators who believed they were incompetent proved less likely than others to pursue rewarding relationships and more likely to sabotage their existing relationships than did people who were less critical of themselves.[39] On the other hand, students who perceived themselves as capable achieved more academically.[40] In another study, subjects who were sensitive to social rejection tended to expect rejection, perceive it where it might not have existed, and over-react to their exaggerated perceptions in ways that jeopardized the quality of their relationships.[41] Research also suggests that communicators who feel anxious about giving speeches seem to create self-fulfilling prophecies about doing poorly that cause them to perform less effectively.[42]

Self-imposed prophecies operate in many ways that affect everyday communication. You've had the experience of waking up in a cross mood and saying to yourself, "This will be a bad day." After you made such a decision, you may have acted in ways that made it come true. If you approached a class expecting to be bored, you most probably did lose interest, owing partly to a lack of attention on your part. If you avoided the company of others because you expected they had nothing to offer, your expectations would have been confirmed—nothing exciting or new did happen to you. On the other hand, if you approached the same day with the idea that it could be a good one, this expectation probably would have been met also. Researchers have found that putting a smile on your face, even if you're not in a good mood, can lead to a more positive disposition.[43] Likewise, if you approach a class determined to learn something, you probably will—even if it's how not to instruct students. In these cases and ones like them, your attitude has a great deal to do with how you see yourself and how you will behave.

A second category of self-fulfilling prophecies is imposed by one person on another, so that the expectations and behaviors of one person govern another's actions. The classic example was demonstrated by Robert Rosenthal and Lenore Jacobson in a study they described in their book *Pygmalion in the Classroom*.[44] The experimenters told teachers that 20 percent of the children in a certain elementary school showed unusual potential for intellectual growth. The names of these 20 percent were drawn by means of a table of random numbers, which is to say that the names were drawn out of a hat. Eight months later these unusual or "magic" children showed significantly greater gains in IQ than did the remaining children, who had not been singled out for the teachers' attention. The change in the teachers' behavior toward these allegedly "special" students led to changes in the intellectual performance of these randomly selected children. Among other things, the teachers gave the "smart" students more time to answer questions, more feedback, and more praise. In other words, the selected children did better—not because they were any more intelligent than their classmates, but because their teachers held higher expectations for them and treated them accordingly.

To put this phenomenon in context with the self-concept, we can say that when a teacher communicates to a child the message "I think you're bright," the child accepts that evaluation and changes her self-concept to include it. Unfortunately, we can assume that the same principle holds for students whose teachers send the message "I think you're stupid."

This type of self-fulfilling prophecy has been shown to be a powerful force for shaping the self-concept and thus the behavior of people in a wide range of settings outside the schools.[45] In psychotherapy, patients who believe they will benefit from treatment often do so regardless of the type of treatment they receive. In the same vein, when a doctor believes that a patient will improve, the patient may do so precisely because of this expectation, whereas another person for whom the doctor has little hope often fails to recover. Apparently the patient's self-concept as sick or well—as shaped by the doctor—plays an important role in determining the actual state of health.

Notice that the observer must do more than just *believe* to create a self-fulfilling prophecy for the person who is the target of the expectations. The observer also must *communicate* that belief in order for the prediction to have any

The difference between a lady and a flower girl is not how she behaves, but how she's treated. I shall always be a flower girl to Professor Higgins, because he always treats me as a flower girl, and always will; but I know I can be a lady to you, because you always treat me as a lady, and always will.

Eliza Doolittle, in G. B. Shaw's *Pygmalion*

"I don't sing because I am happy. I am happy because I sing."

effect. If parents have faith in their children, but the kids aren't aware of that confidence, they won't be affected by their parents' expectations. If a boss has concerns about an employee's ability to do a job but keeps those concerns to herself, the employee won't be influenced. In this sense, the self-fulfilling prophecies imposed by one person on another are as much a communication phenomenon as a psychological one.

Changing Your Self-Concept

After reading this far, you know more clearly just what the self-concept is, how it is formed, and how it affects communication. But we still haven't focused directly on perhaps the most important question of all: How can you change the parts of your self-concept with which you aren't happy? As you read earlier, a significant part of our communication style is part of our genetic makeup. Still, we have the power to change a great deal of our communication-related traits.[46] There's certainly no quick method for becoming the person you'd like to be: Personal growth and self-improvement are a lifetime process. But we can offer several suggestions that will help you move closer to your goals.

Have a Realistic Perception of Yourself   As you've already read, unrealistic perceptions sometimes come from giving yourself more credit than you deserve. Others come from being overly self-critical. By showing the self-concept list you developed on page 41 to others who know you, you can see whether you have been selling yourself short. A periodic session of recognizing your strengths such as you tried earlier in this chapter is often a good way to put your strengths and weaknesses into perspective.

An unrealistically poor self-concept can also arise from the inaccurate feedback of others. Perhaps you are in an environment where you receive an excessive number of prickly messages, many of which are undeserved, and a minimum of fuzzy messages. We've known many homemakers, for example, who have returned to college after many years spent in homemaking, where they received virtually no recognition for their intellectual strengths. It's amazing that these people have the

---

There is a joke which goes right to the heart of this matter. It is about a man whose tire goes flat on a dark and lonely country road. When he discovers that he doesn't have a jack, he recalls seeing a farm house about a mile back. And so he starts to walk there in the hopes of borrowing one. While he is walking, he talks to himself about his situation: "Wow, I'm really stranded here. The guy will probably want a few dollars to lend me his jack. Why should he do it for nothing? Everyone wants to make a few bucks. A few bucks! If I don't get the jack, I'll never get out of here. He'll realize that, and probably want fifteen dollars, maybe twenty-five dollars. Twenty-five dollars? This guy's really got me by the old cashews. He'll ask fifty dollars, for sure— maybe a hundred."

Well, he goes on in this way until he reaches the farm house. He knocks at the door. An elderly farmer answers and with a cheerful smile asks, "Is there something I can do for you, young man?" "Do for me? Do for me?" says the man, "I'll tell you what you can do, you can take your god-damn jack and shove it!"

. . . If, as in this case, you predict that you will not be lent a jack in a spirit of gracious cooperation, you prepare yourself for the confrontation in such a way that you guarantee the jack will not be lent in a spirit of gracious cooperation. Your prediction is transformed into a fact, which then becomes the reality.

From Neil Postman, *Crazy Talk, Stupid Talk*

There is an old joke about a man who was asked if he could play a violin and answered, "I don't know. I've never tried." This is psychologically a very wise reply. Those who have never tried to play a violin really do not know whether they can or not. Those who say too early in life and too firmly, "No, I'm not at all musical," shut themselves off prematurely from whole areas of life that might have proved rewarding. In each of us there are unknown possibilities, undiscovered potentialities—and one big advantage of having an open self-concept rather than a rigid one is that we shall continue to expose ourselves to new experiences and therefore we shall continue to discover more and more about ourselves as we grow older.

S. I. Hayakawa

courage to come to college at all, so low are their self-concepts; but come they do, and most are thrilled to find that they are much brighter and more competent intellectually than they suspected. In the same way, workers with overly critical supervisors, children with cruel "friends," and students with unsupportive teachers all are prone to low self-concepts owing to excessively negative feedback.

If you fall into this category, it's important to put the unrealistic evaluations you receive into perspective and then to seek out more supportive people who will acknowledge your assets as well as point out your liabilities. Doing so is often a quick and sure boost.

Have Realistic Expectations It's important to realize that some of your dissatisfaction might come from expecting too much of yourself. If you demand that you handle every act of communication perfectly, you're bound to be disappointed. Nobody is able to handle every conflict productively, to be totally relaxed and skillful in conversations, or to be 100 percent helpful when others have problems. Expecting yourself to reach such unrealistic goals is to doom yourself to unhappiness at the start.

Sometimes it's easy to be hard on yourself because everyone around you seems to be handling themselves so much better than you. It's important to recognize that much of what seems like confidence and skill in others is a front to hide uncertainty. Others may be suffering from the same self-imposed demands of perfection that you impose on yourself.

Even in cases where others definitely seem more competent than you, it's best to judge yourself against your own growth and not against the behavior of others. Rather than feel miserable because you're not as talented as an expert, realize that you probably are a better, wiser, or more skillful person than you used to be and that this is a legitimate source of satisfaction.

Have the Will to Change Often we say we want to change, but we aren't willing to do the necessary work. In such cases it's clear that the responsibility for growing rests squarely on our shoulders, as the exercise on page 63 shows.

As this exercise demonstrates, we often maintain an unrealistic self-concept by claiming that we "can't" be the person we'd like to be when in fact we're simply not willing to do what's required. You *can* change in many ways, if only you are willing to make the effort.

Have the Skill to Change Often trying isn't enough. In some instances you would change if you knew how to do so. To see if this is the case for you, go back to your list of "can'ts" and "won'ts" and see if any items there are more appropriately "don't know hows." If so, then the way to change is to learn how. You can do so in two ways.

First, you can seek advice—from books such as this one, the references listed on the chapter website, and other printed sources. You can also get advice from

Skill Builder

Reevaluating Your "Can'ts"

1. Choose a partner and for 5 minutes or so take turns making and listing statements that begin with "I can't. . . ." Try to focus your statements on your relationships with family, friends, co-workers, students, and even strangers: anyone with whom you have a hard time communicating. Sample statements:

   "I can't be myself with strangers I'd like to get to know at parties."

   "I can't tell a friend how much I care about her."

   "I can't bring myself to ask my supervisor for the raise I think I deserve."

   "I can't ask questions in class."

2. Notice your feelings as you make each statement: self-pity, regret, concern, frustration, and so on, and reveal these to your partner.

3. Now repeat aloud each statement you've just made, except this time change each "can't" to a "won't." After each sentence, tell your partner whatever thoughts you have about what you've just said.

4. After you've finished, decide whether "can't" or "won't" is more appropriate for each item, and explain your choice to your partner.

5. Are there any instances of the self-fulfilling prophecy in your list—times when your decision that you "can't" do something was the only force keeping you from doing it?

instructors, counselors, and other experts, as well as friends. Of course, not all the advice you receive will be useful, but if you read widely and talk to enough people, you have a good chance of learning the things you want to know.

Second, you can observe models—people who handle themselves in the ways you would like to master. It's often been said that people learn more from models than in any other way, and by taking advantage of this principle you will find that the world is full of teachers who can show you how to communicate more successfully. Become a careful observer. Watch what people you admire do and say, not so that you can copy them, but so that you can adapt their behavior to fit your own personal style.

At this point, you might be overwhelmed at the difficulty of changing the way you think about yourself and the way you act. Remember that we never said that this process would be an easy one (although it sometimes is). But even when change is difficult, you know that it's possible if you are serious. You don't need to be perfect, but you can improve your self-concept if you choose.

"YOU'RE A VERY FINE FELLOW!"

ECHO POINT

© Gahan Wilson

Ethical Challenge

Are We Our Brother's Keeper? Moral Rules Theory

If it is true that our messages help shape others' self-concepts for better or worse, what responsibility do we have to act in their best interests? American philosopher W. D. Ross offered a partial answer to this question by arguing that human beings have certain moral duties: obligations that are self-evident at first glance. Among these are the duties of

1. Fidelity: to keep promises
2. Reparation: to make up for any wrongs committed
3. Gratitude: to feel and express appreciation for the kindness of others
4. Beneficence: to promote goodness and help others
5. Self-improvement: to become the best person we possibly can
6. Justice: to distribute goods fairly, according to what others have earned and deserve
7. Nonmaleficence: to refrain from injuring others and to prevent injury

Of these moral duties, beneficence and nonmaleficence seem most closely related to the question of our responsibility for shaping others' self-concepts. These rules seem to oblige us to communicate in ways that will, at the very least, avoid hurting others and that ideally will help them.

Ross recognized that the obligation to act with beneficence and nonmaleficence would, on occasion, conflict with other duties. Consider a few examples:

• You promise to be honest (following rule 1) but later realize that your candor would hurt the other person's feelings.

• As a boss, you want to hire the most qualified job-seeker (following rule 6), but passing over a less deserving but more needy candidate might demolish his or her self-confidence.

• In order to grow as a person (rule 5) you need to end a romantic relationship, but doing so would demolish the self-confidence of your partner.

In cases like these, Ross reasoned that we should follow two rules: First, to obey the duty that, under the actual circumstances, is most compelling and second, to always do that which has the greatest *prima facie* rightness over wrongness. It seems to follow that the duty of nonmaleficence would generally take precedence over the other duties: At the very least, duty theory suggests, we are obliged to act in ways that do no harm to others.

Duty theory rests on intuition. Ross can offer no reasons to support the claim that these are, indeed, universal duties belonging to all persons, nor can he offer a reasoned way of determining which duty is more compelling. Ross responded to criticisms of this weakness: "To me it seems as self-evident as anything could be, that to make a promise, for instance, is to create a moral claim on us in someone else. Many readers will perhaps say that they do not know this to be true. If so, I certainly cannot prove it to them. I can only ask them to reflect again, in the hope that they will ultimately agree that they also know it to be true."

Duty theory doesn't seem to provide an answer for every situation in which our behavior might affect the way others feel about themselves, but it does present us with a list of questions to ponder as we consider the effects of our messages.

Apply duty theory to your relationship with someone who is important to you and on whose self-concept your behavior is likely to have some impact.

1. What responsibilities do you have to follow the rules of beneficence and nonmaleficence?
2. How can you communicate in ways that honor these rules?

This abstract is based on William D. Ross, *The Right and the Good* (New York: Oxford University Press, 1930).

Presenting the Self: Communication as Identity Management

So far we have described how communication shapes the way communicators view themselves. In the remainder of this chapter we will turn the tables and focus on the topic of **identity management**—the communication strategies that people use to influence how others view them. In the following pages you will see that many of our messages aim at creating a desired identity.

"Hah! This is the Old King Cole nobody ever sees."

Public and Private Selves

To understand how identity management operates, we have to discuss the notion of self in more detail. So far we have referred to the "self" as if each of us had only one identity. In truth, each of us has several selves, some private and others public. Often these selves are quite different.

The **perceived self** is a reflection of the self-concept. Your perceived self is the person you believe yourself to be in moments of honest self examination. We can call the perceived self "private" because you are unlikely to reveal all of it to another person. You can verify the private nature of the perceived self by reviewing the self-concept list you developed while reading page 41. You'll probably find some elements of yourself there that you would not disclose to many people and some that you would not share with anyone. You might, for example, be reluctant to share some feelings about your appearance ("I think I'm rather unattractive"), your intelligence ("I'm not as smart as I wish I were"), your goals ("The most important thing to me is becoming rich"), or your motives ("I care more about myself than about others").

In contrast to the perceived self, the **presenting self** is a public image— the way we want others to view us. The presenting self is sometimes called one's **face**. In most cases the presenting self that we seek to create is a socially approved image: diligent student, loving partner, conscientious worker, loyal friend, and so on. Social norms often create a gap between the perceived and presenting selves. For instance, Table 2.4 shows that the self-concepts of one group of male and female college students were quite similar but that their public selves were different in several respects from both their private selves and from the public selves of the opposite sex.[47]

You can recognize the difference between public and private behaviors by recalling a time when you observed a driver, alone in his or her car, behaving in ways that would never be acceptable in public. All of us engage in backstage ways of acting that we would never do in public. Just recall how you behave in front of the bathroom mirror when the door is locked, and you will appreciate

Table 2.4	Self-Selected Adjectives Describing Perceived and Presenting Selves of College Students			
	PERCEIVED SELF		**PRESENTING SELF**	
Men	Women	Men	Women	
1. Friendly	1. Friendly	1. Wild	1. Active	
2. Active	2. Responsible	2. Able	2. Responsible	
3. Responsible	3. Independent	3. Active	3. Able	
4. Independent	4. Capable	4. Strong	4. Bright	
5. Capable	5. Sensible	5. Proud	5. Warm	
6. Polite	6. Active	6. Smart	6. Funny	
7. Attractive	7. Happy	7. Brave	7. Independent	
8. Smart	8. Curious	8. Capable	8. Proud	
9. Happy	9. Faithful	9. Responsible	9. Sensible	
10. Funny	10. Attractive	10. Rough	10. Smart	

Adapted from C. M. Shaw and R. Edwards, "Self-Concepts and Self-Presentations of Males and Females: Similarities and Differences," *Communication Reports* 10 (1997): 55–62.

the difference between public and private behaviors. If you knew that someone were watching, would you behave differently?

Characteristics of Identity Management

Now that you have a sense of what identity management is, we can look at some characteristics of this process.

We Strive to Construct Multiple Identities   It is an oversimplification to suggest that each of us uses identity management strategies to create just one identity. In the course of even a single day, most people perform a variety of roles: "respectful student," "joking friend," "friendly neighbor," and "helpful worker," to suggest just a few.

The ability to construct multiple identities is one element of communication competence. For example, the style of speaking or even the language itself can reflect a choice about how to construct one's identity. We recall a black colleague who was also minister of a southern Baptist congregation consisting mostly of black members. On campus his manner of speaking was typically professorial; but a visit to hear him preach one Sunday revealed a speaker whose style was much more animated and theatrical, reflecting his identity in that context. Likewise, one scholar pointed out that bilingual Latinos in the United States often choose whether to use English or Spanish depending on the kind of identity they are seeking in a given conversation.[48]

We strive even to construct different identities with the same person. As you grew up you almost certainly changed characters as you interacted with your parents. In one context you acted as responsible adult ("You can trust me with the car!"), and in another context you were the helpless child ("I can't find my socks!"). At some times—perhaps on birthdays or holidays— you were a dedicated family member, and at other times you may have played the role of rebel. Likewise, in romantic relationships we switch among many ways of behaving, depending on the context: friend, lover, business partner, scolding critic, apologetic child, and so on.

Invitation to Insight

Your Many Identities

You can get a sense of the many roles you try to create by keeping a record of the situations in which you communicate over a one- or two-day period. For each situation, identify a dramatic title to represent the image you try to create. A few examples might be "party animal," "helpful housekeeper," "wise older sibling," and "sophisticated film critic."

Identity Management Is Collaborative   Sociologist Erving Goffman used a dramatistic metaphor to describe identity management.[49] He suggested that each of us is a kind of playwright who creates roles that reflect how we want others to see us, as well as a performer who acts out those roles. But unlike the audience for most forms of acting, our "audience" is made up of other actors who are trying to create their own characters. Identity-related communication can be viewed as a kind of process theater in which we collaborate with other actors to improvise scenes in which our characters mesh.

You can appreciate the collaborative nature of identity management by thinking about how you might handle a gripe with a friend or family member who has failed to pass along a phone message that arrived while you were away from home. Suppose that you decide to raise the issue tactfully in an effort to avoid seeming like a nag (desired role for yourself: "nice person") and also to save the other person from the embarrassment of being confronted (hoping to avoid suggesting that the other person's role is "screw-up"). If your tactful bid is accepted, the dialog might sound like this:

You: ". . . By the way, Jenny told me she called yesterday. If you wrote a note, I guess I missed seeing it."

Other: "Oh . . . sorry. I meant to write a note, but as soon as I hung up the doorbell rang, and then I had to run off to class."

You: (*in friendly tone of voice*): "That's okay. I sure would appreciate from now on if you'd leave me a note."

Other: "No problem."

Looking at Diversity

Kim Dugan: Multiple Identities

When I was 23 months old, my American parents brought me from a foster family in Seoul, Korea, to my new home in Albuquerque, New Mexico.

My mom and dad raised me and my Korean brothers and sisters so we would understand and appreciate our heritage. They took us to a Korean church and Korean heritage camps as children, and they gave us all sorts of other cultural experiences. For example, I remember driving 45 minutes across town to the only Korean restaurant in Albuquerque so we could learn about the wonders of kim chee, shinsollo, bulgogi, and other delicious foods.

Juggling my Korean appearance and heritage along with my American self has always been a challenge. In elementary school I was the only Asian in my classes. Some of the kids were both cruel and inaccurate, calling me "Suzie Wong," even though I was no more Chinese than they were. I remember some teachers assuming that, because I was Korean, I couldn't speak English—when in fact it's my first language.

In high school and college, people who didn't know me also were confused about my identity. At UCLA some Asian students who saw my last name asked me about my husband. When I told them I wasn't married, they assumed I was divorced and expressed sympathy! It never occurred to them that I was an adoptee with Euro American parents.

My mixed heritage has also led to a few problems with dating. Some Anglo guys have stereotyped ideas that Asian women are shy and submissive, which is just the opposite of my personality. It didn't take long for them to realize that they weren't getting into the kind of relationship they imagined!

The communication challenges don't just come when I communicate with native-born Euro Americans. Some Koreans also have trouble figuring out how to treat me. My last name, non-accented speech, and assertive style don't jibe with my appearance and my knowledge of Korean culture. I am very glad I stayed involved with the community of Korean adoptees, because they are the only ones who can fully understand the unusual situation I'm in.

My mixture of Korean and U.S. identities presents both challenges and blessings. Sometimes I get tired of having to explain my history, and being stuck with Asian stereotypes (like being smart and submissive) can be a drag. On the other hand, I am also blessed by being part of two cultures.

Photo courtesy of Kim Dugan

In this upbeat conversation, both you and the other person accepted one another's bids for identity. As a result, the conversation ran smoothly. Imagine, though, how differently the outcome would be if the other person didn't accept your role as "nice person":

You: ". . . By the way, Jenny told me she called yesterday. If you wrote a note, I guess I missed seeing it."

Other: (*defensively*): "OK, so I forgot. It's not that big a deal. You're not perfect yourself, you know!"

Your first bid as "nice, face-saving person" was rejected. At this point you have the choice of persisting in trying to play the original role: "Hey, I'm not mad at you, and I know I'm not perfect!" Or, you might switch to the new role of "unjustly accused person," responding with aggravation, "I never said I was perfect. But we're not talking about me here. . . ."

As this example illustrates, *collaboration* in identity management doesn't mean the same thing as *agreement*.[50] The small issue of the phone message might mushroom into a fight in which you and the other person both adopt the role of combatants. The point here is that virtually all conversations provide an arena in which communicators construct their identities in response to the behavior of others. As you read in Chapter 1, communication isn't made up of discrete events that can be separated from one another. Instead, what happens at one moment is influenced by what each party brings to the interaction and what happened in their relationship up to that point.

Identity Management Can Be Deliberate or Unconscious There's no doubt that sometimes we are highly aware of managing impressions. Most job interviews and first dates are clear examples of deliberate identity management. But in other cases we unconsciously act in ways that are really small public performances.[51] For example, experimental subjects expressed facial disgust in reaction to eating sandwiches laced with a supersaturated saltwater solution only when there was another person present: When they were alone, they made no faces while eating the same sandwiches.[52]

Another study showed that communicators engage in facial mimicry (such as smiling or looking sympathetic in response to another's message) in face-to-face settings only when their expressions can be seen by the other person. When they are speaking over the phone, and their reactions cannot be seen, they do not make the same expressions.[53] Studies like these suggest that most of our behavior is aimed at sending messages to others—in other words, identity management.

Chill out what cha yelling for
Lay back it's all been done before
And if you could only let it be
You will see

I like you the way you are
When we're driving in your car
And you're talking to me one
On one but you become

Somebody else round everyone else
You're watching your back like
You can't relax you're trying to
Be cool you look like a fool
To me. Tell me

Why'd you have to go and make things so
Complicated see the way you're acting

Like you're somebody else gets me frustrated . . .

You come over unannounced dressed up
Like you're something else where you are
Ain't where it's at you see you're
Making me laugh out when you
Strike your pose take off all
Your preppy clothes! You know
You're not fooling anyone when you become
Somebody else
Round everyone else
You're watchin your back
Like you can't relax you're trying
To be cool you look like a fool to me . . .

Avril Lavigne, "Complicated"

The experimental subjects described in the preceding paragraph didn't consciously think, "Somebody is watching me eat this salty sandwich, so I'll make a face" or "Because I'm in a face-to-face conversation, I'll show I'm sympathetic by mimicking the facial expressions of my conversational partner." Decisions like these are often instantaneous and outside of our conscious awareness. In the same way, many of our choices about how to act in the array of daily interactions aren't highly considered strategic decisions. Rather, they rely on "scripts" that we have developed over time. You probably have a variety of roles for managing your identity from which to choose in familiar situations such as dealing with strangers, treating customers at work, interacting with family members, and so on. When you find yourself in familiar situations like these, you probably slip into these roles quite often. Only when those roles don't seem quite right do you deliberately construct an approach that reflects how you want the scene to play out.

Despite the pervasiveness of identity management, it seems like an exaggeration to suggest that *all* behavior is aimed at making impressions. Young children certainly aren't strategic communicators. A baby spontaneously laughs when pleased and cries when sad or uncomfortable without any notion of creating an impression in others. Likewise, there are times when we, as adults, act spontaneously.

Despite these exceptions, most people consciously or unconsciously communicate in ways that help construct desired identities for themselves and others.

Identity Management Varies by Situation   The degree to which we consciously manage our identities varies from one situation to another. Not surprisingly, most of us work harder at creating a desired impression in the early stages of a relationship—especially one where we are seeking the approval of people whose opinion we value. If you have ever been in an employment interview where you tried to impress a potential boss, you know how carefully you presented yourself.[54] The same principle operates in courtship situations. For example, college men changed their self-presentation more when they were talking to women they found attractive than they did when talking to less attractive women.[55] After we get to know others, we don't work as hard at managing impressions. The gender of the other person seems to make a difference, though: Research suggests that we are less concerned with identity management among familiar people of the same sex than with less familiar people of the same sex or people of the opposite sex, regardless of how well we know them.[56]

People Differ in Their Degree of Identity Management   Some people are much more aware of their identity management behavior than others. These high self-monitors have the ability to pay attention to their own behavior and others' reactions, adjusting their communication to create the desired impression. By contrast, low self-monitors express what they are thinking and feeling without much attention to the impression their behavior creates.[57] You can get an idea of whether you are a high or a low self-monitor by answering the on page 71.

What is the ideal score for this self-quiz? There are certainly advantages to being a high self-monitor.[58] People who pay attention to themselves are generally good actors who can create the identity they want, acting interested when bored or friendly when they really feel the opposite. This allows them to handle social situations smoothly, often putting others at ease. They are also good "people readers" who can adjust their behavior to get the desired reaction from others. Along with these advantages, there are some potential disadvantages to being an extremely high self-monitor. The analytical nature of such people may prevent them from experiencing events completely because a portion of their attention will always be viewing the situation from a detached position. High self-monitors' ability to act means that it is difficult to tell how they are really feeling. In fact, because high self-monitors change roles often, they may have a hard time knowing *themselves* how they really feel.

People who score low on the self-monitoring scale live life differently from their more self-conscious counterparts. They have a more simple, focused idea of who they are and who they want to be. Low self-monitors are likely to have a narrower repertoire of behaviors, and thus they can be expected to act in more or less the same way regardless of the situation. This means that low self-monitors are easy to read. "What you see is what you get" might be their motto. Although this lack of flexibility may make their social interaction less smooth in many situations, low self-monitors can be counted on to be straightforward communicators.

By now it should be clear that neither extremely high nor low self-monitoring is the ideal. There are some situations when paying attention to yourself and adapting your behavior can be useful, and there are other situations when reacting without considering the effect on others is a better approach. This need for a range of behaviors demonstrates again the notion of communicative competence outlined in Chapter 1: Flexibility is the key to successful relationships. In the

Invitation to Insight

Self-Monitoring Inventory

These statements concern personal reactions to a number of situations. No two statements are exactly alike, so consider each statement carefully before answering. If a statement is true, or mostly true, as applied to you, circle the T. If a statement is false, or not usually true, as applied to you, circle the F.

1. I find it hard to imitate the behavior of other people.   T   F

2. I guess I put on a show to impress or entertain people.   T   F

3. I would probably make a good actor.   T   F

4. I sometimes appear to others to be experiencing deeper
   emotions than I actually am.   T   F

5. In a group of people I am rarely the center of attention.   T   F

6. In different situations and with different people, I often act
   like very different persons.   T   F

7. I can argue only for ideas I already believe.   T   F

8. In order to get along and be liked, I tend to be what people
   expect me to be rather than anything else.   T   F

9. I may deceive people by being friendly when I really dislike them.   T   F

10. I'm not always the person I appear to be.   T   F

Scoring: Give yourself one point for each of questions 1, 5, and 7 that you answered *F*. Give yourself one point for each of the remaining questions that you answered T. Add up your points. If you are a good judge of yourself and scored 7 or above, you are probably a high self-monitoring individual; 3 or below, you are probably a low self-monitoring individual.

Source: Mark Snyder, "The Many Me's of the Self-Monitor," *Psychology Today* (March 1983): 34.

reading on pages 73–74 writer Barry Stevens describes the challenges of managing identities while being true to oneself.

Why Manage Identities?

Why bother trying to shape others' opinions of you? Social scientists have identified several overlapping reasons.[59]

To Start and Manage Relationships   Think about times when you have consciously and carefully managed your approach when meeting someone you would like to know better. You may do your best to appear charming and witty—or perhaps cool and suave. You don't need to be a phony to act this way: You simply are trying to show your best side. Once relationships are up and running, we still manage our identities—perhaps not as much, but often.

To Gain Compliance of Others   We often manage our identity to get others—both those we know and strangers—to act in ways we want. You might, for example, dress up for a visit to traffic court in hope that your image (responsible citizen) will convince the judge to treat you sympathetically. You might chat sociably with neighbors you don't find especially interesting so that you can exchange favors or solve problems as they come up.

To Save Others' Face   We often modify the way we present ourselves to support the way other people want to be seen. For example, able-bodied people often mask their discomfort upon encountering someone who is disabled by acting nonchalant or stressing similarities between themselves and the disabled person.[60] Young children who haven't learned about the importance of face-saving often embarrass their parents by behaving inappropriately ("Mommy, why is that man so fat?"); but by the time they enter school, behavior that might have been excusable or even amusing just isn't acceptable.

"Not the 'real you?' Well, of course it's not the real you. The real you is bald."

How Do We Manage Identities?

How do we create a public face? In an age in which technology provides many options for communicating, the answer depends in part on the communication channel chosen.

Face-to-Face Impression Management   In face-to-face interaction, communicators can manage their front in three ways: manner, setting, and appearance.[61] *Manner* consists of a communicator's words and nonverbal actions. Physicians, for example, display a wide variety of manners as they conduct physical examinations. Some are friendly and conversational, whereas others adopt a brusque and impersonal approach. Still others are polite but businesslike. Much of a communicator's manner comes from what he or she says. A doctor who remembers details about your interests and hobbies is quite different from one who sticks to clinical questions. One who explains a medical procedure creates a different impression than another who reveals little to the patient. Along with the content of speech, nonverbal behaviors play a big role in creating impressions. A doctor who greets you with a smile and a handshake comes across differently from one who gives nothing more than a curt nod. Manner varies widely in other professional and settings—professors, salespeople, hair stylists, and so on—and the impressions they create vary accordingly. The same principle holds in personal relationships. Your manner plays a major role in shaping how others view you. Chapters 5 and 6 will describe in detail how your words and nonverbal behaviors create impres-

Among the People, every person possessed a Shield of one kind or another. One of the most important things to understand about these Shields is that they were never intended to give physical protection in battle. They were not made to turn away arrows or bullets, or for people to hide behind . . .

Sometimes they were made from the tough hides of bears or buffalo bulls, but more often they were covered only with the soft skins of deer, antelope, coyote, otter, weasel, or even mice. They were then hung with eagle plumes, cedar pouches, tassels of animal fur, and many other things. They were also painted with various symbolic figures. These signs told who the man was, what he sought to be, and what his loves, fears, and dreams were. Almost everything about him was written there, reflected in the Mirror of his Shield . . .

These Shields were carried by the men among the People in order that anyone they met might know them.

Hyemeyohsts Storm, *Seven Arrows*

Will the Real Me Please Stand Up?

In the beginning, I was one person, knowing nothing but my own experience.

Then I was told things, and I became two people: the little girl who said how terrible it was that the boys had a fire going in the lot next door where they were roasting apples (which was what the woman said)—and the little girl who, when the boys were called by their mothers to go to the store, ran out and tended the fire and the apples because she loved doing it.

So then there were two of I. One I always doing something that the other I disapproved of. Or other I said what I disapproved of. All this argument in me so much.

In the beginning was I, and I was good.

Then came in other I. Outside authority. This was confusing. And then other I became very confused because there were so many different outside authorities.

Sit nicely. Leave the room to blow your nose. Don't do that, that's silly. Why, the poor child doesn't even know how to pick a bone! Flush the toilet at night because if you don't it makes it harder to clean. DON'T FLUSH THE TOILET AT NIGHT—you wake people up! Always be nice to people. Even if you don't like them, you mustn't hurt their feelings. Be frank and honest. If you don't tell people what you think of them, that's cowardly. Butter knives. It is important to use butter knives. Butter knives? What foolishness! Speak nicely. Sissy! Kipling is wonderful! Ugh! Kipling (turning away).

The most important thing is to have a career. The most important thing is to get married. The hell with everyone. Be nice to everyone. The most important thing is sex. The most important thing is to have everyone like you. The most important thing is to be sophisticated and say what you don't mean and don't let anyone know what you feel. The most important thing is a black seal coat and china and silver. The most important thing is to be clean. The most important thing is to always pay your debts. The most important thing is not to be taken in by anyone else. The most important thing is to love your parents. The most important thing is to work. The most important thing is to be independent. The most important thing is to speak correct English. The most important thing is to go to the right plays and read the right books. The most important thing is to do what others say. And others say all these things.

All the time, I is saying, live with life. That is what is important.

But when I lives with life, other I says no, that's bad. All the different other I's say this. It's dangerous. It isn't practical. You'll come to a bad end. Of course . . . everyone felt that way once, the way you do, but *you'll learn*.

Out of all the other I's some are chosen as a pattern that is me. But there are all the other possibilities of patterns within what all the others say which come into me and become other I which is not myself, and sometimes these take over. Then who am I?

© Diana Ong/SuperStock

Continued

I does not bother about who am I. I is, and is happy being. But when I is happy being, other I says get to work, do something worthwhile! I is happy doing dishes. "You're weird!" I is happy being with people saying nothing. Other I says talk. Talk, talk, talk. I gets lost.

I knows that things are to be played with, not possessed. I likes putting things together, lightly. Taking things apart, lightly. "You'll never have anything!" Making things of things in a way that the things themselves take part in, putting themselves together with surprise and delight to I. "There's no money in that!"

I is human. If someone needs, I gives. "You can't do that! You'll never have anything for yourself! We'll have to support you!"

I loves. I loves in a way that other I does not know. I loves. "That's too warm for friends!" "That's too cool for lovers!" "Don't feel so bad, he's just a friend. It's not as though you loved him." "How can you let him go? I thought you loved him." So cool the warm for friends and hot up the love for lovers, and I gets lost.

So both I's have a house and a husband and children and all that, but both I's are confused because other I says, "You see? You're lucky," while I goes on crying. "What are you crying about? Why are you so ungrateful?" I doesn't know gratitude or ingratitude, and cannot argue. I goes on crying. Other I pushes it out, says, "I am happy! I am very lucky to have such a fine family and a nice house and good neighbors and lots of friends who want me to do this, do that." I is not reasonable either. I goes on crying.

Other I gets tired, and goes on smiling because that is the thing to do. Smile, and you will be rewarded. Like the seal who gets tossed a piece of fish. Be nice to everyone and you will be rewarded. People will be nice to you, and you can be happy with that. You know they like you. Like a dog who gets patted on the head for good behavior. Tell funny stories. Be gay. Smile, smile, smile. . . . I is crying. . . . "Don't be sorry for yourself! Go out

and do things for people!" "Go out and be with people!" I is still crying, but now, that is not heard and felt so much.

Suddenly: "What am I doing?" "Am I to go through life playing the clown?" "What am I doing, going to parties that I do not enjoy?" "What am I doing, being with people who bore me?" "Why am I so hollow and the hollowness filled with emptiness?" A shell. How has this shell grown around me? Why am I proud of my children and unhappy about their lives which are not good enough? Why am I disappointed? Why do I feel so much waste?

I comes through, a little. In moments. And gets pushed back by other I.

I refuses to play the clown any more. Which I is that? "She used to be fun, but now she thinks too much about herself." I lets friends drop away. Which I is that? "She's being too much by herself. That's bad. She's losing her mind." Which mind?

Barry Stevens, Person to Person

sions. Because you have to speak and act, the question isn't *whether* your manner sends a message but rather *what* message it will send.

Along with manner, a second dimension of identity management is *appearance*—the personal items that people use to shape an image. Sometimes appearance is part of creating a professional image. A physician's white lab coat and a police officer's uniform both set the wearers apart as someone special. A tailored suit or a rumpled outfit creates very different impressions in the business world. Off the job, clothing is just as important. We choose clothing that sends a message about ourselves, sometimes trendy and sometimes traditional. Some people dress in ways that accent their sexuality, whereas others hide it. Clothing can say, "I'm an athlete," "I'm wealthy," or "I'm an environmentalist." Along with dress, other aspects of appearance play a strong role in identity management. Do you wear makeup? What is your hairstyle? Do you make an effort to look friendly and confident?

Tattoos offer an interesting example of how appearance can help create an identity. The very act of decorating one's skin makes a statement, and the design or words chosen say even more. One fascinating study explored the communicative function of tattoos worn by some people to announce their HIV-positive condition.[62] At the most obvious level, such tattoos convey important information about the health status of the wearer to medical workers. Beyond being a practical announcement, though, such tattoos can be a vehicle for identity management, intended for both the wearer and others. One tattoo wearer listed the messages that his visible label conveys: the refusal to internalize shame, a commitment to safer sex practices, a challenge to stereotypes about weak "AIDS victims," and an educational tool that generates discussion by making the condition visible.

> We may be born naked, but we waste little time correcting the oversight. Almost from the moment we wriggle into the world, we start getting dressed. Conventional wisdom claims that clothing is simply a means of survival, but clearly there's more to it. Whether it's a couple of strategically placed shells or a suit of armor, a G-string or a caribou parka, clothing is a set of signals to all we meet. And though clothes may indeed protect us from the elements, their real job is to protect us from social opprobrium, or to make a statement—to a potential boss, a potential bride, or a very real enemy.
>
> Banana Republic Catalog

A final way to manage identities is through the choice of *setting*—physical items that we use to influence how others view us. In modern western society the automobile is a major part of identity management. This explains why many people lust after cars that are far more expensive and powerful than they really need. A sporty convertible or fancy imported sedan doesn't just get drivers from one place to another: It also makes statements about the kind of people they are. The physical setting we choose and the way we arrange it are another important way to manage identities. What colors do you choose for the place you live? What artwork? What music do you play? Of course, we choose a setting that we enjoy; but in many cases we create an environment that will present the desired front to others. If you doubt this fact, just recall the last time you straightened up the house before important guests arrived. Backstage you might be comfortable with a messy place, but your public front—at least to some people—is quite different.

Impression Management in Mediated Communication

Most of the preceding examples involve face-to-face interaction, but impression management is just as common and important in other types of communication. Consider the care you probably take when drafting a resume for a potential employer, a thank-you letter in response to a gift, or a love note to a sweetheart. Besides giving careful thought to the wording of your message, you probably make strategic decisions about its appearance. Will you use plain white paper or something more distinctive? Will you type out your words or write them in longhand? People think carefully about considerations like these because they instinctively know that the *way* a message is presented can say as much as the words it contains.

Along with personal correspondence, communicators sometimes manage their identity in the mass print media. Personal newspaper ads in which people

"On the Internet, nobody knows you're a dog."

seek romantic partners are an obvious case of deliberate identity management. Younger people who describe themselves to potential dating partners emphasize physical appearance and are more likely to play up sexuality. By contrast, ads by people over age 50 are more likely to focus on personality features.[63]

At first glance, the technology of computer-mediated communication (CMC) seems to limit the potential for impression management. IM and e-mail messages, for example, appear to lack the "richness" of other channels. They don't convey the tone of your voice, postures, gestures, or facial expressions. However, communication scholars recognize that what is missing in computer-mediated communication can actually be an *advantage* for communicators who want to manage the impressions they make.[64]

CMC generally gives us more control over managing impressions than we have in face-to-face communication. Asynchronous forms of CMC like e-mail, blogs, and web pages allow you to edit your messages until your create just the desired impression. With e-mail (and, to a lesser degree with IMing) you can compose difficult messages without forcing the receiver to respond immediately, and ignore others' messages rather than give an unpleasant response. Perhaps most important, with CMC you don't have to worry about stammering or blushing, apparel or appearance, or any other unseen factor that might detract from the impression you want to create.

CMC allows strangers to change their age, history, personality, appearance, and other matters that would be impossible to hide in person.[65] A quarter of teens have pretended to be a different person online, and a third confess to having given false information about themselves while e-mailing and instant messaging. A survey of one online dating site's participants found that 86 percent felt others misrepresented their physical appearance in their posted descriptions.[66] We'll talk about the ethics of such misrepresentations in the following section.

Like the one-to-one and small group channels of e-mail and instant messaging, "broadcasting" on the media is also a tool for managing one's identity. Blogs, personal web pages, and profiles on social networking websites like MySpace, FaceBook, and Friendster all provide opportunities for communicators to construct an identity.[67] As the reading on page 77 suggests, the words, images, and sounds that self-publishers choose make a statement about who they are—or at least how they want to be regarded by others.

Communicators who want to manage impressions don't always prefer computer-mediated channels. People are generally comfortable with face-to-face interaction when they feel confident that others support the image they want to present. On the other hand, people are more likely to prefer mediated channels when their own self-presentation is threatened.[68]

Identity Management and Honesty

After reading this far, you might think that identity management sounds like an academic label for manipulation or phoniness. There certainly are situations where identity management is dishonest. A manipulative date who pretends to be affectionate in order to gain sexual favors is clearly unethical and deceitful. So are job applicants who lie about academic records to get hired or salespeople who pretend to be dedicated to customer service when their real goal is to make a quick buck. But managing impressions doesn't necessarily make you a liar. In fact, it is almost impossible to imagine how we could communicate effectively without making decisions about which front to present in one situation or

Do I contradict myself?
Very well then I contradict myself.
(I am large, I contain multitudes.)

Walt Whitman, *Song of Myself*

Here I Am Taking My Own Picture

© age fotostock/SuperStock

Morgan Adams, a recent college graduate, decided that her picture on her homepage at MySpace.com had lingered a little too long, a full month. To snap a new one she called on the only photographer she thought she could trust: herself.

In her bedroom in Lubbock, Tex., Ms. Adams, 21, tried out a variety of poses—coy, friendly, sultry, goofy—in the kind of performance young people have engaged in privately for generations before a mirror. But Ms. Adams's mirror was a web cam, and her journey of self-expression, documented in five digital self-portraits, was soon visible to the 56 million registered users of MySpace.

Psychologists and others who study teenagers say the digital self-portraiture is an extension of behavior typical of the young, which earlier generations might have expressed through clothing and hairstyles. "Most of what I've been seeing is taking place in the bedroom," said Kathryn C. Montgomery, a professor of communication at American University, referring to teenage self-portraits. Dr. Montgomery studies the relation of teenagers to the digital media. "It's a locus of teen life where they are forming their identities, and now it's also a private studio where they can develop who they are. What better tool could they have than one that allows them to take pictures of themselves and manipulate them like never before?"

"When I was a kid I didn't want my picture taken," said Jim Taylor, a trend consultant at the Harrison Group in Waterbury, Conn. "But these kids are fabulous self-marketers. Self-branding is a big deal for kids, and self-produced entertainment is a big deal," Mr. Taylor said.

In their pictures, ordinary young women metamorphose into glamour queens or pinup girls, thanks to a few well-rehearsed come-hither poses and mood lighting reminiscent of an old Hollywood studio portrait. Average boys turn themselves into brooding antiheroes by gazing intently into their camera lens in a darkened room, face half-buried in shadow. "There's always a theatrical quality to these shots," Mr. Taylor said. "Kids love melancholy and sadness. There is lots of obvious symbolism about whether they see themselves as an actress, a model, a Christ figure, or a Hamlet."

Amber Davidson, 19, a freshman at Concordia College in Moorhead, Minn., refreshes her self-portrait on MySpace every couple of weeks and puts a lot of thought into it. Her MySpace homepage contains five self-portraits created by pointing the camera toward herself, arm outstretched. She composed each shot so that the arm holding the camera is invisible. In one, Ms. Davidson wears a black-and-white spaghetti-strap dress and peers up winsomely at a camera over her head. It took about 15 tries to get it right, she said.

"I don't want people to think I'm sitting there taking all these pictures of myself, even though I kind of am."

Alex Williams

another. It would be ludicrous to act the same way with strangers as you do with close friends, and nobody would show the same face to a two-year-old as he or she would to an adult.

Each of us has a repertoire of faces—a cast of characters—and part of being a competent communicator is choosing the best face for the situation. Consider a few examples:

- You offer to teach a friend a new skill: playing the guitar, operating a computer program, or sharpening up a tennis backhand. Your friend is making slow progress with the skill, and you find yourself growing impatient.
- You've been IMing for several weeks with someone you met online, and the relationship is starting to turn romantic. You have a physical trait you haven't mentioned.
- At work you face a belligerent customer. You don't believe anyone has the right to treat you this way.
- A friend or family member makes a joke about your appearance that hurts your feelings. You aren't sure whether to make an issue of the joke or to pretend that it doesn't bother you.

In each of these situations—and in countless others every day—you have a choice about how to act. It is an oversimplification to say that there is only one honest way to behave in each circumstance and that every other response would be insincere and dishonest. Instead, identity management involves deciding which face—which part of yourself—to reveal. For example, when teaching a new skill, you choose to display the "patient" instead of the "impatient" side of yourself. In the same way, at work you have the option of acting defensive or nondefensive in difficult situations. With strangers, friends, or family you can choose whether to disclose your feelings. Which face to show to others is an important decision, but in any case you are sharing a real part of yourself. You may not be revealing everything—but as you will learn in Chapter 9, complete self-disclosure is rarely appropriate.

Summary

The self-concept is a relatively stable set of perceptions that individuals hold about themselves. Some of the characteristics of the self are due to inherited personality traits. In addition, the self-concept is created through messages from significant others—reflected appraisal—and through social comparison with reference groups. The self-concept is subjective and may vary from the way a person is perceived by others. Although the self evolves over time, the self-concept resists change. Other factors that affect the self-concept are culture, and sex/gender.

A self-fulfilling prophecy occurs when a person's expectations of an event influence the outcome. One type of prophecy consists of predictions by others, whereas another type is self-imposed. Self-fulfilling prophecies can be both positive and negative.

It is possible to change one's self-concept in ways that lead to more-effective communication. It is necessary to have realistic expectations about how much change is possible and a realistic assessment of oneself. Willingness to exert the effort to change is important, and in some cases change requires new information or skill.

Identity management consists of strategic communication designed to influence others' perceptions of an individual. Identity management aims at presenting to others one or more faces, which may be different from private, spontaneous behavior that occurs outside of others' presence. Some communicators are high self-monitors who are highly conscious of their own behavior, whereas others are less aware of how their words and actions affect others.

Identity management occurs for two reasons. Many times it aims at following social rules and conventions. At other times it aims at achieving a variety of content and relational goals. In either case, communicators engage in creating an identity by managing their manner, appearance, and the settings in which they interact with others. Identity management occurs both in face-to-face and mediated communication. Although identity management might seem manipulative, it can be an authentic form of communication. Because each person has a variety of faces that he or she can reveal, choosing which one to present need not be dishonest.

Key Terms

cognitive conservatism (53)
face (65)
identity management (64)
perceived self (65)
personality (44)

presenting self (65)
reference groups (51)
reflected appraisal (46)
self-concept (41)
self-esteem (43)

self-fulfilling prophecy (58)
significant others (47)
social comparison (48)

Media Resources

ThomsonNOW For quick access to the online resources that accompany this chapter, access ThomsonNOW for *Looking Out/Looking In* at www.thomsonedu.com.

The ThomsonNOW online study system helps you identify concepts you don't fully understand, allowing you to put your study time to the best use. Using chapter-by-chapter diagnostic pre-tests, the system creates a **personalized study plan** for each chapter. Each plan directs you to specific resources designed to improve your understanding, including pages from the text in ebook format. Chapter post-tests give you an opportunity to measure how much you've learned and let you know if you are ready for graded quizzes and exams.

ThomsonNOW for *Looking Out/Looking In* also includes **vocabulary activities** to help you master key terms; self-study **review quizzes** to test your comprehension of the material in this chapter and prepare for exams; **online exercises**, including the Skill Builder and Invitation to Insight activities in the book; **web links** you can use to further explore topics in this chapter; access to a **feature film database** where you can locate information about movies that illustrate communication principles;

and access to the **InfoTrac College Edition** searchable database of over 10 million articles from both scholarly journals and the popular press.

Films

ThomsonNOW In addition to the films described here, use the link to the ThomsonNOW for *Looking Out/Looking In* to link to the **Film in Communication Database**, where you can locate movie clips that illustrate various aspects of interpersonal communication.

Influences on the Self-Concept

Akeelah and the Bee (2006) Rated PG
Eleven-year-old Akeelah Anderson (Keke Palmer) is a really good speller—maybe good enough to win the national championship. But she is also desperately afraid of being ridiculed as a "brainiac" by her classmates at their inner-city middle school. Akeelah is encouraged to excel by her teachers, her principal, and her new mentor, UCLA professor Dr. Joshua Larabee (Laurence Fishburne).

Will Akeelah hide her talents to fit in, or will she think and act like a potential champion? This film illustrates how struggles of self-definition are shaped by both our own desires and the messages we receive from significant others.

Bridget Jones's Diary (2001) Rated R
Unmarried and in her early 30s, Bridget Jones (Renée Zellweger) measures her self-worth by whether men pay attention to her. She worries about dying "fat and alone."

Bridget's obsession with losing weight and finding a partner are due in part to the media appraisals and comparisons that surround her. She has photos of thin models on her refrigerator, self-help books ("What Men Want") on the shelf, glamour magazines on her coffee table, and cry-in-your-beer music ("All By Myself") blaring on the stereo. These media messages scream that she has been weighed in the balance and found wanting.

After years of self-loathing, a suitor named Mark (Colin Firth) offers an appraisal that is water on the desert of Bridget's self-concept: "I like you very much, just as you are." She has spent much of her life trying to live up to social expectations of attractiveness, but Mark accepts her imperfections and appreciates her many positive attributes. Bridget finally embraces the notion that she is fine "just as she is."

Self-Fulfilling Prophecies

Stand and Deliver (1988) Rated PG-13
Jaime Escalante (Edward James Olmos) is a mild-mannered math teacher who is commissioned to the tough classrooms of Garfield High. He is soft-spoken, cerebral, and demanding—in other words, the kind of teacher street-hardened students would normally despise and ignore. Although the students do, in fact, regard him suspiciously at first, by the story's end they adore him. Perhaps more important, they achieve top-flight scores on their advanced-placement calculus exam, which is their ticket to a college education.

How can we account for the students' success? The film suggests that the key is not Escalante's knowledge of math, his lecture techniques, or his classroom charisma. The key is that he believes in his students, who hadn't been believed in before. Because he believes in them, they stop thinking of themselves as losers. Escalante helps them master a subject they thought was impossible and in so doing radically changes their self-concepts. This is a powerful story that offers contemporary support for the "Pygmalion" theory of the self-fulfilling prophecy.

Identity Management

Brokeback Mountain (2005) Rated R
In the summer of 1963, Ennis Del Mar (Heath Ledger) and Jack Twist (Jake Gyllenhaal) are hired to tend sheep on the slopes of Montana's Brokeback Mountain. In their remote campsite, the two men surprise themselves by becoming lovers. After the summer ends, they return to their separate lives. Both marry and have children, managing to ignore their feelings for one another until they meet again. This tragic story of denial shows the extent to which people are willing to go to hide parts of their identity in order to avoid social disapproval.

Catch Me If You Can (2003) Rated PG-13
Frank Abagnale (Leonardo DiCaprio) learns to escape his family's financial and interpersonal woes by creating false identities. He impersonates a teacher, a pilot, a doctor, and a lawyer. These false fronts allow him to become rich, admired, and respected—and very lonely. The more faces and façade he constructs, the more he loses his sense of self. More significantly, his unwillingness to disclose his real identity isolates him from significant others—including his fiancée.

The person who knows Frank best is FBI agent Carl Hanratty (Tom Hanks), who is trying to capture and arrest him. By story's end, Carl becomes something of a father figure to Frank, helping him reestablish a legitimate identity. This entertaining story illustrates how identity management, when used unethically, can lead to strained relationships and a loss of self.

Perception: What You See Is What You Get

3

Study M. C. Escher's drawing *Relativity* in this chapter opener. It pictures a strange universe in which the inhabitants of each world exist at right angles, using the same staircase but oblivious to one another's existence. Each has his or her own conception of up and down, right and left. If these characters were introduced to the residents of other worlds, they would find them odd, defying the rule of gravity.

This surreal vision provides a useful metaphor for challenges we encounter every day. Each of us experiences a different reality, and failing to understand other people's point of view can lead to problems on both practical and relational levels. But perceptual differences can enhance as well as interfere with relationships. By seeing the world through others' eyes you can gain insights that are different—and often more valuable—than those arising out of your own experiences.

This chapter will help you deal with the challenge of communicating in the face of perceptual differences. We will begin by looking at some of the reasons why the world appears different to each of us. In our survey we'll explore several areas: how our psychological makeup, personal needs, interests, and biases shape our perceptions; the physiological factors that influence our view of the world;

I've always admired those reporters who can descend on an area, talk to key people, ask key questions, take samplings of opinions, and then set down an orderly report very much like a road map. I envy this technique and at the same time do not trust it as a mirror of reality. I feel that there are too many realities. What I set down here is true until someone else passes that way and rearranges the world in his own style. In literary criticism the critic has no choice but to make over the victim of his attention into something the size and shape of himself. . . . So much there is to see, but our morning eyes describe a different world than do our afternoon eyes, and surely our wearied evening eyes can only report a weary evening world.

John Steinbeck, *Travels with Charley*

the social roles that affect our image of events; and finally the role that culture plays in creating our ideas of what behavior is proper. In doing so, we'll cover many of the types of physiological and psychological noise you read about in Chapter 1. After examining the perceptual factors that can drive us apart, we will look at two useful skills for bridging the perceptual gap.

The Perception Process

We need to begin our discussion of perception by examining the gap between "what is" and what we know. At one time or another you've probably seen photos of sights invisible to the unaided eye: perhaps an infrared photo of a familiar area or the vastly enlarged image of a minute object taken by an electron microscope. You've also noticed how certain animals are able to hear sounds and smell odors that are not apparent to humans. Experiences like these remind us that there is much more going on in the world than we are able to experience with our limited senses, that our idea of reality is in fact only a partial one.

Even within the realm of our senses we're aware of only a small part of what is going on around us. A simple walk in the park would probably be a different experience for companions with different interests. A botanist might notice the vegetation; a fashion designer might pay attention to the way people are dressed; and an artist might be aware of the colors and forms of the people and surroundings. On a personal level, we've all had the experience of failing to notice something unusual about a friend—perhaps a new hairstyle or a sad expression—until it's called to our attention. Sometimes our failure to recognize some events while recognizing others comes from not paying attention to important information. But in other cases it's simply impossible to be aware of everything, no matter how attentive we might be: There is just too much going on.

William James said, "To the infant the world is just a big blooming, buzzing confusion." One reason for this is the fact that infants are not yet able to sort out the myriad impressions with which we're all bombarded. As we grow, we learn to manage all this data, and as we do so, we begin to make sense out of the world.

Because this ability to organize our perceptions in a useful way is such a critical factor in our ability to function, we need to begin our study of perception by taking a closer look at this process. We can do so by examining the four steps by which we attach meaning to our experiences: selection, organization, interpretation, and negotiation.

Selection

Because we're exposed to more input than we can possibly manage, the first step in perception is the **selection** of which impressions we will attend to. There are several factors that cause us to notice some things and ignore others.

Stimuli that are *intense* often attract our attention. Something that is louder, larger, or brighter stands out. This explains why—other things being equal—we're more likely to remember extremely tall or short people and why someone who laughs or talks loudly at a party attracts more attention (not always favorable) than do quiet guests.

Repetitious stimuli, repetitious stimuli, repetitious stimuli, repetitious stimuli, repetitious stimuli, repetitious stimuli also attract attention.[1] Just as a quiet but steadily dripping faucet can come to dominate our awareness, people to whom we're frequently exposed become noticeable.

ATTENTION IS ALSO FREQUENTLY RELATED TO contrast OR change IN STIMULATION. Put differently, unchanging people or things become less noticeable. This principle gives an explanation (excuse?) for why we take wonderful people for granted when we interact with them frequently. It's only when they stop being so wonderful or go away that we appreciate them.

Motives also determine what information we select from our environment. If you're anxious about being late for a date, you'll notice whatever clocks may be around you; and if you're hungry, you'll become aware of any restaurants, markets, and billboards advertising food in your path. Motives also determine how we perceive people. For example, someone on the lookout for a romantic adventure will be especially aware of attractive potential partners, whereas the same person at a different time might be oblivious to anyone but police or medical personnel in an emergency.

Selection isn't just a matter of attending to some stimuli: It also involves ignoring other cues. If, for example, you decide that someone is a terrific person, you may overlook his or her flaws. If you are focused on examples of unfair male bosses, you might not recognize unfair female bosses.

> We usually see only the things we are looking for— so much that we sometimes see them where they are not.
>
> Eric Hoffer

Organization

Along with selecting information from the environment, we must arrange it in some meaningful way. You can see how the principle of **organization** works by looking at Figure 3.1. You can view the picture either as one of a vase or as one of two twins, depending on whether you focus on the light or the dark areas. In instances such as this we make sense of stimuli by noticing some data that stand out as a *figure* against a less striking *ground*. The "vase-face" drawing is interesting because it allows us to choose between two sets of figure-ground relationships.

This principle of figure-ground organization operates in communication, too. Recall, for instance, how certain speech can suddenly stand out from a babble of voices. Sometimes the words are noticeable because they include your name, whereas at other times they might be spoken by a familiar voice.

The vase-face drawing suggests that there are only two ways to organize impressions. In fact, there are usually many more. Consider, for example, Figure 3.2. How many ways can you view the boxes? One? Two? Three? Keep looking. If you're stumped, Figure 3.3 will help.

Just as you were inclined to view these boxes in one way, each of us can organize our impressions of other communicators using a number of schemes (called *perceptual schema* by social scientists). Sometimes we classify people according to their *appearance:* male or female, beautiful or ugly, heavy or thin, young or old, and so on. At other times we classify people according to their *social roles:* student, attorney,

FIGURE 3.1

FIGURE 3.2

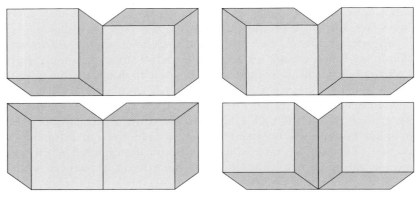

FIGURE 3.3

wife, and so on. Another way we classify people is by their *interaction style:* friendly, helpful, aloof, and sarcastic are examples. In other cases we classify people by their *psychological traits:* curious, nervous, insecure, and so on. Finally, we can use others' *membership*, classifying them according to the group to which they belong: Republican, immigrant, Christian, and so on.

The perceptual schemas we use shape the way we think about and communicate with others. If you've classified a professor, for example, as "friendly," you'll handle questions or problems one way; if you've classified a professor as "mean," your behavior will probably be quite different. What constructs do you use to classify the people you encounter in your life? Consider how your relationship might change if you used different schemas.

Invitation to Insight

Your Perceptual Filters

1. Identify the perceptual schema described in the preceding section that you would use to classify people in each of the following contexts.

   a. Spending time with new acquaintances at a party

   b. Socializing with fellow workers on the job

   c. Choosing teammates for an important class project

   d. Offering help to a stranded motorist

   Describe both the *general type of organizing scheme* (for example, "physical," "membership") and the *specific category* within each type (such as, "attractive," "roughly the same age as me").

2. Consider

   a. other schema you might use in each context.

   b. the different consequences of using the schema you originally chose and the alternative you identified in the preceding step.

   c. how your relationships might change if you used different constructs.

Looking at Diversity

Christa Kilvington: Socioeconomic Stereotyping

What comes to mind when you hear the description "4.0 college student"? How about when you hear "welfare mom"? Most likely you get two very different mental pictures. Perhaps you imagine those kinds of people as complete opposites. And yet, I am both: A college student with straight-A grades who is also a single mother on public assistance.

To some people, the combination doesn't fit. They figure that anyone smart enough to earn a 4.0 GPA shouldn't have ended up on welfare, or that anybody on welfare is probably too dumb and lazy to be in college and have straight-A grades.

The stereotypes people use to classify me shape the way they communicate. Most people who only know me from school and have no idea of my economic situation think of me as intelligent and ambitious—an academic standout. They speak to me formally and respectfully. Those who know me only by my income level—caseworkers, healthcare workers, grocery store clerks—tend to communicate with me in quite a different way. When I go to the welfare office, present my Medicaid card for a prescription, or pay for groceries with food stamps I am often treated as unintelligent, lazy, and dishonest. People speak to me in condescending and disrespectful tones.

Why do some people equate income level with intelligence? Why do they treat me and others differently based on our economic status? Why is it all right to treat people disrespectfully just because they are poor? Stereotypes exist for a reason, but it's important to go beyond them to find out each person's unique story. When you leave your mind open to the possibility that there is more to a person than meets the eye, that is when you grow as a person yourself.

Photo courtesy of Christa Kilvington

Stereotyping   After we have chosen an organizing scheme to classify people, we use that scheme to make generalizations and predictions about members of the groups who fit the categories we use. For example, if you were especially aware of gender, you might be alert to the differences between the way men and women behave or the way they are treated. If religion played an important part in your life, you might think of members of your faith differently from others. If ethnicity was an important issue for you, you would probably tune in to the differences between members of various ethnic groups. There's nothing wrong with generalizations as long as they are accurate. In fact, it would be impossible to get through life without them.

But when generalizations lose touch with reality, they lead to **stereotyping**—exaggerated generalizations associated with a categorizing system.[2] Stereotypes may be based on a kernel of truth, but they go beyond the facts at hand and make claims that usually have no valid basis.

You can begin to get a sense of your tendency to make generalizations and to stereotype by completing the following sentences:

1. Women are _____.
2. Men are _____.
3. Hispanics _____.
4. Anglos _____.
5. Blacks _____.
6. Older people _____.

It's likely that you were able to complete each sentence without much hesitation. Does this mean you were stereotyping? You

Farcus
by David Waisglass
Gordon Coulthart

WAISGLASS/COULTHART

© 1993 Farcus Cartoons

"Kid, there are two types of people in this world . . . those who generalize, and those who don't."

The Magic Wand

Quick-change artist
extraordinaire,
I whip out my folded cane
and change from black
man to blind man with a
flick of the wrist.

It is a profound
metamorphosis
From God gifted wizard of
roundball
dominating backboards
across America,
To God-gifted idiot savant
pounding out chart-busters
on a cock-eyed whim;
From sociopathic gang-
banger with death for eyes
To all seeing soul with
saintly spirit;

From rape deranged
misogynist
to poor motherless child;
From welfare-rich pimp
to disability-rich gimp;
And from 'white man's
burden'
to every man's burden.

It is always a profound
metamorphosis.
Whether from cursed by
man to cursed by God
or from scripture con-
demned to God ordained,
my final form is never of
my choosing.
I only wield the wand;
You are the magician.

Lynn Manning

can answer this question by deciding whether your generalizations fit the three characteristics of stereotypes:

- You often categorize people on the basis of this easily recognized characteristic. For example, the first thing you notice about a person is his or her skin color.
- You ascribe a set of characteristics to most or all members of a category. For example, you assume that all older people are doddering or all men are insensitive to women's concerns.
- You apply the set of characteristics to any member of the group. For example, when you meet an older person, you expect him or her to be slow-witted and confused.[3]

Once we buy into stereotypes like these, we seek out isolated behaviors that support our inaccurate beliefs. For example, men and women in conflict often remember only behaviors of the opposite sex that fit their gender stereotypes.[4] They then point to these behaviors—which might not be representative of how the other person typically behaves—as "evidence" to suit their stereotypical and inaccurate claims: "Look! There you go criticizing me again. Typical for a woman!"

Stereotypes can plague interracial communication.[5] Surveys of college student attitudes show that many blacks characterize whites as "demanding" and "manipulative," whereas many whites characterize blacks as "loud" and "ostentatious." Brent Staples describes how being a black man leads some people—particularly white women—to be afraid of him for no good reason (see p. 208 in Chapter 6). Stereotypes like these can hamper professional relationships as well as personal ones. For example, doctor-patient communication in the United States—particularly between white physicians and minority patients—can suffer from stereotyping on both sides. Physicians may fail to provide important information because they think their patients won't understand, and patients may not ask important questions because they believe their doctors don't have time for them. These kinds of expectations lead to self-fulfilling spirals and poorer health care.[6]

Stereotyping doesn't always arise from bad intentions. In some cases, careless generalizations can grow from good intentions, and even from a little bit of knowledge. For example, knowing that people raised in collectivistic cultures (see pp. 56–57 in Chapter 2) tend to conform to group norms may lead you to mistakenly assume that anyone you meet from such a background is likely to be a selfless team player. But not all members of a group are equally collectivistic, or individualistic for that matter. For example, a close look at Americans of European and Latin descent showed differences within each group.[7] Some Latinos were more independent than some Euro-Americans, and vice versa. Moreover, teens in Japan (a traditionally collectivist culture) say they often feel torn between individualism and collectivism, between time-honored traditions and contemporary trends.[8] As our world's "global village" becomes more connected by technology and media, generalizations about specific cultures are likely to become less accurate.

Stereotypes don't always lead to communication problems. If the person with whom you are interacting happens to fit the pattern in your mind, there may be no difficulties. But if your mental image does not happen to match the characteristics of the other person, problems can arise. A fascinating series of experiments on perceptions of prejudice and gender bias illustrates this point.[9] In one phase of the experiments, white and black students were presented with stories in which a prejudicial act might or might not have taken place. For example, a man who has been promised a hotel room over the phone is later denied the room when he shows up in person. Four race combinations were used for each story: white perpetrator/black victim, white perpetrator/white victim, black perpetrator/white victim, and black perpetrator/black victim. In almost all instances, participants were more likely to label white-on-black behavior (white perpetrator and black victim) as prejudice than any other combination. In addition, females were more likely than males, and blacks were more likely than whites, to label an action as prejudiced. From these results, the researchers conclude that a prototypic or "model" stereotype exists regarding racism

THE INVESTIGATION

John Honik

(whites oppress blacks, men oppress women, and not the reverse) and that "participants who belong to traditionally oppressed groups (blacks, women) may be more sensitive to potential prejudice." In other words, we select, organize, and interpret behavior in ways that fit our existing notions about others' motives.

One way to avoid the kinds of communication problems that come from excessive stereotyping is to "decategorize" others, giving yourself a chance to treat them as individuals instead of assuming that they possess the same characteristics as every other member of the group to which you assign them.

Invitation to Insight

Exploring Your Biases

ThomsonNOW You can explore your hidden biases toward race, gender, age, disability, and other issues by taking a series of self-tests online. You can find the link to these tests through your ThomsonNOW for *Looking Out/Looking In.*

Punctuation   The process of organizing goes beyond our generalized perceptions of people. We also can organize our interactions with others in different ways, and these differing organizational schemas can have a powerful effect on our relationships with others. Communication theorists use the term **punctuation** to describe the determination of causes and effects in a series of interactions.[10] You can begin to understand how punctuation operates by visualizing a running quarrel between a husband and wife. The husband accuses the wife of being too critical, whereas she complains that he is withdrawing from her. Notice that the order in which each partner punctuates this cycle affects how the quarrel looks. The husband begins by blaming the wife: "I withdraw because you're so critical." The wife organizes the situation differently, starting with the husband: "I criticize because you withdraw." After the cycle gets rolling, it is impossible to say which accusation is accurate. The answer depends on how the sentence is punctuated. Figure 3.4 illustrates how this process operates.

FIGURE 3.4
The Same Event Can Be Punctuated in More than One Way

Differing punctuations can lead to a variety of communication problems. Notice how the following situations seem different depending on how they're punctuated:

"I don't like your friend because he never has anything to say."
"He doesn't talk to you because you act like you don't like him."

"I keep talking because you interrupt so much."
"I interrupt because you don't give me a chance to say what's on my mind."

The kind of finger pointing that goes along with arguing over which punctuation scheme is correct will probably make matters worse. It's far more productive to recognize that a dispute can look different to each party and then move on to the more important question of "What can we do to make things better?"

Skill Builder

Punctuation Practice

You can appreciate how different punctuation patterns can influence attitudes and behavior by following these directions.

1. Use the format pictured in Figure 3.4 to diagram the following situations:

   a. A father and daughter are growing more and more distant. The daughter withdraws because she interprets her father's coolness as rejection. The father views his daughter's aloofness as a rebuff and withdraws further.

   b. The relationship between two friends is becoming strained. One jokes to lighten up the tension, and the other becomes more tense.

   c. A dating couple is on the verge of breaking up. One partner frequently asks the other to show more affection. The other withdraws physical contact.

2. Identify two punctuating schemes for each of the situations described in step 1. Consider how the differing schemes would affect the way the two people in each situation respond to one another.

Now identify a difficult communication issue in your own life. Punctuate it in two ways: how you would punctuate it and how the other person might punctuate it. Discuss how seeing the issue from the other person's point of view might change the way you communicate as you discuss the issue.

Interpretation

After we have selected and organized our perceptions, we interpret them in a way that makes some sort of sense. **Interpretation** plays a role in virtually every interpersonal act. Is the person who smiles at you across a crowded room interested in romance or simply being polite? Is a friend's kidding a sign of affection or irritation? Should you take an invitation to "drop by any time" literally or not?

Several factors cause us to interpret an event in one way or another:

Degree of involvement with the other person We sometimes view people with whom we have or seek a relationship more favorably than those whom we observe from a detached perspective.[11] One recent study revealed how this principle operates in everyday life. A group of male subjects was asked to critique presentations by women who allegedly owned restaurants. Half of these presentations were designed to be competent and half to be incompetent. The men who were told they would be having a casual date with the female speakers judged their presentations—whether competent or not—more highly than those who didn't expect any involvement with the speakers.[12]

Personal experience What meaning have similar events held? If, for example, you've been gouged by landlords in the past, you might be skeptical about an apartment manager's assurances that careful housekeeping will assure you the refund of your cleaning deposit.

Assumptions about human behavior "People generally do as little work as possible to get by." "In spite of their mistakes, people are doing the best they can." Beliefs like these will shape the way we interpret another's actions.

Attitudes The attitudes we hold shape the way we make sense of others' behaviors. For example, what would you think if you overheard one man say "I love you" to another? In one study, people with a high degree of homophobia (the fear of or discrimination against homosexuals) were likely to interpret this comment as an indication that the speaker was gay. Those with lower levels of homophobia were more likely to regard the affectionate statement as platonic rather than romantic.[13]

Expectations Anticipation shapes interpretations. If you imagine that your boss is unhappy with your work, you'll probably feel threatened by a request to "see me in my office first thing Monday morning." On the other hand, if you imagine that your work will be rewarded, your weekend will probably be pleasant.

Knowledge If you know that a friend has just been jilted by a lover or been fired from a job, you'll interpret his aloof behavior differently than you would if you were unaware of what had happened. If you know that an instructor speaks sarcastically to all students, you won't be as likely to take her remarks personally.

Self-concept When you're feeling insecure, the world is a very different place from the world you experience when you're feeling secure. For example, the recipient's self-concept has proven to be the single greatest factor in determining whether people who are on the receiving end of being teased interpret the teaser's motives as being friendly or hostile, and whether they respond with comfort or defensiveness.[14] The same goes for happiness and sadness or any other opposing emotions. The way we feel about ourselves strongly influences how we interpret others' behavior.

Relational satisfaction The behavior that seems positive when you are happy with a partner might seem completely different when you are unhappy with a partner. For example, unsatisfied partners in a couple are more likely than satisfied partners to blame one another when things go wrong.[15] They are also more likely to believe that their partners are selfish and have negative

We don't see things as they are. We see things as we are.

Anais Nin

intentions. Unhappy spouses are more likely than happy ones to make negative interpretations of their mate's behavior. To see how this principle operates, recall the husband-wife quarrel we discussed earlier. Suppose the wife suggests that they get away for a weekend vacation. If the marriage has been troubled, the husband might interpret his wife's suggestion as more criticism ("You never pay attention to me"), and the fight will continue. If the marriage is solid, he is more likely to view the suggestion as a bid for a romantic getaway. It wasn't the event that shaped the reaction, but rather the way the husband interpreted the event.

Although we have talked about selection, organization, and interpretation separately, the three phases of perception can occur in differing sequences. For example, a parent or babysitter's past interpretations (such as "Jason is a troublemaker") can influence future selections (his behavior becomes especially noticeable) and the organization of events (when there's a fight, the assumption is that Jason started it). As with all communication, perception is an ongoing process in which it is hard to pin down beginnings and endings.

Negotiation

So far our discussion has focused on the components of perception—selection, organization, and interpretation—that take place in each individual's mind. But perception isn't just a solitary activity: A big part of sense-making occurs between and among people as they influence one another's perceptions and try to achieve a shared perspective. This process is known as **negotiation**.

One way to understand how negotiation operates is to view interpersonal communication as an exchange of stories. Scholars call the stories we use to describe our personal worlds **narratives**.[16] Virtually every interpersonal situation can be described by more than one narrative. These narratives often differ: Ask two quarreling children why they're fighting and they'll each describe how the other person is responsible for launching the conflict. Likewise, courtrooms are filled with opponents who tell very different narratives about who is the "villain" and who is the "hero." Even happy families have stories that place members in particular roles. (Think of the roles in some families you know: "scatterbrain," "the smart one," "athlete," and so on.) In best-case scenarios, family storytelling can actually enhance perspective-taking and lead to family satisfaction and functioning.[17]

When our narratives clash with those of others, we can either hang on to our own point of view and refuse to consider anyone else's (usually not productive), or we can try to negotiate a narrative that creates at least some common ground. Shared narratives provide the best chance for smooth communication. For example, romantic partners who celebrate their successful struggles against relational obstacles are happier than those who don't have this shared appreciation.[18] Likewise, couples that agree about the important turning points in their relationships are more satisfied than those who have different views of what incidents were most important.[19]

Shared narratives don't have to be accurate to be powerful. Couples who report being happily married after fifty or more years seem to collude in a relational narrative that doesn't jibe with the facts.[20] They agree that they rarely have conflict, although objective analysis reveals that they have had their share of struggles. Without overtly agreeing to do so, they choose to blame outside forces or unusual circumstances for problems instead of blaming each other. They offer the most charitable interpretations of each other's behavior, believing that their spouse acts with good intentions when things don't go well. They seem willing to forgive, or even forget, transgressions. Communication researcher Judy Pearson evaluates these findings:

> Should we conclude that happy couples have a poor grip on reality? Perhaps they do, but is the reality of one's marriage better known by outside onlookers than by the players themselves? The conclusion is evident. One key to a long happy marriage is to tell yourself and others that you have one and then to behave as though you do![21]

Influences on Perception

Now that we've explored the processes by which we perceive, it's time to look at some of the influences that cause us to select, organize, interpret, and negotiate information.

Physiological Influences

The first set of influences we need to examine involves our physical makeup. Within the wide range of human similarities, each of us perceives the world in a unique way because of physiological factors. In other words, although the same events exist "out there," each of us receives different images because of our unique perceptual hardware. Consider the long list of factors that shapes our views of the world:

The Senses   The differences in how each of us sees, hears, tastes, touches, and smells stimuli can affect interpersonal relationships. Consider the following everyday situations:

"Turn down that radio! It's going to make me go deaf."

"It's not too loud. If I turn it down, it will be impossible to hear it."

"It's freezing in here."

"Are you kidding? We'll suffocate if you turn up the heat!"

"Why don't you pass that truck? The highway is clear for a mile."

"I can't see that far, and I'm not going to get us killed."

These disputes aren't just over matters of opinion. The sensory data we receive are different. Differences in vision and hearing are the easiest to recognize, but other differences exist as well. There is evidence that identical foods taste differently to different individuals.[22] Scents that please some people repel others. Likewise, temperature variations that leave some of us uncomfortable are inconsequential to others. Recognizing these differences won't eliminate them, but it will make it easier to remember that the other person's preferences aren't crazy, just different.

Age   Older people often view the world differently from younger ones because they have a greater scope and number of experiences. There are also developmental differences that shape perceptions. Swiss psychologist Jean Piaget described a series of stages that children pass through on their way to adulthood.[23] According to

SALLY FORTH   by Greg Howard

To a Laplander, a temperature of fifty-eight degrees may be "hot," to a South African it may be "cold." The statement "It is hot (or cold)" is a statement about what is going on inside one's body. The statement "The temperature is now ninety degrees (or fifty-eight degrees)" is a statement about what is going on outside one's body. . . .

This distinction is by no means trivial. . . . I can never prove to a Laplander that fifty-eight degrees is "cool," but I can prove to him that it is fifty-eight degrees. In other words, there is no paradox in two different people's concluding that the weather is both "hot" and "cold" at the same time. As long as they both know that each of them is talking about a different reality, their conversation can proceed in a fairly orderly way.

From Neil Postman, *Crazy Talk, Stupid Talk*

Piaget, younger children are incapable of performing mental feats that are natural to the rest of us. Until they approach the age of 7, for example, they aren't able to take another person's point of view. This fact helps explain why children often seem egocentric, selfish, and uncooperative. A parent's exasperated plea, "Can't you see I'm too tired to play?" just won't make sense to a 4-year-old full of energy who imagines that everyone else must feel the same.

Health   Recall the last time you came down with a cold, flu, or some other ailment. Do you remember how different you felt? You probably had much less energy. It's likely that you felt less sociable and that your thinking was slower than usual. These kinds of changes have a strong impact on how you relate to others. It's good to realize that someone else may be behaving differently because of illness. In the same way, it's important to let others know when you feel ill so that they can give you the understanding you need.

Fatigue   Just as being ill can affect your relationships, so can being overly tired. Again it's important to recognize the fact that you or someone else may behave differently when fatigued. Trying to deal with important issues at such a time can get you into trouble.

Hunger   People often get grumpy when they haven't eaten and get sleepy after stuffing themselves. A number of physiological changes occur as we eat and become hungry again. Research confirms our own experience that being hungry (and getting grumpy) or having overeaten (and getting tired) affects how we interact with others. In one study, teenagers who reported that their family did not get enough food to eat were almost three times as likely to have been suspended from school, almost twice as likely to have difficulty getting along with others, and four times as likely to have no friends.[24]

Biological Cycles   Are you a "morning person" or a "night person"? Most of us can answer this question easily, and there's a good physiological reason behind our answer. Each of us is in a daily cycle in which all sorts of changes constantly occur, including body temperature, sexual drive, alertness, tolerance to stress, and mood.[25] Most of these changes are due to hormonal cycles. For instance, adrenal hormones, which affect feelings of stress, are secreted at higher rates during some hours. In the same manner, the male and female sex hormones enter our systems at variable rates. We often aren't conscious of these changes, but they surely influence the way we relate to one another. After we're aware that our own daily cycles and those of others govern our feelings and behavior, it becomes possible to manage our lives so that we deal with important issues at the most effective times.

Psychological Challenges   Some differences in perception are rooted in neurology. For instance, people with AD/HD (attention-deficit/hyperactivity disorder) are easily distracted from tasks and have difficulty delaying gratification. It's easy to imagine how those with AD/HD might find a long lecture boring and tedious, while other audience members are fascinated by the same lecture. People with bipolar disorder experience significant mood swings in which their perceptions of events, friends, and even family members shift dramatically. The National Institute of Mental Health estimates that between 5 and 7 million Americans are affected by these two disorders alone—and there are many other psychological conditions that influence people's perceptions.[26] It's important to remember that when others see and respond to the world differently than we do, there may be causes beyond what we immediately recognize.

Invitation to Insight

New Body, New Perspective

You can get a clearer idea of how physiology influences perception by trying the following exercise.

1. Choose one of the following situations:

   An evening in a singles bar

   A volleyball game

   A doctor's physical examination

2. How would the event you chose seem different if:

   Your eyesight were much worse (or better).

   You had a hearing loss.

   You were 8 inches taller (or shorter).

   You were coming down with a serious cold.

   You were a member of the opposite sex.

   You were ten years older (or younger).

   You had AD/HD.

Cultural Differences

So far you have seen how physical factors can make the world a different place for each of us. But there's another kind of perceptual gap that often blocks communication—the gap between people from different backgrounds. Every culture has its own worldview, its own way of looking at the world. Keeping in mind these differing cultural perspectives can be a good way of learning more about both ourselves and others. But at times it's easy to forget that people everywhere don't see things the way we do.

Father, Mother, and Me,
    Sister
    and Auntie say
All the people like us
    are We,
And everyone else
    is They.
And They live over
    the sea
While we live over
    the way,
But—would you
    believe it?—
They look upon We
As only a sort of They!
We eat pork and beef
With cow-horn-handled
    knives.

They who gobble Their
    rice off a leaf
Are horrified out of
    Their lives;
While They who live up
    a tree,
Feast on grubs and clay,
(Isn't it scandalous?) look
    upon We
As a simply disgusting
    They!
We eat kitcheny food.
We have doors that latch.
They drink milk and blood
Under an open thatch.
We have doctors to fee.
They have wizards
    to pay.

And (impudent heathen!)
They look upon We
As a quite impossible
    They!
All good people agree,
And all good people say,
All nice people, like us,
    are We
And everyone else is
    They:
But if you cross over
    the sea,
Instead of over the way,
You may end by (think
    of it!)
looking on We
As only a sort of They!

Rudyard Kipling, *We and They*

The power of culture to shape perceptions was demonstrated in studies over forty years ago exploring the domination of vision in one eye over the other.[27] Researchers used a binoculars-like device that projects different images to each eye. The subjects were twelve natives of the United States and twelve Mexicans. Each was presented with ten pairs of photographs, each pair containing one picture from U.S. culture (for example, a baseball game) and one from Mexican culture (for instance, a bullfight). After viewing each pair of images, the subjects reported what they saw. The results clearly indicated the power of culture to influence perceptions: Subjects had a strong tendency to focus on the image from their own background.

The range of cultural differences is wide. In Middle Eastern countries, personal scents play an important role in interpersonal relationships. Arabs consistently breathe on people when they talk. As anthropologist Edward Hall explains:

> To smell one's friend is not only nice, but desirable, for to deny him your breath is to act ashamed. Americans, on the other hand, trained as they are not to breathe in people's faces, automatically communicate shame in trying to be polite. Who would expect that when our highest diplomats are putting on their best manners they are also communicating shame? Yet this is what occurs constantly, because diplomacy is not only "eyeball to eyeball" but breath to breath.[28]

Even beliefs about the very value of talk differ from one culture to another.[29] Western cultures view talk as desirable and use it for social purposes as well as for task performance. Silence has a negative value in these cultures. It is likely to be interpreted as lack of interest, unwillingness to communicate, hostility, anxiety, shyness, or a sign of interpersonal incompatibility. Westerners are uncomfortable with silence, which they find embarrassing and awkward.

On the other hand, Asian cultures perceive talk differently. For thousands of years, Asian cultures have discouraged the expression of thoughts and feelings. Silence is valued, as Taoist sayings indicate: "In much talk there is great weariness," or "One who speaks does not know; one who knows does not speak." Unlike most North Americans who are uncomfortable with silence, Japanese and Chinese believe that remaining quiet is the proper state when there is nothing to be said. In Asian cultures, a talkative person is often considered a show-off or insincere.

It's easy to see how these different views of speech and silence can lead to communication problems when people from different cultures meet. Both the talkative American and the silent Asian are behaving in ways they believe are proper; yet each views the other with disapproval and mistrust. This may require them to recognize and deal with their **ethnocentrism**—the attitude that one's own culture is superior to others. An ethnocentric person thinks—either privately or openly—that anyone who does not belong to his or her in-group is somehow strange, wrong, or even inferior. Travel writer Rick Steves describes

A woman from Texas went to Washington, D.C., for a job in dormitory administration. When the dorm staff got together for meetings, she kept searching for the right time to break in— and never found it. Although back home she was considered outgoing and confident, in Washington she was perceived as shy and retiring. When she was evaluated at the end of a year, she was told to take an assertiveness-training course because of her inability to speak up.

That's why slight differences in conversational style—tiny little things like microseconds of a pause— can have enormous impact on your life. These little signals make up the mechanics of conversation, and when they're even slightly off, conversation is thrown off—or even cut off. The result in this case was a judgment of psychological problems—even in the mind of the woman herself, who really wondered what was wrong with her and signed up for assertiveness training.

Deborah Tannen, *That's Not What I Meant*

how an ethnocentric point of view can interfere with respect for other cultural practices:

> . . . we [Americans] consider ourselves very clean and commonly criticize other cultures as dirty. In the bathtub we soak, clean, and rinse, all in the same water. (We would never wash our dishes that way.) A Japanese visitor, who uses clean water for each step, might find our way of bathing strange or even disgusting. Many cultures spit in public and blow their nose right onto the street. They couldn't imagine doing that into a small cloth, called a hanky, and storing that in their pocket to be used again and again. Too often we think of the world in terms of a pyramid of "civilized" (us) on the top and "primitive" groups on the bottom. If we measured things differently (maybe according to stress, loneliness, heart attacks, hours spent in traffic jams, or family togetherness) things stack up differently.[30]

The way we communicate with strangers can reflect ethnocentric thinking. Author Anne Fadiman explains why Hmong immigrants from the mountains of Laos prefer their traditional shamanistic healers, called *txiv neeb*, to American doctors. Notice that both perspectives make sense, and that neither the American physicians nor the Hmong immigrants were able to get beyond their familiar set of perceptions to see the encounter from the other culture's point of view:

> A *txiv neeb* might spend as much as eight hours in a sick person's home; doctors forced their patients, no matter how weak they were, to come to the hospital, and then might spend only twenty minutes at their bedsides. *Txiv neebs* were polite and never needed to ask questions; doctors asked about their sexual and excretory habits. *Txiv neebs* could render an immediate diagnosis; doctors often demanded samples of blood (or even urine or feces, which they liked to keep in little bottles), took X rays, and waited for days for the results to come back from the laboratory—and then, after all that, sometimes they were unable to identify the cause of the problem. *Txiv neebs* never undressed their patients; doctors asked patients to take off all their clothes, and sometimes dared to put their fingers inside women's vaginas. *Txiv neebs* knew that to treat the body without treating the soul was an act of patent folly; doctors never even mentioned the soul.[31]

It isn't necessary to travel overseas to encounter differing cultural perspectives. Within this country there are many subcultures, and the members of each one have backgrounds that cause them to see things in different ways. Failure to recognize these differences can lead to unfortunate and unnecessary misunderstandings. For example, an uninformed Anglo teacher or police officer might interpret the downcast expression of a Latino female as a sign of avoidance, or even dishonesty, when in fact this is the proper behavior in her culture for a female being addressed by an older man. To make direct eye contact in such a case would be considered undue brashness or even a sexual come-on.

Along with ethnicity, geography also can influence perception. A fascinating series of studies revealed that climate and geographic latitude are remarkably accurate predictors of communication predispositions.[32] People living in southern latitudes of the United States are more socially isolated, less tolerant of ambiguity, higher in self-esteem, more likely to touch others, and more likely to verbalize their thoughts and feelings. This sort of finding helps explain why communicators who travel from one part of a country to another find that their old patterns of communicating don't work as well in their new location. A southerner whose relatively talkative, high-touch style seemed completely normal at home might be viewed as pushy and aggressive in a new northern home.

It's encouraging to know that open-minded communicators can overcome preexisting stereotypes and learn to appreciate people from different backgrounds as individuals. In one study, college students who were introduced to strangers from different cultural backgrounds developed attitudes about their new conversational partners based more on their personal behavior than on preexisting expectations about how people from those backgrounds might behave.[33]

Social Roles

So far you have seen how cultural and physiological differences can affect communication. Along with these differences, another set of perceptual factors can lead to communication difficulties. From almost the time we're born, each of us is indirectly taught a whole set of roles that we'll be expected to play. In one sense this set of prescribed parts is necessary because it enables a society to function smoothly and provides the security that comes from knowing what's expected of you. But in another sense, having roles defined in advance can lead to wide gaps in understanding. When roles become unquestioned and rigid, people tend to see the world from their own viewpoint, having no experiences that show them how other people see it. Naturally, in such a situation communication suffers.

Gender Roles   Although people use the terms *sex* and *gender* as if they were identical, there is an important difference. *Sex* refers to biological characteristics of a man or woman, whereas *gender* refers to the social and psychological dimensions of masculine and feminine behavior.

In every society gender is one of the most important factors in determining how people perceive one another. **Gender roles** are socially approved ways that men and women are expected to behave. Children learn the importance of gender roles by watching other people and by being exposed to media, as well as by receiving reinforcement.[34] After members of a society learn these customary roles, they tend to regard violations as unusual—or even undesirable.

Some theorists have suggested that stereotypical masculine and feminine behaviors are not opposite poles of a single continuum, but rather two separate sets of behavior.[35] With this view, an individual can act in a masculine manner or a feminine manner or exhibit both types of characteristics. The male–female dichotomy, then, is replaced with four psychological sex types: masculine, feminine, **androgynous** (combining masculine and feminine traits), and undifferentiated (neither masculine nor feminine). Combining the four psychological sex types with the traditional physiological sex types produces the eight categories listed in Table 3.1.

Table 3.1	Gender Roles	
	Male	**Female**
Masculine	Masculine males	Masculine females
Feminine	Feminine males	Feminine females
Androgynous	Androgynous males	Androgynous females
Undifferentiated	Undifferentiated males	Undifferentiated females

Each of these eight psychological sex types perceives interpersonal relationships differently. For example, masculine males may be likely to see their interpersonal relationships as opportunities for competitive interaction, as opportunities to win something. Feminine females probably see their interpersonal relationships as opportunities to be nurturing, to express their feelings and emotions. Androgynous males and females, on the other hand, differ little in their perceptions of their interpersonal relationships.

Androgynous individuals tend to see their relationships as opportunities to behave in a variety of ways, depending on the nature of the relationships themselves, the context in which a particular relationship takes place, and the myriad other variables affecting what might constitute appropriate behavior. These variables are usually ignored by the sex-typed masculine males and feminine females, who have a smaller repertoire of behaviors.

Occupational Roles   The kind of work we do often influences our view of the world. Imagine five people taking a walk through the park. One, a botanist, is fascinated by the variety of trees and other plants. Another, a zoologist, is looking for interesting animals. The third, a meteorologist, keeps an eye on the sky, noticing changes in the weather. The fourth companion, a psychologist, is totally unaware of nature, instead concentrating on the interaction among the people in the park. The fifth person, being a pickpocket, quickly takes advantage of the others' absorption to make some money. There are two lessons in this little scenario. The first, of course, is to watch your wallet carefully. The second is that our occupational roles shape our perceptions.

Even within the same occupational setting, the different roles that participants have can affect their perceptions. Consider a typical college classroom, for example: The experiences of the instructor and students often are dissimilar. Having dedicated a large part of their lives to their work, most instructors see their subject matter—whether French literature, physics, or communication—as vitally important. Students who are taking the course to satisfy a general education requirement may view the subject differently: maybe as one of many obstacles that stand between them and a degree, maybe as a chance to meet new people. Another difference centers on the amount of knowledge possessed by the parties. To an instructor who has taught the course many times, the material probably seems extremely simple; but to students encountering it for the first time, it may seem strange and confusing. We don't need to spell out the interpersonal strains and stresses that come from such differing perceptions.

Perhaps the most dramatic illustration of how occupational roles shape perception occurred in 1971.[36] Stanford psychologist Philip Zimbardo recruited a group of middle-class, well-educated young men. He randomly chose eleven to serve as "guards" in a mock prison set up in the basement of Stanford's psychology building. He issued the guards uniforms, handcuffs, whistles, and billy clubs. The remaining ten subjects became "prisoners" and were placed in rooms with metal bars, bucket toilets, and cots.

Zimbardo let the guards establish their own rules for the experiment. The rules were tough: No talking during meals, rest periods, and after lights-out. Head counts at 2:30 A.M. Troublemakers received short rations.

Faced with these conditions, the prisoners began to resist. Some barricaded their doors with beds. Others went on hunger strikes. Several ripped off their identifying number tags. The guards reacted to the rebellion by clamping down hard on protesters. Some turned sadistic, physically and verbally abusing the prisoners. They threw prisoners into solitary confinement. Others forced prisoners to call each other names and clean out toilets with their bare hands.

Within a short time the experiment had become reality for both prisoners and guards. Several inmates had stomach cramps and lapsed into uncontrollable weeping. Others suffered from headaches, and one broke out in a head-to-toe rash after his request for early "parole" was denied by the guards.

The experiment was scheduled to go on for two weeks, but after six days Zimbardo realized that what had started as a simulation had become too intense. "I knew by then that they were thinking like prisoners and not like people," he said. "If we were able to demonstrate that pathological behavior could be produced in so short a time, think of what damage is being done in 'real' prisons. . . ."

This dramatic exercise in which twenty-one well-educated, middle-class citizens turned almost overnight into sadistic bullies and demoralized victims tells us that how we think is a function of our roles in society. It seems that what we are is determined largely by society's designation of who we are. Fortunately, many officials in the field of law enforcement are aware of the perceptual blindness that can come with one's job. These professionals have developed programs that help to overcome the problem, as the "Operation Empathy" reading illustrates.

Invitation to Insight

Role Reversal

Walk a mile in another person's shoes. Find a group that is foreign to you, and try to become a member of it for a while.

- If you're down on the police, see if your local department has a ride-along program where you can spend several hours on patrol with one or two officers.

- If you think the present state of education is a mess, become a teacher yourself. Maybe an instructor will give you the chance to plan one or more classes.

- If you're adventuresome, follow the example of the police officers in the article on page 102 and become a homeless person for a day. See how you're treated.

- If you're a political conservative, try getting involved in a radical organization; if you're a radical, check out the conservatives.

Whatever group you join, try to become part of it as best you can. Don't just observe. Get into the philosophy of your new role and see how it feels. You may find that all those weird people aren't so weird after all.

Self-Concept

Another factor that influences how we think of ourselves and interact with others is the self-concept. Extensive research shows that a person with high self-esteem is more likely to have a high opinion of others, whereas a person with low self-esteem is likely to have a low opinion of others.[37] Your own experience may bear this out: People with low self-esteem are often cynical and quick to ascribe the worst possible motives to others, whereas people with high self-esteem often think favorably about others. As one writer put it, "What we find 'out there' is what we put there with our unconscious projections. When we think we are looking out a window, it may be, more often than we realize, that we are really gazing into a looking glass."[38]

Operation Empathy: Preparation for the Changing Police Role

We are all aware that it is extremely difficult to immerse the average police officer into situations that will reveal the feelings of the down-and-outer, the social outcast, the have-nots, and show us their perspective of normal law-enforcement procedures. Obviously the officer, in his or her police role, would not fit into a ghetto of any kind. But suppose he or she was a person with a great deal of courage, willing for the sake of experimentation to become a bum, a skid row habitant.

Our Covina officers who were willing to become skid row habitants were carefully selected and conditioned for the role they were about to play. Each was given three dollars with which to purchase a complete outfit of pawn shop clothing. Among other props were such items as a shopping bag filled with collected junk, and a wine bottle camouflaged with a brown paper sack.

Conditioned and ready, our officers, assigned in pairs, moved into the Los Angeles skid row district. They soon discovered that when they tried to leave the area, walking a few blocks into the legitimate retail sections, they were told, "Go back where you belong!" Our officers knew in reality they were not "bums," but they found that other citizens quickly categorized them and treated them accordingly.

During the skid row experiment, our officers ate in the rescue missions and sat through the prayer services with other outcasts and derelicts. They roamed the streets and the alleys and discovered many leveling experiences. Some were anticipated, others were not. Perhaps the most meaningful experience of the skid row exercise occurred to Tom Courtney, a young juvenile officer with five years' police service.

It was dusk, and Tom and his partner were sauntering back to a pre-arranged gathering place. Feeling a little sporty, the pair decided to "polish off" the bottle of wine. They paused in a convenient parking lot, and Tom tipped the bottle up. As if from nowhere, two uniformed policemen materialized before the surprised pair. Tom and his partner were spread-eagled against a building and searched. Forgetting the admonishment not to reveal identities and purpose unless absolutely necessary, Tom panicked and identified himself. Later, Tom found it difficult to explain why he was so quick in his revelation. "You wouldn't understand," he told me; then blurted he "thought he might get shot."

I found it difficult to receive this as a rational explanation, especially since Tom stated that the officers, while firm, were courteous at all times. With some additional prodding, Tom admitted that as he was being searched, he suddenly thought of every negative thing he had ever heard about a policeman. He even perceived a mental flash of a newspaper headline: "Police Officer Erroneously Shot While on Field Experiment."

"I know better now," Tom continued, "but when you feel that way about yourself, you believe—you believe."

I attempted to rationalize with Tom his reason for fear. I asked if he was certain that the officers were courteous. He replied in the affirmative, but added, "They didn't smile, or tell me what they were going to do next." Tom had discovered a new emotional reaction within his own personal makeup, and it left a telling impression.

Today, Tom Courtney is still telling our department personnel, "For God's sake, smile when you can. And above all, tell the man you're shaking down what you are going to do. Take the personal threat out of the encounter, if you can." Equally important as Tom's experience, I believe, is the lesson we learned about personal judgments. Our men in the "Operation Empathy" experiment found they were adjudged by the so-called normal population as "being like" all the other inmates of skid row, simply because their appearance was representative.

Perhaps we would all do well to heed the lesson, for now, more than at any other time in our history, police officers must guard against the natural tendency to lump people into categories simply because they look alike.

Fred Ferguson, "Field Experiment: Preparation for the Changing Police Role"

Common Tendencies in Perception

By now it's obvious that many factors affect the way we interpret the world. Social scientists use the term **attribution** to describe the process of attaching meaning to behavior. We attribute meaning both to our own actions and to the actions of others, but we often use different yardsticks. Research has uncovered several perceptual tendencies that can lead to attribution errors.[39]

We Judge Ourselves More Charitably than Others

In an attempt to convince ourselves and others that the positive face we show to the world is true, we tend to judge ourselves in the most generous terms possible. Social scientists have labeled this tendency the **self-serving bias**.[40] On one hand when others suffer, we often blame the problem on their personal qualities. On the other hand, when we suffer, we blame the problem on forces outside ourselves. Consider a few examples:

> When *they* botch a job, we might think they weren't listening well or trying hard enough; when *we* botch a job, the problem was unclear directions or not enough time.

> When *he* lashes out angrily, we say he's being moody or too sensitive; when *we* lash out angrily, it's because of the pressure we've been under.

> When *she* gets caught speeding, we say she should have been more careful; when *we* get caught speeding, we deny that we were driving too fast or we say, "Everybody does it."

> When *she* uses profanity, it's because of a flaw in her character; when *we* swear, it's because the situation called for it.[41]

The egocentric tendency to rate ourselves more favorably than others rate us has been demonstrated experimentally.[42] In one study, members of a random sample of men were asked to rank themselves on their ability to get along with others.[43] Defying mathematical laws, all subjects—every last one—put themselves in the top half of the population. Sixty percent rated themselves in the top 10 percent of the population, and an amazing 25 percent rated themselves in the top 1 percent. In the same study, 70 percent of the men ranked their leadership in the top quarter of the population, whereas only 2 percent ranked their leadership as below average. Sixty percent said they were in the top quarter in athletic abilities, whereas only 6 percent said they were below average.

We Pay More Attention to Others' Negative Characteristics

What do you think of Harvey? He's handsome, hardworking, intelligent, and honest. He's also very conceited.

Did the last characteristic listed make a difference in your judgment? If it did, you're not alone. Research shows that when people are aware of both positive and negative personal characteristics, they tend to be more influenced by the less desirable characteristics. For example, one

I have heard students say things like, "It was John's fault, his speech was so confusing nobody could have understood it." Then, two minutes later, the same student remarked, "It wasn't my fault, what I said could not have been clearer. John must be stupid." Poor John! He was blamed when he was the sender and when he was the receiver. John's problem was that he was the other person, and that's who is always at fault.

Stephen W. King

"The truth is, Cauldwell, we never see ourselves as others see us."

study revealed that job interviewers were likely to reject a candidate who revealed negative information, even when the rest of the information about the candidate was positive.

We Are Influenced by the Obvious

The error of being influenced by what is most obvious is understandable. As you read at the beginning of this chapter, we select stimuli from our environment that are noticeable: intense, repetitive, unusual, or otherwise attention-grabbing. The problem is that the most obvious factor is not necessarily the only one—or the most significant one for an event. For example,

- When two children (or adults, for that matter) fight, it may be a mistake to blame the one who lashes out first. Perhaps the other one was at least equally responsible, teasing or refusing to cooperate.
- You might complain about an acquaintance whose malicious gossiping or arguing has become a bother, forgetting that by putting up with such behavior in the past you have been at least partially responsible.
- You might blame an unhappy working situation on the boss, overlooking other factors beyond her control such as a change in the economy, the policy of higher management, or demands of customers or other workers.

We Cling to First Impressions

Labeling people according to our first impressions is an inevitable part of the perception process. These labels are a way of making interpretations: "She seems cheerful." "He seems sincere." "They sound awfully conceited."

If such first impressions are accurate, they can be useful ways of deciding how to respond best to people in the future. Problems arise, however, when the labels we attach are inaccurate; after we form an opinion of someone, we tend to hang on to it and make any conflicting information fit our opinion.

Social scientists have coined the term **halo effect** to describe the tendency to form an overall positive impression of a person on the basis of one positive characteristic. Most typically, the positive impression comes from physical attractiveness, which can lead people to attribute all sorts of other virtues to the good-looking person.[44] For example, employment interviewers rate mediocre but attractive job applicants higher than their less attractive candidates.[45] And once employers form positive impressions, they often ask questions that confirm their image of the applicant.[46] For example, when an interviewer forms a positive impression, she might ask leading questions aimed at supporting her positive views ("What lessons did you learn from that setback?"), interpret answers in a positive light ("Ah, taking time away from school to travel was a good idea!"), encourage the applicant ("Good point!"), and sell the company's virtues ("I think you would like working here"). Likewise, applicants who create a negative first impression are operating under a cloud that may be impossible to dispel—a phenomenon sometimes referred to as "the devil effect."[47]

The power of first impressions is also important in personal relationships. A study of college roommates found that those who had positive initial impressions of each other were likely to have positive subsequent interactions, manage their conflicts constructively, and continue living together.[48] The converse was also true: Roommates who got off to a bad start tended to spiral negatively. This reinforces the wisdom and importance of the old adage, "You never get a second chance to make a first impression."

Given the almost unavoidable tendency to form first impressions, the best advice we can give is to keep an open mind and to be willing to change your opinion as events prove it mistaken.

We Assume that Others Are Similar to Us

In Chapter 2 you read one example of this principle: that people with low self-esteem imagine that others view them unfavorably, whereas people with high self-esteem imagine that others view them favorably, too. The frequently mistaken assumption that others' views are similar to our own applies in a wide range of situations:

- You've heard a slightly raunchy joke that you think is pretty funny. You assume that it won't offend a somewhat straitlaced friend. It does.
- You've been bothered by an instructor's tendency to get off the subject during lectures. If you were an instructor, you'd want to know if anything you were doing was creating problems for your students, so you decide that your instructor will probably be grateful for some constructive criticism. Unfortunately, you're wrong.
- You lost your temper with a friend a week ago and said some things you regret. In fact, if someone said those things to you, you'd consider the relationship finished. Imagining that your friend feels the same way, you avoid making contact. In fact, your friend has avoided you because she thinks *you're* the one who wants to end things.

Examples like these show that others don't always think or feel the way we do and that assuming that similarities exist can lead to problems. How can you find out the other person's real position? Sometimes by asking directly, sometimes by checking with others, and sometimes by making an educated guess after you've thought the matter out. All these alternatives are better than simply assuming that everyone would react as you do.

Invitation to Insight

Understanding Your Personality Type

What personality factors influence how you see the world? Find out how you rank on the Myers-Briggs Inventory. You can find the link to this site through your ThomsonNOW for *Looking Out/Looking In*.

After taking the test, you can read explanations of how your personality type is reflected in the way you communicate. You may find it valuable to encourage others with whom you have relationships to take the test too. Read together how your styles differ from each other. Understanding how each of you perceives events differently can be a good start toward adapting your communication to reflect each other's styles.

Perception Checking

Serious problems can arise when people treat interpretations as if they were matters of fact. Like most people, you probably resent others jumping to conclusions about the reasons for your behavior.

"Of course I care about how you imagined I thought you perceived I wanted you to feel."

"Why are you mad at me?" (Who said you were?)

"What's the matter with you?" (Who said anything was the matter?)

"Come on now. Tell the truth." (Who said you were lying?)

As you'll learn in Chapter 9, even if your interpretation is correct, a dogmatic, mind-reading statement is likely to generate defensiveness. The skill of **perception checking** provides a better way to handle your interpretations.[49]

Elements of Perception Checking

A complete perception check has three parts:

■ A description of the behavior you noticed
■ At least two possible interpretations of the behavior
■ A request for clarification about how to interpret the behavior

Perception checks for the preceding three examples would look like this:

> "When you stomped out of the room and slammed the door," (*behavior*) "I wasn't sure whether you were mad at me" (*first interpretation*) "or just in a hurry." (*second interpretation*) "How *did* you feel?" (*request for clarification*)

> "You haven't laughed much in the last couple of days." (*behavior*) "It makes me wonder whether something's bothering you" (*first interpretation*) "or whether you're just feeling quiet." (*second interpretation*) "What's up?" (*request for clarification*)

> "You said you really liked the job I did." (*behavior*) "On the other hand, there was something about your voice that made me think you may not like it." (*first interpretation*) "Maybe it's just my imagination, though." (*second interpretation*) "How do you really feel?" (*request for clarification*)

Perception checking is a tool for helping you understand others accurately instead of assuming that your first interpretation is correct. Because its goal is mutual understanding, perception checking is a cooperative approach to communication. Besides leading to more accurate perceptions, it minimizes defensiveness by preserving the other person's face. Instead of saying, in effect, "I know what you're thinking . . ." a perception check takes the more respectful approach that states or implies, "I know I'm not qualified to judge you without some help."

Perception Checking Considerations

Like every communication skill outlined in *Looking Out/Looking In*, perception checking isn't a mechanical formula that will work in every situation. As you develop the ability to check your perceptions, consider the following factors in deciding when and how to use this approach.

Completeness   Sometimes a perception check won't need all the parts listed earlier to be effective:

> "You haven't dropped by lately. Is anything the matter?" (*single interpretation combined with request for clarification*)
>
> "I can't tell whether you're kidding me about being cheap or if you're serious." (*behavior combined with interpretations*) "Are you mad at me?"
>
> "Are you sure you don't mind driving? I can use a ride if it's no trouble, but I don't want to take you out of your way." (*no need to describe behavior*)

Sometimes even the most skimpy perception check—a simple question like "What's going on?"—will do the job. You might also rely on other people to help you make sense of confusing behavior: "Rachelle has been awfully quiet lately. Do you know what's up?" A complete perception check is most necessary when the risk of sounding judgmental is highest.

Nonverbal Congruency   A perception check can succeed only if your nonverbal behavior reflects the open-mindedness of your words. An accusing tone of voice or a hostile glare will contradict the sincerely worded request for clarification, suggesting that you have already made up your mind about the other person's intentions.

Cultural Rules   The straightforward approach of perception checking has the best chance of working in what Chapter 5 identifies as *low-context cultures:* ones in which members use language as clearly and logically as possible. The dominant cultures of North America and Western Europe fit into this category, and members of these groups are most likely to appreciate the kind of straight talking that perception checking embodies. On the other hand, members of *high-context cultures* (more common in Latin America and Asia) value social harmony over clarity. High-context communicators are more likely to regard candid approaches like perception checking as potentially embarrassing, preferring instead less direct ways of understanding one another. Thus, a "let's get this straight" perception check that might work well with a Euro American manager who was raised to value clarity could be a serious mistake with a Mexican American or Asian American boss who has spent most of his or her life in a high-context culture.

Face Saving   Along with clarifying meaning, perception checking can sometimes be a face-saving way to raise an issue without directly threatening or attacking the other person. Consider these examples:

> "Are you planning on doing those dishes later, or did you forget that it's your turn?"
>
> "Am I boring you, or do you have something else on your mind?"

In the first case you might have been quite confident that the other person had no intention of doing the dishes, and in the second that the other person was bored. Even so, a perception check is a less threatening way of pointing out their behavior than direct confrontation. Remember—one element of competent communication is the ability to choose the best option from a large repertoire, and perception checking can be a useful strategy at times.

Perception Checking in Everyday Life

Perception checking only works if it is sincere and fits your personal style. The following examples show how perception checking sounds in everyday life and may help you find ways to use it when you are faced with ambiguous messages.

My Staring Boyfriend

My boyfriend and I had plans to spend a day sailing. While we were at the wharf waiting for boat, three pretty girls walked by and he stared at them and then said "I wish they were coming sailing with us!"

My feelings were hurt. After keeping quiet for a while, I decided to try a perception check. I said "When you said you wished those girls could come with us, I didn't know whether you were just joking or whether you think I'm plain and boring compared to them." Then I said to him, "I really want to know."

He got embarrassed and said he was just joking around. I'm not stupid or blind: I know he looks at other women sometimes, and I know some of them are prettier than I am. (I look at guys myself sometimes, but I don't think I stare as much as he does.) Even though I was pretty sure I knew what was going on here, I think the perception check was a good way to let him know that his staring does have an effect on me.

My Boss's Jokes

I get confused by my boss's sense of humor. Sometimes he jokes just to be funny, but other times he uses humor to make a point without coming right out and saying what's on his mind. Last week he was talking about the upcoming work schedule and he said with a laugh, "I own you all weekend!" I have a life besides work, so his comment left me worried.

I used a perception check to figure out what he meant: "Brad, when you told me 'I own you all weekend,' I wasn't sure whether you were kidding or whether you really expect me to work Saturday and Sunday. Were you serious?"

He kind of smiled and said, "No, I was just kidding. You only have to work Saturday and Sunday."

I still couldn't be sure whether or not he was serious, so I checked again: "You're kidding, right?"

My boss replied, "Well, I do need you at least one day, and two would be better." Once I figured

out what he really meant, we worked out a schedule that had me work Friday evening and Saturday morning, which gave me the time off I needed.

If I hadn't used the perception check, I would have wound up worrying about being tied up all weekend, and getting mad at my boss for no good reason. I'm glad I spoke up.

My Nervous Friend

My friend and I have been planning to spend a month in Europe next summer. We've had fun surfing the web for sites and getting the advice of people we know who have gone to places we want to visit.

We decided it would be simpler for one of us to handle all the reservations, and that's been my job. I really don't mind doing this, except my friend started to interrogate me about every detail. "Did you lock in the airfare?" "Did you remember to get the Eurail passes?" "What about a hotel in Rome?" "What about phone cards so we can call home?"

I kept my growing irritation inside, but finally it got to be more than I could handle. Fortunately, I used a perception check instead of attacking my friend: "Look, you've been asking me about every detail of our plan, even though I told you I would take care of everything. Do you think I'm going to mess up the planning? Do you want to take over the planning? What's going on?"

When I confronted her, my friend was embarrassed. She said she trusts me completely, but she is so excited that she has a hard time controlling herself. She told me that having the reservations made will leave her feeling like the trip is more of a reality and less of a dream.

Since we've talked, my friend still asks me how the plans are coming. But now that I know why she is so insistent, I find it more amusing than annoying.

My Dad's Affection

My father and I have a great relationship. A while back I picked him up at the airport after a week-long business trip and a long cross-country flight. On the way home, he was quiet—not his usual self. He said he was exhausted, which I understood. When we got home, he brightened up and started joking and playing with my younger brother. This left me feeling unhappy. I thought to myself, "Why is he so happy to see my brother when he hardly said a word to me?" I didn't say anything at the time. The next day I found myself feeling resentful toward my dad, and it showed. He said, "What's up with you?" But I was too embarrassed to say anything.

After learning this approach in class, I tried a perception check. I said, "Dad—when you were quiet on the way home after your business trip and then you perked up when you got home and saw Jaime, I wasn't sure what was up. I thought maybe you were happier to see him than me, or that maybe I'm imagining things. How come you said you were tired with me and then you perked up with Jaime?"

My dad felt awful. He said he was tired in the car, but once he got back to the house he was glad to be home and felt like a new man. I was too wrapped up in my mind to consider this alternative. Because I didn't use a perception check, I was unhappy and I started an unnecessary fight.

Communication Scenarios

Using your ThomsonNOW for *Looking Out/Looking In*, access "Communication Scenarios" and then click on "Perception Checking in Everyday Life" to watch and analyze video examples of perception checking. **ThomsonNOW**

Skill Builder

Perception Checking Practice

Practice your perception checking ability by developing three-part verifications for the following situations:

1. You made what you thought was an excellent suggestion to an instructor. The instructor looked uninterested but said she would check on the matter right away. Three weeks have passed, and nothing has changed.

2. A neighbor and good friend has not responded to your "Good morning" for three days in a row. This person is usually friendly.

3. You haven't received the usual weekly phone call from the folks back home in over a month. The last time you spoke, you had an argument about where to spend the holidays.

4. An old friend with whom you have shared the problems of your love life for years has recently changed when around you: The formerly casual hugs and kisses have become longer and stronger, and the occasions where you "accidentally" brush up against each other have become more frequent.

Empathy and Communication

Perception checking is a valuable tool for clarifying ambiguous messages. But ambiguity isn't the only cause of perceptual problems. Sometimes we understand *what* people mean without understanding *why* they believe as they do. At times like this we are short on the vital ability to empathize.

Empathy Defined

Empathy is the ability to re-create another person's perspective, to experience the world from the other's point of view. It may be impossible to ever experience another person's perspective completely, but with enough effort we can certainly gain a better idea of how the world appears to him or her. As we'll use the term here, empathy involves three dimensions.[50] In one dimension, empathy involves *perspective taking*—an attempt to take on the viewpoint of another person. This requires a suspension of judgment so that for the moment you set aside your own opinions and try to understand the other person. Empathy also has an *emotional* dimension that helps us get closer to experiencing others' feelings: to gain a sense of their fear, joy, sadness, and so on. A third dimension of empathy is a genuine *concern* for the welfare of the other person. When we empathize we go beyond just thinking and feeling as others do and genuinely care about their well-being.

The ability to empathize seems to exist in a rudimentary form in even the youngest children.[51] Research sponsored by the National Institute of Mental Health revealed what many parents know from experience: Virtually from birth, infants become visibly upset when they hear another baby crying, and children who are a few months old cry when they observe another child in tears. Young children have trouble distinguishing others' distress from their own. If, for example, one child hurts its finger, another baby might put its own finger into her mouth as if she were feeling pain. Researchers report cases in which children who see their parents in tears wipe their own eyes, even though they are not crying.

Although children may have a basic capacity to empathize, studies with twins suggest that the degree to which we are born with the ability to sense how others are feeling seems to vary according to genetic factors.[52] Although some people may have an inborn edge, environmental experiences are the key to developing the ability to understand others. Specifically, the way in which parents communicate with their children seems to affect their ability to understand

"How would you feel if the mouse did that to you?"

others' emotional states.[53] When parents point out to children the distress that others feel from their misbehavior ("Look how sad Jessica is because you took her toy. Wouldn't you be sad if someone took away your toys?"), those children gain a greater appreciation that their acts have emotional consequences than when parents simply label such behavior as inappropriate ("That was a mean thing to do!").

It is easy to confuse empathy with **sympathy**, but the concepts are different. With sympathy, you view the other person's situation from *your* point of view. With empathy, you view it from *the other person's* perspective. Consider the difference between sympathizing and empathizing with an unwed mother or a homeless person. When you sympathize, it is the other person's confusion, joy, or pain. When you empathize, the experience becomes your own, at least for the moment. On one hand, empathy is more profound than sympathy, because you experience the other's perspective. Nonetheless, empathy doesn't require you to *agree* with the other person. You can empathize with a difficult relative or a rude stranger without endorsing their behavior.

There is no consistent evidence that suggests that the ability to empathize is better for one sex or the other.[54] Some people, however, seem to have a hereditary capacity for greater empathizing than do others.[55] Studies of identical and fraternal twins indicate that identical female twins are more similar to each other in their ability to empathize than are fraternal twins. Interestingly, there seems to be no difference between male twins. Although empathy may have a biological basis, the role of environment can still play an important role. For example, parents who are sensitive to their children's feelings tend to have children who also are sensitive to the feelings of others.[56]

Total empathy is impossible to achieve. Completely understanding another person's point of view is simply too difficult a task for humans with different backgrounds and limited communication skills. Nonetheless, it is possible to get a strong sense of what the world looks like through another person's eyes.[57]

Invitation to Insight

Your EQ (Empathy Quotient)

ThomsonNOW View the ABC News video "Ned." You can find the link to this site through your ThomsonNOW for *Looking Out/Looking In* Online.

This is the story of how a woman named Norah Vincent spent 18 months disguised as a man whom she called Ned. Vincent makes it clear this wasn't a stunt: Her goal was to learn how men interact, and she was convinced that becoming a male herself was the closest she could come to gaining this perspective. Few people go as far as Vincent to become more empathic; but tales like hers can help less adventurous people better understand one another.

The Pillow Method: A Tool for Building Empathy

Perception checking is a relatively quick, easy tool for clarifying potential misunderstandings. But some issues are too complex and serious to be handled with this approach. Writer Paul Reps describes a tool for boosting empathy when finding merit in another's position seems impossible.[58]

Ethical Challenge

Empathy and the Golden Rule

Virtually everyone is familiar with the Golden Rule, which most of us learned in the form "Do unto others as you would have them do unto you." By obliging us to treat others as well as we would treat ourselves, this maxim seems to offer the foundation for a civil society in which everyone would behave with consideration.

Some ethicists have pointed out that the Golden Rule doesn't work well in situations where others don't want to be treated the same way you would. You may like to blast hip-hop music at top volume at 3 A.M., but appeals to the Golden Rule probably won't placate your neighbors who don't share your musical tastes or late night hours. Likewise, just because you enjoy teasing banter, you aren't entitled to banter with others who might find this type of humor offensive or hurtful.

The Golden Rule presents special problems in cases of intercultural contacts, where norms for what is desirable vary dramatically. For example, most speakers from low-context cultures where English is the first language value honesty and explicit communication, but this level of candor would be offensive in the high-context cultures of Asia or the Middle East. A naive communicator following the Golden Rule might justify social blunders by claiming, "I was just communicating the way I'd like to be treated." This sort of ethnocentrism is a recipe for unsuccessful communication and perhaps for very unpleasant consequences.

In response to the challenge of differing wants, Milton Bennett proposed a "Platinum Rule": "Do unto others as they themselves would have done unto them." Unlike the Golden Rule, this rule requires us to understand how others think and what they want before we can determine how to act ethically. Put differently, the Platinum Rule implies that empathy is a prerequisite for moral sensitivity.

Despite its initial appeal, the Platinum Rule poses its own problems. There are certainly cases where doing unto others what they want might compromise our own needs or even our ethical principles. It is easy to imagine cases in which the Platinum Rule would oblige us to cheat, steal, or lie on others' behalf.

Even if acting on the Platinum Rule is problematic, the benefit of thinking about it seems clear. An essential requirement for benign behavior is the ability to empathize, helping us recognize that what others want may be different than what we would want under the same circumstances.

Describe how applying the Golden Rule and the Platinum Rule would affect one of your important interpersonal relationships.

1. What communication is necessary before you could put each rule into practice?
2. Which rule seems to be preferable?

For a discussion of the Golden and Platinum rules, see M. Bennett, "Overcoming the Golden Rule: Sympathy and Empathy," in D. Nimmo, ed., *Communication Yearbook 3* (New Brunswick, N.J.: Transaction Books, 1979), pp. 407–422; and J. A. Jaksa and M. S. Pritchard, *Communication Ethics: Methods of Analysis*, 2nd ed. (Belmont, Calif.: Wadsworth, 1994), pp. 101–105.

Apart from abstract propositions of comparison (such as two and two make four), propositions which tell us nothing by themselves about concrete reality, we find no proposition ever regarded by any one as evidently certain that has not either been called a falsehood, or at least had its truth sincerely questioned by someone else.

William James, *The Will to Believe*

Developed by a group of Japanese schoolchildren, the **pillow method** gets its name from the fact that a problem has four sides and a middle, just like a pillow (Figure 3.5). As the examples on pages 115–116 show, viewing the issue from each of these perspectives almost always leads to valuable insights.

Position 1: I'm Right, You're Wrong   This is the perspective that we usually take when viewing an issue. We immediately see the virtues in our position and find fault with anyone who happens to disagree with us. Detailing this position takes little effort and provides little new information.

Position 2: You're Right, I'm Wrong   At this point you switch perspectives and build the strongest possible arguments to explain how another person can view the issue differently from you. Besides identifying the strengths in the other's position, this is the time to play the devil's advocate and find flaws in yours.

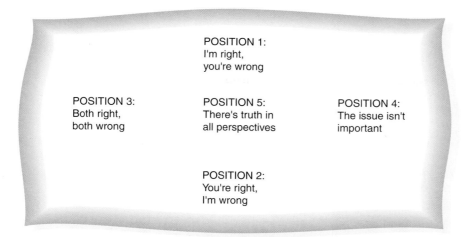

FIGURE 3.5
The Pillow Method

Finding flaws in your position and trying to support the other's position requires discipline and a certain amount of courage, even though this is only an exercise, and you will soon be able to retreat to position 1 if you choose. But most people learn that switching perspectives reveals there is some merit to the other person's perspective.

There are some issues where it seems impossible to call the other position "right." Criminal behavior, deceit, and disloyalty often seem beyond justification. At times like these it is possible to arrive at position 2 by realizing that the other person's behavior is understandable. For example, without approving, you may be able to understand how someone would resort to violence, tell lies, or cheat. Whatever the particulars, the goal of position 2 is to find some way of comprehending how anyone could behave in a way that you originally found impossible to defend.

Position 3: Both Right, Both Wrong   From this position you acknowledge the strengths and weaknesses of each person's arguments. If you have done a good job with position 2, it should be clear that there is some merit in both points of view and that each side has its demerits. Taking a more evenhanded look at the issue can lead you to be less critical and more understanding of another's point of view.

Position 3 can also help you find the commonalities between your position and the other's. Perhaps you've both been right to care so much about the issue, but both wrong to fail to recognize the other person's concerns. Perhaps there are underlying values that you both share and similar mistakes that you've both made. In any case, the perspective of position 3 should help you see that the issue isn't as much a matter of complete right and wrong as it first appeared to be.

Position 4: The Issue Isn't as Important as It Seems   This perspective will help you realize that the issue isn't as important as you thought. Although it is hard to think of some issues as unimportant, a little thought will show that most aren't as important as we make them out to be. The impact of even the most traumatic events—the death of a loved one or the breakup of a relationship, for example—usually lessens over time. The effects may not disappear, but we learn to accept them and get on with life. The importance of a dispute can also fade when you realize that you've let it overshadow other equally important parts of

The test of a first-rate intelligence is the ability to hold two opposed ideas in mind at the same time and still retain the ability to function.

F. Scott Fitzgerald

It was six men of Indostan
To learning much inclined,
Who went to see the
    elephant
Though all of them were
    blind
That each by observation
Might satisfy his mind.
The first approached the
    elephant
And, happening to fall
Against the broad and
    sturdy side,
At once began to bawl:
"Why, bless me! But the
    elephant
Is very much like a wall!"
The second, feeling of the
    tusk,

Cried: "Ho! What have we
    here
So very round and smooth
    and sharp?
To me, 'tis very clear,
This wonder of an elephant
Is very like a spear!"
The third approached the
    animal,
And, happening to take
The squirming trunk within
    his hands
Thus boldly up he spake:
"I see," quoth he, "the ele-
    phant
Is very like a snake!"
The fourth reached out his
    eager hand
And felt about the knee:

"What most this wondrous
    beast is like
Is very plain," quoth he:
" 'Tis clear enough the ele-
    phant
Is very like a tree!"
The fifth who chanced to
    touch the ear
Said: "E'en the blindest man
Can tell what this resembles
    most—
Deny the fact who can:
This marvel of an elephant
Is very like a fan!"
The sixth no sooner had
    begun
About the beast to grope
Than, seizing on the
    swinging tail
That fell within his scope,
"I see," quoth he, "the
    elephant
Is very like a rope!"
And so these men of
    Indostan
Disputed loud and long,
Each in his own opinion
Exceeding stiff and strong;
Though each was partly in
    the right,
And all were in the wrong.

John G. Saxe

your relationship. It's easy to become so wrapped up in a dispute about one subject that you forget about the other ways in which you are close to the other person.

Conclusion: There Is Truth in All Four Perspectives

After completing the first four positions, a final step is to recognize that each of them has some merit. Although logic might suggest that it's impossible for a position to be both right and wrong, both important and unimportant, your own experience will show that there is some truth in each of the positions you have explored. This fifth is very different from the "I'm right and you're wrong" attitude that most people bring to an issue. After you have looked at an issue from these five perspectives, it is almost certain that you will gain new insights. These insights may not cause you to change your mind or even solve the problem at hand. Nonetheless, they can increase your tolerance for the other person's position and thus improve the communication climate.

> The belief that one's own view of reality is the only reality is the most dangerous of all delusions.
>
> Paul Watzlawick

Communication Transcript

The Pillow Method in Action

Example 1: Planning a Wedding
Background
Who would have thought that planning a wedding would be such a nightmare? My fiancée and I are struggling to decide whether we should have a large, festive wedding or a small, intimate one. I'm in favor of having a big, expensive ceremony and party. He wants a smaller, more affordable one.

Position 1: I'm Right, and He Is Wrong
I have a big family, and I would feel guilty not inviting everyone. Also, we have lots of friends who would really miss not being present to celebrate our special day. If we invite one friend or relative, I say we have to invite them all to avoid hurting anybody's feelings. Otherwise, where do you draw the line? As far as money goes, I say that you get married only once, and this is no time to scrimp. My parents are willing to help pay the expenses because they want our entire family to be there at the wedding.

Position 2: He's Right, and I'm Wrong
My fiancé is right to say that we really don't have the funds to spend on a fancy wedding. Every dollar we spend on a lavish event will be one less dollar we have to buy a house, which we hope to do soon. My fiancé is right to say that a big wedding could postpone our house purchase for a year or two—maybe even longer, if real estate prices go up before we can buy. Even if my

parents help pay for the event, our portion would still be more than we can afford. He's also right to say that no matter how many people we invite, someone is always going to be left out. It's just a case of where we draw the line. Finally, he's right to say that planning a big wedding will be a very stressful process.

Position 3: Both of Us Are Right, and Both Are Wrong
Both of us are right, and both are wrong. I'm right to want to include our extended families and friends on this joyous day, and I'm right to say that a special wedding would be a lifetime memory. He's right that doing so could still leave some hurt feelings and that it will postpone our house purchase. He also has a good point when he says that planning a big event could drive us crazy and distract us from the real importance of joining our lives.

Position 4: The Issue Isn't Important
After thinking about it, I've realized that *getting* married is different from *being* married. The decision about what kind of ceremony to have is important, but ultimately it won't affect the kind of marriage we have. How we behave *after* we're married will be much more important. And we are going to face a lot of decisions together—about children and jobs, for example—that will have much bigger consequences than this ceremony.

Conclusion

Before using the pillow method to think through all sides of this issue, I was focused on getting my way. This attitude was creating some feelings between my fiancée and I that were not what we should be having as we faced this most important event. I've realized that if one or the other of us "wins" but the result is injured feelings, it won't be much of a victory. I don't know what kind of ceremony we will finally decide to have, but I'm determined to keep my focus on the really important goal of keeping our relationship positive and respectful.

Example 2: Exotic Dancing

Background

My best friend is an exotic dancer. I have tried to persuade her to find a less degrading way to earn a living, but she doesn't see the need to stop yet. She knows I don't agree with her decision to dance for money, but she tells me it's the only way she can make a decent income at this point in her life.

Position 1: I'm Right, and She Is Wrong

My friend is exaggerating when she says this job is the *only* way she can get the money to put herself through school. She could get a job that doesn't pay as well and make it through until she graduates. It wouldn't be perfect, but other people manage this way, and so can she. My friend is wrong to say this job doesn't intrude into her life away from work. When we lived together, she had some arguments with her boyfriend about a strange man who would send her gifts at the club where she dances. This was really affecting their relationship. Also, sometimes she comes home at 4 A.M. after eight hours of dancing. I don't see how she can go on like this.

Position 2: She's Right, and I'm Wrong

She is right to say that there is no other job where she can make this much money in so little time, at her age, and with her credentials. No one else provides financial support for my friend. She earns enough money to cover rent, food, and pay off some of her loans. She is still physically OK. She is a straight-A student, so it's true that the job isn't affecting her school work. The club where she works is clean and safe.

Position 3: Both of Us Are Right, and Both Are Wrong

I'm right to worry about her and encourage her to think about other options besides exotic dancing. She's right when she says there's no other job that pays so well. She's also right to say that her family doesn't support her in any way, which puts additional pressure on her that I can't imagine.

Position 4: The Issue Isn't Important

My friend and I both love each other and won't let this disagreement affect that. My friend hasn't let the dancing affect her self-worth. The dancing is just a chapter in her life, and it will be over soon.

Conclusion

Now I can see that this dispute has many sides. I still wish my friend would quit her dancing job, and I'm still going to keep trying to persuade her to stop. But this method makes it easier for us to talk about the issue without either of us shutting down or rejecting the other.

Communication Scenarios

Using your ThomsonNOW for *Looking Out/Looking In*, access "Communication Scenarios" and then click on either "Pillow Method: Wedding" or "Pillow Method: Dancing" to watch and analyze video examples of the pillow method. **ThomsonNOW**

Skill Builder

Pillow Talk

Try using the pillow method in your life. It isn't easy, but after you begin to understand it, the payoff in increased understanding is great.

1. Choose a person or viewpoint with whom or which you strongly disagree. If you've chosen a person, it's best to have him or her there with you; but if that's not possible, you can do it alone.

2. What disagreement should you choose? No doubt there are many in your life:

   Parent–child   Friend–friend
   Teacher–student   Nation–nation

Employer–employee   Republican–Democrat
Brother–sister

3. For each disagreement you choose, really place yourself in each position on the pillow as you encounter it:

   a. Your position is correct, and your opponent's is wrong.

   b. Your opponent's position is correct, and yours is wrong.

   c. Both your positions are correct, and both are wrong.

   d. It isn't important which position is right or wrong.

   e. Finally, affirm the fact that there is truth in all four positions.

4. The more important the disagreement is to you, the harder it will be to accept positions 2 through 5 as valid. But the exercise will work only if you can suspend your present position and imagine how it would feel to hold the other ones.

5. How can you tell if you've been successful with the pillow method? The answer is simple: If, after going over all the steps, you can understand—not necessarily *accept*, but just understand —the other person's position, you've done it. After you've reached this *understanding*, do you notice any change in how you feel about the other person?

Summary

There is more to the world "out there" than any person is capable of understanding. We make sense of our environment by the four-step process of selecting certain stimuli from the environment, organizing them into meaningful patterns, interpreting them in a manner that is shaped by a variety of factors, and negotiating them through narratives we share with others.

A number of factors affect the way we select, organize, interpret, and negotiate information. Physiological factors such as our senses, age, and health play an important role. Cultural background also influences the way we view the world, as do social roles and self-concept. In addition to these factors, there are a number of common tendencies that affect the way we assign meaning to others' behavior.

Perception checking can be a useful tool for verifying interpretations of others' behavior instead of assuming that the first hunch is correct. A complete perception check includes a description of the other's behavior, at least two plausible interpretations of its meaning, and a request for clarification about what the behavior does mean.

Empathy is the ability to experience another person's point of view. Empathy differs from sympathy because it involves seeing the situation from the other person's perspective rather than your own. One means for boosting empathy is the pillow method, which involves viewing an issue from five different perspectives.

Key Terms

androgynous (99)
attribution (103)
empathy (109)
ethnocentrism (97)
gender role (99)
halo effect (104)

interpretation (90)
narrative (92)
negotiation (92)
organization (85)
perception checking (106)
pillow method (112)

punctuation (89)
selection (84)
self-serving bias (103)
stereotyping (87)
sympathy (110)

Media Resources

Online Textbook Resources

ThomsonNOW For quick access to the online resources that accompany this chapter, access ThomsonNOW for *Looking Out/Looking In* at www.thomsonedu.com.

The ThomsonNOW online study system helps you identify concepts you don't fully understand, allowing you to put your study time to the best use. Using chapter-by-chapter diagnostic pre-tests, the system creates a **personalized study plan** for each chapter. Each plan directs you to specific resources designed to improve your understanding, including pages from the text in ebook format. Chapter post-tests give you an opportunity to measure how much you've learned and let you know if you are ready for graded quizzes and exams.

Your ThomsonNOW for *Looking Out/Looking In* also includes the ABC News video clip described on page 111; the Communication Scenario videos described on pages 108–109 and 115–116; **vocabulary activities** to help you master key terms; self-study **review quizzes** to test your comprehension of the material in this chapter and prepare for exams; **online exercises**, including the Skill Builder and Invitation to Insight activities in the book; **web links** you can use to further explore topics in this chapter; access to a **feature film database** where you can locate information about movies that illustrate communication principles; and access to the **InfoTrac**® College Edition searchable database of over 10 million articles from both scholarly journals and the popular press.

Films and Television

ThomsonNOW In addition to the films discussed here, use the link to the ThomsonNOW for *Looking Out/Looking In* to link to the **Film in Communication Database**, where you can locate movie clips that illustrate various aspects of interpersonal communication.

Stereotyping

Crash (2004) Rated R
Over 36 hours in Los Angeles, the lives of several strangers collide. Because they come from such different backgrounds, this diverse group of people relies on stereotypes—usually relating to race—to form snap judgments of each other. Unfortunately, their judgments are almost always wrong.

Again and again, the characters' assumptions keep them from understanding the human beings they are encountering. Matt Dillon plays an angry cop who goes out of his way to humiliate a black citizen. An upper-class housewife (Sandra Bullock) believes a Mexican-American locksmith (Michael Pena) is a gangbanger who plans to burgle her home, even though he is actually a gentle man struggling to build a safe life for his family. An Iranian businessman (Shaun Toub) keeps being misidentified as an Arab. Two clean-cut young black men (Larenz Tate and Ludacris) bemoan the fact that they are regarded with fear by whites in an upscale neighborhood.

Since childhood, most of us have been reminded not to judge a book by its cover. *Crash* provides a dramatic example of the problems that can result from ignoring this maxim.

Lost (TV series, on DVD) Rated TV-14
This television series chronicles the mostly desperate lives of survivors of a plane crash that left 48 passengers stranded on a remote island in the South Pacific. The survivors include a doctor, a former prisoner, a rock semi-star, an Iraqi military vet, a mysterious man named Locke, and plenty of others.

The show illustrates the problems of jumping to quick conclusions about strangers. Just about the time the characters—and the viewers—are ready to vilify one of the survivors, a "back story" helps explain the character's motives and provides a measure of empathy for that person. Conversely, some survivors who are initially seen as heroic become less so after their life stories are told.

To paraphrase an old adage, *Lost* illustrates that people are typically more than their worst moments, and often less than their best ones.

Narratives

Don Juan DeMarco (1995) Rated PG-13
Dressed in a cape and mask like Zorro and speaking a faux Spanish accent, Johnny Depp insists that he is the great lover Don Juan De Marco. As his last job before retiring, psychiatrist Jake Mickler (Marlon Brando) takes on the challenge of persuading this oddly charming patient to give up his delusions. But an interesting thing happens during

the treatment: Don Juan's charm and conviction leave the doctor wondering whether life might be better if he adopted his patient's take on reality.

As the film progresses, we see Dr. Mickler struggle to decide which narrative to accept: the clinical approach that has led to his professional success but has left his 32-year marriage in a state of pleasant dullness, or Don Juan's romantic illusion that rekindles Mickler's romance with his wife (Faye Dunaway).

Playful as it is, this film helps us see that reality is socially constructed through the sharing of narratives. It invites us to consider whether the story we have co-created with others is truly the most satisfying as we ponder Don Juan's four essential questions about existences: "What is sacred?"; "Of what is the spirit made?"; "What is worth living for?"; and "What is worth dying for?" Don Juan says the answer to all is "love," and this film makes it hard to dispute the claim.

Building Empathy

The Doctor (1991) Rated PG-13
Jack McKee (William Hurt) is an ace surgeon and a first-class egotist. He treats his patients with a breezy self-assurance, brushing aside their concerns with jokes and indifference. It's not that McKee is mean-spirited: He just views his patients as objects upon which he can practice his skill and not as human beings with feelings.

McKee receives a major attitude adjustment when his nagging cough is diagnosed as throat cancer, and his surgeon treats him with the same mechanical indifference that he had bestowed on his patients. As McKee suffers the indignities of a hospital patient and confronts his mortality, his attitude toward the human side of medical care predictably changes.

The film should become a part of the medical school curriculum, but it also shows other viewers how walking a mile in another person's shoes can lead to greater tolerance and understanding.

30 Days (TV Series, on DVD) Rated TV-PG-MA
In each episode, a person spends one month immersed in an environment that is dramatically different from his or her usual life: A Christian lives with a Muslim family; a 24-year-old straight man moves to San Francisco's gay community; an anti-immigrant activist lives with a family of undocumented workers from Mexico; a man who has lost his job to outsourcing is the house guest of a family in India that works in a customer support call center; the show's producer does jail time, living like an inmate, and so on. Although most participants retain their own values, they gain empathy and respect for lifestyles and beliefs different from their own.

Emotions: Thinking, Feeling, and Communicating

4

It's impossible to talk about communication without acknowledging the importance of emotions. Think about it: Feeling confident can make the difference between success and failure in everything from giving a speech to asking for a date, whereas feeling insecure can ruin your chances. Feeling angry or defensive can spoil your time with others, whereas feeling and acting calm will help prevent or solve problems. The way you share or withhold your feelings of affection can affect the future of your relationships. On and on goes the list of feelings: appreciation, loneliness, joy, insecurity, curiosity, irritation. The point is clear: Communication shapes our feelings, and feelings shape our communication.

The role of emotions in human affairs is apparent to social scientists and lay people alike. When Yale University psychologist Robert Sternberg asked people to describe an "intelligent person," one of the skills listed was the ability to understand and get along with others.[1] This ability to get along was characterized by psychologist Daniel Goleman as one aspect of "emotional intelligence."[2] Goleman makes the claim that intellectual ability is not the only way to measure one's talents and that success in the world depends in great part on the ability to understand and manage one's own emotions and be sensitive to others' feelings.

Because emotions play such an important role in virtually all types of relationships, this chapter takes a closer look at analyzing and expressing them. The following pages will clarify what feelings are, and how to recognize them. You'll

"Honey, let's play 'emoting.' It will give you an edge in business."

read guidelines about when and how to best share feelings with others. Finally, we will explore what causes feelings, and how to enhance ones that make communication more rewarding and decrease ones that interfere with effective relationships. In later chapters we'll discuss how to interpret others' emotional states, but for now we'll focus on identifying and expressing your own emotions.

What Are Emotions?

Suppose that an extraterrestrial visitor asked you to explain emotions. How would you answer? You might start by saying that emotions are things that we feel. But this doesn't say much because in turn you would probably describe feelings as synonymous with emotions. Social scientists generally agree that there are several components to the phenomena we label as feelings.

Physiological Factors

When a person has strong emotions, many bodily changes occur. For example, the physical components of fear include an increased heart rate, a rise in blood pressure, an increase in adrenaline secretions, an elevated blood sugar level, a slowing of digestion, and a dilation of pupils. Marriage researcher John Gottman notes that symptoms like these also occur when couples are in intense conflicts.[3] He calls the condition "flooding" and has found that it impedes effective problem-solving.

Some physiological changes are recognizable to the person having them: a churning stomach or tense jaw, for example. These cues can offer a significant clue to your emotions after you become aware of them.

Every thought, gesture, muscle tension, feeling, stomach gurgle, nose scratch, fart, hummed tune, slip of the tongue, illness— everything is significant and meaningful and related to the now. It is possible to know and understand oneself on all these levels, and the more one knows the more he is free to determine his own life.

If I know what my body tells me, I know my deepest feelings and I can choose what to do. . . . Given a complete knowledge of myself, I can determine my life; lacking that mastery, I am controlled in ways that are often undesirable, unproductive, worrisome, and confusing.

William Schutz,

Here Comes Everybody

Nonverbal Reactions

Not all physical changes that accompany emotions are internal. Feelings are often apparent by observable changes. Some of these changes involve a person's appearance: blushing, sweating, and so on. Other changes involve behavior: a distinctive facial expression, posture, gestures, different vocal tone and rate, and so on.

Although it's reasonably easy to tell when someone is feeling a strong emotion, it's more difficult to be certain exactly what that emotion might be. A slumped posture and sigh may be a sign of sadness, or they may be a sign of fatigue. Likewise, trembling hands might indicate excitement, or they may indicate fear. As you'll learn in Chapter 6, nonverbal behavior is usually ambiguous, and it's dangerous to assume that it can be "read" with much accuracy.

Although we usually think of nonverbal behavior as the reaction to an emotional state, there may be times when the reverse is true—when nonverbal behavior actually *causes* an emotional state. In one study, experimental subjects were able to create various emotional states by altering their facial expressions.[4] When subjects were coached to move their facial muscles in ways that appeared afraid, angry, disgusted, amused, sad, surprised, and contemptuous, the subjects' bodies responded as if they were having these feelings. In another experiment, subjects who were coached to smile actually reported feeling better, and when they altered their expressions to look unhappy, they felt worse than before.[5]

Cognitive Interpretations

Although there may be situations in which there is a direct connection between physical behavior and emotional states, in most situations the mind plays an important role in determining emotional states. As you read earlier, some physiological components of fear are a racing heart, perspiration, tense muscles, and elevated blood pressure. Interestingly enough, these symptoms are similar to the physical changes that accompany excitement, joy, and other emotions. In other words, if we were to measure the physical condition of someone having a strong emotion, we would have a hard time knowing whether that person was trembling with fear or quivering with excitement. The recognition that the bodily components of most emotions are similar led some psychologists to conclude that the experience of fright, joy, or anger comes primarily from the *label* we give to the same physical symptoms at a given time.[6] Psychologist Philip Zimbardo offers a good example of this principle:

> I notice I'm perspiring while lecturing. From that I infer I am nervous. If it occurs often, I might even label myself a "nervous person." Once I have the label, the next question I must answer is "Why am I nervous?" Then I start to search for an appropriate explanation. I might notice some students leaving the room, or being inattentive. I am nervous because I'm not giving a good lecture. That makes me nervous. How do I know it's not good? Because I'm boring my audience. I am nervous because I am a boring lecturer and I want to be a good lecturer. I feel inadequate. Maybe I should open a delicatessen instead. Just then a student says, "It's hot in here, I'm perspiring and it makes it tough to concentrate on your lecture." Instantly, I'm no longer "nervous" or "boring."[7]

In his book *Shyness,* Zimbardo discusses the consequences of making inaccurate or exaggerated attributions. In a survey of more than five thousand subjects, over 80 percent described themselves as having been shy at some time in their lives, whereas more than 40 percent described themselves as being presently shy. Most significantly, those who described themselves as "not shy" behaved in virtually the *same way* as their shy counterparts. They would blush, perspire, and feel their hearts pounding in certain social situations. The biggest difference between the two groups seemed to be the label with which they described themselves.[8] This is a significant difference. Someone who notices the symptoms we've described and thinks, "I'm such a shy person!" will most likely feel more uncomfortable and communicate less effectively than another person with the same symptoms who thinks, "Well, I'm a bit shaky (or excited) here, but that's to be expected."

We'll take a closer look at ways to reduce unpleasant emotions through cognitive processes later in this chapter.

Verbal Expression

As you will read in Chapter 6, nonverbal behavior is a powerful way of communicating emotion. In fact, nonverbal actions are better at conveying emotions than they are at conveying ideas. But sometimes words are necessary to express feelings. Is your friend's uncharacteristically short temper a sign of anger at you, or does it mean something less personal? Is a lover's unenthusiastic response a sign of boredom with you or the result of a long workday? Is a new acquaintance mistaking your friendliness as a come-on? There are times—especially in our low-context culture—when you can't rely on perceptiveness to be sure that a message is communicated and understood accurately.

Some researchers believe there are several "basic" or "primary" emotions.[9] However, there isn't much agreement among scholars about what those emotions are, or about what makes them "basic."[10] Moreover, emotions that are primary in one culture may not be primary in others, and some emotions have no direct equivalent in other cultures.[11] For example, "shame" is a central emotion in the Chinese experience,[12] while it's much less familiar to most people from western cultures. Despite this debate, most scholars acknowledge that *anger*, *joy*, *fear*, and *sadness* are common and typical human emotions.

We experience most emotions with different degrees of intensity, and it's important to use language that represents these differences. Figure 4.1 illustrates this point clearly. To say you're "annoyed" when a friend breaks an important promise, for example, would probably be an understatement. In other cases, people chronically overstate the strength of their feelings. To them, everything is "wonderful" or "terrible." The problem with this sort of exaggeration is that when a truly intense emotion comes along, they have no words left to describe it adequately. If chocolate chip cookies from the local bakery are "fantastic," how does it feel to fall in love?

Researchers have identified a wide range of problems that arise for people who aren't able to talk about emotions constructively, including social isolation, unsatisfying relationships, feelings of anxiety and depression, and misdirected aggression.[13] Furthermore, the way parents talk to their children about emotions has a powerful effect on the chil-

Emotional Weather Report

Late night and early morning low clouds
    with a chance of fog;
    Chance of showers into the afternoon
    with variable high cloudiness
    and gusty winds, gusty winds . . .
Things are tough all over
    when the thunderstorms start;
    Increasing over the southeast
    and south central portions
    of my apartment.
I get upset and a line of thunderstorms was
    developing in the early morning,
    ahead of a slow moving cold front.
    Cold blooded, with tornado watches issued
    shortly before noon Sunday
    for the areas including the western region
    of my mental health
    and the northern portions of my
    ability to deal rationally with my
    disconcerted precarious emotional situation.

Tom Waits

dren's development.[14] The researchers identified two distinct parenting styles: "emotion coaching" and "emotion dismissing." They show how the coaching approach gives children skills for communicating about feelings in later life that lead to much more satisfying relationships. Later in this chapter you will find some guidelines for effectively communicating about emotions.

Furious	Grieving	Ecstatic	Terrified	Adoring
Angry	Sad	Happy	Afraid	Loving
Annoyed	Pensive	Content	Anxious	Liking

FIGURE 4.1
Intensity of Emotions

Invitation to Insight

Recognizing Your Emotions

Keep a three-day record of your feelings. You can do this by spending a few minutes each evening recalling what emotions you felt during the day, what other people were involved, and the circumstances in which the emotions occurred.

At the end of the three-day period you can understand the role that emotions play in your communication by answering the following questions:

1. How did you recognize the emotions you felt: through physiological stimuli, nonverbal behaviors, or cognitive processes?

2. Did you have any difficulty deciding which emotions you were feeling?

3. What emotions do you have most often? Are they primary or mixed? Mild or intense?

4. In what circumstances do you or don't you show your feelings? What factors influence your decision to show or not show your feelings? The type of feeling? The person or persons involved? The situation (time, place)? The subject that the feeling involves (money, sex, and so on)?

5. What are the consequences of the type of communicating you just described in step 4? Are you satisfied with these consequences? If not, what can you do to become more satisfied?

Influences on Emotional Expression

Most people rarely express their emotions, at least verbally. People are generally comfortable making statements of fact and often delight in expressing their opinion, but they rarely disclose how they feel. Why is it that people fail to express their emotions? Let's take a look at several reasons.

Personality

There is an increasingly clear relationship between personality and the way we experience and communicate emotions.[15] For example, extraverted people—those with a tendency to be upbeat, optimistic, and to enjoy social contact—report

The Unexpressed

© Kurt Van Wagner

The unexpressed,
    the unarticulated
    are frightening,
    when as fragments
    they burn
    beneath the skin,
    with no way at all
    to be scratched out,
    plucked out,

or brought to reason.
Events
    bricked up inside
    cry out in despair:
"We've been forgotten.
We'll be eliminated from
    history:
Let us out!
Let us out!

Suffering rises up
    like a lump in the throat:
We are like stifled sobs.
We long so for our
    liberation:
    express us!
    express us!"

Yevgeny Yevtushenko

more positive emotions in everyday life than less extraverted individuals.[16] Likewise, people with neurotic personalities (those with a tendency to worry, feel anxious, and be apprehensive) report more negative emotions in everyday life than less neurotic individuals.

These personality traits are at least partially biological in nature. Psychologists have used magnetic imaging to measure the relation between personality type and brain activity.[17] People who tested high on measures of extraversion had greater brain reactivity to positive stimuli than did less extraverted people. Those who scored high on the neuroticism measures had more brain reactions to negative stimuli. Research like this confirms the familiar belief that some people see the cup being half (or more) full, while others see it as being more empty.

While personality can be a powerful force, it doesn't have to govern your communication satisfaction. Consider shyness, which can be considered the opposite of extroversion. Introverted people can devise comfortable and effective strategies for reaching out. For example, the Internet has proven to be an effective way for reticent communicators to make contact. Chat rooms, instant messaging, e-mail, and computer dating services all provide a low-threat way to approach others and get acquainted.[18]

Culture

While people around the world generally experience the same emotions, the same events can generate quite different feelings in different cultures.[19] The notion of eating snails might bring a smile of delight to some residents of France, whereas it would cause many North Americans to grimace in disgust. More to the point of this book, research has shown that fear of strangers and risky situations is more likely to frighten people living in the United States and Europe than those living in Japan, whereas Japanese are more apprehensive about relational communication than Americans and Europeans.[20] Culture also has an effect on how emotions are valued. One study found that Asian Americans and Hong Kong Chinese value "low arousal positive affect" (such as "calm") more than do European Americans, who tend to value "high arousal positive affect" (such as "excitement").[21]

There are also differences in the degree to which people in various cultures display their feelings. For example, social scientists have found support for the notion that people from warmer climates are more emotionally expressive than those who live in cooler climates.[22] Over twenty-nine hundred respondents representing twenty-six nationalities reported that people from the southern part of their countries were more emotionally expressive than were northerners.

One of the most significant factors that influences emotional expression is the position of a culture on the individualism-collectivism spectrum. Members of collectivistic cultures (such as Japan and India) prize harmony among members of their "in-group" and discourage expression of any negative emotions that might upset relationships among people who belong to it. By contrast, members of highly individualistic cultures like the United States and Canada feel comfortable revealing their emotions to people with whom they are close.[23] Individualists and collectivists also handle emotional expression with members of outgroups differently: Whereas collectivists are frank about expressing negative emotions toward outsiders, individualists are more likely to hide such emotions as dislike.[24] It's easy to see how differences in display rules can lead to communication problems. For example, individualistic North Americans might view

Looking At Diversity

Todd Epaloose: A Native American Perspective on Emotional Expression

Todd Epaloose was raised on the Zuñi pueblo, New Mexico. He spent part of his childhood on the reservation and part attending school in the city. He now lives in Albuquerque, where he studies environmental protection technology and works in a medical lab. As an urbanite who still spends time with his family on the reservation, Todd alternates between two worlds. On the reservation he is surrounded by his Native American culture, whereas in the city he has developed the skills necessary to succeed in a technological society. In this profile, Todd reflects on the differences between the ways Zuñi and Anglo cultures deal with emotional expression.

Zuñi and Anglo cultures are as different as night and day in the ways they treat communication about emotions. In mainstream U.S. culture, speaking up is accepted, or even approved. This is true from the time you are a child. Parents are proud when their child speaks up—whether that means showing affection, being curious, or even expressing unhappiness in a way that the parents approve. Being quiet gets a child labeled as "shy," and is considered a problem. Assertiveness is just as important in school, at work, and in adult relationships.

In Zuñi culture, emotions are much less public. We are a private people, who consider a public display of feelings embarrassing. Self-control is considered a virtue. I think a lot of our emotional reticence comes from a respect for privacy. Your feelings are your own, and showing them to others is just as wrong as taking off your clothes in public. It's not that traditional Zuñis have fewer or less intense feelings than people in the city: It's just that there is less value placed on showing them in obvious ways.

The way we express affection is a good example of Zuñi attitudes and rules for sharing emotions. Our families are full of love—at least as much as families in mainstream American culture. But someone from the city might not recognize this love, since it isn't displayed very much. There isn't a lot of hugging and kissing, even between children and parents. Also, there isn't a lot of verbal expression: People don't say "I love

you" to one another very much. The feeling is there, but it's understood without being mentioned. We show our emotions by our actions: by helping one another, by caring for the people we love when they need us. That's enough to keep us happy.

One way to summarize the difference between the two cultures has to do with talking and listening. Anglo culture places an emphasis on talking—on expressing yourself clearly and completely. Zuñis aren't such great talkers, but that helps make us better listeners. Because we don't speak so much, we have both the need and the time to be better at paying attention to what other people say and what they do to show their emotions. This listening can be helpful in school, where we care less about competing for a teacher's recognition than in understanding what we are supposed to learn. It also makes us good, steady workers who learn our jobs, concentrate on our duties, and work extremely hard to perfect our efficiency. We may not get the recognition that comes from being good talkers, but in the long run I am confident that our restraint will be rewarded. As the saying goes, "What goes around comes around."

Which approach is best? I think both cultures have strengths. Many Zuñis and other Native Americans who want to join the mainstream culture are at a disadvantage. They aren't very good at standing up for their rights, and so they get taken advantage of. Even at home, there are probably times when it's important to express feelings to prevent misunderstandings. On the other hand, I think some Native American emotional restraint might be helpful for people who are used to Anglo communication styles. Respecting others' privacy can be important: Some feelings are nobody else's business, and prying or demanding that they open up seems pushy and rude. Native American self-control can also add some civility to personal relationships. I'm not sure that "letting it all hang out" is always the best way.

One final word: I believe that in order to really understand the differences between emotional expression in Native American and Anglo cultures you have to live in both. If that isn't possible, at least realize that the familiar one isn't the only good approach. Try to respect what you don't understand.

Photo courtesy of Todd Epaloose

collectivistic Asians as less than candid, whereas Asians could easily regard North Americans as overly demonstrative.

The phrase "I love you" offers an interesting case study of cultural differences in emotion expression. Researchers found that Americans say "I love you" more frequently (and to more people) than do members of most other cultures.[25] It's not that love isn't a universal experience; rather, there are significant cultural differences about when, where, how often, and with whom the phrase should be used. For instance, Middle Easterners in the study said that "I love you" should only be expressed between spouses—and they warned that American men who use the phrase cavalierly with Middle Eastern women might be misinterpreted as making a marriage proposal. They were not alone—study participants from a variety of backgrounds (e.g., Eastern Europe, India, Korea) said they use the phrase quite sparingly, believing that its power and meaning would be lost if used too often. However, one factor was consistent across cultures: Women tend to say "I love you" more often than men. For more examples of the effect that gender has on emotion expression, read on.

Gender

Even within a culture, biological sex and gender roles often shape the ways in which men and women experience and express their emotions.[26] In fact, biological sex is the best predictor of the ability to detect and interpret emotional expressions—better than academic background, amount of foreign travel, cultural similarity, or ethnicity.[27] For example, research suggests that women are more attuned to emotions than men,[28] both within and across cultures.[29] A team of psychologists tested men and women's recall of emotional images and found that females were 10 to 15 percent more accurate in remembering them. Furthermore, women's reactions to these emotion-producing stimuli were significantly more intense than men's.

Research on emotional expression suggests that there is at least some truth in the cultural stereotype of the unexpressive male and the more expressive female.[30] As a group, women are more likely than men to express both positive emotions (love, liking, joy, and contentment) and feelings of vulnerability (including fear, sadness, loneliness, and embarrassment). On the other hand, men are less bashful about revealing their strengths.[31] On the Internet, the same differences between male and female emotional expressiveness apply. For example, women were more likely than men to use emoticons, such as the symbol :), to express their feelings than were men.[32] Chapter 9 will discuss how men often express their feelings through actions and activities rather than in words.

One's gender isn't the only factor that affects emotional sensitivity. A second factor is whether the other person is of the same or different sex. For example, men are more likely to express feelings (especially positive ones) with women than with other men.[33] Of course, these gender differences are statistical averages, and many men and women don't fit these profiles.

A third factor that influences sensitivity to others' emotions is the person or people with whom we are communicating. For example, dating and married couples are significantly better at recognizing each other's emotional cues than are strangers, just as people from the same culture seem to be better at recognizing each other's emotions.[34] Not surprisingly, people in close relationships are likely to experience and express more emotions than those in less-close relationships.[35] For example, we have stronger feelings about romantic partners than about people we're less involved with. Of course, not all of those

"It was a time when men regularly performed great feats of valor but were rarely in touch with their feelings."

emotions are positive. The potential for feeling hurt and neglected is stronger in romantic relationships than in other types of relationships.[36]

A final factor is the difference in power between the two parties. People who are less powerful learn—probably from necessity—to read the more powerful person's signals. One experiment revealed that "women's intuition" should be relabeled "subordinate's intuition." In opposite-sex twosomes, the person with less control—regardless of sex—was better at interpreting the leader's nonverbal signals than vice versa.[37]

Social Conventions

In mainstream U.S. society the unwritten rules of communication discourage the direct expression of most emotions.[38] Count the number of genuine emotional expressions that you hear over a two- or three-day period and you'll discover that emotional expressions are rare.

Not surprisingly, the emotions that people *do* share directly are usually positive. Communicators are reluctant to send messages that embarrass or threaten the "face" of others.[39] Historians offer a detailed description of the ways by which contemporary society discourages expressions of anger.[40] When compared to past centuries, Americans today strive to suppress this "unpleasant" emotion in almost every context, including child-raising, the workplace, and personal relationships. Research supports this analysis. One study of married couples revealed that the partners often shared complimentary feelings ("I love you") or face-saving ones ("I'm sorry I yelled at you"). They also willingly disclosed both positive and negative feelings about absent third parties ("I like Fred," "I'm uncomfortable around Gloria"). On the other hand, the husbands and wives rarely verbalized face-threatening feelings ("I'm disappointed in you") or hostility ("I'm mad at you").[41]

Social rules even discourage too much expression of positive feelings.[42] A hug and a kiss for Mother are all right, though a young man should shake hands with Dad. Affection toward friends becomes less and less frequent as we grow older, so that even a simple statement such as "I like you" is seldom heard between adults. Just because we don't express our feelings toward others verbally doesn't mean that we don't communicate them at all. As Chapter 6 explains in detail, a tremendous amount of the information carried via nonverbal communication involves relational messages, including our feelings of affinity (or lack of it) toward others.

Expression of emotions is also shaped by the requirements of many social roles. Salespeople are taught always to smile at customers, no matter how obnoxious. Teachers and managers are expected to behave rationally and keep their emotions under control. Students are rewarded for asking "acceptable" questions and otherwise being submissive and respectful.

Fear of Self-Disclosure

In a society that discourages the expression of emotions, revealing them can seem risky.[43] For a parent, boss, or teacher whose life has been built on the image of confidence and certainty, it may be frightening to say, "I'm sorry. I was wrong." A person who has made a life's work out of not relying on others has a hard time saying, "I'm lonesome. I want your friendship."

Moreover, someone who musters up the courage to share feelings such as these still risks unpleasant consequences. Others might misunderstand: An expression of affection might be construed as a romantic invitation,[44] and a confession of uncertainty might look like a sign of weakness. Another risk is that emotional honesty might make others feel uncomfortable. Finally, there's always a risk that emotional honesty could be used against you, either out of cruelty or thoughtlessness. Chapter 9 discusses alternatives to complete disclosure and suggests circumstances when it can be both wise and ethical to keep your feelings to yourself.

Emotional Contagion

Cultural rules and social roles aren't the only factors that affect our feelings. Our emotions are also influenced by the feelings of those around us through **emotional contagion**: the process by which emotions are transferred from one person to another.[45] As one commentator observed, "We catch feelings from one another as though they were some kind of social virus."[46] There is evidence that students "catch" the mood of their teachers,[47] and that husbands and wives directly influence each other's emotions.[48]

Invitation to Insight

Measuring Your EQ

ThomsonNOW™ You can get a clearer picture of your emotional intelligence by taking a simple online test. You can find the link to this site at your ThomsonNOW for *Looking Out/Looking In*.

Most of us recognize the degree to which emotions are "infectious." You can almost certainly recall instances when being around a calm person leaves you feeling more at peace, or when your previously sunny mood was spoiled by contact with a grouch. Researchers have demonstrated that this process occurs quickly and doesn't require much, if any, verbal communication.[49] In one study, two volunteers completed a survey that identified their moods. Then they sat quietly, facing each other for a 2-minute period, ostensibly waiting for the researcher to return to the room. At the end of that time, they completed another emotional survey. Time after time, the

"I'm not in one of my moods. I'm in one of your moods."

brief exposure resulted in the less expressive partner's moods coming to resemble the moods of the more expressive one. If an expressive communicator can shape another person's emotions with so little input in such a short time, it's easy to understand how emotions can be even more "infectious" with more prolonged contact. In just a few months, the emotional responses of both dating couples and college roommates become dramatically more similar.[50]

Guidelines for Expressing Emotions

As you just read, there aren't any universal rules for the best way to communicate emotions. Personality, culture, gender roles, and social conventions all govern what approach will feel right to the people involved and what is most likely to work in a given situation.

It's easy to think of times when it's *not* smart to express emotions clearly and directly. You usually can't chew out authority figures like difficult bosses or professors, and it's probably not wise to confront dangerous looking strangers who are bothering you.

In spite of all the qualifiers and limitations, there will be times when you can benefit from communicating your feelings clearly and directly—even if you aren't normally an expressive person. When those times come, the guidelines in the following pages can help you explain how you feel.

A wide range of research supports the value of expressing emotions appropriately (see Table 4.1 for a partial list of benefits). At the most basic physiological level, people who know how to express their emotions are healthier than those who don't. On one hand, under-expression of feelings can lead to serious ailments. Inexpressive people—those who value rationality and self-control, try to control their feelings and impulses, and deny distress—are more likely to get a host of ailments, including cancer, asthma, and heart disease.[51]

Communicators who overexpress their negative feelings also suffer physiologically. When people lash out verbally, their blood pressure jumps an average of twenty points, and in some people it increases by as much as one hundred points.[52] The key to health, then, is to learn how to express emotions *constructively.*

Beyond the physiological benefits, another benefit of expressing emotions effectively is the chance of improving relationships.[53] As Chapter 9 explains, self-disclosure is one path (though not the only one) to intimacy. Even on the job, many managers and organizational researchers are contradicting generations of tradition by suggesting that constructively expressing emotions can lead to career success as well as help workers feel better.[54] Of course, the rules for expressing emotions in the workplace are usually more strict than those in personal relationships, so handle with care.[55]

Despite its benefits, expressing emotions effectively isn't a simple matter. It's obvious that showing every feeling of boredom, fear, anger, or frustration would get you into trouble. Even the indiscriminate sharing of positive feelings—love, affection, and so on—isn't always wise. On the other hand, withholding emotions can be personally frustrating and can keep relationships from growing and prospering.

The following suggestions can help you decide when and how to express your emotions. Combined with the guidelines for self-disclosure in Chapter 9, they can improve the effectiveness of your emotional expression.

An emotion without social rules of containment and expression is like an egg without a shell: a gooey mess.

Carol Tavris

Table 4.1	**Some Differences between High and Low Affection Communicators**

Compared to low affection communicators, high affection communicators are:

1. Happier
2. More self-assured
3. More comfortable with interpersonal closeness
4. Less likely to be depressed
5. Less stressed
6. In better mental health
7. More likely to engage in regular social activity
8. Less likely to experience social isolation
9. More likely to receive affection from others
10. More likely to be in satisfying romantic relationships

Adapted from Kory Floyd, "Human Affection Exchange V: Attributes of the Highly Affectionate," *Communication Quarterly* 50 (2002): 135–152.

Recognize Your Feelings

Answering the question "How do you feel?" isn't as easy for some people as others. Some people (researchers call them "affectively oriented") are much more aware of their emotional states and use information about those emotional states when making important decisions.[56] By contrast, people with a low affective orientation usually aren't aware of their emotional states and tend to regard feelings as useless and unimportant information.

Beyond being *aware* of one's feelings, research shows that it's valuable to be able to *identify* one's emotions. Researchers have found that college students who can pinpoint the negative emotions they experience (such as "nervous," "angry," "sad," "ashamed," and "guilty") also have the best strategies for managing those emotions.[57] This explains why the ability to distinguish and label emotions is a vital component of emotional intelligence, both within and across cultures.[58]

As you read earlier in this chapter, feelings become recognizable in a number of ways. Physiological changes can be a clear sign of your feelings. Monitoring nonverbal behaviors is another excellent way to keep in touch with your emotions. You can also recognize your feelings by monitoring your thoughts as well as the verbal messages you send to others. It's not far from the verbal statement "I hate this!" to the realization that you're angry (or bored, nervous, or embarrassed).

Recognize the Difference between Feeling, Talking, and Acting

Just because you feel a certain way doesn't mean you must always talk about it, and talking about a feeling doesn't mean you must act on it. In fact, there is compelling evidence that people who act out angry feelings—whether by lashing out, or even by hitting an inanimate punching bag—actually feel worse than those who experience anger without lashing out.[59]

Understanding the difference between having feelings and acting them out can help you express yourself constructively in tough situations. If, for instance, you recognize that you are upset with a friend, it becomes possible to explore exactly why you feel so upset. Sharing your feeling ("Sometimes I get so mad at you that I could scream") might open the door to resolving whatever is bothering you. Pretending that nothing is bothering you, or lashing out at the other person, is unlikely to diminish your resentful feelings, which can then go on to contaminate the relationship.

Expand Your Emotional Vocabulary

Most people suffer from impoverished emotional vocabularies. Ask them how they're feeling, and the response will almost always include the same terms: *good* or *bad, terrible* or *great,* and so on. Take a moment now to see how many feelings you can write down. After you've done your best, look at Table 4.2 and see which ones you've missed.

Many communicators think they are expressing feelings when, in fact, their statements are emotionally counterfeit. For example, it sounds emotionally revealing to say, "I feel like going to a show" or "I feel we've been seeing too much of each other." But in fact, neither of these statements has any emotional content. In the first sentence the word *feel* really stands for an intention: "I *want* to go to a show." In the second sentence the "feeling" is really a thought: "I *think* we've been seeing too much of each other." You can recognize the absence of emotion in each case by adding a genuine word of feeling to it. For instance, "I'm *bored,* and I want to go to a show" or "I think we've been seeing too much of each other, and I feel *confined.*"

Relying on a small vocabulary to describe feelings is as limiting as relying on a small vocabulary to describe colors. To say that the ocean in all its moods, the

Table 4.2	Some Feelings				
afraid	concerned	exhausted	hurried	nervous	sexy
aggravated	confident	fearful	hurt	numb	shaky
amazed	confused	fed	hysterical	optimistic	shocked
ambivalent	content	fidgety	impatient	paranoid	shy
angry	crazy	flattered	impressed	passionate	sorry
annoyed	defeated	foolish	inhibited	peaceful	strong
anxious	defensive	forlorn	insecure	pessimistic	subdued
apathetic	delighted	free	interested	playful	surprised
ashamed	depressed	friendly	intimidated	pleased	suspicious
bashful	detached	frustrated	irritable	possessive	tender
bewildered	devastated	furious	jealous	pressured	tense
bitchy	disappointed	glad	joyful	protective	terrified
bitter	disgusted	glum	lazy	puzzled	tired
bored	disturbed	grateful	lonely	refreshed	trapped
brave	ecstatic	happy	loving	regretful	ugly
calm	edgy	harassed	lukewarm	relieved	uneasy
cantankerous	elated	helpless	mad	resentful	up
carefree	embarrassed	high	mean	restless	vulnerable
cheerful	empty	hopeful	miserable	ridiculous	warm
cocky	enthusiastic	horrible	mixed	romantic	weak
cold	envious	hostile	mortified	sad	wonderful
comfortable	excited	humiliated	neglected	sentimental	worried

sky as it varies from day to day, and the color of your true love's eyes are all "blue" tells only a fraction of the story. Likewise, it's overly broad to use a term like *good* or *great* to describe how you feel in situations as different as earning a high grade, finishing a marathon, and hearing the words "I love you" from a special person.

There are several ways to express a feeling verbally:[60]

- By using *single words:* "I'm angry" (or "excited," "depressed," "curious," and so on)
- By describing *what's happening to you:* "My stomach is tied in knots," "I'm on top of the world"
- By describing *what you'd like to do:* "I want to run away," "I'd like to give you a hug," "I feel like giving up"

Sometimes communicators inaccurately minimize the strength of their feelings—"I'm a *little* unhappy" or "I'm *pretty* excited" or "I'm *sort of* confused." Of course, not all feelings are strong ones. We do feel degrees of sadness and joy, for example, but some people have a tendency to discount almost every feeling. Do you?

In other cases, communicators express feelings in a coded manner. This happens most often when the sender is uncomfortable about revealing the feeling in question. Some codes are verbal ones, as when the sender hints more or less subtly at the message. For example, an indirect way to say, "I'm lonesome" might be "I guess there isn't much happening this weekend, so if you're not busy, why don't you drop by." Such a message is so indirect that your real feeling may not be recognized. For this reason, people who send coded messages stand less of a chance of having their feelings understood—and their needs met.

If you do decide to express your feeling, you can be most clear by making sure that both you and your partner understand that your feeling is centered on a specific set of circumstances rather than being indicative of the whole relationship. Instead of saying, "I resent you," say, "I resent you when you don't keep your promises." Rather than saying, "I'm bored with you," say, "I'm bored when you talk about your money."

Invitation to Insight

Expanding Your Emotional Vocabulary

ThomsonNOW Use the online activity "Expressing Emotions by Expanding Your Feelings Vocabulary " to expand your emotional vocabulary. (For more suggestions, see Table 4.2 on page 134.) Using the guidelines for expressing emotions on pages 133–140, practice describing your feelings by writing statements for each of the hypothetical situations listed at the website. You can find the link to this site at your ThomsonNOW for *Looking Out/Looking In*.

Share Multiple Feelings

Many times the feeling you express isn't the only one you're experiencing. For example, you might often express your anger but overlook the confusion, disappointment, frustration, sadness, or embarrassment that preceded it. To understand why, consider the following examples. For each one, ask yourself two questions: How would I feel? What feelings might I express?

An out-of-town friend has promised to arrive at your house at six o'clock. When he hasn't arrived by nine, you are convinced that a terrible accident has occurred. Just as you pick up the phone to call the police and local hospitals, your friend breezes in the door with an offhand remark about getting a late start.

You and your companion have a fight just before leaving for a party. Deep inside, you know that you were mostly to blame, even though you aren't willing to admit it. When you arrive at the party, your companion leaves you to flirt with several other attractive guests.

In situations like these you would probably feel mixed emotions. Consider the case of the overdue friend. Your first reaction to his arrival would probably be relief—"Thank goodness, he's safe!" But you would also be likely to feel anger—"Why didn't he phone to tell me he'd be late?" The second example would probably leave you with an even greater number of mixed emotions: guilt at contributing to the fight, hurt and perhaps embarrassment at your friend's flirtations, and anger at this sort of vengefulness.

Despite the commonness of mixed emotions, we often communicate only one feeling—usually the most negative one. In both of the preceding examples you might show only your anger, leaving the other person with little idea of the full range of your feelings. Consider the different reaction you would get by showing *all* your emotions in these cases and in others.

Consider When and Where to Express Your Feelings

Anyone can become angry. That is easy. But to be angry with the right person to the right degree, at the right time for the right purpose, and in the right way: This is not easy.

Aristotle

Often the first flush of a strong feeling is not the best time to speak out. If you're awakened by the racket caused by a noisy neighbor, storming over to complain might result in your saying things you'll regret later. In such a case, it's probably wiser to wait until you have thought out carefully how you might express your feelings in a way that would most likely be heard. Research shows that "imagined interactions" in advance of actual conversations can enhance relationships by allowing communicators to rehearse what they will say and to consider how others might respond.[61]

Even after you've waited for the first wave of strong feeling to subside, it's still important to choose the time that's best suited to the message. Being rushed or tired or disturbed by some other matter is probably a good reason for postponing the expression of your feeling. Often, dealing with your emotions can take a great amount of time and effort, and fatigue or distraction will make it difficult to follow through on the matter you've started. In the same manner, you ought to be sure that the recipient of your message is ready to hear you out before you begin.

There are also cases where you may choose to never express your feelings. Even if you're dying to tell an instructor that her lectures leave you bored to a stupor, you might decide it's best to answer her question "How's class going?" with an innocuous "Okay." And even though you may be irritated by the arrogance of a police officer stopping you for speeding, the smartest approach might be to keep your feelings to yourself. In cases where you experience strong emotions but don't want to share them verbally (for whatever reason), writing out your feelings and thoughts has been shown to have mental, physical, and emotional benefits.[62]

Accept Responsibility for Your Feelings

It's important to make sure that your language reflects the fact that you're responsible for your feelings. Instead of saying, "You're making me angry," say,

Ethical Challenge

Aristotle's Golden Mean

Almost two and a half millennia ago, the philosopher Aristotle addressed issues that are just as important today as they were in classical Greece. In his *Nicomachean Ethics*, Aristotle examines the question of "moral virtue": What constitutes good behavior, and what ways of acting enable us to function effectively in the world? One important part of his examination addresses the management and expression of emotion: what he defines as "passions and actions."

According to Aristotle, an important dimension of virtuous behavior is moderation, which he defines as "an intermediate between excess and deficit . . . equidistant from the extremes . . . neither too much nor too little." Aristotle introduces the concept of virtue through moderation with a mathematical analogy: If ten is many and two is few, then six is the intermediate. Applying this line of reasoning to emotional expression would eveal that, for example, the preferred form of expressing affection would fall equally between the extremes of being completely unexpressive and passionately animated.

Aristotle points out that a formulaic approach to calculating the "golden mean" doesn't work in human affairs by illustrating the flaws in his mathematical analogy: "If ten pounds are too much for a particular person to eat and two too little, it does not follow that the trainer will order six pounds, for this also is perhaps too much for the person who is to take it." In other words, Aristotle recognizes that people have different personalities; and he acknowledges that it isn't realistic or desirable for a passionate person to strive for the same type of behavior as a dispassionate person. After all, a world in which everyone felt and acted identically would be boring.

Instead of a "one approach fits all" approach to emotional expression, Aristotle urges communicators to moderate their own style, to be "intermediate not in the object, but relative to us." Following Aristotle's injunction, a person with a hot temper would strive to cool down, whereas a person who rarely expresses his or her feelings ought to aim at becoming more expressive. The result would still be two people with different styles, but each of whom behaved better than before seeking the golden mean.

According to Aristotle, moderation also means that emotions should be suited to the occasion: We should feel (and express) them "at the right times, with reference to the right objects, towards the right people, with the right motive, and in the right way." We can imagine times when even a normally restrained person could reasonably act with anger and times when a normally voluble person could reasonably behave with restraint. Even then, too much emotion (rage, for example) or too little emotion falls outside the range of virtue. In Aristotle's words, when it comes to "passions and actions . . . excess is a form of failure and so is deficit."

How would your emotional expression be different if you strived for moderation? Answer this question by identifying which parts of your emotional expression are most extreme, either in their intensity or their absence.

1. How might your relationships change if you acted more moderately?
2. Are there any situations in your life when more-extreme forms of emotional expression are both moral and effective?

To read Aristotle's full discussion of the golden mean, see Book Two of his *Nicomachean Ethics*, translated by H. Rachman and published by Harvard University Press in 1934.

"I'm getting angry." Instead of saying, "You hurt my feelings," say, "I feel hurt when you do that." As you'll soon read, people don't make us like or dislike them, and believing that they do denies the responsibility that each of us has for our own emotions. Chapter 5 introduces "I" language, which offers a responsible way to express your feelings.

Be Mindful of the Communication Channel

As Chapter 1 explained, the channels we use to communicate make a difference in how others interpret our messages. This is particularly true when expressing emotions.

Communicators today have many more channel choices than they did a few decades ago, and the decision about when to use mediated channels—such as e-mail, instant messaging, cell phones, and blogging—call for a level of analysis that wasn't required in the past.[63] For instance, is it appropriate to signal your desire to end a relationship in a voice mail message? When is it acceptable to use CAPITAL LETTERS in an instant message to express displeasure? If you're excited about some good news, should you first tell your family and friends in person before publishing it in your blog?

Most people intuitively recognize that the selection of a channel depends in part on the kind of message they're sending. In one survey, students identified which channel they would find best for delivering a variety of messages.[64] Most respondents said they would have little trouble expressing positive messages in person, but preferred mediated channels for negative messages.

"Flaming" is an extreme example of how computer-mediated channels lend themselves to expressing negative emotions. As the reading on page 139 points out, the kind of civility that most people honor in other communication channels seems to have less of a hold on the Internet—certainly among strangers, but

---

Skill Builder

Feelings and Phrases

You can try this exercise alone or with a group.

1. Choose a situation from column A and a receiver from column B.

2. Develop an approach for communicating your feelings for this combination.

3. Now create approaches for the same situation with other receivers from column B. How are the statements different?

4. Repeat the process with various combinations, using other situations from column A.

Column A: Situations	**Column B: Receivers**
a. You have been stood up for a date or appointment	An instructor
b. The other person pokes fun at your schoolwork	A family member (you decide which one)
c. The other person compliments you on your appearance, then says, "I hope I haven't embarrassed you."	A classmate you don't know well
d. The other person gives you a hug and says, "It's good to see you."	Your best friend

My First Flame

© Dave Plunkert/Getty Images

I got flamed for the first time a couple of months ago. To flame, according to "Que's Computer User's Dictionary," is "to lose one's self-control and write a message that uses derogatory, obscene, or inappropriate language."

My flame arrived on a windy Friday morning. I got to work at nine, removed my coat, plugged in my PowerBook, and, as usual, could not resist immediately checking my E-mail. I saw I had a message from a technology writer who does a column about personal computers for a major newspaper, and whom I knew by name only. I had recently published a piece about Bill Gates, the chairman of Microsoft, and as I opened his E-mail to me it was with the pleasant expectation of getting feedback from a colleague. Instead, I got:

> Crave this, a**hole: Listen, you toady-ing dips**t scumbag . . . remove your head from your rectum long enough to look around and notice that real reporters don't fawn over their subjects, pretend that their subjects are making some sort of special contact with them, or, worse, curry favor by telling their subjects how great the a**-licking profile is going to turn out and then brag in print about doing it.

I felt cold. People whose bodies have been badly burned begin to shiver, and the flame seemed to put a chill in the center of my chest which I could feel spreading slowly outward. The insults, being pre-meditated, were more forceful than insults spoken in the heat of the moment.

I had assumed, without really articulating the thought, that while talking to other people through my computer I was going to be sheltered by the same customs and laws that shelter me when I'm talking on the telephone or listening to the radio or watching TV. Now, for the first time, I understood the novelty and power of the technology I was dealing with.

No one had ever said something like this to me before, and no one could have said this to me before: in any other medium, these words would be, literally, unspeakable. The guy couldn't have said this to me on the phone, because I would have hung up and not answered if the phone rang again, and he couldn't have said it to my face, because I wouldn't have let him finish. If this had happened to me in the street, I could have used my status as a physically large male to threaten the person, but in the on-line world my size didn't matter. I suppose the guy could have written me a nasty letter: he probably wouldn't have used the word "rectum," though, and he probably wouldn't have mailed the let-ter; he would have thought twice

while he was addressing the envelope. But the nature of E-mail is that you don't think twice. You write and send.

What would Emily Post advise me to do? Flame the dips**t scumbag right back? I did spend most of that Friday in front of the screen composing the most vile insults I could dream up—words I have never spoken to another human being, and would never speak in any other medium, but which I found easy to type into the computer. I managed to restrain myself from sending my reply until I got home and asked my wife to look at it. She had the good sense to be horrified.

I wanted to talk about my flame with someone else who had been flamed, but I didn't know anyone in my real-world life who had been. Then it occurred to me that I could use the net. People who gather on the net to discuss a specific topic are called newsgroups. I went to alt. flame, thinking this might be the site where people talk about flaming, but it turned out to be a place where peo-ple go to flame each other.

In the absence of rules, there is a natural tendency toward anarchy on the net anyway, and in some stretches I'd come upon sites that were in com-plete chaos, where people had been flaming each other non-stop, absolutely scorching everything around them, and driving all the civilized people away. Sometimes I'd arrive at a dead site long after a flame war broke out; it was like walking through what was once a forest after a wildfire. Some-times I came upon voices that were just howling at the world; you could feel the rage and savagery pouring out through people's fingers.

I asked [computer expert John Norstad] to look at it. He said, "My

Continued

thirteen-year-old daughter is a Pearl Jam fan, and the other night she asked me if there might be some Pearl Jam stuff on the net. So we logged on and looked around, and we were able to download some Pearl Jam posters, some music, some song lyrics—really neat stuff. But then we came to the Pearl Jam newsgroup, and there was a really terrible flame war going on in there. People were saying really awful things to each other, things I was embarrassed to be sitting next to my daughter reading. . . . Terrible things. After a while, my daughter looked over at me and asked, 'Daddy, do these people have a life?' And I said, 'No, darling, most of them don't have a life.'"

John Seabrook

even among people who belong to the same personal networks. Before saying something you may later regret, it's worth remembering the principle stated in Chapter 1 that communication is irreversible. Once you hit the "Send" button, you can't retract an emotional outburst.

Managing Difficult Emotions

Although feeling and expressing many emotions add to the quality of interpersonal relationships, not all feelings are beneficial. For instance, rage, depression, terror, and jealousy do little to help you feel better or improve your relationships. The following pages will give you tools to minimize these unproductive emotions.

Facilitative and Debilitative Emotions

> I can't choose how I feel, but I can choose what I do about it.
>
> Andy Rooney

First, we need to make a distinction between **facilitative emotions**, which contribute to effective functioning, and **debilitative emotions**, which detract from effective functioning.

© The Bridgeman Art Library/Getty Images

One difference between the two types is their *intensity*. For instance, a certain amount of anger or irritation can be constructive because it often provides the stimulus that leads you to improve the unsatisfying conditions. Rage, on the other hand, will usually make matters worse—especially when driving, as illustrated by the problems associated with "road rage."[65] The same holds true for fear. A little bit of fear before an important athletic contest or job interview might give you the boost that will improve your performance. (Mellow athletes or employees usually don't do well.) But total terror is something else. Even a little suspicion can make people more effective communicators. One study revealed that mates who doubted that their relational partners were telling the truth were better at detecting deception than were trusting mates.[66] Of course, an extreme case of paranoia would have the opposite and debilitative effect, reducing the ability to interpret the partner's behavior accurately.

Not surprisingly, debilitative emotions like communication apprehension can lead to a variety of problems in personal, business, educational, and even medical settings.[67] When people become anxious, they generally speak less, which means that their needs aren't met; and when they do manage to speak up, they are less effective than their more confident counterparts.[68]

A second characteristic that distinguishes debilitative feelings from facilitative ones is their extended *duration*. Feeling depressed for a while after the breakup of a relationship or the loss of a job is natural. But spending the rest of your life grieving over your loss would accomplish nothing. In the same way, staying angry at someone for a wrong inflicted long ago can be just as punishing to you as to the wrongdoer.

Many debilitative emotions involve communication. Here are a few examples, offered by readers of *Looking Out/Looking In:*

> When I first came to college, I had to leave my boyfriend. I was living with three girls, and for most of the first semester I was so lonesome and unhappy that I was a pretty terrible roommate.

> I got so frustrated with my overly critical boss that I lost my temper and quit one day. I told him what a horrible manager he was and walked off the job right then and there. Now I'm afraid to list my former boss as a reference, and I'm afraid my temper tantrum will make it harder for me to get a new job.

> I've had ongoing problems with my family, and sometimes I get so upset that I can't concentrate on my work or school, or even sleep well at night.

In the following pages you will learn a method for dealing with debilitative feelings like these that can improve your effectiveness as a communicator. This method is based on the idea that one way to minimize debilitative feelings is to minimize unproductive thinking.

Sources of Debilitative Emotions

For most people, feelings seem to have a life of their own. You wish you could feel calm when approaching strangers, yet your voice quivers. You try to appear confident when asking for a raise, yet your eye twitches nervously. Where do feelings like these come from?

Physiology   One answer lies in our genetic makeup. As you read in Chapter 2, temperament is, to a large degree, inherited. Communication traits like shyness, verbal aggressiveness, and assertiveness are rooted in biology. Fortunately, biology isn't destiny. As you'll soon read, it is possible to overcome debilitative feelings.

Beyond heredity, cognitive scientists tell us that the cause of some debilitative feelings—especially those involving "fight" or "flight" responses—lies deep inside the brain, in an almond-sized cluster of interconnected structures called the amygdala (pronounced "uh MIG duh luh"). The amygdala acts as a kind of sentinel that scans every experience, looking for threats. In literally a split second, it can sound an alarm that triggers a flood of physiological reactions: speeding heart rate, elevating blood pressure, heightening the senses, and preparing the muscles to react.[69]

This defense system has obvious value when we are confronted with real physical dangers. But in social situations the amygdala can hijack the brain, triggering emotions like fear and anger when there is no real threat. You might find yourself feeling uncomfortable when somebody stands too close to you or angry when someone cuts in front of you in line. As you'll soon read, thinking clearly is the way to avoid overreacting to non-threats like these.

Emotional Memory   The source of some threats lies in what neuroscientists have termed our *emotional memory*. Seemingly harmless events can trigger debilitative feelings if they bear even a slight resemblance to troublesome experiences from the past. A few examples illustrate the point:

- Ever since being teased when he moved to a new elementary school, Trent has been uncomfortable in unfamiliar situations.
- Alicia feels apprehensive around men, especially those with deep, booming voices. As a child, she was mistreated by a family member with a loud baritone voice.
- Paul feels a wave of insecurity whenever he is around women who use the same perfume worn by a former lover who jilted him.

Self-Talk

Beyond neurobiology, what we think can have a profound effect on how we feel. It's common to say that strangers or your boss *make* you feel nervous just as you would say that a bee sting makes you feel pain. The apparent similarities between physical and emotional discomforts become clear if you look at them in the following way:

Event	Feeling
Bee sting	physical pain
Meeting strangers	nervous feelings

When looking at your emotions in this way, you seem to have little control over how you feel. However, this apparent similarity between physical pain and emotional discomfort (or pleasure) isn't as great as it seems to be. Cognitive psychologists argue that it is not *events* such as meeting strangers or being jilted by a lover that cause people to feel bad, but rather the *beliefs they hold* about these events.

Albert Ellis, who developed the cognitive approach called *rational-emotive therapy,* tells a story that makes this point clear. Imagine yourself walking by a friend's house and seeing your friend stick his head out of a window and call you a string of vile names. (You supply the friend and the names.) Under these circumstances it's likely that you would feel hurt and upset. Now imagine that instead of walking by the house you were passing a mental institution when the same friend, who was obviously a patient there, shouted the same vile names at you. In this case, your feelings would probably be quite different—most likely sadness and pity. You can see that in this story the activating event of being called names was the same in both cases, yet the emotional consequences were very different. The reason for your different feelings has to do with your thinking in each case. In the first case, you would most likely think that your friend was very angry with you; further, you might imagine that you must have done something terrible to deserve such a response. In the second case, you would probably assume that your friend had some psychological difficulty, and most likely you would feel sympathetic.

From this example you can start to see that it's the *interpretations* that people make of an event, during the process of **self-talk**, that determine their feelings.[70] Thus, the model for emotions looks like this:

Event	Thought	Feeling
Being called names	"I've done something wrong."	hurt, upset
Being called names	"My friend must be sick."	concern, sympathy

The same principle applies in more common situations. In job interviews, for example, people who become nervous are likely to use negative self-talk when they think about their performance: "I won't do well," "I don't know why I'm doing this."[71] In romantic relationships, thoughts shape satisfaction. The words "I love you" can be interpreted in a variety of ways. They could be taken at face value as a genuine expression of deep affection:

Event	Thought	Feeling
Hearing "I love you"	"This is a genuine statement."	delight (perhaps)

The same words might be decoded as a sincere but mistaken declaration uttered in a moment of passion, an attempt to make the recipient feel better, or an attempt at manipulation. For example,

Hearing "I love you"	"S/he's just saying this to manipulate me."	anger

One study revealed that women are more likely than men to regard expressions of love as genuine statements rather than attribute them to some other cause.[72] Other research shows the importance of self-talk in relationships. Members of couples who are unhappy with one another have more negative self-talk about their partner and fewer positive thoughts about their partner and the relationship.[73]

One powerful form of debilitative self-talk is **rumination**: Dwelling persistently on negative thoughts that, in turn, intensify negative feelings. A substantial body of research confirms that self-focused rumination increases feelings of sadness, anxiety, and depression.[74] Just as bad, people who ruminate are more likely to lash out with displaced aggression at innocent bystanders.[75]

The mind is its own place, and in itself can make a Heav'n of Hell, a Hell of Heav'n.

John Milton, *Paradise Lost*

Talking to Yourself

You can become better at understanding how your thoughts shape your feelings by completing the following steps.

1. Take a few minutes to listen to the inner voice you use when thinking. Close your eyes now and listen to it. . . . Did you hear the voice? Perhaps it was saying, "What voice? I don't have any voice. . . ." Try again, and pay attention to what the voice is saying.

2. Now think about the following situations, and imagine how you would react in each. How would you interpret them with your inner voice? What feelings would follow from each interpretation?

   a. While sitting on a bus, in class, or on the street, you notice an attractive person sneaking glances at you.

   b. During a lecture your professor asks the class, "What do you think about this?" and looks toward you.

   c. You are telling friends about your vacation, and one yawns.

   d. You run into a friend on the street and ask how things are going. "Fine," she replies and rushes off.

3. Now recall three recent times when you felt a strong emotion. For each one, recall the activating event and then the interpretation that led to your emotional reaction.

Irrational Thinking and Debilitative Emotions

Focusing on the self-talk that we use to think is the key to understanding debilitative emotions. Many debilitative emotions come from accepting a number of irrational thoughts—we'll call them *fallacies* here—that lead to illogical conclusions and in turn to debilitative emotions. We usually aren't aware of these thoughts, which makes them especially powerful.[76]

1. The Fallacy of Perfection   People who accept the **fallacy of perfection** believe that a worthwhile communicator should be able to handle every situation with complete confidence and skill.

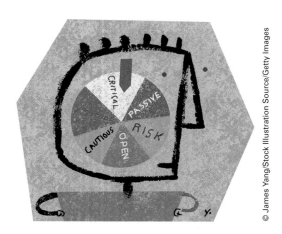

© James Yang/Stock Illustration Source/Getty Images

If you accept the belief that it's desirable and possible to be a perfect communicator, you'll probably assume that people won't appreciate you if you are imperfect. Admitting your mistakes, saying, "I don't know," and sharing feelings of uncertainty seem like social defects when viewed in this manner. Given the desire to be valued and appreciated, it's tempting to try to *appear* perfect, but the costs of such deception are high. If others ever find you out, they'll see you as a phony. Even when your act isn't uncovered, such an act uses up a great deal of psychological energy and thus makes the rewards of approval less enjoyable.

Subscribing to the myth of perfection not only can keep others from liking you, but also can act as a force to diminish your own self-esteem. How can you like yourself when you don't measure up to the way you ought to be? How liberated you become when you can comfortably accept the idea that you are not perfect! That,

> Like everyone else, you sometimes have a hard time expressing yourself.
>
> Like everyone else, you make mistakes from time to time, and there is no reason to hide this.
>
> You are honestly doing the best you can to realize your potential, to become the best person you can be.

Invitation to Insight

Type A Behavior and the Fallacy of Perfection

ThomsonNOW™ View the ABC News feature "Type A Behavior." You can find the link to this site through your ThomsonNOW for *Looking Out/Looking In*.

This profile illustrates how the compulsion to perform perfectly can add stress to close relationships. We see that the challenge perfectionists face is how to set their sights high, without succumbing to an excessive need to handle every situation perfectly.

---

2. The Fallacy of Approval   The **fallacy of approval** is based on the idea that it is not only desirable but also *vital* to get the approval of virtually every person. People who accept this idea go to incredible lengths to seek approval from others even when they have to sacrifice their own principles and happiness to do so. Accepting this fallacy can lead to some ludicrous situations:

> Feeling nervous because people you really don't like seem to disapprove of you
>
> Feeling apologetic when others are at fault
>
> Feeling embarrassed after behaving unnaturally to gain another's approval

In addition to the obvious discomfort that arises from denying your own principles and needs, the fallacy of approval is irrational because it implies that others will respect and like you more if you go out of your way to please them. Often this simply isn't true. How is it possible to respect people who have compromised important values just to gain acceptance? How is it possible to think highly of people who repeatedly deny their own needs as a means of buying approval? Though others may find it tempting to use these individuals to suit their ends, these individuals hardly deserve genuine affection and respect.

Striving for universal approval is irrational because it's simply not possible. Sooner or later a conflict of expectations is bound to occur; one person will approve if you behave only in a certain way, but another will accept only the opposite behavior. What are you to do then?

Don't misunderstand: Abandoning the fallacy of approval doesn't mean living a life of selfishness. It's still important to consider the needs of others and to meet them whenever possible. It's also pleasant—we might say even necessary— to strive for the respect of those people you value. The point here is that when you must abandon your own needs and principles in order to seek these goals, the price is too high.

> I never was what you would call a fancy skater—and while I seldom actually fell, it might have been more impressive if I had. A good resounding fall is no disgrace. It is the fantastic writhing to avoid a fall which destroys any illusion of being a gentleman. How like life that is, after all!
>
> Robert Benchley

3. The Fallacy of Shoulds   The **fallacy of shoulds** is the inability to distinguish between what *is* and what *should be*. You can see the difference by imagining a person who is full of complaints about the world:

"There should be no rain on weekends."

"People ought to live forever."

"Money should grow on trees."

"We should all be able to fly."

Complaints like these are obviously foolish. However pleasant wishing may be, insisting that the unchangeable should be changed won't affect reality one bit. And yet many people torture themselves by engaging in this sort of irrational thinking when they confuse *is* with *should*. They say and think things like this:

"My friend should be more understanding."

"She shouldn't be so inconsiderate."

"They should be more friendly."

"You should work harder."

The message in each of these cases is that you would *prefer* people to behave differently. Wishing that things were better is perfectly legitimate, and trying to change them is, of course, a good idea; but it's unreasonable to *insist* that the world operate just as you want it to or to feel cheated when things aren't ideal.

Imposing the fallacy of shoulds on yourself can also lead to unnecessary unhappiness. Psychologist Aaron Beck points out some unrealistic self-imposed "shoulds":[77]

"I should be able to find a quick solution to every problem."

"I should never feel hurt; I should always be happy and serene."

"I should always demonstrate the utmost generosity, considerateness, dignity, courage, unselfishness."

Becoming obsessed with "shoulds" like these has three troublesome consequences. First, it leads to unnecessary unhappiness because people who are constantly dreaming about the ideal are seldom satisfied with what they have or who they are. Second, merely complaining without acting can keep you from doing anything to change unsatisfying conditions. Third, this sort of complaining can build a defensive climate with others, who will resent being nagged. It's much more effective to tell people about what you'd like than to preach: Say, "I wish you'd be more punctual" instead of "You should be on time." We'll discuss ways of avoiding defensive climates in Chapter 10.

4. The Fallacy of Overgeneralization   The **fallacy of overgeneralization** comprises two types. The first occurs when we base a belief on a *limited amount of evidence*. For instance, how many times have you found yourself saying something like this:

"I'm so stupid! I can't even understand how to do my income tax."

"Some friend I am! I forgot my best friend's birthday."

In cases like these, we focus on a limited type of shortcoming as if it represented everything about us. We forget that along with encountering our difficulties we have solved tough problems and that though we're sometimes forgetful, at other times we're caring and thoughtful.

A second type of overgeneralization occurs when we *exaggerate* shortcomings:

"You *never* listen to me."

"You're *always* late."

"I can't think of *anything*."

On closer examination, absolute statements like these are almost always false and usually lead to discouragement or anger. You'll feel far better when you replace overgeneralizations with more accurate messages to yourself and others:

"You often don't listen to me."

"You've been late three times this week."

"I haven't had any ideas I like today."

5. The Fallacy of Causation   The **fallacy of causation** is based on the irrational belief that emotions are caused by others rather than by one's own self-talk.

This fallacy causes trouble in two ways. The first plagues people who become overly cautious about communicating because they don't want to "cause" any pain or inconvenience for others. This attitude occurs in cases such as:

Visiting friends or family out of a sense of obligation rather than a genuine desire to see them

Keeping quiet when another person's behavior is bothering you

Pretending to be attentive to a speaker when you are already late for an appointment or feeling ill

Praising and reassuring others who ask for your opinion, even when your honest response would be negative

There's certainly no excuse for going out of your way to say things that will result in pain for others, and there will be times when you choose to inconvenience yourself to make life easier for those you care about. It's essential to realize, however, that it's an overstatement to say that you are the one who causes others' feelings. It's more accurate to say that they *respond* to your behavior with feelings of their own. For example, consider how strange it sounds to suggest that you make others fall in love with you. Such a statement simply doesn't make sense. It would be closer to the truth to say that you act in one way or another, and some people might fall in love with you as a result of these actions, whereas others wouldn't. In the same way, it's incorrect to say that you *make* others angry, upset—or happy, for that matter. It's better to say that others create their own responses to your behavior.

The fallacy of causation also operates when we believe that others cause *our* emotions. Sometimes it certainly seems as if they do, either raising or lowering our spirits by their actions. But think about it for a moment: The same actions that will cause you happiness or unhappiness one day have little effect at other times. The insult or compliment that affected your mood strongly yesterday leaves you unaffected today. Why? Because in the latter case you attached less importance to either. You certainly wouldn't feel some emotions without others' behavior; but it's your reaction, not their actions, that determines how you feel.

6. The Fallacy of Helplessness   The **fallacy of helplessness** suggests that satisfaction in life is determined by forces beyond your control. People who continuously see themselves as victims make such statements as:

"There's no way a woman can get ahead in this society. It's a man's world, and the best thing I can do is to accept it."

No one can make you feel inferior unless you agree to it.

Eleanor Roosevelt

© Andrew Bordwin/Images.com

"I was born with a shy personality. I'd like to be more out-going, but there's nothing I can do about that."

"I can't tell my boss that she is putting too many demands on me. If I did, I might lose my job."

The mistake in statements like these becomes apparent after you realize that there are many things you can do if you really want to. As you read in Chapter 2, most "can't" statements can be more correctly rephrased either as "won't" ("I can't tell him what I think" becomes "I won't be honest with him") or as "don't know how" ("I can't carry on an interesting conversation" becomes "I don't know what to say"). After you've rephrased these inaccurate "can'ts," it becomes clear that they're either a matter of choice or an area that calls for your action—both quite different from saying that you're helpless.

When viewed in this light, it's apparent that many "can'ts" are really rationalizations to justify not wanting to change. Lonely people, for example, tend to attribute their poor interpersonal relationships to uncontrollable causes. "It's beyond my control," they think. Also, they expect their relational partners to reject them. Notice the self-fulfilling prophecy in this attitude: Believing that your relational prospects are dim can lead you to act in ways that make you an unattractive prospect. On the other hand, acknowledging that there is a way to change—even though it may be difficult—puts the responsibility for your predicament on your shoulders. You *can* become a better communicator—this book is one step in your movement toward that goal. Don't give up or sell yourself short.

7. The Fallacy of Catastrophic Expectations   Fearful communicators who subscribe to the irrational **fallacy of catastrophic expectations** operate on the assumption that if something bad can possibly happen, it will. Typical catastrophic expectations include:

"If I invite them to the party, they probably won't want to come."

"If I speak up in order to try to resolve a conflict, things will probably get worse."

"If I apply for the job I want, I probably won't be hired."

"If I tell them how I really feel, they'll probably laugh at me."

After you start expecting catastrophic consequences, a self-fulfilling prophecy can begin to build. One study revealed that people who believed that their romantic partners would not change for the better were likely to behave in ways that contributed to the breakup of the relationship.[78]

Although it's naive to assume that all your interactions with others will meet with success, it's just as naive to assume that you'll fail. One way to escape from the fallacy of catastrophic expectations is to think about the consequences that would follow even if you don't communicate successfully. Keeping in mind the folly of trying to be perfect and of living only for the approval of others, realize that failing in a given instance usually isn't as bad as it might seem. What if people do laugh at you? Suppose you don't get the job? What if others do get angry at your remarks? Are these matters really *that* serious?

Before moving on, we need to add a few thoughts about thinking and feeling. First, you should realize that thinking rationally won't completely eliminate debilitative emotions. Some debilitative emotions, after all, are very rational:

grief over the death of someone you love, euphoria over getting a new job, and apprehension about the future of an important relationship after a serious fight, for example. Thinking rationally can eliminate many debilitative emotions from your life, but not all of them.

Invitation to Insight

How Irrational Are You?

1. Return to the situations described in the exercise "Talking to Yourself" on page 144. Examine each one to see whether your self-talk contains any irrational thoughts.

2. Keep a two- or three-day record of your debilitative emotions. Are any of them based on irrational thinking? Examine your conclusions, and see if you repeatedly use any of the fallacies described in the preceding section.

3. Take a class poll to see which fallacies are most "popular." Also, discuss what subjects seem to stimulate most of this irrational thinking (for example, schoolwork, dating, jobs, family).

Minimizing Debilitative Emotions

How can you overcome irrational thinking? Social scientists have developed a simple yet effective approach.[79] When practiced conscientiously, it can help you cut down on the self-defeating thinking that leads to many debilitative emotions.

1. *Monitor your emotional reactions.* The first step is to recognize when you're feeling debilitative emotions. (Of course, it's also nice to recognize pleasant emotions when they occur!) As we suggested earlier, one way to recognize emotions is through proprioceptive stimuli: butterflies in the stomach, racing heart, hot flashes, and so on. Although such stimuli might be symptoms of food poisoning, more often they are symptoms of a strong emotion. You can also recognize certain ways of behaving that suggest your feelings: stomping instead of walking normally, being unusually quiet, or speaking in a sarcastic tone of voice are some examples.

    It may seem strange to suggest that it's necessary to look for emotions—they ought to be immediately apparent. The fact is, however, that we often suffer from debilitative emotions for some time without noticing them. For example, at the end of a trying day you've probably caught yourself frowning and realized that you've been wearing that mask for some time without realizing it.

2. *Note the activating event.* After you're aware of how you're feeling, the next step is to figure out what activating event triggered your response. Sometimes it is obvious. For instance, a common source of anger is being accused unfairly (or fairly) of foolish behavior; a common source of hurt is being rejected by somebody important to you. In other cases, however, the activating event isn't so apparent.

    Sometimes there isn't a single activating event but rather a series of small events that finally builds toward a critical mass and triggers a debilitative emotion. This happens when you're trying to work or sleep and are continually interrupted by a string of interruptions, or when you suffer a series of small disappointments.

    The best way to begin tracking down activating events is to notice the circumstances in which you have debilitative emotions. Perhaps they occur

The thought manifests as the word; The word manifests as the deed; The deed develops into habit; And the habit hardens into character. So watch the thought and its ways with care . . . As we think, so we become.

From the *Dhammapada* (The sayings of the Buddha)

when you're around *specific* people. In other cases, you might be bothered by certain *types of individuals* owing to their age, role, background, or some other factor. Or perhaps certain *settings* stimulate unpleasant emotions: parties, work, school. Sometimes the *topic* of conversation is the factor that sets you off, whether it be politics, religion, sex, or some other topic.

3. *Record your self-talk.* This is the point at which you analyze the thoughts that are the link between the activating event and your feeling. If you're serious about getting rid of debilitative emotions, it's important actually to write down your self-talk when first learning to use this method. Putting your thoughts on paper will help you see whether they actually make any sense.

   Monitoring your self-talk might be difficult at first. This is a new activity, and any new activity seems awkward. If you persevere, however, you'll find that you will be able to identify the thoughts that lead to your debilitative emotions. After you get in the habit of recognizing this internal monologue, you'll be able to identify your thoughts quickly and easily.

4. *Dispute your irrational beliefs.* Disputing your irrational beliefs is the key to success in the rational-emotive approach. Use the list of irrational fallacies on pages 144–149 to discover which of your internal statements are based on mistaken thinking.

   You can do this most effectively by following three steps. First, decide whether each belief you've recorded is rational or irrational. Next, explain why the belief is rational or irrational. Finally, if the belief is irrational, you should write down an alternative way of thinking that is more rational and that can leave you feeling better when faced with the same activating event in the future.

Replacing self-defeating self-talk with more constructive thinking is an especially effective tool for improving self-confidence and relational communication.[80] Nonetheless, this approach triggers objections from some readers.

"So, when he says, 'What a good boy am I,' Jack is really reinforcing his self-esteem."

"The rational-emotive approach sounds like nothing more than trying to talk yourself out of feeling bad." This accusation is totally correct. After all, because we talk ourselves into feeling bad, what's wrong with talking ourselves out of feeling bad, especially when such feelings are based on irrational thoughts? Rationalizing may be an excuse and a self-deception, but there's nothing wrong with being rational.

"The kind of disputing we just read sounds phony and unnatural. I don't talk to myself in sentences and paragraphs." There's no need to dispute your irrational beliefs in any special literary style. You can be just as colloquial as you want. The important thing is to clearly understand what thoughts led you into your debilitative emotions so that you can clearly dispute them. While the approach is new to you, it's a good idea to write or

talk out your thoughts in order to make them clear. After you've had some practice, you'll be able to do these steps in a quicker, less formal way.

"This approach is too cold and impersonal. It seems to aim at turning people into cold-blooded, calculating, emotionless machines." This is simply not true. A rational thinker can still dream, hope, and love: There's nothing necessarily irrational about feelings like these. Basically rational people even indulge in a bit of irrational thinking once in a while. But they usually know what they're doing. Like healthy eaters who occasionally allow themselves a snack of junk food, rational thinkers occasionally indulge in irrational thoughts, knowing that they'll return to their healthy lifestyle soon with no real damage done.

"This technique promises too much. There's no chance I could rid myself of all unpleasant feelings, however nice that might be." We can answer this objection by assuring you that rational-emotive thinking probably won't totally solve your emotional problems. What it can do is to reduce their number, intensity, and duration. This method is not the answer to all your problems, but it can make a significant difference—which is not a bad accomplishment.

Skill Builder

Rational Thinking

1. Return to the diary of irrational thoughts you recorded on page 149. Dispute the self-talk in each case, and write a more rational interpretation of the event.

2. Now try out your ability to think rationally on the spot. You can do this by acting out the scenes listed in step 4. You'll need three players for each one: a subject, the subject's "little voice"—his or her thoughts—and a second party.

3. Play out each scene by having the subject and second party interact while the "little voice" stands just behind the subject and says what the subject is probably thinking. For example, in a scene where the subject is asking an instructor to reconsider a low grade, the little voice might say, "I hope I haven't made things worse by bringing this up. Maybe he'll lower the grade after rereading the test. I'm such an idiot! Why didn't I keep quiet?"

4. Whenever the little voice expresses an irrational thought, the observers who are watching the skit should call out, "Foul." At this point the action should stop while the group discusses the irrational thought and suggests a more rational line of self-talk. The players should then replay the scene with the little voice speaking in a more rational way.

Here are some scenes. Of course, you can invent others as well.

a. Two people are just beginning their first date.

b. A potential employee has just begun a job interview.

c. A teacher or boss is criticizing the subject for showing up late.

d. A student and instructor run across each other in the market.

Communication Transcript

Rational Thinking in Action

The following scenarios demonstrate how the rational thinking method described on pages 149–150 applies in everyday challenges. Notice that thinking rationally doesn't eliminate debilitative emotions. Instead, it helps keep them in control, making effective communication more possible.

Situation 1: Dealing with Annoying Customers
Activating Event

I work in a shopping mall that swarms with tourists and locals. Our company's reputation is based on service, but lately I've been losing my patience with the customers. The store is busy from the second we open until we close. Many of the customers are rude, pushy, and demanding. Others expect me to be a tour guide, restaurant reviewer, medical consultant, and even a baby-sitter. I feel like I'm ready to explode.

Beliefs and Self-Talk

1. I'm sick of working with the public. People are really obnoxious!
2. The customers should be more patient and polite instead of treating me like a servant.
3. This work is driving me crazy! If I keep working here, I'm going to become as rude as the customers.
4. I can't quit: I could never find another job that pays this well.

Disputing Irrational Beliefs

1. It's an overgeneralization to say that *all* people are obnoxious. Actually, most of the customers are fine. Some are even very nice. About 10 percent of them cause most of the trouble. Recognizing that most people are OK leaves me feeling less bitter.
2. It's true that obnoxious customers *should* be more polite, but it's unrealistic to expect that everybody will behave the way they ought to. After all, it's not a perfect world.
3. By saying that the customers are driving me crazy, I suggest that I have no control over the situation. I'm an adult, and I am able to keep a grip on myself. I may not like the way some people behave, but it's my choice how to respond to them.
4. I'm not helpless. If the job is too unpleasant, I can quit. I probably wouldn't find another job that pays as well as this one, so I have to choose which is

more important: money or peace of mind. It's my choice.

Situation 2: Meeting My Girlfriend's Family
Activating Event

Tracy and I are talking about marriage—maybe not soon, but eventually. Her family is very close, and they want to meet me. I'm sure I'll like them, but I am not sure what they will think about me. I was married once before, at a young age. It was a big mistake, and it didn't last. Furthermore, I was laid off two months ago, and I'm between jobs. The family is coming to town next week, and I am very nervous about what they will think of me.

Beliefs and Self-Talk

1. They've *got* to like me! This is a close family, and I'm doomed if they think I'm not right for Tracy.
2. No matter how sensibly I act, all they'll think of is my divorce and unemployment.
3. Maybe the family is right. Tracy deserves the best, and I'm certainly not that!

Disputing Irrational Beliefs

1. The family's approval is definitely important. Still, my relationship with Tracy doesn't depend on it. She's already said that she's committed to me, no matter what they think. The sensible approach is to say I *want* their approval, but I don't *need* it.
2. I'm expecting the absolute worst if I think that I'm doomed no matter what happens when we meet. There is a chance that they will dislike me, but there's also a chance that things will work out fine. There's no point in dwelling on catastrophes.
3. Just because I've had an imperfect past doesn't mean I'm wrong for Tracy. I've learned from my past mistakes, and I am committed to living a good life. I know I can be the kind of husband she deserves, even though I'm not perfect.

Communication Scenarios

Go to your ThomsonNOW for *Looking Out/Looking In,* access "Communication Scenarios" and then click on either "Rational Thinking: Annoying Customers" or "Rational Thinking: Meeting My Girlfriend's Family" to watch and analyze dramatized versions of the scenarios described here. **ThomsonNOW**

ZITS — **BY JERRY SCOTT AND JIM BORGMAN**

Summary

Emotions have several dimensions. They are signaled by internal physiological changes, manifested by nonverbal reactions, and defined in most cases by cognitive interpretations. We can use this information to make choices about whether or not to verbalize our feelings.

There are several reasons why people do not verbalize many of the emotions they feel. Some people have personalities that are less prone toward emotional expression. Culture and gender also have an effect on the emotions we do and don't share with others. Social rules and roles discourage the expression of some feelings, particularly negative ones. Fear of consequences leads people to withhold expression of some emotions. Finally, contagion can lead us to experience emotions that we might not otherwise have had.

Because total expression of emotions is not appropriate for adults, several guidelines help define when and how to express emotions effectively. Expanding your emotional vocabulary, becoming more self-aware, and expressing mixed feelings are important. Recognizing the difference between feeling, thinking, and acting, as well as accepting responsibility for feelings instead of blaming them on others, lead to better reactions. Choosing the proper time and place to share feelings is also important, as is choosing the best channel for expressing emotions.

Whereas some emotions are facilitative, others are debilitative and inhibit effective functioning. Many of these debilitative emotions are biological reactions rooted in the amygdala portion of the brain, but their negative impact can be altered through rational thinking. It is often possible to communicate more confidently and effectively by identifying troublesome emotions, identifying the activating event and self-talk that triggered them, and replacing any irrational thoughts with a more logical analysis of the situation.

Key Terms

debilitative emotions (140)
emotional contagion (131)
facilitative emotions (140)
fallacy of approval (145)
fallacy of catastrophic
   expectations (148)

fallacy of causation (147)
fallacy of helplessness (147)
fallacy of
   overgeneralization (146)
fallacy of perfection (144)
fallacy of shoulds (146)

rumination (143)
self-talk (143)

Media Resources

Online Textbook Resources

ThomsonNOW For quick access to the online resources that accompany this chapter, access ThomsonNOW for *Looking Out/Looking In* at www.thomson.edu.com.

The ThomsonNOW online study system helps you identify concepts you don't fully understand, allowing you to put your study time to the best use. Using chapter-by-chapter diagnostic pre-tests, the system creates a **personalized study plan** for each chapter. Each plan directs you to specific resources designed to improve your understanding, including pages from the text in ebook format. Chapter post-tests give you an opportunity to measure how much you've learned and let you know if you are ready for graded quizzes and exams.

Your ThomsonNOW for *Looking Out/Looking In* also includes the **ABC News video clip** described on page 145; a **communication scenario video** of the transcript on page 152; **vocabulary activities** to help you master key terms; self-study **review quizzes** to test your comprehension of the material in this chapter and prepare for exams; **online exercises**, including the Skill Builder and Invitation to Insight activities in this chapter; **web links** you can use to further explore topics in this chapter; access to a **feature film database** where you can locate information about movies that illustrate communication principles; and access to the **InfoTrac** College Edition searchable database of over 10 million articles from both scholarly journals and the popular press.

Films

ThomsonNOW In addition to the films suggested here, go to your ThomsonNOW for *Looking Out/ Looking In* to link to the **Film in Communication Database**, where you can locate movie clips that illustrate various aspects of interpersonal communication.

The Significance of Expressing Emotions

Garden State (2004) Rated R

Andrew Largeman (Zach Braff) is living an emotionally numb life, due in part to the belief that he may have been responsible for a paralyzing injury to his mother. When his mother dies, Andrew returns home to New Jersey for the first time in nine years—and he confronts the ghosts of his past.

While home, Andrew meets a young woman named Sam (Natalie Portman) and falls for her quirky charm. With the help of Sam and some of his friends, Andrew realizes that he must acknowledge and purge the pain he's been carrying. Andrew also discovers that the road to emotional health runs through his father, Gideon (Ian Holm), who holds Andrew responsible for the breach between them. Gideon represses his own feelings of anger and pain, and epitomizes the approach to life from which Andrew needs to escape.

Andrew ultimately tells his father that even negative feelings are better than suppressed ones: "What I want more than anything in the world is for it to be okay with you for me to feel something again, even if it's pain. . . ." By movie's end, Andrew is transformed. He discovers that confronting pain can lead to joy, and that the road to emotional health is most easily traveled with loving companions.

Debilitative and Facilitative Emotions

The Upside of Anger (2005) Rated R

Terry Ann Wolfmeyer (Joan Allen) becomes embittered when her husband disappears, apparently having skipped the country with his Swedish secretary. Terry and her four daughters act out their anger in a variety of unproductive ways, including chronic drinking, eating disorders, drug use, poor relational choices, passive aggression, and emotional withdrawal. Many words of anger go unspoken or are said behind closed doors—or come spewing out during alcoholic rages.

Ultimately the characters realize their resentment is eating them alive, both personally and relationally, and they begin to choose facilitative rather than debilitative responses to the issues in their lives. With help from neighbor Denny Davies (Kevin Costner)—who is dealing with problems of his own—they come to a place of wholeness and restoration after several years of upheaval. By the film's end, the Wolfmeyers recognize that they, not the event, were responsible for the many negative emotions they experienced.

Expressing Emotions (Ir)responsibly

Riding in Cars with Boys (2001) Rated PG-13
Beverly Donofrio (Drew Barrymore) is an ambitious teenager who becomes pregnant, much to her parents' chagrin. Her hurt and angry father (James Woods) tells her, "You were special, and [now] you ruined your life"—and then he severs his relationship with her. Beverly adopts her father's hurtful emotional style, blaming others and denying responsibility when things don't go her way. For instance, she says "You just ruined our lives" to her young son Jason in a moment of anger—echoing what her father said to her. Later in life, Jason complains to Beverly, "If something bad happens to you, then it's all my fault."

By the time the film ends, it becomes clear that poorly expressed emotions—and the belief that others cause how we feel—have led to strained relationships among people who love and care about one another. The relatively happy ending also suggests that with some work and some new communication patterns, there is hope for change.

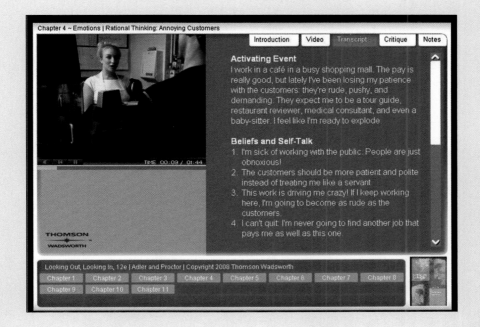

Chapter 4 ~ Emotions | Rational Thinking: Annoying Customers

Introduction   Video   Transcript   Critique   Notes

Activating Event
I work in a café in a busy shopping mall. The pay is really good, but lately I've been losing my patience with the customers: they're rude, pushy, and demanding. They expect me to be a tour guide, restaurant reviewer, medical consultant, and even a baby-sitter. I feel like I'm ready to explode.

Beliefs and Self-Talk
1. I'm sick of working with the public. People are just obnoxious!
2. The customers should be more patient and polite instead of treating me like a servant.
3. This work is driving me crazy! If I keep working here, I'm going to become as rude as the customers.
4. I can't quit. I'm never going to find another job that pays me as well as this one.

TIME 00:09 / 01:44

THOMSON
WADSWORTH

Looking Out, Looking In, 12e | Adler and Proctor | Copyright 2008 Thomson Wadsworth

Chapter 1   Chapter 2   Chapter 3   Chapter 4   Chapter 5   Chapter 6   Chapter 7   Chapter 8
Chapter 9   Chapter 10   Chapter 11

Now the whole world had one language and a common speech.

As men moved eastward, they found a plain in Shinar and settled there.

They said to each other, "Come, let's make bricks and bake them thoroughly." They used brick instead of stone, and tar for mortar.

Then they said, "Come, let us build ourselves a city, with a tower that reaches to the heavens, so that we may make a name for ourselves and not be scattered over the face of the whole earth."

But the Lord came down to see the city and the tower that the men were building.

The Lord said, "If as one people speaking the same language they have begun to do this, then nothing they plan to do will be impossible for them.

Come, let us go down and confuse their language so they will not understand each other."

So the Lord scattered them from there over all the earth, and they stopped building the city.

That is why it was called Babel—because there the Lord confused the language of the whole world.

Genesis 11:1–9

Language: Barrier and Bridge

5

The problems that began with Babel live on today. Sometimes it seems as if none of us speaks the same language. Yet, despite its frustrations and challenges, there is no question that language is a marvelous tool. It is the gift that allows us to communicate in a way that no other animals appear to match. Without language we would be more ignorant, ineffectual, and isolated.

In this chapter we will explore the nature of language, looking at how to take advantage of its strengths and minimize its weaknesses. After a quick explanation of the symbolic nature of language, we will examine the sources of most misunderstandings. We will then move beyond the challenges of simply understanding one another and explore how the language we use affects the climate of interpersonal relationships. Finally, we will broaden our focus even more to look at how linguistic practices shape the attitudes of entire cultures.

Language Is Symbolic

In the natural world, *signs* have a direct connection with the things they represent. For example, smoke is a sign that something's burning, and a high fever is a sign of illness. There's nothing arbitrary about the relationship between natural signs and the things they represent: Nobody made them up, and they exist independent of human opinions.

In human language, the connection between signs and the things they represent isn't so direct. Instead, language is *symbolic:* There's only an arbitrary

I was meeting a friend in a bar, and as I went in, I noted two pretty girls looking at me. "Nine," I heard one whisper as I passed. Feeling pleased with myself, I swaggered over to my buddy and told him a girl had just rated me a nine out of ten.

"I don't want to ruin it for you," he said, "but when I walked in, they were speaking German."

Richard Mogridge

"What part of oil lamp next to double squiggle over ox don't you understand?"

connection between words and the ideas or things to which they refer. For example, there is nothing particularly fivelike in the number five. The word represents the number of fingers on your hand only because English speakers agree that it does. To a speaker of French, the symbol "cinq" would convey the same meaning; to a computer programmer, the same value would be represented by the coded symbol "00110101."

Even sign language, as "spoken" by most deaf people, is symbolic in nature and not the pantomime it might seem. Because this form of communication is symbolic and not literal, hundreds of sign languages around the world have evolved independently whenever significant numbers of deaf people are in contact.[1] These distinct languages include American Sign Language, British Sign Language, French Sign Language, Danish Sign Language, Chinese Sign Language—even Australian Aboriginal and Mayan Sign Languages.

The symbolic nature of language is a blessing. It enables us to communicate in ways that wouldn't otherwise be possible: about ideas, reasons, the past, the future, and things not present. Without symbolic language, none of this would be possible. On the other hand, the indirect relationship between symbols and the things they represent leads to communication problems only hinted about in the tower of Babel story.

If everyone used symbols the same way, language would be much easier to manage and understand. However, your own experience shows that this isn't always the case. Messages that seem perfectly clear to you prove confusing or misleading to others. You tell the hair stylist to "take a little off the top," and then are stunned to discover that her definition of "a little" was equivalent to your definition of "a lot." You have a heated argument about the merits of feminism without realizing that you and the other person have been using the word to represent entirely different ideas. Misunderstandings like these serve to remind us that meanings are in people, not in words.

In Washington, D.C., an uproar developed when the city's ombudsman, David Howard, used the word *niggardly* to describe an approach to budgeting.[2] Howard, who is white, was accused by some African American critics of uttering an unforgivable racial slur. His defenders pointed out that the word, which means "miserly," is derived from Scandinavian languages, and has no link to the racial slur it resembles. Even though the criticisms eventually died away, they illustrate that, correct or not, the meanings that people associate with words have far more significance than do their dictionary definitions.

Understandings and Misunderstandings

Language is rather like plumbing: We pay the most attention to it when something goes wrong. Because misunderstandings are the greatest cause of concern for most people who study language, we'll begin our study by looking at sets of rules we use to understand—and sometimes misunderstand—one another's speech.

Understanding Words: Semantic Rules

Semantic rules reflect the ways in which users of a language assign meaning to a particular linguistic symbol, usually a word. Semantic rules make it possible for us to agree that "bikes" are for riding and "books" are for reading, and they help us know whom we will and won't encounter when we use rooms marked "men" or "women." Without semantic rules, communication would be impossible because each of us would use symbols in unique ways, without sharing meaning.

Semantic misunderstandings arise when people assign different meanings to the same words. As the readings on pages 160 and 167 suggest, semantic problems come in several forms. In the next few pages, we will look at some of the most common ones.

Equivocation   **Equivocal language** consists of statements that have more than one commonly accepted definition. Some equivocal misunderstandings are amusing, as the following newspaper headlines illustrate:

> Family Catches Fire Just in Time
>
> Man Stuck on Toilet; Stool Suspected
>
> 20-Year Friendship Ends at the Altar
>
> Trees Can Break Wind

Some equivocal misunderstandings can be embarrassing, as one woman recalls: "In the fourth grade the teacher asked the class what a period was. I raised my hand and shared everything I had learned about girls getting their period. But he was talking about the dot at the end of a sentence. Oops!"[3]

Other equivocal statements can be even more troubling. A nurse gave one of her patients a scare when she told him that he "wouldn't be needing" his robe, books, and shaving materials anymore. The patient became quiet and moody. When the nurse inquired about the odd behavior, she discovered that the poor man had interpreted her statement to mean he was going to die soon. In fact, the nurse meant he would be going home.

The reading "The Many Meanings of 'I Love You'" on page 160 illustrates how a seemingly simple word can be interpreted in many ways. Imagine the troubles that can (and do) arise when people express their love to one another without understanding—at least until it's too late—that they have very different ideas of what their "love" means.

It's difficult to catch every equivocal statement and clarify it while speaking. For this reason, the responsibility for interpreting statements accurately rests in large part with the receiver. Feedback of one sort or another—for example, the kind of perception checking introduced in Chapter 3 and the paraphrasing described in Chapter 7—can help clear up misunderstandings.

Despite its obvious problems, equivocal language has its uses. As Chapter 9 describes in detail, there are times when using language that is open to several interpretations can be useful. It helps people get along by avoiding the kind of honesty and clarity that can embarrass both the speaker and listener. For example, if a friend proudly shows you a newly completed painting and asks your opinion about it, you might respond equivocally by saying, "Gee, it's really unusual. I've never seen anything like it" instead of giving a less ambiguous but more hurtful response such as "This may be the ugliest thing I've ever seen!"

Relative Language   **Relative words** gain their meaning by comparison. For example, do you attend a large or small school? This depends on what you compare

The Many Meanings of "I Love You"

© Hyacinth Manning/SuperStock

"I love you" [is] a statement that can be expressed in so many varied ways. It may be a stage song, repeated daily without any meaning, or a barely audible murmur, full of surrender. Sometimes it means: I desire you or I want you sexually. It may mean: I hope you love me or I hope that I will be able to love you. Often it means: It may be that a love relationship can develop between us or even I hate you. Often it is a wish for emotional exchange: I want your admiration in exchange for mine or I give my love in exchange for some passion or I want to feel cozy and at home with you or I admire some of your qualities. A declaration of love is mostly a request: I desire you or I want you to gratify me, or I want your protection or I want to be intimate with you or I want to exploit your loveliness.

Sometimes it is the need for security and tenderness, for parental treatment. It may mean: My self-love goes out to you. But it may also express submissiveness: Please take me as I am, or I feel guilty about you, I want, through you, to correct the mistakes I have made in human relations. It may be self-sacrifice and a masochistic wish for dependency. However, it may also be a full affirmation of the other, taking the responsibility for mutual exchange of feelings. It may be a weak feeling of friendliness, it may be the scarcely even whispered expression of ecstasy. "I love you"—wish, desire, submission, conquest; it is never the word itself that tells the real meaning here.

J. A. M. Meerloo

it to. Alongside a huge state university, your school may not seem big; but compared with a small college, it may seem quite large. Relative words such as *fast* and *slow, smart* and *stupid, short* and *long* are clearly defined only through comparison.

Some relative terms are so common that we mistakenly assume they have a clear meaning. For instance, if a friend told you it's "likely" she'll show up at your party tonight, what are the chances she's going to come? In one study, students were asked to assign percentages to such terms as *doubtful, toss-up, likely, probable, good chance,* and *unlikely*.[4] There was a tremendous variation in the meaning of most of these terms. For example, the responses for *probable* ranged from 0 to 99 percent. *Good chance* fell between 35 and 90 percent, whereas *unlikely* fell between 0 and 40 percent.

Using relative terms without explaining them can lead to communication problems. Have you ever responded to someone's question about the weather by saying it was "warm," only to find out the person thought it was cold? Have you followed a friend's advice and gone to a "cheap" restaurant, only to find that it was twice as expensive as you expected? Have classes you heard were "easy" turned out to be hard? The problem in each case resulted from failing to link the relative word to a more measurable term.

Static Evaluation   "Mark is a nervous guy." "Karen is short-tempered." "You can always count on Wes." Statements that contain or imply the word *is* lead to the mistaken assumption that people are consistent and unchanging—an incorrect belief known as **static evaluation.** Instead of labeling Mark as permanently and totally nervous, it would be more accurate to outline the particular situations in which he behaves nervously. The same goes for Karen, Wes, and the rest of us: We are more changeable than the way static, everyday language describes us.

Subscripting is a linguistic device to reduce static evaluation. Adding a subscript whenever appropriate shows the transitory nature of many objects and behaviors. For example, a teacher might write as an evaluation of a student: "Susan$_{\text{May 12}}$ had difficulty cooperating with her classmates." Although the actual device of subscripting is awkward in writing and impractical in conversation, the idea it represents can still be used. Instead of saying, "I'm shy," a more accurate statement might be "I haven't approached any new people since I moved here." The first statement implies that your shyness is an unchangeable trait, rather like your height, whereas the second one implies that you are capable of changing.

> **Invitation to Insight**
> ## Avoiding Troublesome Language
>
> **ThomsonNOW™** For practice recognizing and overcoming the kinds of troublesome language and thinking described in a web-based introduction to general semantics, see the series of exercises at thisisnotthat.com. Go to your ThomsonNOW for *Looking Out/Looking In.*

Abstraction   When it comes to describing problems, goals, appreciation, and requests, some language is more specific than others. **Abstract language** is vague in nature, whereas **behavioral language**—as its name implies—refers to specific things that people say or do. The **"abstraction ladder"** in Figure 5.1 illustrates how the same phenomenon can be described at various levels of specificity and abstraction.

We use higher-level abstractions all the time. For instance, rather than saying, "Thanks for washing the dishes," "Thanks for vacuuming the rug," "Thanks for making the bed," it's easier to say, "Thanks for cleaning up." In such everyday situations, abstractions are a useful kind of verbal shorthand.

Although verbal shorthand like this can be useful, highly abstract language can lead to blanket judgments and stereotyping: "Marriage counselors are worthless," "Skateboarders are delinquents," or "Men are no good." Overly abstract expressions like these can cause people to *think* in generalities, ignoring uniqueness. As you learned in Chapter 3, stereotyping can injure interpersonal relationships because it categorizes and evaluates people in ways that may not be accurate.

Overly abstract language can lead to serious problems. For instance, accusations of sexual assault can arise because one person claims to have said "no" when the other person insists that no such refusal was ever conveyed. In response to this sort of disagreement, specific rules of sexual conduct have become more common in work and educational settings. Perhaps the best-known code of this type is the one developed

Most abstract

You need to have a better attitude.

You need to be more positive.

You need to complain less.

You need to quit complaining when we have to work late or come in on weekends.

You need to quit complaining every time we have to work late or come in on weekends.

Most specific

Figure 5.1
Abstraction Ladder

"Be honest with me, Roger. By 'mid-course correction' you mean divorce, don't you."

at Ohio's Antioch College. The code uses low-level abstractions to minimize the chances of anyone claiming confusion about a partner's willingness. For example, the code states:

If sexual contact and/or conduct is not mutually and simultaneously initiated, then the person who initiates sexual contact/conduct is responsible for getting verbal consent of the other individual(s) involved.

If one person wants to initiate moving to a higher level of sexual intimacy, that person is responsible for getting verbal consent of the other person(s) involved before moving to that level.

If someone has initially consented but then stops consenting during a sexual interaction, she/he should communicate withdrawal verbally and/or through physical resistance. The other individual(s) must stop immediately.[5]

Some critics have ridiculed rules like these as being unrealistically legalistic and chilling for romantic relationships. Whatever its weaknesses, the Antioch code illustrates how low-level abstractions can reduce the chance of a serious misunderstanding. Specific language may not be desirable or necessary in many situations, but in an era when misinterpretations can lead to accusations of physical assault, it does seem to have a useful place. You can better understand the value of behavioral descriptions by looking at the examples in Table 5.1. Notice how much more clearly they explain the speaker's thoughts than do the vaguer terms.

Skill Builder

Down-to-Earth Language

You can appreciate the value of nonabstract language by translating the following into behavioral terms:

1. An abstract goal for improving your interpersonal communication (for example, "be more assertive" or "stop being so sarcastic")
2. A complaint you have about another person (for example, that he or she is "selfish" or "insensitive")
3. A request for someone to change (for example, "I wish you'd be more punctual" or "Try to be more positive")
4. An appreciation you could share with another person (for example, "Thanks for being so helpful" or "I appreciate your patience")

In each case, describe the person or persons involved, the circumstances in which the behavior occurs, and the precise behaviors involved. What differences can you expect when you use behavioral descriptions like the ones you have created here?

Understanding Structure: Syntactic Rules

Syntactic rules govern the grammar of a language. You can appreciate how syntax contributes to the meaning of a statement by considering two versions of a letter:

Table 5.1	**Abstract Vs. Behavioral Descriptions**			
	Abstract Description	**Behavioral Description**		**Remarks**
		Who Is Involved	In What Circumstances	Specific Behaviors	
Problem	I talk too much.	People I find intimidating	When I want them to like me	I talk (mostly about myself) instead of giving them a chance to speak or asking about their lives.	Behavioral description more clearly identifies behaviors to change.
Goal	I want to be more constructive.	My roommate	When we talk about household duties	Instead of finding fault with her ideas, suggest alternatives that might work.	Behavioral description clearly outlines how to act, abstract description doesn't.
Appreciation	"You've really been helpful lately."	(Deliver to fellow worker)	"When I've had to take time off work because of personal problems . . ."	". . . you took my shifts without complaining."	Give both abstract and behavioral descriptions for best results.
Request	"Clean up your act!"	(Deliver to target person)	"When we're around my family . . ."	". . . please don't tell jokes that involve sex."	Behavioral description specifies behavior.

Version 1

Dear John:
I want a man who knows what love is all about. You are generous, kind, thoughtful. People who are not like you admit to being useless and inferior. You have ruined me for other men. I yearn for you. I have no feelings whatsoever when we're apart. I can be forever happy—will you let me be yours?
Mary

Version 2

Dear John:
I want a man who knows what love is. All about you are generous, kind, thoughtful people, who are not like you. Admit to being useless and inferior. You have ruined me. For other men, I yearn. For you, I have no feelings whatsoever. When we're apart, I can be forever happy. Will you let me be?
Yours,
Mary

Semantic rules don't explain why these letters send virtually opposite messages. There's no ambiguity about the meaning of the words they contain: "love," "kind," "thoughtful," and so on. The opposite meanings of the letters came from their different syntax.

Although we usually aren't conscious of the syntactic rules that govern our language, we take notice when they are violated. Sometimes, however, apparently ungrammatical speech is simply following a different set of syntactic rules. For example, consider the way in which some members of the African American

'r u online?': The Evolving Lexicon of Wired Teens

© Brook Trout Studio/Images.com

The conversation begins on the computer, nothing too atypical for a pair of teenage boys bored on a Friday night:

Garret: hey
Josh: sup
Garret: j/cu
Josh: same
Garret: wut r u doing 2nite
Josh: n2m
Garret: cool

Need a translation? Not if you're a 13-year-old who's been Internet-connected since birth. For the rest of us, welcome to the world of Net Lingo—the keyboard generation's gift to language and culture. "sup" is not a call to supper, but a query: "What's up?" And Josh's "n2m" reply? "Not too much."

As in every age, teenagers today are adapting the English language to meet their needs for self-expression. But this time, it's happening online—and at lightning speed. To some, it's a creative twist on dialogue, and a new,

harmless version of teen slang. But to anxious grammarians and harried teachers, it's the linguistic ruin of Generation IM (instant messenger).

"This is really an extension of what teenagers have always done: recreate the language in their own image. But this new lingo combines writing and speaking to a degree that we've never seen before," says Neil Randall, an English professor at the University of Waterloo and author of "Lingo Online: A Report on the Language of the Keyboard Generation."

The result, he says, is the use of writing to simulate speech—a skill not formally taught. New acronyms, abbreviations, and emoticons—keyboard characters lined up to resemble human gestures or expressions, such as smiling :)—are coined daily.

A negative, though, is that their grammar is becoming atrocious, and Net lingo is starting to show up on school assignments: "They talk with

these abbreviated words and run-on sentences with no punctuation. I call it speed talking, and it's starting to carry over into their homework," she says. That's an issue that teachers around the country have been struggling with recently as instant messaging grows in popularity.

Garret says he gets onto IM when he's doing homework, and manages about eight different tasks at one time. Showing incredible focus—or frenzy—he flips from one screen to the next, rapidly firing off messages while surfing the Net and gabbing on the phone. (No, IM hasn't replaced the phone entirely.)

Now a high-school freshman, he says most of his friends were on IM by junior high, and he picked up the lingo as he went along. New terms get passed between friends, and different groups and regions of the country have their own IM lexicons, with particular acronyms, abbreviations, and emoticons that mirror their inside jokes and experience.

Tonight, he tells a friend that he's "j/c." She asks, "what is j/c."

"just chillin'," he types, certain that she will use it in the future.

Kris Axtman

Top IM Terms

IMAO	"In My Arrogant Opinion."
AFK	"Away From Keyboard."
(::[ ]::)	Emoticon for a bandage—an offer of comfort.
:-P	Emoticon that means you're being sassy or sticking out your tongue.
8-)	Emoticon showing you're wearing glasses—or acting smart.

Source: www.yourDictionary.com

community speak. African-American English (AAE) treats forms of the verb *to be* differently than does Standard English.[6] An expression like "I be angry" that would be ungrammatical in Standard English is perfectly correct in AAE, where it would be equivalent to the expression "I've been angry for a while." Advocates of using Standard English have argued that people who speak other dialects are at a disadvantage. Even acknowledging this point, it's important to realize that, from an interpersonal perspective, the challenge in cases like this is to look past the different syntax and try to understand what ideas the other communicator is trying to express.[7]

Understanding Context: Pragmatic Rules

Semantic and syntactic problems don't account for all misunderstandings.[8] To appreciate a different type of communication challenge, imagine how a young female employee might struggle to make sense of her older male boss's statement "You look very pretty today." She almost certainly would understand the meaning of the words, and the syntax is perfectly clear. Still, the boss's message could be interpreted in several ways. Was the remark a simple compliment? A come-on? Did it contain the suggestion that she didn't look nice on other days?

If the boss and employee share the same interpretation of the message, their communication would be smooth. But if they bring different perspectives to interpreting it, a problem exists. Table 5.2 shows a number of ways in which different

Table 5.2	Pragmatic Rules Govern the Use and Meaning of a Statement	
	Boss	**Employee**
Statement	"You look very nice today."	
Self-Concept "Who am I?" "Who is s/he?"	Friendly guy	Woman determined to succeed on own merits
Episode "What's going on in this exchange?"	Casual conversation	Possible come-on by boss?
Relationship "Who are we to one another?"	Boss who treats employees like family members	Subordinate employee, dependent on boss's approval for advancement
Culture "What does my background say about the meaning here?"	Euro-American, raised in United States	Latin American, raised in South America

Adapted from W. B. Pearce and V. Cronen, *Communication, Action, and Meaning.* New York: Praeger, 1980, and E. M. Griffin, *A First Look at Communication Theory,* 4th ed. New York: McGraw-Hill, 2000, p. 74.

"I never said 'I love you.' I said 'I love 'ya.' Big difference!"

perspectives of the boss and employee would lead to their attaching different meanings to the same words.

In situations like this we rely on **pragmatic rules** to decide how to interpret messages in a given context. Pragmatic rules govern the way speech operates in everyday interaction. You can't look up pragmatic rules in any dictionary: They are almost always unstated, but they are just as important as semantic and syntactic rules in helping us make sense of one another's messages.

The best way to appreciate how pragmatic rules operate is to think of communication as a kind of cooperative game. Like all games, success depends on all the players understanding and following the same set of rules. This is why communication scholars use the term *coordination* to describe the way conversation operates when everyone involved uses the same set of pragmatic rules.[9]

Some pragmatic rules are shared by most people in a culture. In the United States and Canada, for instance, competent communicators understand that the question "How's it going?" usually isn't really a request for information. Anyone familiar with the rules of conversation knows that the proper answer is something like "Pretty good. How's it going with you?" Likewise, most people understand the pragmatic rule that says that "Would you like a drink?" means "Would you like an alcoholic beverage?" whereas "Would you like something to drink?" is a more open-ended question.

Pragmatic rules can be quite complex, as the reading "It's a 'Girl' Thing for Women" on page 167 shows. The ways in which the word *girl* can be used in today's conversations differ from what was more accepted in the past, and who uses the word helps determine how many women might react to hearing it.

Besides following cultural rules, people in individual relationships create their own sets of pragmatic rules. Consider the use of humor: The teasing and jokes you exchange with gusto with one friend might be considered tasteless or offensive in another relationship.[10] For instance, imagine an e-mail message typed in CAPITAL LETTERS and filled with CURSE WORDS, INSULTS, NAME-CALLING, and EXCLAMATION MARKS!!! How would you interpret such a message? An outside observer may consider this an example of "flaming" and be appalled, when in fact the message might be a fun-loving case of "verbal jousting" between buddies.[11] If you have a good friend whom you call by a less-than-tasteful nickname as a term of endearment, then you understand the concept. Keep in mind, however, that those who aren't privy to your relationship's pragmatic rules are likely to misunderstand you, so you'll want to be wise about when and where to use these "personal codes."

It's a "Girl" Thing for Women

© Smithsonian American Art Museum, Washington DC/Art Resource, NY

When law professor and commentator Susan Estrich sent off her female research assistants after a long day of work, she cheerfully banished them with "Get out of here, girls." When Richard Riordan's press secretary, Noelia Rodriguez, told a TV station official that she was finally taking a week's vacation, the woman executive exclaimed, "You go, girl!"

There was a time when Estrich wouldn't have dreamed of referring to any female adult as anything but a woman. Rodriguez has never used "girl" in her job, and would be stunned if the word ever passed the Los Angeles mayor's lips.

So what's with all the girls? With a significant degree of female equity and parity established in the workplace and other institutions, there has been a gradual social warming among women to the once-ostracized "girl"—a curiously defiant celebration of a word formerly fraught with oppression.

"We've taken back the word and are using it the way we want—girl power, girl talk," said Jane Pratt, the 34-year-old editor of her eponymous new magazine, *Jane.* "It's about girls supporting each other and reveling in what's fun about being a girl. . . . Girl power means something different from feminism."

This is not the old-school, coffee-making, office-slaving, husband's-credit-card-borrowing girl—although the word incorporates a dollop of old-fashioned girlishness. "Girl" has been reborn in the image of a modern woman: It borrows the youthful vigor and spontaneity of female adolescence and discards the meekness of the old-fashioned office girl.

Sometime around the rise of feminism and *Ms.* magazine a quarter of a century ago, "girl" was banned from the vocabulary of smart-thinking men and women when describing any female over 15. It went the way of stewardesses and poetesses. There

were no more office girls fetching coffee, no more college girls getting degrees or career girls working up the job ladder; no more girl Fridays, script girls or hatcheck girls.

So why are "girls" back? "Often after a social movement has been established for a while—like feminism— you can play around with certain terms," said Lynn Chancer, an assistant professor of sociology at Columbia University who studies feminism.

Now "girl" crops up throughout pop culture. "Girls rule" emblazons T-shirts. A college women's crew scrawls, "You row, girl" on the side of the team van.

As murky as the new "girl" may be, it comes with some rules. One is that the conversation should be casual. Neither men—nor women—should be saying, "I'll have my girl call your girl." And no woman wants to use it in a serious office setting—or around impressionable minds. "We have this 'Take Your Daughter to Work Day,'" said Robin Kramer, Riordan's chief of staff, "and the young women range in age from 7 to 17. Listening to both informal conversations and speeches, even those little ones are referred to as young women."

A second rule is that it's generally a woman's prerogative to use the word. Men treading into "girl" territory enter at their own risk. Sometimes a gentle reminder is all it takes to separate the women from the girls. *Ms.* magazine editor Barbara Findlen recalls a recent conversation with a man in which he referred to someone as "the girl who owns that business." "I said, 'God, a girl owns her own company! How old is she?' He laughed. He got it."

Carla Hall

Invitation to Insight

Your Linguistic Rules

To what extent do linguistic rules affect your understanding of and relationships with others? Explore this question by following these steps:

1. Recall a time when you encountered someone whose speech violated the syntactic rules that you are used to. What was your impression of this person? To what degree was this impression influenced by her or his failure to follow familiar linguistic rules? Consider whether this impression was or was not valid.

2. Recall at least one misunderstanding that arose when you and another person followed different semantic rules. Use hindsight to consider whether this misunderstanding (and others like it) could be avoided. If semantic misunderstandings can be minimized, explain what approaches might be useful.

3. Identify at least two pragmatic rules that govern the use of language in one of your relationships. Share these rules with other students. Do they use language in the same way as you and your relational partner?

The Impact of Language

So far we have focused on language only as a medium for helping communicators understand one another. But along with this important function, language can shape our perceptions of the world around us and reflect the attitudes we hold toward one another.

Naming and Identity

"What's in a name?" Juliet asked rhetorically. If Romeo had been a social scientist, he would have answered "A great deal." Research has demonstrated that names are more than just a simple means of identification: They shape the way others think of us, the way we view ourselves, and the way we act.

Different names have different connotations. In one study several decades ago, psychologists asked U.S. college students to rate over one thousand names according to their likability, how active or passive they seemed, and their masculinity or femininity. In spite of the large number of subjects, the responses were quite similar.[12] Michael, John, and Wendy were likable and active and were rated as possessing the masculine or feminine traits of their sex. More widely accepted names were viewed as being more active, stronger, and better than less common ones.[13]

Names are one way to shape and reinforce a child's personal identity, as the reading on page 169 suggests. Naming a baby after a family member (e.g., "Junior" or "Trey") can create a connection between the youngster and his or her namesake. Name choice can also be a powerful way to make a statement about cultural identity. For example, in recent decades a large percentage of names given to African-American babies have been distinctively

Naming a child is not easy for parents in America who come from non-European backgrounds, from cultures where Ashutosh, Chae-Hyun and Naeem are common names. We have to ask ourselves a number of important questions. How will the child's foreign name sound to American ears? (That test ruled out Shiva, my family deity; a Jewish friend put her foot down.) Will it provoke bullies to beat him up on the school playground? (That was the end of Karan, the name of a warrior from the Mahabharata, the Hindu epic. A boy called "Karen" wouldn't stand a chance.) Will it be as euphonic in New York as it is in New Delhi? (That was how Sameer failed to get off the ground. "Like a bagel with a schmear!" said one ruthless well-wisher.)

Tunku Varadarajan

black.[14] In California, over 40 percent of black girls born recently have names that not a single white baby born in the entire state was given. Researchers suggest that distinctive names like these are a symbol of solidarity with the African-American community. Conversely, choosing a less distinctive name can be a way of integrating the baby into the majority culture. Whether common or unusual, the impact of names recedes after communicators become more familiar with one another.[15]

On Naming Baby

© Steve Collier; Collier Studios/Corbis

A rose by any other name may smell as sweet, but would Rose by another name grow up to be the same person?

Most parents who give their children exotic names are striving for individuality. There are certain advantages to being the only Shalice Jadzia Washington in the school, or on the payroll. Unusual names also don't hold a lot of predispositions that common names do. Danelle Duran named her son Ukiah in part because it was the only name everyone could agree to; no one associated the name with jocks, hicks or nerds, she said.

Unique names can have serious consequences, however. They are harder to pronounce, which can be frustrating, especially for younger children and for

teachers coping with a new class at the beginning of the school year. On a more serious note, studies have shown that people tend to negatively judge people with unusual names solely on the basis of the name.

"A very general finding is that people don't react well to things that are new and unusual. They aren't as comfortable with it, and that applies to names," said Dr. Albert Mehrabian, author of *The Name Game* and *The Baby Name Report Card*. For over a decade, Mehrabian has studied how a name changes perceptions of a person's morality, cheerfulness, success and even masculinity or femininity. Compared to names standard for our culture, unusual names are rated dramatically

lower in all categories—even a change of spelling in a common name will negatively affect someone's scores, he said. "I know a lot of people don't like to hear that, because they think they're being creative. They think they're making their kids (individual), but blue hair is unusual. But is it desirable?"

Even bearers of unusual names warn parents not to give their kids "kick-me-in-the-head" names, which will easily lead to teasing in the schoolyard. Regina Koske, a teacher at a private school in California, remembers two of her students, Strawberry and Justice, who had especially hard times. "The other students laughed and teased Strawberry constantly and said things like, 'I'm going to eat you.' Every time we said the Pledge of Allegiance and got to '. . . and justice for all,' many kids would repeat 'And Justice?' and laugh. After a time, (they) got used to the unusual and name and it wasn't unusual any more. However, every time that child enters a new group of peers, he or she will once again have to deal with the stigma of a particularly unusual name."

Even as adults, an unusual name may lead to ridicule. Contrary to the "Boy Named Sue" idea that a nonstandard name will strengthen a child in adulthood, Mehrabian said he's found that the more unusual a person's name is, the harder it is for them to adjust.

Karina L. Fabian

"My mother is black, my father is African American, and my grandfather is Negro. I can hardly wait to find out about me."

The importance of names in defining identity applies to membership in groups. For example, the term *African American* has become the label of choice for people who, in earlier times, would probably have been called "colored," "Negro," "Afro-American," and "black."[16] Each label has its own connotations, which is why naming is so important. In one study, white subjects with a variety of political beliefs said they would be more likely to vote for a candidate who talked about the concerns of "blacks" than one who talked about the concerns of "African Americans."[17] Clearly, the terms used to label social groups can shape the way members of those groups regard themselves and the way others regard them. Some terms may seem familiar and thus innocuous, but their impact on both the namers and those being named can have subtle but profound effects.

Affiliation

Besides shaping an individual's identity, speech can build and demonstrate solidarity with others. Research has demonstrated that communicators are attracted to others whose style of speaking is similar to theirs.[18] Likewise, communicators who want to show affiliation with one another adapt their speech in a variety of ways, including their choice of vocabulary, rate of talking, number and placement of pauses, and level of politeness.[19] Adolescents who all adopt the same vocabulary of slang words and speech mannerisms illustrate the principle of linguistic solidarity. The same process works among members of other groups, ranging from street gangs to military personnel. Communication researchers call the process of adapting one's speech style to match that of others **convergence**.

Communicators can experience convergence in cyberspace as well as in face-to-face interactions. Members of online communities often develop a shared language and conversational style, and their affiliation with each other can be seen in increased uses of the pronoun "we."[20] On a larger scale, IM and e-mail users create and use shortcuts that mark them as Internet-savvy. If you know what ROTFL, IMHO, and JK mean, you're probably part of that group. (For the uninitiated, those acronyms mean "Rolling on the floor laughing," "In my humble opinion," and "Just kidding.") Interestingly, IMers may find that their cyber-language creeps into everyday conversations.[21] (Have you ever said "LOL" instead of the words "laughing out loud"—or instead of actually laughing out loud?)

When two or more people feel equally positive about one another, their linguistic convergence will be mutual. But when communicators want or need approval they often adapt their speech to accommodate the other person's style, trying to say the "right thing" or speak in a way that will help them fit in. We see this process when immigrants who want to gain the rewards of material success in a new culture strive to master the host language. Likewise, employees

Calvin and Hobbes

by Bill Watterson

CALVIN AND HOBBES by Watterson © 1992 by Watterson. Dist. by UNIVERSAL PRESS SYNDICATE. Reprinted with permission. All rights reserved.

who seek advancement tend to speak more like their superiors, superiors adopt the speech style of managers, and managers converge toward their bosses.

The principle of speech accommodation works in reverse, too. Communicators who want to set themselves apart from others adopt the strategy of **divergence**, speaking in a way that emphasizes their differences from others. For example, members of an ethnic group, even though fluent in the dominant language, might use their own dialect as a way of showing solidarity with one another—a sort of "us against them" strategy. The same can occur across ethnic lines, such as teens who adopt the slang of particular subcultures to show divergence with adults and convergence with their peers.[22] Of course, communicators need to be careful about when to—and when not to—converge their language with others. Most of us can remember the embarrassment of hearing a parent using youthful slang and thinking, "You're too old to be saying that—quit trying to sound like us." On a more serious level, using ethnic/racial epithets when you're not a member of that in-group can be inappropriate and even offensive. One of the pragmatic goals of divergence is the creation of norms about who has the "right" to use certain words and who does not. (The film "The N-Word," described at the end of this chapter, offers a good discussion of this topic.)

Power

Communication researchers have identified a number of language patterns that add to or detract from a speaker's power to influence others. Notice the difference between these two statements:

> "Excuse me, sir. I hate to say this, but I . . . uh . . . I guess I won't be able to turn in the assignment on time. I had a personal emergency, and . . . well . . . it was just impossible to finish it by today. I'll have it on your desk on Monday, OK?"

> "I won't be able to turn in the assignment on time. I had a personal emergency, and it was impossible to finish it by today. I'll have it on your desk Monday."

Whether or not the professor finds the excuse acceptable, it's clear that the tone of the second one is more confident, whereas the tone of the first is apologetic and uncertain. Table 5.3 identifies several **powerless speech mannerisms** illustrated in the statements you just read. A number of studies have shown that speakers whose talk is free of these mannerisms are rated as more competent,

Table 5.3	Examples of Powerless Language
Hedges	"I'm *kinda* disappointed . . ."
	"I *think* we should . . ."
	"I *guess* I'd like to . . ."
Hesitations	"*Uh,* can I have a minute of your time?"
	"*Well,* we could try this idea . . ."
	"I wish you would—*er*—try to be on time."
Intensifiers	"I'm *really* glad to see you."
	"I'm not *very* hungry."
Polite forms	"Excuse me, *sir* . . ."
Tag questions	"It's about time we got started, *isn't it?*"
	"*Don't you think* we should give it another try?"
Disclaimers	"*I probably shouldn't say this but . . .*"
	"*I'm not really sure but . . .*"
Rising inflections	(See the reading on page 219 in Chapter 6)

dynamic, and attractive than speakers who sound powerless.[23] Powerful speech can help candidates in job interviews. Employers rate applicants who use a powerful style as more competent and employable than candidates who speak less forcefully.[24] One study revealed that even a single type of powerless speech mannerism can make a person appear less authoritative or socially attractive.[25]

Powerful speech that gets the desired results in mainstream North American and European cultures doesn't succeed everywhere with everyone.[26] In Japan, saving face for others is an important goal, so communicators there tend to speak in ambiguous terms and use hedge words and qualifiers. In most Japanese sentences the verb comes at the end of the sentence so that the "action" part of the sentence can be postponed. Traditional Mexican culture, with its strong emphasis on cooperation, also uses hedging to smooth over interpersonal relationships. By not taking a firm stand with their speech language, Mexicans avoid making others feel ill at ease. The Korean culture represents yet another people who prefer "indirect" (for example, "perhaps," "could be") over "direct" speech.

Even in cultures that value assertiveness, language that is *too* powerful may intimidate or annoy others. Consider these two different approaches to handling a common situation:

"Excuse me. My baby is having a little trouble getting to sleep. Would you mind turning down the music just a little?"

"My baby can't sleep because your music is too loud. Please turn it down."

The more polite, if less powerful, approach would probably produce better results than the stronger statement. How can this fact be reconciled with the research on powerful language? The answer lies in the tension between the potentially opposing goals of getting immediate results and developing positive relationships. If you come across as too powerful, you may get what you're seeking in the short term but alienate the other person in ways that will make your relationship more difficult in the long term. Furthermore, a statement that is *too* powerful can convey relational messages of disrespect and superiority—just as likely to antagonize others as to gain their compliance.

In some situations polite, less apparently powerful forms of speech can even enhance a speaker's effectiveness.[27] For example, a boss might say to a secretary,

"Would you mind retyping this letter?" In truth, both the boss and secretary know that this is an order and not a request, but the questioning form is more considerate and leaves the secretary feeling better about the boss.[28] The importance of achieving both content and relational goals helps explain why a mixture of powerful speech and polite speech is usually most effective.[29]

Disruptive Language

Not all linguistic problems come from misunderstandings. Sometimes people understand one another perfectly and still wind up in a conflict. Of course, not all disagreements can, or should be, avoided. But eliminating three linguistic habits from your communication repertoire can minimize the kind of disagreements that don't need to happen, allowing you to save your energy for the unavoidable and important disagreements.

Fact–Opinion Confusion   Factual statements are claims that can be verified as true or false. By contrast, opinion statements are based on the speaker's beliefs. Unlike factual statements, they can never be proved or disproved. Consider a few examples of the difference between factual and opinion statements:

Fact	Opinion
You forgot my birthday.	You don't care about me.
You keep interrupting me.	You're a control freak.
You tell a lot of ethnic jokes.	You're a bigot.

When factual and opinion statements are set side by side like this, the difference is clear. In everyday conversation, however, we often present our opinions as if they were facts, and in doing so we invite an unnecessary argument. For example:

"That was a dumb thing to say!"

"Spending that much on a pair of shoes is a waste of money!"

"You can't get a fair shake in this country unless you're a white male."

Notice how much less antagonistic each statement would be if it were prefaced by a qualifier that takes responsibility for the opinion such as "I believe . . . ," "In my opinion . . . ," or "It seems to me . . . ." We'll discuss the importance of responsible "I" language later in this chapter.

Fact–Inference Confusion   Problems also arise when we confuse factual statements with inferential statements—conclusions arrived at from an interpretation of evidence.

Arguments often result when we label our inferences as facts:

A: Why are you mad at me?

B: I'm not mad at you. Why have you been so insecure lately?

A: I'm not insecure. It's just that you've been so critical.

B: What do you mean, "critical"? I haven't been critical. . . .

Instead of trying to read the other person's mind, a far better course is to use the skill of perception checking that you learned in Chapter 3: Identify the observable behaviors (facts) that have caught your attention and describe one or more possible interpretations that you have drawn from them. After describing this train of thought, ask the other person to comment on the accuracy of your interpretation.

"When you didn't return my phone call (*fact*), I got the idea that you're mad at me (*interpretation*). Are you?" (*question*)

"You've been asking me whether I still love you a lot lately (*fact*), and that makes me think you're feeling insecure (*inference*). Or maybe I'm behaving differently. What's on your mind?" (*question*)

Emotive Language   **Emotive language** seems to describe something but actually announces the speaker's attitude toward it. If you approve of a friend's roundabout approach to a difficult subject, you might call her "tactful"; if you don't approve of it, you might accuse her of "beating around the bush." Whether the approach is good or bad is more a matter of opinion than of fact, although this difference is obscured by emotive language. Barbra Streisand's tongue-in-cheek description of men and women illustrates how emotive language can describe the same behavior in favorable or unfavorable terms.

You can appreciate how emotive words are really editorial statements when you consider these examples:

If you approve, say	If you disapprove, say
thrifty	cheap
traditional	old-fashioned
extrovert	loudmouth
cautious	cowardly
progressive	radical
information	propaganda
military victory	massacre
eccentric	crazy

The best way to avoid arguments involving emotive words is to describe the person, thing, or idea you are discussing in neutral terms and to label your opinions as such. Instead of saying "Quit making sexist remarks" say, "I really don't like it when you call us 'girls' instead of 'women.'" Not only are nonemotive statements more accurate, but also they have a much better chance of being well received by others.

Conjugating "Irregular Verbs"

The technique is simple: Just take an action or personality trait and show how it can be viewed either favorably or unfavorably, according to the label it's given. For example:

> I'm casual.
>
> You're a little careless.
>
> He's a slob.

Or try this one:

> I'm thrifty.
>
> You're money conscious.
>
> She's a tightwad.

1. Try a few conjugations yourself, using the following statements:

   a. I'm tactful.

   b. I'm conservative.

   c. I'm quiet.

   d. I'm relaxed.

   e. My child is high-spirited.

   f. I have high self-esteem.

2. Now recall at least two situations in which you used emotive language as if it was a description of fact and not an opinion. A good way to recall these situations is to think of a recent disagreement and imagine how the other people involved might have described it differently than you.

The Language of Responsibility

Besides providing a way to make the content of a message clear or obscure, language reflects the speakers' willingness to take responsibility for their beliefs and feelings. This acceptance or rejection of responsibility says a great deal about the speaker and can shape the tone of a relationship. To see how, read on.

"It" Statements   Notice the difference between the sentences of each set:

> "It bothers me when you're late."
>
> "I'm worried when you're late."

> "It's nice to see you."
>
> "I'm glad to see you."

> "It's a boring class."
>
> "I'm bored in the class."

As their name implies, **"it" statements** replace the personal pronoun *I* with the less immediate word *it*. By contrast, **"I" language** clearly identifies the speaker as the source of a message. Communicators who use "it" statements avoid responsibility for ownership of a message, attributing it instead to some unidentified source. This habit isn't just imprecise; more important, it is an unconscious way to avoid taking a position.

"My hand is doing this movement . . ."

"Is it doing the movement?"

"I am moving my hand like this . . . and now the thought comes to me that . . ."

"The thought 'comes' to you?"

"I have the thought."

"You have it?"

"I think. Yes. I think that I use 'it' very much, and I am glad that by noticing it I can bring it all back to me."

"Bring it back?"

"Bring myself back. I feel thankful for this."

"This?"

"Your idea about the 'it.'"

"My idea?"

"I feel thankful towards you."

Claudio Naranjo

"But" Statements   Statements that take the form "X-but-Y" can be confusing. A closer look at **"but" statements** explains why. In each sentence, the word but cancels the thought that precedes it:

> "You're really a great person, but I think we ought to stop seeing each other."

> "You've done good work for us, but we're going to have to let you go."

> "This paper has some good ideas, but I'm giving it a *D* grade because it's late."

These "buts" often are a strategy for wrapping the speaker's real but unpleasant message between more palatable ideas in a psychological sandwich. This approach can be a face-saving strategy worth using at times. When the goal is to be absolutely clear, however, the most responsible approach is to deliver the positive and negative messages separately so they both get heard.

Questions   Some questions are sincere requests for information. Other questions, though, are a linguistic way to avoid making a declaration.

> "What are we having for dinner?" may hide the statement "I want to eat out" or "I want to get a pizza."

> "How many textbooks are assigned in that class?" may hide the statement "I'm afraid to get into a class with too much reading."

> "Are you doing anything tonight?" can be a less risky way of saying, "I want to go out with you tonight."

> "Do you love me?" safely replaces the statement "I love you," which may be too embarrassing, too intimate, or too threatening to say directly.

Sometimes being indirect can be a tactful way to approach a topic that would be difficult to address head on. When used unnecessarily, though, being indirect can be a way to avoid speaking for yourself. See Chapter 9 for more details about the value and risks of indirect communication.

"I" and "You" Language   We've seen that "I" language is a way of accepting responsibility for a message. In contrast, **"you" language** expresses a judgment of the other person. Positive judgments ("You look great today!") rarely cause problems, but notice how each of the following critical "you" statements implies that the subject of the complaint is doing something wrong:

> "You left this place a mess!"

> "You didn't keep your promise!"

> "You're really crude sometimes!"

Despite its name, "you" language doesn't have to contain the pronoun *you,* which is often implied rather than stated outright:

> "That was a stupid joke!" (*"Your jokes are stupid."*)

> "Don't be so critical!" (*"You're too negative."*)

> "Mind your own business!" (*"You're too nosy."*)

Whether the judgment is stated outright or implied, it's easy to see why "you" language can arouse defensiveness. A "you" statement implies that the speaker is qualified to judge the target—not an idea that most listeners are willing to accept, even when the judgment is correct.

Fortunately, "I" language provides a more accurate and less provocative way to express a complaint.[30] "I" language shows that the speaker takes responsibility for the complaint by describing his or her reaction to the other's behavior without making any judgments about its worth.

A complete "I" statement has four elements. It describes

1. the other person's behavior
2. your interpretations
3. your feelings
4. the consequences that the other person's behavior has for you

When you point one accusing finger at someone, three of your own fingers point back at you.

Louis Nizer

These elements can appear in any order. A few examples of "I" statements illustrate how they sound in everyday conversation:

"I get embarrassed (*feeling*) when you talk about my bad grades in front of our friends (*behavior*). I'm afraid they'll think I'm stupid (*interpretation*). That's why I got so worked up last night (*consequence*)."

"When you didn't pick me up on time this morning (*behavior*), I was late for class, and I wound up getting chewed out by the professor (*consequences*). It seemed to me that my being on time didn't seem important to you. That's why I got so mad (*feeling*)."

"I haven't been very affectionate (*consequence*) because you've hardly spent any time with me in the past few weeks (*behavior*). I'm not sure if you're avoiding me, or if you're just busy (*interpretations*). I'm confused (*feeling*) about how you feel about me, and I want to clear it up."

When the risks of being misunderstood or getting a defensive reaction are high, it's a good idea to include all four elements in your "I" message. In some cases, however, only one or two of them will get the job done:

"I went to a lot of trouble fixing this dinner, and now it's cold. Of course, I'm mad!" (*The behavior is obvious.*)

"I'm worried because you haven't called me up." (*"Worried" is both a feeling and a consequence.*)

Even the best "I" statement won't work unless it's delivered in the right way. If your words are nonjudgmental, but your tone of voice, facial expression, and posture all send "you" messages, a defensive response is likely to follow. The best way to make sure that your actions match your words is to remind yourself that your goal is to describe your thoughts, feelings, and wants and to explain how the other's behavior affects you—not to act like a judge and jury.

Some readers have reservations about using "I" language, despite its theoretical appeal. The best way to overcome questions about this communication skill is to answer them.

■ *"I get too angry to use 'I' language."* It's true that when you're angry the most likely reaction is to lash out with a judgmental "you" message. But it's probably smarter to keep quiet until you've thought about the consequences of what you might say than to blurt out something you'll regret later. It's also important to note that there's plenty of room for expressing anger with "I" language. It's just that you own the feeling as yours ("You bet I'm mad at you!") instead of distorting it into an attack ("That was a stupid thing to do!").

■ *"Even with 'I' language, the other person gets defensive."* Like every communication skill described in this book, "I" language won't always work. You may be so upset or irritated that your judgmental feelings contradict your words. Even if you deliver a perfectly worded "I" statement with total sincerity, the other person might be so defensive or uncooperative that nothing you say will make matters better. But using "I" language will almost certainly *improve* your chances for success, with little risk that this approach will make matters worse.

■ *"'I' language sounds artificial."* "That's not the way I talk," you might object. Much of the awkwardness that comes with first using "I" language is due to its novelty. As you become more used to making "I" statements, they will sound more and more natural—and become more effective.

One of the best ways to overcome your initial awkwardness is to practice making "I" statements in a safe way: by trying them out in a class, writing them in letters, and delivering them to receptive people on relatively minor issues. After your skill and confidence have grown, you will be ready to tackle really challenging situations in a way that sounds natural and sincere.

Skill Builder

Practicing "I" Language

You can develop your skill at delivering "I" messages by following these steps:
1. Visualize situations in your life when you might have sent each of the following messages:

    You're not telling me the truth!

    You think only of yourself!

    Don't be so touchy!

    Quit fooling around!

    You don't understand a word I'm saying!

2. Write alternatives to each statement using "I" language.

3. Think of three "you" statements you might make to people in your life. Transform each of these statements into "I" language and rehearse them with a classmate.

Despite its obvious advantages, even the best constructed and delivered "I" message won't always succeed. As author and "I" language advocate Thomas Gordon acknowledges, "Nobody welcomes hearing that his behavior is causing someone a problem, no matter how the message is phrased." Furthermore, "I" language in large doses can start to sound egotistical. Research shows that self-absorbed people, also known as "conversational narcissists," can be identified by their constant use of first-person singular pronouns.[31] For this reason, "I" language works best in moderation.

"We" Language   One way to avoid overuse of "I" language is to consider the pronoun *we*. **"We" language** implies that the issue is the concern and responsibility of both the speaker and receiver of a message. Consider a few examples:

"We need to figure out a budget that doesn't bankrupt us."

"I think we have a problem. We can't seem to talk about money without fighting."

"We aren't doing a very good job of keeping the place clean, are we?"

"I" and "You" Language on the Job

For some time, Rebecca has been frustrated by her fellow worker Tom's frequent absences from the job. She hasn't spoken up because she likes Tom and also because she doesn't want to sound like a complainer. Lately, though, Tom's absences have become longer and more frequent. Today he extended his half-hour lunch an extra 45 minutes. When he returns to the office, Rebecca confronts him with her gripe using "you" language:

Rebecca   Where have you been? You were due back at 12:30, and it's almost 1:30 now.

Tom   *(Surprised by Rebecca's angry tone, which she has never used before with him)* I had a few errands to run. What's the problem?

Rebecca   We all have errands to run, Tom. But it's not fair for you to do yours on company time.

Tom   *(Feeling defensive after hearing Rebecca's accusation)* I don't see why you have to worry about how I do my job. Beth *[their boss]* hasn't complained, so why should you worry?

Rebecca   Beth hasn't complained because all of us have been covering for you. You should appreciate what a tight spot we're in, making excuses every time you come in late or leave early. *(Again, Rebecca uses "you" language to tell Tom how he should think and act.)*

Tom   *(Now too defensive to consider Rebecca's concerns)* Hey, I thought we all covered for one another here. What about the time last year when I worked late for a week so you could go to your cousin's wedding in San Antonio?

Rebecca   That's different! Nobody was lying then. When you take off, I have to make up stories about where you are. You're putting me in a very difficult spot, Tom, and it's not fair. You can't count on me to keep covering for you.

Tom   *(Feeling guilty, but too angry from Rebecca's judgments and threat to acknowledge his mistakes)* Fine. I'll never ask you for a favor again. Sorry to put you out.

Rebecca may have succeeded in reducing Tom's lateness, but her choice of "you" language left him feeling defensive and angry. The climate in the office is likely to be more strained—hardly the outcome Rebecca was seeking. Notice how she could have handled the same issue using "I" language to describe her problem instead of blaming Tom.

Rebecca   Tom, I need to talk to you about a problem. *(Notice how Rebecca identifies the problem as hers instead of attacking Tom.)*

Tom   What's up?

Rebecca   You know how you come in late to work sometimes or take long lunch hours?

Tom   *(Sensing trouble ahead and sounding wary)* Yeah?

Rebecca   Well, I need to tell you that it's putting me in a tight spot. *(Rebecca describes the problem in behavioral terms and then goes on to express her feeling.)* When Beth asks where you are, I don't want to say you're not here because that might get you in trouble. So sometimes I make excuses or even lie. But Beth is sounding suspicious of my excuses, and I'm worried about that.

Tom   *(Feeling defensive because he knows he's guilty but also sympathetic to Rebecca's position)* I don't want you to get in trouble. It's just that I've got to take care of a lot of personal business.

Rebecca   I know, Tom. I just want you to understand that it's getting impossible for me to cover for you.

Tom   Yeah, OK. Thanks for helping out.

Notice how "I" language made it possible for Rebecca to confront Tom honestly but without blaming or attacking him personally. Even if Tom doesn't change, Rebecca has gotten the problem off her chest, and she can feel proud that she did so in a way that didn't sound ugly or annoying.

Communication Scenarios

To see and analyze video examples of "I" language in action, go to your ThomsonNOW for *Looking Out/Looking In*, access "Communication Scenarios," and then click on "'I' and 'You' Language on the Job." **ThomsonNOW**

Table 5.4	Pronoun Use and Its Effects		
	Advantages	**Disadvantages**	**Tips**
"I" language	Takes responsibility for personal thoughts, feelings, and wants. Less defense-provoking than evaluative "you" language.	Can be perceived as egotistical, narcissistic, and self-absorbed.	Use "I" messages when other person doesn't perceive a problem. Combine "I" with "we" language.
"We" language	Signals inclusion, immediacy, cohesiveness, and commitment.	Can speak improperly for others.	Combine with "I" language. Use in group settings to enhance unity. Avoid when expressing personal thoughts, feelings, and wants.
"You" language	Signals other-orientation, particularly when the topic is positive.	Can sound evaluative and judgmental, particularly during confrontations.	Use "I" language during confrontations. Use "you" language when praising or including others.

It's easy to see how "we" language can help build a constructive climate. It suggests a kind of "we're in this together" orientation that reflects the transactional nature of communication. People who use first-person plural pronouns signal their closeness, commonality, and cohesiveness with others.[32] For example, couples who use "we" language are more satisfied than those who rely more heavily on "I" and "you" language.[33] Chapters 10 and 11 offer detailed advice on the value of achieving a "we" orientation.

On the other hand, "we" statements aren't always appropriate. Sometimes using this pronoun sounds presumptuous because it suggests that you are speaking for the other person as well as yourself. It's easy to imagine someone responding to your statement "We have a problem . . ." by saying "Maybe *you* have a problem, but don't tell me *I* do!"

Given the pros and cons of both "I" language and "we" language, what advice can we give about the most effective pronouns to use in interpersonal communication? Researchers have found that "I/we" combinations (for example, "I think that we . . ." or "I would like to see us . . .") have a good chance of being received favorably.[34] Because too much of any pronoun comes across as inappropriate, combining pronouns is generally a good idea. If your "I" language reflects your position without being overly self-absorbed, your "you" language shows concern for others without judging them, and your "we" language includes others without speaking for them, you will probably come as close as possible to the ideal use of pronouns. Table 5.4 summarizes the advantages and disadvantages of each type of language and offers suggestions for approaches that have a good chance of success.

Gender and Language

So far we have discussed language use as if it were identical for both sexes. Some popular writers and researchers believe that men and women speak in distinct ways, as if from different cultures.[35] Other scholars suggest that the differences are few and mostly not significant.[36] What are the similarities and differences between male and female language use?

Content

The first research on conversational topics and gender was conducted two generations ago. Despite the changes in male and female roles since then, the results of several studies are remarkably similar.[37] In these studies, women and men ranging in age from 17 to 80 described the range of topics each discussed with friends of the same sex. Certain topics were common to both men and women: work, movies, and television. Both men and women tended to reserve discussions of sex and sexuality for members of the same sex.

The differences between the men and women in these studies were more striking than the similarities. Female friends spent much more time discussing personal and domestic subjects, relationship problems, family, health and reproductive matters, weight, food and clothing, men, and other women. Men, on the other hand, were more likely to discuss music, current events, sports, business, and other men. Both men and women were equally likely to discuss personal appearance, sex, and dating in same-sex conversations. True to one common stereotype, women were more likely to gossip about close friends and family. By contrast, men spent more time gossiping about sports figures and media personalities. Women's gossip was no more derogatory than men's.

These differences can lead to frustration when men and women try to converse with one another. Researchers report that *trivial* is the word often used by both men and women to describe topics discussed by the opposite sex. "I want to talk about important things," a woman might say, "like how we're getting along. All he wants to do is talk about the news or what we'll do this weekend." Likewise, some men complain that women ask for and offer more details than necessary and focus too often on feelings and emotions.

Computer Program Detects Author Gender

A new computer program can tell whether a book was written by a man or a woman. The simple scan of key words and syntax is around 80 percent accurate.

The program's success seems to confirm the stereotypical perception of differences in male and female language use. Crudely put, men talk more about objects, and women more about relationships. Female writers use more pronouns (I, you, she, their, myself), say the program's developers, Moshe Koppel, and colleagues. Males prefer words that identify or determine nouns (a, the, that) and words that quantify them (one, two, more).

So this article would already, through sentences such as this, have probably betrayed its author as male: there is a prevalence of plural pronouns (they, them), indicating the male tendency to categorize rather than personalize.

If I were female, the researchers imply, I'd be more likely to write sentences like this, which assume that you and I share common knowledge or engage us in a direct relationship.

Philip Ball, *Nature*

Reasons for Communicating

Both men and women, at least in the dominant cultures of North America, use language to build and maintain social relationships. Regardless of the sex of the communicators, the goals of almost all ordinary conversations include making the conversation enjoyable by being friendly, showing interest in what the other person says, and talking about topics that interest the other person.[38] *How* men and women accomplish these goals is often different, though. Although most communicators try to make their interaction enjoyable, men are more likely than women to emphasize making conversation fun. Their discussions involve a

© New Apollo Gallery, Dublin/SuperStock

Consider the marriage of a man who has had most of his conversations with other men, to a woman who has had most of hers with other women. . . . He is used to fast-paced conversations that typically stay on the surface with respect to emotions, that often enable him to get practical tips or offer them to others and that are usually pragmatic or fun. She is used to conversations that, while practical and fun too, are also a major source of emotional support, self-understanding and the understanding of others. Becoming intimate with a man, the woman may finally start expressing her concerns to him as she might to a close friend. But she may find, to her dismay, that his responses are all wrong. Instead of making her feel better, he makes her feel worse. The problem is that he tends to be direct and practical, whereas what she wants more than anything else is an empathetic listener. Used to years of such responses from close friends, a woman is likely to be surprised and angered by her husband's immediate "Here's what ya' do. . . ."

Mark Sherman and Adelaide Haas

greater amount of joking and good-natured teasing. By contrast, women's discussions involve feelings, relationships, and personal problems. In fact, communication researcher Julia Wood flatly states that "for women, talk *is* the essence of relationships."[39] When members of a group of women were surveyed to find out what kinds of satisfaction they gained from talking with their friends, the most common theme mentioned was a feeling of empathy—"To know you're not alone," as some put it.[40] Whereas men commonly described same-sex conversations as something they *liked*, women described their same-sex conversations as a kind of contact they *needed*. The characteristically female orientation for relational communication is supported by studies of married couples showing that wives spend proportionately more time than husbands communicating in ways that help maintain their relationship.[41]

Men's speech is often driven by different goals than women's speech. Men are more likely to use language to accomplish the job at hand than to nourish relationships. This explains why men are less likely than women to disclose their vulnerabilities, which they might perceive as a sign of weakness. When someone is sharing a problem, instead of empathizing, men are prone to offer advice: "That's nothing to worry about . . ." "Here's what you need to do. . . ." Besides taking care of business, men are more likely than women to use conversations to exert control, preserve their independence, and enhance their status. This explains why men are more prone to dominate conversations and one-up their partners. Men interrupt their conversational partners to assert their own experiences or point of view. (Women interrupt, too, but they usually do so to offer support—quite a different goal.) Just because male talk is competitive doesn't mean it's not enjoyable. When researchers asked men what they liked best about their all-male talk, the most frequent answer was its ease.[42] Another common theme was appreciation of the practical value of conversation: new ways to solve problems. Men also mentioned enjoying the humor and rapid pace that characterized their all-male conversations.

Conversational Style

Women tend to behave differently in conversations than do men.[43] For instance, women ask more questions in mixed-sex conversations than do men—nearly three times as many, according to one study. Other research has revealed that in mixed-sex conversations, men interrupt women far more than the other way around. Men are also more likely than women to use judgmental adjectives ("Reading can be a drag"), directives ("Think of some more"), and "I" references ("I have a lot to do").[44] Women are more likely to use intensive adverbs ("He's *really* interested"), emotional references ("If he really cared about you . . ."), uncertainty verbs ("It seems to me . . ."), and contradictions ("It's cold, but that's OK"). Differences like these show that men's speech is more typically direct, succinct, and task-oriented. By contrast, women's speech is more typically indirect, elaborate, and focused on relationships.

Because they use conversation to pursue social needs, women typically use statements showing support for the other person, demonstrations of equality, and efforts to keep the conversation going.[45] With these goals, it's not surprising that traditionally female speech often contains statements of sympathy and empathy: "I've felt just like that myself," "The same thing happened to me!" Women are also inclined to ask questions that invite the other person to share information: "How did you feel about that?" "What did you do next?" The importance of

"Sometimes I think he can understand every word we're saying."

nurturing a relationship also explains why female speech is often somewhat tentative. Saying, "This is just my opinion . . ." is less likely to put off a conversational partner than a more definite "Here's what I think . . ."

An accommodating style isn't always a disadvantage. One study revealed that women who spoke tentatively were actually more persuasive with men than those who used more-powerful speech.[46] On the other hand, this tentative style was less effective in persuading women. (Language use had no effect on men's persuasiveness.) This study suggests that women who are willing and able to be flexible in their approach can persuade both other women and men—as long as they are not dealing with a mixed-sex audience.

Nongender Variables

Despite the differences identified above, the link between gender and language use isn't as clear-cut as it might seem. Several research reviews have found that the ways women and men communicate are much more similar than different. For example, one analysis of over twelve hundred research studies found that only 1 percent of variance in communication behavior resulted from gender difference.[47] According to this research review, there is no significant difference between male speech and female speech in areas such as use of profanity, use of qualifiers ("I guess" or "This is just my opinion"), tag questions, and vocal fluency.[48] Some on-the-job research shows that male and female supervisors in similar positions behave the same way and are equally effective. In light of this research showing considerable similarities between the sexes and the relatively minor differences, one communication scholar suggests that the "Men Are from Mars, Women Are from Venus" metaphor should be replaced by the notion that "Men Are from North Dakota, Women Are from South Dakota."[49]

A growing body of research explains some of the apparent contradictions between the similarities and differences between male speech and female speech. Research has revealed other factors that influence language use as much or more than does gender.[50] For example, social philosophy plays a role. Feminist wives talk longer than their partners, whereas nonfeminist wives speak less than their partners. In addition, cooperative or competitive orientations of speakers have more influence on how they interact than does their gender.[51] The speaker's occupation also influences speaking style. For example, male day-care teachers' speech to their students resembles the language of female teachers more closely than it resembles the language of fathers at home.

To the degree that women use less-powerful language, there may be two explanations. The first involves their historical role in society at large: Powerless speech may reflect the relative lack of power held by women. If this explanation is valid, the male-female differences in powerful speech and powerless speech are likely to diminish as our society treats both sexes the same. A second, equally compelling explanation for the finding that women use less-powerful language comes from scholars who point out that what powerless speech loses in potency it gains by building rapport between speaker and receiver.[52] Because women have historically been more concerned with building harmonious relationships, it follows that typically feminine speech will sound less powerful. Toward that end, so-called powerless speech is actually *quite* powerful when it comes to building and maintaining relationships.

Another powerful force that influences the way individual men and women speak is their gender role. Recall the gender roles described in Chapter 3 (pages 99–100): masculine, feminine, and androgynous. Remember that these gender roles don't necessarily line up neatly with biological sex. There are "masculine" females, "feminine" males, and androgynous communicators who combine traditionally masculine and feminine characteristics. These gender roles can influence a communicator's style more than his or her biological sex. For example, one study revealed that masculine subjects used significantly more dominance language than did either feminine or androgynous subjects.[53] Feminine subjects expressed slightly more submissive behaviors and more equivalence behaviors than did the androgynous subjects, and their submissiveness and equivalence were much greater than those of the masculine subjects, regardless of their biological sex. And in gay and lesbian relationships, the conversational styles of partners reflect power differences in the relationship (e.g., who is earning more money) more than the biological sex of the communicators.[54]

What should we conclude about similarities and differences in the way men and women speak? While there are differences in male and female speech patterns, they may not be as great as some popular books suggest—and some of them may not be due to biological sex at all. In practical terms, the best approach is to recognize that differences in communication style—whether they come from biological sex, gender, culture, or individual factors—present both challenges and opportunities. We need to take different styles into account, but not exaggerate or use them to stigmatize one another.

Invitation to Insight

Exploring Gender Differences in Communication

Some pop culture writers have claimed that the communication styles of men and women are so different that "men are from Mars, women are from Venus." Most researchers believe the differences aren't nearly so dramatic. One argues metaphorically that "men are from North Dakota, women are from South Dakota." Based on the research described in these pages and your personal experience, which approach seems more accurate to you?

Culture and Language

Anyone who has tried to translate ideas from one language to another knows that conveying the same meaning isn't always easy.[55] Sometimes the results of a bungled translation can be amusing. For example, the American manufacturers of Pet milk unknowingly introduced their product in French-speaking markets without realizing that the word *pet* in French means "to break wind."[56] Likewise, the English-speaking representative of a U.S. soft drink manufacturer naively drew laughs from Mexican customers when she offered free samples of Fresca soda pop. In Mexican slang, the word *fresca* means "lesbian."

Even choosing the right words during translation won't guarantee that nonnative speakers will use an unfamiliar language correctly. For example, Japanese insurance companies warn their policyholders who are visiting the United States to avoid their cultural tendency to say "excuse me" or "I'm sorry" if they are involved in a traffic accident.[57] In Japan, apologizing is a traditional way to express goodwill and maintain social harmony, even if the person offering the apology is not at fault. But in the United States an apology can be taken as an admission of fault and result in Japanese tourists being wrongly held responsible for accidents.

Difficult as it may be, translation is only a small part of the differences in communication between members of different cultures. Differences in the way language is used and the worldview that a language creates make communicating across cultures a challenging task.

Verbal Communication Styles

Using language is more than just choosing a particular group of words to convey an idea. Each language has its own unique style that distinguishes it from others. Matters like the amount of formality or informality, precision or vagueness, and brevity or detail are major ingredients in speaking competently. And when a communicator tries to use the verbal style from one culture in a different one, problems are likely to arise.[58]

One way in which verbal styles vary is in their *directness*. Anthropologist Edward Hall identified two distinct cultural ways of using language.[59] **Low-context cultures** generally value using language to express thoughts, feelings, and ideas as clearly and logically as possible. Low-context communicators look for the meaning of a statement in the words spoken. By contrast, **high-context cultures** value using language to maintain social harmony. Rather than upset others by speaking clearly, high-context communicators learn to discover meaning from the context in which a message is delivered: the nonverbal behaviors of the speaker, the history of the relationship, and the general social rules that govern interaction between people. Table 5.5 summarizes some key differences between the way low- and high-context cultures use language.

North American culture falls toward the low-context end of the scale. Residents of the United States and Canada value straight talk and grow impatient with "beating around the bush." By contrast, most Asian and Middle Eastern cultures fall toward the high-context end of the scale. In many Asian cultures, for example, maintaining harmony is important, so communicators will avoid speaking clearly if that would threaten another person's face. For this reason, Japanese and Koreans are less likely than Americans to offer a clear "no" to an undesirable request. Instead they will probably use roundabout expressions like "I agree with you in principle, but . . ." or "I sympathize with you. . . ."

What mattered to Abu was the music of the sentence . . . in general, it was the poetics, the music of things that tossed his confetti . . . Everywhere, the Arabic alphabet wiggled and popped . . . with outbursts of linguistic jazz, notations from the DNA songbook, energetic markings as primal as grunts and as modern as the abstract electricity of synthesizer feedback.

Tom Robbins,
Skinny Legs and All

Table 5.5	Low- and High-Context Communication Styles
Low Context	**High Context**
Majority of information carried in explicit cues verbal messages, with less focus on the situational context.	Important information carried in contextual (time, place, relationship). Less reliance on explicit verbal messages.
Self-expression valued. Communicators state opinions and desires directly and strive to persuade others to accept their own viewpoint.	Relational harmony valued and maintained by indirect expression of opinions. Communicators abstain from saying "no" directly.
Clear, eloquent speech considered praiseworthy. Verbal fluency admired.	Communicators talk "around" the point, allowing the other to fill in the missing pieces. Ambiguity and use of silence admired.

The same sort of clash between directness and indirectness can aggravate problems between straight-talking, low-context Israelis, who value speaking clearly, and Arabs, whose high-context culture stresses smooth interaction. It's easy to imagine how the clash of cultural styles could lead to misunderstandings and conflicts between Israelis and their Palestinian neighbors. Israelis could view the Palestinians as evasive, whereas the Palestinians could view the Israelis as insensitive and blunt.

It's worth noting that even generally straight-talking residents of the United States raised in the low-context Euro-American tradition often rely on context to make their point. When you decline an unwanted invitation by saying, "I can't make it," it's likely that both you and the other person know that the choice of attending isn't really beyond your control. If your goal was to be perfectly clear, you might say, "I don't want to get together." As Chapter 9 explains in detail, we often equivocate precisely because we want to obscure our true thoughts and feelings.

Besides their degrees of clarity and vagueness, another way in which language styles can vary across cultures is whether they are *elaborate* or *succinct*. Speakers of Arabic, for instance, commonly use language that is much richer and more expressive than that of most communicators who use English. Strong assertions and exaggerations that would sound ridiculous in English are a common feature of Arabic. This contrast in linguistic styles can lead to misunderstandings between people from different backgrounds. As one observer put it,

> First, an Arab feels compelled to overassert in almost all types of communication because others expect him [or her] to. If an Arab says exactly what he [or she] means without the expected assertion, other Arabs may still think that he [or she] means the opposite. For example, a simple "no" by a guest to the host's requests to eat more or drink more will not suffice. To convey the meaning that he [or she] is actually full, the guest must keep repeating "no" several times, coupling it with an oath such as "By God" or "I swear to God." Second, an Arab often fails to realize that others, particularly foreigners, may mean exactly what they say even though their language is simple. To the Arabs, a simple "no" may mean the indirectly expressed consent and encouragement of a coquettish woman. On the other hand, a simple consent may mean the rejection of a hypocritical politician.[60]

Succinctness is most extreme in cultures where silence is valued. In many Native American cultures, for example, the favored way to handle ambiguous

Looking at Diversity

Zarina Kolah: Training Non-Native Customer Service Reps

I train representatives in India to give phone support to customers of large American computer manufacturers. If you call for help with your laptop or desktop PC, you may find yourself speaking with one of the men and women I have helped train.

Our representatives are all smart, educated people. Many have university degrees in engineering and other technical fields. They have studied English in school for several years, but they need to learn the "soft skills" to give the kind of service U.S. customers want and deserve.

Many of the soft skills our reps learn involve speaking and understanding everyday English. That can be quite different from what's taught in Indian schools. For example, we have to teach our reps the meaning of phrases like "Let's touch base," "bottom line" and "yada yada."

One way our reps learn everyday American speech is by watching television programs like Oprah and CNN news. The speech in these shows is much closer to everyday language than what's been taught in Indian schools. Also, we train our reps in American traditions and cultural life. That way, when a caller says "Happy Thanksgiving" or asks "How about those Yankees?" our reps will know what to say.

Understanding Standard English can be challenging enough for our reps, but regional or ethnic accents can be even harder. Think about how different the same statements sound when spoken by a Texan, someone with a Hispanic accent, or a native Chinese English speaker. Our reps have to understand them all.

When Indian call centers began serving customers in the US and Canada, many reps took on Western-sounding names instead of using their real ones. Samik became Sam, Patel was Pat, and Kalyani identified herself as Kate. Nowadays most call centers prefer that their reps use their own names, as customers realize that the reps are in India and would rather have a conversation that reflects this fact.

Language skills are obviously important. But we never forget that the most important "soft skills" are the ones that show we value our customers: politeness, empathy, patience, a sense of humor, and above all, helpfulness. That's true in any language.

social situations is to remain quiet.[61] When you contrast this silent style to the talkativeness that is common in mainstream American cultures when people first meet, it's easy to imagine how the first encounter between an Apache or Navajo and an Anglo might feel uncomfortable to both people.

A third way in which languages differ from one culture to another involves *formality* and *informality*. The informal approach that characterizes relationships in countries like the United States, Canada, Australia, and the Scandinavian countries is quite different from the great concern for using proper speech in many parts of Asia and Africa. Formality isn't so much a matter of using correct grammar as of defining social position. In Korea, for example, the language reflects the Confucian system of relational hierarchies.[62] It has special vocabularies for different sexes, for different levels of social status, for different degrees of intimacy, and for different types of social occasions. For example, there are different degrees of formality for speaking with old friends, nonacquaintances whose background one knows, and complete strangers. One sign of being a learned person in Korea is the ability to use language that recognizes these relational distinctions. When you contrast these sorts of distinctions with the casual friendliness that many North Americans use even when talking with complete strangers, it's easy to see how a Korean might view communicators in the United States as boorish and how an American might view communicators in Korea as stiff and unfriendly.

Language and Heritage

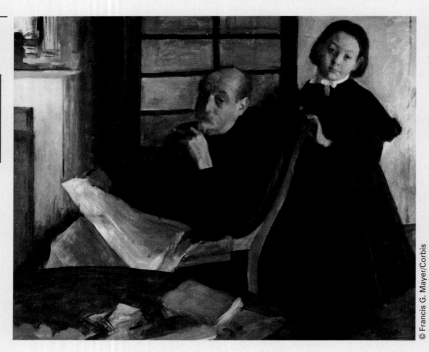

© Francis G. Mayer/Corbis

"Mi'ja, it's me. Call me when you wake up." It was a message left on my phone machine from a friend. But when I heard that word *mi'ja*, a pain squeezed my heart. My father was the only one who ever called me this.

Because his death is so recent, the word overwhelmed me and filled me with grief.

Mi'ja (MEE-ha) from *mi hija* (me ee-HA). The words translate as "my daughter." Daughter, my daughter,

daughter of mine: They're all stiff and clumsy, and have nothing of the intimacy and warmth of the word *mi'ja*— "daughter of my heart," maybe. Perhaps a more accurate translation of *mi'ja* is "I love you." Sometimes a word can be translated into more than a meaning. In it is the translation of a worldview, a way of looking at things, and, yes, even a way of accepting what others might not perceive as beautiful. *Urraca*, for example, instead of "grackle." Two ways of looking at a black bird. One sings, the other cackles. Or, *tocayola*, your name-twin, and therefore, your friend. Or the beautiful *estrenar*, which means to wear something for the first time. There is no word in English for the thrill and pride of wearing something new.

Spanish gives me a way of looking at myself and the world in a new way. For those of us living between worlds, our job in the universe is to help others see with more than their eyes during this period of chaotic transition.

Sandra Cisneros

Language and Worldview

Different linguistic styles are important, but there may be even more-important differences that separate speakers of various languages. For almost a 150 years, theorists have put forth the notion of **linguistic relativism**: that the worldview of a culture is shaped and reflected by the language its members speak.[63] The best-known example of linguistic relativism is the notion that Eskimos have a large number of words (estimated at everything from 17 to 100) for what we

Invitation to Insight

High- and Low-Context Communication

ThomsonNOW Check your knowledge of high- and low-context communication styles with a self-test and sample dialogues available through your ThomsonNOW for *Looking Out/Looking In*. Click "next page" for further explanations, examples and exercises that illustrate these direct and indirect communication styles.

simply call "snow." Different terms are used to describe conditions like a driving blizzard, crusty ice, and light powder. This example suggests how linguistic relativism operates. The need to survive in an Arctic environment led Eskimos to make distinctions that would be unimportant to residents of warmer environments, and after the language makes these distinctions, speakers are more likely to see the world in ways that match the broader vocabulary.

Even though there is some doubt that Eskimos really have so many words for snow,[64] other examples do seem to support the principle of linguistic relativism.[65] For instance, bilingual speakers seem to think differently when they change languages. In one study, French American people

"The Eskimos have eighty-seven words for snow and not one for malpractice."

were asked to interpret a series of pictures. When they described the pictures in French, their descriptions were far more romantic and emotional than when they described the pictures in English. Likewise, when students in Hong Kong were asked to complete a values test, they expressed more traditional Chinese values when they answered in Cantonese than when they answered in English. In Israel, both Arab and Jewish students saw greater distinctions between their group and "outsiders" when using their native language than when they used English, a neutral tongue for them. Examples like these, and like those in the reading on the opposite page show the power of language to shape cultural identity—sometimes for better and sometimes for worse.

The best-known declaration of linguistic relativism is the **Sapir–Whorf hypothesis**, formulated by Edward Sapir and Benjamin Whorf.[66] Following Sapir's theory, Whorf observed that the language spoken by Hopi Native Americans represents a view of reality that is dramatically different from that of more familiar tongues. For example, the Hopi language makes no distinction between nouns and verbs. Therefore, the people who speak it describe the entire world as being constantly in process. Whereas in English we use nouns to characterize people or objects as being fixed or constant, Hopi view them more as verbs, constantly changing. In this sense English represents much of the world rather like a snapshot camera, whereas Hopi language represents the world more like a motion picture.

Some languages contain terms that have no English equivalents.[67] For example, consider a few words in other languages that have no English equivalents:

nemawashi (Japanese): The process of informally feeling out all the people involved with an issue before making a decision

lagniappe (French/Creole): An extra gift given in a transaction that wasn't expected by the terms of a contract

lao (Mandarin): A respectful term used for older people, showing their importance in the family and in society *dharma* (Sanskrit): Each person's unique, ideal path in life and knowledge of how to find it

koyaanisquatsi (Hopi): Nature out of balance; a way of life so crazy it calls for a new way of living

After words like these exist and become a part of everyday life, the ideas that they represent are easier to recognize. But even without such words, each of the ideas just listed is still possible to imagine. Thus, speakers of a language that includes the notion of *lao* would probably treat its older members respectfully, and those who are familiar with *lagniappe* might be more generous. Despite these differences, it is possible to follow these principles without knowing or using these words. Although language may shape thoughts and behavior, it doesn't dominate them absolutely.

Summary

Language is both a marvelous communication tool and the source of many interpersonal problems. Every language is a collection of symbols, governed by a variety of rules: semantic, syntactic, and pragmatic. Because of its symbolic nature, language is not a precise vehicle: Meanings rest in people, not in words themselves.

Language both reflects and shapes the perceptions of its users. Terms used to name people influence the way the people are regarded. The terms used to name speakers and the language they use reflect the level of affiliation of a speaker toward others. Language patterns also reflect and shape a speaker's perceived power.

When used carelessly, language can lead to a variety of interpersonal problems. The level of precision or vagueness of messages can affect a receiver's understanding of them. Both precise messages and vague, equivocal ones have their uses in interpersonal relationships, and a competent communicator has the ability to choose the optimal level of precision for the situation at hand. Some language habits—such as confusing facts with opinions or inferences and using emotive terms—can lead to unnecessary disharmony in interpersonal relationships. Language also acknowledges or avoids the speaker's acceptance of responsibility for his or her positions, and competent communicators know how to use "I" and "we" language to accept the optimal level of responsibility and relational harmony.

The relationship between gender and language is a complex one. There are some differences in the ways men and women speak: The content of their conversations varies, as do their reasons for communicating and their conversational styles. However, not all differences in language use can be accounted for by the speaker's biological sex. Gender roles, occupation, social philosophy, and orientation toward problem solving also influence people's use of language.

Different languages often shape and reflect the views of a culture. Low-context cultures like the United States use language primarily to express feelings and ideas as clearly and unambiguously as possible. High-context cultures such as Japan and Saudi Arabia, however, avoid specificity in order to promote social harmony. Some cultures value brevity and the succinct use of language, whereas others value elaborate forms of speech. In some societies formality is important, whereas in others informality is important. Beyond these differences, there is evidence to support linguistic relativism—the notion that language exerts a strong influence on the worldview of the people who speak it.

Key Terms

abstraction ladder (161)
abstract language (161)
behavioral language (161)
"but" statements (176)
convergence (170)
divergence (171)
emotive language (174)
equivocal language (159)

high-context cultures (185)
"I" language (175)
"it" statements (175)
linguistic relativism (188)
low-context cultures (185)
powerless speech
 mannerisms (171)
pragmatic rules (166)

relative words (159)
Sapir–Whorf hypothesis (189)
semantic rules (159)
static evaluation (161)
syntactic rules (162)
"we" language (178)
"you" language (176)

Media Resources

Online Textbook Resources

ThomsonNOW For quick access to the online resources that accompany this chapter, access ThomsonNOW for *Looking Out/Looking In* at www.thomsonedu.com.

The ThomsonNOW online study system helps you identify concepts you don't fully understand, allowing you to put your study time to the best use. Using chapter-by-chapter diagnostic pre-tests, the system creates a **personalized study plan** for each chapter. Each plan directs you to specific resources designed to improve your understanding, including pages from the text in ebook format. Chapter post-tests give you an opportunity to measure how much you've learned and let you know if you are ready for graded quizzes and exams.

Your ThomsonNOW for *Looking Out/Looking In* also includes the **ABC News video clip** described on page 165; a **communication scenario video** of the transcript on page 179; **vocabulary activities** to help you master key terms; self-study **review quizzes** to test your comprehension of the material in this chapter and prepare for exams; **online exercises**, including the Skill Builder and Invitation to Insight activities in this chapter; **web links** you can use to further explore topics in this chapter; access to a **feature film database** where you can locate information about movies that illustrate communication principles; and access to the **InfoTrac** College Edition searchable database of over 10 million articles from both scholarly journals and the popular press.

Films

In addition to the films suggested here, go to your ThomsonNOW for *Looking Out/Looking In* to link to the **Film in Communication Database**, where you can locate movie clips that illustrate language.

The Importance of Language

Nell (1994) Rated PG-13
The Miracle Worker (1962) Not rated
Nell is the story of a young woman (played by Jodie Foster) raised in virtual isolation in the backwoods of North Carolina. When her mother dies, Nell is discovered and cared for by small-town doctor Jerry Lovell (Liam Neeson) and big-city psychologist Paula Olsen (Natasha Richardson). Much of the film centers on conflicts within and between Lovell and Olsen as they try, from differing perspectives, to understand and help Nell.

At first Nell's utterances sound like gibberish to Lovell and Olsen. But they soon discover that, in her isolation, she learned a strange version of English as spoken by her mother (a stroke victim who read to Nell from the King James version of the Bible) and her twin sister (with whom Nell shared a secret linguistic code). Now that both the mother and sister have died, Nell's linguistic isolation is as profound as her physical distance from the rest of the world.

Nell's story is reminiscent in many ways of Helen Keller's early childhood as described in the well-known film *The Miracle Worker*. Both Nell and Helen were intelligent young women, misunderstood and misdiagnosed by "experts" who assumed that their lack of ability to communicate was a sign of limited mental abilities. Both were cut off from the rest of the world until they developed the ability to communicate with others by a shared language system.

The Miracle Worker and *Nell* are by no means identical tales. Helen Keller's story is biographical, while Nell's is a work of fiction. Furthermore, the films' different conclusions show that linguistic skill is no guarantee of living happily ever after. While learning to communicate through sign language opened the door to live a rich and productive life for Helen Keller, Nell found the "civilized world" a less hospitable place. Despite their differences, both movies offer profound insights into the potential and power of language in the human experience.

Cultural Rules for Language

The N-Word (2004) Not Rated
It is possibly the most inflammatory word in American culture—so much so that the letter "N" is substituted for the actual word in most public discussions of the term. But as this documentary shows, the "N word" has many and varied meanings, ranging from a degrading slur to a term of endearment. A host of scholars and celebrities (including Chris Rock, Whoopi Goldberg, George Carlin, Ice Cube, and Quincy Jones) discuss and debate when, where, how, by whom, and even whether the "N word" should be used.

The film offers a vivid illustration of how pragmatic rules and linguistic convergence/divergence operate in interpersonal and intercultural communication. It also shows how failing to know and abide by cultural meanings and rules can lead to significant misunderstandings and conflict.

Linguistic Convergence

Mean Girls (2004) Rated PG-13
Cady Heron (Lindsay Lohan) was raised in African bush country by her zoologist parents. Back in the U.S.A., Cady has her first experience in formal schooling when she enrolls at North Shore High. She soon learns that high school social life can be every bit as vicious as anything she witnessed among the primates. Her new school is rife with social cliques including the high status Plastics and the geeky Mathletes.

At the urging of her unpopular friends Janis (Lizzy Caplan) and Damian (Daniel Franzese), Cady infiltrates the Plastics to get information so they can demolish the prestige of the popular girls.

For Cady, part of fitting in is to learn and use the vocabulary of the in-group Plastics. In an early conversation with these popular girls, their leader Regina (Rachel McAdams) exclaims to Cady, "Shut up!" Unfamiliar with the slang use of this term, Cady replies, "I didn't say anything." Soon Cady speaks Plastic fluently, tossing about words like "fetch" (cool), "word vomit" (babbling), and the self-explanatory "fugly."

In an interesting example of linguistic convergence, the more Cady "talks the talk" of being a Plastic, the more her values and behaviors become like theirs. By movie's end, she makes some important decisions about herself and her friends—including the decision not to talk or act like a "mean girl."

Gender and Language

When Harry Met Sally (1989) Rated R
Harry Burns (Billy Crystal) and Sally Albright (Meg Ryan) are strangers who get together for purely functional reasons: a cross-country car ride in which they share gas costs and driving. She sizes him up as crude and insensitive; he views her as naive and obsessive. By the time they finish their journey, they are glad to part ways.

But the car ride is just the start of their relationship—and the beginning of a look at male and female communication styles. In their conversations, Harry and Sally often exhibit communication patterns similar to those found in gender-related research. For instance, Harry tends to treat discussions as debates. He regularly tells jokes and enjoys having the first and last word. He rarely asks questions but is quick to answer them. Harry self-discloses with his buddy Jess (Bruno Kirby) but only while watching a football game or taking swings at a batting cage.

Sally, on the other hand, self-discloses with her female friends at restaurants, by phone, while shopping—just about any place. She regularly asks questions of Harry but seems troubled by his competitive answers and approach to sex (Sally: "So you're saying that a man can be friends with a woman he finds unattractive?" Harry: "No, you pretty much want to nail them too"). In the language of Deborah Tannen, Sally's communication is about "rapport" while Harry's is about "report."

The story ends with a strong sense of hope for cross-sex communication. This is due in part to Harry's learning to "speak a different language." The rancor of his early interactions with Sally softens when he expresses empathy (much to her surprise) in a chance bookstore meeting. By movie's end, he offers warm and detailed descriptions of why he enjoys being with and around her. Clearly they are friends as well as lovers, which seems to make their communication stronger. It also helps them fulfill a goal of most movies: the ending suggests they have a good chance to live "happily ever after."

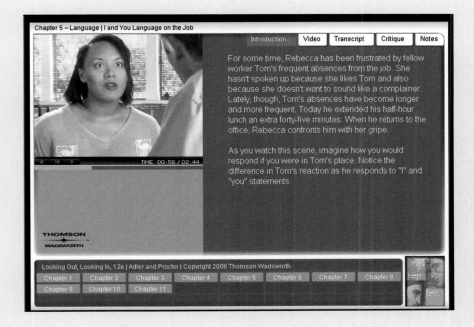

Chapter 5 ~ Language | I and You Language on the Job

Introduction | Video | Transcript | Critique | Notes

For some time, Rebecca has been frustrated by fellow worker Tom's frequent absences from the job. She hasn't spoken up because she likes Tom and also because she doesn't want to sound like a complainer. Lately, though, Tom's absences have become longer and more frequent. Today he extended his half-hour lunch an extra forty-five minutes. When he returns to the office, Rebecca confronts him with her gripe.

As you watch this scene, imagine how you would respond if you were in Tom's place. Notice the difference in Tom's reaction as he responds to "I" and "you" statements.

TIME 00:56 / 02:44

THOMSON
WADSWORTH

Looking Out, Looking In, 12e | Adler and Proctor | Copyright 2008 Thomson Wadsworth

Chapter 1 | Chapter 2 | Chapter 3 | Chapter 4 | Chapter 5 | Chapter 6 | Chapter 7 | Chapter 8
Chapter 9 | Chapter 10 | Chapter 11

Nonverbal Communication: Messages beyond Words

6

Characteristics of Nonverbal Communication

Nonverbal Skills Are Important
All Behavior Has Communicative Value
Nonverbal Communication Is Primarily Relational
Nonverbal Communication Serves Many Functions
Nonverbal Communication Is Ambiguous

Influences on Nonverbal Communication

Gender
Culture

Types of Nonverbal Communication

Body Movement
Voice
Touch
Appearance
Physical Space
Physical Environment
Time

Summary

Key Terms

Media Resources

Sherlock Holmes said the way to understand people is to watch them—not only to see, but also to observe. Observing yourself and others is what this chapter is about. In the following pages you'll become acquainted with the field of nonverbal communication—the way we express ourselves, not by what we say but rather by what we *do*. Some social scientists have argued that 93 percent of the emotional impact of a message comes from nonverbal sources. Others have reasoned more convincingly that the figure is closer to 65 percent.[1] Whatever the precise figure, the point remains: Nonverbal communication plays an important role in how we make sense of one another's behavior.

We need to begin our study of nonverbal communication by defining that term. At first this might seem like a simple task: If *non* means "not" and *verbal* means "words," then *nonverbal communication* means "communicating without words." In fact, this literal definition isn't completely accurate. For instance, most communication scholars do not define American Sign Language as nonverbal even though the messages are unspoken. On the other hand, you'll soon read that certain aspects of the voice aren't really verbal, although they are vocal. (Can you think of any? Table 6.1 will help you.)

What you are speaks so loudly I cannot hear what you say.

Ralph Waldo Emerson

The Adventures of Sherlock Holmes

I was seized with a keen desire to see Holmes again, and to know how he was employing his extraordinary powers. His rooms were brilliantly lit, and, even as I looked up, I saw his tall, spare figure pass twice in a dark silhouette against the blind. He was pacing the room swiftly, eagerly, with his head sunk upon his chest and his hands clasped behind him. To me, who knew his every mood and habit, his attitude and manner told their own story. He was at work again. He had risen out of his drug-created dreams and was hot upon the scent of some new problem. I rang the bell and was shown up to the chamber which had formerly been in part my own.

His manner was not effusive. It seldom was; but he was glad, I think, to see me. With hardly a word spoken, but with kindly eye, he waved me to an armchair, threw across his case of cigars, and indicated a spirit case and a gasogene in the corner. Then he stood before the fire and looked me over in his singular introspective fashion.

"Wedlock suits you," he remarked. "I think, Watson, that you have put on seven and a half pounds since I saw you."

"Seven!" I answered.

"Indeed, I should have thought a little more. Just a trifle more, I fancy, Watson. And in practice again, I observe. You did not tell me that you intended to go into harness."

"Then, how do you know?"

"I see it, I deduce it. How do I know that you have been getting yourself very wet lately, and that you have a most clumsy and careless servant girl?"

"My dear Holmes," said I, "this is too much. You would certainly have been burned, had you lived a few centuries ago. It is true that I had a country walk on Thursday and came home in a dreadful mess, but as I have changed my clothes I can't imagine how you deduce it. As to Mary Jane, she is incorrigible, and my wife has given her notice; but there, again, I fail to see how you work it out."

He chuckled to himself and rubbed his long, nervous hands together.

"It is simplicity itself," said he; "my eyes tell me that on the inside of your left shoe, just where the firelight strikes it, the leather is scored by six almost parallel cuts. Obviously they have been caused by someone who has very carefully scraped round the edges of the sole in order to remove crusted mud from it. Hence, you see, my double deduction that you had been out in vile weather, and that you had a particularly malignant boot-slitting specimen of the London slavey. As to your practice, if a gentleman walks into my rooms smelling of iodoform, with a black mark of nitrate of silver upon his right forefinger, and a bulge on the right side of his top hat to show where he has secreted his stethoscope, I must be dull, indeed, if I do not pronounce him to be an active member of the medical profession."

I could not help laughing at the ease with which he explained his process of deduction. "When I hear you give your reasons," I remarked, "the thing always appears to me to be so ridiculously simple that I could easily do it myself, though at each successive instance of your reasoning I am baffled until you explain your process. And yet I believe that my eyes are as good as yours."

"Quite so," he answered, lighting a cigarette, and throwing himself down into an armchair. "You see, but you do not observe."

Arthur Conan Doyle, *A Scandal in Bohemia*

Table 6.1	**Types of Communication**	
	Vocal Communication	Nonvocal Communication
Verbal Communication	Spoken words	Written words
Nonverbal Communication	Tone of voice, sighs, screams, vocal quality, pitch, loudness, etc.	Gestures, movement, appearance, facial expression, touch, etc.

"Types of Communication," adapted from *Together: Communicating Interpersonally*, by J. Stewart and G. D'Angelo. ©1980 Addison-Wesley. Used courtesy McGraw-Hill Inc.

For our purposes, we'll define **nonverbal communication** as "messages expressed by nonlinguistic means." This rules out sign languages and written words, but it includes messages transmitted by vocal means that don't involve language—the sighs, laughs, and other assorted noises we alluded to earlier. In addition, our definition allows us to explore the nonlinguistic dimensions of the spoken word—volume, rate, pitch, and so on. It also encompasses more-abstract factors such as physical appearance, the environment in which we communicate, how close or far we stand from each other, and the way we use time. And of course, it includes the features most people think of when they consider nonverbal communication: body language, gestures, facial expression, and others.

Characteristics of Nonverbal Communication

The definition in the preceding paragraph only hints at the richness of nonverbal communication. In the following pages, we'll take a look at characteristics that are true of all the many forms and functions of nonverbal communication.

Nonverbal Skills Are Important

It's hard to overemphasize the importance of effective nonverbal expression and the ability to read and respond to others' nonverbal behavior. Nonverbal encoding and decoding skills are a strong predictor of popularity, attractiveness, and socioemotional well-being.[2] Good nonverbal communicators are more persuasive than people who are less skilled, and they have a greater chance of success in settings ranging from careers to poker to romance. Nonverbal sensitivity is a major part of the "emotional intelligence" described in Chapter 4, and researchers have come to recognize that it is impossible to study spoken language without paying attention to its nonverbal dimensions.[3]

All Behavior Has Communicative Value

Suppose you tried not to communicate any messages at all. What would you do? Stop talking? Close your eyes? Withdraw into a ball? Leave the room? You can

Writer [to movie producer Sam Goldwyn]: Mr. Goldwyn, I'm telling you a sensational story. I'm only asking for your opinion, and you fall asleep.

Goldwyn: Isn't sleeping an opinion?

It's called body language, Norman.

Go Figure Reprinted by permission of United Feature Syndicate.

probably see that even these behaviors communicate messages—that you're avoiding contact. One study demonstrated this fact.[4] When communicators were told not to express nonverbal clues, others viewed them as dull, withdrawn, uneasy, aloof, and deceptive.

This impossibility of not communicating is extremely important to understand because it means that each of us is a kind of transmitter that cannot be shut off. No matter what we do, we give off information about ourselves.[5]

Stop for a moment, and examine yourself as you read this. If someone were observing you now, what nonverbal clues would that person get about how you're feeling? Are you sitting forward or reclining back? Is your posture tense or relaxed? Are your eyes wide open, or do they keep closing? What does your facial expression communicate? Can you make your face expressionless? Don't people with expressionless faces communicate something to you?

Of course, we don't always intend to send nonverbal messages. Unintentional nonverbal behaviors differ from intentional ones.[6] For example, we often stammer, blush, frown, and sweat without meaning to do so. Whether or not our nonverbal behavior is intentional, others recognize it and make interpretations about us based on their observations.

Some theorists argue that unintentional behavior may provide information but that it shouldn't count as communication.[7] We draw the boundaries of nonverbal communication more broadly, suggesting that even unconscious and unintentional behavior conveys messages, and thus is worth studying as communication.

Nonverbal Communication Is Primarily Relational

Some nonverbal messages serve utilitarian functions. For example, a police officer directs the flow of traffic, and a team of street surveyors uses hand motions to coordinate its work. But nonverbal communication more commonly expresses the kinds of relational (rather than content) messages discussed in Chapter 1 and the kinds of identity messages that you read about in Chapter 2.[8]

Consider, for example, the role of nonverbal communication in *identity management*. Chapter 2 discussed how we strive to create an image of ourselves as we want others to view us. Nonverbal communication plays an important role in this process—in many cases more important than verbal communication. For instance, think what happens when you attend a party where you are likely to meet strangers you would like to get to know better. Instead of projecting your image verbally ("Hi! I'm attractive, friendly, and easygoing"), you behave in ways that will present this identity. You might smile a lot and perhaps try to strike a relaxed pose. It's also likely that you dress carefully—even if the image involves looking as though you hadn't given a lot of attention to your appearance.

Along with identity management, nonverbal communication allows us to *define the kinds of relationships we want to have with others*. Think about the wide range of ways you could behave when greeting another person. You could wave, shake hands, nod, smile, clap the other person on the back, give a hug, or avoid all contact. Each one of these decisions would send a message about the nature of your relationship with the other person.

Nonverbal behavior can be more powerful than words in defining the kind of relationship you are seeking. Recall all the times and ways you have learned that someone you know is upset with you. Most often the first clues don't come from direct statements but rather from nonverbal clues. Perhaps the message is conveyed through a lack of eye contact, different facial expressions, an increase in distance, or decreased touch. In any case, the change in behavior clearly proves the power of nonverbal communication to define the status of a relationship.

Nonverbal communication performs a third valuable social function: *conveying emotions* that we may be unwilling or unable to express—or ones that we may not even be aware of. In fact, nonverbal communication is much better suited to expressing attitudes and feelings than ideas. You can prove this by imagining how you could express each item on the following list nonverbally:

   a.   You're tired.
   b.   You're in favor of capital punishment.
   c.   You're attracted to another person in the group.
   d.   You think prayer in the schools should be allowed.
   e.   You're angry at someone in the room.

This experiment shows that, short of charades, nonverbal messages are much better at expressing attitudes (a, c, and e) than other sorts of messages (b and d). Among other limitations, nonverbal messages can't convey:

Simple matters of fact ("The book was written in 1997.")

The past or future tenses ("I was happy yesterday"; "I'll be out of town next week.")

An imaginary idea ("What would it be like if . . .")

Conditional statements ("If I don't get a job, I'll have to move out.")

As technology develops, an increasing number of Internet and phone messages will include both visual and vocal dimensions, making communication richer and enhancing understanding.[9] At present, most text, instant, and e-mail messages offer fewer nonverbal cues about the speaker's feelings than do face-to-face encounters, or even telephone voice conversations. New e-mail and IM users soon learn that their messages can be and often are misunderstood. Probably the biggest problems arise from joking remarks being taken as serious statements. To solve these problems, electronic text correspondents have developed a series of symbols—called emoticons or smileys—that can be created using keyboard characters to simulate nonverbal dimensions of a message. The following list contains some of the most common ones. (Because of formatting limitations

---

Proposed Smirking Ban Raises Eyebrows

SAN FRANCISCO
(Reuters)–A raised eyebrow, loud guffaw, smirk or other facial expressions could all be banned in future political debate under new rules proposed for the city council in Palo Alto, California.

In a bid to improve civility in the town's public discourse, a committee on the city council has spent hours debating guidelines for its own behavior.

"Do not use body language or other nonverbal methods of expression, disagreement or disgust," a new list of proposed conduct rules reads.

Another rule calls for council members to address each other with titles followed by last names, a formality not always practiced in laid-back California.

"I don't want to muzzle my colleagues," councilwoman Judy Kleinberg, who headed the committee that drafted the rules, told the San Jose Mercury News. But, she added: "I don't think the people sitting around the cabinet with the president roll their eyes."

Communication Transcript

Recognizing Nonverbal Cues

You can appreciate how nonverbal cues reflect attitudes by reading the following transcript twice. The first time, imagine that Kim's nonverbal behavior signals that she is glad to meet Stacy, and looking forward to getting to know her better. For your second reading, imagine that Kim feels just the opposite: She is put off by Stacy, and feels uncomfortable around her.

Think about all the ways Kim's nonverbal behaviors might change, depending on her attitude toward Stacy. Even though she speaks the same words, imagine how her posture, gestures, facial expressions, voice, and her use of distance might differ, and how these nonverbal cues would reflect her feelings about her new neighbor.

You can watch a video of this transcript through your Looking Out/Looking In *Online Textbook Resources. (See the pages near the inside front and back covers of this book for more about your Online Textbook Resources.)*

Stacy: Hi. I'm new here. Just moved in to Unit 14 yesterday. My name's Stacy. *Extends her hand, ready to shake.*

Kim: Hi! I'm Kim. I'm your next-door neighbor in number 12.

Stacy: Great! This looks like a nice place.

Kim: It is. Everybody's friendly, and we all get along really well.

Stacy (*glancing down at a magazine in Kim's mail*): Hmmm. *American Songwriter.* Are you a musician?

Kim: Yeah, I'm a singer-songwriter. Mostly acoustic. I play around town. Nothing too big yet, but I'm hoping . . .

Stacy (*excitedly*):   Whoa! I'm a musician too!

Kim: Really!

Stacy: Yeah. I play rhythm guitar with The Festering Sores. Have you heard of us?

Kim: Yeah, I think so.

Stacy: Well, you'll have to come hear us some time. And maybe we could even jam together, since we're both guitarists.

Kim: That would be interesting!

Stacy: Wow! I can already tell I'm going to like it here. Hey . . . what's the attitude around here about pets?

Kim: They're pretty strict about the "No dogs or cats" policy.

Stacy: No problem! Jezebel isn't either.

Kim: Well, what *is* Jezebel?

Stacy (*proudly*):   She's a green iguana. A real beauty.

Kim: You're kidding, right?

Stacy: Nope. You'll probably meet her one of these days. In fact, she's kind of a run-away, so you might find her in your place if you leave the door open. Especially when the weather cools down. (*Semi-kidding*) She really likes to snuggle up to a warm body.

Kim: Well, I'm more of a bird person, so . . .

Stacy: She makes friends with everybody. You'll love her!

Kim: Look, I've gotta run. I'm already late for a practice session.

Stacy: I'll see you around. Really glad we're gonna be neighbors!

Kim: Me too.

---

that come with computer-mediated communication, emoticons appear in a side-to-side orientation rather than up and down.) Note that, like most nonverbal messages, emoticons can have multiple meanings.

:-)	Basic smile. Most commonly used to indicate humorous intent. ("No offense intended.")
:- D	Big smile
;-)	Wink and grin. Sometimes used to indicate sarcasm or say, "Don't hit me for what I just said."
:- (	Frown
:- I	Indifference
:- @	Screaming, swearing, very angry

:- |	Disgusted, grim
:˜- (	Crying
:-/ or :-\	Skeptical
:- O	Surprised, yelling, realization of an error. ("Oops!")

As you read in Chapter 5, electronic communicators can also use linguistic shortcuts and acronyms to indicate nonverbal responses, such as <frown> or "WEG" for "wicked evil grin." Of course, it's important to understand that these markers are also identity-management tools, as discussed in Chapter 2. Do writers actually grin when writing <grin>, and do they really scream and swear while typing :-@—or are they simply trying to create an impression of how they think and feel? Toward that end, emoticons and shortcuts like these may be helpful, but they clearly aren't an adequate substitute for the rich mixture of nonverbal messages that flows in face-to-face exchanges. That fact explains why the International Academy of Digital Arts & Sciences offered a $10,000 grant to the person or group that devises "a viable way to infuse digital communication with the same individuality and unspoken cues common in face-to-face interactions."[10]

Nonverbal Communication Serves Many Functions

Just because this chapter focuses on nonverbal communication, don't get the idea that our words and our actions are unrelated. Quite the opposite is true: Verbal and nonverbal communication are interconnected elements in every act of communication. (See Table 6.2 for a comparison of verbal and nonverbal communication.) Nonverbal behaviors can operate in several relationships with verbal behaviors.

Repeating   If someone asked you for directions to the nearest drugstore, you might say, "North of here about two blocks," **repeating** your instructions nonverbally by pointing north. This sort of repetition isn't just decorative: People remember comments accompanied by gestures more than those made with words alone.[11]

Complementing   Even when it doesn't repeat language, nonverbal behavior can reinforce what's been said. **Complementing** nonverbal behaviors match the thoughts and emotions the communicator is expressing linguistically. You can appreciate the value of this function by imagining the difference between saying "thank you" with a sincere facial expression and tone of voice, and saying the same words in a deadpan manner.

Table 6.2	**Some Differences between Verbal and Nonverbal Communication**	
	Verbal Communication	Nonverbal Communication
Complexity	One dimension (words only)	Multiple dimensions (voice, posture, gestures, distance, etc.)
Flow	Intermittent (speaking and silence alternate)	Continuous (it's impossible to not communicate nonverbally)
Clarity	Less subject to misinterpretation	More ambiguous
Impact	Has less impact when verbal and nonverbal cues are contradictory	Has stronger impact when verbal and nonverbal cues are contradictory
Intentionality	Usually deliberate	Often unintentional

Substituting   When a friend asks, "What's up?" you might shrug your shoulders instead of answering in words. Many facial expressions operate as substitutes for speech. It's easy to recognize expressions that function like verbal interjections and say "gosh," "really?" "oh, please!" and so on.[12] Nonverbal **substituting** can be useful when communicators are reluctant to express their feelings in words. Faced with a message you find disagreeable, you might sigh, roll your eyes, or yawn when speaking out would not be appropriate. Likewise, a parent who wants a child to stop being disruptive at a party can flash a glare across the room without saying a word (and what child doesn't know the power of "the look" from Mom or Dad?).

Accenting   Just as we use italics to emphasize an idea in print, we use nonverbal devices to emphasize oral messages. Pointing an accusing finger adds emphasis to criticism (as well as probably creating defensiveness in the receiver). **Accenting** certain words with the voice ("It was *your* idea!") is another way to add nonverbal emphasis.

Regulating   Nonverbal behaviors can serve a **regulating** function by influencing the flow of verbal communication. For example, parties in a conversation often unconsciously send and receive turn-taking cues through the way they use their voice.[13] When you are ready to yield the floor, the unstated rule is this: Create a rising vocal intonation pattern, then use a falling intonation pattern or draw out the final syllable of the clause at the end of your statement. Finally, stop speaking. If you want to maintain your turn when another speaker seems ready to cut you off, you can suppress the attempt by taking an audible breath, using a sustained intonation pattern (because rising and falling patterns suggest the end of a statement), and avoiding any pauses in your speech. We can also regulate conversations nonverbally by nodding (indicating "I understand" or "keep going"), looking away (signaling a lack of attention), or moving toward the door (communicating a desire to end the conversation). Of course, most of us have learned the hard way that nonverbal signals like these don't guarantee that the other party will pay attention to, interpret, or respond to them in the ways we had hoped.

She dresses in flags
comes on
like a mack truck
she paints
her eyelids green
and her mouth
is a loud speaker rasping
  out
profanity
at cocktail parties

she is everywhere
like a sheep dog
working a flock
nipping at your sleeve
spilling your drink
bestowing
wet sloppy kisses
but i
have received
secret messages

carefully written
from the shy
quiet woman
who hides
in this
bizarre
gaudy castle

Ric Masten

I suppose it was something you said That caused me to tighten and pull away. And when you asked, "What is it?" I, of course, said, "Nothing." Whenever I say, "Nothing." You may be very certain there is something. The something is a cold, hard lump of Nothing.

Lois Wyse

Contradicting   People often simultaneously express different and even contradictory messages in their verbal and nonverbal behaviors. A common example of this sort of **mixed message** is the experience we've all had of hearing someone with a red face and bulging veins yelling, "Angry? No, *I'm not angry!*"

Even though some of the ways in which people **contradict** themselves are subtle, mixed messages have a strong impact. As we grow older we become better at interpreting these mixed messages. Children between the ages of 6 and 12 use a speaker's words to make sense of a message. But as adults, we rely more on nonverbal cues to form many impressions. For example, audiences put more emphasis on nonverbal cues than on words to decide whether speakers are honest.[14] They also use nonverbal behaviors to judge the character of speakers as well as their competence and composure; and differences in nonverbal behaviors influence how much listeners are persuaded by a speaker.[15] Even the slightest contradiction in verbal and nonverbal messages may suggest that a speaker is being deceptive, as we'll describe in the following section.

Deceiving   Deception is perhaps the most interesting type of double message. Signals of deception—often called **leakage**—can occur in every type of nonverbal behavior. A strong indicator of deception is inconsistency. Changes in a person's normal pattern of behavior alert us that deception may be occurring.[16] Some nonverbal channels are more revealing than others. Facial expressions are less revealing than body clues, probably because deceivers pay more attention to controlling their faces. Even more useful is the voice, which offers a rich variety of leakage clues.[17] In one experiment, subjects who were encouraged to be deceitful made more speech errors, spoke for shorter periods of time, and had a lower rate of speech than did others who were encouraged to express themselves honestly. Another experiment revealed that the vocal frequency of a liar's voice tends to be higher than that of a truth teller. Research also shows that deceivers delivering a prepared lie responded more quickly than truth tellers, mainly because there was less thinking involved. When unprepared, however, deceivers generally took longer than both prepared deceivers and truth tellers. Table 6.3 outlines some conditions under which liars are likely to betray themselves through nonverbal leakage.

A variety of self-help books and seminars claim that liars can be easily identified by monitoring their nonverbal cues, but scientific research doesn't support that notion. Studies show that most people have only about a coin-flip's chance—50 percent—of accurately identifying someone who is lying.[18] As one writer put it, "There is no unique telltale signal for a fib. Pinocchio's nose just doesn't exist, and that makes liars difficult to spot."[19] Moreover, some popular prescriptions about liars' nonverbal behaviors are less than helpful. For instance, conventional wisdom suggests that liars avert their gaze and fidget more than nonliars. Research,

"I knew the suspect was lying because of certain telltale discrepancies between his voice and nonverbal gestures. Also his pants were on fire."

MANKOFF

Table 6.3	**Leakage of Nonverbal Cues to Deception**

Deception Cues Are Most Likely When the Deceiver
Wants to hide emotions being felt at the moment
Feels strongly about the information being hidden
Feels apprehensive about the deception
Feels guilty about being deceptive
Gets little enjoyment from being deceptive
Needs to construct the message carefully while delivering it

Deception Cues Are Least Likely When the Deceiver
Wants to hide information unrelated to his or her emotions
Has no strong feelings about the information being hidden
Feels confident about the deception
Experiences little guilt about the deception
Enjoys the deception
Knows the deceptive message well and has rehearsed it

Based on "Mistakes When Deceiving" by Paul Ekman, in Thomas A. Sebeok and Robert Rosenthal, eds., *The Clever Hans Phenomenon: Communication with Horses, Whales, Apes, and People* (New York: New York Academy of Sciences, 1981), pp. 269–278.

however, shows just the opposite: Liars often sustain *more* eye contact and fidget *less*, in part because they believe that do otherwise might look deceitful.[20] In other words, while it's possible to make some generalizations about the nonverbal tendencies of liars, caution should be exercised in making evaluations of others' truth-telling based on limited and ambiguous nonverbal cues.

Nonverbal Communication Is Ambiguous

You learned in Chapter 5 that verbal messages are open to multiple interpretations; but nonverbal messages are even more ambiguous. Consider the example of a wink: In one study, college students interpreted this nonverbal signal as meaning a variety of things, including an expression of thanks, a sign of friendliness, a measure of insecurity, a sexual come-on, and an eye problem.[21]

Even the most common nonverbal behavior can be ambiguous. Imagine two possible meanings of silence from a normally talkative friend. Or suppose that a much-admired person with whom you've worked suddenly begins paying more attention to you than ever before. What could some possible meanings of this behavior be? Although nonverbal behavior can be very revealing, it can have so many possible meanings that it's impossible to be certain which interpretation is correct.

The ambiguous nature of nonverbal behavior becomes clear in the area of courtship and sexuality. Does a kiss mean "I like you a lot" or "I want to have sex"? Does pulling away from a romantic partner mean "Stop now" or "Keep trying"?

Safeway Clerks Object to "Service with a Smile" Policy

Twelve Safeway employees have filed grievances over the supermarket chain's smile-and-make-eye-contact rule, complaining that they are being propositioned by shoppers who mistake company-required friendliness for flirting.

Under Safeway's "Superior Service" policy, employees are expected to anticipate customers' needs, take them to items they cannot find, make selling suggestions, thank them by name if they pay by check or credit card and offer to carry out their groceries.

Richelle Roberts, a produce clerk, said she is hit on every day by men who think she is coming on to them. Another produce worker, who spoke on condition of anonymity, said she has hidden in a back room to avoid customers who have harassed her, propositioned her and followed her to her car.

San Francisco Chronicle

Communication researchers explored this question by surveying one hundred college students about sexual consent in twelve dating scenarios in order to discover under what conditions verbal approaches (for example, "Do you want to have sex with me?") were considered preferable to nonverbal indicators (such as, kissing as an indicator of a desire to have sex).[22] In every scenario, verbal consent was seen as less ambiguous than nonverbal consent. This doesn't mean that romantic partners don't rely on nonverbal signals; many of the respondents indicated that they interpret nonverbal cues (such as kissing) as signs of sexual willingness. However, nonverbal cues were far less likely to be misunderstood when accompanied by verbal cues. The conclusions of this research seem obvious: Verbal messages are clearer than nonverbal messages in matters of sexual consent. Just because they are clearer, however, doesn't mean that they are practiced. Using clearer and less ambiguous verbal messages could reduce a variety of unfortunate outcomes.

Not all nonverbal behavior is equally ambiguous. In laboratory settings, subjects are better at identifying positive facial expressions of feelings such as happiness, love, surprise, and interest than negative expressions of feelings such as fear, sadness, anger, and disgust.[23] In real life, however, spontaneous nonverbal expressions are so ambiguous that observers are unable to identify the emotions they convey with accuracy any better than blind guessing.[24] Even the best nonverbal decoders do not approach 100 percent accuracy.

Some people have more difficulty decoding nonverbal signals than do others. For instance, young boys often miss the emotional messages that others send them nonverbally, such as when a teacher attempts to express displeasure through arched eyebrows.[25] For people with a syndrome called nonverbal learning disorder (NVLD), reading facial expression, tone of voice, and other cues is dramatically more difficult.[26] Due to a processing deficit in the right hemisphere of the brain, people with NVLD have trouble making sense of many nonverbal cues. Humor or sarcasm can be especially hard to understand for people—especially children—with NVLD. They often interpret these messages literally, missing the cues that indicate the speaker's real meaning. They have trouble figuring out how to behave appropriately in new situations, so they rely on rote formulas that often don't work. For example,

> . . . if they learn the right way to introduce themselves to an unfamiliar adult (by shaking hands and saying "pleased to meet you") they may attempt the same response in a group of children where it might be viewed as odd or "nerdy." When peers do give them subtle feedback, such as raised eyebrows, they miss the information completely and therefore cannot modify their behavior next time.[27]

Even for those of us who don't suffer from NVLD, the ambiguity of non-verbal behavior can be frustrating. The perception-checking skill you learned in Chapter 3 can be a useful tool for figuring out what meanings you can accurately attach to confusing cues.

Invitation to Insight

Reading "Body Language"

While going through the supermarket checkout stand or waiting for a plane, you've probably noticed books that promise to teach you how to read "body language." These books claim that you can become a kind of mind reader, learning the deepest secrets of everyone around you. But it's not quite as simple as it sounds. Here's an exercise that will both increase your skill in observing nonverbal behavior and show you the dangers of being too sure that you're a perfect reader of body language. You can try the exercise either in or out of class, and the period of time over which you do it is flexible, from a single class period to several days. In any case, begin by choosing a partner, and then follow these directions:

1. For the first period of time (however long you decide to make it), observe the way your partner behaves. Notice movements, mannerisms, postures, style of dress, and so on. To remember your observations, jot them down. If you're doing this exercise out of class over an extended period of time, there's no need to let your observations interfere with whatever you'd normally be doing: Your only job here is to compile a list of your partner's behaviors. In this step you should be careful *not to interpret* your partner's behaviors; just record what you see.

2. At the end of the time period, share what you've seen with your partner, who should do the same with you.

3. For the next period of time your job is not only to observe your partner's behavior but also to *interpret* it. This time in your conference you should tell your partner what you thought his or her behaviors revealed. For example, does careless dressing suggest oversleeping, loss of interest in appearance, or the desire to feel more comfortable? If you noticed frequent yawning, did you think this meant boredom, fatigue after a late night, or sleepiness after a big meal? Don't feel bad if your guesses weren't all correct. Remember that nonverbal clues tend to be ambiguous. You may be surprised how checking out the nonverbal clues you observe can help build a relationship with another person.

This exercise should have shown you the difference between merely observing somebody's behavior and actually interpreting it. Noticing someone's shaky hands or smile is one thing, but deciding what such behaviors mean is quite another. If you're like most people, you probably found that a lot of your guesses were incorrect. Now, if that was true here, it may also be true in your daily life. Being a sharp nonverbal observer can give you some good hunches about how people are feeling, but the only way you can find out if these hunches are correct is to check them out verbally.

Brent Staples: Nonverbal Stereotyping

My first victim was a woman— white, well dressed, probably in her early twenties. I came upon her late one evening on a deserted street in Hyde Park, a relatively affluent neigh- borhood in an otherwise mean, impoverished section of Chicago. As I swung onto the avenue behind her, there seemed to be a discreet, unin- flammatory distance between us. Not so. She cast back a worried glance. To her, the youngish black man—a broad 6 feet 2 inches with a beard and billowing hair, both hands shoved into the pockets of a bulky military jacket—seemed menacingly close. After a few more quick glimpses, she picked up her pace and was soon running in earnest. Within seconds she disappeared into a cross street. As a softy who is scarcely able to take a knife to a raw chicken—let alone hold on to a person's throat—I was surprised, embarrassed, and dis- mayed all at once.

That first encounter, and those that followed, sig- nified that a vast, unnerving gulf lay between nighttime pedestrians—particularly women—and me.

After dark, on the warrenlike streets of Brooklyn where I live, I often see women who fear the worst from me. They seem to have set their faces on neutral, and with their purse straps strung across their chests ban- dolier-style, they forge ahead as though bracing them- selves against being tackled. I understand, of course, that the danger they perceive is not a hallucination. Women are particularly vulnerable to street violence, and young black males are drastically overrepresented

among the perpetrators of that violence. Yet these truths are no solace against the kind of alienation that comes of being ever the suspect, a fearsome entity with whom pedestrians avoid making eye contact.

Over the years, I learned to smother the rage I felt at so often being taken for a criminal. Not to do so would surely have led to madness. I now take precau- tions to make myself less threatening. I move about with care, particularly late in the evening. I give a wide berth to nervous people on subway platforms during the wee hours, particularly when I have exchanged business clothes for jeans. If I happen to be entering a building behind some people who appear skittish, I may walk by, letting them clear the lobby before I return, so as not to seem to be following them. I have been calm and extremely congenial on those rare occasions when I've been pulled over by the police.

And on late-evening constitutionals I employ what has proved to be an excellent tension-reducing meas- ure: I whistle melodies from Beethoven and Vivaldi and the more popular classical composers. Even steely New Yorkers hunching toward nighttime destinations seem to relax, and occasionally they even join in the tune. Virtually everybody seems to sense that a mugger wouldn't be warbling bright, sunny selections from Vivaldi's *Four Seasons*. It is my equivalent of the cow- bell that hikers wear when they know they are in bear country.

Brent Staples, from "Black Men and Public Spaces"

Photo courtesy of Brent Staples

Influences on Nonverbal Communication

The way we communicate nonverbally is influenced to a certain degree by bio- logical sex and to a great degree by the way we are socialized. To learn more about these influences, read on.

Gender

It's easy to identify stereotypical differences in male and female styles of nonver- bal communication. Just think about exaggerated caricatures of macho men and delicate women that appear from time to time. Many humorous films and plays have been created around the results that arise when characters try to act like members of the opposite sex. (For some examples, see the "Films" section under "Media Resources" at the end of this chapter.)

Although few of us behave like stereotypically masculine or feminine movie characters, there are recognizable differences in the way men and women look and act. Some of the most obvious differences are physiological: height, depth and volume of the voice, and so on. Other differences are social. For example, females are usually more nonverbally expressive, and they are better at recognizing others' nonverbal behavior.[28]

Most communication scholars agree that other factors have more influence than biology does in shaping how men and women behave. For example, the ability to read nonverbal cues may have more to do with women's historically less powerful social status: People in subordinate work positions also have better decoding skills.[29] As women continue to gain equal status in the workplace and home, a paradoxical result may be less sensitivity at reading nonverbal cues.

Cultural norms in the western world distinguish male from female behaviors.[30] For example, women make more eye contact than do men with conversational partners. They are more vocally expressive than men. Women interact at closer distances, both with men and with other women, than do men in same-sex conversations. Men are more likely to lean forward in conversations than women; men require and are given more personal space than women. Women are more likely to face conversational partners head on, whereas men more typically stand at an angle. Women express more emotions via facial expressions than men. Most noticeably, women smile considerably more than men.[31] Women gesture more, whereas men use more expansive gestures.

After looking at differences like these, it might seem as if men and women communicate in radically different ways. In fact, men's and women's nonverbal communication is more similar than different in many respects.[32] Differences like the ones described in the preceding paragraph are noticeable, but they are outweighed by the similar rules we follow in areas such as making eye contact, posture, gestures, and so on. You can prove this by imagining what it would be like to use radically different nonverbal rules: standing only an inch away from others, sniffing strangers, or tapping the forehead of someone when you want his or her attention. While biological sex and cultural norms certainly have an influence on nonverbal style, they aren't as dramatic as the Mars-Venus thesis suggests.

Culture

Cultures have different nonverbal languages as well as verbal ones.[33] Fiorello LaGuardia, legendary mayor of New York from 1933 to 1945, was fluent in English, Italian, and Yiddish. Researchers who watched films of his campaign speeches found that they could tell with the sound turned off which language he was speaking by noticing the changes in his nonverbal behavior.[34]

Some nonverbal behaviors have different meanings from culture to culture. The "OK" gesture made by joining the tips of thumb and forefinger to form a circle is a cheery affirmation to most Americans, but it has less positive meanings in other parts of the world.[35] In France and Belgium it means "You're worth zero." In Greece and Turkey it is a vulgar sexual invitation, usually meant as an insult. Given this sort of cross-cultural ambiguity, it's easy to imagine how an innocent tourist might wind up in serious trouble.

Cultural background also influences the way we interpret others' emotions as well as the way we express our own. In one experiment, an ethnically varied

The men walked hand-in-hand, laughing sleepily together under blinding vertical glare. Sometimes they put their arms round each other's necks; they seemed to like to touch each other, as if it made them feel good to know the other man was there. It wasn't love; it didn't mean anything we could understand.

Graham Greene, *Journey without Maps*

group of students—Caucasian, black, Asian, and Hispanic—identified the type, intensity, and appropriateness of emotional expression in fifty-six photos representing eight social situations (such as alone, with a friend, in public, with someone of higher status).[36] Ethnicity led to considerable differences in the way the subjects gauged others' emotional states. For example, blacks perceived the emotions in the photos as more intense than the Caucasian, Asian, and Hispanic subjects; Asians perceived them the least intense. Also, blacks reported a greater frequency of anger expressions than did the other groups. Ethnicity also shaped ideas about appropriate rules for expressing one's own emotions. For example, Caucasians perceived the display of several emotions as more appropriate than did the other groups; Asians perceived the display as less appropriate. These findings remind us that, in a multicultural society, one element of communicative competence is the ability to understand our own cultural filters when judging others' behaviors.

People seem to be aware of differences like these, which explains why we tend to be more comfortable interpreting the behavior of people from backgrounds similar to ours. In one study, immigrants felt more confident about interpreting the facial expressions of people from their home countries than from members of the host country or another cultural group.[37]

Even though we recognize that differences exist in the nonverbal rules of different cultures, subtle differences can damage relationships without the parties ever recognizing exactly what has gone wrong. Anthropologist Edward Hall points out that, whereas Americans are comfortable conducting business at a distance of roughly 4 feet, people from the Middle East stand much closer.[38] It is easy to visualize the awkward advance-and-retreat pattern that might occur when two diplomats or businesspeople from these cultures meet. The Middle Easterner would probably keep moving forward to close the gap, whereas the American would continually back away. Both would feel uncomfortable, probably without knowing why.

Communicators become more tolerant of others after they understand that unusual nonverbal behaviors are the result of cultural differences. In one study, American adults were presented with videotapes of speakers from the United States, France, and Germany.[39] When the sound was eliminated, viewers judged foreigners more negatively than their fellow citizens. But when the speakers' voices were added (allowing viewers to recognize that the speakers were from a different country), the critical ratings dropped. Communicators can also learn to become more aware of other cultures' nonverbal traits. Research shows that training can significantly improve the accuracy of judging facial expressions of emotion, particularly in cross-cultural situations.[40]

Like distance, patterns of eye contact vary around the world.[41] A direct gaze is considered appropriate, if not imperative for speakers seeking power in Latin America, the Arab world, and southern Europe. On the other hand, Asians, Indians, Pakistanis, and northern Europeans gaze at a listener peripherally or not at all.[42] In either case, deviations from the norm are likely to make a listener uncomfortable.

As Table 6.4 shows, differences can lead to misunderstandings. For example, observations have shown that black women in all-black groups are nonverbally more expressive and interrupt one another more than white women in all-white groups. This doesn't mean that black women always feel more intensely than their white counterparts. A more likely explanation is that the two groups follow different cultural rules. The researchers found that in racially mixed groups both black and white women moved closer to each others' style.[43] This nonverbal convergence shows that skilled communicators can adapt their behavior when interacting with members of other cultures or subcultures in order to make the exchange smoother and more effective.

Table 6.4 Cultural Differences in Nonverbal Communication Can Lead to Misunderstandings

Behaviors that have one meaning for members of the same culture or co-culture can be interpreted differently by members of other groups.

Behavior	Probable In-Group Perception	Possible Out-Group Perception
Avoidance of direct eye contact (Latino/a)	Used to communicate attentiveness or respect	A sign of inattentiveness; direct eye contact is preferred
Aggressively challenging a point with which one disagrees (African American)	Acceptable means of dialogue; not regarded as verbal abuse or a precursor to violence	Arguments are viewed as inappropriate and a sign of potential imminent violence
Use of finger gestures to beckon others (Asian)	Appropriate if used by adults for children, but highly offensive if directed at adults	Appropriate gesture to use with both children and adults
Silence (Native American)	Sign of respect, thoughtfulness, and/or uncertainty/ambiguity	Interpreted as boredom, disagreement, or refusal to participate
Touch (Latino/a)	Normal and appropriate for interpersonal interactions	Deemed appropriate for some intimate or friendly interactions; otherwise perceived as a violations of personal space.
Public display of intense emotions (African American)	Accepted and valued as measure of expressiveness; appropriate in most settings	Violates expectations for self-controlled public behaviors; inappropriate in most public settings
Touching or holding hands of same-sex friends (Asian)	Acceptable in behavior that signifies closeness in platonic relationships	Perceived as inappropriate, especially for male friends

From *Interracial Communication Theory into Practice* (with InfoTrac College Edition), 1st ed., by M. P. Orbe and T. M. Harris ©2001. Reprinted with permission of Wadsworth, an imprint of Wadsworth Group, a division of Thomson Learning.

Why Arab Men Hold Hands

When President Bush and Crown Prince Abdullah of Saudi Arabia met in Crawford, Tex., they did something very un-Texan: they walked hand in hand.

Americans may raise an eyebrow at men holding hands, but in the Arab world, affection among men is common, and without sexual connotation.

"Holding hands is the warmest expression of affection between men," said Samir Khalaf, a professor at American University of Beirut in Lebanon. "It's a sign of solidarity and kinship."

In fact, if a man chooses not to touch another in a greeting, it can be interpreted as a sign of distance or disdain. Kissing cheeks, long handshakes and clutching hands are meant to reflect amity, devotion and most important, equality in status, noted Fuad Ishak Khuri, a social anthropologist, in his book, *The Body in Islamic Culture* (2001).

Strangers, on the other hand, do not kiss or hold hands, and the strong do not kiss the weak, wrote Mr. Khuri. And because the sexes are segregated, men rarely have the chance to touch or show affection toward a woman.

"Arab culture has historically been segregated, so emotions and feelings are channeled to the same sex," said Musa Shteiwi, a professor at the University of Jordan. "Men spend a lot of time together, and these customs grew out of that."

But as the Arab world changes, so do the customs. With growing urbanization and increased contact between the sexes, Professor Shteiwi noted, such gestures are slowly becoming dated. It's rare to see men holding hands in a city like Beirut, where the sexes mingle openly, though it is still commonplace in Saudi Arabia and other countries where sex segregation remains strong.

Some expatriates have learned to blend in. As militants targeted Westerners in Saudi Arabia last year, one Saudi businessman gave a friend advice: "Stroll like you have nowhere important to go, and if you see a friend's hand next to you, grab it."

Hassan M. Fattah

Invitation to Insight

Gestures Around the World

ThomsonNOW Before reading any further, take an online quiz to check your understanding of how nonverbal communication can operate in different cultures around the world. Go to your ThomsonNOW for *Looking Out/Looking In* to access the link to this site.

Despite the many cultural differences, some nonverbal behaviors have the same meanings around the world. Smiles and laughter are universal signals of positive emotions, for example, whereas sour expressions are universal signals of displeasure.[44] Charles Darwin believed that expressions like these are the result of evolution, functioning as survival mechanisms that allowed early humans to convey emotional states before the development of language. The innateness of some facial expressions becomes even clearer when we examine the behavior of children born deaf and blind.[45] Despite a lack of social learning, these children display a broad range of expression. They smile, laugh, and cry in ways virtually identical to those of seeing and hearing children. In other words, nonverbal behavior—like much of our communication—is influenced by both our genetic heritage and our culture.

Types of Nonverbal Communication

Keeping the characteristics of nonverbal communication in mind, let's take a look at some of the ways we communicate in addition to words.

Body Movement

The first area of nonverbal communication we'll discuss is the broad field of **kinesics**, or body position and motion. In this section we'll explore the role that body orientation, posture, gestures, facial expressions, and eye contact play in our relationships with one another.

Body Orientation   We'll start with **body orientation**—the degree to which we face toward or away from someone with our body, feet, and head. To understand how this kind of physical positioning communicates nonverbal messages, imagine that you and a friend are in the middle of a conversation when a third person approaches and wants to join you. You're not especially glad to see this person, but you don't want to sound rude by asking him to leave. By turning your body slightly away from the intruder you can make your feelings very clear. The non-verbal message here is "We're interested in each other right now and don't want to include you in our conversation." The general rule is that facing someone directly signals your interest and facing away signals a desire to avoid involvement.

You can learn a good deal about how people feel by observing the way people position themselves. The next time you're in a crowded place where people can choose whom to face directly, try noticing who seems to be included in the action and who is being subtly shut out. And in the same way, pay attention to your own body orientation. You may be surprised to discover that you're avoiding a certain person without being conscious of it or that at times you're "turning your back" on people altogether. If this is the case, it may be helpful to figure out why.

Posture   Another way we communicate nonverbally is through our **posture**. To see if this is true, stop reading for a moment and notice how you're sitting. What does your position say nonverbally about how you feel? Are there any

Fie, fie upon her! There's language in her eyes, her cheek, her lip. Nay, her foot speaks; her wanton spirits look out at every joint and motive in her body.

William Shakespeare, *Troilus and Cressida*

© Dale Kennington/SuperStock

Nonverbal Communication Means

Smiling, frowning
laughing, crying, sighing
standing close to others
being standoffish
The way you look:
your hair, your clothing
your face, your body
your handshake (sweaty
palms?)
your posture
your gestures
your mannerisms
Your voice:
soft-loud
fast-slow
smooth-jerky
The environment that you
create:
your home, your room
your office, your desk
your kitchen, your car

other people near you now? What messages do you get from their present posture? By paying attention to the postures of those around you, as well as your own, you'll find another channel of nonverbal communication that can furnish information about how people feel about themselves and one another.

An indication of how much posture communicates is shown by our language. It's full of expressions that link emotional states with body postures:

I won't take this lying down! (Nor will I stand for it!)

I feel the weight of the world on my shoulders.

He's a real slouch in the office (but he's no slouch on the basketball court).

She's been sitting on that project for weeks.

Posture may be the least ambiguous type of nonverbal behavior. In one study, 176 computer-generated mannequin figures were created and observers were asked to assign emotions to particular postural configurations. The raters had over 90 percent agreement on postures that were connected with anger, sadness, and happiness.[46] Some postures seem easier to interpret than others. Disgust was the emotion that was hardest to identify from body posture, and some raters thought that surprise and happiness had similar postural configurations.

Tension and relaxation offer other postural keys to feelings. We take relaxed postures in nonthreatening situations and tighten up in threatening situations.[47] Based on this observation, we can tell a good deal about how others feel simply by watching how tense or loose they seem to be. For example, tenseness is a way of detecting status differences: The lower-status person is generally the more rigid, tense-appearing one, whereas the higher-status person is more relaxed. This often happens when an employee sits ramrod straight while the boss leans back in her chair. The same principle applies to social situations, where it's often possible to tell who's uncomfortable by looking at pictures. Often you'll see someone laughing and talking as if he were perfectly at home, but his posture almost shouts nervousness. Some people never relax, and their posture shows it.

Gestures   **Gestures**—movements of the hands and arms—are an important type of nonverbal communication. In fact, they are so basic to our nature that people who have been blind from birth use them.[48] Some social scientists claim that a language of gestures was the first form of human communication, preceding speech by tens of thousands of years.[49]

The most common forms of gestures are what social scientists call **illustrators**—movements that accompany speech but don't stand on their own.[50] For instance, if someone on a street corner asked you how to get to a restaurant across town, you might offer street names and addresses—but all the while, you'd probably point with your fingers and gesture with your hands to illustrate how to get there. Remove the words from your directions and it's unlikely that the other person would ever find the restaurant. Think also of people who like to "talk with their hands," gesturing vigorously even when they're conversing on the phone and can't be seen by the other party. Research shows that North Americans use illustrators more often when they are emotionally aroused—trying to explain ideas that are difficult to put into words when they are furious, horrified, agitated, distressed, or excited.[51] Studies also show that it is easier to comprehend and learn a second language when it is accompanied by illustrators and other nonverbal cues.[52]

A second type of gestures is **emblems**—deliberate nonverbal behaviors that have a precise meaning, known to virtually everyone within a cultural group.

The Look of a Victim

© J. L. Anderson/Robertstock.com

Little Red Riding Hood set herself up to be mugged. Her first mistake was skipping through the forest to grandma's house. Her second mistake was stopping to pick flowers. At this point, as you might remember in the story, the mean, heavy wolf comes along and begins to check her out. He observes, quite perceptively, that she is happy, outgoing, and basically unaware of any dangers in her surrounding environment. The big bad wolf catches these nonverbal clues and splits to grandma's house. He knows that Red is an easy mark. From this point we all know what happens.

Body movements and gestures reveal a lot of information about a person. Like Little Red Riding Hood, pedestrians may signal to criminals that they are easy targets for mugging by the way they walk. When was the last time you assessed your "muggability rating"? In a recent study two psychologists set out to identify those body movements that characterized easy victims. They assembled "muggability ratings" of sixty New York pedestrians from the people who may have been the most qualified to judge— prison inmates who had been convicted of assault.

The researchers unobtrusively videotaped pedestrians on weekdays between 10:00 A.M. and 12:00 P.M. Each pedestrian was taped for 6 to 8 seconds, the approximate time it takes for a mugger to size up an approaching person. The judges (prison inmates) rated the "assault potential" of the sixty pedestrians on a 10-point scale. A rating of 1 indicated someone was "a very easy rip-off," of 2, "an easy dude to corner." Toward the other end of the scale, 9 meant a person "would be heavy; would give you a hard time," and 10 indicated that the mugger "would avoid it, too big a situation, too heavy." The results revealed several body movements that characterized easy victims: "Their strides were either very long or very short; they moved awkwardly, raising their left legs with their left arms (instead of alternating them); on each step they tended to lift their whole foot up and then place it down (less muggable sorts took steps in which their feet rocked from heel to toe). Overall, the people rated most muggable walked as if they were in conflict with themselves; they seemed to make each move in the most difficult way possible."

Loretta Malandro and Larry Barker

Unlike illustrators, emblems can stand on their own and often function as replacements for words. For example, all North Americans know that a head nod means "yes," a head shake means "no," a wave means "hello" or "goodbye," and a hand to the ear means "I can't hear you." And almost every Westerner over the age of 7 knows the meaning of a raised middle finger. It's important to remember, however, that the meanings of emblems like these are not universal. For instance, the "thumbs up" sign means "good" in the U.S. but is an obscene gesture in Iraq and several other countries.[53]

A third type of gestures is **adaptors**—unconscious bodily movements in response to the environment. For instance, shivering when it's cold and folding your arms to get warmer are examples of adaptors. Of course, sometimes we cross our arms when we're feeling "cold" toward another person—and thus adaptors can reveal the climate of our relationships. In particular, self-touching behaviors—sometimes called **manipulators**—are often a sign of discomfort, such as fiddling with your hands or rubbing your arms during an interview.[54] But not *all* fidgeting signals uneasiness. People also are likely to engage in self-touching when relaxed. When they let down their guard (either alone or with friends), they will be more likely to fiddle with an earlobe, twirl a strand of hair, or clean their fingernails. Whether or not the fidgeter is hiding something, observers are likely to interpret these behaviors as a signal of dishonesty. Because not all fidgeters are dishonest, it's important not to jump to conclusions about the meaning of adaptors.

Actually, *too few* gestures may be as significant an indicator of mixed messages as *too many*.[55] Limited gesturing may signal a lack of interest, sadness, boredom, or low enthusiasm. Illustrators also decrease whenever someone is cautious about speaking. For these reasons, a careful observer will look for either an increase or a decrease in the usual level of gestures.

Face and Eyes   The face and eyes are probably the most noticed parts of the body, but this doesn't mean that their nonverbal messages are the easiest to read. The face is a tremendously complicated channel of expression for several reasons.

First, it's hard to describe the number and kind of expressions we produce with our face and eyes. Researchers have found that there are at least eight distinguishable positions of the eyebrows and forehead, eight of the eyes and lids, and ten for the lower face.[56] When you multiply this complexity by the number of emotions we feel, you can see why it's almost impossible to compile a dictionary of facial expressions and their corresponding emotions.

Second, facial expressions are difficult to understand because of the speed with which they can change. For example, slow-motion films show expressions fleeting across a subject's face in as short a time as it takes to blink an eye.[57] Also, it seems that different emotions show most clearly in different parts of the face: happiness and surprise in the eyes and lower face; anger in the lower face, brows, and forehead; fear and sadness in the eyes; and disgust in the lower face.

It was terribly dangerous to let your thoughts wander when you were in any public place or within range of a telescreen. The smallest thing could give you away. A nervous tic, an unconscious look of anxiety, a habit of muttering to yourself—anything that carried with it the suggestion of abnormality, of having something to hide. In any case, to wear an improper expression on your face (to look incredulous when a victory was announced, for example) was itself a punishable offense. There was even a word for it in Newspeak: facecrime, it was called.

George Orwell, *1984*

In spite of the complex way in which the face shows emotions, you can still pick up clues by watching it carefully. One of the easiest ways is to look for expressions that seem too exaggerated to be true. For instance, genuine facial expressions usually last no longer than 5 seconds—anything more and we start to doubt they are real (contestants in pageants with smiles plastered on their faces often come across as "fake" or "plastic").[58] Another way to detect feelings is to watch others' expressions when they aren't likely to be thinking about their appearance. We've all had the experience of glancing into another car while stopped in a traffic jam, or of looking around at a sporting event and seeing expressions that the wearer would probably never show in more guarded moments. At other times, it's possible to see a **microexpression** as it flashes across a person's face. For just a moment we see a flash of emotion quite different from the one a speaker is trying to convey, such as a furrowed brow right before smiling and gamely declaring, "Don't worry, I'm fine." Finally, you may be able to spot contradictory expressions on different parts of someone's face: The eyes say one thing, but the mouth or eyebrows might say something quite different.

The eyes themselves can send several kinds of messages. Meeting someone's glance with your eyes is usually a sign of involvement, whereas looking away is often a sign of a desire to avoid contact. This principle has a practical application in commerce: Customers leave larger tips when their servers (whether male or female) maintain eye contact with them.[59] Research also shows that communicators who make direct eye contact are far more likely to get others to comply with their requests than are those who make evasive glances.[60]

Another kind of message the eyes communicate is a positive or negative attitude. When someone looks toward us with the proper facial expression, we get a clear message that the looker is interested in us—hence the expression "making eyes." At the same time, when our long glances toward someone else are avoided, we can be pretty sure that the other person isn't as interested in a relationship as we are. (Of course, there are all sorts of courtship games in which the receiver of a glance pretends not to notice any message by glancing away, yet signals interest with some other part of the body.) The eyes can also communicate both dominance and submission. We've all played the game of trying to stare down somebody, and there are times when downcast eyes are a sign of giving in.

Even the pupils of our eyes communicate. Researchers measured the amount of pupil dilation while showing men and women various types of pictures.[61] The results of the experiment were interesting: A person's eyes grow larger in proportion to the degree of interest in an object. For example, men's pupils grew

Invitation to Insight

The Role of Smiling in Interpersonal Communication

ThomsonNOW View the ABC News feature "Smile Research." You can find the link to this site through your ThomsonNOW for *Looking Out/Looking In*. This story describes how one communication researcher has uncovered the role of smiling in interpersonal communication, especially as a marker of social status.

Exploring Nonverbal Communication

ThomsonNOW The "Exploring Nonverbal Communication" website previews a video series on nonverbal communication available from the University of California. Scroll down and see sample pictures from the videos. Guess about the meaning in the sample pictures and then scroll down further to get the answers. Go to your ThomsonNOW for *Looking Out/Looking In*.

about 18 percent larger when looking at pictures of a naked woman, and women's pupils grew 20 percent when looking at pictures of a naked man. Interestingly enough, the greatest increase in pupil size occurred when women looked at a picture of a mother and an infant.

Voice

The voice is another channel of nonverbal communication. Social scientists use the term **paralanguage** to describe nonverbal, vocal messages. The way a message is spoken can give the same word or words many meanings. For example, note how many meanings come from a single sentence just by shifting the emphasis from one word to another:

This is a fantastic communication book. (Not just any book, but *this* one in particular.)

This is a *fantastic* communication book. (This book is superior, exciting.)

This is a fantastic *communication* book. (The book is good as far as communication goes; it may not be so great as literature or drama.)

This is a fantastic communication *book*. (It's not a play or album; it's a book.)

There are many other ways we communicate paralinguistically through our tone, speed, pitch, volume, number and length of pauses, and **disfluencies** (such as stammering, use of "uh," "um," "er," and so on). All these factors can do a great deal to reinforce or contradict the message that our words convey.

Researchers have identified the power of paralanguage through the use of content-free speech—ordinary speech that has been electronically manipulated so that the words are

"This is Daddy, honey. That was Daddy's office voice."

The Way You Talk Can Hurt You?

Women also have a distinctive style of speaking: "I was shopping last night? And I saw this wonderful dress? It was so black and slinky?" It's hard to convey intonation in print, but the question marks indicate a rise in pitch at the end of the sentence, as in a question. Many women, especially younger women, use this intonation in declarative sentences: "This is Sally Jones? I have an appointment with Dr. Smith? And I'd like to change it to another day?"

I cringe when I hear this. The rising intonation sounds timid and lacking in self-confidence; the speaker seems to be asking for approval or permission to speak when there's no need to. She should make her point straightforwardly, in an assertion that drops in pitch as it ends.

And I worry that rising intonation harms women. It gets them taken less seriously than they should be in public debates; it encourages salesmen and car mechanics to cheat them when they wouldn't try cheating a man.

A woman friend who studies languages says I've got it wrong. Unlike men, who use conversation to fight for status, she tells me, women see it as co-operative. And they use rising pitch to convey this to their audience. Their tone encourages the supportive interjections, such as "Uh-huh," "Exactly," and "I know what you mean," with which women far more than men interlard each other's speech. And it asks listeners to contribute their ideas on the speaker's topic.

At the very least, women's use of rising intonation involves an ambiguity. It uses a sound that in other contexts conveys timidity, for a very different purpose. Given this ambiguity, we shouldn't be surprised if female speakers who are trying to be co-operative are often heard as hesitant.

It's clearly idiotic to treat conversation as a contest, as so many men do. We'd all benefit from a more cooperative approach. But we need a new symbol to express this, one with no connotations of weakness.

If we find this symbol, we can all, men and women, speak in friendly but firm tones. We can tell anecdotes without lecturing but also without seeming to kowtow. When we call the doctor's, we can say: "This is Sally (or Sam) Jones." (No question about it.) "I have an appointment with Dr. Smith." (I'm reminding you of a fact.) "And I'd like to change it to another day." (Now: Can you help me?)

Thomas Hurka

---

unintelligible, but the paralanguage remains unaffected. (Hearing a foreign language that you don't understand has the same effect.) Subjects who hear content-free speech can consistently recognize the emotion being expressed as well as identify its strength.[62]

The impact of paralinguistic cues is strong. In fact, when asked to determine a speaker's attitudes, listeners pay more attention to paralanguage than to the content of the words. Furthermore, when vocal factors contradict a verbal message (as when a speaker shouts, "I am not angry!"), listeners judge the speaker's intention from the paralanguage, not from the words themselves.[63] Young children respond to the paralanguage of adults, warming up to those who speak warmly and shying away from those who speak in a less friendly manner.[64]

Paralanguage can affect behavior in many ways, some of which are rather surprising. Researchers have discovered that communicators are most likely to comply with requests delivered by speakers whose rate was similar to their own: People who spoke rapidly responded most favorably to rapid talkers, whereas slow speakers preferred others whose rate was also slow.[65] Besides complying with same-rate speakers, listeners also feel more positively about people who speak at their own rate.

A pause in the wrong place, an intonation misunderstood, and a whole conversation went awry.

E. M. Forster,
A Passage to India

MEXICAN IDEAL SPEAKER'S VOICE

Medium in pitch
Medium in rate
Loud in volume

Clear enunciation
Well-modulated
Without regional accent
Cheerful

Firm
Low in pitch
Somewhat slow with pauses

U.S. IDEAL SPEAKER'S VOICE

FIGURE 6.1

A Comparison of the
Ideal Speakers' Voice
Types in Mexico and
the United States

Adapted from "Communicative
Power: Gender and Culture as
Determinants of the Ideal Voice"
in *Women and Communicative
Power: Theory, Research and Practice* edited by Carol A. Valentine
and Nancy Hoar. © 1988 by SCA.
Reprinted by permission.

Sarcasm is one instance in which we use both emphasis and tone of voice to change a statement's meaning to the opposite of its verbal message. Experience this reversal yourself with the following three statements. First say them literally, and then say them sarcastically.

"Thanks a lot!"

"I really had a wonderful time on my blind date."

"There's nothing I like better than lima beans."

As they do with other nonverbal messages, people often ignore or misinterpret the vocal nuances of sarcasm. Members of certain groups—children, people with weak intellectual skills, and poor listeners—are more likely to misunderstand sarcastic messages than others.[66] In one study, children younger than age 10 lacked the linguistic sophistication to tell when a message was sarcastic.[67]

Besides reinforcing or contradicting messages, some vocal factors influence the way a speaker is perceived by others. For example, communicators who speak loudly and without hesitations are viewed as more confident than those who pause and speak quietly.[68] People with more-attractive voices are rated more highly than those with less attractive voices.[69] Just what makes a voice attractive can vary. As Figure 6.1 shows, culture can make a difference. Surveys show that there are both similarities and differences between what Mexicans and Americans view as the "ideal" voice. Accent plays an important role in shaping perceptions. Generally speaking, accents that identify a speaker's membership in a group lead to more positive evaluations (if the group is high status) or to negative evaluations (if the group is low status).[70]

Touch

Social scientists use the word **haptics** to describe the study of touching. Touch can communicate many messages and signal a variety of relationships.[71]

Functional/professional (dental exam, haircut)

Social/polite (handshake)

Friendship/warmth (clap on back, Spanish *abrazo*)

Sexual arousal (some kisses, strokes)

Aggression (shoves, slaps)

You might object to the examples following each of these categories, saying that some nonverbal behaviors occur in several types of relationships. A kiss, for example, can mean anything from a polite but superficial greeting to the most intense arousal. What makes a given touch more or less intense? Researchers have suggested a number of factors:

Which part of the body does the touching

Which part of the body is touched

How long the touch lasts

How much pressure is used

Whether there is movement after contact is made

Whether anyone else is present

The situation in which the touch occurs

The relationship between the people involved[72]

Men and Hugs

© Gene Mollica/Images.com

The hug, long reserved for women, celebrating sports victories, and men from other countries, is muscling its way into everyday American Guydom.

The male hug is complicating everything. Men accustomed to the automatic hand clasp accompanied with a brisk up-and-down pump at dinner parties and college reunions, now must preface their greetings or goodbyes with intricate and split-second calculations based on body language, length of friendship and other factors.

Do I shake or do I hug? Making the right choice matters. If one guy goes for the hug, but the other decides upon a handshake, they might collide. An excruciating dance will follow, as the poor lads work feverishly to determine what to do with their hands, their arms, their bodies.

There's more to the hug decision, however, than an embrace. The next question is: which hug? A popular option is the ubiquitous handshake that has grown a back pat. Other men

opt for the embrace, with one arm around the waist, and the other draped over a shoulder: back-clapping tends to accompany this hug. One of them involves a handshake, a mutual tug inward, and a shoulder-bump.

At least two professors—Kory Floyd at Arizona State University and Mark Morman at Baylor University in Waco, Texas—have dedicated part of their careers to studying the male hug. Floyd, for example, has studied the forms and duration of hugs between men. Rarely do they last much longer than one second. As hugs extend to two seconds or more, men watching the huggers quickly begin assuming the embraces are romantic, instead of just friendly.

Only men engage in the combination handshake-hug, says Floyd. "It follows what we call an 'A-frame' configuration; the only body contact is the shoulders," he says. "Men often do it with their handshake in between them, so there is a physical barrier. The third thing is the aggressive

patting on the back that comes along with it, which is a very combative gesture. It's a way for men to say, 'I have positive feelings for you, but let's show them in a way that is masculine and gender validating.' All of those things—distance, a barrier, the combative movement—are all stereotypically masculine ways of behaving."

While Morman agrees that hugging among American men is spreading, he says it always has occurred in certain contexts. The more "emotionally charged" the environment, he says, the more freedom men feel to hug one another. "If you are in the office, generally there is not a lot of emotion there," he says, and hugging remains taboo. But at a wedding or a funeral, or on a battlefield or basketball court, men for a long time have hugged without much hesitation.

Whether, and how, to hug or not falls along cultural lines. America qualifies as a "medium-touch" culture, Floyd says, with some northern European and Asian cultures—in Japan, for example, where people bow to one another instead of touching—registering as "low touch." In some places, everybody hugs, or everybody bows. In America, it's mixed. The handshake remains the standard greeting, but some guys hug with relish. Others recoil from outstretched male arms. Most men probably sit somewhere in between.

Douglas Brown

From this list you can see that there is, indeed, a complex language of touch. Because nonverbal messages are inherently ambiguous, it's no surprise that this language can often be misunderstood. Is a hug playful or suggestive of stronger feelings? Is a touch on the shoulder a friendly gesture or an attempt at domination? The ambiguity of nonverbal behavior often leads to serious problems.

Touch plays a powerful role in shaping how we respond to others. For instance, in a laboratory task, subjects evaluated partners more positively when they were touched (appropriately, of course) by them.[73] Besides increasing liking, touch also increases compliance. In one study, subjects were approached by a research confederate who requested that they return a dime left in the phone booth from which they had just emerged. When the request was accompanied by a light touch on the subject's arm, the probability that the subject would return the dime increased significantly.[74] In a similar experiment, subjects were asked by a confederate to sign a petition or complete a rating scale. Again, subjects were more likely to cooperate when they were touched lightly on the arm. In the rating-scale variation of the study, the results were especially dramatic: 70 percent of those who were touched complied, whereas only 40 percent of those who were untouched did.[75] An additional power of touch is its on-the-job utility: A restaurant server's fleeting touches on the hand and shoulder result in larger tips,[76] as does squatting down to make eye contact with customers.[77] Both women and men in taverns increase their alcohol consumption when touched by a waitress.[78]

Besides being the earliest means we have of making contact with others, touching is essential to our healthy development. During the nineteenth and early twentieth centuries, a large percentage of children born every year died. In some orphanages the mortality rate was nearly 100 percent, but even children in the most "progressive" homes, hospitals, and other institutions died regularly. When researchers finally tracked down the causes of this mortality, they found that the infants suffered from lack of physical contact with parents or nurses, rather than lack of nutrition, medical care, or other factors. From this knowledge came the practice of "mothering" children in institutions—picking a baby up, carrying it around, and handling it several times each day. At one hospital that began this practice, the death rate for infants fell from between 30 and 35 percent to below 10 percent.[79]

Invitation to Insight

The Rules of Touch

Like most types of nonverbal behavior, touching is governed by cultural and social rules. Imagine that you are writing a guidebook for visitors from another culture. Describe the rules that govern touching in the following relationships. In each case, describe how the gender of the participants affects the rules.

1. An adult and a 5-year-old child

2. An adult and a 12-year-old

3. Two good friends

4. Boss and employee

Contemporary research confirms the relationship between touch and health. Studies at the University of Miami's School of Medicine's Touch Research Institute have shown that premature babies grow faster and gain more weight when massaged.[80] The same institute's researchers demonstrated that massage can help premature children gain weight, help colicky children to sleep better, improve the mood of depressed adolescents, and boost the immune function of cancer and HIV patients. Research shows that touch between therapists and clients has the potential to encourage a variety of beneficial changes: more self-disclosure, client self-acceptance, and more positive client-therapist relationships.[81]

Appearance

Whether or not we're aware of the fact, how we look sends messages to others. There are two dimensions to appearance: Physical attractiveness and clothing.

Physical Attractiveness The importance of physical attractiveness has been emphasized in the arts for centuries. More recently, social scientists have begun to measure the degree to which physical attractiveness affects interaction between people.[82] For example, females who are perceived as attractive have more dates, receive higher grades in college, persuade males with greater ease, and receive lighter court sentences. Both men and women whom others perceive as attractive are rated as being more sensitive, kind, strong, sociable, and interesting than their less fortunate brothers and sisters. Physical attractiveness is also an asset in the professional world, affecting hiring, promotion, and performance evaluation decisions.[83]

The influence of physical attractiveness begins early in life.[84] Preschoolers were shown photographs of children their own age and asked to choose potential friends and enemies. The researchers found that children as young as three agreed as to who was attractive and unattractive. Furthermore, the children valued their attractive counterparts—both of the same and the opposite sex—more highly. Teachers also are affected by students' attractiveness. Physically attractive students are usually judged more favorably—as being more intelligent, friendly, and popular—than their less attractive counterparts.[85] Teacher-student assessments work in both directions—research shows that physically attractive professors receive higher evaluations from their students.[86]

Fortunately, attractiveness is something we can control without having to call a plastic surgeon. If you aren't totally gorgeous or handsome, don't despair: Evidence suggests that, as we get to know more about people and like them, we start to regard them as better looking.[87] Moreover, we view others as beautiful or ugly not just on the basis of their "original equipment" but also on the basis of how they use that equipment. Posture, gestures, facial expressions, and other behaviors can increase the physical attractiveness of an otherwise unremarkable person. Exercise can improve the way each of us looks. Finally, the way we dress can make a significant difference in the way others perceive us, as you'll now see.

Clothing   Besides being a means of protecting us from the elements, clothing is a means of communicating nonverbally. One writer has suggested that clothing conveys at least ten types of messages to others:[88]

© National Portrait Gallery/SuperStock

- Economic level
- Economic background
- Educational level
- Social background
- Trustworthiness
- Educational background
- Social position
- Level of success
- Level of sophistication
- Moral character

Research shows that we do make assumptions about people based on their clothing. Communicators who wear special clothing often gain persuasiveness. For example, experimenters dressed in uniforms resembling police officers were more successful than those dressed in civilian clothing in requesting pedestrians to pick up litter and in persuading them to lend a dime to an overparked motorist.[89] Likewise, solicitors wearing sheriff's and nurse's uniforms increased the level of contributions to law enforcement and health care campaigns.[90] Uniforms aren't the only kind of clothing that carries influence. In one study, a male and a female were stationed in a hallway so that anyone who wished to go by had to avoid them or pass between them. In one condition the couple wore "formal daytime dress"; in the other, they wore "casual attire." Passersby behaved differently toward the couple, depending on the style of clothing: They responded positively with the well-dressed couple and negatively with the casually dressed couple.[91]

Similar results in other situations show the influence of clothing. Pedestrians were more likely to return lost coins to people dressed in high status clothing than to those dressed in low status clothing.[92] We are also more likely to follow the lead of high-status dressers, even when it comes to violating social rules. Eighty-three percent of the pedestrians in one study followed a jaywalker dressed in higher-status clothing who violated a "wait" crossing signal, whereas only 48 percent followed a confederate dressed in lower-status clothing.[93] Women who are wearing a jacket are rated as being more powerful than those wearing only a dress or skirt and blouse.[94]

Despite the frequency with which we make them, our clothing-based assumptions aren't always accurate. The stranger wearing wrinkled, ill-fitting old clothes might be a manager on vacation, a normally stylish person on the way to clean a fireplace, or even an eccentric millionaire. As we get to know others better, the importance of clothing shrinks.[95] This fact suggests that clothing is especially important in the early stages of a relationship, when making a positive first impression is necessary to encourage others to know us better. This fact is equally important in personal situations and in employment interviews. In both cases, our style of dress (and personal grooming) can make all the difference between the chance to progress further and outright rejection.

"Tell me about yourself, Kugelman—your hopes, dreams, career path, and what that damn earring means."

Physical Space

Proxemics is the study of the way people and animals use space. There are at least two dimensions of proxemics: distance and territoriality.

Distance   You can sometimes tell how people feel toward one another simply by noting the distance between them. To begin to understand how this is so, try the "Distance Makes a Difference" exercise on this page. During this exercise your feelings probably changed at least three times. During the first phase, when you were across the room from your partner, you probably felt unnaturally far away. Then, as you neared a point about 3 feet from him or her, you probably felt like stopping; this is the distance at which two people in our culture normally stand while conversing socially. If your partner wasn't someone you're emotionally close to, you may have begun to feel quite uncomfortable as you moved through this normal range and came closer; it's possible that you had to force yourself not to move back. Some people find this phase so uncomfortable that they can't get closer than 20 inches or so to their partner.

Invitation to Insight

Distance Makes a Difference

1. Choose a partner, and go to opposite sides of the room and face each other.

2. Very slowly begin walking toward each other while carrying on a conversation. You might simply talk about how you feel as you follow the exercise. As you move closer, try to be aware of any change in your feelings. Continue moving slowly toward each other until you are only an inch or so apart. Remember how you feel at this point.

3. Now, while still facing each other, back up until you're at a comfortable distance for carrying on your conversation.

4. Share your feelings with each other and/or the whole group.

© T. F. Chen Cultural Center/SuperStock

What was happening here? Each of us carries around a sort of invisible bubble of personal space wherever we go. We think of the area inside this bubble as our private territory—almost as much a part of us as our own bodies. As you moved closer to your partner, the distance between your bubbles narrowed and at a certain point disappeared altogether: Your space had been invaded, and this is the point at which you probably felt uncomfortable. As you moved away again, your partner retreated out of your bubble, and you felt more relaxed.

Of course, if you were to try this experiment with someone very close to you—your mate, for example—you might not have felt any discomfort at all, even while touching. The reason is that our willingness to get close to others—physically as well as emotionally—varies according to the person we're with and the situation we're in. And it's precisely the distance that we voluntarily put between ourselves and others that gives a nonverbal clue about our feelings and the nature of the relationship.

As you read earlier in this chapter, appropriate proxemic distances differ from culture to culture. Anthropologist Edward T. Hall has defined four distances that most North Americans use in their everyday lives.[96] He says we choose a particular distance depending on how we feel toward the other person at a given time, the context of the conversation, and our interpersonal goals.

■ The first of Hall's four spatial zones begins with skin contact and ranges out to about 18 inches. We usually use **intimate distance** with people who are emotionally very close to us, and then mostly in private situations—making love, caressing, comforting, protecting.

■ The second spatial zone, **personal distance**, ranges from 18 inches at its closest point to 4 feet at its farthest. Its closer range is the distance at which most couples stand in public. The far range runs from about 21.2 to 4 feet. As Hall puts it, at this distance we can keep someone "at arm's length." This choice of words suggests the type of communication that goes on at this range: The contacts are still reasonably close, but they're much less personal than the ones that occur a foot or so closer.

■ The third spatial zone, **social distance**, ranges from 4 to about 12 feet. Within it are the kinds of communication that usually occur in business. Its closer range, from 4 to 7 feet, is the distance at which conversations usually occur between salespeople and customers and between people who work together. We use the far range of social distance—7 to 12 feet—for more formal and impersonal situations. Sitting at this distance signals a far different and less relaxed type of conversation than would pulling a chair around to the boss's side of the desk and sitting only 3 or so feet away.

■ **Public distance** is Hall's term for the farthest zone, running outward from 12 feet. The closer range of public distance is the one that most teachers use in the classroom. In the farther ranges of public space—25 feet and beyond—two-way communication is almost impossible. In some cases, it's necessary for speakers to use public distance because of the size of their audience, but we

Some thirty inches
from my nose
The frontier of my
Person goes,
And all the untilled
air between
Is private pagus or
demesne.
Stranger, unless with
bedroom eyes
I beckon you to fraternize,
Beware of rudely
crossing it:
I have no gun, but I
can spit.

W. H. Auden

can assume that anyone who voluntarily chooses to use it when he or she could be closer is not interested in having a dialogue.

Choosing the optimal distance can have a powerful effect on how we regard others and how we respond to them. For example, students are more satisfied with teachers who reduce the distance between themselves and their classes. They also are more satisfied with a course itself, and they are more likely to follow a teacher's instructions.[97] Likewise, medical patients are more satisfied with physicians who operate at the closer end of the social distance zone.[98]

Territoriality Whereas personal space is the invisible bubble we carry around as an extension of our physical being, **territory** remains stationary. Any geographical area such as a work area, room, house, or other physical space to which we assume some kind of "rights" is our territory. What's interesting about territoriality is that there is no real basis for the assumption of proprietary rights of "owning" many areas, but the feeling of ownership exists nonetheless. Your room at home probably feels like *yours* whether you're there or not, unlike personal space, which is carried around with you. In the same way, you may feel proprietary about the seat you always occupy in class, even though you have no illusions about owning that piece of furniture.

The way people use space can communicate a good deal about power and status.[99] Generally we grant people with higher status more personal territory and greater privacy. We knock before entering the boss's office, whereas she can usually walk into our work area without hesitating. In traditional schools professors have offices, dining rooms, and even toilets that are private, whereas students, who are presumably less important, have no such sanctuaries. Among the military greater space and privacy usually come with rank: Privates sleep forty to a barrack, sergeants have their own private rooms, and generals have government-provided houses.

Physical Environment

In this section, we want to emphasize the ways in which physical settings, architecture, and interior design affect our communication. Begin by recalling the different homes you've visited lately. Were some of these homes more comfortable to be in than others? Certainly a lot of these kinds of feelings are shaped by the people you were with, but there are some houses where it seems impossible to relax, no matter how friendly the hosts are. We've spent what seemed like endless evenings in what Mark Knapp calls "unliving rooms," where the spotless ashtrays, furniture coverings, and plastic lamp covers seem to send nonverbal messages telling us not to touch anything, not to put our feet up, and not to be comfortable. People who live in houses like this probably wonder why nobody ever seems to relax and enjoy themselves at their parties. One thing is quite certain: They don't understand that this environment they created can communicate discomfort to their guests.

The impressions that home designs communicate can be remarkably accurate. Researchers showed ninety-nine students slides of the insides or outsides of twelve upper-middle-class homes and then asked them to infer the personality of the owners from their impressions.[100] The students were especially accurate after glancing at interior photos. The decorating schemes communicated accurate information about the homeowners' intellectualism, politeness, maturity, optimism, tenseness, willingness to take adventures, and family orientations. The

A good house is planned from the inside out. First, you decide what it has to do for its occupants. Then, you let the functions determine the form. The more numerous and various those functions, the more responsive and interesting the house should be. And it may not look at all like you expect.

Dan MacMasters,
Los Angeles Times

home exteriors also gave viewers accurate perceptions of the owners' artistic interests, graciousness, privacy, and quietness.

Besides communicating information about the designer, an environment can shape the kind of interaction that takes place in it. In one experiment, subjects working in a "beautiful" room were more positive and energetic than those working in "average" or "ugly" spaces.[101] In another experiment, students perceived professors who occupied well-decorated offices as being more credible than those occupying less attractive offices.[102] Doctors have shaped environments to improve the quality of interaction with their patients. Simply removing a doctor's desk makes patients feel almost five times more at ease during office visits.[103] In another study, redesigning a convalescent ward of a hospital greatly increased the interaction between patients. In the old design, seats were placed shoulder to shoulder around the edges of the ward. By grouping the seats around small tables so that patients faced each other at a comfortable distance, the amount of conversations doubled.

Time

Social scientists use the term **chronemics** to describe the study of how humans use and structure time. The way we handle time can express both intentional and unintentional messages.[104] For instance, in a culture that values time highly, waiting can be an indicator of status. "Important" people (whose time is supposedly more valuable than that of others) may be seen by appointment only, whereas it is acceptable to intrude without notice on lesser beings. A related rule is that low-status people must never make high-status people wait. It would be a serious mistake to show up late for a job interview, whereas the interviewer might keep you cooling your heels in the lobby. Important people are often whisked to the head of a restaurant or airport line, while presumably less-exalted masses are forced to wait their turn.

The use of time depends greatly on culture.[105] Some cultures (e.g., North American, German, and Swiss) tend to be **monochronic**, emphasizing punctuality, schedules, and completing one task at a time. Other cultures (e.g., South American, Mediterrannean, and Arab) are more **polychronic**, with flexible schedules in which multiple tasks are pursued at the same time.[106] One psychologist discovered the difference between North and South American attitudes when teaching at a university in Brazil.[107] He found that some Brazilian students arrived halfway through a 2-hour class and that most of them stayed put and kept asking questions when the class was scheduled to end. A half-hour after the official end of the class, the psychologist finally closed off discussion because there was no indication that the students intended to leave. This flexibility of time is quite different from what is common in most North American colleges!

Even within a culture, rules of time vary. Sometimes the variations are geographic. In New York City, the party invitation may say 9:00, but nobody would think of showing up before 9:30. In Salt Lake City, guests are expected to show up on time, or perhaps even a bit early. Even within the same geographic area, different people, groups, and organizations establish their own rules about the use of time.[108] Consider your own experience. In school, some instructors begin and end class punctually, whereas others are more casual. With some people you feel comfortable talking for hours in person or on the phone, with others time seems to be precious and not "wasted."

Summary

Nonverbal communication consists of messages expressed by nonlinguistic means such as body movement, vocal characteristics, touch, appearance, physical space, physical environment, and time.

Nonverbal skills are vital for competent communicators. Nonverbal communication is pervasive; in fact, it is impossible to not send nonverbal messages. Although many nonverbal behaviors are universal, their use is affected by both culture and gender. Most nonverbal communication reveals attitudes and feelings, in contrast to verbal communication, which is better suited to expressing ideas. Nonverbal communication serves many functions. It can repeat, complement, substitute for, accent, regulate, and contradict verbal communication. When presented with conflicting verbal and nonverbal messages, communicators are more likely to rely on the nonverbal ones. For this reason, nonverbal cues are important in detecting deception. It's necessary to exercise caution in interpreting such cues, however, because nonverbal communication is ambiguous.

Key Terms

accenting (202)
adaptors (216)
body orientation (213)
chronemics (228)
complementing (201)
contradicting (204)
disfluencies (218)
emblems (214)
gestures (214)
haptics (220)

illustrators (214)
intimate distance (226)
kinesics (213)
leakage (204)
manipulators (216)
microexpression (217)
mixed message (204)
monochronic (228)
nonverbal communication (197)
paralanguage (218)

personal distance (226)
polychronic (228)
posture (213)
proxemics (225)
public distance (226)
regulating (202)
repeating (201)
social distance (226)
substituting (202)
territory (227)

Media Resources

Online Textbook Resources

ThomsonNOW For quick access to the online resources that accompany this chapter, access your ThomsonNOW for *Looking Out/Looking In* at www.thomsonedu.com.

The ThomsonNOW online study system helps you identify concepts you don't fully understand, allowing you to put your study time to the best use. Using chapter-by-chapter diagnostic pre-tests, the system creates a **personalized study plan** for each chapter. Each plan directs you to specific resources designed to improve your understanding, including pages from the text in ebook format. Chapter post-tests give you an opportunity to measure how much you've learned and let you know if you are ready for graded quizzes and exams.

Your ThomsonNOW for *Looking Out/Looking In* also includes the **ABC News video clip** described on page 217; **vocabulary activities** to help you master key terms; self-study **review quizzes** to test your comprehension of the material in this chapter and prepare for exams; **online exercises**, including the Skill Builder and Invitation to Insight activities in this chapter; **web links** you can use to further explore topics in this chapter; access to a **feature film database** where you can locate information about movies that illustrate communication principles; and access to the **InfoTrac** College Edition searchable database of over 10 million articles from both scholarly journals and the popular press.

Films and Television

ThomsonNOW™ In addition to the films suggested here, go to your ThomsonNOW for *Looking Out/Looking In* to link to the **Film in Communication Database** to locate movie clips illustrating principles of nonverbal communication.

Personality Expression via Nonverbal Communication

Freaky Friday (2003) Rated PG

In the re-make of this Disney classic, Tess Coleman (Jamie Lee Curtis) and teenage daughter Annabell (Lindsay Lohan) wake up to discover that they inhabit one another's bodies and lives. The film is a light and humorous lesson in empathy. Mother, daughter, and viewers all are reminded that the world looks very different depending on one's point of view.

One of the easiest ways to remember "who's who" during the movie is to monitor the characters' nonverbal cues. Although viewers see Tess's body, it's clear that it's being inhabited by a teenage girl if you watch her mannerisms and facial expressions and listen to her vocal tone, rate, and pitch. Similarly, when Tess inhabits her daughter's body, she suddenly engages in a variety of adult behaviors—such as adjusting her teen friend's blouse so it shows less midriff (something only a mother would do).

Although body-switching only happens in the movies, *Freaky Friday* illustrates that nonverbal mannerisms can tell us lot about a person's age, status, and roles.

Nonverbal Communication in Everyday Life

Seinfeld (TV Series, available on DVD) Not Rated

In this popular television series, familiar characters Jerry, George, Elaine, and Kramer regularly monitor, discuss, and poke fun at people's nonverbal communication traits. Fans of the show remember "The Close Talker" (who infringes on others' personal and intimate space), "The Low Talker" (who whispers everything she says), and "The High Talker" (whose vocal pitch is far higher than normal for a man). Other disputes occur over George's unintentional winking, the size of Elaine's head, Jerry's puffy shirt, and Kramer's body tan. The writers of the show clearly understand that people pay a great deal of attention to nonverbal communication cues.

Masculine and Feminine Nonverbal Behaviors

The Birdcage (1996) Rated R
Boys Don't Cry (1999) Rated R
Mrs. Doubtfire (1993) Rated PG-13
Tootsie (1982) Rated PG

One way to recognize differences between masculine and feminine styles of nonverbal communication is to observe the same person playing different gender-related roles. Filmmakers have found this notion intriguing enough to produce several movies in which characters disguise themselves with makeup and costumes—and nonverbal cues—related to masculine and feminine roles.

In *Tootsie*, Michael Dorsey (Dustin Hoffman) is an aspiring New York actor who can't get any roles—at least as a man. In a flash of inspiration, he transforms himself into Dorothy Michaels, a middle-aged woman, and wins a part in a daytime soap opera.

Robin Williams takes on a Tootsie-like role in *Mrs. Doubtfire*. He plays Daniel Hillard, a divorced man who cannot bear to live without his children. His ex-wife (Sally Field) needs a housekeeper for the kids, so Daniel asks his makeup-artist brother (Harvey Fierstein) to turn him into Mrs. Doubtfire.

In yet another twist on the masculine/feminine theme, Robin Williams plays a man who teaches his gay partner to be more macho in *The Birdcage*. The goal, once again, is disguise: The partners want their soon-to-be in-laws to believe they are brothers, not lovers.

Boys Don't Cry recounts the sad life and tragic death of Brandon Teena (Hilary Swank), a popular teen who charms the girls in his small Nebraska town and convinces his male buddies that he is a regular guy. In fact, he was born female and chose to change genders after moving to a new town.

From *Some Like It Hot* to *Victor/Victoria* (where a woman plays a man playing a woman), films through the years have capitalized on masculine/feminine differences to entertain and intrigue. In each case, the success of the characters is determined not only by what they say, but also by their nonverbal behaviors.

The Power of Touch

Life as a House (2001) Rated R

George Monroe (Kevin Kline) is divorced, lives alone in a crumbling garage, has a son who despises him, and gets fired from his job. Then he learns he has terminal cancer. While in the hospital, something important happens to George: He gets touched. The nurse on duty strokes his face, and he is deeply moved by the event. He confesses that he hasn't been touched in years, so the nurse takes a few more moments to gently caress him. Watching his reactions, it's clear that the physical contact restores something he lost: his desire to reconnect with a world from which he had become emotionally detached. The lack of loving touch is an issue for several characters in the story. By film's end, many of their relationships are restored, in good measure because of their willingness to "reach out and touch" the people who matter most in their lives.

Listening: More than Meets the Ear

7

Ric Masten's poem on the following page shows that there's more to listening than gazing politely at a speaker and nodding your head every so often. As you will soon learn, listening is a demanding and complex activity—and just as important as speaking in the communication process.

If we use frequency as a measure, then listening easily qualifies as the most important kind of communication. We spend more time listening to others than in any other type of communication. One study (summarized in Figure 7.1) revealed that college students spend an average of 14 percent of their communicating time writing, 16 percent speaking, 17 percent reading, and a whopping 53 percent listening.[1] On the job, listening is just as important. Studies show that most employees of major corporations in North America spend about 60 percent of each work day listening to others.[2]

Besides being the most frequent form of communication, listening is at least as important as speaking in terms of making relationships work. In committed relationships, listening to personal information in everyday conversations is considered a vital ingredient of satisfaction.[3] In one survey, marital counselors identified "failing to take the other's perspective when listening" as one of the most frequent communication problems in the couples with whom they worked.[4] When a group of adults was asked what communication skills were most important in family and social settings, listening was ranked first.[5]

Listening well is just as important in the workplace as in personal relationships. A study examining the link between listening and career success revealed

> If you think communication is all talk, you haven't been listening.
>
> Ashleigh Brilliant

> Listening, not imitation, may be the sincerest form of flattery.
>
> Dr. Joyce Brothers

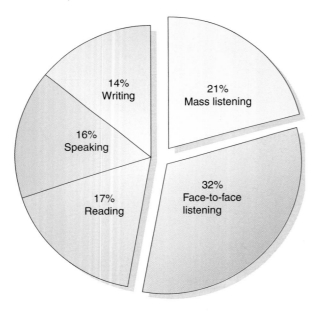

FIGURE 7.1
Types of Communication
Activities

that better listeners rose to higher levels in their organizations.[6] When human resource executives across the country were asked to identify skills of the ideal manager, the ability to listen effectively ranked at the top of the list.[7] In problem-solving groups, effective listeners are judged as having the most leadership skills.[8] Listening is just as important in careers that involve cold facts as in ones that involve lots of one-on-one interaction. For example, in a survey of over 90,000 accountants, effective listening was identified as the most important communication skill for professionals entering that field.[9] When a diverse group of senior executives was asked what skills are most important on the job, listening was identified more often than any other skill, including technical competence, computer knowledge, creativity, and administrative talent.[10]

Just because businesspeople believe listening is important doesn't mean they do it well. A survey in which 144 managers were asked to rate their listening skills illustrates this point. Astonishingly, not one of the managers described himself or herself as a "poor" or "very poor" listener, whereas 94 percent rated themselves as "good" or "very good."[11] The favorable self-ratings contrasted sharply with the perceptions of the managers' subordinates, many of whom said their boss's listening skills were weak. Of course, managers aren't the only people whose listening needs work—all of us could stand to improve our skills. That's why we'll spend an entire chapter talking about this vital communication subject.

This chapter will explore the nature of listening. After defining listening, we will examine the elements that make up the listening process and look at challenges that come with becoming a better listener. Finally, you will read about a variety of listening response styles that you can use to better understand and even help others.

I have just
wandered back
into our conversation
and find
that you
are still
rattling on
about something
or other
i think i must
have been gone
at least
twenty minutes
and you
never missed me
now this might say

something
about my acting ability
or it might say
something about
your sensitivity
one thing
troubles me tho
when it
is my turn
to rattle on
for twenty minutes
which i
have been known to do
have you
been missing too.

Ric Masten

Listening Defined

So far we've used the term "listening" as if it needs no explanation. Actually, there's more to this concept than you might think. We will define **listening**—at least the interpersonal type—as the process of making sense of others' spoken messages. As you'll soon see, this definition excludes some behavior that most people would consider listening.

Hearing versus Listening

People often think of hearing and listening as the same thing, but they are quite different. *Hearing* is the process in which sound waves strike the eardrum and cause vibrations that are transmitted to the brain. (You'll read more about hearing in the following section.) *Listening* occurs when the brain reconstructs these electrochemical impulses

© Zits Partnership. Reprinted by special permission of King Features Syndicate.

into a representation of the original sound and then gives them meaning. Barring illness, injury, or cotton plugs, you can't stop hearing.[12] Your ears will pick up sound waves and transmit them to your brain whether you want them to or not.

Listening, however, isn't automatic. As the cartoon on this page shows, people hear all the time without listening. Sometimes we automatically and unconsciously block out irritating sounds, such as a neighbor's lawnmower or the roar of nearby traffic. We also stop listening when we find a subject unimportant or uninteresting. Boring stories, TV commercials, and nagging complaints are common examples of messages we may tune out.

Mindless Listening

When we move beyond hearing and start to listen, researchers note that we process information in two very different ways.[13] Social scientists use the terms "mindless" and "mindful" to describe these different ways of listening.[14] **Mindless listening** occurs when we react to others' messages automatically and routinely, without much mental investment. Words like "superficial" and "cursory" describe mindless listening better than terms like "ponder" and "contemplate."

While the term "mindless" may sound negative, this sort of low-level information processing is a potentially valuable type of communication, since it frees us to focus our minds on messages that require our careful attention.[15] Given the number of messages to which we're exposed, it's impractical to listen carefully and thoughtfully 100 percent of the time. It's also unrealistic to devote your attention to long-winded stories, idle chatter, or remarks you've heard many times before. The only realistic way to manage the onslaught of messages is to be "lazy" toward many of them. In situations like these, we forego careful analysis and fall back on the schemas—and sometimes the stereotypes—described in Chapter 3 to make sense of a message. If you stop right now and recall the messages you have heard today, it's likely that you processed most of them mindlessly.

Mindful Listening

By contrast, **mindful listening** involves giving careful and thoughtful attention and responses to the messages we receive. You tend to listen mindfully when a message is important to you, and also when someone you care about is speaking about a matter that is important to him or her. Think of how your ears perk up when someone starts talking about your money ("The repairs will cost me *how* much?"), or how you tune in carefully when a close friend tells you about the loss of a loved one. In situations like these, you want to give the message-sender your complete and undivided attention.

Sometimes we respond mindlessly to information that deserves—and even demands—our mindful attention. Ellen Langer's determination to study mindfulness began when her grandmother complained about headaches coming from a "snake crawling around" beneath her skull. The doctors quickly diagnosed the problem as senility—after all, they reasoned, senility comes with old age and makes people talk nonsense. In fact, the grandmother had a brain tumor that eventually took her life. The event made a deep impression on Langer:

> For years afterward I kept thinking about the doctors' reactions to my grandmother's complaints, and about our reactions to the doctors. They went through the motions of diagnosis, but were not open to what they were hearing. Mindsets about senility interfered. We did not question the doctors; mindsets about experts interfered.[16]

Most of our daily decisions about whether to listen mindfully don't have life-and-death consequences, but the point should be clear: There are times when we need to consciously and carefully listen to what others are telling us. That kind of mindful listening will be the focus of the remainder of this chapter.

Elements in the Listening Process

By now, you can begin to see that there is more to listening than sitting quietly while another person speaks. In truth, listening is a process that consists of five elements: hearing, attending, understanding, responding, and remembering.

Hearing

As we have already discussed, **hearing** is the physiological dimension of listening. It occurs when sound waves strike the ear at a certain frequency and loudness. Hearing is influenced by a variety of factors, including background noise. If there are other loud noises, especially at the same frequency as the message we are trying to hear, we find it difficult to sort out the important signals from the background. Hearing is also affected by auditory fatigue, a temporary loss of hearing caused by continuous exposure to the same tone or loudness. If you spend an evening at a loud party, you may have trouble hearing well, even after getting away from the crowd. If you are exposed to loud noise often enough, permanent hearing loss can result—as many rock musicians and fans can attest.

For many communicators, the challenge of hearing is even more difficult due to physiological problems. In the United States alone, more than 13 million people communicate with some degree of hearing impairment. One study revealed that, on any given day, one-fourth to one-third of the children in a typical classroom did not hear normally.[17] As a competent communicator, you need to recognize when you may be speaking to someone with a hearing loss and adjust your approach accordingly. (See the "Looking at Diversity" box on page 237 for tips on how to do so.)

Attending

Whereas hearing is a physiological process, **attending** is a psychological one and is part of the process of selection described in Chapter 3. We would go crazy if we attended to every sound we hear, so we filter out some messages and focus on others. Needs, wants, desires, and interests determine what is attended to. Not surprisingly, research shows that we attend most carefully to messages when there's a payoff for doing so.[18] If you're planning to see a

We should all know this: that listening, not talking, is the gifted and great role, and the imaginative role. And the true listener is much more beloved, magnetic, than the talker, and he is more effective, and learns more and does more good. And so try listening. Listen to your wife, your husband, your father, your mother, your children, your friends; to those who love you and those who don't, to those who bore you, to your enemies. It will work a small miracle. And perhaps a great one.

Brenda Ueland

Bruce C. Anderson: The Challenges of Hearing Disabilities

Bruce Anderson is a student at Minneapolis Community and Technical College, where he is preparing for a career teaching middle school students who are hard of hearing and deaf. He is committed to making sure that nobody is deprived of an education or successful career because of his or her physical condition.

I grew up with a mild hearing disability. The word *mild* doesn't begin to describe how this affected my life. I couldn't hear many of the sounds or tones that are part of most people's voices. You can get an idea what this is like by imagining how hard it would be to listen to a muffled, quiet voice that is being drowned out by loud TV and radio playing at the same time, or trying to understand somebody whispering words while your ears are covered and your head is turned away.

When I flunked the school hearing tests in elementary school, I was put in a "special education" program. The other kids saw us as being different, and we were called the very worst names. I'm not perfect, so I fought back when I was picked on. I knew that I needed to escape this situation, so I devised a plan. In the next hearing test, I just followed the other students. When they heard a tone and raised their hands, I raised mine too. Believe it or not, this satisfied whoever was in charge and I got back into the regular classes. This didn't change the trouble I had hearing and understanding speech.

Back in the regular classes I would sit next to people I knew, and they would let me copy their work. I changed it just enough so it wouldn't look identical. I watched how to do the assignments and either handed them in late or not at all. I also taught myself to read lips. I took all of the shop classes that I could, and I watched the demonstrations carefully so I could follow along. Many of my teachers let me slide by so I could either continue to play on the school athletic teams, or just to move me out of their classroom. The service sector of society needed workers, and I (and people like me) would be filling those jobs.

I was very lucky in some ways: I'm mechanically inclined, and I have been working since I was 14 years old in the maintenance field. Since high school I have been a maintenance engineer, a welder on the railroad, and a service engineer for a commercial laundry equipment company. I have always had to learn things through a hands-on approach because I have never been able to understand completely what a person says to me unless it is in an environment that is quiet.

I chose to become a teacher because I don't want anybody to go through what I did in school. I want to expose hard of hearing and deaf students to options they may never have considered because of their disabilities. I also want to educate hearing people that the hard of hearing and deaf are able to communicate, but as in all communication it must be a two-way process to be successful.

If you're communicating with someone who has a hearing disability, here are a few tips. Have patience when asked to repeat something over once, twice, or even three times. Remember: the deaf and hard of hearing are doing the best they can. Help is very hard to ask for, and it is very difficult to draw attention to yourself by asking others what was said. If this still has not solved the problem try another avenue such as using different words or moving to a quieter location to talk. Even writing something down may be necessary. Hard of hearing and deaf people listen with our eyes, so make sure you're standing or sitting so that the other person can see your face and your gestures.

If you make efforts like these, you will help people with hearing disabilities. And you might also get a new appreciation and respect for their world.

ZITS   **BY JERRY SCOTT AND JIM BORGMAN**

movie, you'll listen to a friend's description more carefully than you would have otherwise. And when you want to get better acquainted with others, you'll pay careful attention to almost anything they say, in hopes of improving the relationship.

Surprisingly, attending doesn't help just the listener: It also helps the message sender. Participants in one study viewed brief movie segments and then described them to listeners who varied in their degree of attentiveness to the speakers. Later on the researchers tested the speakers' long-term recall of details from the movie segments. Those who had recounted the movie to attentive listeners remembered more details of the film.[19]

Understanding

Understanding occurs when we make sense of a message. It is possible to hear and attend to a message without understanding it at all. And, of course, it's possible to misunderstand a message. This chapter describes the many reasons why we misunderstand others—and why they misunderstand us. It also outlines skills that will help you improve your understanding of others.

Responding

Responding to a message consists of giving observable feedback to the speaker. Although listeners don't always respond visibly to a speaker, research suggests they should do so more often. One study of 195 critical incidents in banking and medical settings showed that a major difference between effective and ineffective listening was the kind of feedback offered.[20] Good listeners show they are attentive by nonverbal behaviors such as keeping eye contact and reacting with appropriate facial expressions. Their verbal behavior—answering questions and exchanging ideas, for example—also demonstrate their attention. It's easy to imagine how other responses would signal less effective listening. A slumped posture, bored expression, and yawning send a clear message that you are not tuned in to the speaker.

Adding responsiveness to our listening model demonstrates a fact that we discussed in Chapter 1: Communication is *transactional* in nature. Listening isn't just a passive activity. As listeners we are active participants in a communication transaction. At the same time we receive messages, we also send them. Responding is such an integral part of good listening that we'll devote an entire section to listening responses at the end of this chapter.

Remembering

Remembering is the ability to recall information. If we don't remember a message, listening is hardly worth the effort. Research suggests that most people remember only about 50 percent of what they hear *immediately* after hearing it. Within 8 hours the 50 percent remembered drops to about 35 percent. After two months, the average recall is only about 25 percent of the original message. Given the amount of information we process every day—from teachers, friends, the radio, TV, and other sources—the *residual message* (what we remember) is a small fraction of what we hear. Although the tendency to forget information is common, there are ways to improve your retention and recall. You'll learn some of those ways later in this chapter. For now, though, you can begin to get a sense of how tough it is to listen effectively by trying this exercise.

Invitation to Insight

Listening Breakdowns

You can overcome believing in some common myths about listening by recalling specific instances when

1. you heard another person's message but did not attend to it.

2. you attended to a message but forgot it almost immediately.

3. you attended to and remembered a message but did not understand it accurately.

4. you understood a message but did not respond sufficiently to convey your understanding to the sender.

5. you failed to remember some or all of an important message.

The Challenge of Listening

It's easy to acknowledge that listening is important and to describe the steps in the listening process. What's hard is to actually become a better listener. This section will describe the challenges that listeners must face and overcome to become more effective communicators. We'll look at various types of ineffective listening, then we'll explore the many reasons we don't listen better. As you read this material, think to yourself, "How many of these describe *me*?" The first step to becoming a better listener is to recognize areas that need improvement.

Not comprehending, they hear like the deaf.

Heraclitus

"Someday, you'll act like you understand."

Types of Ineffective Listening

Your own experience will probably confirm the fact that poor listening is all too common. Although a certain amount of ineffective listening is inescapable and sometimes even understandable, it's important to be aware of these types of problems so you can avoid them when listening well really counts.

Pseudolistening   Whereas mindless listening may be a private matter, **pseudolistening** is an imitation of the real thing—an act put on to fool the speaker. Pseudolisteners give the appearance of being attentive: They look you in the eye; they may even nod and smile. But the show of attention is a polite façade because their minds are somewhere else. Paradoxically, pseudolistening can take more effort than simply tuning out the other person.

Stage-hogging   Stage-hogs (sometimes called "conversational narcissists") try to turn the topic of conversations to themselves instead of showing interest in the speaker.[21] One **stage-hogging** strategy is a "shift-response"—changing the focus of the conversation from the speaker to the narcissist: "You think *your* math class is tough? You ought to try my physics class!" Interruptions are another hallmark of stage-hogging. Besides preventing the listener from learning potentially valuable information, they can damage the relationship between the interrupter and the speaker. For example, applicants who interrupt the questions of employment interviewers are likely to be rated less favorably than applicants who wait until the interviewer has finished speaking before they respond.[22]

Selective Listening   Selective listeners respond only to the parts of your remarks that interest them, rejecting everything else. Sometimes **selective listening** is legitimate, as when we screen out radio commercials and music and keep an ear cocked for a weather report or an announcement of the time. Selective listening is less appropriate in personal settings, when your obvious inattention can be a slap in the face to the other person.

Insulated Listening   Insulated listeners are almost the opposite of their selective cousins just described. Instead of looking for specific information, these people avoid it. Whenever a topic arises that they'd rather not deal with, those who use **insulated listening** simply fail to hear or acknowledge it. You remind them about a problem, and they'll nod or answer you—and then promptly ignore or forget what you've just said.

Defensive Listening   Defensive listeners take others' remarks as personal attacks. The teenager who perceives her parents' questions about her friends and activities as distrustful snooping uses **defensive**

Bore, n. A person who talks when you wish him to listen.
Conversation, n. A fair for the display of the minor mental commodities, each exhibitor being too intent upon arrangement of his own wares to observe those of his neighbor.
Egotist, n. A person of low taste more interested in himself than me.
Heaven, n. A place where the wicked cease from troubling you with talk of their personal affairs, and the good listen with attention while you expound your own.

Ambrose Bierce,
The Devil's Dictionary

listening, as do touchy parents who view any questioning by their children as a threat to their authority and parental wisdom. As Chapter 10 will suggest, it's fair to assume that many defensive listeners are suffering from shaky presenting images and avoid admitting it by projecting their own insecurities onto others.

Ambushing   Ambushers listen carefully to you, but only because they're collecting information that they'll use to attack what you say. The technique of a cross-examining prosecution attorney is a good example of **ambushing**. Needless to say, using this kind of strategy will justifiably initiate defensiveness in the other person.

Insensitive Listening   Those who use **insensitive listening** respond to the superficial content in a message but miss the more important emotional information that may not be expressed directly. "How's it going?" an insensitive listener might ask. When you reply by saying "Oh, okay I guess" in a dejected tone, he or she responds "Well, great!" Insensitive listeners tend to ignore the nonverbal cues described in Chapter 6 and lack the empathy described in Chapter 3.

Why We Don't Listen Better

After thinking about the styles of ineffective listening described above, most people begin to see that they listen carefully only a small percentage of the time. Sad as it may be, it's impossible to listen well *all* the time, for several reasons which we'll outline here.

Message Overload   The first reason is that the amount of speech that most of us encounter every day makes careful listening to everything we hear impossible. As you have already read, many of us spend almost half the time we're awake listening to verbal messages. It's impossible to keep our attention totally focused for this amount of time. As a result, we often choose—understandably and sometimes wisely—to listen mindlessly rather than mindfully.

Everybody's talkin'
at me
I don't hear a word
they're sayin'

Fred Neil

Preoccupation   Another reason why we don't always listen carefully is that we're often wrapped up in personal concerns that seem more important than the messages that others are sending. It's hard to pay attention to someone else when you're worrying about an upcoming exam or thinking about the great time you plan to have over the next weekend.

Rapid Thought   Listening carefully is also difficult for a physiological reason. Although we're capable of understanding speech at rates of up to 600 words per minute, the average person only speaks between 100 and 150 words per minute.[23] Thus, we have mental "spare time" while someone is talking. The temptation is to use this time in ways that don't relate to the speaker's ideas: thinking about personal interests, daydreaming, planning a rebuttal, and so on. The trick is to use this spare time to understand the speaker's ideas better rather than to let your attention wander.

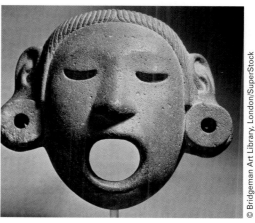

© Bridgeman Art Library, London/SuperStock

At the Party

© Diana Ong/SuperStock

Unrhymed, unrhythmical,
the chatter goes:
Yet no one hears his own
remarks as prose.
Beneath each topic tune-
lessly discussed
The ground-bass is recip-
rocal mistrust.
The names in fashion
shuttling to and fro

Yield, when deciphered,
messages of woe.
You cannot read me like
an open book.
I'm more myself than you
will ever look.
Will no one listen to my
little song?
Perhaps I shan't be with
you very long.

A howl for recognition,
shrill with fear,
Shakes the jam-packed
apartment, but each
ear
Is listening to its hearing,
so none hear.

W. H. Auden

Effort Listening effectively is hard work. The physical changes that occur during careful listening show the effort it takes: The heart rate quickens, respiration increases, and body temperature rises.[24] Notice that these changes are similar to the body's reaction to physical effort. This is no coincidence because listening carefully to a speaker can be just as taxing as a workout—which is why some people choose not to make the effort.[25] If you've come home exhausted after an evening of listening intently to a friend in need, you know how draining the process can be.

External Noise The physical world in which we live often presents distractions that make it hard to pay attention to others. Consider, for example, how the efficiency of your listening decreases when you are seated in a crowded, hot, stuffy room, surrounded by others talking next to you and traffic noises outside. It's not surprising that noisy classrooms often make learning difficult for students.[26] In such circumstances even the best intentions aren't enough to ensure clear understanding.

Faulty Assumptions We often make faulty assumptions that lead us to believe we're listening attentively when quite the opposite is true. When the subject is a familiar one, it's easy to tune out because you think you've heard it all before. A related problem arises when you assume that a speaker's thoughts are too simple or too obvious to deserve careful attention, when in fact they do. At other times just the opposite occurs: You think that another's comments are too complex to be understood (as in some lectures), so you give up trying to make sense of them.

Lack of Apparent Advantages It often seems that there's more to gain by speaking than by listening. When business consultant Nancy Kline asked some of her clients why they interrupted their colleagues, these are the reasons she heard:

My idea is better than theirs.

If I don't interrupt them, I'll never get to say my idea.

I know what they are about to say.

They don't need to finish their thoughts since mine are better.

Nothing about their idea will improve with further development.

It is more important for me to get recognized than it is to hear their idea.

I am more important than they are.[27]

Even if some of these thoughts are true, the egotism behind them is stunning. Furthermore, nonlisteners are likely to find that the people they cut off are

---

Bright-eyed college students in lecture halls aren't necessarily listening to the professor, the American Psychological Association was told yesterday.

If you shot off a gun at sporadic intervals and asked the students to encode their thoughts and moods at that moment, you would discover that:

■ About 20 percent of the students, men and women, are pursuing erotic thoughts.

■ Another 20 percent are reminiscing about something.

■ Only 20 percent are actually paying attention to the lecture; 12 percent actively listen. The others are worrying, daydreaming, thinking about lunch or—surprise—religion (8 percent).

This confirmation of the lecturer's worst fears was reported by Paul Cameron, an assistant professor at Wayne State University in Detroit. Cameron's results were based on a nine-week course in introductory psychology for 85 college sophomores. A gun was fired 21 times at random intervals, usually when Cameron was in the middle of a sentence.

The San Francisco Sunday Examiner and Chronicle

So the first simple feeling I want to share with you is my enjoyment when I can really hear someone. I think perhaps this has been a long-standing characteristic of mine. I can remember this in my early grammar school days. A child would ask the teacher a question, and the teacher would give a perfectly good answer to a completely different question. A feeling of pain and distress would always strike me. My reaction was, "But you didn't hear him!" I felt a sort of childish despair at the lack of communication which was (and is) so common.

Carl R. Rogers

less likely to treat their ideas with respect. Like defensiveness, listening is often reciprocal: You get what you give.

Lack of Training   Even if we want to listen well, we're often hampered by a lack of training. A common but mistaken belief is that listening is like breathing—an activity that people do well naturally. "After all," the common belief goes, "I've been listening since I was a child. I don't need to study the subject in school." The truth is that listening is a skill much like speaking: Virtually everybody does it, though few people do it well. Unfortunately, there is no connection between how competently most communicators *think* they listen and how competent they really are in their ability to understand others.[28] The good news is that listening can be improved through instruction and training.[29] Despite this fact, the amount of time spent teaching listening is far less than that spent on other types of communication. Table 7.1 reflects this upside-down arrangement.

Table 7.1	**Comparison of Communication Activities**			
	Listening	Speaking	Reading	Writing
Learned	First	Second	Third	Fourth
Used	Most	Next to most	Next to least	Least
Taught	Least	Next to least	Next to most	Most

Hearing Problems   Sometimes a person's listening ability suffers from a physiological hearing problem. In such cases, both the person with the problem and others can become frustrated and annoyed at the ineffective communication that results. If you suspect that you or someone you know suffers from a hearing loss, it's wise to have a physician or audiologist perform an examination.

Invitation to Insight

Speaking and Listening with a "Talking Stick"

Explore the benefits of talking less and listening more by using a "Talking Stick." This exercise is based on the Native American tradition of "council." Gather a group of people in a circle, and designate a particular object as the talking stick. (Almost any manageable object will do.) Participants then pass the object around the circle. Each person may speak

   a. when holding the stick,

   b. for as long as he or she holds the stick, and

   c. without interruption from anyone else in the circle.

When a member is through speaking, the stick passes to the left, and the speaker surrendering the stick must wait until it has made its way around the circle before speaking again.

After each member of the group has had the chance to speak, discuss how this experience differed from more common approaches to listening. Decide how the desirable parts of this method could be introduced into everyday conversations.

Media Influences   A final challenge to serious listening is the influence of contemporary mass media, especially television and radio. A growing amount of programming consists of short segments: news items, commercials, music videos, and so on. (Think of CNN, *Sesame Street,* and MTV.) These trends discourage the kind of focused attention that is necessary for careful listening, especially to complicated ideas and feelings.[30]

Learn to listen. Opportunity could be knocking at your door very softly.

Frank Tyger

Meeting the Challenge of Listening Better

After reading the last few pages, you might decide that listening well is next to impossible. Fortunately, with the right combination of attitude and skill, you can indeed listen better. The following guidelines will show you how.

Talk Less   Zeno of Citium put it most succinctly: "We have been given two ears and but a single mouth, in order that we may hear more and talk less." If your

Deafness Lite

So slight is the bereftness of my elated ear-fault
that "Deafness Lite" became the name that I call it.
In a simpler word: things heard are blurred
on the left as well (or as weakly) as right.
Neither half's loss is a matter too drastic
both partly "cured" by batteries in plastic.
But if eyeing such signs of silence, Hearer,
or (harder to do) spying a less visible clue
try, by turning your speech slow and clearer
to reach those few who must communicate anew.
And so
that is why
as their advocate I
ask you unafflicted this:
Make me your talking's target
and practice, practice, practice.
Address then the wise assistive eyes
of sisters and brothers with hindered ear
and so come to know, then to de-stranger-ize
those kindred other souls who less than I can hear.
Repeat. Reword. For patience may reward yourself;
Not by some sense of the charity kind
but by sharing the very daringest adventure:
eyes meeting eyes and mind mating with mind.

Sal Parlato, Jr.

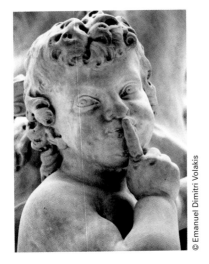

To be heard, there are times
you must be silent.

Chinese Proverb

true goal is to understand the speaker, avoid the tendency to hog the
stage and shift the conversation to your ideas. Talking less doesn't
mean you must remain completely silent. As you'll soon read, giving
feedback that clarifies your understanding and seeks new information is
an important way to understand a speaker. Nonetheless, most of us
talk too much when we're claiming to understand others. Other cultures, including many Native American ones, value listening at least as
much as talking.[31] You can appreciate the value of this approach by
trying the exercise on page 244.

Get Rid of Distractions   Some distractions are external: ringing telephones, radio or television programs, friends dropping in, and so on.
Other distractions are internal: preoccupation with your own problems, an empty stomach, and so on. If the information you're seeking
is really important, do everything possible to eliminate the internal and
external distractions that interfere with careful listening. This might
mean turning off the TV, taking the phone off the hook, or moving to
a quiet room where you won't be bothered by the lure of the computer, the
work on your desk, or the food on the counter.

Don't Judge Prematurely   Most people would agree that it's essential to understand a speaker's ideas before judging them. In spite of this fact, all of us are
guilty of forming snap judgments, evaluating others before hearing them out.
This tendency is greatest when the speaker's ideas conflict with our own. Conversations that ought to be exchanges of ideas turn into verbal battles, with the
"opponents" trying to ambush one another in order to win a victory. It's also
tempting to judge prematurely when others criticize you, even when those criticisms may contain valuable truths and when understanding them may lead to a
change for the better. Even if there is no criticism or disagreement, we tend to
evaluate others based on sketchy first
impressions, forming snap judgments
that aren't at all valid. The lesson contained in these negative examples is
clear: Listen first. Make sure you
understand. *Then* evaluate.

Look for Key Ideas   It's easy to lose
patience with long-winded speakers
who never seem to get to the point—
or *have* a point, for that matter.
Nonetheless, most people do have a
central idea. By using your ability to
think more quickly than the speaker
can talk, you may be able to extract
the central idea from the surrounding
mass of words you're hearing. If you
can't figure out what the speaker is
driving at, you can always use a variety
of response skills, which we'll examine
now.

"You haven't been listening. I keep telling you that
I don't want a product fit for a king."

Lend an Ear

"The first time the car broke down we were somewhere in North Carolina," my mother-in-law told me over the phone. "We had it fixed, and then it stalled again in Delaware. But the worst was on the Verrazano Bridge during rush hour. It seemed as if we'd never get home."

"That sounds horrible," I said, ready to launch into my own horror story—a car that conked out at 9:30 P.M. in a deserted mall parking lot.

But someone knocked at her door, so she had to say good-bye. "Thank you for listening," she added, "but most of all for not telling me your worst car story."

My cheeks burning, I hung up. In the days ahead I found myself thinking about the wisdom of her parting words. I can't count the number of times I've begun to complain—about a fight, a professional disappointment, or even car problems—only to have my friend cut me off with "The same thing just happened to me." Suddenly we're talking about *her* ungrateful kid, *her* leaky fuel line. And I'm left nod-ding my head in all the right places, wondering if we haven't all come down with a bad case of emotional attention deficit disorder.

What we all hope for when we're feeling low or agitated or wildly happy is to find a friend who sounds as if he or she has all the time in the world to listen. We don't always want answers or advice. Sometimes we just want company.

Roberta Isrealoff

EAR
EYES
UNDIVIDED ATTENTION
HEART

Calligraphy by Angie Au. Used by permission.

The Chinese characters that make up the verb *to listen* tell us something significant about this skill.

How Well Do You Listen?

ThomsonNOW You can evaluate your own listening effectiveness by taking a quiz developed for the *Wall Street Journal*. Go to your ThomsonNOW for *Looking Out/ Looking In* to link to this site. Check the accuracy of your self-evaluation by asking someone who knows you well to rate you, using the same set of questions.

Types of Listening Responses

Of the five components of listening (hearing, attending, understanding, responding, and remembering), it's responding that lets us know how well others are tuned in to what we're saying. Think for a moment of someone you consider a good listener. Why did you choose that person? It's probably because of the way she or he responds while you are speaking: making eye contact and nodding when you're talking, staying attentive while you're telling an important story, reacting with an exclamation when you say something startling, expressing empathy and support when you're hurting, and offering another perspective or advice when you ask for it.[32]

The rest of this chapter will describe a variety of response styles. We'll begin by describing responses that are focused on gathering more information to better understand the speaker. By chapter's end, our focus will be on listening responses that offer a speaker our assessment and direction.

Prompting

In some cases, the best response a listener can give is a small nudge to keep the speaker talking. **Prompting** involves using silences and brief statements of encouragement to draw others out. Besides helping you to better understand the speaker, prompting can also help others clarify their thoughts and feelings. Consider this example:

Pablo: Julie's dad is selling a complete computer system for only $600, but if I want it I have to buy it now. He's got another interested buyer. It's a great deal. But buying it would wipe out my savings. At the rate I spend money, it would take me a year to save up this much again.

Tim: Uh-huh.

Pablo: I wouldn't be able to take that ski trip over winter break . . . but I sure could save time with my schoolwork . . . and do a better job, too.

Tim: That's for sure.

Pablo: Do you think I should buy it?

Tim: I don't know. What do *you* think?

Pablo: I just can't decide.

Tim: (*silence*)

Pablo: I'm going to do it. I'll never get a deal like this again.

In cases like this, your prompting can be a catalyst to help others find their own answers. Prompting will work best when it's done sincerely. Your nonverbal behaviors—eye contact, posture, facial expression, tone of voice—have to show that you are concerned with the other person's problem. Mechanical prompting is likely to irritate instead of help.

The greatest compliment that was ever paid me was when one asked me what I thought, and attended to my answer.

Henry David Thoreau

Questioning

It's easy to understand why **questioning** has been called "the most popular piece of language."[33] Asking for information can help both the person doing the asking and the one providing answers.

Questioning can help you, the asker, in at least three ways. Most obviously, the answers you get can fill in facts and details that will sharpen your understanding ("Did he give you any reasons for doing that?" "What happened next?"). Also, by asking questions you can learn what others are thinking and feeling ("What's on your mind?" "Are you mad at me?"), as well as what they might want ("Are you asking me to apologize?").

Besides being useful to the person doing the asking, questions can also be a tool for the one who answers. As people in the helping professions know, questions can encourage self-discovery. Playing counselor can be a dangerous game, but there are times when you can use questions to encourage others to explore their thoughts and feelings. "So, what do you see as your options?" may prompt an employee to come up with creative problem-solving alternatives. "What would be your ideal solution?" might help a friend get in touch with various wants and needs. Most importantly, encouraging discovery rather than dispensing advice indicates you have faith in others' ability to think for themselves. This may be the most important message that you can communicate as an effective listener.

Despite their apparent benefits, not all questions are equally helpful. Whereas **sincere questions** are aimed at understanding others, **counterfeit questions** are aimed at sending a message, not receiving one. Counterfeit questions come in several varieties:

- *Questions that trap the speaker.* When your friend says, "You didn't like that movie, did you?" you're being backed into a corner. It's clear that your friend disapproves, so the question leaves you with two choices: You can disagree and defend your position, or you can devalue your reaction by lying or equivocating—"I guess it wasn't perfect." Consider how much easier it would be to respond to the sincere question, "What did you think of the movie?"

- *A tag question.* Phrases like "did you?" or "isn't that right?" at the end of a question can be a tip-off that the asker is looking for agreement, not information. Although some tag questions are genuine requests for confirmation, counterfeit ones are used to coerce agreement: "You said you'd call at 5 o'clock, but you forgot, didn't you?" Similarly, leading questions that begin with "Don't you" (such as, "Don't you think he would make a good boss?") direct others toward a desired response. As a simple solution, changing "Don't you?" to "Do you?" makes the question less leading.

- *Questions that make statements.* "Are you *finally* off the phone?" is more of a statement than a question—a fact unlikely to be lost on the targeted person. Emphasizing certain words can also turn a question into a statement: "You lent money to *Tony?*" We also use questions to offer advice. The person who asks "Are you going to stand up to him and give him what he deserves?" clearly has stated an opinion about what should be done.

- *Questions that carry hidden agendas.* "Are you busy Friday night?" is a dangerous question to answer. If you say "No," thinking the person has something fun in mind, you won't like hearing, "Good, because I need some help moving my

"I have a pet at home."

"Oh, what kind of a pet?"

"It is a dog."

"What kind of a dog?"

"It is a cocker spaniel."

"Grown up or a puppy?"

"It is full grown."

"What color is it?"

"It is black and white."

"Why didn't you say you had a full-grown, black-and-white cocker spaniel as a pet in the first place?"

From *Communication: The Transfer of Meaning* by Don Fabun.

piano." Obviously, such questions are not designed to enhance understanding: They are setups for the proposal that follows. Other examples include, "Will you do me a favor?" and "If I tell you what happened, will you promise not to get mad?" Wise communicators answer questions that mask hidden agendas cautiously, with responses like "It depends" or "Let me hear what you have in mind before I answer."

■ *Questions that seek "correct" answers.* Most of us have been victims of questioners who want to hear only a particular response. "Which shoes do you think I should wear?" can be a sincere question—unless the asker has a predetermined preference. When this happens, the asker isn't interested in listening to contrary opinions, and "incorrect" responses get shot down. Some of these questions may venture into delicate territory. "Honey, do you think I look ugly?" can be a request for a "correct" answer.

■ *Questions based on unchecked assumptions.* "Why aren't you listening to me?" assumes that the other person isn't paying attention. "What's the matter?" assumes that something is wrong. As Chapter 3 explains, perception checking is a much better way of checking out assumptions. As you recall, a perception check offers a description and interpretations, followed by a sincere request for clarification: "When you kept looking over at the TV, I thought you weren't listening to me, but maybe I was wrong. Were you paying attention?"

Paraphrasing

For all its value, questioning won't always help you understand or help others. As the cartoon on this page shows, questions can even lead to greater confusion. For another example, consider what might happen when you ask for directions to a friend's home. Suppose that you've received these instructions: "Drive about a mile and then turn left at the traffic signal." Now imagine that a few common problems exist in this simple message. First, suppose that your friend's idea of "about a mile" differs from yours: Your mental picture of the distance is actually closer to 2 miles, whereas your friend's is closer to 300 yards. Next, consider that "traffic signal" really means "stop sign"; after all, it's common for us to think one thing and say another. Keeping these problems in mind, suppose that you tried to verify your understanding of the directions by asking, "After I turn at the signal, how far should I go?" to which your friend replies that the house is the third from the corner. Clearly, if you parted after this exchange, you would encounter a lot of frustration before finding the elusive residence.

Because questioning doesn't always provide the information you need, consider another kind of listening response—one that would tell you whether you understood what had already been said before you asked additional questions. This type of feedback involves restating in your own words the message you thought the speaker just sent, without adding anything new. Statements that reword the listener's interpretation of a message are commonly termed **paraphrasing** or *active listening*. If the listener in the preceding scenario had offered this paraphrase—"You're telling me to drive down to the traffic light by the high school and turn toward the mountains, is that it?"—it probably would have led the speaker to clarify the message.

The key to success in paraphrasing is to restate the other person's comments in your own words as a way of cross-checking the information. If you simply repeat the other person's comments verbatim, you will sound foolish—and you still might well be misunderstanding what has been said. Notice the difference between simply parroting a statement and true paraphrasing:

Speaker: I'd like to go, but I can't afford it.
Parroting: You'd like to go, but you can't afford it.
Paraphrasing: So if we could find a way to pay for you, you'd be willing to come. Is that right?
Speaker: You look awful!
Parroting: You think I look terrible.
Paraphrasing: Sounds like you think I've put on too much weight.

There are two levels at which you can paraphrase messages. The first involves paraphrasing *factual information* that will help you understand the other person's ideas more clearly. At the most basic level, this sort of reflecting can prevent frustrating mixups: "So you want to meet *this* Tuesday, not next week, right?"

You can also paraphrase *personal information*: "So my joking makes you think I don't care about your problem." This sort of nondefensive response may be difficult when you are under attack, but it can short-circuit defensive arguments. Chapter 10 will explain in more detail how to use paraphrasing when you're being criticized.

Paraphrasing personal information can also be a tool for helping others, as the Communication Transcript on page 252 shows.[34] Reflecting the speaker's thoughts and feelings (instead of judging or analyzing, for example) shows your involvement and concern. The nonevaluative nature of paraphrasing encourages the problem-holder to discuss the matter further. Reflecting thoughts and feelings allows the problem-holder to unload more of the concerns he or she has been carrying around, often leading to the relief that comes from catharsis. Finally, paraphrasing helps the problem-holder to sort out the problem. The clarity that comes from this sort of perspective can make it possible to find solutions that weren't apparent before. These features make paraphrasing a vital skill in the human services professions, leadership training, and even hostage negotiation.[35]

Effective paraphrasing is a skill that takes time to develop. You can make your paraphrasing sound more natural by taking any of three approaches, depending on the situation:

1. Change the speaker's wording:

Speaker: Bilingual education is just another failed idea of bleeding heart liberals.
Paraphrase: Let me see if I've got this right. You're mad because you think bilingual ed sounds good, but it doesn't work?

> The reality of the other person is not in what he reveals to you, but in what he cannot reveal to you. Therefore, if you would understand him, listen not to what he says but rather to what he does not say.
>
> Kahlil Gibran

Communication Transcript

Paraphrasing on the Job

This conversation between two co-workers shows how paraphrasing can help people solve their own problems. Notice how Jill comes to a conclusion without Mark's advice. Notice also how the paraphrasing sounds natural when combined with sincere questions and other helping styles.

Jill: I've had the strangest feeling about John *(their boss)* lately.

Mark: What's that? *(A simple question invites Jill to go on.)*

Jill: I'm starting to think maybe he has this thing about women—or maybe it's just about me.

Mark: You mean he's coming on to you? *(Mark paraphrases what he thinks Jill has said.)*

Jill: Oh, no, not at all! But it seems like he doesn't take women—or at least me—seriously. *(Jill corrects Mark's misunderstanding and explains herself.)*

Mark: What do you mean? *(Mark asks another simple question to get more information.)*

Jill: Well, whenever we're in a meeting or just talking around the office and he asks for ideas, he always seems to pick men. He gives orders to women—men, too—but he never asks the women to say what they think.

Mark: So you think maybe he doesn't take women seriously, is that it? *(Mark paraphrases Jill's last statement.)*

Jill: He sure doesn't seem interested in their ideas. But that doesn't mean he's a total woman-hater. I know he counts on some women in the office. Teresa has been here forever, and he's always saying he couldn't live without her. And when Brenda got the new computer system up and running last month, I know he appreciated that. He gave her a day off and told everybody how she saved our lives.

Mark: Now you sound confused. *(Reflects her apparent feeling)*

Jill: I am confused. I don't think it's just my imagination. I mean I'm a good producer, but he has never—not once—asked me for my ideas about how to improve sales or anything. And I can't remember a time when he's asked any other women. But maybe I'm overreacting.

Mark: You're not positive whether you're right, but I can tell that this has you concerned. *(Mark paraphrases both Jill's central theme and her feeling.)*

Jill: Yes. But I don't know what to do about it.

Mark: Maybe you should . . . *(Starts to offer advice but catches himself and decides to ask a question instead.)* So what are your choices?

Jill: Well, I could just ask him if he's aware that he never asks women's opinions. But that might sound too aggressive and angry.

Mark: And you're not angry? *(Tries to clarify how Jill is feeling)*

Jill: Not really. I don't know whether I should be angry because he's not taking ideas seriously, or whether he just doesn't take my ideas seriously, or whether it's nothing at all.

Mark: So you're mostly confused. *(Reflects Jill's apparent feeling again)*

Jill: Yes! I don't know where I stand with John, and not being sure is starting to get to me. I wish I knew what he thinks of me. Maybe I could just tell him I'm confused about what is going on here and ask him to clear it up. But what if it's nothing? Then I'll look insecure.

Mark: *(Mark thinks Jill should confront the boss, but he isn't positive that this is the best approach, so he paraphrases what Jill seems to be saying.)* And that would make you look bad.

Jill: I'm afraid maybe it would. I wonder if I could talk it over with anybody else in the office and get their ideas . . .

Mark: . . . see what they think . . .

Jill: Yeah. Maybe I could ask Brenda. She's easy to talk to, and I do respect her judgment. Maybe she could give me some ideas about how to handle this.

Mark: Sounds like you're comfortable with talking to Brenda first. *(Paraphrases)*

Jill: *(Warming to the idea)* Yes! Then if it's nothing, I can calm down. But if I do need to talk to John, I'll know I'm doing the right thing.

Mark: Great. Let me know how it goes.

Communication Scenarios

To see and analyze video examples of paraphrasing in action, go to your ThomsonNOW for *Looking Out/ Looking In,* access "Communication Scenarios," and then click on "'Paraphrasing on the Job." **ThomsonNOW**

2. Offer an example of what you think the speaker is talking about:

Speaker: Lee is such a jerk. I can't believe the way he acted last night.
Paraphrase: You think those jokes were pretty offensive, huh?

3. Reflect the underlying theme of the speaker's remarks:

Paraphrase: You keep reminding me to be careful. Sounds like you're wor-
                 ried that something might happen to me. Am I right?

Paraphrasing won't always be accurate. But expressing your restatement *ten-tatively* gives the other person a chance to make a correction. (See the examples above for illustrations of open-minded paraphrasing.)

Because it's an unfamiliar way of responding, paraphrasing may feel awkward at first; but if you start by paraphrasing occasionally and then gradually increase the frequency of such responses, you can begin to learn the benefits. You can begin practicing paraphrasing by trying the following Skill Builder.

Skill Builder

Paraphrasing Practice

This exercise will help you see that it is possible to understand someone who disagrees with you, without arguing or sacrificing your point of view.

1. Find a partner. Designate one person as *A* and the other as *B*.

2. Find a subject on which you and your partner apparently disagree—a current events topic, a philosophical or moral issue, or perhaps simply a matter of personal taste.

3. Person *A* begins by making a statement on the subject. Person *B*'s job is then to par-aphrase the statement. *B*'s job is simply to understand here, and doing so in no way should signify agreement or disagreement with *A*'s remarks.

4. *A* then responds by telling *B* whether her response was accurate. If there was some misunderstanding, *A* should make the correction, and *B* should feed back her new understanding of the statement. Continue this process until you're both sure that *B* understands *A*'s statement.

5. Now it's *B*'s turn to respond to *A*'s statement and for *A* to help the process of under-standing by correcting *B*.

6. Continue this process until each partner is satisfied that she has explained herself fully and has been understood by the other person.

7. Now discuss the following questions:

   a. How did your understanding of the speaker's statement change after you used active listening?

   b. Did you find that the gap between your position and that of your partner nar-rowed as a result of active listening?

   c. How did you feel at the end of your conversation? How does this feeling compare to your usual feeling after discussing controversial issues?

   d. How might your life change if you used paraphrasing at home? At work? With friends?

There are several factors to consider before you decide to paraphrase:

1. *Is the issue complex enough?* If you're fixing dinner, and someone wants to know when it will be ready, it would be exasperating to hear, "You're interested in knowing when we'll be eating." Likewise, reflecting emotions probably isn't necessary when a friend says, "I hate getting that traffic ticket!"

2. *Do you have the necessary time and concern?* Paraphrasing can take a good deal of time. Therefore, if you're in a hurry, it's wise to avoid starting a conversation you won't be able to finish. Even more important than time is concern: Paraphrasing that comes across as mechanical or insincere reflecting can do more harm than good.[36]

3. *Can you withhold judgment?* Use paraphrasing only if you are willing to focus on the speaker's message without injecting your own judgments. It can be tempting to rephrase others' comments in a way that leads them toward the position you think is best without ever clearly stating your intentions. If you think the situation meets the criteria for advice described earlier in this chapter, you should offer your advice openly.

4. *Is your paraphrasing in proportion to other responses?* Paraphrasing can become annoying when it's overused. This is especially true if you suddenly add this approach to your style. A far better way to use paraphrasing is gradually to introduce it into your repertoire.

Skill Builder

Listening for Feelings

Use the Communication Toolkit Website to practice your skill at recognizing and responding to a speaker's feelings. Go to your ThomsonNOW for *Looking Out/Looking In* to access the link to this site.

Supporting

There are times when other people want to hear more than a reflection of how *they* feel: They would like to know how *you* feel. **Supportive responses** reveal a listener's solidarity with the speaker's situation. One scholar describes supporting as "expressions of care, concern, affection, and interest, especially during times of stress or upset."[37]

There are several types of support:

Empathizing	"I can understand why you'd be upset about this"
	"Yeah, that class was tough for me, too."
Agreement	"You're right—the landlord is being unfair."
	"Sounds like the job is a perfect match for you."
Offers to help	"I'm here if you need me."
	"I'd be happy to study with you for the next test if you'd like."
Praise	"Wow—you did a fantastic job!"
	"You're a terrific person, and if she doesn't recognize it, that's her problem!"
Reassurance	"The worst part seems to be over. It will probably get easier from here."
	"I'm sure you'll do a great job."

There's no question about the value of receiving comfort and support in the face of personal problems. One survey showed that "comforting ability" was among the most important communication skills a friend could have.[38] The value of receiving support with personal problems is clear when big problems arise, but research shows that the smaller, everyday distresses and upsets can actually take a bigger toll on mental health and physical wellbeing.[39] The research is clear: Receiving emotional support during times of stress is good for one's health.[40]

© Len Abbott/Deljou Art Group

It's easy to identify what effective support *doesn't* sound like. Some scholars have called these messages "cold comfort."[41] See Table 7.2 on this page for real cold-comfort messages found in an online discussion. As these examples suggest, you're probably *not* being supportive if you:

■ *Deny others the right to their feelings.* Consider the stock remark "Don't worry about it." Although it may be intended as a reassuring comment, the underlying message is that the speaker wants the person to feel differently. The irony is that the suggestion probably won't work—after all, it's unlikely that people can or will stop worrying just because you tell them to do so. Research about such responses is clear: "Messages that explicitly acknowledge, elaborate, and legitimize the feelings and perspective of a distressed person are perceived as more helpful messages than those which only implicitly recognize or deny the feelings and perspective of the other."[42]

■ *Minimize the significance of the situation.* Consider the times you've been told, "Hey, it's only _____." You can probably fill in the blank in a variety of ways: "a job," "her opinion," "a test," "puppy love," "a party." To someone who has been the victim of verbal abuse, the hurtful message isn't "just words"; to a child who didn't get an invitation, it isn't "just a party"; to a worker who has been chewed out by the boss, it isn't "just a job."

■ *Focus on "then and there" rather than "here and now."* Although it is sometimes true that "you'll feel better tomorrow," it sometimes isn't. Even if the prediction that "ten years from now you won't remember her name" proves correct, it provides little comfort to someone experiencing heartbreak today.

Table 7.2 Cold Comfort: Messages That Don't Help

■ Don't take it so hard. She was a slut anyway.

■ That's nothing! Want to hear how I got dumped?

■ I don't know what you ever saw in him anyway. He's ugly. You can do much better.

■ You know you had this coming—you were overdue for payback.

■ S/he was way too young (old) for you.

■ You can't have everything you want in this life.

■ Now that it's finally over, I can tell you she's been cheating on you, dude!

■ He was just using you for sex.

■ She was always a jerk about you behind your back. Who needs that?

■ Now we'll have more time to hang out together, just like we used to!

■ I'm so glad that this happened to you. I heard a story once about a guy whose significant other left him, and he begged and begged and begged for her to come back. Finally she did, and 20 years later she was a drug addict and committed suicide and left him with nothing but heartache. So you never know what you're saved from.

It is hard to know what to say to a person who has been struck by tragedy, but it is easier to know what not to say. Anything critical of the mourner ("don't take it so hard," "try to hold back your tears, you're upsetting people") is wrong. Anything which tries to minimize the mourner's pain ("it's probably for the best," "it could be a lot worse," "she's better off now") is likely to be misguided and unappreciated. Anything which asks the mourner to disguise or reject his feelings ("we have no right to question God," "God must love you to have selected you for this burden") is wrong as well.

Harold S. Kushner,
When Bad Things Happen to Good People

- *Cast judgment.* It usually isn't encouraging to hear "You know, it's your own fault—you really shouldn't have done that" after you've confessed to making a poor decision. As you'll learn in Chapter 10, evaluative and condescending statements are more likely to engender defensiveness than to help people change for the better.
- *Defend yourself.* When your response to others' concerns is to defend yourself ("Don't blame me; I've done my part"), it's clear that you are more concerned with yourself than with supporting the other person.

How often do people fail to provide appropriate supportive responses? One survey of mourners who had recently suffered from the death of a loved one reported that 80 percent of the statements made to them were unhelpful.[43] Nearly half of the "helpful" statements were advice: "You've got to get out more." "Don't question God's will." Despite their frequency, these suggestions were helpful only 3 percent of the time. The next most frequent response was reassurance, such as "She's out of pain now." Like advice, this kind of support was helpful only 3 percent of the time. Far more helpful were expressions that acknowledged the mourner's feelings.

When handled correctly, supporting responses *can* be helpful. Guidelines for effective support include:

1. *Recognize that you can support another person's struggles without approving of his or her decisions.* Suppose, for instance, that a friend has decided to quit a job that you think she should keep. You could still be supportive by saying, "I know you've given this a lot of thought and that you're doing what you think is best." Responses like this can provide support without compromising your principles.
2. *Monitor the other person's reaction to your support.* If it doesn't seem to help, consider other types of responses that let him or her explore the issue.
3. *Realize that support may not always be welcome.* In one survey, some people reported occasions when social support wasn't necessary because they felt capable of handling the problem themselves.[44] Many regarded uninvited support as an intrusion, and some said it left them feeling more nervous than before. The majority of respondents expressed a preference for being in control of whether their distressing situation should be discussed with even the most helpful friend.

Analyzing

In an **analyzing response**, the listener offers an interpretation of a speaker's message. Analyses like these are probably familiar to you:

"I think what's really bothering you is . . ."

"She's doing it because . . ."

"I don't think you really meant that."

"Maybe the problem started when she . . ."

Interpretations are often effective ways to help people with problems consider alternative meanings—meanings they would have never thought of without your

So Penseroso

Come, megrims, mollygrubs
    and collywobbles!
Come, gloom that limps and
    misery that hobbles!
Come also, most exquisite
    melancholiage,
As dank and decadent as
    November foliage!
I crave to shudder in your
    moist embrace,

To feel your oystery
    fingers on my face.
This is my hour of sad-
    ness and of soulful-
    ness,
And cursed be he who
    dissipates my dole-
    fulness.
I do not desire to be
    cheered,
I desire to retire, I am
    thinking of growing
    a beard,
A sorrowful beard,
    with a mournful, a
    dolorous hue in it,
With ashes and glue
    in it.
I want to be drunk
    with despair,
I want to caress my care,
I do not wish to be blithe,
I wish to recoil and writhe,
I will revel in cosmic woe,
And I want my woe to show.
This is the morbid moment,
This is the ebony hour.
Anoint thee, sweetness and
    light!

I want to be dark and sour!
Away with the bird that
    twitters!
All that glitters is jitters!
Roses, roses are gray,
Violets cry Boo! and frighten
    me.
Sugar is stimulating,
And people conspire to
    brighten me.
Go hence, people, go
    hence!
Go sit on a picket fence!
Go gargle with mineral oil,
Go out and develop a boil!
Melancholy is what I brag
    and boast of,
Melancholy I mean to make
    the most of,
You beaming optimists shall
    not destroy it.
But while I am at it, I intend
    to enjoy it.
Go, people, stuff your
    mouths with soap,
And remember, please, that
    when I mope, I mope!

Ogden Nash

help. Sometimes a clear analysis will make a confusing problem suddenly clear, either suggesting a solution or at least providing an understanding of what is occurring.

In other cases, an analysis can create more problems than it solves. There are two problems with analyzing. First, your interpretation may not be correct, in which case the speaker may become even more confused by accepting it. Second, even if your analysis is correct, telling it to the problem-holder might not be useful. There's a chance that it will arouse defensiveness (because analysis implies superiority). Even if it doesn't, the person may not be able to understand your view of the problem without working it out personally.

How can you know when it's helpful to offer an analysis? There are several guidelines to follow:

1. *Offer your interpretation as tentative rather than as absolute fact.* There's a big difference between saying "Maybe the reason is . . ." or "The way it looks to me . . ." and insisting, "This is the truth."
2. *Your analysis ought to have a reasonable chance of being correct.* An incorrect interpretation—especially one that sounds plausible—can leave a person more confused than before.
3. *You ought to be sure that the other person will be receptive to your analysis.* Even if you're completely accurate, your thoughts won't help if the problem-holder isn't ready to consider them.
4. *Be sure that your motive for offering an analysis is truly to help the other person.* It can be tempting to offer an analysis to show how brilliant you are or even to make the other person feel bad for not having thought of the right answer in the first place. Needless to say, an analysis offered under such conditions isn't helpful.

Advising

When we are approached with another's problem, a common tendency is to offer an **advising response**: to help by offering a solution.[45] Advice can sometimes be helpful, as long as it's given in a respectful, caring way.[46]

Despite its apparent value, advice has its limits: Research has shown that it is actually *unhelpful* at least as often as it's helpful.[47] One limitation on advice involves expertise: Your suggestion may not offer the best course to follow, in which case it can be even harmful. A related consequence of advising is that it often allows others to avoid responsibility for their decisions. A partner who follows advice of yours that doesn't work out can always pin the blame on you. Finally, often people simply don't want advice.

Before offering advice, then, you need to be sure that four conditions are present:[48]

1. *Be confident that the advice is accurate.* You may be certain about some matters of fact, such as the proper way to solve a school problem or the cost of a piece of merchandise, but resist the temptation to act like an authority on matters you know little about. Realize that just because a course of action worked for you doesn't guarantee that it will work for everybody.
2. *Ask yourself whether the person seeking your advice seems willing to accept it.* In this way you can avoid the frustration of making good suggestions, only to find that the person with the problem had another solution in mind all the time. Perhaps the best way to know that a person is willing to accept your advice is when that person *requests* it. Forcing advice on someone who hasn't asked for it often leads to defensiveness and resentment from the advisee.

3. *Be confident that the receiver won't blame you if the advice doesn't work out.* You may be offering advice, but the choice and responsibility for accepting it are up to the recipient.
4. *Deliver your advice supportively, in a face-saving manner.* Advice that is perceived as being offered constructively, in the context of a solid relationship, is much better received than critical comments offered in a way that signals a lack of respect for the receiver.[49]

I've learned that it is best to give advice in only two circumstances: When it is requested and when it is a life-threatening situation.

Andy Rooney

Judging

A **judging response** evaluates the sender's thoughts or behaviors in some way. The judgment may be favorable—"That's a good idea" or "You're on the right track now"—or unfavorable—"An attitude like that won't get you anywhere." But in either case it implies that the person doing the judging is in some way qualified to pass judgment on the speaker's thoughts or actions.

Sometimes negative judgments are purely critical. How many times have you heard such responses as "Well, you asked for it!" or "I *told* you so!" or "You're just feeling sorry for yourself"? Although responses like these can sometimes serve as a verbal slap that brings problem-holders to their senses, they usually make matters worse.

In other cases negative judgments are less critical. These involve what we usually call *constructive criticism*, which is intended to help the problem-holder improve in the future. This is the sort of response given by friends about everything from the choice of clothing to jobs to friends. Another common setting for constructive criticism occurs in school, where instructors evaluate students' work to help them master concepts and skills. But whether it's justified or not, even constructive criticism runs the risk of arousing defensiveness because it may threaten the self-concept of the person at whom it is directed.

Judgments have the best chance of being received when two conditions exist:

1. *The person with the problem should have requested an evaluation from you.* Occasionally an unsolicited evaluation may bring someone to his or her senses, but more often unsolicited evaluation will trigger a defensive response.
2. *The intent of your judgment should be genuinely constructive and not designed as a put-down.* If you are tempted to use judgments as a weapon, don't fool yourself into thinking that you are being helpful. Often the statement "I'm telling you this for your own good . . ." simply isn't true.

Now that you're aware of all the possible listening responses, try the following exercise to see how you might use them in everyday situations.

Invitation to Insight

What Would You Say?

1. In each situation below, describe what you would say in response to the problem being shared.

   a. My family doesn't understand me. Everything I like seems to go against their values, and they just won't accept my feelings as being right for me. It's not that they don't love me—they do. But they don't accept me.

   b. I've been pretty discouraged lately. I just can't get a good relationship going with any guys. I've got plenty of male friends, but that's always as far as it goes. I'm tired of being just a pal. . . . I want to be more than that.

   c. (Child to parents) I hate you guys! You always go out and leave me with some stupid sitter. Why don't you like me?

   d. I don't know what I want to do with my life. I'm tired of school, but there aren't any good jobs around. I could just drop out for a while, but that doesn't really sound very good, either.

   e. Things really seem to be kind of lousy in my marriage lately. It's not that we fight much, but all the excitement seems to be gone. We're in a rut, and it keeps getting worse. . . .

   f. I keep getting the idea that my boss is angry at me. It seems as if lately he hasn't been joking around very much, and he hasn't said anything at all about my work for about three weeks now. I wonder what I should do.

2. After you've written your response to each of these messages, imagine the probable outcome of the conversation that would have followed. If you've tried this exercise in class, you might have two group members role-play each response. Based on your idea of how the conversation might have gone, decide which responses were productive and which were unproductive.

Choosing the Best Listening Response

By now you can see that there are many ways to respond as a listener. Research shows that, in the right circumstances, *all* response styles can help others accept their situation, feel better, and have a sense of control over their problems.[50] But there is enormous variability in which style will work with a given person.[51] This fact explains why communicators who use a wide variety of response styles are usually more effective than those who use just one or two styles.[52] However, there are other factors to consider when choosing how to respond to a speaker.

Gender   Research shows that men and women differ in the way they listen and respond to others.[53] Women are more likely than men to give supportive responses when presented with another person's problem,[54] are more skillful at composing such messages,[55] and are more likely to seek out such responses from listeners.[56] By contrast, men are less skillful at providing emotional support to those who are distressed,[57] and they tend to respond to others' problems by

They Aid Customers by Becoming Good Listeners

© Butler Institute of American Art, Youngstown, Ohio/Dale Kennington/SuperStock

Do you need someone to listen to your troubles?

Have your hair done. Beauty salon chairs may be to today's women what conversation-centered backyard fences were to their grandmothers and psychiatrists' couches are to their wealthier contemporaries.

"We are not as family-oriented as our ancestors were," says counselor-trainer Andy Thompson. "They listened to and helped each other. Now that we have become a society of individuals isolated from one another by cars, telephones, jobs and the like, we have had to find other listeners." Community training program director for Crisis House, Thompson has designed and is conducting human relations training sessions for workers to whom customers tend to unburden their woes most frequently—cosmetologists, bartenders and cabdrivers.

"People can definitely help others just by letting them talk," he said. "Relatives, friends or spouses who

listen do a lot to keep the mental health of this country at a reasonable rate. Workers in situations that encourage communications can make the same meaningful contribution."

Thompson explained that his training is not meant to replace, or be confused with, professional treatment or counseling. His students fill a gap between family and professionals.

"There are not enough psychiatrists or psychologists to go around," he said. "And some professionals become so technical that their help doesn't mean much to persons who just need someone who will let them get problems and questions out in the open where they can look at them."

Thompson's first course of training, completed recently, was for cosmetologists.

The human relations training program attempts to make the most of these built-in assets by using a method Thompson calls "reflective listening."

"The purpose is to let the customer talk enough to clarify her own thinking," he said. "We are not interested in having cosmetologists tell women what to do, but to give them a chance to choose their own course of action.

"There is a tendency among listeners to try to rescue a person with problems and pull them out of negative situations. People don't really want that. They just want to discuss what is on their minds and reach their own conclusions."

Cosmetologists are taught to use phrases that aid customers in analyzing their thoughts. Some of the phrases are, "You seem to think . . ." "You sound like . . ." "You appear to be . . ." "As I get it, you . . ." and "It must seem to you that . . ." There also are barriers to conversation that the cosmetologists are taught to avoid.

"A constant bombardment of questions can disrupt communications," Thompson said. "Commands will have the same effect. Many of them are impossible to follow anyway."

"How many can respond to orders to 'Stop feeling depressed,' 'Don't be so upset,' or 'Don't think about it.' "

"The same applies to negative criticism, 'That's dumb,' for instance; and evaluations, such as 'Oh, you're just confused.' "

"Comments that seem threatening—'You had better stop feeling sad,' as an example—will end a conversation as quickly as changing the subject or not paying attention."

San Diego Union

Ethical Challenge

Unconditional Positive Regard

Carl Rogers is the best-known advocate of paraphrasing as a helping tool. As a psychotherapist, Rogers focused on how professionals can help others, but he and his followers were convinced that the same approach can work in all interpersonal relationships.

Rogers used several terms to describe his approach: Sometimes he labeled it "nondirective," sometimes "client-centered," and at other times "person-centered." All these terms reflect his belief that the best way to help another is to offer a supportive climate in which the people seeking help can find their own answers. Rogers believed that advising, judging, analyzing, and questioning are not the best ways to help others solve their problems. Instead, Rogers and his followers were convinced that people are basically good and that they can improve without receiving any guidance from others, after they accept and respect themselves.

An essential ingredient for person-centered helping is what Rogers called "unconditional positive regard." This attitude requires the helper to treat the speaker's ideas respectfully and nonjudgmentally. Unconditional positive regard means accepting others for who they are, even when you don't approve of their posture toward life. Treating a help-seeker with unconditional

positive regard doesn't oblige you to agree with everything the help-seeker thinks, feels, or does; but it does oblige you to suspend judgment about the rightness or wrongness of the help-seeker's thoughts and actions.

A person-centered approach to helping places heavy demands on the listener. At the skill level, it demands an ability to reflect the speaker's thoughts and feelings perceptively and accurately. Even more difficult, though, is the challenge of listening and responding without passing judgment on the speaker's ideas or behavior.

Unconditional positive regard is especially hard when we are faced with the challenge of listening and responding to someone whose beliefs, attitudes, and values differ profoundly from our own. This approach requires the helper to follow the scriptural injunction of loving the sinner while hating the sin. One of the best models of this approach is illustrated in the movie *Dead Man Walking*. (See the "Films" section under "Media Resources" at the end of this chapter.)

For a better understanding of unconditional positive regard, see the following works of Carl Rogers: *On Becoming a Person* (Boston: Houghton Mifflin, 1961); *Carl Rogers on Personal Power* (New York: Delacorte Press, 1977); "A Theory of Therapy, Personality and Interpersonal Relationships, as Developed in the Client-Centered Framework," in S. Koch, ed., *Psychology: A Study of Science* (New York: McGraw-Hill, 1959).

offering advice or by diverting the topic. In a study of helping styles in sororities and fraternities, researchers found that sorority women frequently respond with emotional support when asked to help; also, they rated their sisters as being better at listening nonjudgmentally, and on comforting and showing concern for them. Fraternity men, on the other hand, fit the stereotypical pattern of offering help by challenging their brothers to evaluate their attitudes and values.[58]

These facts reinforce the importance of choosing a response style that is likely to be appreciated by the other person. Supporting may be a better response when dealing with women, and advice might be more appreciated by men. This doesn't mean that women never value advice or that men don't appreciate emotional support. The challenge is to find the mixture that works best for each person.

The Situation   Sometimes people need your advice. At other times people need encouragement and support, and in still other cases your analysis or judgment will be most helpful. And, as you have seen, sometimes your probes and paraphrasing can help people find their own answers. In other words, a competent communicator needs to analyze the situation and develop an appropriate response.[59] As a rule of thumb, it's often wise to begin with responses that seek understanding and offer a minimum of direction, such as prompting, questioning, paraphrasing, and supporting. Once you've gathered the facts and demonstrated your interest and concern, it's likely that the speaker will be more receptive to (and perhaps even ask for) your analyzing, advising, and evaluating responses.[60]

The Other Person   Besides considering the situation, you should also consider the other person when deciding which style to use. Some people are able to consider advice thoughtfully, whereas others use advice to avoid making their own decisions. Many communicators are extremely defensive and aren't capable of receiving analysis or judgments without lashing out. Still others aren't equipped to think through problems clearly enough to profit from paraphrasing and probing. Sophisticated listeners choose a style that fits the person. One way to determine the most appropriate response is to ask the speaker what s/he wants from you. A simple question such as "Are you looking for my advice, or do you just want a listening ear right now?" can help you give others the kinds of responses they're looking for.

Your Personal Style   Finally, consider yourself when deciding how to respond. Most of us reflexively use one or two response styles. You may be best at listening quietly, offering a prompt from time to time. Or perhaps you are especially insightful and can offer a truly useful analysis of the problem. Of course, it's also possible to rely on a response style that is *unhelpful*. You may be overly judgmental or too eager to advise, even when your suggestions aren't invited or productive. As you think about how to respond to another's messages, consider both your strengths and weaknesses and adapt accordingly.

Summary

Listening is the most common—and perhaps the most overlooked—form of communication. There is a difference between hearing and listening, and there is also a difference between mindless and mindful listening. Listening, defined as the process of making sense of others' spoken messages, consists of five elements: hearing, attending, understanding, responding, and remembering.

A number of responding styles masquerade as listening but actually are only poor imitations of the real thing. We listen poorly for a variety of reasons. Some reasons have to do with the tremendous number of messages that bombard us daily and with the personal preoccupations, noise, media influences, and rapid thoughts that distract us from focusing on the information we are exposed to. Another set of reasons has to do with the considerable effort involved in listening carefully and the mistaken belief there are

more rewards in speaking than in listening. A few listeners fail to receive messages due to physical hearing defects; others listen poorly due to lack of training. Some keys to better listening are to talk less, reduce distractions, avoid making premature judgments, and seek the speaker's key ideas.

Listening responses are the primary way we evaluate whether and how others are paying attention to us. Some listening responses put a premium on gathering information and providing support; these include prompting, questioning, paraphrasing, and supporting. Other listening responses focus more on providing direction and evaluation: analyzing, advising, and judging. The most effective communicators use a variety of these styles, taking into consideration factors such as gender, the situation at hand, the person with the problem, and their own personal style.

Key Terms

advising response (258)
ambushing (241)
analyzing response (256)
attending (236)
counterfeit questions (249)
defensive listening (240)
hearing (236)
insensitive listening (241)

insulated listening (240)
judging response (259)
listening (234)
mindful listening (235)
mindless listening (235)
paraphrasing (251)
prompting (248)
pseudolistening (240)

questioning (249)
remembering (239)
responding (238)
selective listening (240)
sincere questions (249)
stage-hogging (240)
supportive response (254)
understanding (238)

Media Resources

Online Textbook Resources

ThomsonNOW For quick access to the online resources that accompany this chapter, access ThomsonNOW for *Looking Out/Looking In* at www.thomsonedu.com.

The ThomsonNOW online study system helps you identify concepts you don't fully understand, allowing you to put your study time to the best use. Using chapter-by-chapter diagnostic pre-tests, the system creates a **personalized study plan** for each chapter. Each plan directs you to specific resources designed to improve your understanding, including pages from the text in ebook format. Chapter post-tests give you an opportunity to measure how much you've learned and let you know if you are ready for graded quizzes and exams.

Your ThomsonNOW for *Looking Out/Looking In* also includes **Communication Scenario videos** described on page 252; **vocabulary activities** to help you master key terms; self-study **review quizzes** to test your comprehension of the material in this chapter and prepare for exams; **online exercises**, including the Skill Builder and Invitation to Insight activities in this chapter; **web links** you can use to further explore topics in this chapter; access to a **feature film database** where you can locate information about movies that illustrate communication principles; and access to the **InfoTrac** College Edition searchable database of over 10 million articles from both scholarly journals and the popular press.

Films

ThomsonNOW In addition to the films suggested here, go to your ThomsonNOW for *Looking Out/Looking In* to link to the **Film in Communication Database** to locate movie clips illustrating principles of listening.

Ineffective Listening and Its Alternatives

Jerry Maguire (1996) Rated R
Jerry Maguire (Tom Cruise) is a high-powered pro sports agent with a bulging Rolodex and a stable of multimillionaire athletes. Jerry is so successful that he doesn't have time to truly listen to any of his clients. In an early scene, we see him juggle the callers on his multiline office phone, slinging clichés as he switches between athletes. At this point we think that success is the reason Jerry is such an awful listener; but after he loses his job and scrambles to keep his last client, we learn that he is just as inattentive and insensitive when desperate as when successful. Rich or poor, the egocentric Maguire treats people in his life as props. In true Hollywood fashion, Jerry learns the importance of listening only when he is close to losing the most important people in his life.

Supportive Listening

Dead Man Walking (1995) Rated R
Sister Helen Prejean (Susan Sarandon) is a nun who serves in an inner-city neighborhood. She receives a letter from death-row inmate Matthew Poncelet (Sean Penn) and decides to visit him in prison. He fills the profile for everything she is not: uneducated, angry, bigoted, rude, and insecure. Nonetheless, Sister Helen agrees to help Poncelet appeal his murder conviction and death sentence—and her world turns upside down.

Sister Helen's highest goal is to get Matthew to take responsibility for his actions and to come to peace with God, the murder victims' parents, and himself. She does this not by pushing or persuading, but by giving him her time and her ear. In their early meetings, Prejean comes with no agenda; she tells Poncelet, "I'm here to listen. Whatever you want to talk about is fine with me." She asks open-ended questions and allows Poncelet to arrive at his own conclusions. He admits to being surprised that she "didn't come down here preaching fire and brimstone," so he slowly opens his life to her.

As time goes on, Sister Helen comes to realize that Poncelet is, indeed, guilty of the awful crimes for which he has been convicted. Her pain is obvious as she confronts the grieving families of his victims, none of whom can understand or accept why she is willing to help a murderer. What they don't appreciate is that she never wavers in her abhorrence for his deeds, but she remains steadfast in separating her hate for the crime from her concern and love for Poncelet. As such, she provides viewers with proof that unconditional positive regard can be achieved, and can heal.

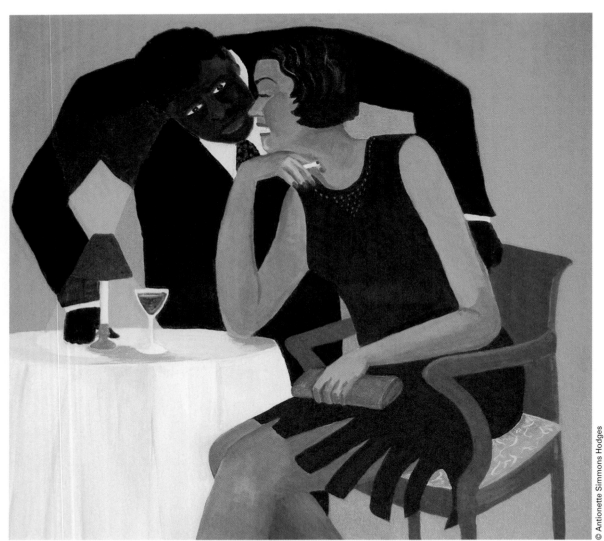

Communication and Relational Dynamics

8

"We have a terrific relationship."

"I'm looking for a better relationship."

"Our relationship has changed a lot."

Relationship is one of those words that people use all the time but have trouble defining. Take a moment to see if you can define the term in your own words. It isn't as easy as it might seem.

The dictionary defines a *relationship* as "the mode in which two or more things stand to one another." This is true enough: You are tall in relationship to some people and short in relationship to others, and we are more or less wealthy only in relationship to others. But physical and economic relationships don't tell us much that is useful about interpersonal communication.

Interpersonal relationships involve the way people deal with one another *socially*. But what is it about social interaction that defines a relationship? This chapter will offer some insights. It will offer explanations for why we form relationships with some people and not with others. It will look at how communication operates as people form, manage, and sometimes end their relationships. You will see that relationships aren't static, like a painting or photograph. Rather, they change over time, like an ongoing dance or drama. Even the most stable and satisfying relationships wax and wane in a variety of ways as communication patterns change. By the time you finish reading the following pages you will have a better sense of how communication both defines and reflects our interpersonal world.

> For communication to have meaning it must have a life. It must transcend "you" and "me" and become "us". . . . In a small way we then grow out of our old selves and become something new.
>
> Hugh Prather

© Joseph Holston

Why We Form Relationships

What makes us seek relationships with some people and not with others? Sometimes we don't have a choice: Children can't select their parents, and most workers aren't able to choose their bosses or colleagues. In many other cases, however, we seek out some people and actively avoid others. Social scientists have collected an impressive body of research on interpersonal attraction.[1] The following are some of the factors they have identified that influence our choice of relational partners.

Appearance

Most people claim that we should judge others on the basis of how they act, not how they look. However, as Chapter 6 explained (see pages 223–225), the reality is quite the opposite.[2] Appearance is especially important in the early stages of a relationship. In one study, a group of over seven hundred men and women were matched as blind dates, allegedly for a "computer dance." After the party was over, they were asked whether or not they would like to date their partners again. The result? The more physically attractive the person (as judged in advance by independent raters), the more likely he or she was seen as desirable. Other factors—social skills and intelligence, for example—didn't seem to affect the decision.[3]

Even if your appearance isn't beautiful by societal standards, consider these encouraging facts: First, after initial impressions have passed, ordinary-looking people with pleasing personalities are likely to be judged as attractive.[4] Second, physical factors become less important as a relationship progresses.[5] As one social scientist put it, "Attractive features may open doors, but apparently, it takes more than physical beauty to keep them open."[6]

Similarity

A large body of research confirms the fact that we like people who are similar to us, at least in most cases.[7] For example, the more similar a married couple's personalities are, the more likely they are to report being happy and satisfied in their marriage.[8] Friends in middle and high school report being similar to one another in many ways, including having mutual friends, enjoying the same sports, liking the same social activities, and using (or not using) alcohol and cigarettes to the same degree.[9] For adults, similarity is more important to relational happiness than even communication ability: Friends who have equally low levels of communication skills are just as satisfied with their relationships as are friends having high levels of communication skills.[10]

One theory for why we are attracted to similar others is that it provides a measure of ego support. If we judge those who are like us to be attractive, then we must be attractive, too (or so goes the theory). One study described the lengths to which this "implicit egotism" can affect perceptions of attractiveness.[11] Results showed that people are disproportionately likely to marry others whose first or last names resemble their own, and they are also attracted to those with similar birthdays or even jersey numbers.

Attraction is greatest when we are similar to others in a high percentage of important areas. For example, two people who support each other's career goals, enjoy the same friends, and have similar beliefs about human rights can tolerate trivial disagreements about the merits of sushi or rap music. With enough similarity in key areas, they can even survive disputes about more important subjects, such as how much time to spend with their families or whether separate vacations are acceptable. But if the number and content of disagreements become too great, the relationship may be threatened.

Similarity turns from attraction to dislike when we encounter people who are like us in many ways but who behave in a strange or socially offensive manner.[12] For instance, you have probably disliked people others have said were "just like you" but who talked too much, were complainers, or had some other unappealing characteristic. In fact, there is a tendency to have stronger dislike for similar but offensive people than for those who are offensive but different. One likely reason is that such people threaten our self-esteem, causing us to fear that we may be as unappealing as they are. In such circumstances, the reaction is often to put as much distance as possible between ourselves and this threat to our ideal self-image.

Complementarity

The familiar saying that "opposites attract" seems to contradict the principle of similarity we just described. In truth, though, both are valid. Differences strengthen a relationship when they are *complementary*—when each partner's characteristics satisfy the other's needs. Individuals, for instance, are often likely to be attracted to each other when one partner is dominant and the other passive.[13] Relationships also work well when the partners agree that one will exercise control in certain areas ("You make the final decisions about money") and the other will exercise control in different areas ("I'll decide how we ought to decorate the place"). Strains occur when control issues are disputed.

When successful and unsuccessful couples are compared over a twenty-year period, it becomes clear that partners in successful marriages are similar enough to satisfy each other physically and mentally but different enough to meet each other's needs and keep the relationship interesting. Successful couples find ways to keep a balance between their similarities and differences, adjusting to the changes that occur over the years. We'll have more to say about balancing similarities and differences later in this chapter.

Reciprocal Attraction

We like people who like us—usually.[14] The power of reciprocal attraction is especially strong in the early stages of a relationship. At that time we are attracted to people who we believe are attracted to us. Conversely, we will probably not care for people who either attack or seem indifferent toward us.

It's no mystery why reciprocal liking builds attractiveness. People who approve of us bolster our feelings of self-esteem. This approval is rewarding in its own right, and it can also confirm a presenting self-concept that says, "I'm a likable person."

You can probably think of cases where you haven't liked people who seemed to like you. For example, you might think the other person's supposed liking is counterfeit—an insincere device to get something from you. At other times the liking may not fit with your own self-concept. When someone says you're good-looking, intelligent, and kind, but you believe you're ugly, stupid, and mean, you may choose to disregard the flattering information and remain in your familiar state of unhappiness. Groucho Marx summarized this attitude when he said he would never join any club that would consider having him as a member.

Competence

We like to be around talented people, probably because we hope their skills and abilities will rub off on us. On the other hand, we are uncomfortable around those who are *too* competent—probably because we look bad by comparison. Given these contrasting attitudes, it's no surprise that people are generally attracted to those who are talented but who have visible flaws that show that they are human, just like us.[15] There are some qualifications to this principle. People with especially high or low self-esteem find "perfect" people more attractive than those who are competent but flawed, and some studies suggest that women tend to be more impressed by uniformly superior people of both sexes, whereas men tend to be more impressed by desirable but "human" subjects. On the whole, though, the principle stands: The best way to gain the liking of others is to be good at what you do but to admit your mistakes.

Disclosure

Revealing important information about yourself can help build liking.[16] Sometimes the basis of this liking comes from learning about how we are similar, either in experiences ("I broke off an engagement myself") or in attitudes ("I feel nervous with strangers, too"). Self-disclosure also builds liking because it is a sign of regard. When people share private information with you, it suggests that they respect and trust you—a kind of liking that we've already seen increases attractiveness. Disclosure plays an even more important role as relationships develop beyond their earliest stages.

Not all disclosure leads to liking. Research shows that the key to satisfying self-disclosure is *reciprocity:* getting back an amount and kind of information equivalent to that which you reveal.[17] A second important ingredient in successful self-disclosure is *timing.* It's probably unwise to talk about your sexual insecurities with a new acquaintance or express your pet peeves to a friend at your birthday party. The information you reveal ought to be appropriate for the setting and stage of the relationship. Chapter 9 contains more information on the subject of self-disclosure.

Proximity

As common sense suggests, we are likely to develop relationships with people we interact with frequently.[18] In many cases, proximity leads to liking. For instance, we're more likely to develop friendships with close neighbors than with distant ones, and chances are good that we'll choose a mate with whom we cross paths often. Facts like these are understandable when we consider that proximity allows us to get more information about other people and benefit from a relationship with them. Also, people in close proximity may be more similar to us than those not close—for example, if we live in the same neighborhood, odds are we share the same socioeconomic status. And the Internet provides a new means for creating closeness, as users are able to experience "virtual proximity" in cyberspace.[19]

Familiarity, on the other hand, can also breed contempt. Evidence to support this fact comes from police blotters as well as university laboratories. Thieves frequently prey on nearby victims, even though the risk of being recognized is greater. Spousal and child abuse are distressingly common. Most aggravated assaults occur within the family or among close neighbors. Within the law, the same principle holds: You are likely to develop strong personal feelings of either like or dislike regarding others you encounter frequently.

Rewards

Some social scientists have argued that all relationships—both impersonal and personal—are based on a semi-economic model called *social exchange theory*.[20] This model suggests that we often seek out people who can give us rewards that are greater than or equal to the costs we encounter in dealing with them. Rewards may be tangible (a nice place to live, a high-paying job) or intangible (prestige, emotional support, companionship). Costs are undesirable outcomes: unpleasant work, emotional pain, and so on. A simple formula captures the social exchange theory of why we form and maintain relationships:

Rewards − Costs = Outcome

According to social exchange theorists, we use this formula (often unconsciously) to decide whether dealing with another person is a "good deal" or "not worth the effort," based on whether the outcome is positive or negative.

At its most blatant level, an exchange approach seems cold and calculating; but in some types of relationships it seems quite appropriate. A healthy business relationship is based on how well the parties help one another, and some friendships are based on an informal kind of barter: "I don't mind listening to the ups and downs of your love life because you rescue me when the house needs repairs." Even close relationships have an element of exchange. Friends and lovers often tolerate each other's quirks because the comfort and enjoyment they get make the less-than-pleasant times worth accepting. In more-serious cases, social exchange explains why some people stay in abusive relationships. Sadly, these people often report that they would rather be in a bad relationship than have no relationship at all.

"I'd like to buy everyone a drink. All I ask in return is that you listen patiently to my shallow and simplistic views on a broad range of social and political issues."

At first glance, the social exchange approach seems to present a view of relationships very different from one based on the need to seek intimacy. In fact, the two approaches aren't incompatible. Seeking intimacy of any type—whether emotional, physical, or even intellectual—has its costs; and our decision about whether to "pay" those costs is, in great measure, made by considering the likely rewards. If the costs of seeking and maintaining an intimate relationship are too great or the payoffs not worth the effort, we may decide to withdraw.

Relational Development and Maintenance

So far we have looked at some factors that influence why we are attracted to certain people. In the following pages, we'll examine the kinds of communication that we use to start, maintain, and end relationships.

Models of Relational Development

Your own experience demonstrates that relational beginnings are a unique time. How does communication change as we spend time with others and get to know them? Communication scholars have different perspectives on this question. To learn two major perspectives, read on.

Developmental Models   One of the best-known models of relational stages breaks the rise and fall of relationships into ten stages, contained in the two broad phases of "coming together" and "coming apart."[21] Other researchers have suggested that any model of relational communication ought to contain a third phase of **relational maintenance**—communication aimed at keeping relationships operating smoothly and satisfactorily.[22] Figure 8.1 shows how Knapp's ten stages fit into this three-phase view of relational communication.

This model seems most appropriate for describing communication between romantic partners, but in many respects it works well for other types of close relationships.[23] As you read the following section, consider how the stages could describe a long-term friendship, a couple in love, or even business partners.

FIGURE 8.1
Stages of Relational Development

Adapted from *Interpersonal Communication and Human Relationships*, 2nd edition by Mark L. Knapp and Anita L. Vangelisti. Published by Allyn and Bacon, Boston, MA. Copyright © 1992 by Pearson Education. Adapted by permission of the publisher.

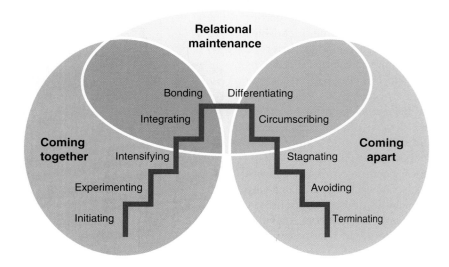

Initiating The goals in the first stage of a relationship are to show that you are interested in making contact and to show that you are the kind of person worth talking to. Communication during this **initiating** stage is usually brief, and it generally follows conventional formulas: handshakes, remarks about innocuous subjects like the weather, and friendly expressions. These kinds of behavior may seem superficial and meaningless, but they are a way of signaling that we're interested in building some kind of relationship with the other person. They allow us to say without saying, "I'm a friendly person, and I'd like to get to know you."

Initiating relationships—especially romantic ones—can be particularly hard for people who are shy. As the "Looking at Diversity" profile on page 274 illustrates, making contact via the Internet can be helpful in cases like this. One study of an online dating service found that participants who identified themselves as shy expressed a greater appreciation for the system's anonymous, nonthreatening environment than did non-shy users.[24] The researchers found that many shy users employed the online service specifically to help overcome their inhibitions about initiating relationships in face-to-face settings.

Experimenting After we have made contact with a new person, the next stage is to decide whether we are interested in pursuing the relationship further. This involves *uncertainty reduction*—the process of getting to know others by gaining more information about them.[25] A usual part of uncertainty reduction is the search for common ground, and it involves the conversational basics such as "Where are you from?" or "What's your major?" From there we look for other similarities: "You're a runner, too? How many miles do you do a week?"

The hallmark of the **experimenting** stage is small talk. Even though we may dislike it, we tolerate the ordeal of small talk because it serves several functions. First, it is a useful way to find out what interests we share with the other person. It also provides a way to "audition" the other person—to help us decide whether a relationship is worth pursuing. In addition, small talk is a safe way to ease into a relationship. You haven't risked much as you decide whether to proceed further.

The willingness to pursue relationships with strangers is partly a matter of personal style. Some people are outgoing, and others are shy, but culture also shapes behavior toward newcomers, especially ones from a different background. Research suggests that members of high-context cultures are more cautious in their first encounters with strangers and make more assumptions about them based on their backgrounds than do members of low-context cultures.[26] This fact might explain why people from certain backgrounds appear reserved or even unfriendly, when in fact they are simply operating by a set of rules different from those common in low-context North America.

For communicators who are interested in one another, the move from initiating to experimenting seems to occur even more rapidly in cyberspace than in person. One study found that people who develop relationships via e-mail begin asking questions about attitudes, opinions, and preferences more quickly than those in face-to-face contact.[27] It probably helps that e-mailers can't see each other's nonverbal reactions—they don't have to worry about blushing,

Looking at Diversity

Matt DeLanoy: Stuttering and Relationship Building

Meeting people can be hard for anybody, but it's especially tough for me because I stutter. The first words out of my mouth in a new situation are usually the most awkward. After I'm comfortable with the other person and the setting, I tend to stutter less—or I just don't worry about it as much.

I enjoy meeting strangers in Internet chat rooms where my stuttering isn't an issue. Many of them become friends over time. On the computer, I can say what I want, the way I want, without worrying about how the words will come out.

I'm okay with my stuttering—it's part of who I am, and I've learned to live with it. But before I phone an Internet friend for the first time, I usually tell them about my stuttering so they aren't surprised. Holding back this kind of personal information can become a problem. I have an Internet friend who was hitting it off with a guy in one of our chat rooms. She kept asking him to phone her and he kept turning her down, and none of us could figure out why. He finally confessed that he was deaf, and all of us were mad that he hadn't told us sooner. It's not like he had to announce "I'm deaf" the first time he got in the chat room, and nobody had a problem with his deafness. But hiding that kind of information for too long is a bad idea. It's better to trust people than keep a secret.

I've learned over the years that cyber-communication is more similar to face-to-face communication than some people think. For instance, in chat rooms our interaction is in "real time"—not delayed like it is when e-mailing. Because of this, I can often sense when others are uncomfortable with a subject, or perhaps even being deceptive, simply by noticing pauses as they are writing their messages. I can also tell a lot from the words and phrases people use, such as whether they know the "lingo" of the Internet, or if their language suddenly becomes more or less formal while they're cyber-chatting.

Most of my communication still takes place in person, so I've had to learn how to manage my stuttering. When I get stuck on a certain word, the best thing for me to do is stop, take a breath, and choose a different word. When that happens, what I need most from others is patience. Most of all, I want people to know that my stuttering doesn't mean I'm unable or unwilling to communicate—it just means I sometimes need to find different ways to make it work.

Photo courtesy of Matt DeLanoy

stammering, or looking away if they realize that they asked for too much information too quickly.

Intensifying   In the **intensifying** stage the kind of truly interpersonal relationship defined in Chapter 1 begins to develop. Several changes in communication patterns occur during intensifying. The expression of feelings toward the other becomes more common. Dating couples use a wide range of communication strategies to describe their feelings of attraction.[28] About one-quarter of the time they express their feelings directly, openly discussing the state of the relationship. More often they use less direct methods of communication: spending an increasing amount of time together, asking for support from one another, doing favors for the partner, giving tokens of affection, hinting and flirting, expressing feelings nonverbally, getting to know the partner's friends and family, and trying to look more physically attractive. In developing friendships, intensifying can include participating in shared activities, hanging out with mutual friends, or taking trips together.[29]

The intensifying stage is usually a time of relational excitement and even euphoria. For romantic partners, it's often filled with starstruck gazes, goosebumps, and daydreaming. As a result, it's a stage that's regularly depicted in movies and romance novels—after all, we love to watch lovers in love. The problem, of course, is that the stage doesn't last forever. Sometimes romantic partners who stop feeling goosebumps begin to question whether they're still in love. Although it's possible that they're not, it's also possible that they've simply moved on to a different stage in their relationship—integrating.

Integrating As a relationship strengthens, the parties begin to take on an identity as a social unit. In romantic relationships, invitations begin to come addressed to the couple. Social circles merge. The partners begin to take on each other's commitments: "Sure, we'll spend Thanksgiving with your family." Common property may begin to be designated—our apartment, our car, our song.[30] Partners develop unique, ritualistic ways of behaving.[31] Close friends may even begin to speak alike, using personal idioms and sentence patterns.[32] In this sense, the **integrating** stage is a time when individuals give up some characteristics of their old selves and develop shared identities.

As we become more integrated with others, our sense of obligation to them grows.[33] We feel obliged to provide a variety of resources such as class notes and money, whether or not the other person asks for them. Surprisingly, although integration is characterized by more relational solidarity, partners make fewer straightforward requests than they did in earlier relational stages. In dating relationships, for example, there is a curvilinear relationship (shown in Figure 8.2) between the relational stage and the number of explicit requests.[34] This pattern isn't as surprising as it might at first seem: As partners become better acquainted, their knowledge of each other makes overt requests less necessary. But later, as the relationship inevitably begins to change, the need for more explicit statements of wants and needs will increase again.

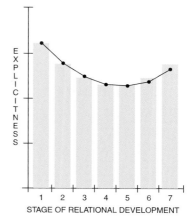

FIGURE 8.2

Explicitness of Requests Varies across Relational Stages

Adapted from D. H. Solomon, "A Developmental Model of Intimacy and Date Request Explicitness." *Communication Monographs* 64 (1997): 99–118.

Bonding During the **bonding** stage, the parties make symbolic public gestures to show the world that their relationship exists. The most common form of bonding in romantic relationships is a wedding ceremony and the legal ties that come with it. Given the importance of bonding in validating relationships and taking them to a different level, it's not surprising that the gay and lesbian communities are striving for this kind of recognition.

Bonding marks a turning point in a relationship. Up to now the relationship may have developed at a steady pace: Experimenting gradually moved into intensifying and then into integrating. Now, however, there is a spurt of commitment. The public display and declaration of exclusivity make this a distinct stage in the relationship.

Relationships don't have to be romantic to achieve bonding. Consider, for example, the contracts that formalize a business partnership or the initiation ceremony in a fraternity or sorority. As one author notes, even friendships can achieve bonding with acts that "officialize" the relationship:

> Some Western cultures have rituals to mark the progress of a friendship and to give it public legitimacy and form. In Germany, for example, there's a small ceremony called *Duzen*, the name itself signifying the transformation in the relationship. The ritual calls for the two friends, each holding a glass of wine or beer, to entwine arms, thus bringing each other physically close, and to drink up after making a promise of eternal brotherhood with the word *Bruderschaft*. When it's over, the

© Francis G. Mayer/Corbis

friends will have passed from a relationship that requires the formal *Sie* mode of address to the familiar *du*.

Differentiating   Bonding is the peak of what Knapp calls the "coming together" phase of relational development. But people in even the most committed relationships need to assert their individual identities. This **differentiating** stage is the point where the "we" orientation that has developed shifts, and more "me" messages begin to occur. Instead of talking about "our" weekend plans, differentiating conversations focus on what "I" want to do. Relational issues that were once agreed upon (such as, "You'll be the breadwinner and I'll manage the home") now become points of contention: "Why am *I* stuck at home when I have better career potential than *you*?" The root of the term "differentiating" is the word "different," suggesting that change plays an important role in this stage.

Differentiating is likely to occur when a relationship begins to experience the first, inevitable feelings of stress. This need for autonomy and change needn't be a negative experience, however. People need to be individuals as well as parts of a relationship, and differentiation is a necessary step toward autonomy. Think, for instance, of young adults who want to forge their own unique lives and identity, even while maintaining their relationships with their parents.[35] And as the model on page 272 illustrates, differentiating is often a part of normal relational maintenance, in which partners manage the inevitable changes that come their way. The key to successful differentiating is maintaining a commitment to the relationship while creating the space for being an individual as well. (This is a challenge that we will discuss in more detail later in this chapter when we discuss dialectical tensions in relationships.)

Circumscribing   So far we have been looking at the growth of relationships. Although some reach a plateau of development, going on successfully for as long as a lifetime, others pass through several stages of decline and dissolution.

In the **circumscribing** stage, communication between members decreases in quantity and quality. Restrictions and restraints characterize this stage. Rather than discuss a disagreement (which requires energy on both sides), members opt for withdrawal—either mental (silence or daydreaming and fantasizing) or physical (where people spend less time together). Circumscribing doesn't involve total avoidance, which may come later. Rather, it involves a shrinking of interest and commitment—the opposite of what occurred in the integrating stage.

Stagnating   If circumscribing continues, the relationship enters the **stagnating** stage. The excitement of the intensifying stage is long gone, and the partners behave toward each other in old, familiar ways without much feeling. No growth occurs. The relationship is a hollow shell of its former self. We see stagnation in many workers who have lost enthusiasm for their job yet continue to go through the motions for years. The same sad event occurs for some couples who unenthusiastically have the same conversations, see the same people, and follow the same routines without any sense of joy or novelty.

Avoiding   When stagnation becomes too unpleasant, parties in a relationship begin to create physical distance between each other. This is the **avoiding** stage. Sometimes they do it indirectly under the guise of excuses ("I've been sick lately and can't see you"); sometimes they do it directly ("Please don't call me; I don't want to see you now"). In either case, by this point the handwriting is on the wall about the relationship's future.

The deterioration of a relationship from bonding through circumscribing, stagnating, and avoiding isn't inevitable. One of the key differences between marriages that end in separation and those that are restored to their former intimacy is the communication that occurs when the partners are unsatisfied.[36] Unsuccessful couples deal with their problems by avoidance, indirectness, and less involvement with each other. By contrast, couples who "repair" their relationship communicate much more directly. They confront each other with their concerns (sometimes with the assistance of a counselor) and spend time and effort negotiating solutions to their problems.

Terminating   Not all relationships end: Many career partnerships, friendships, and marriages last for a lifetime once they've been established. But many do deteriorate and reach the final stage of **terminating**.

Characteristics of this stage include summary dialogues of where the relationship has gone and the desire to dissociate. The relationship may end with a cordial dinner, a note left on the kitchen table, a phone call, or a legal document. Depending on each person's feelings, this stage can be quite short, or it may be drawn out over time.

Relationships don't always move toward termination in a straight line. Rather, they take a back-and-forth pattern, where the trend is toward dissolution.[37] Regardless of how long it takes, termination doesn't have to be totally negative. Understanding each other's investments in the relationship and needs for personal growth may dilute the hard feelings. In fact, many relationships aren't so much terminated as redefined. A divorced couple, for example, may find new, less intimate ways to relate to each other.

In romantic relationships, the best predictor of whether the parties will be friends after reaching the terminating stage is whether they were friends before their emotional involvement.[38] The way the couple splits up also makes a difference. It's no surprise to find that friendships are most possible when communication during the breakup is positive: expressions that there are no regrets for time spent together and other attempts to minimize hard feelings. When communication during termination is negative (manipulative, complaining to third parties), friendships are less likely.

After termination, couples often engage in "grave-dressing"—retrospective attempts to explain why the relationship failed.[39] The narrative each

A happy marriage may be increasingly rare—but so is a good, old-fashioned, face-to-face breakup, where someone cries or gets a drink splashed in his face. The miracles of technology are allowing increasing numbers of single Americans to become chickens. Why deal with the anxiety of giving someone the heave-ho in person when you have e-mail and text messaging?

You'd expect college kids to conduct all human contact via Internet and cell phone. But older Americans are sometimes even more inclined to hit the delete button when it's time to send an ex-lover packing. Online dating service Match.com reports that 48 percent of online daters had experienced an e-mail breakup, and people 55 years old or older are the most likely. The survey of 1,100 Internet daters conducted for the service by Zoomerang showed that only 37 percent thought it appropriate to send a "Dear John" e-mail. But that doesn't seem to be stopping many people.

Los Angeles Times

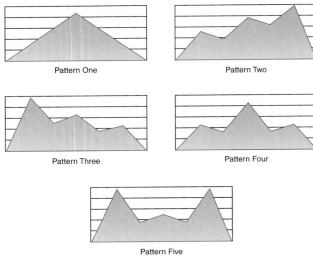

FIGURE 8.3
Patterns of Relational
Development and
Deterioration

Adapted from Johnson, A., Wittenberg, E., Haigh, M., Wigley, S.,
Becker, J., Brown, K., and Craig, E.
"The Process of Relationship Development and Deterioration: Turning
Points in Friendships that Have Terminated," *Communication Quarterly* 52 (2004): 54–67.

partner creates about "what went wrong" has an impact on how the couple will get along after their breakup (imagine the difference between saying and hearing "We just weren't right for each other" versus "He was too selfish and immature for a committed relationship").[40]

While Knapp's model offers insights into relational stages, it doesn't describe the ebb and flow of communication in every relationship. For instance, Knapp suggests that movement among stages is generally sequential, so that relationships typically progress from one stage to another in a predictable manner as they develop and deteriorate. One study found that many terminated friendships did indeed follow a pattern similar to the one described by Knapp and pictured in Pattern One of Figure 8.3.[41] However, several other patterns of development and deterioration were also identified, as seen in Patterns Two through Five. In other words, not all relationships begin, progress, decline, and end in the same linear fashion.

Finally, Knapp's model suggests that a relationship exhibits only the most dominant traits of just one of the ten stages at any given time. Despite this fact, elements of other stages are usually present. For example, two lovers deep in the throes of integrating may still do their share of experimenting ("Wow, I never knew that about you!") and have differentiating disagreements ("Nothing personal, but I need a weekend to myself"). Likewise, family members who spend most of their energy avoiding each other may have an occasional good spell in which their former closeness briefly intensifies. The notion that relationships can experience features of both "coming together" and "coming apart" at the same time is explored in the following section on relational dialectics.

Invitation to Insight

Your Relational Stage

You can gain a clearer appreciation of the accuracy and value of relational stages by answering the following questions.

1. If you are in a relationship, describe its present stage and the behaviors that characterize your communication in this stage. Give specific examples to support your assessment.

2. Discuss the trend of the communication in terms of the stages described on pages 273–278. Are you likely to remain in the present stage, or do you anticipate movement to another stage? Which one? Explain your answer.

3. Describe your level of satisfaction with the answer to question 2. If you are satisfied, describe what you can do to increase the likelihood that the relationship will operate at the stage you described. If you are not satisfied, discuss what you can do to move the relationship toward a more satisfying stage.

4. Because both parties define a relationship, define your partner's perspective. Would she or he say that the relationship is at the same stage as you describe it? If not, explain how

your partner would describe it. What does your partner do to determine the stage at which your relationship operates? (Give specific examples.) How would you like your partner to behave in order to move the relationship to or maintain it at the stage you desire? What can you do to encourage your partner to behave in the way you desire?

5. Now consider a relationship (friendship or romance) you have been in that has terminated. Which of the five graphs on page 278 best describes the development and decline of that relationship? If none of the graphs matches your experience, develop a new graph to illustrate your relationship's pattern.

Dialectical Perspectives   Not all theorists agree that stage-related models like the one described in the preceding pages are the best way to explain interaction in relationships. Some suggest that communicators grapple with the same kinds of challenges whether a relationship is brand new or decades old. They argue that communicators seek important but inherently incompatible goals throughout virtually all of their relationships. The struggle to achieve these goals creates **dialectical tensions**: conflicts that arise when two opposing or incompatible forces exist simultaneously. Communication scholars have identified a number of dialectical forces that make successful communication challenging.[42] They suggest that the struggle to manage these dialectical tensions creates the most powerful dynamics in relational communication. In the following pages we will discuss three powerful dialectical tensions.

Connection versus Autonomy   No one is an island. Recognizing this fact, we seek out involvement with others. But, at the same time, we are unwilling to sacrifice our entire identity to even the most satisfying relationship. The conflicting desires for connection and autonomy are embodied in the **connection-autonomy dialectic**. Research on relational breakups demonstrates the consequences for relational partners who can't find a way to manage these very different personal needs.[43] Some of the most common reasons for relational breakups involve failure of partners to satisfy each other's needs for connection: "We barely spent any time together," "S/he wasn't committed to the relationship," "We had different needs." But other relational complaints involve excessive demands for connection: "I was feeling trapped," "I needed freedom." Perhaps not surprisingly, some research suggests that men value autonomy in relationships more than women do, while women tend to value connection and commitment.[44]

The levels of connection and autonomy that we seek can change over time. In his book *Intimate Behavior,* Desmond Morris suggests that each of us repeatedly goes through three stages: "Hold me tight," "Put me down," and "Leave me alone."[45] This cycle becomes apparent in the first years of life when children move from the "hold me tight" stage that characterizes infancy into a new "put me down" stage of exploring the world by crawling, walking, touching, and tasting. The same 3-year-old who insists "I can do it myself" in August may cling to parents on the first day of preschool in September. As children grow into adolescents, the "leave me alone" orientation becomes apparent. Teenagers who used to happily spend time with their parents now may groan at the thought of a family vacation or even the notion of sitting down at the dinner table each evening. As adolescents move into adulthood, they typically grow closer to their families again.[46]

Love one another, but make not a bond of love:

Let it rather be a moving sea between the shores of your souls. Fill each other's cup but drink not from one cup.

Give one another of your bread but eat not of the same loaf.

Sing and dance together and be joyous, but let each one of you be alone.

Even as the strings of a lute are alone though they quiver with the same music.

Kahlil Gibran, *The Prophet*

In adult relationships, the same cycle of intimacy and distance repeats itself. In marriages, for example, the "hold me tight" bonds of the first year are often followed by a desire for autonomy. This desire can manifest itself in a number of ways, such as wanting to make friends or engage in activities that don't include the spouse or the need to make a career move that might disrupt the relationship. As the discussion of relational stages earlier in this chapter explained, this movement from connection to autonomy may lead to the breakup of relationships, but it can also be part of a cycle that redefines the relationship in a new form that can recapture or even surpass the intimacy that existed in the past.

In accounts of relational turning points, both men and women in heterosexual romantic pairs cite the connection-autonomy dialectic as one of the most significant factors affecting their relationship.[47] This dialectical tension is crucial in negotiating turning points related to commitment, conflict, disengagement, and reconciliation.

Managing the tension between connection and autonomy is also important at the end of a relationship, as partners seek ways to salvage the positive parts of their relationship (if only the good memories) and take steps toward their new independence.[48] Even at the end of life, the connection-autonomy dialectic comes into play. When a loved one is in an extended period of declining health, the partner often feels torn between the desire to stay close and the need to let go. This tension is especially poignant when one partner suffers from a condition like Alzheimer's disease and becomes mentally "absent" while physically "present."[49]

Openness versus Privacy   As Chapter 1 explained, disclosure is one characteristic of interpersonal relationships. Yet, along with the need to disclose, we have an equally important drive to maintain some space between ourselves and others. These conflicting needs create the **openness-privacy dialectic**.

Even the strongest interpersonal relationships require some distance. Lovers may go through periods of much sharing and periods of relative withdrawal. Likewise, they experience periods of passion and then periods of little physical contact. Friends have times of high disclosure when they share almost every feeling and idea and then disengage for days, months, or even longer.

What do you do in an intimate relationship when a person you care about asks an important question that you don't want to answer? "Do you think I'm attractive?" "Are you having a good time?" Your commitment to honesty may compel you toward a candid response, but your concern for the other person's feelings and a desire for privacy may lead you to be less than completely honest. Partners use a variety of strategies to gain privacy from each other.[50] For example, they may confront the other person directly and explain that they don't want to continue a discussion, or they may be less direct and offer nonverbal cues, change the topic, or leave the room. This dialectic raises so many communication challenges that Chapter 9 explores it in depth.

Predictability versus Novelty   Stability is an important need in relationships, but too much of it can

"And do you, Rebecca, promise to make love only to Richard, month after month, year after year, and decade after decade, until one of you is dead?"

lead to feelings of staleness. The **predictability-novelty dialectic** reflects this tension. Humorist Dave Barry exaggerates only slightly when he talks about the boredom that can come when husbands and wives know each other too well:

> After a decade or so of marriage, you know *everything* about your spouse, every habit and opinion and twitch and tic and minor skin growth. You could write a seventeen-pound book solely about the way your spouse *eats*. This kind of intimate knowledge can be very handy in certain situations—such as when you're on a TV quiz show where the object is to identify your spouse from the sound of his or her chewing—but it tends to lower the passion level of a relationship.[51]

Although too much familiarity can lead to the risk of boredom and stagnation, nobody wants a completely unpredictable relational partner. Too many surprises can threaten the foundations upon which the relationship is based ("You're not the person I married!").

The challenge for communicators is to juggle the desire for predictability with the desire for novelty that keeps the relationship fresh and interesting. People differ in their desire for predictability and novelty, so there is no optimal mixture of the two. As you will read shortly, people can use a number of strategies to manage these contradictory drives.

Managing Dialectical Tensions   Although all of the dialectical tensions play an important role in managing relationships, some occur more frequently than others. In one study, young married couples reported that connection-autonomy was the most frequent tension (30.8 percent of all reported contradictions).[52] Predictability-novelty was second (21.7 percent). Least common was openness-privacy (12.7 percent).

Managing the dialectical tensions outlined in these pages presents communication challenges. There are a number of ways to meet these challenges, and some work better than others.[53]

- *Denial.* In the strategy of denial, communicators respond to one end of the dialectical spectrum and ignore the other. For example, a couple caught between the conflicting desires for predictability and novelty might find their struggle for change too difficult to manage and choose to follow predictable, if unexciting, patterns of relating to each other.
- *Disorientation.* In this strategy, communicators feel so overwhelmed and helpless that they are unable to confront their problems. In the face of dialectical tensions they might fight, freeze, or even leave the relationship. Two people who discover soon after the honeymoon that a "happily ever after" conflict-free life isn't realistic might become so terrified that they would come to view their marriage as a mistake.
- *Alternation.* Communicators who use this strategy choose one end of the dialectical spectrum at some times and the other end at other times. Friends, for example, might manage the connection-autonomy dialectic by alternating between times when they spend a large amount of time together and other times when they live independent lives.
- *Segmentation.* Partners who use this tactic compartmentalize different areas of their relationship. For example, a couple might manage the openness-privacy dialectic by sharing almost all their feelings about mutual friends with each other, but keeping certain parts of their past romantic histories private. Segmentation is the most frequently used method for stepchildren to manage openness-privacy tensions with their nonresident parents.[54] In the "Zits" cartoon on the next page,

Jeremy realizes he has forgotten to use his usual approach of segmentation to manage the openness-privacy dialectic with his inquisitive parents.

- *Balance.* Communicators who try to balance dialectical tensions recognize that both forces are legitimate and try to manage them through compromise. As Chapter 11 points out, compromise is inherently a situation in which everybody loses at least a little of what he or she wants. A couple caught between the conflicting desires for predictability and novelty might seek balance by compromising with a lifestyle that is neither as predictable as one wants nor as surprise-filled as the other wants—not an ideal outcome.

- *Integration.* With this strategy, communicators simultaneously accept opposing forces without trying to diminish them. Communication researcher Barbara Montgomery describes a couple who accept the needs for both predictability and novelty by devising a "predictably novel" approach: Once a week they would do something together that they had never done before.[55] In a similar way, some stepfamilies manage the tension between the "old family" and the "new family" by adapting and blending their family rituals.[56]

- *Recalibration.* Communicators can respond to dialectical challenges by reframing them so that the apparent contradiction disappears. For example, a change in thinking can transform your attitude from loving someone *in spite* of your differences to loving him or her *because* of those differences.[57] Or consider how two people who each felt hurt by each other's unwillingness to share parts of his or her past might redefine the secrets as creating an attractive aura of mystery instead of being a problem to be solved. The desire for privacy would still remain, but it would no longer compete with a need for openness about every aspect of the past.

- *Reaffirmation.* This strategy acknowledges that dialectical tensions will never disappear. Instead of trying to make them go away, reaffirming communicators accept—or even embrace—the challenges that the tensions present. The metaphorical view of relational life as a kind of roller coaster reflects this strategy, and communicators who use reaffirmation view dialectical tensions as part of the ride.

Characteristics of Relationships

Whether you analyze a relationship in terms of stages or dialectical tensions, two characteristics are true of every interpersonal relationship. As you read about each, consider how it applies to your own experience.

Your Dialectical Tensions

Describe how each of the dialectical tensions described in these pages operates in one of your important relationships. Which incompatible goals do you and your relational partner(s) seek? Which of the strategies described on pages 281–282 do you use to manage these tensions? Are you satisfied with this strategy, or can you suggest better strategies?

Relationships Are Constantly Changing   Relationships are certainly not doomed to deteriorate. But even the strongest ones are rarely stable for long periods of time. In fairy tales a couple may live "happily ever after," but in real life this sort of equilibrium is less common. Consider a husband and wife who have been married for some time. Although they have formally bonded, their relationship will probably shift from one dimension of a relational dialectic to another, and forward or backward along the spectrum of stages. Sometimes the partners will feel the need to differentiate from each other, and at other times they will need to seek intimacy. Sometimes they will feel secure in the predictable patterns they have established, and at other times one or both will feel hungry for novelty. The relationship may become circumscribed or even stagnant. From this point the marriage may fail, but this fate isn't certain. With effort, the partners may move from the stage of stagnating to experimenting, or from circumscribing to intensifying.

Communication theorist Richard Conville describes the constantly changing, evolving nature of relationships as a cycle in which partners move through a series of stages, returning to ones they previously encountered, although at a new level[58] (see Figure 8.4). In this cycle, partners move from security (integration, in Knapp's terminology) to disintegration (differentiating) to alienation (circumscribing) to resynthesis (intensifying, integrating) to a new level of security. This process repeats itself again and again.

Relationships Are Affected by Culture   Many of the qualities that shape personal relationships are universal.[59] For example, social scientists have found that communication in all cultures has both the task and relational dimensions described on pages 268–272 in this chapter, that the same facial expressions signal the same emotions in all cultures, and that the distribution of power is a factor in every human society. Males in all cultures (in fact, in all species of mammals) are likely to invest less emotionally in sexual relationships, and are typically more competitive.

While the general elements of relationships are universal, the particulars often differ from one culture to another. Consider, for example, how the Western notion of romance and marriage is reflected in the model of relational stages described on pages 273–278. The notion that bonding only follows after experimenting, intensifying, and integrating doesn't apply everywhere.[60] Indeed, in some cultures, the bride and groom may meet only weeks, days, or even minutes before they become husband and wife. Research shows that these relationships can be

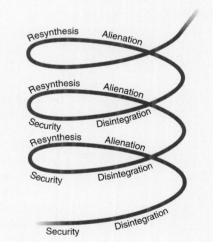

FIGURE 8.4
A Helical Model of Relational Cycles

Technology and Indian Marriage: A Match Made in Heaven

© Brooklyn Museum/Corbis

Some 18 months ago in southern India, the parents of a software engineer working in Chennai began to despair of finding him a suitable bride. They were, truth to tell, rather picky: "Our requirement is a suitable Hindu Nadar girl of Sivakasi/Madurai side origin, preferably employed as a software engineer in Chennai, age between 21 to 24, height 5 feet 2 inches to 5 feet 6 inches and sufficiently good-looking." She also had to speak Tamil.

There was, however, a happy ending. They ventured online, to a website called Bharatmatrimony.com, which now flaunts their story. They identified a girl, received a message from her father, matched horoscopes and, having introduced the happy couple to each other, will celebrate the wedding next month.

Online marriage-broking is one of the successes of Indian e-business, used by the single looking for "love matches" as well as by their parents and siblings. So complex are the requirements of Indians seeking a partner that the Internet might have been designed to meet their needs. Bharatmatrimony's boss, Janakiram Murugavel, says that language is the biggest criterion. His site is divided into 15 linguistic sections. Then comes status and caste, which divides Indians at birth into thousands of groups. About 70% of his customers want to marry within their caste. Most still also use astrology. Bharatmatrimony offers an online horoscope service.

Economist

both successful and satisfying.[61] (See the reading on this page for a perspective on Indian courtship patterns.)

A variety of differences—profound, but not always apparent—can make relationships between people from different cultures challenging.[62] For example, deciding how much (or how little) to share what's on your mind is a challenge in any relationship. This decision can be especially tricky when the cultural rules about self-disclosure vary. (Chapter 9 addresses this subject in detail.) Low-context cultures such as the U.S. value directness, while high-context ones like Japan consider tact far more important. The titles of two self-help books offer a revealing peek at the mindset of these approaches. One American self-help book is titled *How to Say No without Feeling Guilty*,[63] while the Japanese counterpart is titled *16 Ways to Avoid Saying No*.[64] It's easy to see how differing notions of appropriateness could lead to challenges in intercultural relationships.

When challenges arise out of cultural differences, the kinds of intercultural competence described in Chapter 1 (pages 34–36) become especially important. Motivation, tolerance for ambiguity, open-mindedness, knowledge of others' practices, and skill at adapting to others' communication styles are likely to make communication more smooth and relationships more satisfying.

Relationships Require Maintenance   Just as gardens need tending, cars need tune-ups, and bodies need exercise, relationships need ongoing maintenance to keep them successful and satisfying.[65] Communication accounts for as much as 80% of the difference between satisfying and unsatisfying relationships, so it's important to explore the nature of maintenance-related interaction.[66]

What kinds of communication help maintain relationships? Researchers have identified five strategies that couples use to keep their interaction satisfying.[67]

- *Positivity:* Keeping the relational climate polite and upbeat, and also avoiding criticism. (Chapter 10 addresses this topic in detail.)
- *Openness:* Talking directly about the nature of the relationship and disclosing your personal needs and concerns. (Chapter 9 describes the challenges of finding the optimal amount of self-disclosure.)
- *Assurances:* Letting the other person know—both verbally and nonverbally— that he or she matters to you, and that you are committed to the relationship.
- *Social networks:* Communication with others can provide support and relief that helps relational partners understand and appreciate one another. Friends, family, and co-workers also provide companionship that takes pressure off the relationship to satisfy all the partners' needs.
- *Sharing tasks:* Helping one another take care of life's chores and obligations makes life easier and reaffirms the value of the relationship.

Every type of relationship can benefit from these maintenance strategies, but social scientists have found that some couples are more likely than others to use them. For example, a 12-year research program at the Universities of Washington and California explored relational patterns of same-sex couples.[68] While all types of couples—straight, gay, and lesbian—have about the same levels of relational satisfaction, gay and lesbian partners seem to be better at maintaining a positive tone by using some of the maintenance strategies outlined above. For example, compared to straight couples, gay and lesbian partners are more upbeat in the face of conflict. They tend to take disagreements less personally; use fewer controlling, hostile tactics; and get less emotionally aroused when problems arise.

Invitation to Insight

Maintaining Your Relationships

How well are you maintaining your important relationships through constructive communication? Choose one relationship that matters to you: With family members, friends, or a romantic partner. Analyze the degree to which you and the others involved use the maintenance strategies listed above to keep the relationship strong and satisfying. What steps could you take to improve matters?

Table 8.1	Some Types of Relational Transgressions

Lack of Commitment
Failure to honor important obligations (e.g., financial, emotional, task-related)
Self-serving dishonesty
Unfaithfulness
Distance
Physical separation (beyond what is necessary)
Psychological separation (avoidance, ignoring)
Disrespect
Criticism (especially in front of third parties)
Problematic Emotions
Jealousy
Unjustified suspicion
Rage
Aggression
Verbal hostility
Physical violence

Repairing Damaged Relationships

Sooner or later, even the strongest relationships hit a bumpy patch. Some problems arise from outside forces: Work, finances, competing relationships, and so on. At other times, problems arise from differences and disagreements within your relationship. Chapter 11 offers guidelines for dealing with these sorts of challenges.

A third type of relational problem comes from **relational transgressions**, when one partner violates the explicit or implicit terms of the relationship, letting the other one down in some important way.

Types of Relational Transgressions   Table 8.1 lists some types of relational transgressons. Violations like these fall into different categories.[69]

Minor versus Significant   Some of the items listed in Table 8.1 aren't inherently transgressions, and in small doses they can actually aid relationships. For instance, a *little* distance can make the heart grow fonder, a *little* jealousy can be a sign of affection, and a *little* anger can start the process of resolving a gripe. In large and regular doses, however, these acts become serious transgressions that can damage personal relationships.

Social versus Relational   Some transgressions violate *social rules* shared by society at large. For example, almost everyone would agree that ridiculing or humiliating a friend or family member in public is a violation of a fundamental social rule regarding saving others' face. Other rules are *relational* in nature—unique norms constructed by the parties involved. For instance, some families have a rule stating "If I'm going to be more than a little bit late, I'll let you know so you don't worry." Once such a rule exists, failure to honor it feels like a violation, even though outsiders might not view it as such.

Deliberate versus Unintentional   Some transgressions are unintentional. You might reveal something about a friend's past without realizing that this disclosure would be embarrassing. Other violations, though, are intentional. In a fit of anger, you might purposely lash out with a cruel comment, knowing that it will hurt the other person's feelings.

One-time versus Incremental The most obvious transgressions occur in a single episode: An act of betrayal, a verbal assault, or stalking out in anger. But more subtle transgressions can occur over time. Consider emotional withdrawal: Everybody has times of needing isolation, and we usually give one another the space to do just that. But if the withdrawal slowly becomes pervasive, it becomes a violation of the fundamental rule in most relationships that partners should be available to one another.

Strategies for Relational Repair Research confirms the commonsense notion that a first step to repairing a transgression is to talk about the violation.[70] Chapter 10 offers tips for sending clear, assertive messages when you believe you've been wronged: "I was really embarrassed when you yelled at me in front of everybody last night." In other cases, you might be responsible for the transgression and want to raise it for discussion: "What did I do that you found so hurtful?" "Why was my behavior a problem for you?" Asking questions like these—and listening nondefensively to the answers—can be an enormous challenge. Chapter 7 offered guidelines for listening, and Chapter 10 provides tips about how to manage criticism.

Even if you apologize, there are no guarantees that transgressions—especially serious ones—will be forgiven. For the best chance of repairing damaged relationships, the transgressor's message requires three elements:

- An explicit acknowledgment that the transgression was wrong: "I acted like a selfish jerk."
- A sincere apology: "I'm really sorry. I feel awful for letting you down."
- Some type of compensation: "No matter what happens, I'll never do anything like that again."[71]

An apology will only be convincing if the speaker's nonverbal behaviors match his or her words. Even then, it may be unrealistic to expect immediate forgiveness. Sometimes, especially with severe transgressions, expressions of regret and promises of new behavior need to be demonstrated over time before the aggrieved party accepts them as genuine.

Forgiving Transgressions Many people think of forgiveness as a topic for theologians and philosophers. However, social scientists have found that forgiving others has both personal and relational benefits. On a personal level, forgiveness has been shown to reduce emotional distress and aggression,[72] as well as to improve cardiovascular functioning.[73] Interpersonally, extending forgiveness to lovers, friends, and family can help restore damaged relationships.[74]

Not surprisingly, some transgressions are harder to forgive than others. One study of dating partners found that sexual infidelity and breaking up with the partner were the two least forgivable offenses.[75]

"I said I'm sorry."

Even when a sincere apology is offered, forgiving others can be difficult. Research shows that one way to improve your ability to forgive is to recall times when you have mistreated or hurt others in the past—in other words, to remember that you, too, have wronged others and needed their forgiveness.[76] Knowing that it's in our own best interest to be forgiving, communication researcher Douglas Kelley encourages us to remember these words from R.P. Walters: "When we have been hurt we have two alternatives: be destroyed by resentment, or forgive. Resentment is death; forgiving leads to healing and life."[77]

Invitation to Insight

Your Relational Transgressions

1. Identify transgressions you have made in one important relationship. Describe whether these transgressions were minor or significant, social or relational, deliberate or unintentional, and one-time or incremental. (If you think the relationship can handle it, consider asking the "victim" of your transgression to describe your behavior and its effects.)

2. Consider (or ask the other person) whether it's necessary to repair your transgression. Examine the strategies described above, and decide how you could put them into action.

Communicating about Relationships

By now you understand that relationships are complex, dynamic, and important. But what kinds of messages do we exchange as we communicate in those relationships?

Content and Relational Messages

In Chapter 1 you read that every message has a *content* and a *relational* dimension. The most obvious component of most messages is their content—the subject being discussed. The content of such statements as "It's your turn to do the dishes" or "I'm busy Saturday night" is obvious.

Content messages aren't the only thing being exchanged when two people communicate. In addition, almost every message—both verbal and nonverbal—has a second, relational dimension, which makes statements about how the parties feel toward one another.[78] These relational messages deal with one or more social needs, most commonly control, affection, or respect. Consider the two examples we just mentioned:

- Imagine two ways of saying "It's your turn to do the dishes": one that is demanding and another that is matter-of-fact. Notice how the different nonverbal messages make statements about how the sender views control in this part of the relationship. The demanding tone says, in effect, "I have a right to tell you what to do around the house," whereas the matter-of-fact tone suggests, "I'm just reminding you of something you might have overlooked."

■ You can easily visualize two ways to deliver the statement "I'm busy Saturday night": one with little affection and the other with much affection.

Notice that in each of these examples the relational dimension of the message was never discussed. In fact, most of the time we aren't conscious of the many relational messages that bombard us every day. Sometimes we are unaware of relational messages because they match our belief about the amount of respect, control, and affection that is appropriate. For example, you probably won't be offended if your boss tells you to do a certain job because you agree that supervisors have the right to direct employees.

"You say 'off with her head,' but what I'm hearing is, 'I feel neglected.'"

In other cases, however, conflicts arise over relational messages even though content is not disputed. If your boss delivers the order in a condescending, sarcastic, or abusive tone of voice, you probably will be offended. Your complaint wouldn't be with the order itself but rather with the way it was delivered. "I may work for this company," you might think, "but I'm not a slave or an idiot. I deserve to be treated like a human being."

How are relational messages communicated? As the boss–employee example suggests, they are usually communicated nonverbally (which includes tone of voice). To test this fact for yourself, imagine how you could act while saying, "Can you help me for a minute?" in a way that communicates each of the following relationships:

superiority	friendliness	sexual desire
helplessness	aloofness	irritation

Although nonverbal behaviors are a good source of relational messages, they are ambiguous. The sharp tone that you receive as a personal insult might be due to fatigue, and the interruption that you assume is an attempt to ignore your ideas might be a sign of pressure that has nothing to do with you. Before you jump to conclusions about relational clues, it's a good idea to check them out verbally, using the perception-checking skills described in Chapter 3.

Types of Relational Messages

The number and variety of content messages are almost infinite, ranging from black holes to doughnut holes, from rock and roll to *Rock of Ages*. But unlike the range of content messages, there is a surprisingly narrow range of relational messages. Virtually all of them fit into one of four categories.

Affinity   An important kind of relational communication involves **affinity**—the degree to which people like or appreciate one another.[79] Not surprisingly, affection is the most important ingredient in romantic relationships.[80] Not all affinity messages are positive, though: A glare or an angry word shows the level of liking just as clearly as a smile or profession of love.

Drawing by Mike Ewers. Reprinted by permission.

© Jack Vettriano. Courtesy of Portland Gallery, London

Immediacy   **Immediacy** refers to the degree of interest and attention that we feel toward and communicate to others. Not surprisingly, immediacy is an important element of relationships.[81] A great deal of immediacy comes from nonverbal behavior such as eye contact, facial expression, tone of voice, and the distance we put between ourselves and others.[82] Immediacy can also come from our language. For example, saying "we have a problem" is more immediate than saying "you have a problem." Chapters 5 and 6 discuss nonverbal and verbal immediacy in more detail.

Immediacy isn't the same thing as affinity: It's possible to like someone without being immediate with them. For instance, you can convey liking with a high degree of immediacy, such as with a big hug and kiss or by shouting "I really like you!" You can also imagine situations where you like someone but operate with a low degree of immediacy. (Picture a quiet, pleasant evening at home where you and another person each read or work comfortably but independently.) You can also imagine communicating dislike in high-and low-immediacy ways.

The most obvious types of immediacy involve positive feelings, but it's possible to express disapproval and disliking with either high or low intensity. Imagine, for instance, the difference between mild and extreme ways—both verbal and nonverbal—of letting a friend know that you are unhappy about something he or she has done.

Highly immediate communication certainly has its value, but there are also times when a low degree of intensity is desirable. It would be exhausting to interact with full intensity all the time. It would also be inappropriate to communicate with high immediacy in cultures that frown upon such behaviors, particularly in public settings. In most cases, the key to relational satisfaction is to create a level of immediacy that works for you and the other person.

Respect   At first glance respect might seem identical to affinity, but the two attitudes are different.[83] Whereas affinity involves liking, **respect** involves esteem. It's possible to like others without respecting them. For instance, you might like—or even probably love—your 2-year-old cousin without respecting her. In the same way, you might have a great deal of affection for some friends, yet not respect the way they behave. The reverse is also true: It's possible to respect people you don't like. You might hold an acquaintance in high esteem for being a hard worker, honest, talented, or clever, yet not particularly enjoy that person's company.

Respect is an extremely important ingredient in good relationships. In fact, it is a better predictor of relational satisfaction than liking, or even loving.[84] Your own experience will show that being respected is sometimes more important than being liked. Think about occasions in school when you were offended because an instructor or fellow students didn't seem to take your comments or questions seriously. The same principle holds on the job, where having your opinions count often means more than being popular. Even in more personal relationships, conflicts often focus on the issue of respect. Being taken seriously is a vital ingredient of self-esteem.

Control   A final dimension of relational communication involves **control**—the degree to which the parties in a relationship have the power to influence one another. Some types of control involve *conversation*—who talks the most, who interrupts whom, and who changes the topic most often.[85] Another dimension of control involves *decisions:* Who has the power to determine what will happen in the relationship? What will we do Saturday night? Shall we use our savings to fix up the house or to take a vacation? How much time should we spend together and how much should we spend apart?

Relational problems arise when the people involved don't have similar ideas about the distribution of control. If you and a friend each push for your own idea, problems are likely to arise. (It can also be difficult when neither person wants to make a decision: "What do you want to do tonight?" "I don't know . . . why don't you decide." "No, *you* decide.")

Most healthy relationships handle the distribution of control in a flexible way. Rather than clinging to the lopsidedness of one-up/one-down relation-ships or the unrealistic equality of complete shared responsibility, partners shift between one-up, one-down, and straight-across roles. John may handle the decisions about car repairs and menu planning, as well as taking the spotlight at parties with their friends. Mary manages the finances and makes most of the decisions about childcare, as well as controlling the conversation when she and John are alone. When a decision is very important to one partner, the other willingly gives in, knowing that the favor will be returned later. When issues are important to both partners, they try to share power equally. But when an impasse occurs, each will make concessions in a way that keeps the overall bal-ance of power equal.

Metacommunication

Not all relational messages are nonverbal. Social scientists use the term **metacom-munication** to describe messages that people exchange, verbally or nonverbally, about their relationship.[86] In other words, metacommunication is communica-tion about communication. Whenever we discuss a relationship with others, we are metacommunicating: "I hate it when you use that tone of voice," or "I appreciate how honest you've been with me." Verbal metacommunication is an essential ingredient in successful relationships. Sooner or later it becomes necessary to talk about what is going on between you and the other person. The ability to focus on the kinds of issues described in this chapter can keep the relationship on track.

Metacommunication is an important method for solving conflicts in a constructive manner. It provides a way to shift discussion from the content level to relational questions, where the problem often lies. For example, con-sider the conversation between Macon and Muriel in the "Communication Transcript" on the next page. Imagine how the discussion might have been more productive if they had focused on the relational issue of Macon's com-mitment to Muriel and her son. By sticking to the content level—the boy's

Communication Transcript

Content and Relational Messages

Both content and relational communication are important. But when each person in a conversation focuses on a different level, problems are likely to arise. In this excerpt from Anne Tyler's novel The Accidental Tourist, *Muriel tries to turn Macon's content-related remark about her son into a discussion about the future of their relationship. Until Macon and Muriel agree about whether they will focus on content or relational issues, they are likely to remain at an uncomfortable impasse.*

"I don't think Alexander's getting a proper education," he said to her one evening.

"Oh, he's okay."

"I asked him to figure what change they'd give back when we bought the milk today, and he didn't have the faintest idea. He didn't even know he'd have to subtract."

"Well, he's only in second grade," Muriel said.

"I think he ought to switch to a private school."

"Private schools cost money."

"So? I'll pay."

She stopped flipping the bacon and looked over at him. "What are you saying?" she asked.

"Pardon?"

"What are you saying, Macon? Are you saying you're committed?"

Macon cleared his throat. He said, "Committed."

"Alexander's got ten more years of school ahead of him. Are you saying you'll be around for all ten years?"

"Um . . ."

"I can't just put him in a school and take him out again with every passing whim of yours."

He was silent.

"Just tell me this much," she said. "Do you picture us getting married sometime? I mean when your divorce comes through?" He said, "Oh, well, marriage, Muriel . . ."

"You don't, do you. You don't know what you want. One minute you like me and the next you don't. One minute you're ashamed to be seen with me and the next you think I'm the best thing that ever happened to you." He stared at her. He had never guessed that she read him so clearly.

"You think you can just drift along like this, day by day, no plans," she said. "Maybe tomorrow you'll be here, maybe you won't. Maybe you'll just go on back to Sarah. Oh yes! I saw you at Rose's wedding. Don't think I didn't see how you and Sarah looked at each other."

Macon said, "All I'm saying is—"

"All I'm saying," Muriel told him, "is take care what you promise my son. Don't go making him promises you don't intend to keep."

"But I just want him to learn to subtract!" he said.

Anne Tyler, *The Accidental Tourist*

---

math skill—Muriel avoided the kind of metacommunication that is often necessary to keep relationships healthy.

Metacommunication isn't just a tool for handling problems. It is also a way to reinforce the satisfying aspects of a relationship: "I really appreciate it when you compliment me about my work in front of the boss." Comments like this serve two functions: First, they let others know that you value their behavior; second, they boost the odds that others will continue the behavior in the future.

Despite the benefits of metacommunication, bringing relational issues out in the open does have its risks. Your desire to focus on the relationship might look like a bad omen—"Our relationship isn't working if we have to keep talking it over."[87] Furthermore, metacommunication does involve a certain degree of analysis ("It seems like you're angry with me"), and some people resent being analyzed. These cautions don't mean that verbal metacommunication is a bad idea. They do suggest, though, that it's a tool that needs to be used carefully.

Summary

People form interpersonal relationships for a variety of reasons. Some reasons involve the degree of interpersonal attraction that communicators feel for one another. Attraction can come from physical appearance, perceived similarity, complementarity, reciprocal attraction, perceived competence, disclosure of personal information, proximity, and rewards.

Two models offer somewhat different perspectives on how communication operates in the development and maintenance of interpersonal relationships. A stage-related model characterizes communication as exhibiting different characteristics as people come together and draw apart. A dialectical model characterizes communicators in every stage as being driven by the need to manage a variety of mutually incompatible needs. Both models share a variety of characteristics, such as the fact that relationships are constantly changing, are affected by culture, and require maintenance. When relationships become damaged by transgressions, repair strategies and forgiveness become important skills for both parties.

Communication occurs on two levels: content and relational. Relational communication can be both verbal and nonverbal. Relational messages usually refer to one of four dimensions of a relationship: affinity, immediacy, respect, or control. Metacommunication consists of messages that refer to the relationship between the communicators.

Key Terms

affinity (289)
avoiding (276)
bonding (275)
circumscribing (276)
connection-autonomy
    dialectic (279)
control (291)
dialectical tension (279)

differentiating (276)
experimenting (273)
immediacy (290)
initiating (273)
integrating (275)
intensifying (274)
metacommunication (291)
openness-privacy dialectic (280)

predictability-novelty
    dialectic (281)
relational maintenance (272)
relational transgressions (286)
respect (290)
stagnating (276)
terminating (277)

Media Resources

Online Textbook Resources

ThomsonNOW For quick access to the online resources that accompany this chapter, access ThomsonNOW for *Looking Out/Looking In* at www.thomsonedu.com.

The ThomsonNOW online study system helps you identify concepts you don't fully understand, allowing you to put your study time to the best use. Using chapter-by-chapter diagnostic pre-tests, the system creates a **personalized study plan** for each chapter. Each plan directs you to specific resources designed to improve your understanding, including pages from the text in ebook format. Chapter post-tests give you an opportunity to measure how much you've learned and let you know if you are ready for graded quizzes and exams.

Your ThomsonNOW for *Looking Out/Looking In* also includes self-study **review quizzes** to test your comprehension of the material in this chapter and prepare for exams; **online exercises**, including the Skill Builder and Invitation to Insight activities in this chapter; **web links** you can use to further explore topics in this chapter; access to a **feature film database** where you can locate information about movies that illustrate communication principles; and access to the **InfoTrac** College Edition searchable database of over 10 million articles from both scholarly journals and the popular press.

Films and Television

ThomsonNOW In addition to the films and television shows suggested here, go to your Thomson-NOW *Looking Out/Looking In* to link to the **Film in Communication Database** to locate movie clips that illustrate various relational dynamics.

Relational Attraction

TV Reality Shows

Beginning with *The Real World* in the 1990s, many so-called "reality shows" have allowed viewers to watch people create, maintain, and end interpersonal relationships in televised episodes. Some of these programs (such as "The Bachelor/Bachelorette" and "Blind Date") are matchmaking contests in which participants select relational partners. Physical attractiveness plays an important role in initial attraction in these shows, but it is increased proximity and disclosure that allows participants to assess the costs and rewards of an ongoing relationship with their selected partners.

Other reality shows such as "Survivor" and "Big Brother" pit participants against each other, with each person vying not be voted off the show by fellow contestants. In many cases, alliances form based on similarities (women vs. men; older participants vs. younger ones) and proximity (allied teammates spend more time with each other and often—but not always—grow to like each other). Competence is also a factor in that participants are attracted to those who perform well in the shows' survival contests. And complementarity plays a role when participants' differing talents create "odd bedfellow" partnerships.

Although reality shows don't always match most people's real worlds, the interpersonal relationships that develop on these programs often mirror what happens in everyday life.

Developmental Models

50 First Dates (2004) Rated PG-13

When Henry Roth (Adam Sandler) meets Lucy Whitmore (Drew Barrymore) for the first time, they hit it off and make plans to see each other the following day. At their next encounter, Lucy has no memory of having met Henry. It turns out that several years earlier Lucy suffered a head injury that causes her, as she sleeps at night, to forget everything that has happened since the day of her accident.

This fictional premise offers an in-depth look at the relational stages of initiating, experimenting, and intensifying—the stages in which Henry and Lucy are stuck. Henry woos Lucy each day with a variety of techniques, some of which work better than others. After a bevy of first dates, avowed bachelor Henry realizes he needs and wants relational commitment—so he develops a creative method to move the relationship to the integrating and bonding stages.

50 First Dates, like the movie *Groundhog Day*, metaphorically illustrates that relationships can sometimes get stuck in ruts, and that personal growth by one or both parties can be a key for moving relationships forward.

Dialectical Tensions

Bend It Like Beckham (2002) Rated PG-13

Jesminder "Jess" Bhamra (Parminder Nagra) is a young teen struggling to juggle conflicting goals, relationships, and cultures. Her parents want her to embrace her Indian heritage and traditional Sikh upbringing, but she would rather play soccer in the parks of London. Jess knows her parents would never allow her to participate—so she doesn't tell them. She makes up stories so she can attend practices and games.

Secrets are a central theme of this movie, as several characters wrestle with the dialectical tension of openness versus privacy. Throughout the story, discovered secrets often lead to hurt and a sense of betrayal—yet it's easy to see that most of the secrets were kept for good reasons.

Ultimately, Jess decides to openly pursue her goals and dreams, even if it disappoints the people she loves. In all of her relationships—with family, friends, and lovers—Jess finds that she must balance connection with autonomy, predictability with novelty, and privacy with openness. By movie's end, she appears to be up to the challenge.

InfoTrac College Edition/Research

Title: **Why We Communicate**

Instructions: Use PowerTrac to locate the article "Men's and Women's Organizational Peer Relationships: A Comparison" by Janie Harden Fritz.

TAKE ME TO
INFOTRAC

Questions and Answers
Answer the following questions in the fields below.

Question 1: What does the research in this article say about the different ways in which men and women form interpersonal relationships on the job?

Question 2: How well do the findings in this article match your personal experience?

Instructor Email:
Your Name:
Your Email:

Submit Answers   Print Page

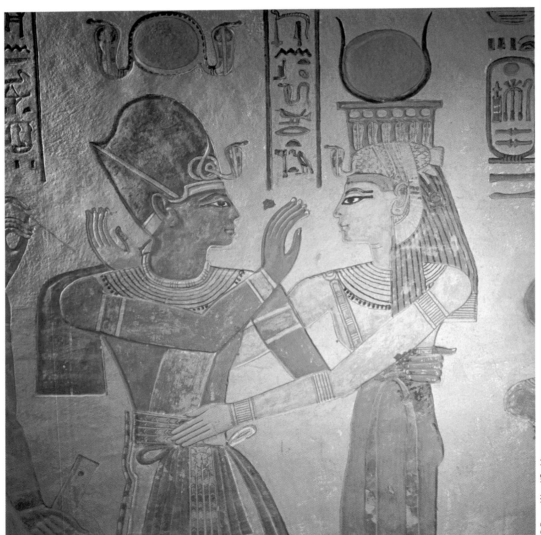

Intimacy and Distance in Relational Communication

9

How are humans like porcupines? Borrowing an analogy from philosopher Arthur Schopenhauer, Deborah Tannen explains:

> [Porcupines] huddle together for warmth, but their sharp quills prick each other, so they pull away. But then they get cold. They have to keep adjusting their closeness and distance to keep from freezing and from getting pricked by their fellow porcupines—the source of both comfort and pain.
>
> We need to get close to each other to have a sense of community, to feel we're not alone in the world. But we need to keep our distance from each other to preserve our independence, so others don't impose on or engulf us. This duality reflects the human condition. We are individual and social creatures. We need other people to survive, but we want to survive as individuals.[1]

Chapter 8 introduced the dialectical tensions that pull us in opposite directions as we try to manage our personal and relational goals. On one hand, we crave connection, but on the other we want autonomy. On one hand we recognize the desire to share personal information with people who matter, but on the other we protect our privacy.

This chapter explores how these opposing drives shape much of our communication. The first half of the chapter explores the nature of intimacy in relationships: What it is, factors that shape it, and the tension between our desire for closeness and distance. The second part examines the nature of self-disclosure: The various types of disclosing communication and how they operate in personal relationships. Finally, we will look at alternatives to revealing our personal thoughts and feelings as we strive to create and manage satisfying relationships.

Intimacy in Relationships

The musical group Three Dog Night said it well: One *can* be the loneliest number. Empirical research confirms the value of intimacy with others. People who report having satisfying intimate relationships have higher self-esteem, a stronger sense of identity, and greater feelings of control over their lives than those without close relationships.[2] In one study, researchers asked people who were dying in hospices and hospitals what mattered most in life. Fully 90 percent of these terminally ill patients put intimate relationships at the top of the list. As a 50-year-old mother of three children who was dying of cancer put it, "You need not wait until you are in my condition to know nothing in life is as important as loving relationships."[3]

Dimensions of Intimacy

Webster's *New Collegiate Dictionary* defines intimacy as a state of "close union, contact, association, or acquaintance." This closeness can occur in a variety of relationships. When researchers asked several hundred college students to identify their "closest, deepest, most involved, and most intimate relationship," the answers were varied.[4] Roughly half (47 percent) identified a romantic partner. About a third (36 percent) chose a friendship. Most of the rest (14 percent) cited a family member.

Intimacy has several dimensions. The first dimension is *physical*. Even before birth, the fetus experiences a physical closeness with its mother that will never happen again, "floating in a warm fluid, curling inside a total embrace, swaying to the undulations of the moving body and hearing the beat of the pulsing heart."[5] As they grow up, fortunate children are continually nourished by physical intimacy: being rocked, fed, hugged, and held. As we grow older, the opportunities for physical intimacy are less regular but still possible and important. Some, but by no means all, physical intimacy is sexual. In one survey, only one-quarter of the respondents (who were college students) stated that intimacy necessarily contains a romantic or sexual dimension.[6] Companions who have endured physical challenges together—in athletics or emergencies, for example—form a bond that can last a lifetime.

A second dimension of intimacy comes from *intellectual* sharing. Not every exchange of ideas counts as intimacy, of course. Talking about next week's midterm with your professor or classmates isn't likely to forge strong relational bonds. But when you engage another person in an exchange of important ideas, a kind of closeness develops that can be powerful and exciting.

A third dimension of intimacy is *emotional:* exchanging important feelings. Sharing personal information can both reflect and create feelings of closeness. Surprisingly, this sort of personal communication needn't happen in face-to-face encounters. One study revealed that

© Kirsten Soderlind/Corbis

almost two-thirds of a randomly selected group of e-mail users said they had formed a personal relationship with someone they met for the first time through an Internet newsgroup.[7] The electronic friends characterized their relationships in ways that sound remarkably similar to traditional friendships: interdependence (for instance, "We would go out of our way to help each other"), breadth ("Our communication ranges over a wide variety of topics"), depth ("I feel I could confide in this person about almost anything"), and commitment ("I am very committed to maintaining this relationship").

If we define intimacy as being close to another person, then *shared activities* is a fourth dimension that can achieve intimacy. Shared activities can include everything from working side by side at a job to meeting regularly for exercise workouts. When partners spend time together, they can develop unique ways of relating that transform the relationship from an impersonal one to an interpersonal one. For example, both friendships and romantic relationships are often characterized by several forms of play. Partners invent private codes, fool around by acting like other people, tease one another, and play games—everything from having punning contests to arm wrestling.[8] Not all shared activities create and express intimacy, of course, but the bond that comes from experiencing significant events with another person is too frequent and significant to ignore.

Some intimate relationships exhibit all four dimensions: physical, intellectual, emotional, and shared activities. Other intimate relationships exhibit only one or two. Some relationships, of course, aren't intimate in any way. Acquaintances, roommates, and co-workers may never become intimate. In some cases even family members develop smooth but relatively impersonal relationships.

Not even the closest relationships always operate at the highest level of intimacy. At times you might share all your thoughts or feelings with a friend, family member, or lover; at other times you might withdraw. You might freely share your feelings about one topic and stay more aloof about another one. The same principle holds for physical intimacy, which waxes and wanes in most relationships.

Masculine and Feminine Intimacy Styles

Until recently most social scientists believed that women are better than men at developing and maintaining intimate relationships.[9] This view grew from the assumption that the disclosure of personal information is the most important ingredient of intimacy. Most research *does* show that women (taken as a group, of course) are somewhat more willing than men to share their thoughts and feelings, although the differences aren't as dramatic as some people might think.[10] In terms of the amount and depth of information exchanged, female–female relationships are at the top of the disclosure list. Male–female relationships come in second, whereas male–male relationships involve less disclosure than any other type. At every age, women disclose more than men, and the information they disclose is more personal and more likely to involve feelings. Although both sexes are equally likely to reveal negative information, men are less likely to share positive feelings.[11]

Through the mid-1980s, many social scientists interpreted the relative lack of male self-disclosure as a sign that men are unwilling or even unable to develop close relationships. Some argued that the female trait of disclosing personal information and feelings makes women more "emotionally mature" and "interpersonally competent" than men. The title of one book captured this attitude of female superiority and male deficiency: *The Inexpressive Male: A Tragedy of American Society*.[12] Personal-growth programs and self-help books urged men to achieve closeness by learning to open up and share their feelings.

DEBBIE, I HAVE A PROBLEM WITH INTIMACY — TONY

But scholarship conducted in the past two decades has shown that emotional expression isn't the *only* way to develop close relationships. Unlike women, who value personal talk, men grow close to one another by doing things together. In one study, more than 75 percent of the men surveyed said that their most meaningful experiences with friends came from activities other than talking.[13] They reported that, through shared activities, they "grew on one another," developed feelings of interdependence, showed appreciation for one another, and demonstrated mutual liking. Likewise, men regarded practical help as a measure of caring. Research like this shows that, for many men, closeness grows from activities that don't depend heavily on disclosure: A friend is a person who does things *for* you and *with* you.

The same pattern holds in communication between fathers and their sons. Whereas mothers typically express their love toward sons directly through words and nonverbal behaviors like hugs and kisses, fathers are less likely to be so direct with their young adult sons.[14] Instead, they often show their sons affection by doing favors and helping the sons with tasks and challenges.

Actually, it isn't biological sex that is most significant in shaping how men express intimacy. Rather, it's the *gender role* that a particular man adopts. Recall that Chapter 3 explained how both men and women can adopt a gender role—masculine, feminine, or androgynous—that may or may not match their biological sex. Applying this range of styles to intimacy reveals that masculine men are most likely to express caring via helping behaviors and shared activities.[15] Men whose communication style includes some stereotypically feminine elements are more likely to express affection more directly, especially to other men.

The difference between male and female measures of intimacy helps explain some of the stresses and misunderstandings that can arise between the sexes. For example, a woman who looks for emotional disclosure as a measure of affection may overlook an "inexpressive" man's efforts to show he cares by doing favors or spending time together. Fixing a leaky faucet or taking a hike may look like ways to avoid getting close, but to the man who proposes them, they may be measures of affection and bids for intimacy. Likewise, differing ideas about the timing and meaning of sex can lead to misunderstandings. Whereas many women think of sex as a way to express intimacy that has already developed, men are more likely to see it as a way to *create* that intimacy.[16] In this sense, the man who encourages sex early in a relationship or after a fight may not be just a testosterone-crazed lecher: He may view the shared activity as a way to build closeness. By contrast, the woman who views personal talk as the pathway to intimacy may resist the idea of physical closeness before the emotional side of the relationship has been discussed.

As always, it's important to realize that generalizations don't apply to every person. Also, notions of what constitutes appropriate male behavior are changing. For example, one analysis of prime-time television sitcoms revealed that male characters who disclose personal information generally receive favorable responses

The locker room had become a kind of home to me . . . I relax, my concerns lost among relationships that are warm and real, but never intimate, lost among the constants of an athlete's life. The lines of communication are clear and simple. . . . We are at ease in the setting of satin uniforms and shower nozzles.

Bill Bradley

from other characters.[17] Researchers also note that a cultural shift is occurring in North America in which fathers are becoming more affectionate with their sons than they were in previous generations—although some of that affection is still expressed through shared activities.[18]

Cultural Influences on Intimacy

Historically, the notions of public and private behavior have changed dramatically.[19] What would be considered private behavior in modern terms was quite public at times in the past. For example, in sixteenth-century Germany, a new husband and wife were expected to consummate their marriage upon a bed carried among witnesses who would validate the marriage![20] Conversely, at the same time in England as well as in colonial America, the customary level of communication between spouses was rather formal: not much different from the way acquaintances or neighbors spoke to one another.

Even today, the notion of intimacy varies from one culture to another. In one study, researchers asked residents of Britain, Japan, Hong Kong, and Italy to describe their use of thirty-three rules that governed interaction in social relationships.[21] The rules governed a wide range of communication behaviors: everything from using humor to shaking hands to managing money. The results showed that the greatest differences between Asian and European cultures focused on the rules for dealing with intimacy: showing emotions, expressing affection in public, conducting sexual activity, respecting privacy, and so on.

Self-disclosure is especially high in mainstream North American society. In fact, people from the United States are more disclosing than members of any culture studied.[22] They are likely to disclose more about themselves to acquaintances and even strangers. One British travel book captured this tendency to disclose personal information with this tongue-in-cheek description:

> Sit next to an American on an airplane and he will immediately address you by your first name, ask "So how do you like it in the States?," explain his recent divorce in intimate detail, invite you home for dinner, offer to lend you money, and wrap you in a warm hug on parting. This does not necessarily mean he will remember your name the next day.[23]

Not all Americans are equally disclosing. Within U.S. culture, intimacy varies from one group to another. For example, working-class African American men are much more disclosing than their white counterparts.[24] By contrast, upwardly mobile black men communicate more like white men with the same social agenda, disclosing less with their male friends.

In some collectivist cultures such as Taiwan and Japan, there is an especially great difference in the way people communicate with members of their "in-groups" (such as family and close friends) and with their "outgroups."[25] They generally do not reach out to outsiders, often waiting until they are properly introduced before entering into a conversation. After they are introduced, they address outsiders with a degree of formality. They go to extremes to hide unfavorable information about in-group members from outsiders, on the principle that one doesn't air dirty laundry in public. By contrast, members of more individualistic cultures like the United States and Australia make less distinction between personal relationships and casual ones. They act more familiar with strangers and disclose more personal information, making them excellent "cocktail party conversationalists." Social psychologist Kurt Lewin captured the difference nicely when he noted that Americans are easy to meet but difficult to get to know, whereas Germans are difficult to meet but easy to get to know.[26]

Cultural differences in intimacy are becoming less prominent as the world becomes more connected through the media, travel, and technology. For instance, romance and passionate love were once seen as particularly "American" concepts of intimacy. Recent evidence shows, however, that men and women in a variety of cultures—individualist and collectivist, urban and rural, rich and poverty-stricken—may be every bit as romantic as Americans. These studies suggest that the large differences that once existed between Western and Eastern cultures may be fast disappearing.[27]

Intimacy in Computer-Mediated Communication

A few decades ago, it would have been hard to conceive that the words "computer" and "intimacy" could be positively linked. Computers were viewed as impersonal machines that couldn't transmit important features of human communication, such as facial expression, tone of voice, and touch. However, as Chapters 1 and 2 described, researchers now know that computer-mediated communication (CMC) can be just as personal as face-to-face (FtF) interaction. In fact, studies show that relational intimacy may develop *more* quickly through CMC than in FtF communication,[28] and that CMC enhances verbal, emotional, and social intimacy in friendships.[29]

Your own experience probably supports these claims. The relative anonymity of chat rooms, blogs, and online dating services provides a freedom of expression that might not occur in FtF meetings,[30] giving relationships a chance to get started. In addition, instant messaging, e-mailing, and text messaging offer more constant contact with friends, family, and partners than might otherwise be possible.[31] The potential for developing and maintaining intimate relationships via computer is captured well by one user's comment (which has a fun double meaning): "I've never clicked this much with anyone in my life."[32]

This doesn't mean that all cyber-relationships are (or will become) intimate. Just as in face-to-face relationships, communicators choose varying levels of self-disclosure with their cyberpartners. Some online relationships are relatively impersonal; others are highly interpersonal. In any case, CMC is an important component in creating and maintaining intimacy in contemporary relationships.

The Limits of Intimacy

It's impossible to have a close relationship with everyone: There just isn't enough time and energy. Even if we could seek intimacy with everyone we encountered, few of us would want that much closeness. Consider the range of everyday contacts that don't require any sort of intimacy. Some are based on economic transactions (the people at work or the shopkeeper you visit several times a week), some are based on group membership (church or school), some on physical proximity (neighbors, carpooling), and some grow out of third-party connections (mutual friends, child care). Simply engaging in conversational give-and-take with both strangers and acquaintances can be enjoyable.

Some scholars have pointed out that an obsession with intimacy can actually lead to *less* satisfying relationships.[33] People who consider intimate communication as the only kind worth pursuing place little value on relationships that don't meet this standard. This can lead them to regard interaction with strangers and casual acquaintances as superficial, or at best as the groundwork for deeper relationships. When you consider the pleasure that can come from polite but distant communication, the limitations of this view become clear. Intimacy is definitely rewarding, but it isn't the only way of relating to others.

Lonely Gay Teen Seeking Same

© Images.com/Corbis

When he was 15, a youth I will refer to by only his first name, Jeffrey, finally admitted to himself that he was gay. Jeffrey knew of no homosexuals in his high school or in his small town in the heart of the South.

It was around this time that Jeffrey first typed the words "gay" and "teen" into a search engine on the computer he'd gotten several months before and was staggered to find himself aswirl in a teeming online gay world, replete with resource centers, articles, advice columns, personals, chat rooms, message boards, porn sites and—most crucially—thousands of closeted and anxious kids like himself. That discovery changed his life.

"The Internet is the thing that has kept me sane," he told me. "I live constantly in fear. I can't be my true self. My mom complains: 'I can see you becoming more detached from us. You're always spending time on the computer.' But the Internet is my refuge."

Jeffrey's computer is in his bedroom, garrisoned inside a thicket of codes and passwords. While he uses the Internet to communicate with high-school friends, he has separate screen names and instant messaging services for these activities. This way, no one from his "straight life" can track his forays into the online gay world.

A brainy, ebullient kid, Jeffrey is an excellent student, active in high-school government, with a number of close friends. He took a girl as his date to homecoming earlier this fall. But his free time belongs largely to the disembodied gay life he pursues online—from 8:30 p.m. to 2 a.m. during the school year, and for even longer stretches in summertime.

For homosexual teenagers with computer access, the Internet has, quite simply, revolutionized the experience of growing up gay. Isolation and shame persist among gay teenagers, of course, but now, along with the inhospitable families and towns in which many find

themselves marooned, there exists a parallel online community—real people like them in cyberspace. Gay teenagers surfing the Net can find Web sites packed with information about homosexuality and about local gay support groups and counseling services, along with coming-out testimonials from young people around the world.

"The Internet is an inferior substitute for real-live human beings," says Kevin Jennings, executive director of the Gay, Lesbian and Straight Education Network, a national organization working to end antigay bias in schools. "But it's frankly better than nothing, which is what gay youth have had before."

Online boyfriends and girlfriends were common among the gay teenagers I spoke with. In some cases, the relationships had a sexual component, but what startled me was the level of closeness and intimacy teenagers derived from these cyber relationships. Jeffrey explained how he and C. sustained that intimacy without ever meeting. "We were in search of things we could do and share that were very personal and very intimate," he said. "We'd come up with little nicknames and little jokes between ourselves." They planned to attend the same college, he said, and had even discussed marriage and the adoption of children.

Jeffrey told me once, speaking of his relationship with C.: "I think it's almost like an accelerated relationship. You can't go out to the movies, so there's nothing to fill the space. You have to talk. It creates this intimacy between you; it draws you closer. Our relationship isn't based on looks or financial status or anything physical. There's no space fillers, because you can't just sit there for 15 minutes and not say anything."

Jennifer Egan

Invitation to Insight

Your IQ (Intimacy Quotient)

What is the level of intimacy in your important relationships? Find out by following these directions.

1. Identify the point on each scale below that best describes one of your important relationships.

   a. Your level of physical intimacy

       1 *2* *3* *4* *5*

       low   high

   b. Your amount of emotional intimacy

       1 *2* *3* *4* *5*

       low   high

   c. The extent of your intellectual intimacy

       1 *2* *3* *4* *5*

       low   high

   d. The degree of shared activities in your relationship

       1 *2* *3* *4* *5*

       low   high

2. Now answer the following questions:

   a. What responses to each dimension of intimacy seem most significant to you?

   b. Are you satisfied with the intimacy profile outlined by your responses?

   c. If you are not satisfied, what steps can you take to change your degree of intimacy?

© Blue Lantern Studio/Corbis

Self-Disclosure in Relationships

One way by which we judge the strength of our relationships is the amount of information we share with others. "We don't have any secrets," some people proudly claim. Opening up certainly is important. As you read in Chapter 1, one ingredient in qualitatively interpersonal relationships is disclosure. Given the obvious importance of self-disclosure, we need to take a closer look at the subject. Just what is it? When is it desirable? How can it best be done?

The best place to begin is with a definition. **Self-disclosure** is the process of deliberately revealing information about oneself that is significant and would not normally be known by others. Let's take a closer look at this definition. Self-disclosure must be *deliberate*. If you accidentally mention to a friend that you're thinking about quitting a job, or if your facial expression reveals irritation you wanted to hide, that information doesn't qualify as self-disclosure. Besides being deliberate, the information must also be *significant*. Volunteering trivial facts, opinions, or feelings—that you like fudge, for example—hardly counts as disclosure. The third requirement is that the information being disclosed is *not known by others*. There's nothing noteworthy about telling others that you are depressed or elated if they already know that. Table 9.1 describes some characteristics of self-disclosure in personal relationships.

Table 9.1	Characteristics of Self-Disclosure
Characteristic	**Comments**
Usually occurs in dyads	One-on-one disclosures are usually more comfortable than more public revelations.
Incremental	Small disclosures build confidence to reveal more important information later.
Relatively scarce	Most common early in relationships and at crucial times later. Not frequent in mature relationships (where partners know each other well).
Best in context of positive relationships	Most productive when delivered in a constructive manner, even if the information is difficult. Positive relationships have the strength to handle such revelations.

Degrees of Self-Disclosure

Although our definition of self-disclosure is helpful, it doesn't reveal the important fact that not all self-disclosure is equally revealing—that some disclosing messages tell more about us than others.

Social psychologists Irwin Altman and Dalmas Taylor describe two ways in which communication can be more or less disclosing.[34] Their model of **social penetration** is pictured in Figure 9.1. The first dimension of self-disclosure in this model involves the **breadth** of information volunteered—the range of subjects being discussed. For example, the breadth of disclosure in your relationship with a fellow worker will expand as you begin revealing information about your life away from the job as well as on-the-job information. The second dimension of self-disclosure is the **depth** of information volunteered, the shift from relatively impersonal messages to more personal ones.

Depending on the breadth and depth of information shared, a relationship can be casual or intimate. In a casual relationship the breadth may be great, but not the depth. A more intimate relationship is likely to have high depth in at least one area. The most intimate relationships are those in which disclosure is great in both breadth and depth. Altman and Taylor see the development of a relationship as a progression from the periphery of their model to its center, a process that typically occurs over time. Each of your personal relationships probably has a different combination of breadth of subjects and depth of disclosure. Figure 9.2 pictures a student's self-disclosure in one relationship.

FIGURE 9.1
Social Penetration Model

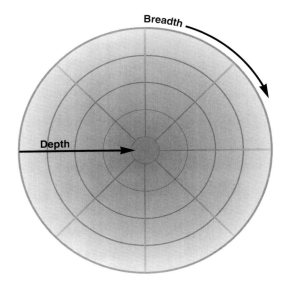

What makes the disclosure in some messages deeper than others? One way to measure depth is by how far it goes on two of the dimensions that define self-disclosure. Some revelations are certainly more *significant* than others. Consider the difference between saying, "I love my family" and "I love you." Other revelations qualify as deep disclosure because they are *private*. Sharing a secret that you've told to only a few close friends is certainly a revealing act of self-disclosure, but it's even more revealing to divulge information that you've never told anyone.

Another way to measure the depth of disclosure is to look at the types of information we share.

FIGURE 9.2
Sample Model of Social Penetration

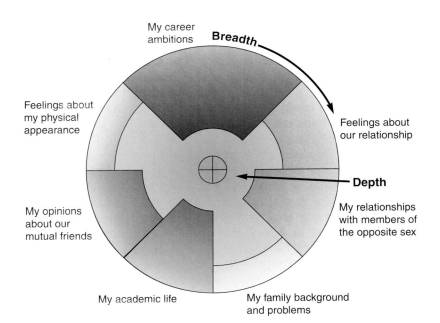

Clichés   **Clichés** are ritualized, stock responses to social situations—virtually the opposite of self-disclosure: "How are you doing?" "Fine!" "We'll have to get together soon."

Although they sound superficial, clichés can also serve as codes for messages we don't usually express directly, such as "I want to acknowledge your presence" (for instance, when two acquaintances walk past each other). Additional unstated messages often contained in clichés are "I'm interested in talking if you feel like it" or "Let's keep the conversation light and impersonal; I don't feel like disclosing much about myself right now." Accompanied by a different set of nonverbal cues, a cliché can say, "I don't want to be impolite, but you'd better stay away from me for now." Whatever valuable functions they may serve, it's clear that clichés don't qualify as self-disclosure.

Facts   Not all facts qualify as self-disclosure. They must fit the criteria of being intentional, significant, and not otherwise known:

"This isn't my first try at college. I dropped out a year ago with terrible grades."

"I'm practically engaged." *(On meeting a stranger while away from home)*

"That idea that everyone thought was so clever wasn't really mine. I read it in a book last year."

Facts like these can be meaningful in themselves, but they also have a greater significance in a relationship. Disclosing important information suggests a level of trust and commitment to the other person that signals a desire to move the relationship to a new level.

Opinions   Still more revealing is the level of opinions:

"I used to think abortion was no big deal, but lately I've changed my mind."

"I really like Karen."

"I don't think you're telling me what's on your mind."

Opinions like these usually reveal more about a person than facts alone. If you know where the speaker stands on a subject, you can get a clearer picture of how your relationship might develop. Likewise, every time you offer a personal opinion, you are giving others information about yourself.

Feelings   The fourth level of self-disclosure—and usually the most revealing one—is the realm of feelings. At first glance, feelings might appear to be the same as opinions, but there is a big difference. As we saw, "I don't think you're telling me what's on your mind" is an opinion. Now notice how much more we learn about the speaker by looking at three different feelings that might accompany this statement:

"I don't think you're telling me what's on your mind, *and I'm suspicious.*"

"I don't think you're telling me what's on your mind, *and I'm angry.*"

"I don't think you're telling me what's on your mind, *and I'm hurt.*"

The difference between these four levels of communication suggests why relationships can be frustrating. Sometimes the communicators might never get to the levels of personal opinions and feelings. At other times communicators can spend too much time at these more personal levels. Just as a diet of rich foods can become unappealing if carried to excess, too much personal information can also become unappealing. Another sort of problem occurs when two communicators want to disclose on different levels. If one person is willing to deal only with facts and perhaps an occasional opinion, and the other insists on revealing personal feelings, the results are likely to be uncomfortable for both.

Invitiation to Insight

Self-Disclosure Test for Couples

ThomsonNOW If you are in a committed relationship, this test will help you explore the degree to which you share your thoughts and feelings with your partner. To take this test, go to your ThomsonNOW for *Looking Out/Looking In.*

A Model of Self-Disclosure

One way to look at the important part that self-disclosure plays in interpersonal communication is by means of a device called the **Johari Window**.[35] (The window takes its name from the first names of its creators, Joseph Luft and Harry Ingham.) Imagine a frame like Figure 9.3 that contains everything there is to know about you: your likes and dislikes, your goals, your secrets, your needs—everything.

Of course, you aren't aware of everything about yourself. Like most people, you're probably discovering new things about yourself all the time. To represent this, we can divide the frame containing everything about you into two parts: the part you know about and the part you do not know about, as in Figure 9.4.

We can also divide this frame containing everything about you in another way. In this division one part represents the things about you that others know, and the second part represents the things about you that you keep to yourself. Figure 9.5 represents this view.

When we impose these two divided frames one atop the other, we have a Johari Window. By looking at Figure 9.6 you can see everything about you divided into four parts.

Part 1 represents the information of which both you and the other person are aware. This part is your *open area.* Part 2 represents the *blind area:* information of which you are unaware but of which the other person is aware. You learn about information in the blind area primarily through feedback from others. Part 3 represents your *hidden area:* information that you know but aren't willing to reveal to others. Items in this hidden area become public primarily through self-disclosure, which is the focus of this chapter. Part 4 represents information that is *unknown* to both you

FIGURE 9.3

FIGURE 9.4

FIGURE 9.5

and others. At first the unknown area seems impossible to verify. After all, if neither you nor others know what it contains, how can you be sure it exists? We can deduce its existence because we are constantly discovering new things about ourselves. It is not unusual to discover, for example, that you have an unrecognized talent, strength, or weakness.

	Known to self	Not known to self
Known to others	1 OPEN	2 BLIND
Not known to others	3 HIDDEN	4 UNKNOWN

FIGURE 9.6

Benefits and Risks of Self-Disclosure

Occasionally we may blurt out a piece of revealing personal information, but most of the time our decision to self-disclose is conscious and deliberate. What are the risks and benefits of opening up?

Benefits of Self-Disclosure   There are several reasons why people choose to share personal information. As you read about each of them, see which apply to you.

Catharsis   Sometimes you might disclose information in an effort to "get it off your chest." In a moment of candor you might, for instance, reveal your regrets about having behaved badly in the past. Later in this chapter you'll read guidelines for disclosing that increase the odds that you can achieve catharsis in a way that helps, instead of harming relationships.

Reciprocity   A well-documented conclusion from research is that one act of self-disclosure begets another.[36] There is no guarantee that your self-disclosures will trigger self-disclosures by others, but your own honesty can create a climate that makes others feel safer and perhaps even obligated to match your level of honesty. Sometimes revealing personal information will cause the other person to do so. It's easy to imagine how telling a partner how you feel about the relationship ("I've been feeling bored lately . . .") would generate the same degree of candor ("You know, I've felt the same way!"). Reciprocity doesn't always occur on a turn-by-turn basis: Telling a friend today about your job-related problems might help her feel comfortable opening up to you later about her family history, when the time is right for this sort of disclosure.

Self-Clarification   Sometimes you can clarify your beliefs, opinions, thoughts, attitudes, and feelings by talking about them with another person. This sort of "talking the problem out" occurs with psychotherapists, but it also goes on with others, all the way from good friends to bartenders or hairdressers.

"Bob, as a token of my appreciation for this wonderful lunch I would like to disclose to you my income-tax returns for the past four years."

Stephanie Dalton Cowan. © Thomson

he stripped
the dark circles
of mystery off
revealed his eyes
and thus
he waited
exposed
and I
did sing the song

around
until I found
the chorus
that speaks
    of windows
looking out
    means looking in
my friend

Ric Masten

Self-Validation   If you disclose information ("I think I did the right thing . . .") with the hope of obtaining the listener's agreement, you are seeking validation of your behavior—confirmation of a belief that you hold about yourself. On a deeper level, this sort of self-validating disclosure seeks confirmation of important parts of your self-concept. Self-validation through self-disclosure is an important part of the "coming out" process through which gay people recognize their sexual preference and choose to integrate this knowledge into their personal, family, and social lives.[37]

Identity Management   Sometimes we reveal personal information to make ourselves more attractive. Some observers have made this point bluntly, asserting that self-disclosure has become another way of "marketing" ourselves.[38] Consider two people on their first date. It's not hard to imagine how one or both partners might share personal information to appear more sincere, interesting, sensitive, or interested in the other person. The same principle applies in other situations. A salesperson might say, "I'll be honest with you . . ." primarily to show that she is on your side, and a new acquaintance might talk about the details of his past to seem more friendly and likable.

Relationship Maintenance and Enhancement   A large body of research supports the role of self-disclosure in relational success.[39] For example, there is a strong relationship between the quality of self-disclosure and marital satisfaction.[40] The same principle applies in other personal relationships. The bond between grandparents and grandchildren, for example, grows stronger when the honesty and depth of sharing between them are high.[41]

Social Influence   Revealing personal information may increase your control over the other person and sometimes over the situation in which you and the other person find yourselves. For example, an employee who tells the boss that another firm has made overtures probably will have an increased chance of getting raises and improvements in working conditions.

Although most of the preceding motives might strike you as being manipulative, they often aren't premeditated. There are cases, however, when an act of self-disclosure is calculated to achieve a desired result. Of course, if a disclosure's hidden motive ever becomes clear to the receiver, the results can be negative.

The motives for disclosing vary from one situation to another, depending on several factors. The strongest factor in why we disclose seems to be how well we know the other person.[42] When the target of disclosure is a friend, the most important reason that people give for disclosing is relationship maintenance and enhancement. In other words, we disclose to friends in order to strengthen the relationship. The second important reason is self-clarification—to sort out confusion to understand ourselves better.

With strangers, reciprocity becomes the most common reason for disclosing. We offer information about ourselves to strangers to learn more about them, so that we can decide whether and how to continue the relationship. The second-most common reason is impression formation. In other words, we often reveal information about ourselves to strangers to make ourselves look good. This information, of course, is usually positive—at least in the early stages of a friendship.

My stupid mouth,
Has got me in
trouble.
I said too much
again . . .

John Mayer

Risks of Self-Disclosure   While the benefits of disclosing are certainly important, opening up can also involve risks that make the decision to disclose a difficult and sometimes painful one.[43] The risks of self-disclosure fall into several categories.[44]

Rejection   John Powell summed up the risks of disclosing in answering the question that forms the title of his book, *Why Am I Afraid to Tell You Who I Am?*: "I am afraid to tell you who I am, because, if I tell you who I am, you may not like who I am, and that's all I have."[45] The fear of disapproval is powerful. Sometimes it is exaggerated and illogical, but there are real dangers in revealing personal information:

A: I'm starting to think of you as more than a friend. To tell the truth, I love you.

B: I think we should stop seeing one another.

Negative Impression   Even if disclosure doesn't lead to total rejection, it can create a negative impression.

A: I've been thinking that we should get another dog.

B: To tell you the truth, I really don't like dogs. I haven't said so before because I know how much you love them.

A: Really? I can't imagine living with somebody who doesn't love dogs as much as I do.

Decrease in Relational Satisfaction   Besides affecting others' opinions of you, disclosure can lead to a decrease in the satisfaction that comes from a relationship.

A: I need to tell you something. I really don't like it when you want to cuddle so much.

B: But I want to be close to you. . . .

Loss of Influence   Another risk of disclosure is a potential loss of influence in the relationship. Once you confess a secret weakness, your control over how the other person views you can be diminished.

A: (Manager to employee) I'd like to give you the weekend off, but to tell you the truth, I don't get to make any judgment calls around here. My boss makes all the decisions. In fact, he doesn't respect my opinions at all.

B: No kidding. I guess I know who to ask when I want to get anything done around here.

Hurting the Other Person   Even if revealing hidden information leaves you feeling better, it might hurt others—cause them to be upset, for example. It's probably easy to imagine yourself in a situation like this:

A: I'm so ugly! I can't think of anything that will change the way I look.

B: Neither can I.

Guidelines for Self-Disclosure

By now it should be clear that deciding when and how much personal information to disclose is not a simple matter. The following guidelines can help you choose the level of self-disclosure that is appropriate in a given situation.

Do You Have a Moral Obligation to Disclose?   Sometimes we are morally obliged to disclose personal information. For example, surveys reveal that a majority of HIV-positive patients believe they have a "duty" to reveal their status to healthcare providers and partners, even when doing so risks their pride, dignity, and being stigmatized.[46]

Is the Other Person Important to You? There are several ways in which someone might be important to you. Perhaps you have an ongoing relationship deep enough so that sharing significant parts of yourself justifies keeping your present level of togetherness intact. Or perhaps the person to whom you're considering disclosing is someone with whom you've previously related on a less personal level. But now you see a chance to grow closer, and disclosure may be the path toward developing that personal relationship.

"Since we're both being honest, I should tell you I have fleas."

Are the Amount and Type of Disclosure Appropriate?   It is usually a mistake to share too much information too soon. Research shows that in most relationships the process of disclosure is gradual.[47] At first most of the information that is exchanged is relatively superficial. As the parties move into the intensifying, integrating, and bonding stages of the relationship, the rate of disclosure begins to grow—but not in all situations. Most conversations—even among friends—focus on everyday, mundane topics and disclose little or no personal information.[48] Even partners in intimate relationships rarely talk about personal information.[49] One good measure of happiness is how well the level of disclosure matches the expectations of communicators: If we get what we believe is a reasonable amount of candor from others, we are satisfied. If they tell us too little—or too much—we become less satisfied.

Besides being moderate in amount, self-disclosure should consist of positive information as well as negative information. Hearing nothing but a string of dismal confessions or complaints can be discouraging. In fact, people who disclose an excess of negative information are often considered "negatively adjusted."[50]

Finally, when considering the appropriateness of disclosure in any relationship, timing is also important. If the other person is tired, preoccupied, or in a bad mood it may be best to postpone an important conversation.

Is the Risk of Disclosing Reasonable?   Take a realistic look at the potential risks of self-disclosure. Even if the probable benefits are great, opening yourself up to almost certain rejection may be asking for trouble. On the other hand, knowing that your partner is trustworthy and supportive makes the prospect of disclosing more reasonable.

Revealing personal thoughts and feelings can be especially risky on the job.[51] The politics of the workplace sometimes requires communicators to keep feelings to themselves in order to accomplish both personal and organizational goals. You might, for example, find the opinions of a boss or customer personally offensive but decide to bite your tongue rather than risk your job or lose goodwill for the company.

In anticipating risks, be sure that you are realistic. It's sometimes easy to indulge in catastrophic expectations and imagine all sorts of disastrous consequences when in fact such horrors are unlikely to occur.

Is the Disclosure Relevant to the Situation at Hand?   The kind of disclosure that is often a characteristic of highly personal relationships usually isn't appropriate in less personal settings. For instance, a study of classroom communication revealed that sharing all feelings—both positive and negative—and being completely honest resulted in less cohesiveness than did a "relatively" honest climate in which pleasant but superficial relationships were the norm.[52]

Even in personal relationships—with close friends, family members, and so on—constant disclosure isn't a useful goal. Even during a phase of high disclosure, sharing *everything* about yourself isn't necessarily constructive. Usually the subject of appropriate self-disclosure involves the relationship rather than personal information. Furthermore, it is usually most constructive to focus your disclosure about the relationship on the "here and now" as opposed to "there and then." "How am I feeling now?" "How are we doing now?" These are appropriate topics for sharing personal thoughts and feelings. At times it's relevant to bring up the past, but only as it relates to what's going on in the present.

Will the Effect Be Constructive?   Self-disclosure can be a vicious tool if it's not used carefully. As Chapter 11 explains, every person has a psychological "beltline." Below that beltline are areas about which the person is extremely sensitive. Below-the-belt jabs are a powerful way to disable another person, though usually at great cost to the relationship. It's important to consider the effects of your candor before opening up to others. Comments such as "I've always thought you were pretty unintelligent" or "Last year I made love to your best friend" may sometimes resolve old business and thus be constructive, but they also can be devastating—to the listener, to the relationship, and to your self-esteem.

Is the Self-Disclosure Clear and Understandable?   When you are expressing yourself to others, it's important that you reveal yourself in a way that's intelligible. This means using the guidelines for clear language outlined in Chapter 5. For instance, it's far better to describe another's behavior by saying, "When you don't answer my phone calls or drop by to visit anymore . . ." than to complain vaguely, "When you avoid me. . . ."

Is the Self-Disclosure Reciprocated?   The amount of personal information you reveal will usually depend on how much the other person reveals. As a rule, disclosure is a two-way street. For example, couples are happiest when their levels of openness are roughly equal.[53]

There are a few times when one-way disclosure is acceptable. Most of them involve formal, therapeutic relationships in which a client approaches a trained professional with the goal of resolving a problem. For instance, you wouldn't necessarily expect to hear about your doctor's personal ailments during a physical checkup.

Communication Transcript

Appropriate and Inappropriate Self-Disclosure

Ramon has been working in an entry-level sales job for almost a year after graduating from the university. He likes the company, but he is growing frustrated at his lack of advancement. After much thought, he decides to share his concerns with his boss, Julie. Notice that Ramon's self-disclosure has the potential to enhance or jeopardize personal goals and relationships, depending on how well it follows the guidelines on pages 313–314.

Ramon   Do you have a few minutes to talk?

Julie   Sure, no problem. Come on in.

Ramon   Do you mind if we close the door?

Julie   *(looking a bit surprised)* Sure.

Ramon   I'd like to talk to you about the future.

Julie   The future?

Ramon   Well, it's been over a year since I started to work here. One of the things you told me in the interview back then was that people move up fast here . . .

Julie   Well, . . .

Ramon   . . . and I'm confused because I've been doing pretty much the same work since I was hired.

Julie   Well, we do think a lot of your work.

Ramon   I'm glad to hear that. But I'm starting to wonder how much of a chance I'll have to grow with this company. *(Ramon is disclosing his concerns about career advancement—a very appropriate topic to raise with his boss. There is some risk in this sort of disclosure, but given Ramon's apparently good standing with his boss, it seems reasonable.)*

Julie   I can understand that you're anxious about taking on more responsibility. I can tell you that you've got a good shot at advancing, if you can just hang in there for a little while.

Ramon   *(Impatiently)* That sounds good, but I've been waiting—longer than I expected to. I'm starting to wonder if some of the things I've heard around here are true.

Julie   *(suspiciously)* What kinds of things are you talking about, Ramon?

Ramon   Well, Bill and Latisha were telling me about some people who left here because they didn't get the promotions they were promised. *(Ramon discloses information that was told to him in confidence, jeopardizing the standing of two co-workers with Julie.)*

Julie   *(firmly)* Ramon, I'm sure you understand that I can't talk about personnel decisions involving former employees. I can tell you that we try to give people all the challenges and rewards they deserve, though it can take a while.

Ramon   A year seems like more than "a while." I'm starting to think this company is more interested in having somebody with a Hispanic name on the payroll than giving me a real shot at promotion. *(Ramon's concern may be legitimate, but the sarcastic tone of his disclosure isn't constructive.)*

Julie   Look: I probably shouldn't be saying this, but I'm as frustrated as you are that it's taking so long to get a promotion arranged for you. I can tell you that there will be some personnel changes soon that will give you a good chance to make the kinds of changes you want. I think you can expect to see some changes in the next six weeks. *(Julie offers two items of self-disclosure that encourage Ramon to reciprocate.)*

Ramon   That's really good to hear! I have to tell you that I've started to think about other career options. Not because I want to leave here, but because I just can't afford to stand still. I really need to start bringing home more money. I don't want to be one of those losers who still can't afford to buy his own house by the time he's 40. *(Ramon makes a big mistake disclosing his opinion about home ownership—a topic that has no relevance to the discussion at hand.)*

Julie   Gee, I'm still renting . . .

Ramon   Oh. I didn't mean that the way it sounded . . . *(But the damage from the inappropriate disclosure is already done.)*

Julie   Anyway, I'm glad you let me know about your concerns. I hope you can hang in there for just a little while longer.

Ramon   Sure. Six weeks, huh? I'll keep an eye on the calendar!

After the conversation, Julie still thinks Ramon is a candidate for promotion, but some of his inappropriate disclosures have left her with doubts about his maturity and good judgment, which she didn't have before they spoke. Julie makes a mental note to keep an eye on Ramon and to reconsider the amount of responsibility she gives him until he has demonstrated the ability to share his personal feelings and concerns more constructively.

Communication Scenarios

To see and analyze a dramatized version of the conversation between Ramon and Julie, go to your Thomson-NOW for *Looking Out/Looking In*, access "Communication Scenarios," and then click on "Appropriate and Inappropriate Self-Disclosure." **ThomsonNOW™**

Appropriate Self-Disclosure

Use the guidelines on pages 313–314 to develop one scenario where you might reveal a self-disclosing message. Create a message of this type, and use the information in this chapter to discuss the advantages and disadvantages of sharing this message.

Alternatives to Self-Disclosure

Although self-disclosure plays an important role in interpersonal relationships, it isn't the only type of communication available. To understand why complete honesty isn't always an easy or ideal choice, consider some familiar dilemmas:

> A new acquaintance is much more interested in becoming friends than you are. She invites you to a party this weekend. You aren't busy, but you don't want to go. What would you say?

> Your boss asks you what you think of his new wardrobe. You think it's cheap and flashy. Would you tell him?

> You're attracted to your best friend's mate, who has confessed that s/he feels the same way about you. You both agreed that you won't act on your feelings and that even bringing up the subject would make your friend feel terribly insecure. Now your friend has asked whether you're attracted at all to the mate. Would you tell the truth?

> You've just been given a large, extremely ugly painting as a gift by a relative who visits your home often. How would you respond to the question, "Where will you put it?"

Situations like these highlight some of the issues that surround deceptive communication. On one hand, our moral education and common sense lead us to abhor anything less than the truth. Ethicists point out that the very existence of a society seems based on a foundation of truthfulness.[54]

Although honesty is desirable in principle, it can have potentially unpleasant consequences. It's tempting to avoid situations where self-disclosure would be difficult, but examples like the preceding ones show that evasion isn't always possible. Research and personal experience show that communicators—even those with the best intentions—aren't always completely honest when they find themselves in situations in which honesty would be uncomfortable.[55] Four common alternatives to self-disclosure are silence, lying, equivocating, and hinting. We will take a closer look at each one.

Silence

One alternative to self-disclosure is to keep your thoughts and feelings to yourself. You can get a sense of how much you rely on silence instead of disclosing by keeping a record of when you do and don't express your opinions. You're likely to find that withholding thoughts and feelings is a common approach for you.

Silence can be in the best interest of both you and the other person. Telling the whole truth may be honest, but it can jeopardize you, the other person, and your relationship. (See the risks of self-disclosure outlined on page 312.)

As the Ethical Challenge on page 324 shows, many ethicists argue that silence isn't necessarily dishonorable, especially when total candor is likely to cause pain. Most thoughtful communicators would keep quiet rather than blurt out unsolicited opinions like "You look awful" or "You talk too much." Social scientists have found that people often make distinctions between "lies of omission" and "lies of commission"—and that saying nothing (omission) is usually judged less harshly than telling an outright lie (commission).[56]

Lying

To most of us, lying appears as a breach of ethics. Although lying to gain unfair advantage over an unknowing victim seems clearly wrong, another kind of mistruth—the "benevolent lie"—isn't so easy to dismiss as completely unethical. A **benevolent lie** is defined (at least by the teller) as unmalicious, or even helpful, to the person to whom it is told. Whether or not they are innocent, benevolent lies are quite common. In several studies spanning four decades, a significant majority of people surveyed acknowledge that even in their closest relationships, there are times when lying is justified.[57] In one study, 130 subjects were asked to keep track of the truthfulness of their everyday conversational statements.[58] Only 38.5 percent of these statements—slightly more than a third—proved to be totally honest. In another experiment, subjects recorded their conversations over a two-day period and later counted their own deceptions. The average lie rate: three fibs for every ten minutes of conversation.[59]

Reasons for Lying   What reasons do people give for being deceitful? When subjects in one study were asked to provide a lie-by-lie account of their reasons for concealing or distorting the truth, five major reasons emerged.[60]

1. *To save face.* Over half the lies were justified as a way to prevent embarrassment. Such lying is often given the approving label "tact" and is used "when it would be unkind to be honest, but dishonest to be kind."[61] Sometimes a face-saving lie protects the recipient, as when you pretend to remember someone at a party in order to save that person from the embarrassment of being forgotten. At other times a lie protects the teller from humiliation. You might, for instance, cover up your mistakes by blaming them on outside forces: "You didn't receive the check? It must have been delayed in the mail."
2. *To avoid tension or conflict.* Sometimes it seems worthwhile to tell a small lie to prevent a large conflict. You might, for example, say you're not annoyed at a friend's teasing in order to prevent the hassle that would result if you expressed your annoyance. It's often easier to explain your behavior in dishonest terms than to make matters worse. You might avoid further tension by saying, "I'm not mad at you; it's just been a tough day."
3. *To guide social interaction.* Sometimes we lie to make everyday relationships run smoothly. You might, for instance, pretend to be glad to see someone you actually dislike or fake interest in a dinner companion's boring stories to make a social event pass quickly. Children who aren't skilled or interested in these social lies are often a source of embarrassment for their parents.
4. *To expand or reduce relationships.* Some lies are designed to make relationships grow: "You're going downtown? I'm headed that way. Can I give you a

The injunction against bearing false witness, branded in stone and brought down by Moses from the mountaintop, has always provoked ambivalent, conflicting emotions. On the one hand, nearly everyone condemns lying. On the other, nearly everyone does it every day. How many of the Ten Commandments can be broken so easily and with so little risk of detection over the telephone?

Paul Gray

ride?" In one study, a majority of college students (both men and women) willingly lied to improve their chances of getting a date with an attractive partner. Their exaggerations and untruths covered a wide range of topics, including their attitudes about love, personality traits, income, past relationships, career skills, and intelligence—all in the direction of making themselves more similar to the attractive prospects.[62]

Sometimes we tell untruths to *reduce* interaction with others: "I really have to go. I should be studying for a test tomorrow." At other times people lie to end a relationship entirely: "You're really great, but I'm just not ready to settle down yet."

5. *To gain power.* Sometimes we tell lies to show that we're in control of a situation. Turning down a last-minute request for a date by claiming you're busy can be one way to put yourself in a one-up position, saying in effect, "Don't expect me to sit around waiting for you to call." Lying to get confidential information—even for a good cause—also falls into the category of lying to gain power.

This five-part scheme isn't the only way to categorize lies. The taxonomy outlined in Table 9.2 is more complicated and covers some types of lies that don't fit into the categories above. Exaggerations, for example, are lies told to boost the effect of a story. In exaggerated tales the fish grow larger, hikes grow longer and more strenuous, and so on. The stories may be less truthful, but they become more interesting—at least to the teller.

Most people think that benevolent lies are told for the benefit of the recipient. In the study cited earlier, the majority of subjects claimed that such lying is "the right thing to do." Other research paints a less flattering picture of who benefits most from lying. One study found that two out of every three lies are told for "selfish reasons."[63] A look at Table 9.2 seems to make this figure too conservative. Of the 322 lies recorded, 75.8 percent were for the benefit of the liar. Less than 22 percent were for the benefit of the person hearing the lie, whereas a mere 2.5 percent were intended to aid a third party.

Before we become totally cynical, however, the researchers urge a charitable interpretation. After all, most intentional communication behavior—truthful or not—is designed to help the speaker achieve a goal. Therefore, it's unfair to judge benevolent lies more harshly than other types of messages. If we define selfishness as the extent to which some desired resource or interaction is denied to the person hearing the lie or to a third party, then only 111 lies (34.5 percent) can be considered truly selfish. This figure may be no worse than the degree of selfishness in honest messages.

Effects of Lies   What are the consequences of discovering you've been lied to? In an interpersonal relationship, the discovery can be traumatic. As we grow closer to others, our expectations about

"Remember when I said I was going to be honest with you, Jeff? That was a big, fat lie."

Table 9.2	Types of Lies and Their Frequency		
	BENEFIT SELF	BENEFIT OTHER	BENEFIT THIRD PARTY
BASIC NEEDS	68	I	I
A. Acquire resources	29	0	0
B. Protect resources	39	I	I
AFFILIATION	128	I	6
A. Positive	65	0	0
I. Initiate interaction	8	0	0
2. Continue interaction	6	0	0
3. Avoid conflict	48	0	0
4. Obligatory acceptance	3	0	0
B. Negative	43	I	3
I. Avoid interaction	34	I	3
2. Leave-taking	9	0	0
C. Conversational control	20	0	3
I. Redirect conversation	3	0	0
2. Avoid self-disclosure	17	0	3
SELF-ESTEEM	35	63	I
A. Competence	82	6	0
B. Taste	0	18	I
C. Social desirability	27	19	0
OTHER	13	5	0
A. Dissonance reduction	3	5	0
B. Practical joke	2	0	0
C. Exaggeration	8	0	0

From "White Lies in Interpersonal Communication: A Taxonomy and Preliminary Investigation of Social Motivations," *Western Journal of Speech Communication* 48 (1984): 315.

their honesty grow stronger. After all, discovering that you've been lied to requires you to redefine not only the lie you just discovered, but also many of the messages you previously took for granted. Was last week's compliment really sincere? Was your joke really funny, or was the other person's laughter a put-on? Does the other person care about you as much as he or she claimed?

Research has shown that lying does, in fact, threaten relationships.[64] Not all lies are equally devastating, however. Research suggests that a liar's motives make a significant difference in whether the deception is perceived as acceptable by others.[65] If a lie appears to be self-serving and exploitive, it will most likely be treated as a relational transgression. On the other hand, if a mistruth seems aimed at sparing another's feelings, the chances of being forgiven increase.

Feelings like dismay and betrayal are greatest when the relationship is most intense, when the importance of the subject is high, and when there is previous suspicion that the other person isn't being completely honest. Of these three factors, the importance of the information lied about proved to be the key factor in provoking a relational crisis. We may be able to cope with "misdemeanor" lying, but "felonies" are a grave threat. In fact, the discovery of major deception can lead to the end of the relationship. More than two-thirds of the subjects in

Is Misleading Your Spouse Fraud or Tact?

How could I **POSSIBLY** STAY IN LOVE WITH SOMEONE I COULDN'T TRUST ??

I'LL NEVER LIE TO YOU AGAIN, DARLING... **NEVER !!**

When their marriage of more than a decade ended in divorce, Anaheim banker Ronald Askew sued his ex-wife for fraud because she admittedly concealed the fact that she had never felt sexually attracted to him. On Wednesday, an Orange County jury agreed, and ordered Bonnette Askew to pay her ex-husband $242,000 in damages.

"I'm astonished by this verdict and I've looked at divorce in 62 societies," said Helen Fisher, an American Museum of Natural History anthropologist who authored the recent book *Anatomy of Love: The Natural History of Monogamy, Adultery and Divorce.*

Bonnette Askew, 45, acknowledged in court that she had never been sexually attracted to her husband. But she said she always loved him and noted that their marriage was not sexless and that they had two children together.

She first admitted her lack of sexual desire for him during a joint therapy session in 1991. "I guess he confused sex with love," Bonnette Askew said, adding that she concealed her lack of desire because she "didn't want to hurt his male ego."

But Ronald Askew, 50, said his lawsuit had more to do with honesty and integrity than sex. He felt deceived, especially because he said he repeat-

edly asked her before their marriage to be honest with him and reveal any important secrets.

If Ronald Askew believes total honesty is the foundation of good marriages, Fisher has a message for him: "Grow up."

"Since when is anyone truly honest with anyone?" Fisher said. "Did this man really want her to say: 'You're short, fat and you're terrible in bed'? Much of the world is amazed at what they see as brutal honesty in America. She was operating on an entirely different set of social values, which much of the world operates on—delicacy as opposed to brutal honesty."

Maria Cone, Los Angeles Times

one study reported that their relationship had ended because they discovered a lie. Furthermore, they attributed the breakup directly to the lie.

The lesson here is clear: Lying about major parts of your relationship can have the gravest consequences. If preserving a relationship is important, honesty—at least about important matters—really does appear to be the best policy.

Equivocating

Lying isn't the only alternative to self-disclosure. When faced with the choice between lying and telling an unpleasant truth, communicators can—and often do—equivocate. As Chapter 5 explained, *equivocal language* has two or more equally plausible meanings. Sometimes people send equivocal messages without meaning to, resulting in confusion. "I'll meet you at the apartment" could refer to more than one place. But at other times we are deliberately vague. For instance, when a friend asks what you think of an awful outfit, you could say "It's really unusual—one of a kind!" Likewise, if you are too angry to accept a friend's apology but don't want to appear petty, you might say, "Don't worry about it." One humorous set of suggestions shows how equivocation can help a reluctant business contact provide ambiguous references for an incompetent job applicant:

> For a lazy worker "You will be lucky to get this person to work for you."
>
> For someone with no talent: "I recommend this candidate with no qualifications."
>
> For a candidate who should not be hired under any circumstances: "Waste no time hiring this person."

The value of equivocation becomes clear when you consider the alternatives. Consider the dilemma of what to say when you've been given an unwanted present—that ugly painting we mentioned before, for example—and the giver asks what you think of it. How can you respond? On one hand, you need to choose between telling the truth and lying. On the other hand, you have a choice of whether to make your response clear or vague. Figure 9.7 displays these choices. After considering the choices, it's clear that the first—an equivocal, true response—is far preferable to the others in several respects.

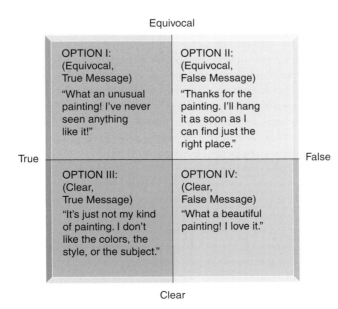

FIGURE 9.7

Dimensions of Truthfulness and Equivocation

From *Equivocal Communication* by Bavelas, et al.

- *It spares the receiver from embarrassment.* For example, rather than flatly saying "No" to an unappealing invitation, it may be kinder to say, "I have other plans"—even if those plans are to stay home and watch TV.
- *It can save face for both the sender and receiver.* Because equivocation is often easier to take than the cold, hard truth, it spares the teller from feeling guilty. It's less taxing on the conscience to say, "I've never tasted anything like this" than to say, "This meal tastes terrible," even though the latter comment is more precise. Few people want to lie, and equivocation provides an alternative to deceit.

    A study by communication researcher Sandra Metts and her colleagues shows how equivocation can save face in difficult situations.[66] Several hundred college students were asked how they would turn down unwanted sexual overtures from a person whose feelings were important to them: either a close friend, a prospective date, or a dating partner. The majority of students chose a diplomatic reaction ("I just don't think I'm ready for this right now") as being more face-saving and comfortable than a direct statement ("I just don't feel sexually attracted to you"). The diplomatic reaction seemed sufficiently clear to get the message across but not so blunt as to embarrass or even humiliate the other person.
- *It provides an alternative to lying.* If a potential employer asks about your grades during an interview, you would be safe saying, "I had a B average last semester," even though your overall grade average is closer to C. The statement isn't a complete answer, but it is honest as far as it goes. As one team of researchers put it, "equivocation is neither a false message nor a clear truth, but rather an alternative used precisely when both of these are to be avoided."[67]

Given these advantages, it's not surprising that most people will usually choose to equivocate rather than tell a lie. In a series of experiments, subjects chose among telling a face-saving lie, telling the truth, and equivocating. Only 6 percent chose the lie, and only between 3 and 4 percent chose the hurtful truth. By contrast, over 90 percent chose the equivocal response.[68] People *say* they prefer truth telling to equivocating, but given the choice, they prefer to finesse the truth.[69]

Hinting

Hints are more direct than equivocal statements. Whereas an equivocal statement isn't necessarily aimed at changing others' behavior, a hint does aim to get a desired response from others.[70]

Direct Statement	Face-Saving Hint
I'm too busy to continue with conversation.	I know you're busy; I'd better let you go.
Please don't smoke in here because it is bothering me.	I'm pretty sure that smoking isn't permitted here.
I'd like to invite you out for lunch, but I don't want to risk a "no" answer.	Gee, it's almost lunchtime. Have you ever eaten at that new Italian restaurant around the corner?

As Emily Dickinson's poem on this page suggests, hinting can spare others discomfort that comes with the undiluted truth. The face-saving value of hints explains why communicators are more likely to be indirect than fully disclosing when they deliver a potentially embarrassing message.[71] The success of a hint depends on the other person's ability to pick up the unexpressed message. Your subtle remarks might go right over the head of an insensitive receiver—or one who chooses not to respond. If this happens, you may decide to be more direct. On the other hand, if the costs of a direct message seem too high, you can withdraw without risk.

> Tell all the Truth but tell it slant—
> Success in Circuit lies
> Too bright for our infirm Delight
> The Truth's superb surprise
>
> Emily Dickinson

The Ethics of Evasion

It's easy to see why people choose hints, equivocations, and benevolent lies instead of complete self-disclosure. These strategies provide a way to manage difficult situations that is easier than the alternatives for both the speaker and the receiver of the message. In this sense, successful liars, equivocators, and hinters can be said to possess a certain kind of communicative competence. On the other hand, there are certainly times when honesty is the right approach, even if it's painful. At times like these, evaders could be viewed as lacking the competence or the integrity to handle a situation most effectively.

Are hints, benevolent lies, and equivocations ethical alternatives to self-disclosure? Some of the examples in these pages suggest that the answer is a qualified "yes." Many social scientists and philosophers agree. As the "Ethical Challenge" on page 324 shows, some argue that the morality of a speaker's *motives* for lying, not the lie itself, ought to be judged, and others ask whether the *effects* of a lie will be worth the deception.

Another measure of the acceptability of some lies is the fact that most people are willing to accept them without challenging the person who they know is lying. In fact, there are some circumstances when lies are judged as *more* appropriate than the undiluted truth.[72] For example, there are some circumstances when we are likely to not challenge statements that we know are untruthful:[73]

- When we expect others tell a fib. (You listen with amusement to a friend's or relative's tall tales, even though you know they are exaggerations.)
- When the lie is mutually advantageous. (A fellow employee's self-serving account of a job mixup might get you off the hook, too.)

Must We Always Tell the Truth?

"Is there really a Santa Claus?"

"Am I talking too much?"

"Isn't this the cutest baby you've ever seen?"

"Was it good for you?"

Questions like these often seem to invite answers that are less than totally honest. The research summarized on page 317 reveals that, at one time or another, virtually everyone avoids telling the complete truth. Sometimes we remain silent, sometimes we tell benevolent lies, and sometimes we equivocate. We seem to be caught between the time-honored commandment "Thou shall not lie" and the fact that everybody *does* seem to bend the truth, if only for altruistic reasons. What, then, are the ethics of honesty?

Philosopher Immanuel Kant had a clear answer: We may be able to evade unpleasant situations by keeping quiet, but we must always tell the complete truth when there is no way to avoid speaking up. He said that "truthfulness in statements which cannot be avoided is the formal duty of an individual . . . however great may be the disadvantage accruing to himself or another." Kant's unbending position didn't make any exception for lies or equivocations told in the best interests of the receiver. In his moral code, lying is wrong—period.

Kant's unbending position grows from his *categorical imperative*: the dictum that the morality of an action is determined by whether it could be practiced universally. At one level, the categorical imperative demands that we ask, "What if everybody lied?" Because it would be intolerable—even impossible—to function in a world in which everyone lied, we have an ethical obligation to refrain from lying, even once.

Not all ethicists have shared Kant's rigid standards of truth telling. Utilitarian philosophers claim that the way to determine the morality of a behavior is to explore whether it leads to the greatest happiness for the greatest number of people. Philosopher Sissela Bok adopts this stance when she argues that the morality (or immorality) of an untruth can be calculated only by comparing its effect to that of telling the unvarnished truth. She offers some circumstances in which deception may be justified: doing good, avoiding harm, and protecting a larger truth.

Despite her tolerance for some lies, Bok doesn't consider benign falsehoods to be just as acceptable as the truth. Her *principle of veracity* asserts that "truthful statements are preferable to lying in the absence of special considerations." In other words, she encourages truth telling whenever possible. Of course, the phrase "wherever possible" is open to interpretation, and Bok is realistic enough to recognize that liars are prone to self-deceptive justifications. For this reason, she tempers her utilitarian position with a *test of publicity*. She suggests that we ask how others would respond if they knew that we were being untruthful. If most disinterested observers with all the facts supported untruthful speech as the best course, then it passes the test of publicity.

Submit your case for avoiding the truth to a "court of self-disclosure":

1. Recall recent situations in which you have used each of the following evasive approaches: lying, equivocating, and hinting.

2. Write an anonymous description of each situation, including a justification for your behavior, on a separate sheet of paper. Submit the cases to a panel of "judges" (most likely fellow students), who will evaluate the morality of these decisions.

Read Kant's own words on truth telling in the following works: "On a Supposed Right to Lie from Altruistic Motives," in Lewis White Beck, trans. and ed., *Critique of Practical Reason and Other Writings in Moral Philosophy* (Chicago: University of Chicago Press, 1964); and H. J. Paton, trans., *Groundwork of the Metaphysics of Morals* (New York: Harper Torchbooks, 1964). Bok's arguments are detailed in her book *Lying: Moral Choice in Public and Private Life* (New York: Vintage, 1979). See also Charles Fried's essay "The Evil of Lying," in *Right and Wrong* (Cambridge, Mass.: Harvard University Press, 1978).

- When a lie helps us avoid embarrassment. (You assure your host that a meal was delicious, even though it tasted awful.)
- When the lie helps us avoid confronting an unpleasant truth. (A family acts as if there is nothing wrong when they know that one member is an alcoholic.)
- When we have asked the other person to lie. (One partner tells the other: "If you're ever unfaithful to me, I don't want to know about it.")

In light of these facts, perhaps the right questions to ask are whether an indirect message is truly in the interests of the receiver and whether this sort of evasion is the only, or the best, way to behave in a given situation.

Summary

Intimacy in interpersonal relationships has four dimensions: physical, intellectual, emotional, and shared activities. Both gender and culture affect the way intimacy is expressed. Intimacy can occur in computer-mediated communication as well as in face-to-face interaction. Not all relationships are intimate; communicators must make choices about when, where, and with whom they will be intimate.

An important issue in interpersonal relationships is the appropriate type and degree of self-disclosure: honest, revealing messages about the self that are intentionally directed toward others. A number of factors govern whether a communicator will be judged as being a high- or low-level discloser. The social penetration model describes two dimensions of self-disclosure: breadth and depth. Disclosure of feelings is usually more revealing than disclosure of opinions, and disclosure of opinions is usually more revealing than disclosure of facts. Clichés are the least revealing.

The Johari Window model is a useful way to illustrate self-disclosure. A window representing a single person can illustrate the amount of information that an individual reveals to others, hides, is blind to, and is unaware of. Communicators disclose personal information for a variety of reasons and benefits: catharsis, reciprocity, self-clarification, self-validation, identity management, relationship maintenance and enhancement, and social influence. The risks of self-disclosure include the possibility of rejection, making a negative impression, a decline in relational satisfaction, a loss of influence, and hurting the other person.

Four alternatives to revealing personal facts, feelings, and opinions are silence, lying, equivocating, and hinting. Nonmalicious benevolent lies serve a variety of functions: saving face for the sender or receiver, avoiding tension or conflict, guiding social interaction, managing relationships, and gaining power. Equivocal messages are an attractive alternative to lies and direct honesty. Hints, which are more direct than equivocal statements, are used primarily to avoid embarrassment. Lies, equivocations, and hints may be ethical alternatives to self-disclosure; however, whether they are depends on the speaker's motives and the effects of the deception.

Key Terms

benevolent lie (317)
breadth (305)
clichés (307)

depth (305)
intimacy (298)
Johari Window (308)

self-disclosure (304)
social penetration (305)

Media Resources

Online Textbook Resources

ThomsonNOW For quick access to the online resources that accompany this chapter, access ThomsonNOW for *Looking Out/Looking In* at www.thomsonedu.com.

The ThomsonNOW online study system helps you identify concepts you don't fully understand, allowing you to put your study time to the best use. Using chapter-by-chapter diagnostic pre-tests, the system creates a **personalized study plan** for each chapter. Each plan directs you to specific resources designed to improve your understanding, including pages from the text in ebook format. Chapter post-tests give you an opportunity to measure how much you've learned and let you know if you are ready for graded quizzes and exams.

Your ThomsonNOW for *Looking Out/Looking In* also includes a **communication scenario video** of the transcript on page 315; **vocabulary activities** to help you master key terms; self-study **review quizzes** to test your comprehension of the material in this chapter and prepare for exams; **online exercises**, including the Skill Builder and Invitation to Insight activities in this chapter; **web links** you can use to further explore topics in this chapter; access to a **feature film database** where you can locate information about movies that illustrate communication principles; and access to the **InfoTrac College Edition** searchable database of over 10 million articles from both scholarly journals and the popular press.

Films

ThomsonNOW In addition to the films suggested here, go to your ThomsonNOW for *Looking Out/Looking In* and access the **Film in Communication Database** to locate movie clips that illustrate various relational dynamics.

The Need for Intimacy

About a Boy (2002) Rated PG-13
Bachelor Will Freeman (Hugh Grant) prides himself on being free of any emotional commitments. "I'm on my own," Will proclaims. "There's just me. I'm not putting myself first, because there isn't anybody else there."

Marcus (Nicholas Hoult), who is 12, also has little intimacy in his life, but not by choice. His bad haircut, nerdy clothing, and visible love for his mother make him a constant target of teasing by the kids at school. Marcus has no friends, but plenty of pluck and determination.

A series of events leads Will into Marcus's life, where both decide they can use each other for their own devices. Marcus wants Will to marry his mother; Will wants Marcus to feign the role of son to help Will score points with single mothers. Neither plan works—but in the process, Will and Marcus slowly creep inside each other's lives. The intimacy they experience as friends changes both of them for the better. Ultimately they learn that, indeed, no person is meant to be an island.

Intimacy and Self-Disclosure in Family Relationships

In Her Shoes (2005) Rated PG-13
Descriptions of intimacy often focus on romances or friendships, but experience tells us that many of our closest relationships are with family members. Such is the case with the Feller sisters. Maggie (Cameron Diaz) is a flirty, flaky party girl, while her sister Rose (Toni Collette) is a plain, hardworking, responsible lawyer. The sisters have nothing in common except their family history—and, despite their differences, their fierce love for one another.

Maggie and Rose have a major falling out, but over time they (re)discover how much they care for and need each other. They know each other's secrets; they cover each other's weaknesses; they value each other's strengths. Near movie's end, Maggie shares with Rose an e.e. cummings poem whose final line captures the intimacy shared by these sisters: "I carry your heart. I carry it in my heart."

Transamerica (2006) Rated R
A week before surgery that will finally complete her transformation from a man to a woman, Bree Osbourne (Felicity Huffman) discovers that, as a young man, he fathered a son who is now 17 years old. Before authorizing the surgery, Bree's therapist insists that Bree must meet and come to terms with the son.

Bree reluctantly travels to New York where she discovers that Toby (Kevin Zegers) is a street hustler. Understandably hesitant to reveal her true identity, Bree presents herself as a Christian missionary dedicated to helping sex workers live a more healthy life. She offers to drive Toby to Los Angeles, where he hopes to become a porn star. During their cross-country trip, parent and child find points of connection. Still, Bree cannot bring herself to disclose her true identity until events force her to reveal the truth.

While Bree's secret is far more explosive than most, her struggle to protect her most precious and private feelings while honoring relational obligations is familiar and touching.

The Process of Self Disclosure

Before Sunset (2004) Rated R
Nine years earlier, American Jesse (Ethan Hawke) and Parisian Céline (Julie Delpy) spent an intensely romantic twelve hours in Vienna. Now in their early 30s, they meet again in a Paris bookstore. Jesse's flight back to New York leaves in a few hours and they use the time to reconnect.

At first, Jesse and Céline banter superficially, but we know unspoken questions are on their minds: Is either one married? Are they happy? Is the mutual attraction still there?

As their conversation goes on, Céline and Jesse slowly and cautiously begin to open up. Their prudence comes from both being in relationships they both take seriously, from the desire to avoid hurting one another, and also the fear of revealing painful information about themselves. Over and over they touch on a risky topic, then back off with a joke. Still, the trajectory is toward revealing important feelings. Each act of self-disclosure evokes a reciprocal sharing from the other, and the breadth and depth of personal information increases. Slowly, they address the fact that their experience in Vienna was the central point in their emotional lives.

Jesse and Céline's conversations reflect the real-world dance of disclosure. Better than almost any other film, *Before Sunset* captures the nervous hesitations, false starts, confessions and retreats that occur when revealing important information to people who matter. The film captures both the risks of opening up, and the costs of not doing so.

Alternatives to Self-Disclosure

Liar, Liar (1997) Rated PG-13
Fletcher Reed (Jim Carrey) is a charming, smooth-talking attorney who says whatever is necessary to get what he wants, regardless of the truth. Reed tells expedient lies away from work, too, and now his 5-year-old son Max (Justin Cooper) no longer believes a word his father says. "My dad's a liar," the boy announces in school. "You mean a *lawyer*," his teacher says. Max shrugs his shoulders, as if to say, "What's the difference?"

When Fletcher fails to show up for Max's birthday party, the boy makes a wish as he blows out the candles: that for just one day his dad won't tell a single lie. This wish comes true, and we are treated to a vision of what life would be like if people were totally honest. Much of the film draws laughs by presenting humorous scenarios arising from the fantasy of an attorney telling the entire truth. But the film isn't just an exercise in lawyer bashing: Viewers also get an amusing look at why total self-disclosure is unrealistic in everyday situations. "How are you today?" a judge asks Fletcher. "I'm a little upset about a bad sexual episode last night," he replies. In a hilarious scene, Fletcher creates an uproar at work by telling his colleagues and bosses his true opinion of them.

At the most simplistic level, *Liar, Liar* argues that healthy relationships demand honesty and attention. But, for more sophisticated communication analysts, it also argues that total honesty can be as risky as lying.

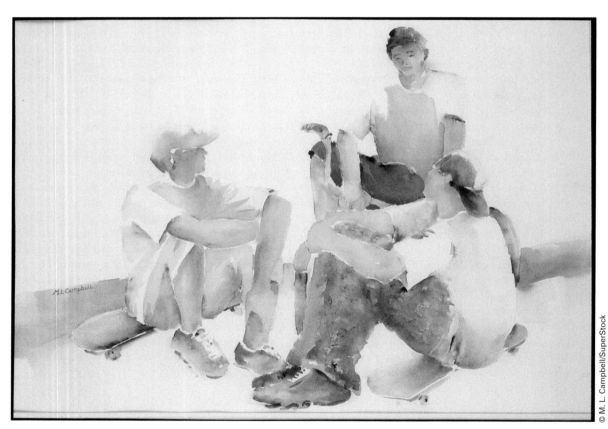

Improving Communication Climates

10

Personal relationships are a lot like the weather. Some are fair and warm, whereas others are stormy and cold; some are polluted, and others healthy. Some relationships have stable climates, whereas others change dramatically—calm one moment and turbulent the next. You can't measure the interpersonal climate by looking at a thermometer or glancing at the sky, but it's there nonetheless. Every relationship has a feeling, a pervasive mood that colors the interactions of the participants.

Although we can't change the external weather, we *can* change an interpersonal climate. This chapter will explain the forces that make some relationships pleasant and others unpleasant. You will learn what kinds of behavior contribute to defensiveness and hostility and what kinds lead to more positive feelings. After reading these pages you will have a better idea of the climate in each of your important relationships—and even more important, how to improve it.

Communication Climate: The Key to Positive Relationships

The term **communication climate** refers to the emotional tone of a relationship. A climate doesn't involve specific activities as much as the way people feel about each other as they carry out those activities. Consider two interpersonal communication classes, for example. Both meet for the same length of time and follow the same syllabus. It's easy to imagine how one of these classes might be a friendly, comfortable place to learn, whereas the other could be cold and tense—even hostile. The same principle holds in other contexts. The role of climate in families and friendships is obvious. So is the impact of climate in the workplace. Have you ever held a job where backbiting, criticism, and suspicion were the norm? Or have you been lucky enough to hold a job where the atmosphere was positive, encouraging, and supportive? If you've experienced both, you know what a difference climate makes.

It's hard to overstate the importance of a positive communication climate. For starters, it is the best predictor of marital satisfaction.[1] Satisfied couples communicate a 5 to 1 ratio of positive to negative statements, whereas the ratio for dissatisfied couples is 1 to 1.[2] Positive, confirming messages are just as important in families. For example, the communication climate that parents create for their children affects the way they interact,[3] and the satisfaction that siblings feel with one another drops sharply as aggressive, disconfirming messages increase.[4] The same principle holds on the job: Employees have a higher level of commitment to organizations where they experience a positive communication climate,[5] both on the job site and in virtual work environments.[6] Studies also show that performance and job satisfaction increase when the communication climate is positive.[7] In school, teacher confirmation plays a significant role in college students' learning.[8] Whether it's the workplace, the classroom, or the home, people thrive in communication climates that affirm and support them.

Like their meteorological counterparts, communication climates are shared by everyone involved. It's rare to find one person describing a relationship as open and positive while another describes it as cold and hostile. Also, just like the weather, communication climates can change over time. A relationship can be overcast at one time and sunny at another. Carrying the analogy to its conclusion, we need to acknowledge that communication climate forecasting is not a perfect science. Unlike the weather, however, people can change the communication climates in their relationships.

Confirming and Disconfirming Communication

What makes a communication climate positive or negative? In large part, the answer is surprisingly simple. The climate of a relationship is shaped by the degree to which the people believe themselves to be *valued* by one another.

Social scientists use the term **confirming communication** to describe messages that convey valuing, and **disconfirming communication** to describe those that show a lack of regard. In one form or another, confirming messages say "you exist," "you matter," "you're important." By contrast, disconfirming communication signals a lack of regard. In one form or another, disconfirming messages say, "I don't care about you," "I don't like you," "You're not important to me."

Like beauty, the decision about whether a message is confirming or disconfirming is up to the beholder.[9] Consider, for example, times when you took a comment that might have sounded unsupportive to an outsider ("You turkey!") as a sign of affection within the context of your personal relationship. Likewise, a comment that the sender might have meant to be helpful ("I'm telling you this for your own good . . .") could easily be regarded as a disconfirming attack.

It's obvious that confirming messages are more desirable than disconfirming ones. But what characteristics distinguish them?

Types of Confirming Messages   Research shows that three increasingly positive types of messages have the best chance of being confirming.[10]

Recognition   The most fundamental act of confirmation is to recognize the other person. Recognition seems easy and obvious, and yet there are many times when we do not respond to others on this basic level. Failure to write or visit a friend is a common example. So is failure to return a phone message. Avoiding eye contact and not approaching someone you know on campus at a party or on the street sends a negative message. Of course, this lack of recognition may simply be an oversight. You might not notice your friend, or the pressures of work and school might prevent you from staying in touch. Nonetheless, if the other person *perceives* you as avoiding contact, the message has the effect of being disconfirming.

Acknowledgment   Acknowledging the ideas and feelings of others is a stronger form of confirmation. Listening is probably the most common form of acknowledgment. Of course, counterfeit listening—ambushing, stage-hogging, pseudolistening, and so on—has the opposite effect of acknowledgment. More active acknowledgment includes asking questions, paraphrasing, and reflecting. Not surprisingly, employees rate highly managers who solicit their opinions—even when the managers don't accept every opinion.[11] As you read in Chapter 7, reflecting the speaker's thoughts and feelings can be a powerful way to offer support when others have problems.

Endorsement   Whereas acknowledgment means that you are interested in another's ideas, endorsement means that you agree with them or otherwise find them important. It's easy to see why endorsement is the strongest type of confirming message because it communicates the highest form of valuing. The most obvious form of endorsement is agreeing. Fortunately, it isn't necessary to agree completely with another person in order to endorse her or his message. You can probably find something in the message that you endorse. "I can see why you were so angry," you might reply to a friend, even if you don't approve of his outburst. Of course, outright praise is a strong form of endorsement and one that you can use surprisingly often after you look for opportunities to compliment others.

Types of Disconfirming Messages   In contrast to confirming communication, disconfirming communication shows a lack of regard for the other person, either by disputing or ignoring some important part of that person's message.[12] Communication researchers have identified seven types of disconfirming messages.[13]

Impervious Responses   As you just read, recognition is the most basic type of confirmation. By contrast, ignoring another person characterizes an **impervious response**.

Being ignored can be more disconfirming than being dismissed or attacked. Most experts agree that it is psychologically healthier to have someone disagree with you than ignore you.[14] In the working world, research shows that employees sometimes nudge unwanted coworkers to quit their jobs by avoiding interaction with them, creating a chilly communication climate.[15]

Verbal Abuse   The most obvious type of disconfirming message is **verbal abuse**: communication that appears to be meant to cause psychological pain to another person. Where verbal abuse exists in a relationship, it is seldom an

> I've learned that being kind is more important than being right.
>
> Andy Rooney

> The worst sin towards our fellow creatures is not to hate them, but to be indifferent to them; that's the essence of inhumanity.
>
> George Bernard Shaw

Communicating with Waiters: A Test of Character

Office Depot CEO Steve Odland remembers like it was yesterday working in an upscale French restaurant in Denver. The purple sorbet in cut glass he was serving tumbled onto the expensive white gown of an obviously rich and important woman. "I watched in slow motion ruining her dress for the evening," Odland says. "I thought I would be shot on sight."

Thirty years have passed, but Odland can't get the stain out of his mind, nor the woman's kind reaction. She was startled, regained composure and, in a reassuring voice, told the teenage Odland, "It's OK. It wasn't your fault." When she left the restaurant, she also left the future Fortune 500 CEO with a life lesson: You can tell a lot about a person by the way he or she treats the waiter.

Odland isn't the only CEO to have made this discovery. Rather, it seems to be one of those rare laws of the land that every CEO learns on the way up. How others treat the CEO says nothing, they say. But how others treat the waiter is like a magical window into the soul.

The Waiter Rule also applies to the way people treat hotel maids, mailroom clerks, bellmen and security guards. Au Bon Pain co-founder Ron Shaich, now CEO of Panera Bread, says he was interviewing a candidate for general counsel in St. Louis. She was "sweet" to Shaich but turned "amazingly rude" to someone cleaning the tables, Shaich says. She didn't get the job.

Shaich says any time candidates are being considered for executive positions at Panera Bread, he asks his assistant, Laura Parisi, how they

treated her, because some applicants are "pushy, self-absorbed and rude" to her before she transfers the call to him.

People view waiters as their temporary personal employees. Therefore, how executives treat waiters probably demonstrates how they treat their actual employees, says Sara Lee CEO Brenda Barnes, a former waitress and postal clerk, who says she is a demanding boss but never shouts at or demeans an employee.

"Sitting in the chair of CEO makes me no better of a person than the forklift operator in our plant," she says. "If you treat the waiter, or a subordinate, like garbage, guess what? Are they going to give it their all? I don't think so."

Del Jones

isolated event. Some abuse is overt, but at other times it can be disguised in malicious humor or sarcasm:.

"Come here, fatty."

"You're such a bitch!"

Generalized Complaining Specific complaints can get problems out in the open, but **generalized complaining** is usually disconfirming because it implies a character fault:

"I wish you would be more friendly."

"Why can't you clean up after yourself?"

"You need to have a more positive attitude."

Interrupting Beginning to speak before the other person has finished speaking can show a lack of concern about what the other person has to say. The occasional **interrupting response** is not likely to be taken as a disconfirmation, but repeatedly interrupting a speaker can be both discouraging and irritating.

Irrelevant Responses A comment unrelated to what the other person has just said is an **irrelevant response**:

A: What a day! I thought it would never end. First the car overheated, and I had to call a tow truck, and then the computer broke down at work.

B: Listen, we have to talk about a present for Ann's birthday. The party is on Saturday, and I have only tomorrow to shop for it.

Fire and Ice

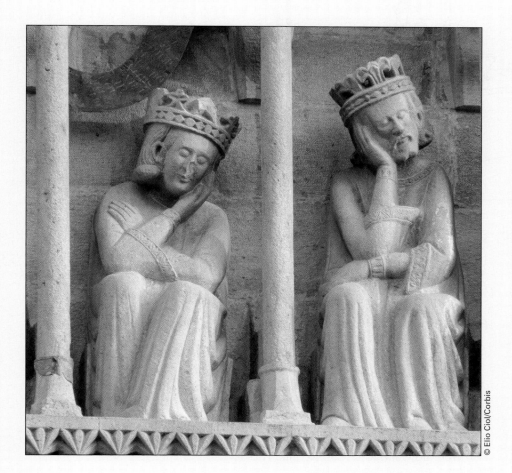

© Elio Ciol/Corbis

Some say the world will end in fire,
Some say in ice.
From what I've tasted of desire
I hold with those who favor fire.

But if it had to perish twice,
I think I know enough of hate
To know that for destruction ice
Is also great
And would suffice.

Robert Frost

"I'll take care of it impersonally."

A: I'm really beat. Could we talk about it in a few minutes? I've never seen a day like this one.

B: I just can't figure out what would suit Ann. She's got everything. . . .

Tangential Responses   Conversational "take-aways" are called **tangential responses**. Instead of ignoring the speaker's remarks completely, the other party uses them as a starting point for a shift to a different topic:

A: I'd like to know for sure whether you want to go skiing during vacation. If we don't decide whether to go soon, it'll be impossible to get reservations anywhere.

B: Yeah. And if I don't pass my botany class, I won't be in the mood to go anywhere. Could you give me some help with this homework?

Impersonal Responses   **Impersonal responses** are loaded with clichés and other statements that never truly respond to the speaker:

A: I've been having some personal problems lately, and I'd like to take off work early a couple of afternoons to clear them up.

B: Ah, yes. We all have personal problems. It seems to be a sign of the times.

Ambiguous Responses   **Ambiguous responses** contain messages with more than one meaning, leaving the other party unsure of the responder's position:

A: I'd like to get together with you soon. How about Tuesday?

B: Uh, maybe so.

A: Well, how about it? Can we talk Tuesday?

B: Oh, probably. See you later.

Incongruous Responses   An **incongruous response** contains two messages that seem to deny or contradict each other. Often at least one of these messages is nonverbal:

A: Darling, I love you.

B: I love you, too. *(said in a monotone while watching TV)*

How Communication Climates Develop

As soon as two people start to communicate, a relational climate begins to develop. If their messages are confirming, the climate is likely to be a positive one. If their messages are disconfirming, the relationship is likely to be hostile, cold, or defensive.

Verbal messages certainly contribute to the climate of a relationship, but many climate-shaping messages are nonverbal. The very act of approaching others is confirming, whereas avoiding them can be disconfirming. Smiles or frowns, the presence or absence of eye contact, tone of voice, the use of personal space—all these and other cues send messages about how the parties feel toward one another.

After a climate is formed, it can take on a life of its own and grow in a self-perpetuating **spiral**: a reciprocating communication pattern in which each person's message reinforces the other's.[16] In positive spirals, one partner's confirming message leads to a similar message from the other person. This positive reaction leads the first person to be even more confirming. Negative spirals are just as powerful, though they leave the partners feeling worse about themselves and each other.

Research shows how spirals operate in relationships to reinforce the principle that "what goes around comes around." In one study of married couples, each spouse's response in conflict situations was similar to the other's statement.[17] Conciliatory statements (for example, supporting, accepting responsibilities, agreeing) were likely to be followed by conciliatory responses. Confrontational acts (such as criticism, hostile questions, and faultfinding) were likely to trigger equally confrontational responses. The same pattern held for other kinds of messages: Avoidance begat avoidance, analysis begat analysis, and so on. Table 10.1 illustrates some reciprocal communication patterns that have the potential to create positive and negative spirals.

Table 10.1	Positive and Negative Reciprocal Communication Patterns

Negative Reciprocal Patterns

Pattern	Example
Complaint-counter complaint	A: I wish you weren't so self-centered. B: Well, I wish you weren't so critical.
Disagreement-disagreement	A: Why are you so hard on Marta? She's a great boss. B: Are you kidding? She's the biggest phony I've ever seen. A: You wouldn't know a good boss if you saw one. B: Neither would you.
Mutual indifference	A: I don't care if you want to stay: I'm exhausted, and I'm getting out of here. B: Go ahead if you want, but find your own way home.
Arguments involving punctuation	A: How can I talk when you won't listen? B: How can I listen when you won't talk?

Positive Reciprocal Patterns

Pattern	Example
Validation of other's perspective	A: This assignment is really confusing. Nobody can figure out what we're supposed to do. B: I can understand how it might be unclear. Let me try to explain . . .
Recognizing similarities	A: I can't believe you want to take an expensive vacation! We should be saving money, not spending more! B: I agree we should be saving. But I think we can take this trip and still save some money. Let me show you what I've figured out . . .
Supportiveness	A: I'm going crazy with this job. It was supposed to be temporary. I have to do something different, and soon. B: I can see how much you hate it. Let's figure out how we can get the project finished soon, so you can get back to your regular work.

Adapted from *Competence and Interpersonal Conflict*, by W. Cupach and D. Canary. Reproduced by permission of The McGraw-Hill Companies.

	1	2	3	4	5	6	7	8	9	10	11	12	13	14	15	16	17	18	19	20	21	22	23	24	25	26	27	28	29	30	31	R	H	E
TAT	3	0	0	1	0	0	0	0	0	0	0	6	0	0	1	0	0	0	0	0	0	8	0	0	3	9	7	1	1	2	6	48	63	6
TIT	3	0	0	1	0	0	0	0	0	0	0	6	0	0	1	0	0	0	0	0	0	8	0	0	3	9	7	1	1	2	6	48	63	6

Game called on account of infinity.

Escalatory conflict spirals are the most visible way that disconfirming messages reinforce one another.[18] One attack leads to another until a skirmish escalates into a full-fledged battle:

A: (*mildly irritated*) Where were you? I thought we agreed to meet here a half-hour ago.

B: (*defensively*) I'm sorry. I got hung up at the library. I don't have as much free time as you do, you know.

A: I wasn't *blaming* you, so don't get so touchy. I do resent what you just said, though. I'm plenty busy. And I've got lots of better things to do than wait around for you!

B: Who's getting touchy? I just made a simple comment. You've sure been defensive lately. What's the matter with you?

Although they are less obvious, **de-escalatory conflict spirals** can also be destructive.[19] Rather than fighting, the parties slowly lessen their dependence on each other, withdraw, and become less invested in the relationship. The good news is that spirals can also be positive. A word of praise can lead to a returned compliment, which can lead to an act of kindness, which can result in an improved relational climate.

Spirals—whether positive or negative—rarely go on indefinitely. Most relationships pass through cycles of progression and regression. If the spiral is negative, partners may find the exchange growing so unpleasant that they switch from negative to positive messages without discussing the matter. In other cases they may engage in metacommunication. "Hold on," one might say. "This is getting us nowhere." This ability to "rebound" from negative spirals and turn them in a positive direction is a hallmark of successful relationships.[20] However,

Invitation to Insight

Evaluating Communication Climates

You can probably recognize the communication climate in each of your relationships without much analysis. But taking the following steps will help explain why these climates exist. Taking these steps may also suggest how to improve negative climates.

1. Identify the communication climate of an important interpersonal relationship. Using weather metaphors (sunny, gloomy, calm) may help.

2. List the confirming or disconfirming communications that created and now maintain this climate. Be sure to list both verbal and nonverbal messages.

3. Describe what you can do either to maintain the existing climate (if positive) or to change it (if negative). Again, list both verbal and nonverbal messages.

if the partners pass the "point of no return" and continue spiraling downward, their relationship may end.

Positive spirals also have their limit: Even the best relationships go through periods of conflict and withdrawal, although a combination of time and communication skills can eventually bring the partners back into greater harmony.

Defensiveness: Causes and Remedies

Researcher John Gottman identifies defensiveness as one of the primary warning signs of a marriage that is in trouble.[21] Defensive responses often include counterattacks ("I'm not the stubborn one—*you* are!"), which lead the other person to become defensive, and soon the communication climate is polluted.

The word **defensiveness** suggests guarding oneself from attack, but what kind of attack? Surely, few if any of the times you become defensive involve a physical threat. If you're not threatened by bodily injury, what *are* you guarding against? To answer this question we need to talk more about the notions of the presenting self and face introduced in Chapter 2.

Recall that a person's face consists of the physical traits, personality characteristics, attitudes, aptitudes, and all the other parts of the image that he or she wants to present to the world. Actually, it is a mistake to talk about a single face: We try to project different faces to different people. You might, for instance, try to impress a potential employer with your seriousness but want your friends to see you as a joker.

When others are willing to accept and acknowledge important parts of our presenting image, there is no need to feel defensive. On the other hand, when others confront us with **face-threatening acts**—messages that seem to challenge the image we want to project—we are likely to resist their messages.[22] Defensiveness, then, is the process of protecting our presenting self, our face.

You can understand how defensiveness operates by imagining what might happen if an important part of your presenting self were attacked. Suppose, for instance, that your boss criticized you for making a stupid mistake. Or consider how you would feel if a friend called you self-centered or your sweetheart called you lazy. You would probably feel threatened if these attacks were unjustified. But notice that you might very well react defensively even if you knew deep inside that the attacks were justified. For instance, you have probably responded defensively at times when you *did* make a mistake, acted selfishly, or cut corners on your work. In fact, we often feel most defensive when criticism is right on target.[23] The drive to defend a presenting image—even when it is false—leads some people to act in destructive ways, such as being sarcastic or verbally abusive.[24]

One reason for such defensiveness has to do with our need for approval. In response to the question "Why am I afraid to tell you who I am?" author John Powell quotes one actual response: "Because if I tell you who I am, you may not like who I am, and that is all I have."[25] So one reason we wear defensive masks is to appear to be the kind of person who will gain the approval of others.

Types of Defensive Reactions

When a part of your presenting self is attacked by others and you aren't willing to accept their judgment, you are faced with what psychologists call **cognitive dissonance**—an inconsistency between two conflicting pieces of information, attitudes, or behavior.[26] Dissonance is an uncomfortable condition, and communicators strive to resolve it by seeking consistency. One way

It is a curious psychological fact that the man who seems to be "egotistic" is not suffering from too much ego, but from too little.

Sydney J. Harris

"Why am I talking this loud? Because I'm wrong."

I seem to get the most defensive when I think something I have done is "bad." The judgment as to what is bad is a judgment of mine as well as others around me. It cuts the most when someone else's judgment of me agrees with my own bad impression of myself.

John T. Wood

to eliminate the dissonance, of course, is to accept the critic's judgment and revise your presenting self accordingly. You could agree that you were stupid or mistaken, for example. Sometimes, however, you aren't willing to accept judgments. The accusations of your critic may be false. And even if they are true, you may be unwilling to admit their truth. It isn't pleasant to admit that you were lazy, unfair, or foolish. There are three broad ways to resolve dissonance without agreeing with a critic. Each of them is characterized by **defense mechanisms**: psychological devices that resolve dissonance by maintaining a positive presenting image.

Attacking the Critic   Counterattacking follows the old maxim that the best defense is a good offense. Attacking defensive maneuvers can take several forms.

- *Verbal aggression* Sometimes the recipient uses **verbal aggression** to assault the critic directly. "Where do you get off calling me sloppy?" you might storm to a roommate. "You're the one who leaves globs of toothpaste in the sink and dirty clothes all over the bedroom!" This sort of response shifts the blame onto the critic, without acknowledging that the original judgment might be true. Other attacks on the critic are completely off the subject: "You're in no position to complain about my sloppiness. At least I pay my share of the bills on time." Again, this response resolves the dissonance without ever addressing the validity of the attack.
- *Sarcasm* Disguising the counterattack in a barbed, humorous message of **sarcasm** is a less-direct form of aggression. "You think I ought to study more? Thanks for taking a break from watching soap operas and eating junk food to run my life." Sarcastic responses might score high on wit and quick thinking, but their hostile, disconfirming nature usually leads to a counterattack and a mutually destructive defensive spiral.

Distorting Critical Information   A second way of defending a perceived self under attack is to somehow distort the critical information in a manner that leaves the presenting self intact—at least in the eyes of the defender. There are a number of ways to distort critical information.

Table 10.2	Rationalization Reader for Students
Situation	**What to Say**
When the course is offered in lecture format:	We never get a chance to say anything.
When the course is offered in discussion format:	The professor just sits there. We don't know how to teach the course.
When all aspects of the course are covered in class:	All she does is follow the text.
When you're responsible for covering part of the course outside class:	She never covers half the things we're tested on.
When you're given objective tests:	They don't allow for any individuality.
When you're given essay tests:	They're too vague. We never know what's expected.
When the instructor gives no tests:	It isn't fair! She can't tell how much we really know.

- *Rationalization* **Rationalization** is the invention of logical but untrue explanations of behavior that is unacceptable to the self. "I would help you out, but I really have to study," you might say as a convenient way to avoid an unpleasant chore. "I'm not overeating," you might protest to another critic who you secretly admit is on target. "I have a busy day ahead, and I need to keep my strength up." (See Table 10.2 for other examples.)
- *Compensation* Those using **compensation** emphasize a strength in one area to cover up a weakness in another. A guilty parent might keep up the façade of being conscientious by protesting, "I may not be around much, but I give those kids the best things money can buy!" Likewise, you might try to convince yourself and others that you are a good friend by compensating: "Sorry I forgot your birthday. Let me give you a hand with that job." There's nothing wrong with most acts of compensation in themselves. The harm comes when they are used not sincerely but rather insincerely to maintain a fictitious presenting image.
- *Regression* Another way to avoid facing attack is to play helpless, claiming you *can't* do something when in truth you *don't want* to do it. "I'd like to have a relationship with you, but I just can't: I'm not ready." "I wish I could do the job better, but I just can't: I just don't understand it." The test for **regression** is to substitute the word *won't* for *can't*. In many cases it becomes clear that "It's not my fault" is a fiction.

Avoiding Dissonant Information A third way to protect a threatened presenting image is to avoid information altogether. Avoidance can take several forms.

- *Physical avoidance* Steering clear of people who attack a presenting self is an obvious way to avoid dissonance. Sometimes **physical avoidance** may be wise. There's little profit in being battered by hostile or abusive criticism. At other times, however, the relationship may be important enough and the criticism valid enough that avoiding the situation only makes matters worse.
- *Repression* Sometimes we mentally block out dissonant information. You might, for instance, know that you ought to discuss a problem with a friend, boss, or instructor, yet you put the idea out of your mind whenever it arises. It's possible even to repress a problem in the face of a critic. Changing the subject, acting as if you don't understand, and even pretending you don't hear the criticism all fall into the category of **repression**.

■ *Apathy* Another avoidance response, **apathy**, involves acknowledging unpleasant information but pretending that you don't care about it. You might, for instance, sit calmly through a friend's criticism and act as if it didn't bother you. Similarly, you might respond to the loss of a job by acting indifferent: "Who cares? It was a dumb job anyhow."

■ *Displacement* **Displacement** occurs when we vent aggressive or hostile feelings against people or objects that are seen as less threatening than the people or objects that threatened us originally. You may be mad at your boss, but rather than risk getting fired, you could displace your aggression by yelling at the people you live with. Despite its obvious costs, displacement almost always lets us preserve (at least to ourselves) the image that we're *potent*—that we're in control and can't be pushed around by forces beyond our control. The very act of displacing proves this a lie, of course—but a lie that the displacer fails to recognize.

Invitation to Insight

Defense Mechanism Inventory

List the three defense mechanisms you use most often, and describe a recent example of each. You can arrive at your list both by thinking about your own behavior and by asking others to share their impressions of you.

Conclude your inventory by describing:

1. The people with whom you become defensive most often

2. The parts of your presenting self you frequently defend

3. The usual consequences of using defense mechanisms

4. Any more-satisfying ways you could act in the future

Preventing Defensiveness in Others

So far, we have talked about defensiveness as if it is the responsibility of only the person who feels threatened. If this were the case, then the prescription would be simple: Grow a thick skin, admit your flaws, and stop trying to manage impressions. This prescription isn't just unrealistic: It ignores the role played by those who send face-threatening messages. In fact, competent communicators protect others' face needs as well as their own.[27]

You probably recognize that the best chances for creating a favorable response come from sending messages that honor the other person's face by supporting his or her presenting self.[28] These facts might leave you caught in an apparent bind, asking yourself how to send a face-honoring message when you have a genuine gripe with someone.

The solution to this dilemma lies in the two-dimensional nature of communication. On a content level you can express dissatisfaction with the other person, but on a relational level you can say—verbally or nonverbally—that you value him or her. The possibility of handling potentially delicate issues in ways that improve your relationships may seem overwhelming, but the influential work of researcher Jack Gibb offers some useful tools for reducing defensiveness.[29] After observing groups for several years, Gibb was able to isolate six types of defense-arousing communication and six contrasting behaviors that lessen the level of threat and defensiveness by conveying face-honoring relational messages of respect. The **Gibb categories** are listed in Table 10.3 and summarized in the following pages.

Evaluation versus Description   The first type of defense-arousing behavior that Gibb noted is **evaluation**. Most people become irritated at judgmental statements, which they are likely to interpret as indicating a lack of regard. One form of evaluation is "you" language, described in Chapter 5.

Unlike evaluative "you" language, **description** focuses on the *speaker's* thoughts and feelings instead of judging the speaker. Descriptive messages often are expressed in "I" language, which tends to provoke less defensiveness than "you" language.[30] Contrast the following evaluative "you" claims with their descriptive "I" counterparts:

Table 10.3	The Gibb Categories of Defensive and Supportive Behaviors
Defensive Behaviors	**Supportive Behaviors**
1. Evaluation	1. Description
2. Control	2. Problem Orientation
3. Strategy	3. Spontaneity
4. Neutrality	4. Empathy
5. Superiority	5. Equality
6. Certainty	6. Provisionalism

Source: Jack Gibb

Evaluation:	"You don't know what you're talking about!"
Description:	"I don't understand how you came up with that idea."
Evaluation:	"This place is a mess!"
Description:	"When you don't clean up, I have to either do it or live with your mess. That's why I'm mad!"
Evaluation:	"Those jokes are disgusting!"
Description:	"When you tell those off-color jokes, I get really embarrassed."

Note how each of the descriptive statements focuses on the speaker's thoughts and feelings without judging the speaker. Despite its value, descriptive language isn't the only element necessary for success. Its effectiveness depends in part on when, where, and how the language is used. You can imagine how each of the preceding descriptive statements would go over if said in front of a room full of bystanders or in a whining tone of voice. Even the best timing and delivery of a descriptive message won't guarantee success. Some people will react defensively to anything you say or do. Nonetheless, it's easy to see that describing how the other person's behavior affects you is likely to produce better results than judgmentally attacking the other person.

Control versus Problem Orientation
A second defense-provoking message involves some attempt to control another. **Controlling communication** occurs when a sender seems to be imposing a solution on the receiver with little regard for the receiver's needs or interests. The object of control can involve almost anything: where to eat dinner, what TV program to watch, whether to remain in a relationship, or how

"If we can just get beyond this 'I'm the boss' mentality and concentrate on a simple 'What I say goes' outlook, I think this will all work out."

to spend a large sum of money. Whatever the situation, people who act in controlling ways create a defensive climate. None of us likes to feel that our ideas are worthless and that nothing we say will change other people's determination to have their way—yet this is precisely the attitude that a controller communicates. Whether it is done through words, gestures, tone of voice, or some other channel, the controller generates hostility wherever he or she goes. The unspoken message that such behavior communicates is "I know what's best for you, and if you do as I say, we'll get along."

In contrast, in **problem orientation** communicators focus on finding a solution that satisfies both their needs and those of the others involved. The goal here isn't to "win" at the expense of your partner but rather to work out some arrangement in which everybody feels like a winner. Chapter 11 has a great deal to say about "win-win" problem-solving as a way to find problem-oriented solutions.

Here are some examples of how some controlling and problem-orientation messages might sound:

Controlling:	"You need to stay off the phone for the next two hours."
Problem orientation:	"I'm expecting some important calls. Can we work out a way to keep the line open?"
Controlling:	"There's only one way to handle this problem . . ."
Problem orientation:	"Looks like we have a problem. Let's work out a solution we can both live with."

Strategy versus Spontaneity   Gibb uses the word **strategy** to characterize defense-arousing messages in which speakers hide their ulterior motives. The words *dishonesty* and *manipulation* capture the essence of strategy. Even if the motives of strategic communication are honorable, the victim of such deception who discovers the attempt to deceive is likely to feel offended at being played for a naive sucker.

Spontaneity is the behavior that contrasts with strategy. Spontaneity simply means being honest with others rather than manipulating them. What it doesn't mean is blurting out what you're thinking as soon as an idea comes to you. As we discussed in Chapter 9, there are appropriate (and inappropriate) times for self-disclosure. You would undoubtedly threaten others' presenting selves if you were "spontaneous" about every opinion that crossed your mind. Gibb's notion of spontaneity involves setting aside hidden agendas that others both sense and resist. These examples illustrate the difference:

Strategy:	"What are you doing Friday after work?"
Spontaneity:	"I have a piano I need to move Friday after work. Can you give me a hand?"
Strategy:	"Tom and Judy go out to dinner every week."
Spontaneity:	"I'd like to go out to dinner more often."

This is a good place to talk about larger issues regarding the Gibb model. First, Gibb's emphasis on being direct is better suited for a low-context culture like the United States, which values straight talk, than for high-context cultures. Second, there are ways in which each of the communication approaches Gibb labels as "supportive" can be used to exploit others and, therefore, violate the spirit of positive climate building. For instance, consider spontaneity. Although it sounds paradoxical at first, spontaneity can be a strategy, too. Sometimes you'll see people using honesty in a calculating way, being just frank enough to win someone's trust or sympathy. This "leveling" is probably the most defense-arousing strategy of all because once you have learned someone is using frankness as a manipulation, you are less likely to trust that person in the future.

Neutrality versus Empathy   Gibb uses the term **neutrality** to describe a fourth behavior that arouses defensiveness. Probably a better descriptive word would be *indifference*. A neutral attitude is disconfirming because it communicates a lack of concern and implies that the welfare of the other person isn't very important to you. This perceived indifference is likely to promote defensiveness because people do not like to think of themselves as worthless, and they'll protect a self-concept that regards them as worthwhile.

Notice the difference between neutral and empathic statements:

Neutral:	"That's what happens when you don't plan properly."
Empathic:	"Ouch—looks like this didn't turn out the way you expected."
Neutral:	"Sometimes things just don't work out. That's the way it goes."
Empathic:	"I know you put a lot of time and effort into this project."

The negative effects of neutrality become apparent when you consider the hostility that most people have for the large, impersonal organizations with which they have to deal: "They think of me as a number instead of a person"; "I felt as if I were being handled by computers and not human beings." These two common statements reflect reactions to being handled in an indifferent way. Gibb found that *empathy* helps rid communication of the quality of indifference. **Empathy** means accepting another's feelings, putting yourself in another's place. This doesn't mean that you need to agree with that person. By simply letting that person know of your care and respect, you'll be acting in a supportive way. Gibb noted the importance of nonverbal messages in communicating empathy. He found that facial and bodily expressions of concern are often more important to the receiver than the words used.

Superiority versus Equality   A fifth behavior that arouses defensiveness is **superiority**. Any message that suggests "I'm better than you" is likely to arouse feelings of defensiveness in the recipients. A body of research confirms that patronizing messages irritate recipients ranging from young students to senior citizens, at least in Western cultures.[31] As humorist Dave Barry suggests in the reading on page 344, some superiority comes from the content of messages. In other cases, the *way* we deliver messages suggests a one-up approach. Consider, for example, how using simplified grammar and vocabulary, talking loudly and slowly, not listening, and varying speaking pitch convey a patronizing attitude.

Here are two examples of the difference between superiority and equality:

Superior:	"You don't know what you're talking about."
Equal:	"I see it a different way."
Superior:	"No, that's not the right way to do it!"
Equal:	"If you want, I can show you a way that has worked for me."

There are certainly times when we communicate with others who possess talents or knowledge lesser than ours, but even then it isn't necessary to communicate an attitude of superiority. Gibb found ample evidence that many people who have superior skills and talents are capable of projecting feelings of **equality** rather

How to Argue Effectively

I argue very well. Ask any of my remaining friends. I can win an argument on any topic, against any opponent. People know this and steer clear of me at parties. Often, as a sign of their great respect, they don't even invite me. You too can win arguments. Simply follow these rules:

Drink Liquor

Suppose you are at a party and some hotshot intellectual is expounding on the economy of Peru, a subject you know nothing about. If you're drinking some health-fanatic drink like grapefruit juice, you'll hang back, afraid to display your ignorance, while the hotshot enthralls your date. But if you drink several large martinis, you'll discover you have *strong views* about the Peruvian economy. You'll be a *wealth* of information. You'll argue forcefully, offering searing insights and possibly upsetting furniture. People will be impressed. Some may leave the room.

Make Things Up

Suppose, in the Peruvian economy argument, you are trying to prove that Peruvians are underpaid, a position you base solely on the fact that *you* are underpaid, and you'll be damned if you're going to let a bunch of Peruvians be better off. *Don't* say: "I think Peruvians are underpaid." Say instead: "The average Peruvian's salary in 1981 dollars adjusted for the revised tax base is $1,452.81 per annum, which is $836.07 below the mean gross poverty level." NOTE: Always make up exact figures. If an opponent asks you where you got your information, make *that* up too. Say: "This information comes from Dr. Hovel T. Moon's study for the Buford Commission published on May

9, 1982. Didn't you read it?" Say this in the same tone of voice you would use to say, "You left your soiled underwear in my bathroom."

Use Meaningless but Weighty-Sounding Words and Phrases

Memorize this list:

Let me put it this way
In terms of
Vis-a-vis
Per se
As it were
Qua
So to speak

You should also memorize some Latin abbreviations such as "Q.E.D.," "e.g.," and "i.e." These are all short for "I speak Latin, and you don't." Here's how to use these words and phrases. Suppose you want to say, "Peruvians would like to order appetizers more often, but they don't have enough money." You never win arguments talking like that. But you WILL win if you say, "Let me put it this way. In terms of appetizers vis-a-vis Peruvians qua Peruvians, they would like to order them more often, so to speak, but they do not have enough money per se, as it were. Q.E.D." Only a fool would challenge that statement.

Use Snappy and Irrelevant Comebacks

You need an arsenal of all-purpose irrelevant phrases to fire back at your opponents when they make valid points. The best are:

You're begging the question.
You're being defensive.
Don't compare apples to oranges.
What are your parameters?

This last one is especially valuable. Nobody (other than engineers and policy wonks) has the vaguest idea what "parameters" means. Here's how to use your comebacks:

You say: "As Abraham Lincoln said in 1873 . . ."
Your opponent says: "Lincoln died in 1865."
You say: "You're begging the question."
You say: "Liberians, like most Asians . . ."
Your opponent says: "Liberia is in Africa."
You say: "You're being defensive."

Compare Your Opponent to Adolf Hitler

This is your heavy artillery, for when your opponent is obviously right and you are spectacularly wrong. Bring Hitler up subtly. Say, "That sounds suspiciously like something Adolf Hitler might say," or "You certainly do remind me of Adolf Hitler."

So that's it. You now know how to out-argue anybody. Do not try to pull any of this on people who generally carry weapons.

Dave Barry

than superiority. Such people convey that, although they may have greater talent in certain areas, they see others as having just as much worth as human beings.

Certainty versus Provisionalism Have you ever run into people who are positive they're right, who know that theirs is the only or proper way of doing something, who insist that they have all the facts and need no additional information? If you have, you've met individuals who project the defense-arousing behavior that Gibb calls **certainty**. Communicators who regard their own opinions with certainty while disregarding the ideas of others demonstrate a lack of regard and respect. It's likely that the receiver will take the certainty as a personal affront and react defensively.

"I understand completely. I like good movies, and you like bad movies."

In contrast to certainty is **provisionalism**, in which people may have strong opinions but are willing to acknowledge that they don't have a corner on the truth and will change their stand if another position seems more reasonable. Consider these examples that contrast certain and provisional approaches:

Certain: "That will never work!"

Provisional: "I think you'll run into problems with that approach."

Certain: "You don't know what you're talking about!"

Provisional: "I've never heard anything like that before. Where did you hear it?"

> The need to be right—the sign of a vulgar mind.
>
> Albert Camus

Invitation to Insight

How Critical Are You?

ThomsonNOW™ You can get a sense of how critical you are by taking a short online test at RateYourself.com. Besides receiving your own score, you can compare your results with the average ratings of other quiz-takers. You can find the link to this site through ThomsonNOW for *Looking Out/Looking In*.

There is no guarantee that using Gibb's supportive, confirming approach to communication will build a positive climate. The other person may simply not be receptive. But the chances for a constructive relationship will be greatest when communication consists of the supportive approach described here. Besides boosting the odds of getting a positive response from others, supportive communication can leave you feeling better in a variety of ways: more in control of your relationships, more comfortable, and more positive toward others.

Defensiveness Feedback

1. Approach an important person in your life and request some help in learning more about yourself. Inform the other person that your discussion will probably take at least an hour, so make sure that both of you are prepared to invest the necessary amount of time.

2. Begin by explaining all twelve of the Gibb behaviors to your partner. Be sure to give enough examples so that each category is clearly understood.

3. When your explanation is complete and you've answered all your partner's questions, ask him or her to tell you which of the Gibb categories you use. Seek specific examples so that you are certain to understand the feedback fully. (Because you are requesting an evaluation, be prepared for a little defensiveness on your own part at this point.) Inform your partner that you are interested in discovering both the defense-arousing and the supportive behaviors you use and that you are sincerely interested in receiving a candid answer. (Note: If you don't want to hear the truth from your partner, don't try this exercise.)

4. As your partner speaks, record the categories that he or she lists in sufficient detail for both of you to be sure that you have understood the comments.

5. When you have finished your list, show it to your partner. Listen to your partner's reactions, and make any corrections that are necessary to reflect an accurate understanding of the comments. When your list is accurate, have your partner sign it to indicate that you have understood it clearly.

6. In a concluding statement note:

   a. how you felt as your partner was describing you

   b. whether you agree with the evaluation

   c. what effect your use of the Gibb categories has on your relationship with your partner

Saving Face: The Clear Message Format

As you've already seen, an essential ingredient in building a supportive climate is to avoid attacking others—to preserve their face, as discussed in Chapter 2. At the same time, we need to share our legitimate concerns when problems arise in a relationship.

The next few pages will describe a method for speaking your mind in a clear, direct, yet nonthreatening **assertive** way that expresses your needs, thoughts, and feelings clearly and directly without judging or dictating to others. This "clear message" format builds on the perception checking skill you learned in Chapter 3 and the "I" language approach you learned in Chapter 5. This new skill works for a variety of messages: your hopes, problems, complaints, and appreciations.[32] Whereas perception checking and "I" statements have three elements, a complete, clear message has five parts. We'll examine each part one by one and then discuss how to combine them in your everyday communication.

Looking at Diversity

Abdel Jalil Elayyadi: Promoting Understanding after 9/11

 I grew up in Morocco and moved to the United States when I was 19. I love the U.S. and have many wonderful friends here—but communicating with strangers became more difficult after the September 11 terrorist attacks in 2001. The fact that I'm an Arab Muslim created a tense climate between some Americans and me since that fateful day.

The good news is that people who knew me before 9/11 have been very supportive. In fact, because they know how I conduct my life—peacefully, morally, responsibly—their immediate reaction to the events of that day was, "How can this be? Muslims don't believe in killing innocent lives." I was happy to learn that my relationship with them made a difference in how they understood the Muslim faith.

Unfortunately, things are different with those who didn't know me before 9/11. I feel as if I'm easily stereotyped and misunderstood by people who prejudge me because of my religion and nationality. When I encounter people who think that all Muslims are terrorists who hate Americans, I try to do three things to change the defensive climate:

First, I quickly explain that Muslims are peace-loving people who abhor the taking of innocent life. I want them to know that I completely agree with their disdain for the terrorists. That builds a bridge of trust that allows us to keep talking.

Second, I try to use examples to help them understand how the 9/11 terrorists don't represent most Muslims or Arabs. I ask them how they would feel if Arabs judged Americans by the acts of Timothy McVeigh, or Christians by the acts of the Ku Klux Klan. This usually helps them view Muslims in a different and more accurate light.

Finally, the more we talk, the more we focus on things we have in common and beliefs we share. The goal is to discover that we are not enemies simply because we have different religions or nationalities—and in fact, there is no reason we can't be friends.

What do these conversations accomplish? In some cases, not a lot—because there are a few people who prefer to keep their prejudices rather than change them. But in other cases, I think I've made a difference, however small, in promoting peace and understanding in the world.

Photo courtesy of Abdel Jalil Elayyadi

Behavior

As you read in Chapter 5, a **behavioral description** describes the raw material to which you react. A behavioral description should be *objective*, describing an event without interpreting it.

Two examples of behavioral descriptions might look like this:

Example 1 "One week ago John promised me that he would ask my permission before smoking in the same room with me. Just a moment ago he lit up a cigarette without asking for my OK."

Example 2 "Chris has acted differently over the last week. I can't remember her laughing once since the holiday weekend. She hasn't dropped by my place like she usually does, hasn't suggested we play tennis, and hasn't returned my phone calls."

Notice that both statements describe only facts. The observer has not attached any meaning. The value of describing the problem without using emotive language was demonstrated by a study examining conflicts between couples. Satisfied partners tend to offer behavioral complaints ("You always throw your socks on the floor"), whereas unsatisfied partners make more complaints aimed at personal characteristics ("You're a slob").[33] Complaining about socks deals with a habit that can be changed; complaining that someone is a slob is a character assault that is unlikely to be forgotten when the conflict is over.

Interpretation

An **interpretation statement** describes the meaning you've attached to the other person's behavior. The important thing to realize about interpretations is that they are *subjective*. As you learned via the skill of perception checking (see Chapter 3), we can attach more than one interpretation to any behavior. For example, look at these two different interpretations of each of the preceding descriptions:

Example 1

Interpretation A: "John must have forgotten about our agreement that he wouldn't smoke without asking me first. I'm sure he's too considerate to go back on his word on something he knows I feel strongly about."

Interpretation B: "John is a rude, inconsiderate person. After promising not to smoke around me without asking, he's just deliberately done so. This shows that he cares only about himself. In fact, I bet he's deliberately doing this to drive me crazy!"

Example 2

Interpretation A: "Something must be bothering Chris. It's probably her family. She'll probably just feel worse if I keep pestering her."

Interpretation B: "Chris is probably mad at me. It's probably because I kidded her about losing so often at tennis. I'd better leave her alone until she cools off."

After you become aware of the difference between observable behavior and interpretation, some of the reasons for communication difficulties become clear. Many problems occur when a sender fails to describe the behavior on which an interpretation is based. For instance, imagine the difference between hearing a friend say

"You are a tightwad!" *(no behavioral description)*

versus explaining

"When you never offer to pay me back for the coffee and snacks I often buy you, I think you're a tightwad." *(behavior plus interpretation)*

The first speaker's failure to specify behavior would probably confuse the receiver, who has no way of knowing what prompted the speaker's remarks. This failure to describe behavior also reduces any chance that the receiver will change the offensive behavior, which, after all, is unknown to that person. In Gibb's terms, these examples show the difference between evaluation and description.

Just as important as specifying behavior is the need to label an interpretation as such instead of presenting it as a matter of fact—or what Gibb would describe as the difference between certainty and provisionalism. Consider the difference between saying

"It's obvious that if you cared for me you'd write more often." (*interpretation presented as fact*)

versus

"When I didn't get a letter or even a postcard from you, I thought that you didn't care for me." (*interpretation made clear*)

Skill Builder

Behaviors and Interpretations

1. Tell two other group members several interpretations that you have recently made about other people in your life. For each interpretation, describe the behavior on which you based your interpretations.

2. With your partners' help, consider some alternate interpretations of the behavior that might be as plausible as your original one.

3. After considering the alternate interpretations, decide

   a. which one was most reasonable

   b. how you might share that interpretation (along with the behavior) with the other person involved in a tentative, provisional way

---

Feeling

Reporting behavior and sharing your interpretations are important, but **feeling statements** add a new dimension to a message. For example, consider the difference between saying

"When you laugh at me (*behavior*), I think you find my comments foolish (*interpretation*), and *I feel embarrassed*."

versus

"When you laugh at me, I think you find my comments foolish, and *I feel angry*."

Skill Builder

Name the Feeling

Add a feeling that you would be likely to have to each of the following messages:

1. I felt _____ when I found out you didn't invite me on the camping trip. You said you thought I wouldn't want to go, but I have a hard time accepting that.

2. I felt _____ when you offered to help me move. I know how busy you are.

3. When you tell me you still want to be a friend but you want to "lighten up a little," I get the idea you're tired of me, and I feel _____.

4. You told me you wanted my honest opinion about your paintings, and then when I tell you what I think, you say I don't understand them. I'm _____.

How would the impact of each message be different if it didn't include a feeling statement?

It's important to recognize that some statements *seem* as if they're expressing feelings but are actually interpretations or statements of intention. For instance, it's not accurate to say "I feel like leaving" (really an intention) or "I feel you're wrong" (an interpretation). Statements like these obscure the true expression of feelings.

Consequence

A **consequence statement** explains what happens as a result of the situation you've described so far. There are three types of consequences:

- What happens to you, the speaker

  "When I didn't get the phone message yesterday (*behavior*), I didn't know that my doctor's appointment was delayed and that I would end up sitting in the office for an hour when I could have been studying or working (*consequences*). It seems to me that you don't care enough about how busy I am to even write a simple note (*interpretation*), and that's why I'm so mad (*feeling*)."

- What happens to the person you're addressing

  "When you have four or five drinks at a party after I've warned you to slow down (*behavior*), you start to act strange: You make crude jokes that offend everybody, and on the way home you drive poorly (*consequences*). For instance, last night you almost hit a phone pole while you were backing out of the driveway (*more behavior*). I don't think you realize how differently you act (*interpretation*), and I'm worried (*feeling*) about what will happen if you don't drink less."

- What happens to others

  "You probably don't know because you couldn't hear her cry (*interpretation*), but when you rehearse your lines for the play without closing the doors (*behavior*), the baby can't sleep (*consequence*). I'm especially concerned (*feeling*) about her because she's had a cold lately."

Consequence statements are valuable for two reasons. First, they help you understand more clearly why you are bothered or pleased by another's behavior. Just as important, telling others about the consequences of their actions can clarify for them the results of their behavior. As with interpretations, we often think that others should be aware of consequences without being told; but the fact is that they often aren't. By explicitly stating consequences, you can be sure that you or your message leaves nothing to the listener's imagination.

When you are stating consequences, it's important simply to describe what happens without moralizing. For instance, it's one thing to say, "When you didn't call to say you'd be late, I stayed up worrying," and another to rant on, "How can I ever trust you? You're going to drive me crazy!" Remember that it's perfectly legitimate to express your thoughts and feelings, but it's important to label them as such. And when you want to request change from someone, you can use intention statements, which we'll now describe.

Intention

Intention statements are the final element of the clear message format. They can communicate three kinds of messages:

- Where you stand on an issue

  "When you call us 'girls' after I've told you we want to be called 'women' (*behavior*), I get the idea you don't appreciate how important the difference is to us (*interpretation*) and how demeaning it feels (*feeling*). Now I'm in an awkward spot: Either I have to keep bringing the subject up, or else drop it and feel bad (*consequence*). I want you to know how much this bothers me (*intention*)."

- Requests of others

  "When I didn't hear from you last night (*behavior*), I thought you were mad at me (*interpretation*). I've been thinking about it ever since (*consequence*), and I'm still worried (*feeling*). I'd like to know whether you are angry (*intention*)."

- Descriptions of how you plan to act in the future

  "I've asked you to repay the twenty-five dollars I lent you three times now (*behavior*). I'm getting the idea that you've been avoiding me (*interpretation*), and I'm pretty angry about it (*feeling*). I want you to know that unless we clear this up now, you shouldn't expect me ever to lend you anything again (*intention*)."

As in the preceding cases, we are often motivated by one single intention. Sometimes, however, we act from a combination of intentions, which may even be in conflict with each other. When this happens, our conflicting intentions often make it difficult for us to reach decisions:

"I want to be truthful with you, but I don't want to violate my friend's privacy."

"I want to continue to enjoy your friendship and company, but I don't want to get too attached right now."

"I want to have time to study and get good grades, but I also want to have a job with some money coming in."

Using the Clear Message Format

Before you try to deliver messages by using the clear message format, there are a few points to remember.

1. *The elements may be delivered in mixed order.* As the examples on the preceding pages show, it's sometimes best to begin by stating your feelings. At other times you can start by sharing your intentions or interpretations or by describing consequences.
2. *Word the message to suit your personal style.* Instead of saying, "I interpret your behavior to mean . . ." you might choose to say "I think . . ." or "It seems to me . . ." or perhaps "I get the idea. . . ." In the same way, you can express your intentions by saying, "I hope you'll understand (or do) . . ." or perhaps, "I wish you would. . . ." The words that you choose should sound authentic in order to reinforce the genuineness of your statement.
3. *When appropriate, combine two elements in a single phrase.* The statement ". . . and ever since then I've been wanting to talk to you" expresses both a consequence and an intention. In the same way, saying, ". . . and after you said that, I felt confused" expresses a consequence and a feeling. Whether you combine elements or state them separately, the important point is to be sure that each one is present in your statement.
4. *Take your time delivering the message.* It isn't always possible to deliver messages such as the ones here all at one time, wrapped up in neat paragraphs. It will often be necessary to repeat or restate one part before the other person understands what you're saying. As you've already read, there are many types of psychological and physical noise that make it difficult for us to understand each other. In communication, as in many other activities, patience and persistence are essential.

Now try your hand at combining all these elements in the exercise on the next page.

Putting Your Message Together

1. Join with two other class members. Each person in turn should share a message that he or she might want to send to another person, being sure to include behavior, interpretation, feeling, consequence, and intention statements in the message.

2. The others in the group should help the speaker by offering feedback about how the message could be made clearer if there is any question about the meaning.

3. After the speaker has composed a satisfactory message, he or she should practice actually delivering it by having another group member play the role of the intended receiver. Continue this practice until the speaker is confident that he or she can deliver the message effectively.

4. Repeat this process until each group member has had a chance to practice delivering a message.

Responding Nondefensively to Criticism

The world would be a happier place if everyone communicated supportively and assertively, as described in the previous two sections. But how can you respond nondefensively when others send aggressive messages and use evaluation, control, superiority, and all the other attacking behaviors that Gibb identified? Despite your best intentions, it's difficult to be reasonable when you're being attacked. Being attacked is hard enough when the criticism is clearly unfair, but it's often even harder when the criticism is on target. Despite the accuracy of your critic, the tendency is either to counterattack aggressively with a barrage of verbal aggression or to withdraw nonassertively.

Because neither of these counterattacks is likely to resolve a dispute, we need alternative ways of behaving. There are two such ways. Despite their apparent simplicity, they have proven to be among the most valuable skills many communicators have learned.[34]

Seek More Information

The response of seeking more information makes good sense when you realize that it's foolish to respond to a critical attack until you understand what the other person has said. Even attacks that on first consideration appear to be totally unjustified or foolish often prove to contain at least a grain of truth and sometimes much more.

Many readers object to the idea of asking for details when they are criticized. Their resistance stems from confusing the act of *listening openmindedly* to a speaker's comments with *accepting* the comments. After you realize that you can listen to, understand, and even acknowledge the most hostile comments without necessarily accepting them, it becomes much easier to hear another person out. If you disagree with a person's criticism, you will be in a much better position to explain yourself after you understand the criticism. On the other hand, after carefully listening to the person's criticism, you might just see that it is valid, in which case you have learned some valuable information about yourself. In either case, you have everything to gain and nothing to lose by paying attention to the critic.

Of course, after one has spent years instinctively resisting criticism, learning to listen to the other person will take some practice. To make matters clearer, here are several ways in which you can seek additional information from your critics.

Ask for Specifics   Often the vague attack of a critic is virtually useless even if you sincerely want to change. Abstract attacks such as "You're being unfair" or "You never help out" can be difficult to understand. In such cases it is a good idea to request more specific information from the sender. "What do I *do* that's unfair?" is an important question to ask before you can judge whether the attack is correct. "When haven't I helped out?" you might ask before agreeing with or disagreeing with the attack.

If you have already asked for specifics and are still accused of reacting defensively, the problem may be in the *way* you ask. Your tone of voice and facial expression, posture, and other nonverbal clues can give the same words radically different connotations. For example, think of how you could use the words "Exactly what are you talking about?" to communicate either a genuine desire to know or your belief that the speaker is crazy. It's important to request specific information only when you genuinely want to learn more from the speaker because asking under any other circumstances will make matters only worse.

Nothing is weaker than water;
Yet, for attacking what is hard and tough,
Nothing surpasses it, nothing equals it.
The principle, that what is weak overcomes what is strong,
And what is yielding conquers what is resistant, is known to everyone.
Yet few utilize it profitably in practice . . .

Lao Tzu, *Tao Te Ching*

© Beata Szpura/Getty Images

Guess about Specifics On some occasions even your sincere and well-phrased requests for specific information won't meet with success. Sometimes your critics won't be able to define precisely the behavior they find offensive. At these times, you'll hear such comments as "I can't tell you exactly what's wrong with your sense of humor—all I can say is that I don't like it." At other times, your critics may know the exact behaviors they don't like but for some reason seem to get a perverse satisfaction out of making you struggle to figure it out. At times like this, you hear such comments as, "Well, if you don't know what you did to hurt my feelings, I'm certainly not going to tell you!"

Needless to say, failing to learn the specifics of another's criticism when you genuinely want to know can be frustrating. In instances like these, you can often learn more clearly what is bothering your critic by *guessing* at the specifics of a criticism. In a sense you become both detective and suspect, the goal being to figure out exactly what "crime" you have committed. Like the technique of asking for specifics, guessing must be done with goodwill if it's to produce satisfying results. You need to convey to the critic that for both your sakes you're truly interested in finding out what is the matter. After you have communicated this intention, the emotional climate generally becomes more comfortable because, in effect, both you and the critic are seeking the same goal.

Here are some typical questions you might hear from someone guessing about the specifics of another's criticism:

> "So you object to the language I used in writing the paper. Was my language too formal?"

> "OK, I understand that you think the outfit looks funny. What is it that's so bad? Is it the color? Does it have something to do with the fit? The fabric?"

> "When you say that I'm not doing my share around the house, do you mean that I haven't been helping enough with the cleaning?"

Paraphrase the Speaker's Ideas Another strategy is to draw out confused or reluctant speakers by paraphrasing their thoughts and feelings and using the active listening skills described in Chapter 7. Paraphrasing is especially good in helping others solve their problems; and because people generally criticize you because your behavior creates some problem for them, the strategy is especially appropriate at such times.

One advantage of paraphrasing is that you don't have to guess about the specifics of your behavior that might be offensive. By clarifying or amplifying what you understand critics to be saying, you'll learn more about their objections. A brief dialogue between a disgruntled customer and an especially talented store manager using paraphrasing might sound like this:

Customer: The way you people run this store is disgusting! I just want to tell you that I'll never shop here again.

Manager: (*reflecting the customer's feeling*) It seems that you're quite upset. Can you tell me your problem?

Customer:	It isn't *my* problem; it's the problem your salespeople have. They seem to think it's a great inconvenience to help a customer find anything around here.
Manager:	So you didn't get enough help locating the items you were looking for, is that it?
Customer:	Help? I spent 20 minutes looking around in here before I even talked to a clerk. All I can say is that it's a hell of a way to run a store.
Manager:	So what you're saying is that the clerks seemed to be ignoring the customers?
Customer:	No. They were all busy with other people. It just seems to me that you ought to have enough help around to handle the crowds that come in at this hour.
Manager:	I understand now. What frustrated you most was the fact that we didn't have enough staff to serve you promptly.
Customer:	That's right. I have no complaint with the service I get after I'm waited on, and I've always thought you had a good selection here. It's just that I'm too busy to wait so long for help.
Manager:	Well, I'm glad you brought this to my attention. We certainly don't want loyal customers going away mad. I'll try to see that it doesn't happen again.

> Placing the blame is a bad habit, but taking the blame is a sure builder of character.
>
> O. A. Battista

This conversation illustrates two advantages of paraphrasing. First, the critic often reduces the intensity of the attack after he or she realizes that the complaint is being heard. Often criticism grows from the frustration of unmet needs—which in this case was partly a lack of attention. As soon as the manager genuinely demonstrated interest in the customer's plight, the customer began to feel better and was able to leave the store relatively calm. Of course, this sort of reflective listening won't always mollify your critic, but even when it doesn't, there's still another benefit that makes the strategy worthwhile. In the sample conversation, for instance, the manager learned some valuable information by taking time to understand the customer. The manager discovered that there were certain times when the number of employees was insufficient to help the crowd of shoppers and also that the delays at these times seriously annoyed at least some shoppers, thus threatening a loss in business. This knowledge is certainly important, and by reacting defensively to the customer's complaint, the manager would not have learned from it.

Ask What the Critic Wants

Sometimes your critic's demand will be obvious:

"Turn down that music!"

"I wish you'd remember to tell me about phone messages."

"Would you clean up your dirty dishes *now!*"

At other times, however, you'll need to do some investigating to find out what the critic wants from you:

Alex:	I can't believe you invited all those people over without asking me first!
Barb:	Are you saying you want me to cancel the party?
Alex:	No, I just wish you'd ask me before you make plans.

Cynthia: You're so critical! It sounds like you don't like anything about this paper.

Donna: But you asked for my opinion. What do you expect me to do when you ask?

Cynthia: I want to know what's wrong, but I don't *just* want to hear criticisms. If you think there's anything good about my work, I wish you'd tell me that, too.

This last example illustrates the importance of accompanying your questions with the right nonverbal behavior. It's easy to imagine two ways in which Donna could have nonverbally supported her response, "What do you expect me to do when you ask?" One would show a genuine desire to clarify what Cynthia wanted, whereas the other would have been clearly hostile and defensive. As with all the styles in this section, your responses to criticism have to be sincere to work.

Ask about the Consequences of Your Behavior   As a rule, people criticize your behavior only when some need of theirs is not being met. One way to respond to this kind of criticism is to find out exactly what troublesome consequences your behavior has for them. You'll often find that behaviors that seem perfectly legitimate to you cause some difficulty for your critic; after you have understood this, criticisms that previously sounded foolish take on a new meaning.

Neighbor A: You say that I ought to have my cat neutered. Why is that important to you?

Neighbor B: Because at night he picks fights with my cat, and I'm tired of paying the vet's bills.

Worker A: Why do you care whether I'm late to work?

Worker B: Because when the boss asks, I feel obligated to make up some story so you won't get in trouble, and I don't like to lie.

Husband: Why does it bother you when I lose money at poker? You know I never gamble more than I can afford.

Wife: It's not the cash itself. It's that when you lose, you're in a grumpy mood for two or three days, and that's no fun for me.

Ask What Else Is Wrong   It might seem crazy to invite more criticism, but sometimes asking about other complaints can uncover the real problem:

Raul: Are you mad at me?

Tina: No. Why are you asking?

Raul: Because the whole time we were at the picnic you hardly spent any time talking to me. In fact, it seemed like whenever I came over to where you were, you went off somewhere else.

Tina: Is anything else wrong?

Raul: Well, I've been wondering lately if you're tired of me.

This example shows that asking if anything else bothers your critic isn't just an exercise in masochism. If you can keep your defensiveness in check, probing further can lead the conversation to issues that are the source of the critic's real dissatisfaction.

Sometimes soliciting more information from a critic isn't enough. What do you do, for instance, when you fully understand the other person's criticism and still feel a defensive response on the tip of your tongue? You know that if you try

Ethical Challenge

Nonviolence: A Legacy of Principled Effectiveness

Among the most familiar and challenging biblical injunctions is Christ's mandate, "If someone strikes you on one cheek, turn to him the other. . . ."

The notion of meeting aggression with nonviolence is an ancient one. The Taoist doctrine of *wu-wei*, promulgated over twenty-four hundred years ago in China, advocates nonaction in the face of an attack. In ancient India, the principle of *ahimsa*—nonharming— was shared by Buddhists, Jains, and many Hindus. In the West, some Greek stoics advocated nonaction in the face of threats.

Pacifism has a moral foundation, but by the nineteenth century it was used as a potent strategy for achieving political goals. In the United States, abolitionist William Lloyd Garrison advocated the use of nonviolence to protest slavery. On both sides of the Atlantic, the suffragette movement used nonviolent resistance as a tool to secure rights for women. In czarist Russia, Count Leo Tolstoy led a pacifist movement rejecting war and advocating civil disobedience as a tool for inhibiting violence.

In the twentieth century, nonviolence proved to be a powerful tool for political change. Mahatma Gandhi was demonstrably the most successful practitioner of this tool, first in South Africa and later in India, where his approach of *satyagraha* (truth-force) played a decisive role in the 1947 withdrawal of imperial Britain from India. In the 1950s and 1960s, Martin Luther King and his followers used nonviolence to demonstrate the evils of racial segregation, contributing to the passage of groundbreaking civil rights laws.

The effectiveness of nonviolence in achieving social change can also be effective in interpersonal situations. Nonconfrontational strategies provide communicators with an approach that is both principled and pragmatic.

For more information on nonviolent strategies, see Peter Ackerman and Christopher Kruegler, *Strategic Nonviolent Conflict: The Dynamics of People Power in the Twentieth Century* (Westport, Conn.: Praeger, 1994); and Robert L. Holmes, ed., *Nonviolence in Theory and Practice* (Belmont, Calif.: Wadsworth, 1990).

to defend yourself, you'll wind up in an argument; on the other hand, you simply can't accept what the other person is saying about you. The solution to such a dilemma is outrageously simple and is discussed in the following section.

Agree with the Critic

But, you protest, how can you honestly agree with criticisms that you don't believe are true? The following pages will answer this question by showing that in virtually every situation you can honestly accept the other person's point of view while still maintaining your own position. To see how this can be so, you need to realize that there are two different types of agreement you can use in almost any situation.

> Love your enemies, for they tell you your faults.
>
> Benjamin Franklin

Agree with the Facts This is the easiest type of agreement to understand, though not always to practice. Research suggests that it is also highly effective in restoring a damaged reputation with a critic.[35] You agree with your critic when the accusation is factually correct:

"You're right, I am angry."

"I suppose I *was* being defensive."

"Now that you mention it, I did get pretty sarcastic."

Agreeing with the facts seems sensible when you realize that certain facts are indisputable. If you agree to be somewhere at 4:00 and don't show up until 5:00, you *are* tardy, no matter how good your explanation for tardiness. If you've broken a borrowed object, run out of gas, or failed to finish a job you started, there's no point in denying it. In the same way, if you're honest, you may have to agree with

"When will he be able to sit up and take criticism?"

many interpretations of your behavior even when they're not flattering. You do get angry, act foolishly, fail to listen, and behave inconsiderately. After you rid yourself of the myth of perfection, it's much easier to acknowledge these truths.

If many criticisms aimed at you are accurate, why is it so difficult to accept them without being defensive? The answer to this question lies in a confusion between agreeing with the *facts* and accepting the *judgment* that so often accompanies them. Most critics don't merely describe the action that offends them; they also evaluate it, and it's this evaluation that we resist:

"It's silly to be angry."

"You have no reason for being defensive."

"You were wrong to be so sarcastic."

It's evaluations like these that we resent. By realizing that you can agree with—and even learn from—the descriptive part of many criticisms and still not accept the accompanying evaluations, you'll often have a response that is both honest and nondefensive.

Of course, in order to reduce defensiveness, your agreements with the facts must be honest ones admitted without malice. It's humiliating to accept descriptions that aren't accurate, and maliciously manipulatively pretending to accept these leads only to trouble. You can imagine how unproductive the conversation given earlier would have been if the manager had spoken the same words in a sarcastic tone. Agree with the facts only when you can do so sincerely. Though this won't always be possible, you'll be surprised at how often you can use this simple response.

Agree with the Critic's Perception   Agreeing with your critics may be fine when you acknowledge that the criticisms are justified, but how can you agree when they seem to be completely unjustified? You've listened carefully and asked questions to make sure you understand the criticisms, but the more you listen, the more positive you are that the critics are totally out of line. Even in these cases there is a way of agreeing—this time not with the critics' conclusions but with their right to see things their way.

A: I don't believe that you've been all the places you were just describing. You're probably just making all this up to impress us.

B: Well, I can see how you might think that. I've known people who lie to get approval.

C: I want to let you know right from the start that I was against hiring you for the job. I think you got it because you're a woman.

D: I can understand why you'd believe that with all the antidiscrimination laws on the books. I hope that after I've been here for a while, you'll change your mind.

E: I don't think you're being totally honest about your reason for wanting to stay home. You say it's because you have a headache, but I think you're avoiding Mary.

F: I can see why that would make sense to you because Mary and I got into an argument the last time we were together. All I can say is that I do have a headache.

One key to feeling comfortable with acknowledging accurate criticism is to understand that *agreeing* with a critic doesn't necessarily oblige you to *apologize*. Sometimes you aren't responsible for the behavior that your critic finds objectionable, in which case an explanation might be more appropriate than an apology:

> "I know I'm late. There was an accident downtown, and the streets are jammed." *(Spoken in an explanatory, nondefensive tone)*

In other cases, your behavior might be understandable, if not perfect. When this happens, you can acknowledge the validity of the criticism without apologizing:

> "You're right. I *did* lose my temper. I've had to remind you three or four times, and I guess I finally used up all my patience." *(Again, delivered as an explanation, not a defense or counterattack)*

In still other cases, you can acknowledge your critic's right to see things differently than you without backing off from your position.

> "I can understand why you think I'm overreacting. I know this doesn't seem as important to you as it does to me. I hope you can understand why I think this is such a big deal."

Apologizing is fine if you can do so sincerely; but you will be able to agree with critics more often if you understand that doing so doesn't require you to grovel.

Some critics don't seem to deserve the kinds of respectful responses outlined here. They seem more interested in attacking you than explaining themselves. Before you counterattack these hostile critics, ask yourself whether a defensive response will be worth the consequences.

Skill Builder

Coping with Criticism

Take turns practicing nondefensive responses with a partner:

1. Choose one of the following criticisms, and brief your partner on how it might be directed at you:

   a. You're so selfish sometimes. You think only of yourself.

   b. Don't be so touchy!

   c. You say you understand me, but you don't really.

   d. I wish you'd do your share around here.

   e. You're so critical!

2. As your partner criticizes you, answer with the appropriate response from the preceding pages. As you do so, try to adopt an attitude of genuinely wanting to understand the criticism and finding parts that you can sincerely agree with.

3. Ask your partner to evaluate your response. Does it follow the forms described in the previous pages? Does it sound sincere?

4. Replay the same scene, trying to improve your response.

Communication Transcript

Responding Nondefensively to Criticism

Defending yourself—even when you're right—isn't always the best approach. This dialogue shows the importance of using self-control and thinking before responding when you are being criticized. The employee realizes that arguing won't change his boss's mind, so he decides to reply as honestly as he can without becoming defensive.

Boss   How'd things go while I was out?

Employee   Pretty well, except for one thing. Mr. Macintosh—he said you knew him—came in and wanted to buy about $200 worth of stuff. He wanted me to charge him wholesale, and I asked him for his tax resale number, just like you told me. He said he didn't have it, so I told him he'd have to pay retail. He got pretty mad.

Boss   He's a good customer. I hope you gave him the discount.

Employee   *(beginning to sound defensive)* Well, I didn't. You told me last week that the law said we had to charge full price and sales tax unless the customer had a resale number.

Boss   Oh, my gosh! Didn't Macintosh tell you he had a number?

Employee   *(becoming more defensive)* He did, but he didn't have it with him. I didn't want to get you mad at me for breaking the law.

Boss   *(barely concealing his exasperation)* Well, customers don't always have their resale numbers memorized. Macintosh has been coming here for years, and we just fill in his number on the records later.

Employee   *(deciding to respond nondefensively instead of getting into an argument that he knows he can't win)* I can see why it looks like I gave Mr. Macintosh a hard time. You don't ask him for the number, and I insisted on having it. *(agrees with the boss's perception)*

Boss   Yes! There's a lot of competition in this business, and we have to keep our customers happy—especially the good ones—or we'll lose them. Macintosh drives across town to do business with us. There are places right near him. If we jerk him around he'll go there, and we'll lose a good customer.

Employee   That's true. *(agrees with the fact that it is important to keep customers happy)* And I want to know how to treat customers right. But I'm confused about how to handle people who want a discount and don't have resale numbers. What should I do? *(asks what the boss wants)*

Boss   Well, you need to be a little flexible with good customers.

Employee   How should I do that? *(asks for specifics)*

Boss   Well, it's OK to trust people who are regulars.

Employee   So I don't need to ask regular customers for their resale numbers. I should look them up later? *(paraphrases to clarify boss's ambiguous directions to "trust" regular customers)*

Boss   That's right. You've got to use your head in business!

Employee   *(ignores the indirect accusation about not "using his head," recognizing that there's no point in defending himself)* OK, so when regular customers come in, I won't even ask them for their resale numbers . . . right? *(paraphrases again to be sure he has the message correct; the employee has no desire to get criticized again about this matter)*

Boss   No, go ahead and ask for the number. If they have it, we won't have to look it up later. But if they don't have the number, just say OK and give them the discount.

Employee   Got it. I only have one question: How can I know who the regular customers are? Should I take their word for it? *(asks for specifics)*

Boss   Well, you'll get to know most of them after you've been here a while. But it's OK to trust them until then. If they say they're regulars, just take their word for it. You've got to trust people sometimes, you know!

Employee   *(ignores the fact that the boss originally told him not to trust people but rather to insist on getting their number; decides instead to agree with the boss)* I can see how important it is to trust good customers.

Boss   Right.

Employee   Thanks for clearing up how to handle the resale numbers. Is there anything else I ought to know so things will run smoothly when you're not in the store? *(asks if anything else is wrong)*

Boss   I don't think so. *(patronizingly)* Don't get discouraged; you'll catch on. It took me twenty years to build this business. Stick with it, and some day you could be running a place like this.

Employee   *(trying to agree with his boss without sounding sarcastic)* That would be great.

The employee's refusal to act defensively turned what might have been a scolding into a discussion about how to handle a business challenge in the future. The employee might not like the boss's patronizing attitude and contradictory directions, but his communication skill kept the communication climate positive—probably the best possible outcome for this situation.

Communication Scenarios
To see and analyze a dramatized version of this conversation, go to ThomsonNOW for *Looking Out/Looking In*, access "Communication Scenarios," and then click on "Responding Nondefensively to Criticism." **ThomsonNOW**

Summary

Every relationship has a communication climate. Positive climates are characterized by confirming messages, which make it clear that the parties value one another. Negative climates are usually disconfirming. In one way or another, messages in disconfirming relationships convey indifference or hostility. Communication climates develop early in a relationship, from both verbal and nonverbal messages. After they are created, reciprocal messages create either positive or negative spirals in which the frequency and intensity of either positive or negative messages are likely to grow.

Defensiveness hinders effective communication. Most defensiveness occurs when people try to protect key parts of a presenting self-image that they believe is under attack. Defensive communicators respond by attacking their critic, distorting critical information, or avoiding critical messages. Using the supportive behaviors defined by Jack Gibb when expressing potentially threatening messages can reduce the likelihood of triggering defensive reactions in others. In addition, we can share our thoughts and feelings with others in face-saving ways by using the clear message format. A complete clear message describes the behavior in question, at least one interpretation, the speaker's feelings, the consequences of the situation, and the speaker's intentions in making the statement.

When faced with criticism by others, it is possible to respond nondefensively by attempting to understand the criticism and by agreeing with either the facts or the critic's perception.

Key Terms

ambiguous response (334)
apathy (340)
assertive (346)
behavioral description (347)
certainty (345)
cognitive dissonance (337)
communication climate (329)
compensation (339)
confirming
    communication (330)
consequence statement (350)
controlling
    communication (341)
de-escalatory conflict
    spiral (336)
defense mechanism (338)
defensiveness (337)

description (341)
disconfirming
    communication (330)
displacement (340)
empathy (343)
equality (343)
escalatory conflict spiral (336)
evaluation (341)
face-threatening act (337)
feeling statement (349)
generalized complaining (332)
Gibb categories (341)
impersonal response (334)
impervious response (331)
incongruous response (334)
intention statement (350)
interpretation statement (348)

interrupting response (332)
irrelevant response (332)
neutrality (343)
physical avoidance (339)
problem orientation (342)
provisionalism (345)
rationalization (339)
regression (339)
repression (339)
sarcasm (338)
spiral (335)
spontaneity (342)
strategy (342)
superiority (343)
tangential response (334)
verbal abuse (331)
verbal aggression (338)

Media Resources

Online Textbook Resources

ThomsonNOW For quick access to the online resources that accompany this chapter, access ThomsonNOW for *Looking Out/Looking In* at www.thomsonedu.com.

The ThomsonNOW online study system helps you identify concepts you don't fully understand, allowing you to put your study time to the best use. Using chapter-by-chapter diagnostic pre-tests, the system creates a **personalized study plan** for each chapter. Each plan directs you to specific resources designed to improve your understanding, including pages from the text in ebook format. Chapter post-tests give you an opportunity to measure how much you've learned and let you know if you are ready for graded quizzes and exams.

Your ThomsonNOW for *Looking Out/Looking In* also includes a **communication scenario video** of the transcript on pages 360–361; **vocabulary activities** to help you master key terms; self-study **review quizzes** to test your comprehension of the material in this chapter and prepare for exams; **online exercises**, including the Skill Builder and Invitation to Insight activities in this chapter; **web links** you can use to further explore topics in this chapter; access to a **feature film database** where you can locate information about movies that illustrate communication principles; and access to the **InfoTrac** College Edition searchable database of over 10 million articles from both scholarly journals and the popular press.

Films and Television

ThomsonNOW In addition to the films suggested here, go to your ThomsonNOW for *Looking Out/Looking In* and access the **Film in Communication Database** to locate movie clips that illustrate various communication climates.

Confirming Communication

Antwone Fisher (2002) Rated PG-13
Antwone Fisher (Derek Luke) is an angry young sailor. A shipboard fight lands him in the office of base psychiatrist Jerome Davenport (Denzel Washington), whose job is to help Antwone manage his temper. After several sessions of stubborn silence, Antwone reveals that he was abandoned at birth by his imprisoned mother. He never knew his father, who was murdered two months before he was born. Raised by a cruel foster family, Antwone feels rootless and angry at the world. Davenport becomes a father figure to Antwone and assures him of his value and worth. On Davenport's advice, Antwone travels home to Cleveland in search of his roots.

The movie, based on a true story, is a powerful example of how being ignored is the ultimate form of disconfirmation. The fact that Antwone's mother never sought him out during or after her imprisonment communicated to Antwone that his existence didn't matter. When he finally tracks her down and confronts her with the pain of his abandonment, she sits in guilty silence and doesn't respond (it appears she is emotionally incapable of doing so). The good news is that his father's family—who didn't even know Antwone existed before he shows up on their doorstep—gives him a royal welcome home. The movie offers hope for turning around a tough life through the confirmation and love of people who care.

Communication Spirals

Changing Lanes (2002) Rated R
Gavin Banek (Ben Affleck) and Doyle Gipson (Samuel L. Jackson) are strangers who literally meet by accident. Both are running late for court appointments when their cars collide. Gipson wants to exchange insurance information and file an accident report; Banek only cares about getting to court on time. Banek hands Gipson a blank check and drives away yelling "Better luck next time"—leaving Gipson stranded in the middle of the road with a disabled car.

This event begins a negative spiral that quickly spins out of control. Gipson sends Banek a fax with the phrase "Better luck next time" scrawled on an important document that Banek accidentally left with Gipson. Banek retaliates by finding ways to ruin Gipson's credit rating. Gipson counterattacks and so does Banek—and in one day's time, these two men wreak havoc on each other's lives. *Changing Lanes* offers a sobering look at how the ineffective handling of a communication episode between strangers can lead to a destructive communication spiral.

Defensive Communication Climate

Office Space (1999) Rated R

Peter Gibbons (Ron Livingston) hates his job—with good reason. He works for a computer firm that treats its employees like cogs in a machine. The company is top-heavy with impersonal managers who bombard their supervisees with memos and pounce on the smallest infractions of office policy. As a result, the employees lack motivation and feel little commitment to the organization. They also feel defensive any time they are approached by a manager.

Peter's boss is Bill Lumbergh (Gary Cole), who on the surface talks a good game. He doesn't raise his voice or use abusive language when correcting Peter; in fact, he offers suggestions in positive terms ("If you could go ahead and make sure to do that from now on, that would be great"). Unfortunately, he delivers these messages in a syrupy tone of voice that reeks of condescension. Moreover, Lumbergh doesn't listen or respond to his employees, nor does he ask for their input or participation. He simply delivers monologues and walks away. In Gibb's terms, Lumbergh uses control, neutrality, and superiority (and most of the other defense-provoking components as well)—and the result is that Peter and the other employees hide when they see the boss coming their way.

Office Space is a good example of a toxic communication climate. For anyone who has had the misfortune of working in a dysfunctional organization, the movie will probably elicit a chuckle—because the office communication will look and sound all too familiar.

Giving and Receiving Criticism

American Idol (Television Series)

The popular television show *American Idol* requires contestants to perform songs not only in front of millions of viewers, but also before a panel of judges who publicly critique the performers and their talents (or lack thereof). Receiving criticism is always a face-threatening process, but particularly so when a huge audience is listening in.

It's interesting to watch how the *Idol* judges offer their criticisms and how the contestants respond. When the verdict is negative, some judges are curt and evaluative ("That was awful!") or broad and vague ("That didn't work"). The most helpful criticisms focus on specific behaviors and suggestions for change ("I think you need a song in a lower range—you seemed to be straining for the high notes").

Of course, performers don't always respond well to suggestions. Many quickly defend themselves ("I thought I did just fine") or shift the blame ("I didn't choose the song"). Others follow principles described in this chapter, such as seeking more information or agreeing with the critic, hoping to improve their next performance.

Shows like *American Idol* are designed for entertainment, not education—but from a communication perspective, they offer valuable lessons about giving and receiving criticism.

Chapter 10 ~ Improving Communication Climates | Responding to Criticism

Introduction | Video | Transcript | Critique | Notes

1. Which of the Gibb categories outlined in the textbook's Chapter 9 does the boss exhibit when she criticizes the employee's behavior?

2. Does the employee ever seem defensive during this discussion? How successful is her defensive reaction?

3. Why can it be a good idea to use non-defensive responses in the face of unjustified attacks, such

TIME   01:07 / 02:28

THOMSON WADSWORTH

Looking Out, Looking In, 12e | Adler and Proctor | Copyright 2008 Thomson Wadsworth

Chapter 1 | Chapter 2 | Chapter 3 | Chapter 4 | Chapter 5 | Chapter 6 | Chapter 7 | Chapter 8
Chapter 9 | Chapter 10 | Chapter 11

Managing Interpersonal Conflicts

11

The Nature of Conflict

Conflict Defined
Conflict Is Natural
Conflict Can Be Beneficial

Conflict Styles

Avoiding
Accommodating
Competing
Compromising
Collaborating
Which Style to Use?

Conflict in Relational Systems

Complementary, Symmetrical,
   and Parallel Styles
Intimate and Aggressive Styles
Conflict Rituals

Variables in Conflict Styles

Gender
Culture

Constructive Conflict Skills

Identify Your Problem and Unmet Needs
Make a Date
Describe Your Problem and Needs
Consider Your Partner's Point of View
Negotiate a Solution
Follow Up the Solution

Constructive Conflict: Questions and Answers

Isn't the Win-Win Approach Too Good
   to Be True?
Isn't the Win-Win Approach
   Too Elaborate?
Isn't Win-Win Negotiating Too Rational?
Is It Possible to Change Others?

Summary

Key Terms

Media Resources

For most people, conflict has about the same appeal as a trip to the dentist. A quick look at a thesaurus offers a clue about the distasteful nature of conflict. Synonyms for the term include *battle, brawl, clash, competition, discord, disharmony, duel, fight, strife, struggle, trouble,* and *violence.* Even the metaphors we use to describe our conflicts show that we view conflict as something to be avoided.[1] We often talk about conflict as a kind of war: "He shot down my arguments." "OK, fire away." "Don't try to defend yourself!" Other metaphors suggest that conflict is explosive: "Don't blow up!" "I needed to let off steam." "You've got a short fuse." Sometimes conflict seems like a kind of trial, in which one party accuses another: "Come on, admit you're guilty." "Stop accusing me!" "Just listen to my case." Language that suggests that conflict is a mess is also common: "Let's not open this can of worms." "That's a sticky situation." "Don't make such a stink!" Even the metaphor of a game implies that one side has to defeat the other: "That was out of bounds." "You're not playing fair." "I give up; you win!"

Despite images like these, the truth is that conflict *can* be constructive. With the right set of communication skills, conflict can be less like a struggle and more like a kind of dance in which partners work together to create something that would be impossible without their cooperation. You may have to persuade the other person to become your partner rather than your adversary, and you may be clumsy at first; but with enough practice and goodwill, you can work together instead of at cross-purposes.

The attitude you bring to your conflicts can make a tremendous difference between success and failure. One study revealed that college students in close romantic relationships who believed that conflicts are destructive were most likely to neglect or quit the relationship and less likely to seek a solution than couples who had less-negative attitudes.[2] Of course, attitudes alone won't always guarantee satisfying solutions to conflicts—but the kinds of skills you will learn in this chapter can help well-intentioned partners handle their disagreements constructively.

The Nature of Conflict

Before focusing on how to solve interpersonal problems constructively, we need to take a brief look at the nature of conflict. What is it? Why is it an inevitable part of life? How can it be beneficial?

Conflict Defined

Before reading farther, make a list of the interpersonal conflicts in your life. They probably involve many different people, revolve around very different subjects,

© Marie Bertrand/Corbis

and take many different forms. Some become loud, angry arguments. Others may be expressed in calm, rational discussions. Still others might simmer along most of the time with brief but bitter flare-ups.

Whatever form they may take, all interpersonal conflicts share certain characteristics. William Wilmot and Joyce Hocker provide a thorough definition when they define **conflict** as *an expressed struggle between at least two interdependent parties who perceive incompatible goals, scarce resources, and interference from the other party in achieving their goals.*[3] A closer look at the key parts of this definition will help you recognize how conflict operates in your life.

Expressed Struggle   A conflict can exist only when both parties are aware of a disagreement. For instance, you may be upset for months because a neighbor's loud stereo keeps you awake at night, but no conflict exists between the two of you until the neighbor learns of your problem. Of course, the expressed struggle doesn't have to be verbal. A dirty look, the silent treatment, and avoiding the other person are all ways of expressing yourself. One way or another, both parties must know that a problem exists before they're in conflict.

Perceived Incompatible Goals   All conflicts look as if one party's gain would be another's loss. For instance, consider the neighbor whose stereo keeps you awake at night. Doesn't somebody have to lose? If the neighbor turns down the noise, she loses the enjoyment of hearing the music at full volume; but if the neighbor keeps the volume up, you're still awake and unhappy.

The goals in this situation really aren't completely incompatible—there are solutions that allow both parties to get what they want. For instance, you could achieve peace and quiet by closing your windows or getting the neighbor to close hers. You might use a pair of earplugs, or perhaps the neighbor could get a set of earphones, allowing the music to be played at full volume without bothering anyone. If any of these solutions prove workable, the conflict disappears.

Unfortunately, people often fail to see mutually satisfying solutions to their problems. As long as they *perceive* their goals to be mutually exclusive, a conflict exists.

Perceived Scarce Resources   Conflicts also exist when people believe there isn't enough of something to go around. The most obvious example of a scarce resource is money—a cause of many conflicts. If a worker asks for a raise in pay and the boss would rather keep the money or use it to expand the business, the two parties are in conflict.

Time is another scarce commodity. As authors and family men, we authors of this textbook constantly face struggles about how to use the limited time we have at home. Should we work on this book? Chat with our wives? Spend time with our children? Enjoy the luxury of being alone? With only 24 hours in a day, we're bound to wind up in conflicts with our families, editors, students, and friends—all of whom want more of our time than we have to give.

Interdependence   However antagonistic they might feel, the parties in conflict are usually dependent on each other. The welfare and satisfaction of one depend on the actions of another. If not, then even in the face of scarce resources and incompatible goals there would be no need for conflict. Interdependence exists between conflicting nations, social groups, organizations, friends, and lovers. In

We struggled together, knowing. We prattled, pretended, fought bitterly, laughed, wept over sad books or old movies, nagged, supported, gave, took, demanded, forgave, resented—hating the ugliness of each other, yet cherishing that which we were. . . . Will I ever find someone to battle with as we battled, love as we loved, share with as we shared, challenge as we challenged, forgive as we forgave? You used to say that I saved up all of my feelings so that I could spew forth when I got home. The anger I experienced in school I could not vent there. How many times have I heard you chuckle as you remembered the day I would come home from school and share with you all of the feelings I had kept in. "If anyone had been listening they would have thought you were punishing me, striking out at me. I always survived and you always knew that I would still be with you when you were through." There was an honesty about our relationship that may never exist again.

Vian Catrell

each case, if the two parties didn't need each other to solve the problem, they would go their separate ways. One of the first steps toward resolving a conflict is to take the attitude that "we're all in this together."

Interference from the Other Party   No matter how much one person's position may differ from another's, a full-fledged conflict won't occur until the participants act in ways that prevent one another from reaching their goals. For example, you might let some friends know that you object to their driving after drinking too much alcohol, but the conflict won't escalate until you act in ways that prevent them from getting behind the wheel. Likewise, a parent-child dispute about what clothing and music are appropriate will blossom into a conflict when the parents try to impose their position on the child.

Conflict Is Natural

Every relationship of any depth at all has conflict.[4] No matter how close, how understanding, how compatible you and other people are, there will be times when your ideas or actions or needs or goals won't match. You like rap music, but your companion likes classical; you want to date other people, but your partner wants to keep the relationship exclusive; you think a paper that you've written is fine, but your instructor wants it changed; you like to sleep late on Sunday mornings, but your housemate likes to play the stereo—loudly! There's no end to the number and kinds of disagreements possible.

College students who have kept diaries of their relationships report that they take part in about seven arguments per week. Most have argued with the other person before, often about the same topic.[5] In another survey, 81 percent of the respondents acknowledged that they had conflicts with friends.[6] Even the 19 percent who claimed that their friendships were conflict-free used phrases like "push and pull" or "little disagreements" to describe the tensions that inevitably occurred. Among families, conflict can be even more frequent. Researchers recorded dinner conversations for fifty-two families and found an average of 3.3 "conflict episodes" per meal.[7]

At first this might seem depressing. If problems are inevitable in even the best relationships, does this mean that you're doomed to relive the same arguments, the same hurt feelings, over and over? Fortunately, the answer to this question is a definite "no." Even though conflict is a part of a meaningful relationship, you can change the way you deal with it.

Conflict Can Be Beneficial

Because it is impossible to *avoid* conflicts, the challenge is to handle them well when they do arise. Effective communication during conflicts can actually keep good relationships strong. People who use the constructive skills described in this chapter are more satisfied with their relationships[8] and with the outcomes of their conflicts.[9]

Perhaps the best evidence of how constructive conflict skills can benefit a relationship focuses on communication between husbands and wives. Over twenty years of research shows that both happy and unhappy marriages have conflicts but that they manage conflict in very different ways.[10] One nine-year study revealed that unhappy couples argue in ways that we have catalogued in this book as destructive.[11] They are more concerned with defending themselves than with being problem oriented; they fail to listen carefully to each other, have little or no empathy for their partners, use evaluative "you" language, and ignore each other's nonverbal relational messages.

Many satisfied couples think and communicate differently when they disagree. They view disagreements as healthy and recognize that conflicts need to be faced.[12] Although they may argue vigorously, they use skills like perception checking to find out what the other person is thinking, and they let each other know that they understand the other side of the argument.[13] They are willing to admit their mistakes, both contributing to a harmonious relationship and helping to solve the problem at hand.

In the following pages, we will review communication skills that can make conflicts constructive, and we will introduce still more skills that you can use to resolve the inevitable conflicts you face. Before doing so, however, we need to examine how individuals behave when faced with a dispute.

Conflict Styles

Most people have "default" styles of handling conflict—characteristic approaches they take when their needs appear incompatible with what others want. While our habitual styles work sometimes, they may not work at all in other situations. What styles do you typically use to deal with conflict? Find out by thinking about how two hypothetical characters—Paul and Lucia—manage a problem.

Paul and Lucia have been running partners for over a year. Three times every week, they spend an hour or more together working out. The two runners are equally matched, and they enjoy challenging one another to cover longer distances at a quicker pace. During their time on the road, the friends have grown quite close. Now they often talk about personal matters that they don't share with anyone else.

Recently Lucia has started to invite some of her friends along on the runs. Paul likes Lucia's friends, but they aren't strong athletes, so the outings become a much less satisfying workout. Also, Paul fears losing the special one-on-one time that he and Lucia have had.

Paul shared his concerns with Lucia, but she dismissed them. "I don't see what the problem is," she replied. "We still get plenty of time on the road, and you said you like my friends." "But it isn't the same," replied Paul.

This situation has all the elements of a conflict: Expressed struggle (their differences are in the open and they still disagree), seemingly incompatible goals and interference (Lucia wants to run with her friends; Paul wants to run with just Lucia), apparently scarce resources (they only have so much time for running), and interdependence (they enjoy one another's company and run better together than separately).

Here are five ways Paul and Lucia could handle the matter. Each represents one approach to managing conflict:

Not everything that is faced can be changed, but nothing can be changed until it is faced.

James Baldwin

What counts in making a happy marriage is not so much how compatible you are, but how you deal with incompatibility.

Leo Tolstoy

- They could say "Let's just forget it" and stop running together.
- Paul could give in, sacrificing his desire for one-on-one conversations and challenging runs. Or Lucia could give in, sacrificing her other friendships to maintain her friendship with Paul.
- One or the other could issue an ultimatum: "Either we do it my way, or we stop running together."
- They could compromise, inviting friends along on some runs but excluding them on other days.
- Lucia and Paul could brainstorm ways they could run with her friends and still get their workouts and one-on-one time with each other.

These approaches represent the five styles depicted in Figure 11.1, each of which is described in the paragraphs below.

Avoiding (Lose-Lose)

Avoiding occurs when people nonassertively ignore or stay away from conflict. Avoidance can be physical (steering clear of a friend after having an argument) or conversational (changing the topic, joking, or denying that a problem exists).

Avoidance reflects a pessimistic attitude about conflict under the belief that there is no good way to resolve the issue at hand. Some avoiders believe it's easier to put up with the status quo than to face the problem head-on and try to solve it. Other avoiders believe it's better to quit (on either the topic or the relationship) than to keep facing the same issues without hope of solution. In either case, avoiding often results in *lose-lose* outcomes in which none of the parties get what they want.

In the case of Paul and Lucia, avoiding means that, rather than struggling with their disagreement, they just stop running together. Although it means they'll no longer be fighting, it also means they'll both lose a running partner and an important component of their friendship (and maybe their friendship altogether). This "solution" illustrates how avoiding can produce lose-lose results.

FIGURE 11.1
Conflict Styles

Adapted from William W. Wilmot and Joyce L. Hocker (2007). *Interpersonal Conflict* (7th ed.), pp. 130–175. New York: McGraw-Hill.

© Images.com/Corbis

I was angry with my
   friend.
I told my wrath, my wrath
   did end.
I was angry with my foe:
I told it not, my wrath did
   grow.
And I watered it in fears,
Night and morning with
   my tears;
And I sunned it with
   smiles,
And with soft deceitful
   wiles.
And it grew both day and
   night,
Till it bore an apple
   bright;
And my foe beheld it
   shine,
And he knew that it was
   mine,
And into my garden stole
When the night had
   veiled the pole:
In the morning glad I see
My foe outstretched
   beneath the tree.

William Blake

Although avoiding may keep the peace temporarily, it typically leads to unsatisfying relationships.[14] Chronic misunderstandings, resentments, and disappointments pile up and contaminate the emotional climate. For this reason, we can say that avoiders have a low concern both for their own needs and for the interests of the other person, who is also likely to suffer from unaddressed issues (see Figure 11.1).

Despite its obvious shortcomings, avoiding isn't always a bad idea.[15] You might choose to avoid certain topics or situations if the risk of speaking up is too great, such as triggering an embarrassing fight in public, or even risking physical harm. You might also avoid a conflict if the relationship it involves isn't worth the effort. Even in close relationships, though, avoidance has its logic. If the issue is temporary or minor, you might let it pass. These reasons help explain why the communication of many happily married couples is characterized by "selectively ignoring" the other person's minor flaws.[16] This doesn't mean that a key to successful relationships is avoiding *all* conflicts. Instead, it suggests that it's smart to save energy for the truly important ones.

Accommodating (Lose-Win)

Are there genuinely nice, sweet people in this world? Yes, absolutely yes, and they get angry as often as you and I. They must—otherwise they would be full of vindictive feelings and slush, which would prevent genuine sweetness.

Theodore Isaac Rubin

Accommodating occurs when you allow others to have their way rather than asserting your own point of view. Figure 11.1 depicts accommodators as having low concern for themselves and high concern for others, resulting in *lose-win*, "we'll do it your way" outcomes. In our hypothetical scenario, Paul could accommodate Lucia by letting her friends join in on their runs, even though it means less of a physical challenge and quality time with Lucia—or Lucia could accommodate Paul by running with just him.

The motivation of an accommodator plays a significant role in this style's effectiveness. If accommodation is a genuine act of kindness, generosity, or love, then chances are good that it will enhance the relationship. Most people appreciate those who "take one for the team," "treat others as they want to be treated," or "lose the battle to win the war." However, people are far less appreciative of those who habitually use this style to play the role of "martyr, bitter complainer, whiner, or saboteur."[17]

We should pause here to mention the important role that culture plays in perceptions of conflict styles. People from high-context, collectivist backgrounds (such as many Asian cultures) are likely to regard avoidance and accommodation as face-saving and noble ways to handle conflict.[18] In low-context, individualist cultures (such as the United States), avoidance and accommodation are often viewed less positively. For instance, think of the many unflattering terms that Americans use for people who give up or give in during conflicts ("pushover," "yes man," "doormat," "spineless"). As you will read later in this chapter, collectivist cultures have virtuous words and phrases to describe these same traits. The point here is that all conflict styles have value in certain situations, and that culture plays a significant role in determining how each style is valued.

Competing (Win-Lose, Sometimes Degenerating to Lose-Lose)

The flip side of accommodating is **competing**. This *win-lose* approach to conflict involves high concern for self and low concern for others. As Figure 11.1 shows, competition seeks to resolve conflicts "my way." If Lucia and Paul each tried to force the other to concede, one of them might prevail—but at the other's expense.

People resort to competing when they perceive a situation as being an "either-or" one: Either I get what I want or you get what you want. The most clear-cut examples of win-lose situations are certain games such as baseball or poker, in which the rules require a winner and a loser. Some interpersonal issues seem to fit into this win-lose framework: two co-workers seeking a promotion to the same job, or a couple who disagree on how to spend their limited money.

There are cases when competing can enhance a relationship. One study revealed that some men and women in satisfying dating relationships use competition to enrich their interaction.[19] For example, some found satisfaction by competing in play (who's the better racquetball player?), in achievement (who gets the better job offer?), and in altruism (who's more romantic?). These satisfied couples developed a shared narrative (see Chapter 3) that defined competition as a measure of regard, quite different from conflict that signaled a lack of appreciation and respect. Of course, it's easy to see how these arrangements could backfire if one partner became a gloating winner or a sore loser. Feeling like you've been defeated can leave you wanting to get even, creating a downward competitive spiral that degrades to a *lose-lose* relationship.[20]

Power is the distinguishing characteristic in win-lose problem solving because it is necessary to defeat an opponent to get what one wants. The most obvious kind of power is physical. Some parents threaten their children with warnings such as "Stop misbehaving, or I'll send you to your room." Adults who use physical power to deal with each other usually aren't so blunt, but the legal system is the implied threat: "Follow the rules, or we'll lock you up."

Real or implied force isn't the only kind of power used in conflicts. People who rely on authority of many types engage in win-lose methods without ever threatening physical coercion. In most jobs, supervisors have the authority to assign working hours, job promotions, and desirable or undesirable tasks and, of course, to fire an unsatisfactory employee. Teachers can use the power of grades to coerce students to act in desired ways.

"Well, if it doesn't matter who's right and who's wrong, why don't I be right and you be wrong?"

Even the usually admired democratic system of majority rule is a win-lose method of resolving conflicts. However fair it may seem, with this system one group is satisfied and the other is defeated.

The dark side of competition is that it often breeds aggression.[21] Sometimes aggression is obvious, but at other times it can be more subtle. To understand how, read on.

Passive Aggression   **Passive aggression** occurs when a communicator expresses hostility in an obscure or manipulative way. As the Ethical Challenge on page 375 explains, this behavior has been termed **"crazymaking."** It occurs when people have feelings of resentment, anger, or rage that they are unable or unwilling to express directly. Instead of keeping these feelings to themselves, a crazymaker sends aggressive messages in subtle, indirect ways, thus maintaining the front of kindness. This amiable façade eventually crumbles, leaving the crazymaker's victim confused and angry at having been fooled. The targets of the crazymaker can either react with aggressive behavior of their own or retreat to nurse their hurt feelings. In either case, passive aggression seldom has anything but harmful effects on a relationship.[22] In our scenario, Lucia could take a passive-aggressive approach to Paul's desire to keep their workouts exclusive by showing up late to run, just to annoy him. Paul could become passive-aggressive by agreeing to include Lucia's friends, then pouring on the speed and leaving them behind.

Direct Aggression   **Direct aggression** occurs when a communicator expresses a criticism or demand that threatens the face of the person at whom it is directed. Communication researcher Dominic Infante identified several types of direct aggression: character attacks, competence attacks, physical appearance attacks, maledictions (wishing the other ill fortune), teasing, ridicule, threats, swearing, and nonverbal emblems.[23]

Direct aggression can have a severe impact on the target. Recipients can feel embarrassed, inadequate, humiliated, hopeless, desperate, or depressed. These results can lead to decreased effectiveness in personal relationships, on the job, and in families.[24] There is a significant connection between verbal aggression and physical aggression,[25] but even if the attacks never lead to blows, the psychological effects can be devastating. For example, siblings who were teased by a brother or sister report less satisfaction and trust than those whose relationships were relatively free of this sort of aggression,[26] and high school teams with aggressive coaches lose more games than those whose coaches are less aggressive.[27]

Aggressive behavior can punish the attacker as well as the victim. Men who view conversations as contests and partners as opponents are 60 percent more apt to die earlier than those who are less aggressive.[28] Newly married couples whose disagreements are marked by sarcasm, interruptions, and criticism suffer a drop in the effectiveness of their immune systems.[29]

Ethical Challenge

Dirty Fighting with Crazymakers

Psychologist George Bach uses the term "crazymakers" to describe passive-aggressive behavior. His term reflects the insidious nature of indirect aggression, which can confuse and anger a victim who may not *even* be aware of being victimized. Although a case can be made for using all of the other approaches to conflict described in this chapter, it is difficult to find a justification for passive-aggressive crazymaking.

The following categories represent a nonexhaustive list of crazymaking. They are presented here as a warning for potential victims, who might choose to use perception checking, "I" language, assertion, or other communication strategies to explore whether the user has a complaint that can be addressed in a more constructive manner.

The Avoider Avoiders refuse to fight. When a conflict arises, they leave, fall asleep, pretend to be busy at work, or keep from facing the problem in some other way. Because avoiders won't fight back, this strategy can frustrate the person who wants to address an issue.

The Pseudoaccommodator Pseudoaccommodators pretend to give in and then continue to act in the same way.

The Guiltmaker Instead of expressing dissatisfaction directly, guiltmakers try to make others feel responsible for causing pain. A guiltmaker's favorite line is "It's OK; don't worry about me . . ." accompanied by a big sigh.

The Mind Reader Instead of allowing their partners to express feelings honestly, mind readers go into character analysis, explaining what the partner really means or what's wrong with the partner. By behaving this way, mind readers refuse to handle their own feelings and leave no room for their partners to express themselves.

The Trapper Trappers play an especially dirty trick by setting up a desired behavior for their partners and then, when it's met, attacking the very behavior they requested. An example of this technique is for the trapper to say, "Let's be totally honest with each other," and then attack the partner's self-disclosure.

The Crisis Tickler Crisis ticklers almost bring what's bothering them to the surface but never quite come out and express themselves. Instead of admitting concern about the finances, they innocently ask, "Gee, how much did that cost?" dropping a rather obvious hint but never really dealing with the crisis.

The Gunnysacker These people don't share complaints as they arise. Instead, they put their resentments into a psychological gunnysack, which after a while begins to bulge with both large and small gripes. Then, when the sack is about to burst, the gunnysacker pours out all the pent-up aggressions on the overwhelmed and unsuspecting victim.

The Trivial Tyrannizer Instead of honestly sharing their resentments, trivial tyrannizers do things they know will get their partners' goat—leaving dirty dishes in the sink, clipping fingernails in bed, belching out loud, turning up the television too loud, and so on.

The Beltliner Everyone has a psychological "beltline," and below it are subjects too sensitive to be approached without damaging the relationship. Beltlines may have to do with physical characteristics, intelligence, past behavior, or deeply ingrained personality traits that a person is trying to overcome. In an attempt to "get even" or hurt their partners, beltliners will use intimate knowledge to hit below the belt, where they know it will hurt.

The Joker Because they are afraid to face conflicts squarely, jokers kid around when their partners want to be serious, thus blocking the expression of important feelings.

The Withholder Instead of expressing their anger honestly and directly, withholders punish their partners by keeping back something—courtesy, affection, good cooking, humor, sex. As you can imagine, this is likely to build up even greater resentments in the relationship.

The Benedict Arnold These characters get back at their partners by sabotage, by failing to defend them from attackers, and even by encouraging ridicule or disregard from outside the relationship.

For more information about crazymaking, see George Bach and Peter Wyden, *The Intimate Enemy* (New York: Avon, 1968); and George Bach, *Aggression Lab: The Fair Fight Manual* (Dubuque, Iowa: Kendall-Hunt, 1971).

Compromising (Partial Lose-Lose)

A **compromise** gives both people at least some of what they want, although both sacrifice part of their goals. People usually settle for a compromise when it seems that partial satisfaction is the best they can hope for. In the case of Paul and Lucia, they could strike a "halfway" deal by alternating workouts with and without her friends. Unlike avoidance, where both parties lose because they don't address their problem, compromisers actually negotiate a solution that gives them some of what they want, but also leaves everybody losing something.

Although a compromise may be better than losing everything, this method hardly seems to deserve the positive image that it has with some people. In his valuable book on conflict resolution, Albert Filley makes an interesting observation about our attitudes toward this method.[30] Why is it, he asks, that if someone says, "I will compromise my values," we view the action unfavorably, yet we view favorably parties in a conflict who compromise to reach a solution? Although compromises may be the best obtainable result in some conflicts, it's important to realize that both people in a conflict can often work together to find much better solutions. In such cases *compromise* is a negative word.

Most of us are surrounded by the results of bad compromises. Consider a common example: the conflict between one person's desire to smoke cigarettes and another's need for clean air. The win-lose outcomes of this issue are obvious: Either the smoker abstains, or the nonsmoker gets polluted lungs—neither very satisfying. But a compromise in which the smoker gets to enjoy only a rare cigarette or must retreat outdoors and in which the nonsmoker still must inhale some fumes or feel like an ogre is hardly better. Both sides have lost a considerable amount of both comfort and goodwill. Of course, the costs involved in other compromises are even greater. For example, if a divorced couple compromise on child care by haggling over custody and then grudgingly agree to split the time with their children, it's hard to say that anybody has won.

Some compromises do leave both parties satisfied. You and the seller might settle on a price for a used car that is between what the seller was asking and what you wanted to pay. Although neither of you got everything you wanted, the outcome would still leave both of you satisfied. Likewise, you and your companion might agree to see a film that is the second choice for both of you in order to spend an evening together. As long as everyone is satisfied with an outcome, compromise can be an effective way to resolve conflicts. When compromises are satisfying and successful, it might be more accurate to categorize them as the final style we'll discuss: collaborating.

Collaborating (Win-Win)

> Let us begin anew, remembering on both sides that civility is not a sign of weakness.
>
> John F. Kennedy

Collaborating seeks *win-win* solutions to conflict. Collaborators show a high degree of concern for both themselves and others. Rather than trying to solve problems "my way" or "your way," their focus is on "our way." In the best case, collaborating can lead to a *win-win* outcome, where everybody gets what they want.

If Lucia and Paul were to collaborate, they might determine that the best way for both of them to get what they want is to continue their one-on-one workouts, but invite Lucia's friends to join in for a few miles at the end of each run. They might schedule other, less-challenging workouts that include the friends. Or they might find other ways to get together with Lucia's friends that are fun for both of them.

The goal of collaboration is to find a solution that satisfies the needs of everyone involved. Not only do the partners avoid trying to win at the other's expense, but also they believe that by working together it is possible to find a solution that goes beyond a mere compromise and allows all parties to reach their goals. Consider a few examples:

- A newly married husband and wife find themselves arguing frequently over their budget. The husband enjoys buying impractical and enjoyable items for himself and for the house, whereas the wife fears that such purchases will ruin their carefully constructed budget. Their solution is to set aside a small amount of money each month for "fun purchases." The amount is small enough to be affordable yet gives the husband a chance to escape from their spartan lifestyle. The wife is satisfied with the arrangement because the luxury money is now a budget category by itself, which gets rid of the "out-of-control" feeling that comes when her husband makes unexpected purchases. The plan works so well that the couple continues to use it even after their income rises, by increasing the amount devoted to luxuries.
- Marta, a store manager, hates the task of rescheduling employee work shifts to accommodate their social and family needs. She and her staff develop an arrangement in which employees arrange schedule swaps on their own and notify her in writing after they are made.
- Wendy and Kathy are roommates who have different study habits. Wendy likes to do her work in the evenings, which leaves her days free for other things, but Kathy feels that nighttime is party time. The solution they worked out is that Monday through Wednesday evenings Wendy studies at her boyfriend's place while Kathy does anything she wants; Thursday and Sunday, Kathy agrees to keep things quiet around the house.

The point here isn't that these solutions are the correct ones for everybody with similar problems: The win-win method doesn't work that way. Different people might have found other solutions that suited them better. Collaboration gives you a way of creatively finding just the right answer for your unique problem—and that answer might be one that neither party thought of or expected before collaborating. By generating win-win solutions, you can tailor-make a way of resolving your conflicts that everyone can live with comfortably. Later in this chapter, you'll learn a specific process for arriving at collaborative solutions to problems.

Which Style to Use?

Collaborating might seem like the ideal approach to solving problems; but it's an oversimplification to imagine that there is a single "best" way.[31] Generally speaking, win-win approaches are preferable to win-lose and lose-lose solutions. But we've already seen that there are times when avoiding, accommodating, competing, and compromising are appropriate. Table 11.1 lists some of the issues to consider when deciding which style to use when facing a conflict. As you decide which approach to use, consider several factors:

1. *The Relationship* When someone else clearly has more power than you, accommodating may be the best approach. If the boss tells you to fill that order "*Now!*" it may be smart to do so without comment. A more assertive response ("I'm still tied up with the job you gave me yesterday") might be reasonable, but it could also cost you your job.

Table 11.1	Factors to Consider When Choosing the Most Appropriate Conflict Style			
Avoiding (lose-lose)	Accommodating (lose-win)	Competing (win-lose)	Compromising (partial lose-lose)	Collaborating (win-win)
When the issue is of little importance	When you discover you are wrong	When there is not enough time to seek a win-win outcome	To achieve quick, temporary solutions to complex problems	When the issue is too important for a compromise
When the costs of confrontation outweigh the benefits	When the issue is more important to the other person than it is to you	When the issue is not important enough to negotiate at length	When opponents are strongly committed to mutually exclusive goals	When a long-term relationship between you and the other person is important
To cool down and gain perspective	When the long-term cost of winning isn't worth the short-term gain	When the other person is not willing to cooperate	When the issues are moderately important but not enough for a stalemate	To merge insights with someone who has a different perspective on the problem
	To build up credits for later conflicts	When you are convinced that your position is right and necessary	As a backup mode when collaboration doesn't work	To develop a relationship by showing commitment to the concerns of both parties
	To let others learn by making their own mistakes	To protect yourself against a person who takes advantage of noncompetitive people		To come up with creative and unique solutions to problems

Adapted from William W. Wilmot and Joyce L. Hocker (2007). *Interpersonal Conflict* (7th ed.), pp. 130–175. New York: McGraw-Hill.

2. *The Situation* Different situations call for different conflict styles. After haggling over the price of a car for hours, it might be best to compromise by simply splitting the difference. In other cases, though, it may be a matter of principle for you to "stick to your guns" and attempt to get what you believe is right.

3. *The Other Person* Win-win is a fine ideal, but sometimes the other person isn't willing or able to collaborate. You probably know communicators who are so competitive that they put winning on even minor issues ahead of the well-being of your relationship. In such cases, your efforts to collaborate may have a low chance of success.

4. *Your Goals* Sometimes your overriding concern may be to calm down an enraged or upset person. Accomodating an outburst from your crotchety and sick neighbor, for example, is probably better than standing up for yourself and triggering a stroke. In still other cases, your moral principles might compel an aggressive statement even though it might not get you what you originally sought: "I've had enough of your racist jokes. I've tried to explain why they're so offensive, but you obviously haven't listened. I'm leaving!"

Your Conflict Style

Assess your conflict style by taking the self-test at the website for the Peace and Justice Support Network of the Mennonite Church. This instrument measures the way you deal with issues in both "calm" and "stormy" situations. Go to your ThomsonNOW for *Looking Out/Looking In* to access a link to this site.

Conflict in Relational Systems

So far we have focused on individual conflict styles. Even though the style you choose in a conflict is important, your style isn't the only factor that will determine how a conflict unfolds. In reality, conflict is *relational:* Its character usually is determined by the way the parties interact with each other.[32] You might, for example, be determined to handle a conflict with your neighbor assertively, only to be driven to aggression by his uncooperative nature—or even to nonassertion by his physical threats. Likewise, you might plan to hint to a professor that you are bothered by her apparent indifference, but wind up discussing the matter in an open, assertive way in reaction to her constructive response. Examples like these suggest that conflict doesn't depend on just individual choice. Rather, it depends on how the partners interact. When two or more people are in a long-term relationship they develop their own **relational conflict style**—a pattern of managing disagreements. The mutual influence that parties have on each other is so powerful that it can overcome our disposition to handle conflicts in the manner that comes most easily to one or the other.[33] As we will soon see, some relational conflict styles are constructive, whereas others can make life miserable and threaten relationships.

Complementary, Symmetrical, and Parallel Styles

Partners in interpersonal relationships—and impersonal ones, too—can use one of three styles to manage their conflicts. In relationships with a **complementary conflict style**, the partners use different but mutually reinforcing behaviors. In a **symmetrical conflict style**, both partners use the same behaviors. In a **parallel conflict style**, both partners shift between complementary and symmetrical patterns from one issue to another. Table 11.2 illustrates how the same conflict can unfold in very different ways, depending on whether the partners' communication is symmetrical or complementary. A parallel style would alternate between these two patterns, depending on the situation.

Research shows that a complementary "fight-flight" style is common in many unhappy marriages. One partner—most commonly the wife—addresses the conflict directly, whereas the other—usually the husband—withdraws.[34] It's easy to see how this pattern can lead to a cycle of increasing hostility and isolation because each partner punctuates the conflict differently, blaming the other for making matters worse. "I withdraw because she's so critical," a husband might say. The wife wouldn't organize the sequence in the same way, however. "I criticize because he withdraws" would be her perception.

Complementary styles aren't the only ones that can lead to problems. Some distressed marriages suffer from destructively symmetrical communication. If both

Table 11.2	Complementary and Symmetrical Conflict Styles	
Situation	Complementary Styles	Symmetrical Styles
Example 1: Wife upset because husband is spending little time at home.	Wife complains; husband withdraws, spending even less time at home. (Destructive)	Wife complains. Husband responds angrily and defensively. (Destructive)
Example 2: Female employee offended when male boss calls her "sweetie."	Employee objects to boss, explaining her reasons for being offended. Boss apologizes for his unintentional insult. (Constructive)	Employee maliciously "jokes" about boss at company party. (Destructive)
Example 3: Parents uncomfortable with teenager's new friends.	Parents express concerns. Teen dismisses them, saying "There's nothing to worry about." (Destructive)	Teen expresses discomfort with parents' protectiveness. Parents and teen negotiate a mutually agreeable solution. (Constructive)

partners treat each other with matching hostility, one threat or insult leads to another in an escalatory spiral. If the partners both withdraw from each other instead of facing their problems, a de-escalatory spiral results, in which the satisfaction and vitality ebb from the relationship, leaving it a shell of its former self.

As Table 11.2 shows, both complementary and symmetrical behaviors can produce "good" results as well as "bad" results. If the complementary behaviors are positive, then a positive spiral results and the conflict stands a good chance of being resolved. This is the case in Example 2 in Table 11.2, where the boss is open to hearing the employee's concerns, listening willingly as the employee talks. Here, a complementary talk-listen pattern works well.

Symmetrical styles can also be beneficial. The clearest example of constructive symmetry occurs when both parties communicate assertively, listening to each other's concerns and working together to resolve them. The potential for this sort of solution occurs in Example 3, in the parent-teenager conflict. With enough mutual respect and careful listening, both the parents and their teenager can understand one another's concerns and very possibly find a way to give both parties what they want.

Intimate and Aggressive Styles

Another way to look at conflict styles is to examine the interaction between intimacy and aggression. The following scheme was originally used to describe communication between couples, but it also works well for other types of relationships.

■ *Nonintimate-Aggressive* These partners fight but are unsuccessful at satisfying important content and relational goals. In some relationships aggression is expressed directly: "Forget it. I'm not going to another stupid party with your friends. All they do is gossip and eat." In other relationships, indirect aggression is the norm: (*Sarcastically*) "Sure I'd *love* to go to another party with your friends." Neither of these approaches is satisfying because there are few rewards to justify the costs of the unpleasantness.

- *Nonintimate-Nonaggressive* The parties avoid conflicts—and each other—instead of facing issues head-on: "You won't be coming home for the holidays? Oh, well, I guess that's OK. . . ." Relationships of this sort can be quite stable, but because this pattern of communication doesn't confront and resolve problems, the vitality and satisfaction can decline over time.
- *Intimate-Aggressive* This pattern combines aggression and intimacy in a manner that might seem upsetting to outsiders but that can work well in some relationships. Lovers may argue like cats and dogs, but then make up just as intensely. Co-workers might argue heatedly about how to get the job done, but cherish their association.
- *Intimate-Nonaggressive* This sort of relationship has a low amount of attacking or blaming. Partners may confront each other directly or indirectly, but one way or another they manage to prevent issues from interfering with their relationship.

The pattern that partners choose may reveal a great deal about the kind of relationship they have chosen. Communication researcher Mary Ann Fitzpatrick identified three types of couples, which she descriptively labeled as "separates," "independents," and "traditionals."[35] Further research revealed that partners in each type of relationship approached conflict in a different manner.[36] Separates and independents tended to avoid conflict. Traditionals, by contrast, spent the most time focusing on their interaction. They also felt most secure about their relationships. They expressed negative emotions frequently but also sought and revealed a large amount of personal information. Satisfied traditional couples fit the intimate-nonaggressive pattern, communicating more positive and less negative information than independents.

Findings like this suggest that there's no single "best" relational conflict style.[37] Some families or couples may fight intensely but love one another just as strongly. Others might handle issues more rationally and calmly. Even a nonintimate-nonaggressive style can work well when there's no desire to have an interpersonal relationship. You might, for example, be willing to accommodate the demands of an eccentric professor for a semester because rolling with the punches gets you the education you are seeking without provoking a confrontation that could be upsetting and costly.

"I'm not yelling *at* you, I'm yelling *with* you."

Invitation to Insight

Understanding Conflict Styles

You can gain a clearer idea of how conflict styles differ by completing the following exercise.

1. Join a partner, and choose one of the following conflicts to work on. If you prefer, you may substitute a conflict of your own.

   Roommates disagree about the noise level in their apartment.

   Parents want their college sophomore son or daughter to stay home for the winter vacation. The son or daughter wants to travel with friends.

   One person in a couple wants to spend free time socializing with friends. The other wants to stay at home together.

2. Role-play the conflict four times, reflecting each of the following styles:

   Nonintimate-Aggressive   Intimate-Aggressive

   Nonintimate-Nonaggressive   Intimate-Nonaggressive

3. After experiencing each of these styles, determine which of them characterizes the way conflict is managed in one of your interpersonal relationships. Are you satisfied with this approach? If not, describe what style would be more appropriate.

Conflict Rituals

When people have been in a relationship for some time, their communication often develops into **conflict rituals**—usually unacknowledged but very real patterns of interlocking behavior.[38] Consider a few common rituals:

- A young child interrupts her parents, demanding to be included in their conversation. At first the parents tell the child to wait, but she whines and cries until the parents find it easier to listen than to ignore the fussing.
- A couple fights. One partner leaves. The other accepts the blame for the problem and begs forgiveness. The first partner returns, and a happy reunion takes place. Soon they fight again.
- A boss flies into rage when the pressure builds at work. Recognizing this, the employees avoid him as much as possible. When the crisis is over, the boss compensates for his outbursts by being especially receptive to employee requests.
- Roommates have a blowout over housekeeping responsibilities. One roommate gives the other "the silent treatment" for several days, then begins picking up around the house without admitting being wrong.

There's nothing inherently wrong with the interaction in many rituals, especially when everybody involved accepts them as ways of managing conflict.[39] Consider the preceding examples. In the first, the little girl's whining may be the only way she can get the parents' attention. In the second, both partners might use the fighting as a way to blow off steam, and both might find that the joy of a reunion is worth the grief of the separation. In the third, the ritual might work well for the boss (as a way of releasing pressure) and for employees (as a way of getting their requests met). And in the fourth, at least the house gets cleaned—eventually.

Rituals can cause problems, though, when they become the *only* way relational partners handle their conflicts. As you learned in Chapter 1, competent communicators have a large repertoire of behaviors, and they are able to choose the most effective response for a given situation. Relying on one ritual pattern to handle all conflicts is no more effective than using a screwdriver to handle every home repair or putting the same seasoning on every dish you cook. Conflict rituals may be familiar and comfortable, but they aren't always the best way to resolve the various conflicts that are part of any relationship.

Invitation to Insight

Your Conflict Rituals

Describe two conflict rituals in one of your important relationships. One of your examples should consist of a positive ritual and the other of a negative ritual. For each example, explain

1. A subject that is likely to trigger the conflict (such as, money, leisure time, affection)

2. The behavior of one partner that initiates the ritual

3. The series of responses by both partners that follows the initiating event

4. How the ritual ends

Based on your description, explain an alternative to the unsatisfying ritual, and describe how you might be able to change the way you manage the conflict in a more satisfying way.

Variables in Conflict Styles

By now you can see that every relational system is unique. The communication patterns in one family, business, or classroom are likely to be very different from those in any other. But along with the differences that arise in individual relationships, there are two powerful variables that affect the way people manage conflict: gender and culture. We will now look at each of these variables and see how they affect how conflict is managed.

Gender

Men and women often approach conflicts differently. Even in childhood, males are more likely to be aggressive, demanding, and competitive, whereas females are more likely to be cooperative. Studies of children from preschool to early adolescence have shown that boys try to get their way by ordering one another around: "Lie down." "Get off my steps." "Gimme your arm." By contrast, girls are more likely to make proposals for action, beginning with the word "Let's": "Let's go find some." "Let's ask her, 'Do you have any bottles?' " "Let's move *these* out *first*."[40] Whereas boys tell each other what role to take in pretend play ("Come on, be a doctor"), girls more commonly ask each other what role they want ("Will you be the patient for a few minutes?") or make a joint proposal ("We can both be doctors"). Furthermore, boys often make demands without offering an explanation ("Look, man. I want the wire cutters right now."). By contrast, girls often give reasons for their suggestions ("We gotta *clean* 'em first . . . 'cause they got germs.").

Adolescent girls use aggression in conflicts, but their methods are usually more indirect than those of boys. Whereas teenage boys often engage in verbal showdowns, and may even engage in physical fights, teenage girls typically use gossip, backbiting, and social exclusion.[41] This is not to suggest that girls' aggression is any less destructive than boys'. The film *Mean Girls* (based on the book *Queen Bees and Wannabes*[42]) offers a vivid depiction of just how injurious these indirect assaults can be on the self-concepts and relationships of young women.

Invitation to Insight

ABC News: "Mean Girls"

ThomsonNOW To learn more about how gender rules shape aggression among some American teens, view the ABC News feature "Mean Girls." You can access this video through your ThomsonNOW for *Looking Out/Looking In*.

Gender differences in dealing with conflict often persist into adulthood. One survey of college students revealed that men and women viewed conflicts in contrasting ways.[43] Regardless of their cultural background, female students described men as being concerned with power and more interested in content than relational issues. Phrases used to describe male conflict styles included: "The most important thing to males in conflict is their egos." "Men don't worry about feelings." "Men are more direct." By contrast, women were described as being more concerned with maintaining the relationship during a conflict. Phrases used to describe female conflict styles included: "Women are better listeners." "Women try to solve problems without controlling the other person." "Females are more concerned with others' feelings." When the actual conflict behaviors of both sexes are observed, women turn out to be more assertive than men about expressing their ideas and feelings, and men are more likely to withdraw from discussing issues.[44]

These sorts of differences don't mean that men are incapable of forming good relationships. Instead, their notions of what makes a good relationship are different. For some men, friendship and aggression aren't mutually exclusive. In fact, many strong male relationships are built around competition—at work or in athletics, for example. Women can be competitive, too, but they also are more likely to use logical reasoning and bargaining than aggression.[45] When men communicate with women, they become less aggressive and more cooperative than they are in all-male groups.

In contrast with the "men are from Mars, women are from Venus" view of conflict, a look at the entire body of research on gender and conflict suggests that the differences in how the two sexes handle conflict are relatively small, and sometimes different from the stereotypical picture of aggressive men and passive women.[46] It would appear that people may *think* there are greater differences in male and female ways of handling conflicts than there actually are.[47] People who assume that men are aggressive and women accommodating may notice behavior that fits these stereotypes ("See how much he bosses her around. A typical man!"). On the other hand, behavior that doesn't fit these stereotypes (accommodating men, pushy women) goes unnoticed.

Where men and women do have characteristically different conflict styles, the reasons may have little to do with gender. The situation at hand has a greater influence on shaping the way a person handles conflict.[48] For example, both men and women are more likely to respond aggressively when attacked by the other person. (Recall the discussion of defensive spirals in Chapter 10.) In fact, researchers exploring how married couples handle disagreements found that the importance of gender in determining conflict style is "dwarfed" by the behavior of the other person.[49]

What, then, can we conclude about the influence of gender on conflict? Research has demonstrated that there are, indeed, some small but measurable differences in the two sexes. But, although men and women may have characteristically different conflict styles, the individual style of each communicator—regardless of gender—and the nature of the relationship are more important than gender in shaping the way he or she handles conflict.

Culture

The way in which people manage conflict varies tremendously depending on their cultural background. The straight-talking, assertive approach that characterizes many North Americans is not the universal norm.[50]

Perhaps the most important cultural factor in shaping attitudes toward conflict is an orientation toward individualism or collectivism.[51] In individualistic cultures like the United States, the goals, rights, and needs of each person are considered important, and most people would agree that it is an individual's right to stand up for himself or herself. By contrast, collectivist cultures (more common in Latin America and Asia) consider the concerns of the group to be more important than those of any individual. In these cultures, the kind of assertive behavior that might seem perfectly appropriate to a North American would be regarded as rude and insensitive.

Another factor that distinguishes the assertiveness that is so valued by North Americans and northern Europeans is the difference between high- and low-context cultural styles.[52] Recall from our discussion in Chapter 6 that low-context cultures like the United States place a premium on being direct and literal. By contrast, high-context cultures like Japan value self-restraint and avoid confrontation. Communicators in these cultures derive meaning from a variety of unspoken rules, such as context, social conventions, and hints. Preserving and honoring the face of the other person is a prime goal, and communicators go to great lengths to avoid any communication that might risk embarrassing a conversational partner. For this reason, what seems like "beating around the bush" to an American would be polite to an Asian. In Japan, for example, even a simple request like "close the door" would be too straightforward.[53] A more indirect statement such as "It is somewhat cold today" would be more appropriate. To take a more important example, Japanese are reluctant to say "no" to a request. A more likely answer would be "let me think about it for a while," which anyone familiar with Japanese culture would recognize as a refusal.

© Historical Picture Archive/Corbis

When indirect communication is a cultural norm, it is unreasonable to expect more straightforward approaches to succeed. When people from different cultures face a conflict, their habitual communication patterns may not mesh smoothly. The challenge faced by an American husband and his Taiwanese wife illustrates this sort of problem. The husband would try to confront his wife verbally and directly (as is typical in the United States), leading her to either become defensive or withdraw completely from the discussion. She, on the other hand, would attempt to indicate her displeasure by changes in mood and eye contact (typical of Chinese culture) that were either not noticed or uninterpretable by her husband. Thus, neither "his way" nor "her way" was working and they could not see any realistic way to "compromise."[54]

It isn't necessary to look at Asia to encounter cultural differences in conflict. Americans visiting Greece, for example, often think they are witnessing an argument when they are overhearing a friendly conversation.[55] A comparative study of American and Italian nursery schoolchildren showed that one of the Italian children's favorite pastimes was a kind of heated debating that Italians call *discussione* but that Americans would call arguing. Likewise, research has shown that the conversations of working-class Jewish speakers of eastern European origin used arguments as a means of being sociable.

Within the United States, the ethnic background of communicators also plays a role in their ideas about conflict. When members of a group of African American, Mexican American, and Anglo American college students were asked about their views regarding conflict, some important differences emerged.[56] For example, Anglo Americans seem more willing to accept conflict as a natural part of relationships, whereas Mexican Americans describe the short- and long-term dangers of conflict. Anglos' willingness to experience conflicts may be part of their individualistic, low-context communication style of speaking directly and avoiding uncertainty. It's not surprising that people from more collective, high-context cultures that emphasize harmony among people with close relationships tend to handle conflicts in less direct ways. With differences like these, it's easy to imagine how two friends, lovers, or fellow workers from different cultural backgrounds might have trouble finding a conflict style that is comfortable for them both.

Despite these differences, it's important to realize that culture isn't the only factor that influences the way people approach conflict or how they behave when they disagree. Some research suggests that our approach to conflict may be part of our biological makeup.[57] Furthermore, scholarship suggests that a person's self-concept is more powerful than his or her culture in determining conflict style.[58] For example, an assertive person raised in an environment that downplays conflict is still likely to be more aggressive than an unassertive person who grew up in a culture where conflicts are common. You might handle conflicts calmly in a job where rationality and civility are the norm, but shriek like a banshee at home if that's the way you and a relational partner handle conflicts. Finally, as the Looking at Diversity profile on page 387 illustrates, the way each of us deals with conflict is a matter of personal choice. We can choose to follow unproductive patterns, or we can choose more constructive approaches.

Constructive Conflict Skills

The collaborative, win-win conflict style described earlier in this chapter has many advantages over win-lose and lose-lose approaches. Why, then, is it so rarely used? There are three reasons. The first is lack of awareness. Some people are so used to competition that they mistakenly think that winning requires them to defeat their "opponent."

Even when they know better, another reason prevents many people from seeking win-win solutions. Conflicts are often emotional affairs, in which people react

Looking at Diversity

Manny Raya: Leading by Example

I grew up in a Hispanic neighborhood where almost nobody went to college. If you wanted to be admired and respected, you joined a gang and showed that you were tough and bad.

By the 5th grade, my friends and I were drinking, fighting, and tagging. In the 9th grade I was labeled as a violent offender and sent to probation school. In the next couple of years I was arrested for two felonies: possession of a deadly weapon and gang terrorism. At that point I expected to spend most of my adult life in jail.

While I was on probation, a counselor persuaded me get a job and attend community college. I didn't expect to like either work or school, but that's when my life began to turn around.

Most of the people where I worked were surfers, and just for fun I decided to give it a try. I got a board and wetsuit, and just paddled out. The locals were pretty amazed to see me out there, but they were really friendly and helpful. I discovered that I could be a welcome part of a different world.

About the same time, in my college philosophy class, we read about Plato's allegory of the cave. A prisoner in the cave has only seen reflected shadows of the real world. Once he's released, he sees reality for the first time. I realized that that story described me up to then, and that I had the choice to live in a larger world.

Once he's free, the cave prisoner wants to share that reality with people still trapped in the shadow world. Like that prisoner, I want to show people from backgrounds like mine that there's more to life than fighting and prison. Another gang member-surfer and I started the Homies Turf to Surf camp. Every summer, we try to show kids who are already in trouble that there's an alternative to a lifestyle of fighting and jail.

I'm proud to say that we have turned some young lives around—but not by preaching. I still love my Hispanic community and my gang brothers, and don't ever disrespect them. I've learned that the best way to help people change is to provide a good example and then step back and let them make a choice. Forcing just doesn't work.

Photo courtesy of Manny Raya

combatively without stopping to think of better alternatives. Because this kind of emotional reflex prevents constructive solutions, it's often necessary to stop yourself from speaking out aggressively during a conflict and starting an escalating spiral of defensiveness. The time-honored advice of "counting to ten" applies here. After you've thought about the matter, you'll be able to *act* constructively instead of *reacting* in a way that's likely to produce a lose-lose outcome.

A third reason win-win solutions are rare is that they require the other person's cooperation. It's difficult to negotiate constructively with someone who insists on trying to defeat you. In this case, use your best persuasive skills to explain that by working together you can find a solution that satisfies both of you.

In spite of these challenges, it is definitely possible to become better at resolving conflicts. In the following pages we will outline a method to increase your chances of being able to handle your conflicts in a collaborative, win-win manner. As you read the following steps, try to imagine yourself applying them to a problem that's bothering you now.

Identify Your Problem and Unmet Needs

Before you speak out, it's important to realize that the problem that is causing conflict is yours. Whether you want to return an unsatisfactory piece of merchandise, complain to noisy neighbors because your sleep is being disturbed, or request a change in working conditions from your employer, the problem is yours. Why? Because in each case *you* are the person who "owns" the problem—the one who is dissatisfied. You are the one who has paid for the unsatisfactory merchandise; the merchant who sold it to you has the use of your good money. You are the one who is losing sleep as a result of your neighbors' noise; they are content to go on as before. You are the one who is unhappy with your working conditions, not your employer.[*]

Realizing that the problem is yours will make a big difference when the time comes to approach the other party. Instead of feeling and acting in an evaluative way, you'll be more likely to state your problem in a descriptive way, which will not only be more accurate but also reduce the chance of a defensive reaction.

After you realize that the problem is yours, the next step is to identify the unmet needs that make you dissatisfied. For instance, in the barking dog example, your need may be to get some sleep or to study without interruptions. In the case of a friend who teases you in public, your need would probably be to avoid embarrassment.

Sometimes the task of identifying your needs isn't as simple as it first seems. Behind the apparent content of an issue is often a relational need. Consider this example: A friend hasn't returned some money you lent long ago. Your apparent need in this situation might be to get the money back. But a little thought will probably show that this isn't the only, or even the main, thing you want. Even if you were rolling in money, you'd probably want the loan repaid because of a more important need: *to avoid feeling victimized by your friend's taking advantage of you.*

As you'll soon see, the ability to identify your real needs plays a key role in solving interpersonal problems. For now, the point to remember is that before you voice your problem to your partner, you ought to be clear about which of your needs aren't being met.

"Is this a good time to have a big fight?"

Make a Date

Destructive fights often start because the initiator confronts a partner who isn't ready. There are many times when a person isn't in the right frame of mind to face a conflict, perhaps owing to fatigue, being in too much of a hurry to take the necessary time, being upset over another problem, or not feeling well. At times like these it's unfair to "jump" a person without notice and expect to get full attention for your problem. If you do persist, you'll probably have an ugly fight on your hands.

After you have a clear idea of the problem, approach your partner with a request to try to solve it. For example, "Something's been bothering me. Can we talk about it?"

---

[*] Of course, others involved in the conflict may have problems of their own. For instance, the merchant, the noisy neighbors, and your employer may all be bothered by your requests. But the fact remains that the reason you are speaking up about these matters is because you are dissatisfied. Thus, the problem is at least initially yours.

If the answer is "yes," you're ready to go further. If it isn't the right time to confront your partner, find a time that's agreeable to both of you.

Describe Your Problem and Needs

Your partner can't possibly meet your needs without knowing why you're upset and what you want. Therefore, it's up to you to describe your problem as specifically as possible. The best way to deliver a complete, accurate message is to use the assertive, clear message format discussed in Chapter 10. Notice how well this approach works in the following examples:

Example 1

"I have a problem. It's about your leaving dirty clothes around the house after I've told you how much it bothers me (*behavior*). It's a problem because I have to run around like crazy and pick things up whenever guests come, which is no fun at all (*consequence*). I'm starting to think that either you're not paying attention to my requests or you're trying to drive me crazy (*thoughts*), and either way I'm getting more and more resentful (*feeling*). I'd like to find some way to have a neat place without my having to be a maid or a nag."

Example 2

"I have a problem. When you drop by without calling ahead, and I'm studying (*behavior*), I don't know whether to visit or ask you to leave (*thought*). Either way, I get uncomfortable (*feeling*), and it seems like whatever I do, I lose: Either I have to put you off or get behind in my work (*consequences*). I'd like to find a way to get my studying done and still socialize with you (*intention*)."

Example 3

"Something is bothering me. When you tell me you love me and yet spend almost all your free time with your other friends (*behavior*), I wonder whether you mean it (*thought*). I get insecure (*feeling*), and then I start acting moody (*consequence*). I need some way of finding out for sure how you feel about me (*intention*)."

After stating your problem and describing what you need, it's important to make sure that your partner has understood what you've said. As you can remember from the discussion of listening in Chapter 7, there's a good chance—especially in a stressful conflict—that your words will be misinterpreted.

It's usually unrealistic to insist that your partner paraphrase your statement, and fortunately there are more tactful and subtle ways to make sure that you've been understood. For instance, you might try saying, "I'm not sure I expressed myself very well just now—maybe you should tell what you heard me say so I can be sure I got it right." In any case, be absolutely sure that your partner understands your whole message before going any further. Legitimate agreements are tough enough without getting upset about a conflict that doesn't even exist.

> Our marriage used to suffer from arguments that were too short. Now we argue long enough to find out what the argument is about.
>
> Hugh Prather

Consider Your Partner's Point of View

After you have made your position clear, it's time to find out what your partner needs to feel satisfied about this issue. There are two reasons why it's important to discover your partner's needs. First, it's fair. Your partner has just as much right as you to feel satisfied, and if you expect help in meeting your needs, it's reasonable that you behave in the same way. But in addition to fairness, there's another, practical reason for concerning yourself with what your partner wants. Just as an unhappy partner will make it hard for you to become satisfied, a happy partner will be more likely to cooperate in letting you reach your goals. Thus, it's in your own self-interest to discover and meet your partner's needs.

You can learn about your partner's needs simply by asking about them: "Now I've told you what I want and why. Tell me what you need to feel OK about this." After your partner begins to talk, your job is to use the listening skills discussed earlier in this book to make sure that you understand.

Negotiate a Solution

Now that you and your partner understand each other's needs, the goal becomes finding a way to meet them. This is done by developing as many potential solutions as possible and then evaluating them to decide which one best meets everyone's needs. Probably the best description of the win-win approach was written by Thomas Gordon in his book *Parent Effectiveness Training*.[59] The following steps are a modification of this approach.

1. *Identify and define the conflict.* We've discussed identifying and defining the conflict in the preceding pages. These consist of discovering each person's problem and needs, setting the stage for meeting all of them.
2. *Generate a number of possible solutions.* In this step, the partners work together to think of as many means as possible to reach their stated ends. The key concept here is quantity: It's important to generate as many ideas as you can think of without worrying about which ones are good or bad. Write down every thought that comes up, no matter how unworkable: Sometimes a far-fetched idea will lead to a more workable one.
3. *Evaluate the alternative solutions.* This is the time to talk about which solutions will work and which ones won't. It's important for all parties to be honest about their willingness to accept an idea. If a solution is going to work, everyone involved has to support it.
4. *Decide on the best solution.* Now that you've looked at all the alternatives, pick the one that looks best to everyone. It's important to be sure that everybody understands the solution and is willing to try it out. Remember that your decision doesn't have to be final, but it should look potentially successful.

Follow Up the Solution

You can't be sure that the solution will work until you try it. After you've tested it for a while, it's a good idea to set aside some time to talk over its progress. You may find that you need to make some changes or even rethink the whole problem. The idea is to keep on top of the problem, to keep using creativity to solve it.

As you think about applying this method, it is important to keep two points in mind. First, realize the importance of following every step. Each one is essential to the success of your encounter, and skipping one or more steps can lead to misunderstandings that might cause the conversation to degenerate into a negative spiral. After you have practiced the method a number of times and are familiar with it, this type of problem solving will become almost second nature. You will then be able to approach your conflicts without following this

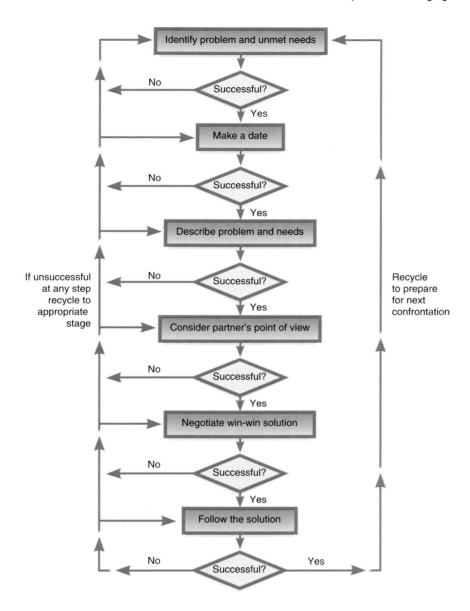

FIGURE 11.2
Flow Chart of the
Win-Win Negotiation
Process

Adapted from Rory Remer and Paul
deMesquita. "Teaching and Learning
Skills of Interpersonal Confrontation,"
in *Intimates in Conflict: A Communication Perspective* edited by Cahn
©1990 p. 227.

step-by-step approach. But for the time being try to be patient and trust the value of the pattern.

You can expect and prepare for a certain amount of resistance from the other person. As Figure 11.2 shows, when a step doesn't meet with success, simply move back and repeat the preceding ones as necessary.

Win-win solutions aren't always possible. There will be times when even the best-intentioned people simply won't be able to find a way of meeting all their needs. In times like these, the process of negotiation has to include some compromises. But even then the preceding steps haven't been wasted. The genuine desire to learn what the other person wants and to try to satisfy those wants will build a climate of goodwill that can help you find the best solution to the present problem and also improve your relationship in the future.

Communication Transcript

Win-Win Problem Solving

It is 7:15 A.M. on a typical school day. Chris enters the kitchen and finds the sink full of dirty dishes. It was her roommate Terry's turn to do them. She sighs in disgust and begins to clean up, slamming pots and pans.

Terry   Can't you be a little more quiet? I don't have a class till 10:00, and I want to catch up on sleep.

Chris   *(Expressing her aggression indirectly in a sarcastic tone of voice)* Sorry to bother you. I was cleaning up last night's dinner dishes.

Terry   *(Misses the message)* Well, I wish you'd do it a little more quietly. I was up late studying last night, and I'm beat.

Chris   *(Decides to communicate her irritation more directly, if aggressively)* Well, if you'd done the dishes last night, I wouldn't have had to wash them now.

Terry   *(Finally realizes that Chris is mad at her, responds defensively)* I was going to do them when I got up. I've got two midterms this week, and I was studying until midnight last night. What's more important, grades or a spotless kitchen?

Chris   *(Perpetuating the growing defensive spiral)* I've got classes, too, you know. But that doesn't mean we have to live like pigs!

Terry   *(Angrily)* Forget it. If it's such a big deal, I'll never leave another dirty dish!

Chris and Terry avoid each other as they get ready for school. During the day Chris realizes that attacking Terry will only make matters worse. She decides on a more constructive approach that evening.

Chris   That wasn't much fun this morning. Want to talk about it?

Terry   I suppose so. But I'm going out to study with Kim and Alisa in a few minutes.

Chris   *(Realizing that it's important to talk at a good time)* If you have to leave soon, let's not get into it now. How about talking when you get back?

Terry   OK, if I'm not too tired.

Chris   Or we could talk tomorrow before class.

Terry   OK.

Later that evening Terry and Chris continue their conversation.

Chris   *(Defines the issue as her problem by using the assertive clear message format)* I hated to start the day with a fight. But I also hate having to do the dishes when it's not my turn *(behavior)*. It doesn't seem fair for me to do my job and yours *(interpretation)*, and that's why I got so mad *(feeling)* and nagged at you *(consequence)*.

Terry   But I was studying! You know how much I have to do. It's not like I was partying.

Chris   *(Avoids attacking Terry by sincerely agreeing with the facts and explaining further why she was upset)* I know. It wasn't just doing the dishes that got me upset. It seems like there have been a lot of times when I've done your jobs and mine, too.

Terry   *(Defensively)* Like when?

Chris   *(Gives specific descriptions of Terry's behavior)* Well, this was the third time this week that I've done the dishes when it's your turn, and I can think of a couple of times lately when I've had to clean up your stuff before people came over.

Terry   I don't see why it's such a big deal. If you just leave the stuff there, I'll clean it up.

Chris   *(Still trying to explain herself, she continues to use "I" language)* I know you would. I guess it's harder for me to put up with a messy place than it is for you.

Terry   Yeah. If you'd just relax, living together would be a lot easier!

Chris   *(Resenting Terry's judgmental accusation that the problem is all hers)* Hey, wait a second! Don't blame the whole thing on me. It's just that we have different standards. It looks to you like I'm too hung up on keeping the place clean . . .

Terry   Right.

Chris   . . . and if we do it your way, then I'd be giving up. I'd have to either live with the place messier than I like it or clean everything up myself. Then I'd get mad at you, and things would be pretty tense around here. *(Describes the unpleasant consequences of not solving the problem in a mutually satisfactory way)*

Terry   I suppose so.

Chris   We need to figure out how to take care of the apartment in a way that we can both live with. *(Describes the broad outline of a win-win solution)*

Terry   Yeah.

Chris   So what could we do?

Terry   *(Sounding resigned)* Look, from now on I'll just do the dishes right away. It isn't worth arguing about.

Chris   Sure it is. If you're sore, the apartment may be clean, but it won't be worth it.

Terry   *(Skeptically)* OK; what do you suggest?

Chris   Well, I'm not sure. You don't want the pressure of having to clean up right away, and I don't want to have to do my jobs and yours, too. Right?

Terry   Yeah. *(Still sounding skeptical)* So what are we going to do—hire a housekeeper to clean up?

Chris   *(Refusing to let Terry sidetrack the discussion)* That would be great if we could afford it. How about using paper plates? That would make cleaning up from meals easier.

Terry   Yeah, but there would still be pots and pans.

Chris   Well, it's not a perfect fix, but it might help a little. *(Goes on to suggest other ideas)* How about cooking meals that don't take a lot of work to clean up—maybe more salads and less fried stuff that sticks to pans. That would be a better diet, too.

Terry   Yeah. I do hate to scrub crusty frying pans. But that doesn't do anything about your wanting the living room picked up all the time, and I bet I still wouldn't keep the kitchen as clean as you like it. Keeping the place super clean just isn't as big a deal to me as it is for you.

Chris   That's true, and I don't want to have to nag you! *(Clarifies the end she's seeking)* You know, it's not really cleaning up that bothers me. It's doing more than my share of work. I wonder if there's a way I could be responsible for keeping the kitchen clean and picking up if you could do something else to keep the workload even.

Terry   Are you serious? I'd love to get out of doing the dishes! You mean you'd do them . . . and keep the place picked up . . . if I did something else?

Chris   As long as the work was equal and you really did your jobs without me having to remind you.

Terry   What kind of work would you want me to do?

Chris   How about cleaning up the bathroom?

Terry   Forget it. That's worse than doing the dishes.

Chris   OK. How about cooking?

Terry   That might work, but then we'd have to eat together all the time. It's nice to do our own cooking when we want to. It's more flexible that way.

Chris   OK. But what about shopping? I hate the time it takes, and you don't mind it that much, do you?

Terry   You mean shop for groceries? You'd trade that for cleaning the kitchen?

Chris   Sure. And picking up the living room. It takes an hour each time we shop, and we make two trips every week. Doing the dishes would be much quicker.

Terry   All right!

The plan didn't work perfectly: At first Terry put off shopping until all the food was gone, and Chris took advantage by asking Terry to run other errands during her shopping trips. But their new arrangement proved much more successful than the old arrangement. The apartment was cleaner and the workload more even, which satisfied Chris. Terry was less the object of Chris's nagging, and she had no kitchen chores, which made her happier. Just as important, the relationship between Chris and Terry was more comfortable—thanks to win-win problem solving.

Communication Scenarios

To see and analyze a dramatized version of the interactions between Chris and Terry, go to your Thomson-NOW for *Looking Out/Looking In*, access "Communication Scenarios," and then click on "Win-Win Problem Solving." **ThomsonNOW**

Constructive Conflict: Questions and Answers

After learning about win-win negotiating, people often express doubts about how well it can work. "It sounds like a good idea," they say, "but . . ." Three questions arise more than any others, and they deserve an answer.

Isn't the Win-Win Approach Too Good to Be True?

Research shows that seeking mutual benefit is not just a good idea—it actually works. In fact, the win-win approach produces better results than a win-lose approach.

In a series of experiments, researchers presented subjects with a bargaining situation called "prisoner's dilemma," in which they could choose either to cooperate or betray a confederate.[60] There are three types of outcomes in prisoner's dilemma: One partner can win big by betraying a confederate, both can win by cooperating, or both can lose by betraying each other. Although cynics might assume that the most effective strategy is to betray a partner (a win-lose approach), researchers found that cooperation is actually the best hard-nosed strategy. Players who demonstrated their willingness to support the other person and not hold grudges did better than those using a more competitive approach.

There are certainly some conflicts that can't be resolved with win-win approaches. Only one suitor can marry the prince or princess, and only one person can be hired for the advertised job. Furthermore, it's impossible to reach a win-win solution when your partner refuses to cooperate. Most of the time, however, good intentions and creative thinking can lead to outcomes that satisfy everyone's needs.

Isn't the Win-Win Approach Too Elaborate?

The win-win approach is detailed and highly structured. In everyday life you may rarely use every step: Sometimes the problem at hand won't justify the effort, and at other times you and your partner might not need to be so deliberate to take care of the problem. Nonetheless, while learning to use the approach try to follow all the steps carefully. After you have become familiar with and skillful at using them all, you will be able to use whichever ones prove necessary in a given situation. For important issues, you are likely to find that every step of the win-win approach is important. If this process seems time-consuming, just consider the time and energy that will likely be required if you *don't* resolve the issue at hand.

Isn't Win-Win Negotiating Too Rational?

Frustrated readers often complain that the win-win approach is so sensible that only a saint could use it successfully. "Sometimes I'm so angry that I don't care about being supportive or empathetic or anything else," they say. "I just want to blow my top!"

At times like this, you might need to temporarily remove yourself from the situation so you don't say or do something you'll later regret. You might feel better confiding in a third party. Or you might blow off steam with physical exercise. There are even cases when an understanding partner might allow you to have what has been called a "Vesuvius"—an uncontrolled, spontaneous explosion. Before you blow your top, though, be sure that your partner understands what you're doing and realizes that whatever you say doesn't call for a response. Your partner should let you rant and rave for as long as you want without getting defensive or "tying in." Then when your eruption subsides, you can take steps to work through whatever still troubles you.

Is It Possible to Change Others?

Readers often agree that win-win problem solving would be terrific—if everyone had read *Looking Out/Looking In* and understood the method. "How can I get the other person to cooperate?" the question goes.

Though you won't always be able to gain your partner's cooperation, a good job of selling can do the trick most of the time. The key lies in showing that it's in your partner's self-interest to work together with you: "Look, if we can't settle this, we'll both feel miserable. But if we can find an answer, think how much better off we'll be." Notice that this sort of explanation projects both the favorable consequences of cooperating and the unfavorable consequences of competing.

You can also boost the odds of getting your partner's cooperation by modeling the communication skills described in this book. You've read that defense-arousing behavior is reciprocal, but so is supportive communication. If you can listen sincerely, avoid evaluative attacks, and empathize with your partner's concerns, for example, there's a good chance that you'll get the same kind of behavior in return. And even if your cooperative attitude doesn't succeed, you'll gain self-respect from knowing that at least you behaved honorably and constructively.

Summary

Conflict is a fact of life in every interpersonal relationship. The way in which conflicts are handled plays a major role in the quality of a relationship. When managed constructively, conflicts can lead to stronger and more satisfying interaction; but when they are handled poorly, relationships will suffer.

Communicators can respond to conflicts in a variety of ways: avoiding, accommodatng, competing, compromising, or collaborating. Each of these approaches can be justified in certain circumstances. The way a conflict is handled is not always the choice of a single person, because the parties influence each other as they develop a relational conflict style. This style may be complementary, symmetrical, or parallel; it can involve a combination of intimate and aggressive elements; and it can involve constructive or destructive rituals. Besides being shaped by the relationship, a conflict style is also shaped by a person's gender and cultural background.

In most circumstances a collaborative, win-win outcome is the ideal, and it can be achieved by following the guidelines outlined on pages 387–390.

Key Terms

accommodating (372)
avoiding (370)
collaborating (376)
competing (372)
complementary conflict
  style (379)

compromising (376)
conflict (367)
conflict ritual (382)
crazymaking (374)
direct aggression (374)
lose-lose problem solving (372)

parallel conflict style (379)
passive aggression (374)
relational conflict style (379)
symmetrical conflict style (379)
win-lose problem solving (372)
win-win problem solving (376)

Media Resources

Online Textbook Resources

ThomsonNOW For quick access to the online resources that accompany this chapter, access ThomsonNOW for *Looking Out/Looking In* at www.thomsonedu.com.

The ThomsonNOW online study system helps you identify concepts you don't fully understand, allowing you to put your study time to the best use. Using chapter-by-chapter diagnostic pre-tests, the system creates a **personalized study plan** for each chapter. Each plan directs you to specific resources designed to improve your understanding, including pages from the text in ebook format. Chapter post-tests give you an opportunity to measure how much you've learned and let you know if you are ready for graded quizzes and exams.

Your ThomsonNOW for *Looking Out/Looking In* also includes the **ABC News video clip** described on page 384; a **communication scenario video** of the transcript on pages 392–393; **vocabulary activities** to help you master key terms; self-study **review quizzes** to test your comprehension of the material in this chapter and prepare for exams; **online exercises**, including the Skill Builder and Invitation to Insight activities in this chapter; **web links** you can use to further explore topics in this chapter; access to a **feature film database** where you can locate information about movies that illustrate communication principles; and access to the **InfoTrac** College Edition searchable database of over 10 million articles from both scholarly journals and the popular press.

Films

ThomsonNOW In addition to the films suggested here, go to your ThomsonNOW for *Looking Out/ Looking In* and access the **Film in Communication Database** to locate movie clips that illustrate different interpersonal communication conflict styles.

Dysfunctional Conflict

American Beauty (1999) Rated R
From outside, Lester and Carolyn Burnham (Kevin Spacey and Annette Bening) look like the perfect couple: attractive, with good jobs and an immaculate suburban home. But we soon learn that life isn't as good as it seems. The Burnhams' relationship with their daughter Jane (Thora Birch) is superficial. Carolyn is in denial about Lester's crisis, and she ignores his pleas to recapture their lost love. As the film relentlessly moves toward a stunning conclusion, we are presented with a portrait of American family members who alternate between avoidance and aggression without demonstrating any apparent skill at managing the serious conflicts that face them.

Conflict Styles

The Secret Lives of Dentists (2002) Rated R
Like the Burnhams in *American Beauty*, David and Dana Hurst appear to be living the American dream. They are successful dentists who share a practice; they have been married for ten years and have three young daughters; they have a home in the suburbs and another in the country.

Under the surface, all is not well. Dana (Hope Davis) is unhappy with the lack of intimacy in their marriage, so she tries to fulfill her passions in other ways. David (Campbell Scott) witnesses his wife in the embrace of another man but chooses not to confront her about it. As a result, Dana, David, and their children go through the motions of being a happy family, even though no one in the family seems happy.

David illustrates several conflict management styles: avoiding, accommodating, passive aggression, direct aggression, and compromising. The one style he never employs is to directly address the problem and collaborate with Dana on a solution, because he believes that confronting her would only lead to bigger problems.

The movie's ending provides no clear verdict on whether the choices David and Dana make are good ones. It's possible that they were wise to "weather the storm" by avoiding their conflict and letting it pass. However, it seems likely that they will encounter similar storms in the future—until and unless they are willing to deal with their conflicts more openly and collaboratively.

Culture and Conflict

The Joy Luck Club (1993) Rated R
The Joy Luck Club tells a series of stories involving four Chinese women and their daughters. The mothers all flee difficult situations in China to start new lives in the United States, where they raise their daughters with a mixture of Chinese and

American styles. Many of the movie's conflicts are rooted in cultural value clashes.

The mothers were raised in the high-context, collectivist environment of China, where open conflict is discouraged, and individual needs (particularly of women) are submerged for the larger good. To achieve their goals, the mothers use a variety of indirect and passive-aggressive methods. Their daughters, raised in the United States, adopt a more low-context, direct form of communication. They are also more assertive and aggressive in their conflict styles, particularly when dealing with their mothers.

The daughters have a harder time dealing with the men in their lives. For example, Rose (Rosalind Chao) begins her relationship with Ted (Andrew McCarthy) very assertively, telling him candidly what she thinks and how she feels about him (he is charmed by her directness). They marry, and she becomes an accommodator, constantly submerging her needs for his. Rather than liking Rose's accommodating, Ted comes to despise it. He exhorts her to be more assertive: "Once in a while, I would like to hear what you want. I'd like to hear your voice, even if we disagree." He then suggests that they separate.

Several of the stories have happy endings. In Rose's case, she fights for her rights with Ted—and ultimately they reconcile. In fact, each woman in the movie takes a stand on an important issue in her life, and most of the outcomes are positive. The women in *The Joy Luck Club* learn to both embrace and reject aspects of their cultural heritage as they attempt to manage their conflicts effectively.

Endnotes

Endnotes for Chapter 1

1. K. D. Williams (2001). *Ostracism: The Power of Silence* (pp. 7–11). New York: Guilford.
2. J. B. Ross & M. M. McLaughlin (Eds.) (1949). *A Portable Medieval Reader*. New York: Viking.
3. S. Schachter (1959). *The Psychology of Affiliation* (pp. 9–10). Stanford, CA: Stanford University Press.
4. UPI, *Wisconsin State Journal*, September 7, 1978.
5. J. McCain (1999). *Faith of My Fathers* (p. 212). New York: Random House.
6. Three articles in *The Journal of the American Medical Association* 267 (January 22/29, 1992) discuss the link between psychosocial influences and coronary heart disease: R. B. Case, A. J. Moss, N. Case, M. McDermott, & S. Eberly (1992). "Living Alone after Myocardial Infarction," pp. 515–519; R. B. Williams, J. C. Barefoot, R. M. Califf, T. L. Haney, W. B. Saunders, D. B. Pryon, M. A. Hlatky, I. C. Siegler, & D. B. Mark (1992). "Prognostic Importance of Social and Economic Resources among Medically Treated Patients with Angiographically Documented Coronary Artery Disease," pp. 520–524; and R. Ruberman (1992). "Psychosocial Influences on Mortality of Patients with Coronary Heart Disease," pp. 559–560; see also J. T. Cacioppo, J. M. Ernst, M. H. Burleson, M. K. McClintock, W. B. Malarkey, L. C. Hawkley, R. B. Kowalewski, A. Paulsen, J. A. Hobson, K. Hugdahl, D. Spiegel, & G. G. Berntson (2000). "Lonely Traits and Concomitant Physiological Processes: The MacArthur Social Neuroscience Studies." *International Journal of Psychophysiology, 35,* 143–154.
7. S. Cohen, W. J. Doyle, D. P. Skoner, B. S. Rabin, & J. M. Gwaltney (1997). "Social Ties and Susceptibility to the Common Cold." *Journal of the American Medical Association, 277,* 1,940–1,944.
8. R. Narem (1980). "Try a Little TLC." *Science, 80,* 15.
9. J. Lynch (1977). *The Broken Heart: The Medical Consequences of Loneliness* (pp. 239–242). New York: Basic Books; see also A. J. Kposowa (2000). "Marital Status and Suicide in The National Longitudinal Mortality Study." *Journal of Epidemiology and Community Health, 54,* 254–261.
10. Lynch, op. cit.
11. W. D. Rees and S. G. Lutkins (1967). "Mortality of Bereavement." *British Medical Journal,: 4,* 13.
12. "Defensiveness and High Blood Pressure" (1997). *Harvard Heart Letter, 4:* 8.
13. R. Shattuck (1980). *The Forbidden Experiment: The Story of the Wild Boy of Aveyron* (p. 37). New York: Farrar, Straus & Giroux.
14. R. B. Rubin, E. M. Perse, & C. A. Barbato (1988). "Conceptualization and Measurement of Interpersonal Communication Motives." *Human Communication Research, 14,* 602–628.
15. S. Duck & G. Pittman (1994). "Social and Personal Relationships." In M. L. Knapp and G. R. Phillips (Eds.), *Handbook of Interpersonal Communication*, 2nd ed. Newbury Park, CA: Sage.
16. S. Ball-Rokeach (2000). "Belonging in the 21st Century: The Case of Los Angeles." (Los Angeles: Annenberg School for Communication). Retrieved September 11, 2006, from http://www.metamorph.org/whitepaper12.html.
17. E. Diener & M. E. P. Seligman (2002). "Very Happy People." *Psychological Science, 13,* 81–84.
18. D. Kahneman, A. B. Krueger, D. A. Schkade, N. Schwartz, & A. A. Stone (n.d.). "A Daily Measure." *Science, 306,* 1645.
19. J. Rochmis (n.d.). "Humans Do Many Things." *Wired Magazine* online. Retrieved June 12, 2000, from http://www.wired.com/news/culture/0,1284,34387,00.html.

20. National Communication Association, *How Americans Communicate*, 1999. Retrieved September 11, 2006, from http://www.natcom.org/research/Roper/how_americans_communicate.htm.

21. W. Goldschmidt (1990). *The Human Career: The Self in the Symbolic World*. Cambridge, MA: Basil Blackwell.

22. J. L. Winsor, D. B. Curtis, & R. D. Stephens (1997). "National Preferences in Business and Communication Education: An Update." *Journal of the Association for Communication Administration*, 3, 170–179; see also M. S. Peterson (1997). "Personnel Interviewers' Perceptions of the Importance and Adequacy of Applicants' Communication Skills." *Communication Education, 46*, 287–291.

23. J. Flanigan, "For All of Us, the Future of Labor Lies in Learning." *Los Angeles Times* (Sept. 5, 1993): D5.

24. A. H. Maslow (1968). *Toward a Psychology of Being*. New York: Van Nostrand Reinhold.

25. See, for example, R. K. Shelly (1997). "Sequences and Cycles in Social Interaction." *Small Group Research, 28*, 333–356.

26. M. Dainton & L. Stafford (1993). "The Dark Side of 'Normal' Family Interaction." In B. H. Spitzberg & W. R. Cupach (Eds.), *The Dark Side of Interpersonal Communication*. Hillsdale, NJ: Erlbaum.

27. See R. Buck & C. A. VanLear (2002). "Verbal and Nonverbal Communication: Distinguishing Symbolic, Spontaneous, and Pseudo-Spontaneous Nonverbal Behavior." *Journal of Communication 52*, 522–541; and T. Clevenger, Jr. (1991). "Can One Not Communicate? A Conflict of Models." *Communication Studies 42*, 340–353. For a detailed rationale of the position argued in this section, see G. H. Stamp & M. L. Knapp (1990). "The Construct of Intent in Interpersonal Communication." *Quarterly Journal of Speech 76*, 282–299.

28. For a thorough discussion of communication difficulties, see N. Coupland, H. Giles, & J. M. Wiemann (Eds.) (1991). *Miscommunication and Problematic Talk*. Newbury Park, CA: Sage.

29. J. P. Dillard, D. H. Solomon, & M. T. Palmer (1999). "Structuring the Concept of Relational Communication." *Communication Monographs 66*, 49–65; and P. Watzlawick, J. Beavin, & D. Jackson (1967). *Pragmatics of Human Communication*. New York: Norton.

30. For a similar list of characteristics, see J. C. McCroskey & V. P. Richmond (1996). *Fundamentals of Human Communication: An Interpersonal Perspective*. Prospect Heights, IL: Waveland.

31. A. Sillars (1998). "(Mis)Understanding." In B. H. Spitzberg and W. R. Cupach (Eds.), *The Dark Side of Close Relationships*. Mahwah, NJ: Erlbaum.

32. J. C. McCroskey & L. Wheeless (1976). *Introduction to Human Communication* (p. 5). Boston: Allyn and Bacon. See also D. H. Cloven & M. E. Roloff (1991). "Sense-Making Activities and Interpersonal Conflict: Communicative Cures for the Mulling Blues." *Western Journal of Speech Communication 55*, 134–158. See also D. Stiebel (1997). *When Talking Makes Things Worse! Resolving Problems When Communication Fails*. Kansas City, Mo.: Andrews and McMeel.

33. M. V. Redmond (1995). "Interpersonal Communication: Definitions and Conceptual Approaches." In M. V. Redmond (Ed.), *Interpersonal Communication: Readings in Theory and Research* (pp. 4–11). Fort Worth: Harcourt Brace.

34. See, for example, G. R. Miller & M. Steinberg (1975). *Between People: A New Analysis of Interpersonal Communication*. Chicago: SRA; and J. Stewart & C. Logan (1998). *Together: Communicating Interpersonally*, 5th ed. New York: McGraw-Hill.

35. For further discussion of the characteristics of impersonal and interpersonal communications, see Arthur P. Bochner (1984). "The Functions of Human Communication in Interpersonal Bonding." In C. C. Arnold and J. W. Bowers (Eds.), *Handbook of Rhetorical and Communication Theory* (p. 550). Boston: Allyn and Bacon; S. Trenholm & A. Jensen (1992). *Interpersonal Communication*, 2nd ed. (pp. 27–33). Belmont, CA: Wadsworth; J. Stewart & G. D'Angelo (1998). *Together: Communicating Interpersonally*, 5th ed. (p. 5). New York: McGraw-Hill.

36. J. Wood (1997). *Relational Communication*, 2nd ed. Belmont, CA: Wadsworth.

37. K. J. Gergen (1991). *The Saturated Self: Dilemmas of Identity in Contemporary Life* (p. 158). New York: Basic Books.

38. UCLA Internet Report (2000). "Surveying the Digital Future," UCLA Center for Communication Policy,. Retrieved April 26, 2006, from http://www.digitalcenter.org/pdf/InternetReportYearOne.pdf.

39. "Surveying the Digital Future: Year Four," op. cit.

40. See, for example, J. Boase, J. B. Horrigan, B. Wellman, & L. Rainie (January 2006). *The Strength of Internet Ties*. Washington, DC: Pew Internet & American Life Project; A. Lenhart, M. Madden, & P. Hitlin (July 2005). *Teens and Technology: Youth are Leading the Transition to a Fully Wired and Mobile Nation*. Washington, DC: Pew Internet & American Life Project; and J. Boase & B. Wellman (2006). "Personal Relationships: On and Off the Internet." In D. Perlman & A.L. Vangelisti (Eds.), *The Cambridge Handbook of Personal Relationships*. New York: Cambridge University Press.

41. A. J. Flanagin (2005). "IM Online: Instant Messaging Use Among College Students." *Communication Research Reports, 22*, 175–187.

42. J. Boase, J. B. Horrigan, B. Wellman, & L. Rainie (January 2006). *The Strength of Internet Ties*. Washington, DC: Pew Internet & American Life Project.

43. M. Dainton & B. Aylor (2002). "Patterns of Communication Channel Use in the Maintenance of Long-Distance Relationships." *Communication Research Reports, 19*, 118–129.

44. M. Marriott (1998). "The Blossoming of Internet Chat." *New York Times* online. Retrieved July 2, 1998, from http://www.nytimes.com/library/tech/98/07/circuits/articles/02/chat.html.

45. D. Tannen (1994). "Gender Gap in Cyberspace." *Newsweek* (May 16, 1994): 52–53.

46. D. Kirkpatrick (1992). "Here Comes the Payoff from PCs." *Fortune* (March 23, 1992): 93–102.

47. For a thorough review of this topic, see B. H. Spitzberg & W. R. Cupach (1989). *Handbook of Interpersonal Competence Research*. New York: Springer-Verlag.

48. For a thorough discussion of the nature of communication competence, see B. H. Spitzberg & W. R. Cupach (2002). "Interpersonal Skills." In M. L. Knapp & J. A. Daly (Eds.), *Handbook of Interpersonal Communication*, 3rd ed. Thou-

sand Oaks, CA: Sage.; and S. R. Wilson & C. M. Sabee (2003). "Explicating Communicative Competence as a Theoretical Term." In J. O. Greene & B. R. Burleson (Eds.), *Handbook of Communication and Social Interaction Skills*. Mahwah, NJ: Erlbaum.

49. See Y. Y. Kim (1991). "Intercultural Communication Competence: A Systems-Theoretic View." In S. Ting-Toomey & F. Korzenny (Eds.), *Cross-Cultural Interpersonal Communication*. Newbury Park, CA: Sage; and G. M. Chen & W. J. Sarosta (1996). "Intercultural Communication Competence: A Synthesis." In B. R. Burleson & A. W. Kunkel (Eds.), *Communication Yearbook 19*. Thousand Oaks, CA: Sage.

50. J. K. Burgoon & N. E. Dunbar (2000). "An Interactionist Perspective on Dominance-Submission: Interpersonal Dominance as a Dynamic, Situationally Contingent Social Skill." *Communication Monographs, 67*, 96–121.

51. M. J. Collier (1996). "Communication Competence Problematics in Ethnic Relationships." *Communication Monographs, 63*, 314–336.

52. L. Chen (1997). "Verbal Adaptive Strategies in U.S. American Dyadic Interactions with U.S. American or East-Asian Partners." *Communication Monographs, 64*, 302–323.

53. B. H. Spitzberg (1991). "An Examination of Trait Measures of Interpersonal Competence." *Communication Reports, 4*, 22–29.

54. B. H. Spitzberg (2000). "What Is Good Communication?" *Journal of the Association for Communication Administration, 29*, 103–119.

55. L. K. Guerrero, P. A. Andersen, P. F. Jorgensen, B. H. Spitzberg, & S. V. Eloy (1995). "Coping with the Green-Eyed Monster: Conceptualizing and Measuring Communicative Responses to Romantic Jealousy." *Western Journal of Communication, 59*, 270–304.

56. See B. J. O'Keefe (1988). "The Logic of Message Design: Individual Differences in Reasoning about Communication." *Communication Monographs, 55*, 80–103.

57. See, for example, A. D. Heisel, J. C. McCroskey, & V. P. Richmond (1999). "Testing Theoretical Relationships and Non-Relationships of Genetically-Based Predictors: Getting Started with Communibiology." *Communication Research Reports, 16*, 1–9; and J. C. McCroskey & M. J. Beatty (2000). "The Communibiological Perspective: Implications for Communication in Instruction." *Communication Education, 49*, 1–6.

58. J. Ayres & T. Hopf (1993). *Coping with Speech Anxiety*. Norwood, NJ: Ablex; see also M. Allen, J. Bourhis, T. Emmers-Sommer, & E. Sahlstein (1998). "Reducing Dating Anxiety: A Meta-Analysis." *Communication Reports, 11*, 49–55.

59. M. A. deTurck & G. R. Miller (1990). "Training Observers to Detect Deception: Effects of Self-Monitoring and Rehearsal." *Human Communication Research, 16*, 603–620.

60. R. B. Rubin, E. M. Perse, & C. A. Barbato (1988). "Conceptualization and Measurement of Interpersonal Communication Motives." *Human Communication Research, 14*, 602–628.

61. D. Hemple (in press). "Invitational Capacity." In F. van Emeren & P. Houtlosser, *The Practice of Argumentation*. Amsterdam: John Benjamins.

62. D. B. Wackman, S. Miller, & E. W. Nunnally (1976). *Student Workbook: Increasing Awareness and Communication Skills* (p. 6). Minneapolis: Interpersonal Communication Programs.

63. D. E. Ifert & M. E. Roloff (1997). "The Role of Sensitivity to the Expressions of Others and Ability to Modify Self-Presentation." *Communication Quarterly, 45*, 55–67.

64. R. Martin (1992). "Relational Cognition Complexity and Relational Communication in Personal Relationships." *Communication Monographs, 59*, 150–163; see also B. R. Burleson & S. E. Caplan (1998). "Cognitive Complexity." In J. C. McCroskey, J. A. Daly, M. M. Martin, and M. J. Beatty (Eds.), *Communication and Personality: Trait Perspectives* (pp. 233–286). Creskill, NY: Hampton Press.

65. Burleson & Samter, op. cit., p. 22.

66. B. R. Burleson (1989). "The Constructivist Approach to Person-Centered Communication: Analysis of a Research Exemplar." In B. Dervin, L. Grossberg, B. J. O'Keefe, & E. Wartella (Eds.), *Rethinking Communication: Paradigm Exemplars* (pp. 33–72). Newbury Park, CA: Sage.

67. B. D. Sypher & T. Zorn (1986). "Communication-Related Abilities and Upward Mobility: A Longitudinal Investigation." *Human Communication Research, 12*, 420–431.

68. J. M. Wiemann & P. M. Backlund (1980). "Current Theory and Research in Communication Competence." *Review of Educational Research, 50*, 185–199; S. G. Lakey & D. J. Canary (2002). "Actor Goal Achievement and Sensitivity to Partner as Critical Factors in Understanding Interpersonal Communication Competence and Conflict Strategies." *Communication Monographs, 69*, 217–235; see also M. V. Redmond (December 1985). "The Relationship between Perceived Communication Competence and Perceived Empathy." *Communication Monographs, 52*, 377–382; and M. V. Redmond (1989). "The Functions of Empathy (Decentering) in Human Relations." *Human Relations, 42*, 593–605.

69. Research summarized in D. E. Hamachek (1987). *Encounters with the Self*, 2nd ed. (p. 8.). Fort Worth: Holt, Rinehart and Winston; see also J. A. Daly, A. L. Vangelisti, & S. M. Daughton (1995). "The Nature and Correlates of Conversational Sensitivity." In M. V. Redmond (Ed.), *Interpersonal Communication: Readings in Theory and Research*. Fort Worth: Harcourt Brace.

70. D. A. Dunning & J. Kruger (December 1999). "Unskilled and Unaware of It: "How Difficulties in Recognizing One's Own Incompetence Lead to Inflated Self-Assessments." *Journal of Personality and Social Psychology, 77*, 1,121–1,134.

71. Adapted from the work of R. P. Hart as reported by M. L. Knapp (1984). In *Interpersonal Communication and Human Relationships* (pp. 342–344). Boston: Allyn and Bacon; see also R. P. Hart & D. M. Burks (1972). "Rhetorical Sensitivity and Social Interaction." *Speech Monographs 39*, 75–91; and R. P. Hart, R. E. Carlson, & W. F. Eadie (1980). "Attitudes toward Communication and the Assessment of Rhetorical Sensitivity." *Communication Monographs, 47*, 1–22.

72. J. F. Kikoski & C. K. Kikoski (1996). *Reflexive Communication in the Culturally Diverse Workplace* (p 3). Westport, CT: Quorum.

73. "Tripling of Hispanic and Asian Populations in 50 Years; Non-Hispanic Whites May Drop To Half of Total Population." U.S. Census Bureau publication CB04-44. Retrieved October 13, 2005, from http://www.census.gov/Press-Release/www/releases/archives/population/001720.html.

74. *Directory of Foreign Firms Operating in the U.S.*, 18th ed. (2005). Millis, MA: Uniworld Business Publications.

75. Fidelity Investments (1996). *Fidelity's Targeted International Equity Funds* (pp. 2–4). Boston: Fidelity Distributors.

76. "Employment at U.S.-Based Global Companies." *Workforce Management*, July 2005: 36–46.

77. *Directory of Foreign Firms*, op. cit.

78. See, for example, C. Hajek & H. Giles (2003). "New Directions in Intercultural Communication Competence: The Process Model." In B.R. Burleson & J.O. Greene (Eds.), *Handbook of Communication and Social Interaction Skills.* Mahwah, NJ: Erlbaum; and S. Ting-Toomey & L.C. Chung (2005). *Understanding Intercultural Communication.* Los Angeles: Roxbury.

79. M. Kalliny, K. Cruthirds, & M. Minor (2006). "Differences between American, Egyptian and Lebanese Humor Styles: Implications for International Management." *International Journal of Cross-Cultural Management, 6,* 121–134.

80. L. A. Samovar & R. E. Porter (2004). *Communication Between Cultures,* 5th ed. Belmont, CA: Wadsworth.

81. J. W. Kassing (1997). "Development of the Intercultural Willingness to Communicate Scale." *Communication Research Reports, 14,* 399–407.

82. J. K. Burgoon, C. R. Berger, & V. R. Waldron (2000). "Mindfulness and Interpersonal Communication." *Journal of Social Issues, 56,* 105–128.

83. C. R. Berger (1979). "Beyond Initial Interactions: Uncertainty, Understanding, and the Development of Interpersonal Relationships." In H. Giles & R. St. Clair (Eds.), *Language and Social Psychology* (pp. 122–144). Oxford: Blackwell.

84. L. J. Carrell (1997). "Diversity in the Communication Curriculum: Impact on Student Empathy." *Communication Education, 46,* 234–244.

Endnotes for Chapter 2

1. W. Soldz & G. E. Vaillant (1999). "The Big Five Personality Traits and the Life Course: A 45-Year Longitudinal Study." *Journal of Research in Personality 33,* 208–232.

2. For a summary of research on heritability of personality, see W. Wright, *Born That Way: Genes, Behavior, Personality.* New York: Knopf, 1998.

3. C. E. Schwartz, C. I. Wright, L. M. Shin, J. Kagan, & S. L. Rauch (2003). "Inhibited and Uninhibited Infants 'Grown Up': Adult Amygdalar Response to Novelty." *Science,* (June 20, 2003): 1952–1953.

4. J. G. Cole & J. C. McCroskey (2000). "Temperament and Socio-Communicative Orientation." *Communication Research Reports, 17,* 105–114.

5. A. D. Heisel, J. C. McCroskey, & V. P. Richmond (1999). "Testing Theoretical Relationships and Non-Relationships of Genetically-Based Predictors: Getting Started with Communibiology," *Communication Research Reports, 16,* 1–9.

6. Cole & McCroskey, op. cit.

7. C. J. Wigley 1998). "Vergal Aggressiveness." In J. C. McCroskey, J. A. Daly, M. M. Martin, & M. J. Beatty (Eds.), *Personality and Communication: Trait Perspectives.* New York: Hampton.

8. J. C. McCroskey, A.D. Heisel, & V. P. Richmond (2001). "Eysenck's Big Three and Communication Traits: Three

Correlational Studies." *Communication Monographs, 68,* 360–366.

9. R. R. McCrae & P. T. Costa (1987). "Validation of the Five-Factor Model of Personality across Instruments and Observers." *Journal of Personality and Social Psychology, 52,* 81–90.

10. R. R. McCrae & P. T Costa., Jr. (1997). "Personality Trait Structure as a Human Universal." *American Psychologist, 52,* 509–516.

11. C. H. Cooley (1912). *Human Nature and the Social Order.* New York: Scribner's.

12. A. L. Vangelisti & L. P. Crumley (1998). "Reactions to Messages that Hurt: The Influence of Relational Contexts." *Communication Monographs, 65,* 173–196.

13. L. Leets & Sunwolf (2004). "Being Left Out: Rejecting Outsiders and Communicating Group Boundaries in Childhood and Adolescent Peer Groups." *Journal of Applied Communication Research, 32,* 195–223.

14. A. Sillars, A. Koerner, & M.A. Fitzpatrick (2005). "Communication and Understanding in Parent-Adolescent Relationships." *Human Communication Research, 31,* 107–128.

15. T. Adler (1992). "Personality, Like Plaster, Is Pretty Stable over Time." *APA Monitor* (October 1992): 18.

16. J. and R. W. Robins (1993). "A Longitudinal Study of Consistency and Change in Self-Esteem from Early Adolescence to Early Childhood." *Child Development, 64,* 909–923.

17. J. D. Brown, N. J. Novick, K. A. Lord, & J. M. Richards (1992). "When Gulliver Travels: Social Context, Psychological Closeness, and Self-Appraisals." *Journal of Personality and Social Psychology, 62,* 717–734.

18. M. Han (2003). "Body Image Dissatisfaction and Eating Disturbance among Korean College Female Students: Relationships to Media Exposure, Upward Comparison, and Perceived Reality." *Communication Studies, 34,* 65–78; and K. Harrison & J. Cantor (1997). "The Relationship Between Media Consumption and Eating Disorders." *Journal of Communication, 47,* 40–67.

19. P. N. Myers & F. A. Biocca (1992). "The Elastic Body Image: The Effect of Television Advertising and Programming on Body Image Distortions in Young Women." *Journal of Communication, 42,* 108–134.

20. C. M. Strong (2005). "The Role of Exposure to Media Idealized Male Physiques on Men's Body Image." *Dissertation Abstracts International, 65,* 4306.

21. D. Grodin & T. R. Lindolf (1995). *Constructing the Self in a Mediated World.* Newbury Park, CA: Sage.

22. N. Ellison, R. Heino, & J. Gibbs (2006). "Managing Impressions Online: Self-Presentation Processes in the Online Dating Environment." *Journal of Computer-Mediated Communication* 11: Article 2. Retrieved September 11, 2006, from http://jcmc.indiana.edu/vol11/issue2/ellison.html.

23. J. D. Brown & T. A. Mankowski (1993). "Self-Esteem, Mood, and Self-Evaluation: Changes in Mood and the Way You See You." *Journal of Personality and Social Psychology, 64,* 421–430.

24. M. A. Gara, R. L. Woolfolk, B. D. Cohen, & R. B. Goldston (1993). "Perception of Self and Other in Major Depression." *Journal of Abnormal Psychology, 102,* 93–100.

25. L. C. Miller, L. L. Cooke, J. Tsang, & F. Morgan (1992). "Should I Brag? Nature and Impact of Positive and Boast-

ful Disclosures for Women and Men." *Human Communication Research, 18,* 364–399.

26. B. Bower (1992). "Truth Aches: People Who View Themselves Poorly May Seek the 'Truth' and Find Despair." *Science News* (August 15, 1992): 110–111; and W. B. Swann (2005). "The Self and Identity Negotiation." *Interaction Studies, 6,* 69–83.

27. W. W. Wilmot (1995). *Relational Communication* (pp. 35–54). New York: McGraw-Hill.

28. J. Servaes (1989). "Cultural Identity and Modes of Communication." In J. A. Anderson (Ed.), *Communication Yearbook 12* (p. 396). Newbury Park, CA: Sage.

29. A. Bharti (1985). "The Self in Hindu Thought and Action." In *Culture and Self: Asian and Western Perspectives.* New York: Tavistock.

30. S. Bochner (1994). "Cross-Cultural Differences in the Self Concept: A Test of Hofstede's Individualism/Collectivism Distinction." *Journal of Cross-Cultural Psychology, 25,* 273–283.

31. W. B. Gudykunst & S. Ting-Toomey 1988. *Culture and Interpersonal Communication.* Newbury Park, CA: Sage.

32. L. A. Samovar & R. E. Porter (1991). *Communication between Cultures* (p. 91). Belmont, CA: Wadsworth.

33. D. Klopf (1984). "Cross-Cultural Apprehension Research: A Summary of Pacific Basin Studies." In J. Daly & J. McCroskey (Eds.), *Avoiding Communication: Shyness, Reticence, and Communication Apprehension.* Beverly Hills, CA: Sage.

34. S. Ting-Toomey (1988). "A Face-Negotiation Theory." In Y. Kim & W. Gudykunst (Eds.), *Theory in Interpersonal Communication.* Newbury Park, CA: Sage.

35. L. C. Lederman (1993). "Gender and the Self." In L. P. Arliss & D. J. Borisoff (Eds.), *Women and Men Communicating: Challenges and Changes* (pp. 41–42). Fort Worth: Harcourt Brace.

36. For more examples of gender-related labels, see A. Wittels (1978). *I Wonder . . . A Satirical Study of Sexist Semantics.* Los Angeles: Price Stern Sloan.

37. M. Knox, J. Funk, R. Elliott, & E. G. Bush (2000). "Gender Differences in Adolescents' Possible Selves." *Youth and Society, 31,* 287–309.

38. C. J. Smith, J. A. Noll, & J. B. Bryant (1999). "The Effect of Social Context on Gender Self-Concept." *Sex Roles 40,* 499–512.

39. J. Kolligan, Jr. (1990). "Perceived Fraudulence as a Dimension of Perceived Incompetence." In R. J. Sternberg & J. Kolligen, Jr. (Eds.), *Competence Considered.* New Haven, Conn.: Yale University Press. See also A. L. Vangelisti, S. D. Corbin, A. E. Lucchetti, & R. J. Sprague (1999). "Couples' Concurrent Cognitions: The Influence of Relational Satisfaction on the Thoughts Couples Have as They Converse." *Human Communication Research, 25,* 370–398.

40. B. Zimmerman, A. Bandura, & M. Martinez-Pons (1992). "Self-Motivation for Academic Attainment: The Role of Self-Efficacy Beliefs and Personal Goal Setting." *American Educational Research Journal, 29,* 663–676.

41. G. Downey & S. I. Feldman (1996). "Implications of Rejection Sensitivity for Intimate Relationships." *Journal of Personality and Social Psychology, 70,* 1,327–1,343.

42. P. D. MacIntyre & K. A Thivierge (1995). "The Effects of Speaker Personality on Anticipated Reactions to Public Speaking." *Communication Research Reports, 12,* 125–133.

43. C. L. Kleinke, T. R. Peterson, & T. R. Rutledge (1998). "Effects of Self-Generated Facial Expressions on Mood." *Journal of Personality and Social Psychology, 74,* 272–279.

44. R. Rosenthal & L. Jacobson (1968). *Pygmalion in the Classroom.* New York: Holt, Rinehart and Winston.

45. P. D. Blank (Ed.) (1993). *Interpersonal Expectations: Theory, Research, and Applications* Cambridge, England: Cambridge University Press.

46. For a thorough discussion of this subject, see M. E. P. Seligman (1993). *What You Can Change and What You Can't.* New York: Knopf.

47. C. M. Shaw & R. Edwards (1997). "Self-Concepts and Self-Presentations of Males and Females: Similarities and Differences." *Communication Reports, 10,* 55–62.

48. C. M. Scotton (1983). "The Negotiation of Identities in Conversation: A Theory of Markedness and Code Choice." *International Journal of Sociological Linguistics, 44,* 119–125.

49. E. Goffman (1959). *The Presentation of Self in Everyday Life.* Garden City, NY: Doubleday; and (1971) *Relations in Public.* New York: Basic Books.

50. J. Stewart & C. Logan (1998). *Together: Communicating Interpersonally,* 5th ed. (p. 120). New York: McGraw-Hill.

51. M. R. Leary & R. M. Kowalski (1990). "Impression Management: A Literature Review and Two-Component Model." *Psychological Bulletin, 107,* 34–47.

52. V. Brightman, A. Segal, P. Werther, & J. Steiner (1975). "Ethological Study of Facial Expression in Response to Taste Stimuli." *Journal of Dental Research, 54,* 141.

53. N. Chovil (1991). "Social Determinants of Facial Displays." *Journal of Nonverbal Behavior, 15,* 141–154.

54. See, for example, R. A. Giacalone & P. Rosenfeld (Eds.) (1991), *Applied Impression Management: How Image-Making Affects Managerial Decisions.* Newbury Park, CA: Sage.

55. D. Morier & C. Seroy (1994). "The Effect of Interpersonal Expectancies on Men's Self-Presentation of Gender Role Attitudes to Women." *Sex Roles, 31,* 493–504.

56. M. Leary, J. B. Nezlek, D. Downs, et al. (1994). "Self-Presentation in Everyday Interactions: Effects of Target Familiarity and Gender Composition." *Journal of Personality and Social Psychology 67,* 664–673.

57. M. Snyder (1987). *Public Appearances, Private Realities: The Psychology of Self-Monitoring.* New York: W. H. Freeman.

58. The following discussion is based on material in D. E. Hamachek (1992). *Encounters with the Self,* 3rd ed. (pp. 24–26). Fort Worth, TX: Harcourt.

59. For a more detailed discussion of identity-related goals, see S. Metts & E. Grohskopf 2003). "Impression Management: Goals, Strategies, and Skills." In J. O. Greene and B. R. Burleson (Eds.), *Handbook of Communication and Social Skills.* Mahwah, NJ: Erlbaum.

60. L. M. Coleman & B. M. DePaulo (1991). "Uncovering the Human Spirit: Moving beyond Disability and 'Missed' Communications." In N. Coupland, H. Giles, & J. M. Wiemann (Eds.), *"Miscommunication" and Problematic Talk* (pp. 61–84). Newbury Park, CA: Sage.

61. J. W. Vander Zanden (1984). *Social Psychology,* 3rd ed. (pp. 235–237). New York: Random House.

62. D. Brouwer (1998). "The Precarious Visibility Politics of Self-Stigmatization: The Case of HIV/AIDS Tattoos." *Text and Performance Quarterly, 18,* 114–136.

63. J. Coupland (2000). "Past the 'Perfect Kind of Age'? Styling Selves and Relationships in Over-50s Dating Advertisements." *Journal of Communication, 50*, 9–30.

64. P. B. O'Sullivan (2000). "What You Don't Know Won't Hurt Me: Impression Management Functions of Communication Channels in Relationships." *Communication Monographs 26*, 403–432. See also S. B. Barnes (2003). *Computer-Mediated Communication: Human-to-Human Communication across the Internet* (pp. 136–162). Boston: Allyn and Bacon.

65. J. R. Suler (2002). "Identity Management in Cyberspace." *Journal of Applied Psychoanalytic Studies 4*, 455–459.

66. J. L. Gibbs, N. B. Ellison, & R. D. Heino (2006). "Self-Presentation in Online Personals: The Role of Anticipated Future Interaction, Self-Disclosure, and Perceived Success in Internet Dating." *Communication Research 33*, 1–26.

67. See, for example, D. Chandler (n.d.). "Personal Home Pages and the Construction of Identities on the Web." Retrieved May 8, 2006, from http://www.aber.ac.uk/~dgc/webident.html.

68. O' Sullivan, op. cit.

Endnotes for Chapter 3

1. The graphic demonstrations of factors influencing perception in this and the following paragraph are borrowed from D. Coon (2004). *Introduction to Psychology*, 10th ed. Belmont, CA: Wadsworth.

2. G. W. Allport (1958). *The Nature of Prejudice* (p. 185). New York: Doubleday Anchor.

3. M. Hewstone & R. Brown (1986). "Contact Is Not Enough." In M. Hewstone & R. Brown (Eds.), *Contact and Conflict in Intergroup Encounters* (p. 29). Oxford, England: Basil Blackwell. See also H. Giles, N. Coupland, J. Coupland, A. Williams, & J. Nussbaum (1992). "Intergenerational Talk and Communication with Older People." *International Journal of Aging and Human Development, 33*, 251–297.

4. M. Allen (1998). "Methodological Considerations When Examining a Gendered World." In D. Canary and K. Dindia (Eds.), *Handbook of Sex Differences and Similarities in Communication* (pp. 427–444). Mahwah, NJ: Erlbaum.

5. B. Allen (1995). "Diversity and Organizational Communication." *Journal of Applied Communication Research, 23*, 143–155. See also R. Buttny (1997). "Reported Speech in Talking Race on Campus." *Human Communication Research, 23*, 477–506; and P. C. Hughes & J. R. Baldwin (2002). "Communication and Stereotypical Impressions." *Howard Journal of Communications, 13*, 113–128.

6. R. M. Perloff, B. Bonder, G. B. Ray, E. B. Ray, & L. A. Siminoff (2006). "Doctor-Patient Communication, Cultural Competence, and Minority Health: Theoretical and Empirical Perspectives." *American Behavioral Scientist, 49*, 835–852; M. N. Oliver, M. A. Goodwin, R. S. Gotler, & K. C. Strange (2001). "Time Use in Clinical Encounters: Are African-American Patients Treated Differently?" *Journal of the National Medical Association, 93*, 380–385.

7. J. Oetzel (1998). "The Effects of Self-Construals and Ethnicity on Self-Reported Conflict Styles." *Communication Reports, 11*, 133–144.

8. N. Nishizawa (2004). "The 'Self' of Japanese Teenagers: Growing Up in the Flux of a Changing Culture and Society." *Dissertation Abstracts International, 65*, 2642.

9. M. L. Inman & R. S. Baron (1996). "Influence of Prototypes on Perceptions of Prejudice." *Journal of Personality and Social Psychology, 70*, 727–739.

10. P. Watzlawick, J. Beavin, & D. D. Jackson (1967). *Pragmatics of Human Communication* (p. 65). New York: Norton.

11. V. Manusov (1993). "It Depends on Your Perspective: Effects of Stance and Beliefs about Intent on Person Perception." *Western Journal of Communication, 57*, 27–41.

12. T. Adler (1992). "Enter Romance, Exit Objectivity." *APA Monitor*, (June 1992), 18.

13. K. Floyd & M. T. Morman (2000). "Reacting to the Verbal Expression of Affection in Same-Sex Interaction." *Southern Communication Journal, 65*, 287–299.

14. J. K. Alberts, U. Kellar-Guenther, & S. R. Corman (1996). "That's Not Funny: Understanding Recipients' Responses to Teasing." *Western Journal of Communication, 60*, 337–357. See also R. Edwards, R. Bello, F. Brandau-Brown, & D. Hollems (2001). "The Effects of Loneliness and Verbal Aggressiveness on Message Interpretation." *Southern Communication Journal, 66*, 139–150.

15. See T. N. Bradbury & F. D. Fincham (1990). "Attributions in Marriage: Review and Critique." *Psychological Bulletin, 107*, 3–33; and V. Manusov (1990). "An Application of Attribution Principles to Nonverbal Behavior in Romantic Dyads." *Communication Monographs, 57*, 104–118.

16. C. L. M. Shaw (1997). "Personal Narrative: Revealing Self and Reflecting Other." *Human Communication Research, 24*, 302–319.

17. J. K. Kellas (2005). "Family Ties: Communicating Identity Through Jointly Told Family Stories." *Communication Monographs, 72*, 365–389.

18. J. Flora & C. Segrin (2000). "Relationship Development in Dating Couples: Implications for Relational Satisfaction and Loneliness." *Journal of Social and Personal Relationships, 17*, 811–825.

19. L. A. Baxter & G. Pittman (2001). "Communicatively Remembering Turning Points of Relational Development in Heterosexual Romantic Relationships." *Communication Reports, 14*, 1–17.

20. J. M. Martz, J. Verette, X. B. Arriaga, L. F. Slovik, C. L. Cox, & C. E. Rosbult (1998). "Positive Illusion in Close Relationships." *Personal Relationships, 5*, 159–181. See also S. L. Murray, J. G. Holmes, & D. W. Griffin (1996). "The Benefits of Positive Illusions: Idealization and the Construction of Satisfaction in Close Relationships." *Journal of Personality and Social Psychology, 70*, 79–98.

21. J. C. Pearson (1996). "Positive Distortion: 'The Most Beautiful Woman in the World.'" In K. M. Galvin and P. Cooper (Eds.), *Making Connections: Readings in Interpersonal Communication* p. 177. Beverly Hills, CA: Roxbury.

22. For a detailed description of how the senses affect perception, see N. Ackerman (1990). *A Natural History of the Senses*. New York: Random House.

23. J. Piaget (1952). *The Origins of Intelligence in Children*. New York: International Universities Press.

24. K. Alaimo, C. M. Olson, & E. A. Frongillo (2001). "Food Insufficiency and American School-Aged Children's

Cognitive, Academic, and Psychosocial Development." *Pediatrics, 108,* 44–53.

25. C. Cooper & C. McConville (1990). "Interpreting Mood Scores: Clinical Implications of Individual Differences in Mood Variability." *British Journal of Medical Psychology, 63,* 215–225. See also J. Mendlewicz & H. M. van Praag (Eds.) (1983). *Biological Rhythms and Behavior.* New York: Karger.

26. For descriptions of various psychological disorders and their treatments, visit the National Institute of Mental Health website at http://www.nimh.nih.gov/.

27. J. W. Bagby (1957). "A Cross-Cultural Study of Perceptual Predominance in Binocular Rivalry." *Journal of Abnormal and Social Psychology, 54,* 331–334.

28. E. T. Hall (1969). *The Hidden Dimension* (p. 160). New York: Doubleday Anchor.

29. H. Giles, N. Coupland, & J. M. Wiemann (1992). "Talk Is Cheap . . . But 'My Word Is My Bond': Beliefs about Talk." In K. Bolton & H. Kwok (Eds.), *Sociolinguistics Today: International Perspectives.* London: Routledge & Kegan Paul.

30. R. Steves (May–September 1996). "Culture Shock." *Europe Through the Back Door Newsletter, 50,* 20.

31. A. Fadiman (1997). *The Spirit Catches You and You Fall Down* (p. 33). New York: Farrar, Straus, and Giroux.

32. P. Andersen, M. Lustig, & J. Anderson (1987). *Changes in Latitude, Changes in Attitude: The Relationship between Climate, Latitude, and Interpersonal Communication Predispositions.* Paper presented at the annual convention of the Speech Communication Association, Boston; and P. Andersen, M. Lustig, & J. Andersen (1988). *Regional Patterns of Communication in the United States: Empirical Tests.* Paper presented at the annual convention of the Speech Communication Association, New Orleans.

33. V. Manusov, M. R. Winchatz, & L. M. Manning (1997). "Acting Out of Our Minds: Incorporating Behavior Into Models of Stereotype-Based Expectancies for Cross-Cultural Interactions." *Communication Monographs, 64,* 119–139.

34. See S. A. Rathus (1993). *Psychology,* 5th ed. (pp. 640–643) Fort Worth: Harcourt Brace Jovanovich; and C. Wade & C. Tavris (1987). *Psychology* (pp. 488–490). New York: Harper & Row.

35. S. L. Bem (1985). "Androgyny and Gender Schema Theory: A Conceptual and Empirical Integration." In T. B. Sonderegger (Ed.), *Nebraska Symposium on Motivation: Psychology and Gender.* Lincoln, Neb.: University of Nebraska Press.

36. P. G. Zimbardo, C. Haney, & W. C. Banks (1973). "A Pirandellian Prison." *New York Times Magazine,* April 8, 1973.

37. See, for example, P. Baron (1974). "Self-Esteem, Ingratiation, and Evaluation of Unknown Others." *Journal of Personality and Social Psychology,* 104–109.

38. D. E. Hamachek (1982). *Encounters with Others: Interpersonal Relationships and You* (p. 3). New York: Holt, Rinehart and Winston.

39. D. Hamachek (1992). *Encounters with the Self,* 3rd ed. Fort Worth, TX: Harcourt Brace Jovanovich.

40. For a review of these perceptual biases, see Hamachek, *Encounters with the Self.* See also Bradbury & Fincham, op. cit. For an example of the self-serving bias in action, see R.

Buttny (1997). "Reported Speech in Talking Race on Campus." *Human Communication Research, 23,* 477–506.

41. S. L. Young (2004). "What the _____ Is Your Problem?: Attribution Theory and Perceived Reasons for Profanity Usage During Conflict." *Communication Research Reports, 21,* 338–347.

42. B. Sypher & H. E. Sypher (January 1984). "Seeing Ourselves as Others See Us." *Communication Research, 11,* 97–115.

43. Reported by D. Myers (May 1980). "The Inflated Self." *Psychology Today, 14,* 16.

44. K. Dion, E. Berscheid, & E. Walster (1972). "What Is Beautiful Is Good." *Journal of Personality and Social Psychology, 24,* 285–290.

45. L. Watkins & L. Johnston (2000). "Screening Job Applicants: The Impact of Physical Attractiveness and Application Quality." *International Journal of Selection and Assessment, 8,* 76–84.

46. T. Dougherty, D. Turban, & J. Collander (1994). "Confirming First Impressions in the Employment Interview." *Journal of Applied Psychology, 79,* 659–665.

47. G. I. Cook, R. L. Marsh, & J. L. Hicks (2003). "Halo and Devil Effects Demonstrate Valenced-Based Influences on Source-Mentoring Decisions." *Consciousness and Cognition, 12,* 257–278.

48. C. I. Marek, M. B. Wanzer, & J. L. Knapp (2004). "An Exploratory Investigation of the Relationship between Roommates' First Impressions and Subsequent Communication Patterns." *Communication Research Reports, 21,* 210–220.

49. See, for example, A. Sillars, W. Shellen, A. McIntosh, & M. Pomegranate (1997). "Relational Characteristics of Language: Elaboration and Differentiation in Marital Conversations." *Western Journal of Communication, 61,* 403–422.

50. J. B. Stiff, J. P. Dillard, L. Somera, H. Kim, & C. Sleight (1988). "Empathy, Communication, and Prosocial Behavior." *Communication Monographs, 55,* 198–213.

51. This research is described by D. Goleman (1995) in *Emotional Intelligence* (p. 98). New York: Bantam.

52. M. Davis (1994). "The Heritability of Characteristics Associated with Dispositional Empathy." *Journal of Personality, 62.*

53. B. Burleson, J. Delia, & J. Applegate (1995). "The Socialization of Person-Centered Communication: Parental Contributions to the Social-Cognitive and Communication Skills of Their Children." In M. A. Fitzpatrick & A. Vangelisti (Eds.), *Perspectives in Family Communication.* Thousand Oaks, CA: Sage.

54. R. Lennon & N. Eisenberg (1987). "Gender and Age Differences in Empathy and Sympathy." In N. Eisenberg & J. Strayer (Eds.), *Empathy and Its Development.* Cambridge, England: Cambridge University Press.

55. T. Adler (1990). "Look at Duration, Depth in Research on Emotion." *APA Monitor,* (October 1990), 10.

56. N. D. Feshbach, "Parental Empathy and Child Adjustment/ Maladjustment." In Eisenberg & Strayer, op. cit.

57. See, for example, "Diversity in the Communication Curriculum: Impact on Student Empathy." *Communication Education, 46* (1977), 234–244.

58. P. Reps (1967). "Pillow Education in Rural Japan." In *Square Sun, Square Moon.* New York: Tuttle.

Endnotes for Chapter 4

1. R. J. Sternberg (1985). *Beyond I.Q.* New York: Cambridge University Press.
2. D. Goleman (1995). *Emotional Intelligence: Why It Can Matter More Than I.Q.* New York: Bantam.
3. J. M. Gottman & N. Silver (1999). *The Seven Principles for Making Marriages Work.* New York: Three Rivers Press.
4. P. Ekman, R. W. Levenson, & W. V. Friesen (September 16, 1983). "Autonomic Nervous System Activity Distinguishes among Emotions." *Science, 221,* 1,208–1,210.
5. C. L. Kleinke, T. R. Peterson, & T. R. Rutledge (1998). "Effects of Self-Generated Facial Expressions on Mood." *Journal of Personality and Social Psychology, 74,* 272–279.
6. S. Valins (1966). "Cognitive Effects of False Heart-Rate Feedback." *Journal of Personality and Social Psychology, 4,* 400–408.
7. P. Zimbardo (1977). Shyness: *What It Is, What to Do about It* (p. 53). Reading, MA: Addison-Wesley.
8. Ibid., p. 54.
9. R. Plutchik (1980). *Emotion: A Psychoevolutionary Synthesis.* New York: Harper & Row; P. R. Shaver, S. Wu, & J. C. Schwartz (1992). "Cross-Cultural Similarities and Differences in Emotion and its Representation: A Prototype Approach." In M. S. Clark (Ed.), *Emotion* (pp. 175–212). Newbury Park, CA: Sage.
10. P. Ekman (1999). "Basic Emotions." In T. Dalgleish & T. Power (Eds.), *The Handbook of Cognition and Emotion* (pp. 45–60). Sussex, U.K.: John Wiley & Sons; A. Ortony &d T. J. Turner (1990). "What's Basic about Basic Emotions?" *Psychological Review, 97,* 315–331.
11. M. Ferrari & E. Koyama (2002). "Meta-Emotions about Anger and Amae: A Cross-Cultural Comparison." *Consciousness and Emotion, 3,* 197–211.
12. Shaver et al., op. cit.
13. Goleman, op. cit.
14. J. M. Gottman, L. F. Katz, & C. Hooven (1997). *Meta-Emotion: How Families Communicate Emotionally.* Mahwah, NJ: Erlbaum.
15. J. C. McCroskey, V. P. Richmond, A. D. Heisel, & J. L Hayhurst (2004). "Eysenck's Big Three and Communication Traits: Communication Traits as Manifestations of Temperament." *Communication Research Reports, 21,* 404–410; J. J. Gross, S. K. Sutton, & T. V. Ketelaar (1998). "Relations between Affect and Personality: Support for the Affect-Level and Affective-Reactivity Views." *Personality and Social Psychology Bulletin, 24,* 279–288.
16. P. T. Costa & R. R. McCrae (1980). "Influence of Extraversion and Neuroticism on Subjective Well-Being: Happy and Unhappy People." *Journal of Personality and Social Psychology, 38,* 668–678.
17. T. Canli, Z. Zhao, J. E. Desmond, E. Kang, J. Gross, & J. D. E. Gabrieli (2001). "An MRI Study of Personality Influences on Brain Reactivity to Emotional Stimuli." *Behavioral Neuroscience, 115,* 33–42.
18. L. Kelly, R. L. Duran, & J. J. Zolten (2001). "The Effect of Reticence on College Students' Use of Electronic Mail to Communicate with Faculty." *Communication Education, 50,* 170–176. See also B. W. Scharlott & W. G. Christ (2001). "Overcoming Relationship-Initiation Barriers: The Impact of a Computer-Dating System on Sex Role, Shyness, and Appearance Inhibitions." *Computers in Human Behavior, 11,* 191–204.

19. C. Goddard (2002). "Explicating Emotions across Languages and Cultures: A Semantic Approach." In S. R. Fussell (Ed.), *The Verbal Communication of Emotions.* Mahwah, NJ: Erlbaum.
20. S. Ting-Toomey (1991). "Intimacy Expressions in Three Cultures: France, Japan, and the United States." *International Journal of Intercultural Relations, 15,* 29–46. See also C. Gallois (1993). "The Language and Communication of Emotion: Universal, Interpersonal, or Intergroup?" *American Behavioral Scientist, 36,* 309–338.
21. J. L. Tsai, B. Knutson, & H. H. Fung (2006). "Cultural Variation in Affect Valuation." *Journal of Personality and Social Psychology, 90,* 288–307.
22. J. W. Pennebaker, B. Rime, & V. E. Blankenship (1996). "Stereotypes of Emotional Expressiveness of Northerners and Southerners: A Cross-Cultural Test of Montesquieu's Hypotheses." *Journal of Personality and Social Psychology, 70,* 372–380.
23. Ibid., p. 176. See also Gallois, op. cit.
24. H. C. Triandis (1994). *Culture and Social Behavior* (p. 169). New York: McGraw-Hill. See also F. M. Moghaddam, D. M. Taylor, & S. C. Wright (1993) *Social Psychology in Cross-Cultural Perspective.* New York: Freeman.
25. R. Wilkins & E. Gareis (2006). "Emotion Expression and the Locution 'I Love You': A Cross-Cultural Study." *International Journal of Intercultural Relations, 30,* 51–75.
26. L. K. Guerrero, S. M. Jones, & R. R. Boburka (2006). "Sex Differences in Emotional Communication." In K. Dindia & D. J. Canary (Eds.), *Sex Differences and Similarities in Communication,* 2nd ed. Mahweh, NJ: Erlbaum; S. R. Wester, D. L. Vogel, P. K. Pressly, & M. Heesacker (2002). "Sex Differences in Emotion: A Critical Review of the Literature and Implications for Counseling Psychology." *Counseling Psychologist, 30,* 630–652.
27. J. Swenson & F. L. Casmir (1998). "The Impact of Culture-Sameness, Gender, Foreign Travel, and Academic Background on the Ability to Interpret Facial Expression of Emotion in Others." *Communication Quarterly, 46,* 214–230.
28. T. Canli, J. E. Desmond, Z. Zhao, & J. D. E. Gabrieli (2002). "Sex Differences in the Neural Basis of Emotional Memories." *Proceedings of the National Academy of Sciences, 10,* 10,789–10,794.
29. J. Merten (2005). "Culture, Gender and the Recognition of the Basic Emotions." *Psychologia: An International Journal of Psychology in the Orient, 48,* 306–316.
30. See, for example, A. W. Kunkel & B. R. Burleson (1999). "Assessing Explanations for Sex Differences in Emotional Support: A Test of the Different Cultures and Skill Specialization Accounts." *Human Communication Research, 25,* 307–340.
31. D. J. Goldsmith & P. A. Fulfs (1999). "'You Just Don't Have the Evidence': An Analysis of Claims and Evidence in DeborahTannen's *You Just Don't Understand.*" In M. E. Roloff (Ed.), *Communication Yearbook 22* (pp. 1–49). Thousand Oaks, CA: Sage.
32. D. F. Witmer & S. L. Katzman (1999). "On-Line Smiles: Does Gender Make a Difference in the Use of Graphic Accents?" *Journal of Computer-Mediated Communication, 2* (online, domain name expired).
33. K. Floyd (1997). "Communication Affection in Dyadic Relationships: An Assessment of Behavior and Expectancies." *Communication Quarterly, 45,* 68–80.

34. H. A. Elfenbein & N. Ambady (2002). "On the Universality and Cultural Specificity of Emotion Recognition: A Meta-Analysis." *Psychological Bulletin, 128,* 203–235.

35. M. S. Clark & E. J. Finkel (2005). "Willingness to Express Emotion: The Impact of Relationship Type, Communal Orientation, and Their Interaction." *Personal Relationships, 12,* 169–180.

36. J. A. Feeney (2005). "Hurt Feelings in Couple Relationships: Exploring the Role of Attachment and Perceptions of Personal Injury." *Personal Relationships, 12,* 253–271.

37. S. E. Snodgrass (1985). "Women's Intuition: The Effect of Subordinate Role on Interpersonal Sensitivity." *Journal of Personality and Social Psychology, 49,* 146–155.

38. S. B. Shimanoff (1984). "Commonly Named Emotions in Everyday Conversations." *Perceptual and Motor Skills, 58,* 514. See also J. M. Gottman (1982). "Emotional Responsiveness in Marital Conversations." *Journal of Communication, 32,* 108–120.

39. S. B. Shimanoff (1988). "Degree of Emotional Expressiveness as a Function of Face-Needs, Gender, and Interpersonal Relationship." *Communication Reports, 1,* 43–53.

40. C. A. Stearns & P. Stearns (1986). *Anger: The Struggle for Emotional Control in America's History.* Chicago: University of Chicago Press.

41. S. B. Shimanoff (1985). "Rules Governing the Verbal Expression of Emotions between Married Couples." *Western Journal of Speech Communication, 49,* 149–165.

42. S. Duck (1992). "Social Emotions: Showing Our Feelings about Other People." *Human Relationships.* Newbury Park, CA: Sage. See also S. B. Shimanoff (1985). "Expressing Emotions in Words: Verbal Patterns of Interaction." *Journal of Communication, 35,* 16–31.

43. L. B. Rosenfeld (1979). "Self-Disclosure Avoidance: Why I Am Afraid To Tell You Who I Am." *Communication Monographs, 46,* 63–74.

44. L. A. Erbert & K. Floyd (2004). "Affectionate Expressions as Face-Threatening Acts: Receiver Assessments." *Journal of Social and Personal Relationships, 17,* 230–246.

45. E. Hatfield, J. T. Cacioppo, R. L. Rapson, & K. Oatley (1984). *Emotional Contagion.* Cambridge, England: Cambridge University Press; see also S. Colino (2006) "That Look—It's Catching." *The Washington Post,* (May 30, 2006), HE01.

46. Goleman, op. cit., p. 115.

47. A. B. Bakker (2005). "Flow Among Music Teachers and Their Students: The Crossover of Peak Experiences." *Journal of Vocational Behavior, 66,* 822–833.

48. C. R. Goodman & R. A. Shippy (2002). "Is it Contagious? Affect Similarity Among Spouses." *Aging and Mental Health, 6,* 266–274.

49. E. S. Sullins (1991). "Emotional Contagion Revisited: Effects of Social Comparison and Expressive Style on Mood Convergence." *Personality and Social Psychology Bulletin, 17,* 166–174.

50. C. Anderson, D. Keltner, & O. P. John (May 2003). "Emotional Convergence between People over Time." *Journal of Personality and Social Psychology, 84,* 1,054–1,068.

51. T. DeAngelis (1992). "Illness Linked with Repressive Style of Coping." *APA Monitor, 23(12),* 14–15.

52. A. W. Seigman & T. W. Smith (1994). *Anger, Hostility, and the Heart.* Hillsdale, NJ: Erlbaum.

53. E. Kennedy-Moore & J. C. Watson (1999). *Expressing Emotion: Myths, Realities, and Therapeutic Strategies.* New York: Guilford.

54. S. Nelton (1996). "Emotions in the Workplace." *Nation's Business,* (February 1996), 25–30.

55. M. W. Kramer & J. A. Hess (2002). "Communication Rules for the Display of Emotions in Organizational Settings." *Management Communication Quarterly, 16,* 66–80.

56. M. Booth-Butterfield & S. Booth-Butterfield (1998). "Emotionality and Affective Orientation." In J. C. McCroskey, J. A. Daly, M. M. Martin, & M. J. Beatty (Eds.), *Communication and Personality: Trait Perspectives.* Creskill, NY: Hampton.

57. L. F. Barrett, J. Gross, T. Christensen, & M. Benvenuto (2001). "Knowing What You're Feeling and Knowing What to Do About It: Mapping the Relation Between Emotion Differentiation and Emotion Regulation." *Cognition and Emotion, 15,* 713–724.

58. D. Grewal & P. Salovey (2005). "Feeling Smart: The Science of Emotional Intelligence." *American Scientist, 93,* 330–339; S. H. Yoo, D. Matsumoto, & J. LeRoux (2006). "The Influence of Emotion Recognition and Emotion Regulation on Intercultural Adjustment." *International Journal of Intercultural Relations, 30,* 345–363.

59. B. J. Bushman, R. F. Baumeister, & A. D. Stack (1999). "Catharsis, Aggression, and Persuasive Influence: Self-Fulfilling or Self-Defeating Prophecies?" *Journal of Personality and Social Psychology, 76,* 367–376.

60. For an extensive discussion of ways to express emotions, see S. R. Fussell (2002). *The Verbal Communication of Emotions.* Mahwah, NJ: Erlbaum.

61. J. M. Honeycutt (2003). *Imagined Interactions: Daydreaming About Communication.* Cresskill, NJ: Hampton Press; J. M. Honeycutt & S. G. Ford (2001). "Mental Imagery and Intrapersonal Communication: A Review of Research on Imagined Interactions (IIs) and Current Developments." *Communication Yearbook, 25,* 315–338.

62. J. Pennebaker (2004). *Writing to Heal: A Guided Journal for Recovering from Trauma and Emotional Upheaval.* Oakland, CA: Harbinger.

63. B. H. Spitzberg (2006). "Preliminary Development of a Model and Measure of Computer-Mediated Communication (CMC) Competence." *Journal of Computer-Mediated Communication, 11,* article 12. Retrieved September 11, 2006, from http://jcmc.indiana.edu/vol11/issue2/spitzberg.html.

64. P. B. O'Sullivan (2000). "What You Don't Know Won't Hurt Me: Impression Management Functions of Communication Channels in Relationships." *Human Communication Research, 26,* 403–431.

65. T. E. Galovski, L. S. Malta, & E. B. Blanchard (2005). *Road Rage: Assessment and Treatment of the Angry, Aggressive Driver.* Washington, DC: American Psychological Association.

66. S. A. McCornack & T. R. Levine (1990). "When Lovers Become Leery: The Relationship between Suspicion and Accuracy in Detecting Deception." *Communication Monographs, 57,* 219–230.

67. J. Bourhis & M. Allen (1992). "Meta-Analysis of the Relationship between Communication Apprehension and Cognitive Performance." *Communication Education, 41,* 68–76.

68. M. L. Patterson & V. Ritts (1997). "Social and Communicative Anxiety: A Review and Meta-Analysis." In B. R. Burleson (Ed.), *Communication Yearbook 20.* Thousand Oaks, CA: Sage.

69. For a thorough discussion of how neurobiology shapes feelings, see J. E. LeDoux (1996). *The Emotional Brain.* New York: Simon and Schuster.

70. D. R. Vocate (1994). "Self-Talk and Inner Speech." In D. R. Vocate (Ed.), *Intrapersonal Communication: Different Voices, Different Minds.* Hillsdale, NJ: Erlbaum.

71. J. Ayers, T. Keereetaweep, P. Chen, & P. A. Edwards (1998). "Communication Apprehension and Employment Interviews." *Communication Education, 47,* 1–17.

72. M. Booth-Butterfield & M. R. Trotta (1994). "Attributional Patterns for Expressions of Love." *Communication Reports, 7,* 119–129.

73. A. L. Vangelisti, S. D. Corgin, A. E. Lucchetti, & R. J. Sprague (1999). "Couples' Concurrent Cognitions: The Influence of Relational Satisfaction on the Thoughts Couples Have as They Converse." *Human Communication Research, 25,* 370–398.

74. C. L. Rusting & S. Nolen-Hoeksema (1998). "Regulating Responses to Anger." *Journal of Personality and Social Psychology, 74,* 790–803.

75. B. J. Bushman, A. M. Bonacci, W. C. Pedersen, E. A. Vasquez, & N. Miller (2005). "Chewing on It Can Chew You Up: Effects of Rumination on Triggered Displaced Aggression." *Journal of Personality and Social Psychology, 88,* 969–983.

76. J. A. Bargh (1988). "Automatic Information Processing: Implications for Communication and Affect." In H. E. Sypher & E. T. Higgins (Eds.), *Communication, Social Cognition, and Affect.* Hillsdale, NJ: Erlbaum.

77. A. Beck (1976). *Cognitive Therapy and the Emotional Disorders.* New York: International Universities Press.

78. S. Metts & W. R. Cupach (1990). "The Influence of Relationship Beliefs and Problem-Solving Relationships on Satisfaction in Romantic Relationships." *Human Communication Research, 17,* 170–185.

79. A. Meichenbaum (1977). *Cognitive Behavior Modification.* New York: Plenum. See also A. Ellis & R. Greiger (1977). *Handbook for Rational-Emotive Therapy.* New York: Springer; and M. Wirga & M. DeBernardi (March 2002)."The ABCs of Cognition, Emotion, and Action." *Archives of Psychiatry and Psychotherapy, 1,* 5–16.

80. A. Chatham-Carpenter & V. DeFrancisco (1997). "Pulling Yourself Up Again: Women's Choices and Strategies for Recovering and Maintaining Self-Esteem." *Western Journal of Communication, 61,* 164–187.

Endnotes for Chapter 5

1. O. W. Sacks (1989). *Seeing Voices: A Journey into the World of the Deaf* (p. 17). Berkeley, CA: University of California Press.

2. M. Henneberger (January 29, 1999). "Misunderstanding of Word Embarrasses Washington's New Mayor." *New York Times* online, http://www.nyt.com (no longer in database).

3. T. L. Scott (2000). "Teens before Their Time." *Time,* (November 27, 2000), 22.

4. T. Wallsten (1986). "Measuring the Vague Meanings of Probability Terms." *Journal of Experimental Psychology, 115,* 348–365.

5. Reprinted in *Newsweek,* March 7, 1994, p. 54, and *Time,* October 11, 1993, p. 24.

6. M. L. Hecht, M. J. Collier, & S. A. Ribeau (1993). *African American Communication: Ethnic Identity and Cultural Interpretation* (pp. 84–89). Newbury Park, CA: Sage.

7. For a discussion of linguistic and political issues surrounding African American English, see the *Journal of English Linguistics, 32* (September 2004), a special issue devoted to this topic.

8. N. Coupland, J. M. Wiemann, & H. Giles (1991). "Talk as 'Problem' and Communication as 'Miscommunication': An Integrative Analysis." In N. Coupland, J. M. Wiemann, &d H. Giles, (Eds.), *"Miscommunication" and Problematic Talk.* Newbury Park, CA: Sage.

9. W. B. Pearce & V. Cronen (1980). *Communication, Action, and Meaning.* New York: Praeger. See also V. Cronen, V. Chen, & W. B. Pearce (1988). "Coordinated Management of Meaning: A Critical Theory." In Y. Y. Kim & W. B. Gudykunst (Eds.), *Theories in Intercultural Communication.* Newbury Park, CA: Sage.

10. E. K. E. Graham, M. Papa, & G. P. Brooks (1992). "Functions of Humor in Conversation: Conceptualization and Measurement." *Western Journal of Communication, 56,* 161–183.

11. P. B. O'Sullivan & A. Flanagin (2003). "Reconceptualizing 'Flaming' and Other Problematic Communication.," *New Media and Society, 5,* 67–93.

12. M. G. Marcus (October 1976) "The Power of a Name." *Psychology Today, 9,* 75–77, 106.

13. A. Mehrabian (1992). "Interrelationships among Name Desirability, Name Uniqueness, Emotion Characteristics Connoted by Names, and Temperament." *Journal of Applied Social Psychology, 22,* 1,797–1,808.

14. R. G. Fryer & S. D. Levitt (2004). "The Causes and Consequences of Distinctively Black Names," *Quarterly Journal of Economics, 119,* 767–805.

15. C. A. VanLear (1991). "Testing a Cyclical Model of Communicative Openness in Relationship Development." *Communication Monographs, 58,* 337–361.

16. D. Niven & J. Zilber (2000). "Preference for African American or Black." *Howard Journal of Communications, 11,* 267–277.

17. J. Zilber & D. Niven (1995). "'Black' versus 'African American': Are Whites' Political Attitudes Influenced by the Choice of Racial Labels?" *Social Science Quarterly, 76,* 655–664.

18. See, for example, R. K. Aune & Toshiyuki Kikuchi (1993). "Effects of Language Intensity Similarity on Perceptions of Credibility, Relational Attributions, and Persuasion." *Journal of Language and Social Psychology, 12,* 224–238.

19. H. Giles, J. Coupland, & N. Coupland (Eds.) (1991). *Contexts of Accommodation: Developments in Applied Sociolinguistics.* Cambridge, England: Cambridge University Press.

20. J. Cassell & D. Tversky (2005). "The Language of Online Intercultural Community Formation.," *Journal of Computer-Mediated Communication, 10,* Article 2.

21. "OMG: IM Slang is Invading Everyday English." NPR Weekend Edition, February 18, 2006. Retrieved September

11, 2006, from http://www.npr.org/templates/story/story.php?storyId=5221618.

22. A. Reyes (2005). "Appropriation of African American Slang by Asian American Youth." *Journal of Sociolinguistics, 9,* 509–532.

23. J. J. Bradac, J. M. Wiemann, & K. Schaefer (1994). "The Language of Control in Interpersonal Communication." In J. A. Daly & J. M. Wiemann (Eds.), *Strategic Interpersonal Communication* (pp. 102–104). Hillsdale, NJ: Erlbaum. See also S. H. Ng & J. J. Bradac (1993). *Power in Language: Verbal Communication and Social Influence* (p. 27). Newbury Park, CA: Sage.

24. S. Parton, S. A. Siltanen, L. A. Hosman, & J. Langenderfer (2002). "Employment Interview Outcomes and Speech Style Effects." *Journal of Language and Social Psychology, 21,* 144–161.

25. L. A. Hosman (1989). "The Evaluative Consequences of Hedges, Hesitations, and Intensifiers: Powerful and Powerless Speech Styles." *Human Communication Research, 15,* 383–406.

26. L. A. Samovar & R. E. Porter (2001). *Communication between Cultures,* 4th ed. (pp. 58–59). Belmont, CA: Wadsworth.

27. J. Bradac & A. Mulac (1984). "Attributional Consequences of Powerful and Powerless Speech Styles in a Crisis-Intervention Context." *Journal of Language and Social Psychology, 3,* 1–19.

28. J. J. Bradac (1983). "The Language of Lovers, Flovers [sic], and Friends: Communicating in Social and Personal Relationships." *Journal of Language and Social Psychology, 2,* 141–162.

29. D. Geddes (1992). "Sex Roles in Management: The Impact of Varying Power of Speech Style on Union Members' Perception of Satisfaction and Effectiveness." *Journal of Psychology, 126,* 589–607.

30. E. S. Kubany, D. C. Richard, G. B. Bauer, & M. Y. Muraoka (1992). "Impact of Assertive and Accusatory Communication of Distress and Anger: A Verbal Component Analysis." *Aggressive Behavior, 18,* 337–347.

31. R. Raskin & R. Shaw (1988). "Narcissism and the Use of Personal Pronouns." *Journal of Personality, 56,* 393–404; and A. L. Vangelisti, M. L. Knapp, & J. A. Daly (1990). "Conversational Narcissism." *Communication Monographs, 57,* 251–274.

32. A. S. Dreyer, C. A. Dreyer, & J. E. Davis (1987). "Individuality and Mutuality in the Language of Families of Field-Dependent and Field-Independent Children." *Journal of Genetic Psychology, 148,* 105–117.

33. J. M. Honeycutt (1999). "Typological Differences in Predicting Marital Happiness from Oral History Behaviors and Imagined Interactions." *Communication Monographs, 66,* 276–291.

34. R. F. Proctor & J. R. Wilcox (1993). "An Exploratory Analysis of Responses to Owned Messages in Interpersonal Communication." *ETC: A Review of General Semantics, 50,* 201–220; and Vangelisti et al., *Conversational Narcissism,* op. cit.

35. See, for example, D. Tannen (1990). *You Just Don't Understand: Women and Men in Conversation.* New York: William Morrow; and J. Gray (1992). *Men Are from Mars; Women Are from Venus.* New York: HarperCollins.

36. K. Dindia (2006). "Men are From North Dakota, Women are From South Dakota." In K. Dindia and D. J. Canary (Eds.), *Sex Differences and Similarities in Communication:*

Critical Essays and Empirical Investigations of Sex and Gender in Interaction, 2nd ed. Mahwah, NJ: Erlbaum; D. J. Goldsmith & P. A. Fulfs (1999). "'You Just Don't Have the Evidence': An Analysis of Claims and Evidence in Deborah Tannen's *You Just Don't Understand.*" In M. E. Roloff, (Ed.), *Communication Yearbook 22.* Thousand Oaks, CA: Sage.

37. See, for example, A. Haas & M. A. Sherman (1982). "Conversational Topic as a Function of Role and Gender." *Psychological Reports, 51,* 453–454; and B. Fehr (1996). *Friendship Processes.* Thousand Oaks, CA: Sage.

38. R. A. Clark (1998). "A Comparison of Topics and Objectives in a Cross Section of Young Men's and Women's Everyday Conversations." In D. J. Canary & K. Dindia, (Eds.), *Sex Differences and Similarities in Communication: Critical Essays and Empirical Investigations of Sex and Gender in Interaction.* Mahwah, NJ: Erlbaum.

39. J. T. Wood (1994). *Gendered Lives: Communication, Gender, and Culture* (p. 141). Belmont, CA: Wadsworth.

40. M. A. Sherman & A. Haas (June 1984). "Man to Man, Woman to Woman." *Psychology Today, 17,* 72–73.

41. J. D. Ragsdale (1996). "Gender, Satisfaction Level, and the Use of Relational Maintenance Strategies in Marriage." *Communication Monographs 63,* 354–371.

42. Haas & Sherman, op. cit.

43. For a summary of research on differences between male and female conversational behaviors, see H. Giles & R. L. Street Jr. (1985). "Communication Characteristics and Behavior." In M. L. Knapp & G. R. Miller (Eds.), *Handbook of Interpersonal Communication* (pp. 205–261). Beverly Hills, CA: Sage; and A. Kohn (February 1988). "Girl Talk, Guy Talk." *Psychology Today, 22,* 65–66.

44. A. Mulac (2006). "The Gender-Linked Language Effect: Do Language Differences Really Make a Difference?" In K. Dindia & D. J. Canary (Eds.), *Sex Differences and Similarities in Communication: Critical Essays and Empirical Investigations of Sex and Gender in Interaction,* 2nd ed. Mahwah, NJ: Erlbaum.

45. Clark, op. cit.

46. L. L. Carli (1990). "Gender, Language, and Influence." *Journal of Personality and Social Psychology, 59,* 941–951.

47. D. J. Canary & K. S. Hause (1993). "Is There Any Reason to Research Sex Differences in Communication?" *Communication Quarterly, 41,* 129–144.

48. C. J. Zahn (1989). "The Bases for Differing Evaluations of Male and Female Speech: Evidence from Ratings of Transcribed Conversation." *Communication Monographs, 56,* 59–74. See also L. M. Grob, R. A. Meyers, & R. Schuh (1997). "Powerful/ Powerless Language Use in Group Interactions: Sex Differences or Similarities?" *Communication Quarterly, 45,* 282–303.

49. K. Dindia, op. cit.

50. C. J. Zahn (1989). "The Bases for Differing Evaluations of Male and Female Speech: Evidence from Ratings of Transcribed Conversation." *Communication Monographs, 56,* 59–74.

51. B. A. Fisher (1983). "Differential Effects of Sexual Composition and Interactional Content on Interaction Patterns in Dyads." *Human Communication Research, 9,* 225–238.

52. See, for example, D. Tannen (1994). *Talking from 9 to 5: Women and Men in the Workplace: Language, Sex and Power.* New York: William Morrow; and Wood, op. cit.

53. D. G. Ellis & L. McCallister (1980). "Relational Control Sequences in Sex-Typed and Androgynous Groups." *Western Journal of Speech Communication, 44,* 35–49.

54. S. Steen & P. Schwarz (1995). "Communication, Gender, and Power: Homosexual Couples as a Case Study." In M. A. Fitzpatrick & A. L. Vangelisti (Eds.), *Explaining Family Interactions* (pp. 310–343). Thousand Oaks, CA: Sage.

55. For a thorough discussion of the challenges involved in translation from one language to another, see L. A. Samovar & R. E. Porter (1991). *Communication between Cultures* (pp. 165–169). Dubuque, IA: W.C. Brown.

56. The examples in this paragraph are taken from D. Ricks (1983). *Big Business Blunders: Mistakes in International Marketing* (p. 41). Homewood, IL: Dow Jones-Irwin.

57. N. Sugimoto (1991, March) *"Excuse Me" and "I'm Sorry": Apologetic Behaviors of Americans and Japanese.* Paper presented at the Conference on Communication in Japan and the United States, California State University, Fullerton, CA.

58. A summary of how verbal style varies across cultures can be found in Chapter 5 of W. B. Gudykunst & S. Ting-Toomey (1988). *Culture and Interpersonal Communication.* Newbury Park, CA: Sage.

59. E. Hall (1959). *Beyond Culture.* New York: Doubleday, 1959.

60. A. Almaney & A. Alwan (1982). *Communicating with the Arabs.* Prospect Heights, IL: Waveland.

61. K. Basso (1970). "To Give Up on Words: Silence in Western Apache Culture." *Southern Journal of Anthropology, 26,* 213–230.

62. J. Yum (1987). "The Practice of Uye-ri in Interpersonal Relationships in Korea." In D. Kincaid (Ed.), *Communication Theory from Eastern and Western Perspectives.* New York: Academic Press.

63. T. Seinfatt (1989). "Linguistic Relativity: Toward a Broader View." In S. Ting-Toomey and F. Korzenny (Eds.), *Language, Communication, and Culture: Current Directions.* Newbury Park, CA: Sage.

64. L. Martin & G. Pullum (1991). *The Great Eskimo Vocabulary Hoax.* Chicago: University of Chicago Press.

65. H. Giles & A. Franklyn-Stokes (1989). "Communicator Characteristics." In M. K. Asante & W. B. Gudykunst (Eds.), *Handbook of International and Intercultural Communication.* Newbury Park, CA: Sage.

66. B. Whorf (1956). "The Relation of Habitual Thought and Behavior to Language." In J. B. Carrol (Ed.), *Language, Thought, and Reality.* Cambridge, MA: MIT Press.

67. H. Rheingold (1988). *They Have a Word for It.* Los Angeles: Jeremy P. Tarcher.

Endnotes for Chapter 6

1. Research summarized by J. K. Burgoon (1994). "Nonverbal Signals." In M. L. Knapp & G. R. Miller (Eds.), *Handbook of Interpersonal Communication* (p. 235). Newbury Park, CA: Sage.

2. Research supporting these claims is cited in J. K. Burgoon & G. D. Hoobler (2002). "Nonverbal Signals." In M. L. Knapp & J. A. Daly (Eds.), *Handbook of Interpersonal Communication,* 3rd ed. Thousand Oaks, CA: Sage.

3. S. E. Jones & C. D. LeBaron (2002). "Research on the Relationship between Verbal and Nonverbal Communication: Emerging Interactions." *Journal of Communication, 52,* 499–521.

4. B. M. DePaulo (1994). "Spotting Lies: Can Humans Learn to Do Better?" *Current Directions in Psychological Science, 3,* 83–86.

5. Not all communication theorists agree with the claim that all nonverbal behavior has communicative value. For a contrasting opinion, see Burgoon, "Nonverbal Signals," pp. 229–232.

6. F. Manusov (Summer 1991). "Perceiving Nonverbal Messages: Effects of Immediacy and Encoded Intent on Receiver Judgments." *Western Journal of Speech Communication, 55,* 235–253. See also R. Buck and C. A. VanLear (2002). "Verbal and Nonverbal Communication: Distinguishing Symbolic, Spontaneous, and Pseudo-Spontaneous Nonverbal Behavior." *Journal of Communication, 52,* 522–541.

7. See, for example, T. Clevenger Jr. (1991). "Can One Not Communicate? A Conflict of Models." *Communication Studies, 42,* 340–353.

8. J. K. Burgoon & B. A. LePoire (1999). "Nonverbal Cues and Interpersonal Judgments: Participant and Observer Perceptions of Intimacy, Dominance, Composure, and Formality." *Communication Monographs, 66,* 105–124. See also Burgoon & Hoobler, op. cit.

9. A. Ramirez & J. K. Burgoon (2004). "The Effect of Interactivity on Initial Interactions: The Influence of Information Valence and Modality and Information Richness on Computer-Mediated Interaction." *Communication Monographs, 71,* 442–447.

10. "Smile When You Write That." *Los Angeles Times,* March 18, 1999, p. C2.

11. E. S. Cross & E. A. Franz (2003, April). *Talking Hands: Observation of Bimanual Gestures as a Facilitative Working Memory Mechanism.* Cognitive Neuroscience Society 10th Annual Meeting, New York.

12. M. T. Motley (1993). "Facial Affect and Verbal Context in Conversation: Facial Expression as Interjection." *Human Communication Research, 20,* 3–40.

13. See, for example, K. Drummond and R. Hopper (1993). "Acknowledgment Tokens in Series," *Communication Reports, 6,* 47–53; and H. M. Rosenfeld (1987). "Conversational Control Functions of Nonverbal Behavior." In A. W. Siegman and S. Feldstein (Eds.), *Nonverbal Behavior and Communication,* 2nd ed. Hillsdale, NJ: Erlbaum.

14. J. Hale & J. B. Stiff (1990). "Nonverbal Primacy in Veracity Judgments." *Communication Reports, 3,* 75–83; and J. B. Stiff, J. L. Hale, R. Garlick, & R. G. Rogan (1990). "Effect of Individual Judgments of Honesty and Deceit." *Southern Speech Communication Journal, 55,* 206–229.

15. J. K. Burgoon, T. Birk, & M. Pfau (1990). "Nonverbal Behaviors, Persuasion, and Credibility." *Human Communication Research, 17,* 140–169.

16. D. D. Henningsen, M. G. Cruz, & M. C. Morr (2000). "Pattern Violations and Perceptions of Deception." *Communication Reports, 13,* 1–9.

17. See, for example, B. M. DePaulo (1980). "Detecting Deception Modality Effects." In L. Wheeler (Ed.), *Review of Personality and Social Psychology,* vol. 1. Beverly Hills, CA: Sage; and J. Greene, D. O'Hair, M. Cody, & C. Yen (1985). "Planning and Control of Behavior during Deception." *Human Communication Research, 11,* 335–364.

18. B. M. DePaulo, J. J. Lindsay, B. E. Malone, L. Muhlenbruck, K. Charlton, & H. Cooper (2003). "Cues to Deception." *Psychological Bulletin, 129,* 74–118; A. Vrig,

K. Edward, K. P. Roberts, & R. Bull (2000). "Detecting Deceit Via Analysis of Verbal and Nonverbal Behavior." *Journal of Nonverbal Behavior, 24,* 239–263.

19. C. Lock (2004). "Deception Detection: Psychologists Try to Learn How to Spot a Liar." *Science News Online, 166,* 72.

20. L. Caso, A. Vrij, S. Mann, & G. DeLeo (2006). "Deceptive Responses: The Impact of Verbal and Non-Verbal Countermeasures." *Legal and Criminological Psychology, 11,* 99–111; A. Vrig (2004). "Why Professionals Fail to Catch Liars and How They Can Improve." *Legal and Criminological Psychology, 9,* 159–181.

21. A. E. Lindsey & V. Vigil (1999). "The Interpretation and Evaluation of Winking in Stranger Dyads." *Communication Research Reports, 16,* 256–265.

22. G. Y. Lim, G. Y. & M. E. Roloff (1999). "Attributing Sexual Consent." *Journal of Applied Communication Research, 27,* 1–23.

23. D. Druckmann, R. Rozelle, & J. Baxter 1982). *Nonverbal Communication: Survey, Theory, and Research* (p. 52). Beverly Hills, CA: Sage.

24. M. Motley & C. Camden (1988). "Facial Expression of Emotion: A Comparison of Posed versus Spontaneous Expressions in an Interpersonal Communication Setting." *Western Journal of Speech Communication, 52,* 1–22.

25. J. Amos (2005). "How Boys Miss Teacher's Reprimand." *BBC News* (September 8, 2005). Retrieved September 11, 2006, from http://news.bbc.co.uk/1/hi/sci/tech/4227296.stm.

26. B. P. Rourke (1989). *Nonverbal Learning Disabilities: The Syndrome and the Model.* New York: Guilford.

27. E. S. Fudge (n.d.). "Nonverbal Learning Disorder Syndrome?" Retrieved September 11, 2006, from http://www.nldontheweb.org/fudge.htm.

28. J. C. Rosip & J. A. Hall (2004). "Knowledge of Nonverbal Cues, Gender, and Nonverbal Decoding Accuracy.," *Journal of Nonverbal Behavior, 28,* 267–286; J. A. Hall (1985). "Male and Female Nonverbal Behavior." In A. W. Siegman & S. Feldstein (Eds.), *Multichannel Integrations of Nonverbal Behavior.* Hillsdale, NJ: Erlbaum.

29. J. A. Hall, J. D. Carter, & T. G. Horgan (2001). "Status Roles and Recall of Nonverbal Cues." *Journal of Nonverbal Behavior, 25,* 79–100.

30. For a comprehensive summary of male-female differences and similarities in nonverbal communication, see P. A. Andersen (1999). *Nonverbal Communication: Forms and Functions* (p. 107). Mountain View, CA: Mayfield. For a detailed summary of similarities and differences, see D. J. Canary & T. M. Emmers-Sommer (1997). *Sex and Gender Differences in Personal Relationships.* New York: Guilford.

31. J. A. Hall, T. G. Horgan, & J. D. Carter (2002). "Assigned and Felt Status in Relation to Observer-Coded and Participant-Reported Smiling." *Journal of Nonverbal Behavior, 26,* 63–81.

32. Andersen, op. cit., p. 107.

33. D. Matsumoto & S. H. Yoo (2005). "Culture and Applied Nonverbal Communication." In R. S. Feldman & R. E. Riggio (Eds.), *Applications of Nonverbal Communication* (pp. 255–277). Mahweh, NJ: Erlbaum.

34. R. Birdwhistell (1970). *Kinesics and Context* (Chap. 9). Philadelphia: University of Pennsylvania Press.

35. P. Ekman, W. V. Friesen, & J. Baer (May 1984). "The International Language of Gestures." *Psychology Today, 18,* 64–69.

36. D. Matsumoto (1993). "Ethnic Differences in Affect Intensity, Emotion Judgments, Display Rule Attitudes, and Self-Reported Emotional Expression in an American Sample." *Motivation and Emotion, 17,* 107–123.

37. M. G. Beaupré & U. Hess (2006). "An Ingroup Advantage for Confidence in Emotion Recognition Judgments: The Moderating Effect of Familiarity with the Expressions of Outgroup Members." *Personality and Social Psychology Bulletin, 32,* 16–26.

38. E. Hall (1969). *The Hidden Dimension.* Garden City, NY: Anchor Books.

39. A. M. Warnecke, R. D. Masters, & G. Kempter (1992). "The Roots of Nationalism: Nonverbal Behavior and Xenophobia." *Ethnology and Sociobiology, 13,* 267–282.

40. H. A. Elfenbein (2006). "Learning in Emotion Judgments: Training and the Cross-Cultural Understanding of Facial Expressions." *Journal of Nonverbal Behavior, 30,* 21–36.

41. Hall, *The Hidden Dimension.*

42. J. B. Bavelas, L. Coates, & T. Johnson (2002). "Listener Responses as a Collaborative Process: The Role of Gaze." *Journal of Communication, 52,* 566–579.

43. M. Booth-Butterfield & F. Jordan (1998). *"Act Like Us": Communication Adaptation among Racially Homogeneous and Heterogeneous Groups.* Paper presented at the Speech Communication Association meeting, New Orleans, LA.

44. S. Weitz (Ed.) (1974). *Nonverbal Communication: Readings with Commentary.* New York: Oxford University Press.

45. J. Eibl-Eibesfeldt (1972). "Universals and Cultural Differences in Facial Expressions of Emotions." In J. Cole (Ed.), *Nebraska Symposium on Motivation.* Lincoln: University of Nebraska Press.

46. M. Coulson (2004). "Attributing Emotion to Static Body Postures: Recognition Accuracy, Confusions, and Viewpoint Dependence." *Journal of Nonverbal Behavior, 28,* 117–139.

47. A. Mehrabian (1981). *Silent Messages,* 2nd ed. (pp. 47–48, 61–62). Belmont, CA: Wadsworth.

48. J. M. Iverson (1999). "How to Get to the Cafeteria: Gesture and Speech in Blind and Sighted Children's Spatial Descriptions." *Developmental Psychology, 35,* 1,132–1,142.

49. M. C. Corballis (2002). *From Hand to Mouth: The Origins of Language.* Princeton, NJ: Princeton University Press.

50. Andersen, op. cit., p. 37.

51. P. Ekman & W. V. Friesen (1969). "The Repertoire of Nonverbal Behavior: Categories, Origins, Usage, and Coding." *Semiotica, 1,* 49–98.

52. A. Sueyoshi & D. M. Hardison (2005). "The Role of Gestures and Facial Cues in Second Language Listening Comprehension." *Language Learning, 55,* 661–699.

53. B. I. Koerner (2003). "What Does a 'Thumbs Up' Mean in Iraq?" *Slate* (March 28, 2003). Retrieved September 11, 2006, from http://www.slate.com/id/2080812.

54. P. Ekman & W. V. Friesen (1974). "Nonverbal Behavior and Psychopathology." In R. J. Friedman & M. N. Katz (Eds.), *The Psychology of Depression: Contemporary Theory and Research.* Washington, DC: J. Winston.

55. Ekman, *Telling Lies,* p. 107.

56. P. Ekman & W. V. Friesen (1975). *Unmasking the Face: A Guide to Recognizing Emotions from Facial Clues.* Englewood Cliffs, NJ: Prentice-Hall.

57. Ibid., p. 150.

58. E. Krumhuber & A. Kappas (2005). "Moving Smiles: The Role of Dynamic Components for the Perception of the

Genuineness of Smiles." *Journal of Nonverbal Behavior, 29,* 3–24.

59. S. F. Davis & J. C. Kieffer (1998). "Restaurant Servers Influence Tipping Behavior." *Psychological Reports, 83,* 223–226.

60. N. Gueguen & C. Jacob (2002). "Direct Look versus Evasive Glance and Compliance With a Request." *Journal of Social Psychology, 142,* 393–396.

61. E. H. Hess & J. M. Polt (1960). "Pupil Size as Related to Interest Value of Visual Stimuli." *Science, 132,* 349–350.

62. For a summary, see Knapp and Hall, op. cit., pp. 344–346.

63. A. Mehrabian & M. Wiener (1967). "Decoding of Inconsistent Communications." *Journal of Personality and Social Psychology, 6,* 109–114; see also A. Mehrabian & S. Ferris (1967). "Interference of Attitudes from Nonverbal Communication in Two Channels." *Journal of Consulting Psychology, 31,* 248–252.

64. A. R. Trees (2000). "Nonverbal Communication and the Support Process: Interactional Sensitivity in Interactions between Mothers and Young Adult Children." *Communication Monographs, 67,* 239–261.

65. D. Buller & K. Aune (1992). "The Effects of Speech Rate Similarity on Compliance: Application of Communication Accommodation Theory." *Western Journal of Communication, 56,* 37–53. See also D. Buller, B. A. LePoire, K. Aune, & S. V. Eloy (1992). "Social Perceptions as Mediators of the Effect of Speech Rate Similarity on Compliance." *Human Communication Research, 19,* 286–311; D. B. Buller & R. K. Aune (1988). "The Effects of Vocalics and Nonverbal Sensitivity on Compliance: A Speech Accommodation Theory Explanation." *Human Communication Research, 14,* 301–332.

66. P. A. Andersen (1984). "Nonverbal Communication in the Small Group." In R. S. Cathcart & L. A. Samovar (Eds.), *Small Group Communication: A Reader,* 4th ed. Dubuque, IA: W.C. Brown.

67. M. Harris, S. Ivanko, S. Jungen, S. Hala, & P. Pexman (2001, October). 2001 *You're Really Nice: Children's Understanding of Sarcasm and Personality Traits.* Poster presented at the 2nd Biennial Meeting of the Cognitive Development Society, Virginia Beach, VA.

68. K. J. Tusing & J. P. Dillard (2000). "The Sounds of Dominance: Vocal Precursors of Perceived Dominance during Interpersonal Influence." *Human Communication Research, 26,* 148–171.

69. M. Zuckerman & R. E. Driver (1989). "What Sounds Beautiful Is Good: The Vocal Attractiveness Stereotype." *Journal of Nonverbal Behavior, 13,* 67–82.

70. S. H. Ng & J. J. Bradac (1993). *Power in Language: Verbal Communication and Social Influence* (p. 40). Newbury Park, CA: Sage.

71. R. Heslin & T. Alper (1983). "Touch: A Bonding Gesture." In J. M. Wiemann & R. P. Harrison (Eds.), *Nonverbal Interaction* (pp. 47–75). Beverly Hills, CA: Sage.

72. Ibid.

73. J. Burgoon, J. Walther, & E. Baesler (1992). "Interpretations, Evaluations, and Consequences of Interpersonal Touch." *Human Communication Research, 19,* 237–263.

74. C. R. Kleinke (1977). "Compliance to Requests Made by Gazing and Touching Experimenters in Field Settings.," *Journal of Experimental Social Psychology, 13,* 218–223.

75. F. N. Willis & H. K. Hamm (1980). "The Use of Interpersonal Touch in Securing Compliance." *Journal of Nonverbal Behavior, 5,* 49–55.

76. A. H. Crusco & C. G. Wetzel (1984). "The Midas Touch: Effects of Interpersonal Touch on Restaurant Tipping." *Personality and Social Psychology Bulletin, 10,* 512–517.

77. M. Lynn & K. Mynier (1993). " Effect of Server Posture on Restaurant Tipping." *Journal of Applied Social Psychology, 23,* 678–685.

78. D. Kaufman & J. M. Mahoney (1999). "The Effect of Waitresses' Touch on Alcohol Consumption in Dyads." *Journal of Social Psychology, 139,* 261–267.

79. H. Bakwin (1949). "Emotional Deprivation in Infants." *Journal of Pediatrics, 35,* 512–521.

80. T. Adler (1993). "Congressional Staffers Witness Miracle of Touch." *APA Monitor* (February 1993), 12–13.

81. M. S. Driscoll, D. L. Newman, & J. M. Seal (1988). "The Effect of Touch on the Perception of Counselors." *Counselor Education and Supervision, 27,* 344–354; and J. M. Wilson (1982). "The Value of Touch in Psychotherapy." *American Journal of Orthopsychiatry, 52,* 65–72.

82. For a summary, see Knapp & Hall, *Nonverbal Communication in Human Interaction,* pp. 93–132.

83. M. Hosoda, E. F. Stone-Romero, & G. Coats (2003). "The Effects of Physical Attractiveness on Job-Related Outcomes: A Meta-Analysis of Experimental Studies." *Personnel Psychology, 56,* 431–462.

84. K. K. Dion (1973). "Young Children's Stereotyping of Facial Attractiveness." *Developmental Psychology, 9,* 183–188.

85. V. Ritts, M. L. Patterson, & M. E. Tubbs (1992). "Expectations, Impressions, and Judgments of Physically Attractive Students: A Review." *Review of Educational Research, 62,* 413–426.

86. T. C. Riniolo, K. C. Johnson, & T. R. Sherman (2006). "Hot or Not: Do Professors Perceived as Physically Attractive Receive Higher Student Evaluations?" *Journal of General Psychology, 133,* 19–35.

87. K. F. Albada, M. L. Knapp, & K. E. Theune (2002). "Interaction Appearance Theory: Changing Perceptions of Physical Attractiveness Through Social Interaction." *Communication Theory, 12,* 8–40.

88. W. Thourlby (1978). *You Are What You Wear* (p. 1). New York: New American Library.

89. L. Bickman (1974). "The Social Power of a Uniform." *Journal of Applied Social Psychology, 4,* 47–61.

90. S. G. Lawrence & M. Watson (1991). "Getting Others to Help: The Effectiveness of Professional Uniforms in Charitable Fund Raising." *Journal of Applied Communication Research, 19,* 170–185.

91. H. Fortenberry, J. Maclean, P. Morris, & M. O'Connell (1978). "Mode of Dress as a Perceptual Cue to Deference." *The Journal of Social Psychology, 104.*

92. L. Bickman (April 1974). "Social Roles and Uniforms: Clothes Make the Person." *Psychology Today, 7,* 48–51.

93. M. Lefkowitz, R. R. Blake, & J. S. Mouton (1955). "Status of Actors in Pedestrian Violation of Traffic Signals." *Journal of Abnormal and Social Psychology, 51,* 704–706.

94. L. E. Temple & K. R. Loewen (1993). "Perceptions of Power: First Impressions of a Woman Wearing a Jacket." *Perceptual and Motor Skills, 76,* 339–348.

95. T. F. Hoult (1954). "Experimental Measurement of Clothing as a Factor in Some Social Ratings of Selected American Men." *American Sociological Review, 19,* 326–327.

96. Hall, *The Hidden Dimension.*

97. M. Hackman & K. Walker (1990). "Instructional Communication in the Televised Classroom: The Effects of System Design and Teacher Immediacy." *Communication Education, 39,* 196–206. See also J. C. McCroskey & V. P. Richmond (1992). "Increasing Teacher Influence through Immediacy." In V. P. Richmond & J. C. McCroskey (Eds.), *Power in the Classroom: Communication, Control, and Concern.* Hillsdale, NJ: Erlbaum.

98. C. Conlee, J. Olvera, & N. Vagim (1993). "The Relationships among Physician Nonverbal Immediacy and Measures of Patient Satisfaction with Physician Care." *Communication Reports, 6,* 25–33.

99. G. Brown, T. B. Lawrence, & S. L. Robinson, (2005). "Territoriality in Organizations." *Academy of Management Review, 30,* 577–594.

100. E. Sadalla (1987). "Identity and Symbolism in Housing." *Environment and Behavior, 19,* 569–587.

101. A. Maslow & N. Mintz (1956). "Effects of Aesthetic Surroundings: Initial Effects of Those Aesthetic Surroundings upon Perceiving 'Energy' and 'Well-Being' in Faces." *Journal of Psychology, 41,* 247–254.

102. J. J. Teven & M. E. Comadena (1996). "The Effects of Office Aesthetic Quality on Students' Perceptions of Teacher Credibility and Communicator Style." *Communication Research Reports, 13,* 101–108.

103. R. Sommer (1969). *Personal Space: The Behavioral Basis of Design.* Englewood Cliffs, NJ: Prentice-Hall.

104. D. I. Ballard & D. R. Seibold (2000). "Time Orientation and Temporal Variation across Work Groups: Implications for Group and Organizational Communication." *Western Journal of Communication, 64,* 218–242.

105. R. Levine (1988). "The Pace of Life across Cultures." In J. E. McGrath (Ed.), *The Social Psychology of Time.* Newbury Park, CA: Sage.

106. E. T. Hall & M. R. Hall (1987). *Hidden Differences: Doing Business with the Japanese.* Garden City, NY: Anchor Press.

107. R. Levine & E. Wolff (March 1985). "Social Time: The Heartbeat of Culture." *Psychology Today, 19,* 28–35.

108. D. I. Ballard & D. R. Seibold (2004). "Organizational Members' Communication and Temporal Experience" *Communication Research, 31,* 135–172; C. Kaufman-Scarborough & J. D. Lindquist (1999). "Time Management and Polychronicity: Comparisons, Contrasts, and Insights for the Workplace." *Journal of Managerial Psychology, 14,* 288–312.

Endnotes for Chapter 7

1. L. Barker, R. Edwards, C. Gaines, K. Gladney, & R. Holley (1981). "An Investigation of Proportional Time Spent in Various Communication Activities by College Students." *Journal of Applied Communication Research, 8,* 101–109.

2. Research summarized in A. D. Wolvin & C. G. Coakley (1981). "A Survey of the Status of Listening Training in Some Fortune 500 Corporations," *Communication Education, 40,* 152–164.

3. K. J. Prager & D. Buhrmester (1998). "Intimacy and Need Fulfillment in Couple Relationships." *Journal of Social and Personal Relationships. 15,* 435–469.

4. A. L. Vangelisti (1994). "Couples' Communication Problems: The Counselor's Perspective." *Journal of Applied Communication Research. 22,* 106–126.

5. A. D. Wolvin (1984). "Meeting the Communication Needs of the Adult Learners." *Communication Education, 33,* 267–271.

6. B. D. Sypher, R. N. Bostrom, & J. H. Seibert (1989). "Listening Communication Abilities and Success at Work." *Journal of Business Communication 26,* 293–303. See also E. R. Alexander, L. E. Penley, & I. E. Jernigan (1992). "The Relationship of Basic Decoding Skills to Managerial Effectiveness." *Management Communication Quarterly, 6,* 58–73.

7. J. L. Winsor, D. B. Curtis, & R. D. Stephens (1999). "National Preferences in Business and Communication Education: An Update." *Journal of the Association for Communication Administration. 3,* 170–179.

8. S. Johnson & C. Bechler (1998). "Examining the Relationship between Listening Effectiveness and Leadership Emergence: Perceptions, Behaviors, and Recall." *Small Group Research, 29,* 452–471.

9. D. Christensen & D. Rees (October, 2002). "Communication Skills Needed by Entry-Level Accountants." *The CPA Letter, 82.* Retrieved July 5, 2006, from http://www.aicpa.org/pubs/cpaltr/Oct2002/AUDIT/audit.htm.

10. V. Marchant (June 28, 1999). "Listen Up!" *Time 153,* 74. See also *Job Outlook 2006,* summarized at http://www.naceweb.org/press/display.asp?year=&prid=235.

11. J. Brownell (1990). "Perceptions of Effective Listeners: A Management Study." *Journal of Business Communication, 27,* 401–415.

12. A. Fernald (2001). "Hearing, Listening, and Understanding: Auditory Development in Infancy." In G. Bemner & A. Fogel (Eds.), *Blackwell Handbook of Infant Development* (pp. 35–70). Malden, MA: Blackwell.

13. S. Chaiken & Y. Trope (Eds.) (1999). *Dual-Process Theories in Social Psychology.* New York: Guilford; A. Todorov, S. Chaiken, & M. D. Henderson (2002). "The Heuristic-Systematic Model of Social Information Processing." In J. P. Dillard & M. Pfau (Eds.), *The Persuasion Handbook: Developments in Theory and Practice* (pp. 137–167). Thousand Oaks, CA: Sage.

14. E. Langer (1990). *Mindfulness.* Reading, MA: Addison-Wesley.

15. J. K. Burgoon, C. R. Berger, & V. R. Waldron (2000). "Mindfulness and Interpersonal Communication." *Journal of Social Issues, 56,* 105–127.

16. Langer, op. cit., p. 90.

17. C. Flexer (1997). "Commonly-Asked Questions about Children with Minimal Hearing Loss in the Classroom." *Hearing Loss* (February 1997), 8–12.

18. L. R. Smeltzer & K. W. Watson (1984). "Listening: An Empirical Comparison of Discussion Length and Level of Incentive." *Central States Speech Journal, 35,* 166–170.

19. M. Pasupathi, L. M. Stallworth, & K. Murdoch (1998). "How What We Tell Becomes What We Know: Listener Effects on Speakers' Long-Term Memory for Events." *Discourse Processes, 26,* 1–25.

20. M. H. Lewis & N. L. Reinsch, Jr. (1988). "Listening in Organizational Environments." *Journal of Business Communication, 23,* 49–67.

21. A. L. Vangelisti, M. L. Knapp, & J. A. Daly (1990). "Conversational Narcissism." *Communication Monographs, 57,* 251–274. See also J. C. McCroskey & V. P. Richmond (1993). "Identifying Compulsive Communicators: The Talkaholic Scale." *Communication Research Reports, 10,* 107–114.

22. K. B. McComb & F. M. Jablin (1984). "Verbal Correlates of Interviewer Empathic Listening and Employment Interview Outcomes." *Communication Monographs, 51,* 367.

23. A. Wolvin & C. G. Coakley (1988). *Listening,* 3rd ed. (p. 208). Dubuque, IA: W.C. Brown.

24. R. Nichols (September 1987). "Listening Is a Ten-Part Skill." *Nation's Business, 75,* 40.

25. S. Golen (1990). "A Factor Analysis of Barriers to Effective Listening," *Journal of Business Communication, 27,* 25–36.

26. P. Nelson, K. Kohnert, S. Sabur, & D. Shaw (2005). "Noise and Children Learning Through a Second Language: Double Jeopardy?" *Language, Speech, & Hearing Services in Schools, 36,* 219–229.

27. N. Kline (1999). *Time to Think: Listening to Ignite the Human Mind* (p. 21). London: Ward Lock.

28. L. J. Carrell & S. C. Willmington (1996). "A Comparison of Self-Report and Performance Data in Assessing Speaking and Listening Competence." *Communication Reports, 9,* 185–191.

29. N. Spinks & B. Wells (1991). "Improving Listening Power: The Payoff." *Bulletin of the Association for Business Communication, 54,* 75–77.

30. M. Elias (2005). "So Much Media, So Little Attention Span." *USA Today* (March 30, 2005). Retrieved September 11, 2006, from http://www.usatoday.com/news/education/2005-03-30-kids-attention_x.htm.

31. D. Carbaugh (1999). "'Just Listen': 'Listening' and Landscape among the Blackfeet." *Western Journal of Communication, 63,* 250–270.

32. A. M. Bippus (2001). "Recipients' Criteria for Evaluating the Skillfulness of Comforting Communication and the Outcomes of Comforting Interactions." *Communication Monographs, 68,* 301–313.

33. G. Goodman & G. Esterly (1990). "Questions—The Most Popular Piece of Language." In J. Stewart (Ed.), *Bridges Not Walls* (5th ed). New York: McGraw-Hill.

34. Adapted from B. R. Burleson (1994). "Comforting Messages: Features, Functions, and Outcomes." In J. A. Daly & J. M. Wiemann (Eds.), *Strategic Interpersonal Communication* (p. 140). Hillsdale, NJ: Erlbaum.

35. S. Myers (2000). "Empathic Listening: Reports on the Experience of Being Heard." *Journal of Humanistic Psychology, 40,* 148–173; S. G. Grant (1998). "A Principal's Active Listening Skills and Teachers' Perceptions of the Principal's Leader Behaviors." *Dissertation Abstracts International Section A: Humanities and Social Sciences, 58,* 2933; V. B. Van Hasselt, M. T. Baker, & S. J. Romano (2006). "Crisis (Hostage) Negotiation Training: A Preliminary Evaluation of Program Efficacy." *Criminal Justice and Behavio, 33,* 56–69.

36. See J. Bruneau (1989). "Empathy and Listening: A Conceptual Review and Theoretical Directions," *Journal of the International Listening Association, 3,* 1–20; and K. N. Cissna & R. Anderson (1990). "The Contributions of Carl R. Rogers to a Philosophical Praxis of Dialogue." *Western Journal of Speech Communication, 54,* 137–147.

37. B. R. Burleson (2003). "Emotional Support Skills." In J. O. Greene and B. R. Burleson (Eds.), *Handbook of Communication and Social Interaction Skills* (p. 552). Mahwah, NJ: Erlbaum.

38. B. Burleson & W. Samter (1987, August). *Cognitive Complexity, Communication Skills, and Friendship.* Paper presented at the 7th International Congress on Personal Construct Psychology, Memphis, TN.

39. See, for example, J. Ekenrode (1984). "Impact of Chronic and Acute Stressors on Daily Reports of Mood." *Journal of Personality and Social Psychology, 46,* 907–918; A. D. Kanner, J. C. Coyne, C. Schaefer, & R. S. Lazarus (1981). "Comparison of Two Modes of Stress Measurement: Daily Hassles and Uplifts versus Major Life Events." *Journal of Behavioral Medicine, 4,* 1–39; A. DeLongis, J. C. Coyne, G. Dakof, S. Polkman, & R. S. Lazarus (1982). "Relation of Daily Hassles, Uplifts, and Major Life Events to Health Status." *Health Psychology, 1,* 119–136.

40. E. L. MacGeorge, W. Samter, & S. J. Gillihan (2005). "Academic Stress, Supportive Communication, and Health." *Communication Education, 54,* 365–372; B. R. Burleson 2003). "Emotional Support Skills." In J. O. Greene & B. R. Burleson (Eds.), *Handbook of Communication and Social Interaction Skills* (pp. 551–594). Mahwah, NJ: Erlbaum.

41. "D. Hample (2006). "Anti-Comforting Messages." In K. M. Galvin & P. J. Cooper (Eds.), *Making Connections: Readings in Relational Communication,* 4th ed. (pp. 222–227). Los Angeles: Roxbury; see also B. R. Burleson & E. L. MacGeorge (2002). "Supportive Communication." In M. L. Knapp & J. A. Daly (Eds.), *Handbook of Interpersonal Communication,* 3rd ed. Thousand Oaks, CA: Sage.

42. W. Samter, B. R. Burleson, & L. B. Murphy (1987). "Comforting Conversations: The Effects of Strategy Type on Evaluations of Messages and Message Producers." *Southern Speech Communication Journal, 52,* 263–284.

43. M. Davidowitz & R. D. Myrick (1984). "Responding to the Bereaved: An Analysis of 'Helping' Statements." *Death Education, 8,* 1–10.

44. R. A. Clark & J. G. Delia (1997). "Individuals' Preferences for Friends' Approaches to Providing Support in Distressing Situations." *Communication Reports, 10,* 115–121.

45. C. J. Notarius & L. R. Herrick (1988). "Listener Response Strategies to a Distressed Other." *Journal of Social and Personal Relationships, 5,* 97–108.

46. S. J. Messman, D. J. Canary, & K. S. Hause (2000). "Motives to Remain Platonic, Equity, and the Use of Maintenance Strategies in Opposite-Sex Friendships." *Journal of Social and Personal Relationships, 17,* 67–94.

47. D. J. Goldsmith & K. Fitch (1997). "The Normative Context of Advice as Social Support." *Human Communication Research, 23,* 454–476. See also D. J. Goldsmith & E. L. MacGeorge (2000). "The Impact of Politeness and Relationship on Perceived Quality of Advice about a Problem." *Human Communication Research, 26,* 234–263. See also B. R. Burleson (1992). "Social Support." In M. L. Knapp & J. A. Daly (Eds.), *Handbook of Interpersonal Communication,* 3rd ed. CA: Sage.

48. D. J. Goldsmith (2000). "Soliciting Advice: The Role of Sequential Placement in Mitigating Face Threat." *Communication Monographs, 67,* 1–19.

49. D. J. Goldsmith & E. L. MacGeorge (2000). "The Impact of Politeness and Relationship on Perceived Quality of Advice about a Problem." *Human Communication Research, 26,* 234–263.

50. See, for example, R. Silver & C. Wortman (1981). "Coping with Undesirable Life Events." In J. Garber & M. Seligman (Eds.), *Human Helplessness: Theory and Applications* (pp. 279–340). New York: Academic Press; and C. R. Young, D. E. Giles, & M. C. Plantz (1982). "Natural Networks: Help-Giving and Help-Seeking in Two Rural Communities." *American Journal of Community Psychology, 10,* 457–469.

51. Clark & Delia, op. cit.

52. See research cited in B. Burleson (1990). "Comforting Messages: Their Significance and Effects." In J. A. Daly & J. M. Wiemann (Eds.), *Communicating Strategically: Strategies in Interpersonal Communication.* Hillside, NJ: Erlbaum. See also J. L. Chesbro (1999). "The Relationship between Listening Styles and Conversational Sensitivity." *Communication Research Reports, 16,* 233–238.

53. M. Johnston, M. Kirtley, J. B. Weaver, K. Watson, & L. Barker (2000). "Listening Styles: Biological or Psychological Differences?" *International Journal of Listening, 14,* 32–47.

54. W. Samter (2002). "How Gender and Cognitive Complexity Influence the Provision of Emotional Support: A Study of Indirect Effects." *Communication Reports, 15,* 5–17; J. L. Hale, M. R. Tighe, & P. A. Mongeau (1997). "Effects of Event Type and Sex on Comforting Messages." *Communication Research Reports, 14,* 214–220.

55. B. R. Burleson (1982). "The Development of Comforting Communication Skills in Childhood and Adolescence." *Child Development, 53,* 1,578–1,588.

56. R. Lemieux & M. R. Tighe (2004). "Attachment Styles and the Evaluation of Comforting Responses: A Receiver Perspective." *Communication Research Reports, 21,* 144–153.

57. B. R. Burleson, A. J. Holmstrom, & C. M. Gilstrap (2005). "'Guys Can't Say That to Guys:' Four Experiments Assessing the Normative Motivation Account for Deficiencies in the Emotional Support Provided by Men." *Communication Monographs, 72,* 468–501.

58. M. S. Woodward, L. B. Rosenfeld, & S. K. May (1996). "Sex Differences in Social Support in Sororities and Fraternities." *Journal of Applied Communication Research, 24,* 260–272.

59. L. M. Horowitz, E. N. Krasnoperova, & D. G. Tatar (2001). "The Way to Console May Depend on the Goal: Experimental Studies of Social Support." *Journal of Experimental Social Psychology, 37,* 49–61.

60. R. W. Young & C. M. Cates (2004). "Emotional and Directive Listening in Peer Mentoring." *International Journal of Listening, 18,* 21–33.

Endnotes for Chapter 8

1. D. Byrne (1997). "An Overview (and Underview) of Research and Theory Within the Attraction Paradigm." *Journal of Social and Personal Relationships, 17,* 417–431.

2. E. Hatfield & S. Sprecher (1986). *Mirror, Mirror: The Importance of Looks in Everyday Life.* Albany, NY: State University of New York Press.

3. E. Walster, E. Aronson, D. Abrahams, & L. Rottmann (1966). "Importance of Physical Attractiveness in Dating Behavior." *Journal of Personality and Social Psychology, 4,* 508–516.

4. E. Berscheid & E. H. Walster (1978). *Interpersonal Attraction,* 2nd ed. Reading, MA: Addison-Wesley.

5. K. F. Albada (2002). "Interaction Appearance Theory: Changing Perceptions of Physical Attractiveness Through Social Interaction." *Communication Theory, 12,* 8–41.

6. D. Hamachek (1982). *Encounters with Others: Interpersonal Relationships and You.* New York: Holt, Rinehart and Winston.

7. See, for example, D. Byrne (1999). "An Overview (and Underview) of Research and Theory within the Attraction Paradigm." *Journal of Social and Personal Relationships, 14,* 417–431.

8. S. Luo & E. Klohnen (2005). "Assortative Mating and Marital Quality in Newlyweds: A Couple-Centered Approach," *Journal of Personality and Social Psychology, 88,* 304–326; see also D. M. Amodio & C. J. Showers (2005). "Similarity Breeds Liking Revisited: The Moderating Role of Commitment." *Journal of Social and Personal Relationships, 22,* 817–836.

9. F. E. Aboud & M. J. Mendelson (1998). "Determinants of Friendship Selection and Quality: Developmental Perspectives." In W. M. Bukowski & A. F. Newcomb (Eds.), *The Company They Keep: Friendship in Childhood and Adolescence.* New York: Cambridge University Press.

10. B. R. Burleson & W. Samter (1996). "Similarity in the Communication Skills of Young Adults: Foundations of Attraction, Friendship, and Relationship Satisfaction." *Communication Reports, 9,* 127–139.

11. J. T. Jones, B. W. Pelham, & M. Carvallo (2004) "How Do I Love Thee? Let Me Count the J's: Implicit Egotism and Interpersonal Attraction." *Journal of Personality and Social Psychology, 87,* 665–683.

12. D. Mette & S. Taylor (1971). "When Similarity Breeds Contempt." *Journal of Personality and Social Psychology, 20,* 75–81.

13. L. Heatherington, V. Escudero, & M. L. Friedlander (2005). "Couple Interaction During Problem Discussions: Toward an Integrative Methodology." *Journal of Family Communication, 5,* 191–207.

14. S. Specher (1998). "Insiders' Perspectives on Reasons for Attraction to a Close Other." *Social Psychology Quarterly, 61,* 287–300.

15. E. Aronson (2004). *The Social Animal,* 9th ed. New York: Bedford, Freeman, & Worth. See Chapter 9: Liking, Loving, and Interpersonal Sensitivity.

16. K. Dindia (2002). "Self-Disclosure Research: Knowledge Through Meta-Analysis." In M. Allen & R. W. Preiss (Eds.), *Interpersonal Communication Research: Advances Through Meta-Analysis* (pp. 169–185). Mahwah, NJ: Erlbaum.

17. Dindia, op cit.

18. C. Flora, (Jan/Feb2004). "Close Quarters." *Psychology Today, 37,* 15–16.

19. C. Haythornthwaite, M. M. Kazmer, & J. Robbins (2000). "Community Development Among Distance Learners: Temporal and Technological Dimensions." *Journal of Computer-Mediated Communication, 6,* Issue 1, Article 2. Retrieved September 11, 2006, from http://jcmc.indiana.edu/vol6/issue1/haythornthwaite.html.

20. See, for example, M. E. Roloff (1981). *Interpersonal Communication: The Social Exchange Approach.* Beverly Hills, CA: Sage.

21. M. L. Knapp & A. L. Vangelisti (2006). *Interpersonal Communication and Human Relationships,* 6th ed. Boston: Allyn & Bacon. See also T. A. Avtgis, D. V. West, & T. L. Anderson (1998). "Relationship Stages: An Inductive Analysis Identifying Cognitive, Affective, and Behavioral Dimensions of Knapp's Relational Stages Model." *Communication Research Reports 15,* 280–287; and S. A. Welch & R. B. Rubin (2002). "Development of Relationship Stage Measures." *Communication Quarterly, 50,* 34–40.

22. K. Dindia (2003). "Definitions and Perspectives on Relational Maintenance Communication." In D. J. Canary and M. Dainton, (Eds.), *Maintaining Relationships through Communication.* Mahwah, NJ: Erlbaum.

23. A. J. Johnson, E. Wittenberg, M. Haigh, S. Wigley, J. Becker, K. Brown, & E. Craig (2004). "The Process of Relationship Development and Deterioration: Turning Points in Friendships That Have Terminated." *Communication Quarterly, 52,* 54–67.

24. B. W. Scharlott & W. G. Christ (1995). "Overcoming Relationship-Initiation Barriers: The Impact of a Computer-Dating System on Sex Role, Shyness, and Appearance Inhibitions." *Computers in Human Behavior, 11,* 191–204.

25. C. R. Berger (1987). "Communicating under Uncertainty." In M. E. Roloff & G. R. Miller (Eds.), *Interpersonal Processes: New Directions in Communication Research.* Newbury Park, CA: Sage. See also C. R. Berger & R. J. Calabrese (1975). "Some Explorations in Initial Interaction and Beyond: Toward a Developmental Theory of Interpersonal Communication." *Human Communication Research, 1,* 99–112.

26. W. B. Gudykunst & S. Ting-Toomey (1988). *Culture and Interpersonal Communication* (p. 193). Newbury Park, CA: Sage.

27. L. Pratt, R. L. Wiseman, M. J. Cody, & P. F. Wendt (1999). "Interrogative Strategies and Information Exchange in Computer-Mediated Communication." *Communication Quarterly, 47,* 46–66.

28. J. H. Tolhuizen (1989). "Communication Strategies for Intensifying Dating Relationships: Identification, Use and Structure." *Journal of Social and Personal Relationships, 6,* 413–434.

29. Johnson et al., op. cit.

30. L. A. Baxter (1987). "Symbols of Relationship Identity in Relationship Culture." *Journal of Social and Personal Relationships, 4,* 261–280.

31. C. J. S. Buress & J. C. Pearson (1997). "Interpersonal Rituals in Marriage and Adult Friendship," *Communication Monographs, 64,* 25–46.

32. R. A. Bell & J. G. Healey (1992) "Idiomatic Communication and Interpersonal Solidarity in Friends' Relational Cultures." *Human Communication Research, 18,* 307–335.

33. M. Roloff, C. A. Janiszewski, M. A. McGrath, C. S. Burns, & L. A. Manrai (1988). "Acquiring Resources from Intimates: When Obligation Substitutes for Persuasion." *Human Communication Research 14,* 364–396.

34. D. H. Solomon (1997). "A Developmental Model of Intimacy and Date Request Explicitness." *Communication Monographs, 64,* 99–118.

35. L. G. Ferdinand (2005). "The Influence of Differentiation of Self and Family of Origin on Individual and Relationship Functioning in Young Adults." *Dissertation Abstracts International: Section B: The Sciences and Engineering, 66,* 1,715.

36. J. A. Courtright, F. E. Miller, L. E. Rogers, & D. Bagarozzi (1990). "Interaction Dynamics of Relational Negotiation: Reconciliation versus Termination of Distressed Relationships." *Western Journal of Speech Communication, 54,* 429–453.

37. D. M. Battaglia, F. D. Richard, D. L. Datteri, & C. G. Lord (1998). "Breaking Up Is (Relatively) Easy to Do: A Script for the Dissolution of Close Relationships." *Journal of Social and Personal Relationships, 15,* 829–845.

38. S. Metts, W. R. Cupach, & R. A. Bejllovec (1989). "'I Love You Too Much to Ever Start Liking You': Redefining Romantic Relationships." *Journal of Social and Personal Relationships, 6,* 259–274.

39. S. Duck (1982). "A Topography of Relationship Disengagement and Dissolution." In S. Duck (Ed.), *Personal Relationships 4: Dissolving Personal Relationships* (pp. 1–30). New York: Academic Press.

40. A. L. Weber, J. H. Harvey, & T. L. Orbuch (1992). "What Went Wrong: Communicating Accounts of Relationship Conflict." In M. L. McLaughlin, M. J. Cody, & S. J. Read (Eds.), *Explaining One's Self to Others: Reason-Giving in a Social Context* (pp. 261–280). Hillsdale, NJ: Erlbaum.

41. A. Johnson, E. Wittenberg, M. Haigh, S. Wigley, J. Becker., K. Brown, & E. Craig (2004). "The Process of Relationship Development and Deterioration: Turning Points in Friendships that Have Terminated." *Communication Quarterly, 52,* 54–67.

42. See, for example, L. A. Baxter & B. M. Montgomery (1992). *Relating: Dialogues and Dialectics.* New York: Guilford; W. K. Rawlins (1996). *Friendship Matters: Communication, Dialectics, and the Life Course.* New York: Aldine de Gruyter; B. H. Spitzberg (1993). "The Dark Side of (In)Competence." In W. R. Cupach & B. H. Spitzberg (Eds.), *The Dark Side of Interpersonal Communication.* Hillsdale, NJ: Erlbaum.

43. Summarized by L. A. Baxter (1994). "A Dialogic Approach to Relationship Maintenance." In D. J. Canary & L. Stafford (Eds.), *Communication and Relational Maintenance.* San Diego: Academic Press.

44. A. P. Buunk (2005). "How Do People Respond to Others with High Commitment or Autonomy in their Relationships?" *Journal of Social and Personal Relationships, 22,* 653–672.

45. Morris, *Intimate Behavior,* pp. 21–29.

46. T. D. Golish (2000). "Changes in Closeness between Adult Children and Their Parents: A Turning Point Analysis." *Communication Reports, 13,* 78–97.

47. L. A. Baxter & L. A. Erbert (1999). "Perceptions of Dialectical Contradictions in Turning Points of Development in Heterosexual Romantic Relationships." *Journal of Social and Personal Relationships, 16,* 547–569.

48. E. E. Graham (2003). "Dialectic Contradictions in Postmarital Relationships." *Journal of Family Communication, 3,* 193–215.

49. L. A. Baxter, D. O. Braithwaite, T. D. Golish, & L. N. Olson (2002). "Contradictions of Interaction for Wives of Elderly Husbands with Adult Dementia." *Journal of Applied Communication Research, 30,* 1–20.

50. S. Petronio (2000). "The Boundaries of Privacy: Praxis of Everyday Life." In S. Petronio (Ed.), *Balancing the Secrets of Private Disclosures* (pp. 37-49). Mahwah, NJ: Erlbaum.

51. D. Barry (1990). *Dave Barry Turns 40* (p. 47). New York: Fawcett.

52. D. R. Pawlowski (1998). "Dialectical Tensions in Marital Partners' Accounts of Their Relationships," *Communication Quarterly, 46*, 396–416.

53. E. M. Griffin (2000). *A First Look at Communication Theory*, 4th ed. New York: McGraw-Hill.

54. D. O. Braithwaite & L. Baxter (2006). "'You're My Parent But You're Not': Dialectical Tensions in Stepchildren's Perceptions About Communicating with the Nonresident Parent." *Journal of Applied Communication Research, 34*, 30–48.

55. B. M. Montgomery (1993). "Relationship Maintenance versus Relationship Change: A Dialectical Dilemma." *Journal of Social and Personal Relationships, 10*, 205–223.

56. D. O. Braithwaite, L. A. Baxter, & A. M. Harper (1998). "The Role of Rituals in the Management of the Dialectical Tension of 'Old' and 'New' in Blended Families." *Communication Studies, 49*, 101–120.

57. See A. Christensen & J. Jacobson (2000). *Reconcilable Differences*. New York: Guilford.

58. R. L. Conville (1991). *Relational Transitions: The Evolution of Personal Relationships* (p. 80). New York: Praeger.

59. For a discussion of similarities across cultures, see D. E. Brown (1991). *Human Universals*. New York: McGraw-Hill.

60. R. R. Hamon & B. B. Ingoldsby (Eds.) (2003), *Mate Selection Across Cultures*. Thousand Oaks, CA: Sage.

61. J. E. Myers, J. Madathil, & L. R. Tingle (2005). " *Journal of Counseling & Development, 83*, 183–190; P. Yelsma & K. Athappilly (1988). "Marriage Satisfaction and Communication Practices: Comparisons Among Indian and American Couples." *Journal of Comparative Family Studies, 19*, 37–54.

62. For a detailed discussion of cultural differences that affect relationships, see M. Sun Kim (2002) *Non-Western Perspectives on Human Communication: Implications for Theory and Practice*. Thousand Oaks, CA: Sage.

63. P. Breitman & C. Hatch (2000). *How To Say No Without Feeling Guilty*. New York: Broadway Books.

64. M. Imami (1981). *16 Ways to Avoid Saying No*. Tokyo: The Nihon Keizai Shimbun.

65. D. J. Canary & L. Stafford (1992). "Relational Maintenance Strategies and Equity in Marriage." *Communication Monographs. 59*, 243–267.

66. D. J. Weigel & D. S. Ballard-Reisch (1999). "Using Paired Data to Test Models of Relational Maintenance and Marital Quality." *Journal of Social and Personal Relationships, 16*, 175–191.

67. L. Stafford & D. J. Canary (1991). "Maintenance Strategies and Romantic Relationship Type, Gender, and Relational Characteristics." *Journal of Personality and Social Psychology, 7*, 217–242.

68. For a description of this ongoing research program, see The Gottman Institute, "Twelve-year study of gay and lesbian couples." Retrieved July 28, 2006, from http://www.gottman.com/research.

69. T. M. Emmers-Sommer (2003). "When Partners Falter: Repair After a Transgression." In D. J. Canary & M. Dainton (Eds.), *Maintaining Relationships through Communication* (pp. 185–205). Mahwah, NJ: Erlbaum.

70. K. Dindia & L. A. Baxter (1987). "Strategies for Maintaining and Repairing Marital Relationships." *Journal of Social and Personal Relationships, 4*, 143–158.

71. D. L. Kelley & V. R. Waldron (2005). "An Investigation of Forgiveness-Seeking Communication and Relational Outcomes." *Communication Quarterly, 53*, 339–358.

72. H. K. Orcutt (2006). "The Prospective Relationship of Interpersonal Forgiveness and Psychological Distress Symptoms Among College Women." *Journal of Counseling Psychology, 53*, 350–361; J. Eaton & C. W. Struthers (2006). "The Reduction of Psychological Aggression Across Varied Interpersonal Contexts Through Repentance and Forgiveness." *Aggressive Behavior, 32*, 195–206.

73. K. A. Lawler, J. W. Younger, R. L. Piferi, et al. (2003). "A Change of Heart: Cardiovascular Correlates of Forgiveness in Response to Interpersonal Conflict." *Journal of Behavioral Medicine, 26*, 373–393.

74. V. R. Waldron & D. L. Kelley (2005). "Forgiving Communication as a Response to Relational Transgressions." *Journal of Social and Personal Relationships, 22*, 723–742.

75. G. F. Bachman & L. K. Guerrero (2006). "Forgiveness, Apology, and Communicative Responses to Hurtful Events." *Communication Reports, 19*, 45–56.

76. S. Takaku, B. Weiner, & K. Ohbuchi (2001). "A Cross-Cultural Examination of the Effects of Apology and Perspective-Taking on Forgiveness." *Journal of Language & Social Psychology, 20*, 144–167.

77. D. Kelley (1998). "The Communication of Forgiveness." *Communication Studies, 49*, 255–272.

78. See P. Watzlawick, J. H. Beavin, & D. D. Jackson (1967). *Pragmatics of Human Communication*. (New York: Norton; and W. J. Lederer & D. D. Jackson 1968). *The Mirages of Marriage*. New York: Norton.

79. See, for example, R. A. Bell & J. A. Daly 1995). "The Affinity-Seeking Function of Communication." In M. V. Redmond (Ed.), *Interpersonal Communication: Readings in Theory and Research*. Fort Worth: Harcourt Brace.

80. M. Dainton (1998). "Everyday Interaction in Marital Relationships: Variations in Relative Importance and Event Duration." *Communication Reports, 11*, 101–143.

81. S. A. Myers & T. A. Avtgis (1997). "The Association of Socio-Communicative Style and Relational Types on Perceptions of Nonverbal Immediacy." *Communication Research Reports, 14*, 339–349.

82. For a thorough examination of this topic, see chap. 11 ("Nonverbal Immediacy") of V. P. Richmond & J. C. McCroskey (2004). *Nonverbal Behavior in Interpersonal Relationships*, 5th ed. Boston: Allyn and Bacon.

83. T. S. Lim & J. W. Bowers (1991). "Facework: Solidarity, Approbation, and Tact" *Human Communication Research, 17*, 415–450.

84. J. R. Frei & P. R. Shaver (2002). "Respect in Close Relationships: Prototype, Definition, Self-Report Assessment, and Initial Correlates." *Personal Relationships, 9*, 121–139.

85. M. T. Palmer (1989). "Controlling Conversations: Turns, Topics, and Interpersonal Control." *Communication Monographs, 56*, 1–18.

86. Watzlawick et al., op. cit.; see also T. Bryant (2001). " *Marriage & Family, 4*, 147–152.

87. D. Tannen (1986). *That's Not What I Meant! How Conversational Style Makes or Breaks Your Relations with Others* (p. 190). New York: Morrow.

Endnotes for Chapter 9

1. D. Tannen (1986). *That's Not What I Meant! How Conversational Style Makes or Breaks Relationships.* (pp. 17–18). New York: Ballantine. For an extended discussion of Schopenhauer's's position, see D. Luepnitz (2003). *Schopenhauer's Porcupines: Intimacy and Its Dilemmas.* (New York: Basic Books).

2. K. J. Prager & D. Buhrmester (1998). "Intimacy and Need Fulfillment in Couple Relationships." *Journal of Social and Personal Relationships, 15,* 435–469.

3. C. E. Crowther & G. Stone (1986). *Intimacy: Strategies for Successful Relationships* (p. 13). Santa Barbara, CA: Capra Press.

4. E. Berscheid, M. Schneider, & A. M. Omoto (1989). "Issues in Studying Close Relationships: Conceptualizing and Measuring Closeness." In C. Hendrick (Ed.), *Close Relationships* (pp. 63–91).Newbury Park, CA: Sage.

5. D. Morris (1973). *Intimate Behavior.* (p. 7). New York: Bantam.

6. K. Floyd (1996). "Meanings for Closeness and Intimacy in Friendship." *Journal of Social and Personal Relationships, 13,* 85–107.

7. M. R. Parks & K. Floyd (1996). "Making Friends in Cyberspace." *Journal of Communication, 46,* 80–97.

8. L. A. Baxter (1994). "A Dialogic Approach to Relationship Maintenance." In D. Canary & L. Stafford (Eds.), *Communication and Relational Maintenance.* San Diego: Academic Press.

9. J. T. Wood & C. C. Inman (1993). "In a Different Mode: Masculine Styles of Communicating Closeness." *Applied Communication Research, 21,* 279–295; K. Floyd (1995). "Gender and Closeness among Friends and Siblings." *Journal of Psychology, 129,* 193–202.

10. See, for example, K. Dindia (2000). "Sex Differences in Self-Disclosure, Reciprocity of Self-Disclosure, and Self-Disclosure and Liking: Three Meta-Analyses Reviewed." In S. Petronio (Ed.), *Balancing Disclosure, Privacy and Secrecy.* Mahwah, NJ: Erlbaum.

11. See, for example, K. Floyd (1995). "Gender and Closeness among Friends and Siblings." *Journal of Psychology, 129,* 193–202.

12. J. O. Balswick (1988). *The Inexpressive Male: A Tragedy of American Society.* Lexington, MA: Lexington Books.

13. S. Swain (1989). "Covert Intimacy in Men's Friendships: Closeness in Men's Friendships." In B. J. Risman & P. Schwartz (Eds.), *Gender in Intimate Relationships: A Microstructural Approach.* Belmont, CA: Wadsworth.

14. M. T. Morman & K. Floyd (1999). "Affection Communication between Fathers and Young Adult Sons: Individual and Relational-Level Correlates." *Communication Studies, 50,* 294–309.

15. L. Stafford, M. Dainton, & S. Haas (2000). "Measuring Routine and Strategic Relational Maintenance: Scale Revision, Sex versus Gender Roles, and the Prediction of Relational Characteristics." *Communication Monographs, 67,* 306–323.

16. C. K. Reissman (1990). *Divorce Talk: Women and Men Make Sense of Personal Relationships.* New Brunswick, NJ: Rutgers University Press.

17. G. E. Good, M. J. Porter, & M. G. Dillon (2002). "When Men Divulge: Men's Self-Disclosure on Prime Time Situation Comedies." *Sex Roles, 46,* 419–427.

18. M. T. Morman & K. Floyd (2002). "A 'Changing Culture of Fatherhood': Effects of Affectionate Communication, Closeness, and Satisfaction in Men's Relationships With Their Fathers and Their Sons." *Western Journal of Communication, 66,* 395–411.

19. J. Adamopoulos (1991). "The Emergence of Interpersonal Behavior: Diachronic and Cross-Cultural Processes in the Evolution of Intimacy." In S. Ting-Toomey & F. Korzenny (Eds.), *Cross-Cultural Interpersonal Communication.* Newbury Park, CA: Sage. See also G. Fontaine (1990). "Cultural Diversity in Intimate Intercultural Relationships." In D. D. Cahn (Ed.), *Intimates in Conflict: A Communication Perspective.* Hillsdale, NJ: Erlbaum.

20. J. Adamopoulos & R. N. Bontempo (1986). "Diachronic Universals in Interpersonal Structures." *Journal of Cross-Cultural Psychology, 17,* 169–189.

21. M. Argyle & M. Henderson (1985). "The Rules of Relationships." In S. Duck & D. Perlman (Eds.), *Understanding Personal Relationships,* Beverly Hills, CA: Sage.

22. W. B. Gudykunst & S. Ting-Toomey (1988). *Culture and Interpersonal Communication* (pp. 197–198). Newbury Park, CA: Sage.

23. S. Faul (1994). *The Xenophobe's Guide to the Americans* (p. 3). London: Ravette.

24. C. W. Franklin (1992). "'Hey Home—Yo Bro': Friendship among Black Men." In P. M. Nardi (Ed.), *Men's Friendships.* Newbury Park, CA: Sage.

25. H. C. Triandis (1994). *Culture and Social Behavior* (p. 230). New York: McGraw-Hill.

26. K. Lewin (1936). *Principles of Topological Psychology.* New York: McGraw-Hill.

27. E. Hatfield & R. L. Rapson (2006). "Passionate Love, Sexual Desire, and Mate Selection: Cross-Cultural and Historical Perspectives." In P. Noller & J. A. Feeney (Eds.), *Close Relationships: Functions, Forms and Processes* (pp. 227–243). Hove, England: Psychology Press/Taylor & Francis.

28. L. B. Hian, S. L. Chuan, T. M. K. Trevor, & B. H. Detenber (2004). "Getting to Know You: Exploring the Development of Relational Intimacy in Computer-Mediated Communication." *Journal of Computer-Mediated Communication, 9,* Issue 3.

29. Y. Hu, J. F. Wood, V. Smith, & N. Westbrook (2004). "Friendships Through IM: Examining the Relationship Between Instant Messaging and Intimacy." *Journal of Computer-Mediated Communication, 10,* Issue 1.

30. A. Ben-Ze'ev (2003). "Privacy, Emotional Closeness, and Openness in Cyberspace." *Computers in Human Behavior, 19,* 451–467.

31. J. Boase, J. B. Horrigan, B. Wellman, & L Rainie (2006). "The Strength of Internet Ties." *Pew Internet & American Life Project.* Retrieved September 11, 2006, from http://www.pewinternet.org/pdfs/PIP_Internet_ties.pdf.

32. S. Henderson & M. Gilding (2004). "_I've Never Clicked This Much With Anyone in my Life': Trust and Hyperpersonal Communication in Online Friendships." *New Media & Society, 6,* 487–506.

33. See, for example, R. Bellah, W. M. Madsen, A. Sullivan, & S. M. Tipton (1985). *Habits of the Heart: Individualism and Commitment in American Life.* Berkeley, CA: University of California Press; R. Sennett (1974). *The Fall of Public Man: On the Social Psychology of Capitalism.* New York: Random House; and S. Trenholm & A. Jensen (1990). *The Guarded Self: Toward a Social History of Interpersonal Styles.*

Paper presented at the Speech Communication Association meeting, San Juan, PR.

34. I. Altman & D. A. Taylor (1973). *Social Penetration: The Development of Interpersonal Relationships* New York: Holt, Rinehart and Winston. See also D. A. Taylor & I. Altman (1987). "Communication in Interpersonal Relationships: Social Penetration Processes." In M. E. Roloff & G. R. Miller (Eds.), *Interpersonal Processes: New Directions in Communication Research*. Newbury Park, CA: Sage.

35. J. Luft (1969). *Of Human Interaction*. Palo Alto, CA: National Press Books.

36. K. Dindia (2002). "Self-Disclosure Research: Advances Through Meta-Analysis." In M. Allen & R. W. Preiss (Eds.), *Interpersonal Communication Research: Advances Through Meta-Analysis* (pp. 169–185). Mahwah, NJ: Erlbaum; V. J. Derlega & A. L. Chaikin (1975). *Sharing Intimacy: What We Reveal to Others and Why*. Englewood Cliffs, NJ: Prentice-Hall.

37. R. C. Savin-Williams (2001). *Mom, Dad. I'm Gay: How Families Negotiate Coming Out*. Washington, DC: American Psychological Association.

38. H. L. Wintrob (1987). "Self-Disclosure as a Marketable Commodity." *Journal of Social Behavior and Personality, 2,* 77–88.

39. E. Aronson (1999). *The Social Animal,* 7th ed. New York: W.H. Freeman.

40. F. D. Fincham & T. N. Bradbury (1989). "The Impact of Attributions in Marriage: An Individual Difference Analysis." *Journal of Social and Personal Relationships, 6,* 69–85.

41. V. G. Downs (1988). "Grandparents and Grandchildren: The Relationship between Self-Disclosure and Solidarity in an Intergenerational Relationship." *Communication Research Reports, 5,* 173–179.

42. L. B. Rosenfeld & W. L. Kendrick (Fall 1984). "Choosing to Be Open: Subjective Reasons for Self-Disclosing." *Western Journal of Speech Communication, 48,* 326–343.

43. K. G. Niederhoffer & J. W. Pennebaker (2002). "Sharing One's Story: On the Benefits of Writing or Talking About Emotional Experience." In C. R. Snyder & S. J. Lopez (Eds.), *Handbook of Positive Psychology* (pp. 573–583). London: Oxford University Press.

44. K. Greene, V. J. Derlega, & A. Mathews (2006). "Self-Disclosure in Personal Relationships." In A. Vangelisti & D. Perlman (Eds.), *The Cambridge Handbook of Personal Relationships*. New York: Cambridge University Press; L. B. Rosenfeld (2000). "Overview of the Ways Privacy, Secrecy, and Disclosure are Balanced in Today's Society." In S. Petronio (Ed.), *Balancing the Secrets of Private Disclosures* (pp. 3–17). Mahweh, NJ: Erlbaum.

45. J. Powell (1969). *Why Am I Afraid to Tell You Who I Am?* Niles, IL: Argus Communications.

46. R. Agne, T. L. Thompson, & L. P. Cusella (2000). "Stigma in the Line of Face: Self-Disclosure of Patients' HIV Status to Health Care Providers." *Journal of Applied Communication Research, 28,* 235–261. V. J. Derlega, B. A. Winstead, & L. Folk-Barron (2000). "Reasons For and Against Disclosing HIV-Seropositive Test Results to an Intimate Partner: A Functional Perspective." In S. Petronio (Ed.), *Balancing the Secrets of Private Disclosures* (pp. 71–82). Mahwah, NJ: Erlbaum.

47. K. Dindia, M. A. Fitzpatrick, & D. A. Kenny (1988). *Self-Disclosure in Spouse and Stranger Interaction: A Social Relations Analysis*. Paper presented at the annual meeting of the International Communication Association, New Orleans, LA; and S. W. Duck & D. E. Miell (1991). "Charting the Development of Personal Relationships." In R. Gilmour & S. W. Duck (Eds.), *Studying Interpersonal Interaction* (pp. 133–144). New York: Guilford.

48. S. Duck (1991). "Some Evident Truths about Conversations in Everyday Relationships: All Communications Are Not Created Equal." *Human Communication Research, 18,* 228–267.

49. C. L. Kleinke (1979). "Effects of Personal Evaluations." In *Self-Disclosure*. San Francisco: Jossey-Bass.

50. E. M. Eisenberg & M. G. Witten (1987). "Reconsidering Openness in Organizational Communication." *Academy of Management Review, 12,* 418–428.

51. L. B. Rosenfeld & J. R. Gilbert (1989). "The Measurement of Cohesion and Its Relationship to Dimensions of Self-Disclosure in Classroom Settings." *Small Group Behavior, 20,* 291–301.

52. T. E. Runge & R. L. Archer (December 1981). "Reactions to the Disclosure of Public and Private Self-Information." *Social Psychology Quarterly, 44,* 357–362.

53. L. B. Rosenfeld & G. I. Bowen (1991). "Marital Disclosure and Marital Satisfaction: Direct-Effect versus Interaction-Effect Models." *Western Journal of Speech Communication, 55,* 69–84.

54. A. Jaksa & M. Pritchard (1993). *Communication Ethics: Methods of Analysis,* 2nd ed. (pp. 65–66). Belmont, CA: Wadsworth.

55. D. O'Hair & M. J. Cody (1993). "Interpersonal Deception: The Dark Side of Interpersonal Communication?" In B. H. Spitzberg & W. R. Cupach (Eds.), *The Dark Side of Interpersonal Communication*. Hillsdale, NJ: Erlbaum.

56. M. Spranca, E. Minsk, & J. Baron (1991). "Omission and Commission in Judgement and Choice." *Journal of Experimental Social Psychology, 27,* 76–105.

57. M. L. Knapp (2006). "Lying and Deception in Close Relationships." In A. Vangelisti & D. Perlman (Eds.), *The Cambridge Handbook of Personal Relationships*. New York: Cambridge University Press.

58. R. E. Turner, C. Edgely, & G. Olmstead (1975). "Information Control in Conversation: Honesty Is Not Always the Best Policy." *Kansas Journal of Sociology, 11,* 69–89.

59. R. S. Feldman, J. A. Forrest, & B. R. Happ (2002). "Self-Presentation and Verbal Deception: Do Self-Presenters Lie More?" *Basic and Applied Social Psychology, 24,* 163–170.

60. B. M. DePaulo, D. A. Kashy, S. E. Kirkendol, & M. M. Wyer (1996). "Lying in Everyday Life." *Journal of Personality and Social Psychology, 70,* 779–795.

61. J. Bavelas (1983). "Situations that Lead to Disqualification." *Human Communication Research, 9,* 130–145.

62. W. C. Rowatt, M. R. Cunningham, & P. B. Druen (1999). "Lying to Get a Date: The Effect of Facial Physical Attractiveness on the Willingness to Deceive Prospective Dating Partners." *Journal of Social and Personal Relationships, 16,* 209–223.

63. D. Hample (1980). "Purposes and Effects of Lying." *Southern Speech Communication Journal, 46,* 33–47.

64. S. A. McCornack & T. R. Levine (1990). "When Lies Are Uncovered: Emotional and Relational Outcomes of Discovered Deception." *Communication Monographs, 57,* 119–138.

65. J. S. Seiter, J. Bruschke, & C. Bai (2002). "The Acceptability of Deception as a Function of Perceivers' Culture, Deceiver's Intention, and Deceiver-Deceived Relationship." *Western Journal of Communication, 66,* 158–181.

66. S. Metts, W. R. Cupach, & T. T. Imahori (1992). "Perceptions of Sexual Compliance-Resisting Messages in Three Types of Cross-Sex Relationships." *Western Journal of Communication, 56,* 1–17.

67. J. B. Bavelas, A. Black, N. Chovil, & J. Mullett (1990). *Equivocal Communication* (p. 171). Newbury Park, CA: Sage.

68. Ibid.

69. W. P. Robinson, A. Shepherd, & J. Heywood (1998). "Truth, Equivocation/Concealment, & Lies in Job Applications & Doctor-Patient Communication." *Journal of Language & Social Psychology, 17,* 149–164.

70. M. T. Motley (1992). "Mindfulness in Solving Communicators' Dilemmas." *Communication Monographs, 59,* 306–314.

71. S. B. Shimanoff (1988). "Degree of Emotional Expressiveness as a Function of Face-Needs, Gender, & Interpersonal Relationship." *Communication Reports 1,* 43–53.

72. A. P. Hubbell (1999, May). *"I Love Your Family—They Are Just Like You": Lies We Tell to Lovers & Perceptions of Their Honesty & Appropriateness.* Paper presented at the annual meeting of the International Communication Association, San Francisco. See also S. A. McCornack (1992). "Information Manipulation Theory." *Communication Monographs, 59,* 1–16.

73. P. Andersen (1999). *Nonverbal Communication: Forms & Functions* (pp. 297–298). Mountain View, CA: Mayfield.

Endnotes for Chapter 10

1. J. Veroff, E. Douvan, T. L. Orbuch, & L. K. Acitelli 1998). "Happiness in Stable Marriages: The Early Years." In T. N. Bradbury (Ed.), *The Developmental Course of Marital Dysfunction.* New York: Cambridge University Press.

2. J. Gottman (2006). "Why Marriages Fail." In K. M. Galvin & P. J. Cooper (Eds.), *Making Connections: Readings in Relational Communication,* 4th ed. (pp. 228–236). Los Angeles: Roxbury.

3. C. A. Barbato, E. E. Graham, & E. E. Perse (2003). "Communicating in the Family: An Examination of the Relationship of Family Communication Climate & Interpersonal Communication Motives." *Journal of Family Communication, 3,* 123–148.

4. J. J. Teven, M. M. Martin, & N. C. Neupauer (1998). "Sibling Relationships: Verbally Aggressive Messages & Their Effect on Relational Satisfaction." *Communication Reports, 11,* 179–186.

5. R. Guzley (1992). "Organizational Climate & Communication Climate: Predictors of Commitment to the Organization." *Management Communication Quarterly, 5,* 379–402.

6. A. D. Akkirman & D. L. Harris (2005). "Organizational Communication Satisfaction in the Virtual Workplace." *Journal of Management Development, 24,* 397–409.

7. D. Pincus (1986). "Communication Satisfaction, Job Satisfaction, & Job Performance." *Human Communication Research, 12,* 395–419.

8. K. Ellis (2000). "Perceived Teacher Confirmation: The Development & Validation of an Instrument & Two Studies of the Relationship to Cognitive & Affective Learning." *Human Communication Research, 26,* 264–291.

9. A. L. Vangelisti & S. L. Young (2000). "When Words Hurt: The Effects of Perceived Intentionality on Interpersonal Relationships." *Journal of Social & Personal Relationship, 17,* 393–424.

10. K. Cissna & E. Seiberg (1995). "Patterns of Interactional Confirmation & Disconfirmation." In M. V. Redmond (Ed.), *Interpersonal Communication: Readings in Theory & Research.* Fort Worth: Harcourt Brace.

11. M. W. Allen (1995). "Communication Concepts Related to Perceived Organizational Support." *Western Journal of Communication, 59,* 326–346.

12. E. Seiberg (1976). "Confirming & Disconfirming Communication in an Organizational Setting." In J. Owen, P. Page, & G. Zimmerman (Eds.), *Communication in Organizations* (pp. 129–149). St. Paul, MN: West.

13. E. Sieberg & C. Larson (1971). *Dimensions of Interpersonal Response.* Paper presented at the meeting of the International Communication Association, Phoenix, AZ.

14. See, for example, A. Holte & L. Wichstrom (1990). "Disconfirmatory Feedback in Families of Schizophrenics." *Scandinavian Journal of Psychology, 31,* 198–211.

15. S. A. Cox (1999). "Group Communication & Employee Turnover: How Coworkers Encourage Peers to Voluntarily Exit." *Southern Communication Journal, 64,* 181–192.

16. W. W. Wilmot, *Dyadic Communication* (New York: R&om House, 1987), pp. 149–158.

17. C. Burggraf & A. L. Sillars (1987). "A Critical Examination of Sex Differences in Marital Communication." *Communication Monographs, 54,* 276–294. See also D. A. Newton & J. K. Burgoon (1990). "The Use & Consequences of Verbal Strategies during Interpersonal Disagreements." *Human Communication Research, 16,* 477–518.

18. J. L. Hocker & W. W. Wilmot (1995). *Interpersonal Conflict,* 4th ed. (p. 34). Dubuque, IA: Brown & Benchmark.

19. Ibid., p. 36.

20. J. M. Gottman & R. W. Levinson (1999). "Rebound for Marital Conflict & Divorce Prediction." *Family Process, 38,* 387–292.

21. J. Gottman (1994). *Why Marriages Succeed or Fail.* New York: Simon & Schuster.

22. M. K. Lapinski & F. J. Boster (2001). "Modeling the Ego-Defensive Function of Attitudes." *Communication Monographs, 68,* 314–324.

23. G. H. Stamp, A. L. Vangelisti, & J. A. Daly (1992). "The Creation of Defensiveness in Social Interaction." *Communication Quarterly, 40,* 177–190.

24. D. R. Turk & J. L. Monahan (1999). "'Here I Go Again': An Examination of Repetitive Behaviors during Interpersonal Conflicts." *Southern Communication Journal, 64,* 232–244.

25. J. Powell (1969). *Why Am I Afraid to Tell You Who I Am?* (p. 12). Chicago: Argus Communications.

26. L. Festinger (1957). *A Theory of Cognitive Dissonance.* Stanford, CA: Stanford University Press.

27. See, for example, W. R. Cupach & S. J. Messman (1999). "Face Predilections & Friendship Solidarity." *Communication Reports, 12,* 117–124.

28. A. M. Nicotera (1993). *Interpersonal Communication in Friend & Mate Relationships.* Albany: State University of New York.

29. J. Gibb (September 1961). "Defensive Communication." *Journal of Communication, 11,* 141–148. See also E. Robertson (2005). "Placing Leaders at the Heart of Organizational Communication." *Communication Management, 9,* 34–37.

30. R. F. Proctor & J. R. Wilcox (1993). "An Exploratory Analysis of Responses to Owned Messages in Interpersonal Communication." *ETC: A Review of General Semantics, 50,* 201–220.

31. Research summarized in J. Harwood, E. B. Ryan, H. Giles, & S. Tysoski (1997). "Evaluations of Patronizing Speech & Three Response Styles in a Non-Service-Providing Context." *Journal of Applied Communication Research, 25,* 170–195.

32. Adapted from S. Miller, E. W. Nunnally, & D. B. Wackman (1975). *Alive & Aware: How to Improve Your Relationships through Better Communication.* Minneapolis, MN: International Communication Programs. See also R. Remer & P. deMesquita (1990). "Teaching & Learning the Skills of Interpersonal Confrontation." In D. D. Cahn (Ed.), *Intimates in Conflict: A Communication Perspective.* Hillsdale, NJ: Erlbaum.

33. J. K. Alberts (1988). "An Analysis of Couples' Conversational Complaints." *Communication Monographs, 55,* 184–197; J. K. Alberts & G. Driscoll (1992). "Containment versus Escalation: The Trajectory of Couples' Conversational Complaints." *Western Journal of Communication, 56,* 394–412.

34. Adapted from M. Smith 1975). *When I Say No, I Feel Guilty* (pp. 93–110). New York: Dial Press.

35. W. L. Benoit & S. Drew (1997). "Appropriateness & Effectiveness of Image Repair Strategies." *Communication Reports, 10,* 153–163. See also Stamp et al., "Creation of Defensiveness."

Endnotes for Chapter 11

1. W. W. Wilmot & J. L. Hocker (2007). *Interpersonal Conflict,* 7th ed. (pp. 39–49). New York: McGraw-Hill. See also P. M. Buzzanell & N. A. Burrell (1997). "Family & Workplace Conflict: Examining Metaphorical Conflict Schemas & Expressions across Context & Sex." *Human Communication Research, 24,* 109–146.

2. S. Metts & W. Cupach (1990). "The Influence of Relationship Beliefs & Problem-Solving Responses on Satisfaction in Romantic Relationships." *Human Communication Research, 17,* 170–185.

3. Wilmot & Hocker, *Interpersonal Conflict,* pp. 8–15.

4. For a summary of research detailing the prevalence of conflict in relationships, see W. R. Cupach & D. J. Canary 1997). *Competence in Interpersonal Conflict* (pp. 5–6). New York: McGraw-Hill.

5. W. L. Benoit & P. J. Benoit (1987). "Everyday Argument Practices of Naive Social Actors." In J. Wenzel (Ed.), *Argument & Critical Practices.* Annandale, VA: Speech Communication Association.

6. W. Samter & W. R. Cupach (1998). "Friendly Fire: Topical Variations in Conflict among Same- & Cross-Sex Friends." *Communication Studies, 49,* 121–138.

7. S. Vuchinich (1987). "Starting & Stopping Spontaneous Family Conflicts." *Journal of Marriage & the Family 49,* 591–601.

8. J. M. Gottman (1982). "Emotional Responsiveness in Marital Conversations." *Journal of Communication, 32,* 108–120.

See also W. R. Cupach (1982, May). *Communication Satisfaction and Interpersonal Solidarity as Outcomes of Conflict Message Strategy Use.* Paper presented at the International Communication Association conference, Boston.

9. P. Koren, K. Carlton, & D. Shaw (1980). "Marital Conflict: Relations among Behaviors, Outcomes, and Distress." *Journal of Consulting and Clinical Psychology, 48,* 460–468.

10. Hocker & Wilmot, *Interpersonal Conflict,* p. 37.

11. J. M. Gottman (1979). *Marital Interaction: Experimental Investigations.* New York: Academic Press. See also D. A. Infante, S. A. Myers, & R. A. Buerkel (1994). "Argument and Verbal Aggression in Constructive and Destructive Family and Organizational Disagreements." *Western Journal of Communication, 58,* 73–84.

12. S. E. Crohan (1992). "Marital Happiness & Spousal Consensus on Beliefs about Marital Conflict: A Longitudinal Investigation." *Journal of Science and Personal Relationships, 9,* 89–102.

13. D. J. Canary, H. Weger, Jr., & L. Stafford (1991). "Couples' Argument Sequences and Their Associations with Relational Characteristics." *Western Journal of Speech Communication, 55,* 159–179.

14. J. P. Caughlin & T. D. Golish (2002). "An Analysis of the Association Between Topic Avoidance and Dissatisfcation: Comparing Perceptual and Interpersonal Explanations." *Communication Monographs, 69,* 275–295.

15. J. P. Caughlin & T. D. Arr (2004). "When is Topic Avoidance Unsatisfying? Examining Moderators of the Association Between Avoidance and Dissatisfaction." *Human Communication Research, 30,* 479–513.

16. D. D. Cahn (1992). *Conflict in Intimate Relationships* (p. 100). New York: Guilford.

17. Wilmot & Hocker, *Interpersonal Conflict,* p. 159.

18. J. G. Oetzel & S. Ting-Toomey (2003). "Face Concerns in Interpersonal Conflict: A Cross-Cultural Empirical Test of the Face Negotiation Theory." *Communication Research, 30,* 599–625; M. U. Dsilva & L. O. Whyte (1998). "Cultural Differences in Conflict Styles: Vietnamese Refugees and Established Residents." *Howard Journal of Communication, 9,* 57–68.

19. S. J. Messman & R. L. Mikesell (2000). "Competition & Interpersonal Conflict in Dating Relationships." *Communication Reports, 13,* 21–34.

20. L. N. Olson & D. O. Braithwaite (2004). "'If You Hit Me Again, I'll Hit You Back': Conflict Management Strategies of Individuals Experiencing Aggression During Conflicts." *Communication Studies, 55,* 271–285.

21. K. Warren, S. Schopplerey, & D. Moberg (2005). "'A Model of Contagion Through Competition in the Aggressive Behaviors of Elementary School Students." *Journal of Abnormal Child Psychology, 33,* 283–292.

22. M. J. Beatty, K. M. Valencic, J. E. Rudd, & J. A. Dobos (1999). "A 'Dark Side' of Communication Avoidance: Indirect Interpersonal Aggressiveness." *Communication Research Reports, 16,* 103–109.

23. D. A. Infante (1987). "Aggressiveness." In J. C. McCroskey & J. A. Daly (Eds.), *Personality & Interpersonal Communication.* Newbury Park, CA: Sage.

24. D. A. Infante, A. S. Rancer, & F. F. Jordan (1996). "Affirming & Nonaffirming Style, Dyad Sex, and the Perception of Argumentation andVerbal Aggression in an Interpersonal Dispute." *Human Communication Research, 22,* 315–334.

25. D. A. Infante, T. A. Chandler, & J. E. Rudd (1989). "Test of an Argumentative Skill Deficiency Model of Interspousal Violence." *Communication Monographs, 56,* 163–177.

26. M. M. Martin, C. M. Anderson, P. A. Burant, & K. Weber (1997). "Verbal Aggression in Sibling Relationships." *Communication Quarterly, 45,* 304–317.

27. J. W. Kassing & D. A. Infante (1999). "Aggressive Communication in the Coach-Athlete Relationship." *Communication Research Reports, 16,* 110–120.

28. B. K. Houston, M. A. Babyak, M. A. Chesney, & G. Black (1997). "Social Dominance and 22-Year All-Cause Mortality in Men." *Psychosomatic Medicine, 59,* 5–12.

29. "Marital Tiffs Spark Immune Swoon." *Science News* (September 4, 1993), 153.

30. A. C. Filley (1975). *Interpersonal Conflict Resolution* (p. 23). Glenview, IL: Scott, Foresman.

31. D. Canary (2003). "Managing Interpersonal Conflict: A Model of Events Related to Strategic Choices." In J. O. Greene & B. R. Burleson (Eds.), *Handbook of Communication and Social Interaction Skills* (pp. 515–549). Mahwah, NJ: Erlbaum.

32. Hocker & Wilmot, *Interpersonal Conflict;* also, M. L. Knapp, L. L. Putnam, & L. J. Davis (1988). "Measuring Interpersonal Conflict in Organizations: Where Do We Go from Here?" *Management Communication Quarterly, 1,* 414–429.

33. C. S. Burggraf & A. L. Sillars (1987). "A Critical Examination of Sex Differences in Marital Communication." *Communication Monographs, 53,* 276–294.

34. J. Gottman & L. J. Krokoff (1989). "Marital Interaction and Satisfaction: A Longitudinal View." *Journal of Consulting and Clinical Psychology, 67,* 47–52; G. R. Pike & A. L. Sillars (1985). "Reciprocity of Marital Communication." *Journal of Social and Personal Relationships, 2,* 303–324.

35. M. A. Fitzpatrick (1977). "A Typological Approach to Communication in Relationships." In B. Rubin (Ed.), *Communication Yearbook 1.* New Brunswick, NJ: Transaction Books.

36. M. A. Fitzpatrick, J. Fey, C. Segrin, & J. L. Schiff (1993). "Internal Working Models of Relationships and Marital Communication." *Journal of Language and Social Psychology, 12,* 103–131. See also M. A. Fitzpatrick, S. Fallis, & L. Vance (1982) . "Multifunctional Coding of Conflict Resolution Strategies in Marital Dyads." *Family Relations, 21,* 61–70.

37. J. Gottman (2006). "Why Marriages Fail." In K. M. Galvin & P. J. Cooper, *Making Connections: Readings in Relational Communication,* 4th ed. Los Angeles: Roxbury.

38. Wilmot & Hocker, *Interpersonal Conflict.*

39. Cupach & Canary, p. 109.

40. Research summarized by D. Tannen (1989). *You Just Don't Understand: Women and Men in Conversation* (pp. 152–157, 162–165). New York: William Morrow.

41. N. H. Hess & E. H. Hagen (2006). *Evolution and Human Behavior, 27,* 231–245; M. K. Underwood (2003). *Social Aggression Among Girls.* New York: Guilford.

42. R. Wiseman (2003). *Queen Bees & Wannabes: Helping Your Daughter Survive Cliques, Gossip, Boyfriends, and Other Realities of Adolescence.* New York: Three Rivers Press.

43. M. J. Collier (1991). "Conflict Competence within African, Mexican, and Anglo-American Friendships." In S. Ting-Toomey & F. Korzenny (Eds.), *Cross-Cultural Interpersonal Communication.* Newbury Park, CA: Sage.

44. D. J. Canary, W. R. Cupach, & S. J. Messman (1995). *Relationship Conflict.* Newbury Park, CA: Sage.

45. See M. J. Papa & E. J. Natalle (1989). "Gender, Strategy Selection, and Discussion Satisfaction in Interpersonal Conflict." *Western Journal of Speech Communication, 52,* 260–272.

46. B. M. Gayle, R. W. Preiss, & M. A. Allen (2001). "A Meta-Analytic Interpretation of Intimate and Non-Intimate Interpersonal Conflict." In M. A. Allen, R. W. Preiss, B. M. Gayle, & N. Burrell (Eds.), *Interpersonal Communication: Advances through Meta-Analysis.* New York: Erlbaum.

47. M. Allen (1998). "Methodological Considerations When Examining a Gendered World." In D. Canary & K. Dindia (Eds.), *Handbook of Sex Differences and Similarities in Communication.* Mahwah, NJ: Erlbaum.

48. Research summarized in W. R. Cupach & D. J. Canary (1997). *Competence in Interpersonal Conflict* (pp. 63–65). New York: McGraw-Hill.

49. C. S. Burggraf & A. L. Sillars (1987). "A Critical Examination of Sex Differences in Marital Communication." *Communication Monographs, 54,* 276–294.

50. For a more detailed discussion of culture, conflict, and context, see W. B. Gudykunst & S. Ting-Toomey (1988). *Culture and Interpersonal Communication* (pp. 153–160). Newbury Park, CA: Sage.

51. S. Ting-Toomey (1994). "Managing Conflict in Intimate Intercultural Relationships." In D. D. Cahn (Ed.), *Conflict in Personal Relationships.* Hillsdale, NJ: Erlbaum.

52. See, for example, S. Ting-Toomey (1988). "Rhetorical Sensitivity Style in Three Cultures: France, Japan, and the United States." *Central States Speech Journal, 39,* 28–36.

53. K. Okabe (1987). "Indirect Speech Acts of the Japanese." In L. Kincaid (Ed.), *Communication Theory: Eastern and Western Perspectives* (pp. 127–136). San Diego, CA: Academic Press.

54. G. Fontaine, "Cultural Diversity in Intimate Intercultural Relationships." In Cahn, *Intimates in Conflict.*

55. The following research is summarized in Tannen, *You Just Don't Understand,* p. 160.

56. Collier, "Conflict Competence."

57. See, for example, K. J. Beatty & J. C. McCroskey (1997). "It's in Our Nature: Verbal Aggressiveness as Temperamental Expression." *Communication Quarterly, 45,* 466–460.

58. J. G. Oetzel (1998). "Explaining Individual Communication Processes in Homogeneous and Heterogeneous Groups through Individualism-Collectivism and Self-Construal." *Human Communication Research, 25,* 202–224.

59. T. Gordon (1970). *Parent Effectiveness Training* (pp. 236–264). New York: Wyden.

60. R. Axelrod (1984). *The Evolution of Cooperation.* New York: Basic Books.

Glossary

Abstraction ladder A range of more to less abstract terms describing an event or object.

Abstract language Language that lacks a description of observable elements. *See also* Behavioral language.

Accenting Nonverbal behaviors that emphasize part of a verbal message.

Accommodating A nonassertive response style in which the communicator submits to a situation rather than attempts to have his or her needs met.

Adaptors Unconscious bodily movements in response to the environment.

Affinity The degree to which persons like or appreciate one another.

Ambiguous response A disconfirming response with more than one meaning, leaving the other party unsure of the responder's position.

Ambushing A style in which the receiver listens carefully in order to gather information to use in an attack on the speaker.

Analyzing response A helping style in which the listener offers an interpretation of a speaker's message.

Androgynous Possessing both masculine and feminine traits.

Apathy A defense mechanism in which a person avoids admitting emotional pain by pretending not to care about an event.

Assertion A direct expression of the sender's needs, thoughts, or feelings, delivered in a way that does not attack the receiver's dignity.

Attending The process of filtering out some messages and focusing on others.

Attribution The process of attaching meaning to behavior.

Avoiding A stage of relational development immediately prior to terminating in which the parties minimize contact with one another.

Behavioral description An account that refers only to observable phenomena.

Behavioral language Language that describes observable behavior. *See also* Abstract language.

Benevolent lie A lie defined by the teller as not malicious, or even helpful, to the person to whom it is told.

Body orientation Type of nonverbal communication characterized by the degree to which we face forward or away from someone.

Bonding A stage of relational development in which the parties make symbolic public gestures to show that their relationship exists.

Breadth First dimension of self-disclosure involving the range of subjects being discussed.

"But" statements Statements in which the word *but* cancels out the expression that preceded it.

Certainty Attitude behind messages that dogmatically imply that the speaker's position is correct and that the other person's ideas are not worth considering. Likely to generate a defensive response.

Channel The medium through which a message passes from sender to receiver.

Chronemics The study of how humans use and structure time.

Circumscribing A stage of relational development in which partners begin to reduce the scope of their contact and commitment to one another.

Clichés Ritualized, stock statements delivered in response to a social situation.

Co-culture A culture that exists within the larger culture of a country or society, such as subgroups defined by age, race/ethnicity, occupation, sexual orientation, physical disability, religion, avocation, and so on.

Cognitive complexity The ability to construct a variety of frameworks for viewing an issue.

Cognitive conservatism The tendency to seek and attend to information that conforms to an existing self-concept.

Cognitive dissonance An inconsistency between two conflicting pieces of information, attitudes, or behaviors. Communicators strive to reduce dissonance, often through defense mechanisms that maintain an idealized presenting image.

Collaborating A stage of relational development that seeks *win-win* solutions to conflict.

Communication A continuous, transactional process involving participants who occupy different but overlapping environments and create relationships through the exchange of messages, many of which are affected by external, physiological, and psychological noise.

Communication climate The emotional tone of a relationship between two or more individuals.

Communication competence The ability to accomplish one's personal goals in a manner that maintains a relationship on terms that are acceptable to all parties.

Compensation A defense mechanism in which a person stresses a strength in one area to camouflage a shortcoming in some other area.

Competing A win-lose approach to conflicts that seeks to resolve them in one's own way.

Complementary conflict style A relational conflict style in which partners use different but mutually reinforcing behaviors.

Complementing Nonverbal behavior that reinforces a verbal message.

Compromising An approach to conflict resolution in which both parties attain at least part of what they wanted through self-sacrifice.

Computer-mediated communication (CMC) Communication between individuals that is conducted via computer channels such as e-mail, chat, and instant messaging.

Confirming communication A message that expresses caring or respect for another person.

Conflict An expressed struggle between at least two interdependent parties who perceive incompatible goals, scarce rewards, and interference from the other party in achieving their goals.

Conflict ritual An unacknowledged repeating pattern of interlocking behavior used by participants in a conflict.

Connection-autonomy dialectic The tension between the need for integration and the need for independence in a relationship.

Consequence statement An explanation of the results that follow from either the behavior of the person to whom the message is addressed or the speaker's interpretation of the addressee's behavior. Consequence statements can describe what happens to the speaker, the addressee, or others.

Content message A message that communicates information about the subject being discussed. *See also* Relational message.

Contradicting Nonverbal behavior that is inconsistent with a verbal message.

Control (conversational and decision) The social need to influence others. *See also* Conversational control, Decision control.

Controlling communication Messages in which the sender tries to impose some sort of outcome on the receiver, usually resulting in a defensive reaction.

Convergence The process of adapting one's speech style to match that of others with whom the communicator wants to identify. *See also* Divergence.

Conversational control The power to determine who speaks in a conversation.

Counterfeit questions Questions that disguise the speaker's true motives, which do not include a genuine desire to understand the other person. *See also* Sincere questions.

Crazymaking *See* Passive aggression.

Debilitative emotions Emotions that prevent a person from functioning effectively.

Decision control The power to influence which person in a relationship decides what activities will take place.

Decoding The process in which a receiver attaches meaning to a message. Synonymous with *interpreting.*

De-escalatory conflict spiral A communication spiral in which the parties slowly lessen their dependence on one another, withdraw, and become less invested in the relationship.

Defense mechanism A psychological device used to maintain a presenting self-image that an individual believes is threatened.

Defensive listening A response style in which the receiver perceives a speaker's comments as an attack.

Defensiveness The attempt to protect a presenting image a person believes is being attacked.

Depth A dimension of self-disclosure involving a shift from relatively nonrevealing messages to more personal ones.

Description Gibb's term for language that describes a complaint in behavioral terms rather than being judgmental, thereby creating a supportive communication climate. *See also* Evaluation, "I" language.

Dialectical tensions Inherent conflicts that arise when two opposing or incompatible forces exist simultaneously.

Differentiating A stage of relational development in which the parties re-establish their individual identities after having bonded together.

Direct aggression A criticism or demand that threatens the face of the person at whom it is directed.

Disconfirming communication A message that expresses a lack of caring or respect for another person.

Disfluencies Nonlinguistic verbalizations, for example, um, er, ah.

Displacement A defense mechanism in which a person vents hostile or aggressive feelings on a target that cannot strike back, instead of on the true target.

Divergence Speaking mannerisms that emphasize a communicator's differences from others. *See also* Convergence.

Dyad Two individuals communicating. The interaction may or may not be interpersonal in nature.

Emblems Deliberate nonverbal behaviors with precise meanings, known to virtually all members of a cultural group.

Emotional contagion The process by which emotions are transferred from one person to another.

Emotive language Language that conveys the sender's attitude rather than simply offers an objective description.

Empathy The ability to project oneself into another person's point of view, so as to experience the other's thoughts and feelings.

Encoding The process of putting thoughts into symbols, most commonly words.

Environment The field of experiences that leads a person to make sense of another's behavior. Environments consist of physical characteristics, personal experiences, relational history, and cultural background.

Equality A type of supportive communication described by Gibb, suggesting that the sender regards the receiver as worthy of respect.

Equivocal language Ambiguous language that has two or more equally plausible meanings.

Escalatory conflict spiral A communication spiral in which one attack leads to another until the initial skirmish escalates into a full-fledged battle.

Ethnocentrism The attitude that one's own culture is superior to others.

Evaluation Gibb's term for judgmental assessments of another person's behavior, thereby increasing the odds of creating a defensive communication climate. *See also* Description, "I" language.

Experimenting An early stage in relational development, consisting of a search for common ground. If the experimentation is successful, the relationship will progress to intensifying. If not, it may go no further.

Face The socially approved identity that a communicator tries to present. *See also* Impression management.

Face-threatening act Behavior by another that is perceived as attacking an individual's presenting image, or face.

Facilitative emotions Emotions that contribute to effective functioning.

Fallacy of approval The irrational belief that it is vital to win the approval of virtually every person a communicator deals with.

Fallacy of catastrophic expectations The irrational belief that the worst possible outcome will probably occur.

Fallacy of causation The irrational belief that emotions are caused by others and not by the person who has them.

Fallacy of helplessness The irrational belief that satisfaction in life is determined by forces beyond one's control.

Fallacy of overgeneralization Irrational beliefs in which (1) conclusions (usually negative) are based on limited evidence, or (2) communicators exaggerate their shortcomings.

Fallacy of perfection The irrational belief that a worthwhile communicator should be able to handle every situation with complete confidence and skill.

Fallacy of shoulds The irrational belief that people should behave in the most desirable way.

Feeling statement An expression of the sender's emotions that results from interpretation of sense data.

Gender role Socially approved ways that men and women are expected to behave.

Generalized complaining A disconfirming response that implicitly or explicitly attributes responsibility for the speaker's displeasure to another party.

Gestures Motions of the body, usually hands or arms, that have communicative value.

Gibb categories Six sets of contrasting styles of verbal and nonverbal behavior. Each set describes a communication style that is likely to arouse defensiveness and a contrasting style that is likely to prevent or reduce it. Developed by Jack Gibb.

Halo effect The power of a first impression to influence subsequent perceptions.

Hearing The physiological dimension of listening.

High-context cultures Cultures that avoid direct use of language, relying on the context of a message to convey meaning.

Identity *See* Presenting self.

Identity management The communication strategies people use to influence how others view them.

"I" language A statement that describes the speaker's reaction to another person's behavior without making judgments about its worth. *See also* "You" language.

Illustrators Nonverbal behaviors that accompany and support verbal messages.

Immediacy The degree of interest and attention that we feel toward and communicate to others.

Impersonal communication Behavior that treats others as objects rather than individuals. *See also* Interpersonal communication.

Impersonal response A disconfirming response that is superficial or trite.

Impervious response A disconfirming response that ignores another person's attempt to communicate.

Impression management *See* Identity management.

Incongruous response A disconfirming response in which two messages, one of which is usually nonverbal, contradict each other.

Influence *See* Control.

Initiating The first stage in relational development, in which the parties express interest in one another.

Insensitive listening Failure to recognize the thoughts or feelings that are not directly expressed by a speaker; instead, accepting the speaker's words at face value.

Instrumental goals Goals aimed at getting others to behave in desired ways.

Insulated listening A style in which the receiver ignores undesirable information.

Integrating A stage of relational development in which the parties begin to take on a single identity.

Intensifying A stage of relational development preceding integrating, in which the parties move toward integration by increasing the amount of contact and the breadth and depth of self-disclosure.

Intention statement A description of where the speaker stands on an issue, what he or she wants, or how he or she plans to act in the future.

Interpersonal communication In a quantitative sense, communication (usually face-to-face) between two individuals. (*See also* Dyad.) In a qualitative sense, communication in which the parties consider one another as unique individuals rather than objects. It is characterized by minimal use of stereotyped labels; unique, idiosyncratic rules; and a high degree of information exchange.

Interpretation The process of attaching meaning to sense data; synonymous with *Decoding*.

Interpretation statement A statement that describes the speaker's interpretation of the meaning of another person's behavior. *See also* Attribution.

Interrupting response A disconfirming response in which one communicator interrupts another.

Intimacy A state of personal sharing arising from physical, intellectual, and/or emotional contact.

Intimate distance One of Hall's four distance zones, ranging from skin contact to 18 inches.

Irrelevant response A disconfirming response in which one communicator's comments bear no relationship to the previous speaker's ideas.

"It" statements Statements that replace the personal pronoun "I" with the less immediate word "it," often reducing the speaker's acceptance of responsibility for the statement.

Johari Window A model that describes the relationship between self-disclosure and self-awareness.

Judging response A reaction in which the receiver evaluates the sender's message either favorably or unfavorably.

Kinesics The study of body position and motion.

Leakage Nonverbal behaviors that reveal information a communicator does not disclose verbally.

Linear communication model A characterization of communication as a one-way event in which a message flows from sender to receiver.

Listening Process that consists of hearing, attending, understanding, responding, and remembering an aural message.

Lose–lose problem solving An approach to conflict resolution in which neither side achieves its goals. Sometimes lose–lose outcomes result from both parties seeking a win–lose victory over each other. In other cases, the parties settle for a lose–lose outcome (for example, compromise) because they cannot find any better alternative.

Low-context cultures Cultures that use language primarily to express thoughts, feelings, and ideas as clearly and logically as possible.

Mannerisms Affected or exaggerated style or manner.

Message Information sent from a sender to a receiver.

Metacommunication Messages (usually relational) that refer to other messages: communication about communication.

Microexpression Brief facial expression.

Mindful listening Giving careful and thoughtful attention and responses to the messages we receive.

Mindless listening Reacting to others' messages automatically and routinely, without much mental investment.

Mixed message Situation in which a person's words are incongruent with his/her nonverbal behavior.

Monochronic Behavior emphasizing punctuality, schedules, and completing one task at a time.

Narrative A perception of the world shared by a collection of people. Narratives can be described in terms of a dramatic theme.

Negotiation A process in which two or more parties discuss specific proposals in order to find a mutually acceptable agreement.

Neutrality A defense-arousing behavior described by Gibb in which the sender expresses indifference toward a receiver.

Noise External, physiological, and psychological distractions that interfere with the accurate transmission and reception of a message.

Nonverbal communication Messages expressed by other than linguistic means.

Openness-privacy dialectic The tension between the need for disclosure and the need for privacy in a relationship.

Paralanguage Nonlinguistic means of vocal expression: rate, pitch, tone, and so on.

Parallel conflict style A relational conflict style in which the approach of the partners varies from one situation to another.

Paraphrasing Restating a speaker's thoughts and/ or feelings in the listener's own words.

Passive aggression An indirect expression of aggression, delivered in a way that allows the sender to maintain a façade of kindness.

Perceived self The person we believe ourselves to be in moments of candor. It may be identical with or different from the presenting and ideal self.

Perception checking A three-part method for verifying the accuracy of interpretations, including a description of the sense data, two possible interpretations, and a request for confirmation of the interpretations.

Personal distance One of Hall's four distance zones, ranging from 18 inches to 4 feet.

Personality A relatively consistent set of traits exhibited by a person across a variety of situations.

Physical avoidance A defense mechanism whereby the person steers clear of people who attack a presenting self to avoid dissonance.

Pillow method A method for understanding an issue from several perspectives rather than with an egocentric "I'm right and you're wrong" attitude.

Polychronic Behavior emphasizing punctuality, schedules, and completing one task at a time.

Posture The way in which individuals carry themselves—erect, slumping, and so on.

Powerless speech mechanisms Ways of speaking that may reduce perceptions of a communicator's power.

Pragmatic rules Linguistic rules that help communicators understand how messages may be used and interpreted in a given context.

Predictability-novelty dialectic The tension between the need for stability and the need for novelty in a relationship.

Presenting self The image a person presents to others. It may be identical with or different from the perceived and ideal self.

Problem orientation A supportive style of communication described by Gibb in which the communicators focus on working together to solve their problems instead of trying to impose their own solutions on one another.

Prompting Using silences and brief statements of encouragement to draw out a speaker.

Provisionalism A supportive style of communication described by Gibb in which the sender expresses a willingness to consider the other person's position.

Proxemics The study of how people and animals use space.

Pseudolistening An imitation of true listening in which the receiver's mind is elsewhere.

Public distance One of Hall's four distance zones, extending outward from 12 feet.

Punctuation The process of determining the causal order of events.

Questioning response A style of helping in which the receiver seeks additional information from the sender. Some questioning responses are really disguised advice.

Rationalization A defense mechanism in which logical but untrue explanations maintain an unrealistic desired or presenting self-image.

Receiver One who notices and attends to a message.

Reference groups Groups against which we compare ourselves, thereby influencing our self-concept and self-esteem.

Reflected appraisal The theory that a person's self-concept matches the way the person believes others regard him or her.

Regression A defense mechanism in which a person avoids assuming responsibility by pretending that he or she is unable to do something instead of admitting to being simply unwilling.

Regulating One function of nonverbal communication, in which nonverbal cues control the flow of verbal communication among individuals.

Relational conflict style A pattern of managing disagreements that repeats itself over time in a relationship.

Relational maintenance Communication aimed at keeping relationships operating smoothly and satisfactorily.

Relational message A message that expresses the social relationship between two or more individuals.

Relational transgressions One partner's violation of the explicit or implicit terms of the relationship, letting the other one down in some important way.

Relative words Words that gain their meaning by comparison.

Remembering Ability to recall information.

Repeating Nonverbal behaviors that duplicate the content of a verbal message.

Repression A defense mechanism in which a person avoids facing an unpleasant situation or fact by denying its existence.

Respect The social need to be held in esteem by others.

Responding Giving observable feedback to the speaker.

Rumination Dwelling persistently on negative thoughts that, in turn intensify negative feelings.

Sapir–Whorf hypothesis Theory of linguistic determinism in which language shapes a culture's perceived reality.

Sarcasm A potential defensive reaction in which an individual redirects a perceived threat to his or her presenting self by attacking the critic with contemptuous, often ironical remarks.

Selection The first stage in the perception process in which some data are chosen to attend to and others to ignore.

Selective listening A listening style in which the receiver responds only to messages that interest him or her.

Self-concept The relatively stable set of perceptions each individual holds of himself or herself.

Self-disclosure The process of deliberately revealing information about oneself that is significant and that would not normally be known by others.

Self-esteem The part of the self-concept that involves an individual's evaluations of his or her self-worth.

Self-fulfilling prophecy A prediction or expectation of an event that makes the outcome more likely to occur than would otherwise have been the case.

Self-monitoring The process of attending to one's behavior and using these observations to shape the way one behaves.

Self-serving bias The tendency to interpret and explain information in a way that casts the perceiver in the most favorable manner.

Self-talk The nonvocal process of thinking. On some level, self-talk occurs as a person interprets another's behavior.

Semantic rules Rules that govern the meaning of language, as opposed to its structure. *See also* Syntactic rules.

Sender The creator of a message.

Significant others People whose opinion is important enough to affect one's self-concept strongly.

Sincere questions Questions that are aimed at soliciting information that enable the asker to understand the other person. *See also* Counterfeit questions.

Social comparison Evaluation of oneself in terms of or by comparison to others.

Social distance One of Hall's distance zones, ranging from 4 to 12 feet.

Social penetration A model that describes relationships in terms of their breadth and depth.

Spiral A reciprocal communication pattern in which each person's message reinforces the other's. *See also* De-escalatory conflict spiral, Escalatory conflict spiral.

Spontaneity A supportive communication behavior described by Gibb in which the sender expresses a message without any attempt to manipulate the receiver.

Stage-hogging A listening style in which the receiver is more concerned with making his or her own point than in understanding the speaker.

Stagnating A stage of relational development characterized by declining enthusiasm and standardized forms of behavior.

Static evaluation The tendency to view people or relationships as unchanging.

Stereotyping Categorizing individuals according to a set of characteristics assumed to belong to all members of a group.

Strategy A defense-arousing style of communication described by Gibb in which the sender tries to manipulate or deceive a receiver.

Substituting Nonverbal behavior that takes the place of a verbal message.

Superiority A defense-arousing style of communication described by Gibb in which the sender states or implies that the receiver is not worthy of respect.

Supportive response Response that demonstrates solidarity with a speaker's situation.

Symmetrical conflict style A relational conflict style in which both partners use the same tactics.

Sympathy Compassion for another's situation. *See also* Empathy.

Syntactic rules Rules that govern the ways symbols can be arranged, as opposed to the meanings of those symbols. *See also* Semantic rules.

Tangential response A disconfirming response that uses the speaker's remark as a starting point for a shift to a new topic.

Terminating The concluding stage of relational development, characterized by the acknowledgement of one or both parties that the relationship is over.

Territory A stationary area claimed by an individual.

Transactional communication model A characterization of communication as the simultaneous sending and receiving of messages in an ongoing, irreversible process.

Understanding Occurs when sense is made of a message.

Verbal abuse A disconfirming response intended to cause psychological pain to another.

Verbal aggression A defense mechanism in which a person avoids facing unpleasant information by verbally attacking the confronting source.

"We" language Statement that implies that the issue is the concern and responsibility of both the speaker and receiver of a message. *See also* "I" language, "You" language.

Win–lose problem solving An approach to conflict resolution in which one party reaches its goal at the expense of the other.

Win–win problem solving An approach to conflict resolution in which the parties work together to satisfy all their goals.

"You" language A statement that expresses or implies a judgment of the other person. *See also* "I" language.

Photo Credits

Literary Credits

This page constitutes an extension of the copyright page. We have made every effort to trace the ownership of all copyrighted material and to secure permission from copyright holders. In the event of any question arising as to the use of any material, we will be pleased to make the necessary corrections in future printings. Thanks are due to the following authors, publishers, and agents for permission to use the material indicated.

Preface PEANUTS: © United Features Syndicate, Inc.

Chapter 1 4: From "The Silencing." *Newsweek,* June 18, 1973, p. 42. Copyright © 1973 Newsweek, Inc. All rights reserved. Reprinted by permission. **12:** © Zits Partnership. Reprinted by special permission of King Features Syndicate. **13:** From Ric Masten, "Let it Be a Dance We Do." Reprinted by permission. **15:** © The New Yorker Collection 1991 Michael Maslin from cartoonbank.com. All rights reserved. **17:** "I Don't Wanna Fight" from the Touchstone Motion Picture *What's Love Got to Do with It?* Words and music by Billy Lawrie, Lulu Frieda and Steve Du Berry. Copyright © 1993 by Famous Music Publishing Company Limited and Chrysalis Music. All rights for Famous Music Company Publishing Company Limited administered in the U.S. by Ensign Music Corporation International. Copyright secured. All rights reserved. © Chrysalis Music Ltd. All rights for United States and Canada are administered by Chrysalis Songs. All rights reserved. Used by permission. **17:** © The New Yorker Collection 1993 Mike Twohy from cartoonbank.com. All rights reserved. **19:** Vlado Uzunangelov, "I Must be 57 Words Heavier." Reprinted by permission. **22:** Ted Anthony, "Internet Messaging Dissolves Distance, Cultural Differences." Associated Press, posted Dec. 24, 2002. Reprinted by permission of the Associated Press. **24:** © Zits Partnership. Reprinted by special permission of King Features Syndicate. **29:** Dilbert © Scott Adams/Dist. by United Feature Syndicate, Inc.

Chapter 2 43: Adapted from H.M. Johnson (1998) *How Do I Love Me?* 3rd ed., Salem, Wisconsin: Sheffield Publishing Co. Used by permission. **45:** © The New Yorker Collection 1971 Lee Lorenz from cartoonbank.com. All rights reserved. **47:** Poem "Premier Artiste" by Lenni Shender Goldstein. Used courtesy of the poet. **48:** © Zits Partnership. Reprinted by special permission of King Features Syndicate. **49:** "Cipher in the Snow" by Jean Mizer from *Today's Education.* Used with permission from the author. **51:** "Incident" by Countee Cullen published in Color © Harper & Bros., N.Y., renewed 1952 Ida M. Cullen. Used by permission. **58:** CATHY © Cathy Guisewite. Reprinted with permission of Universal Press Syndicate. All rights reserved. **60:** © The New Yorker Collection 1991 Edward Frascino from cartoonbank.com. All rights reserved. **61:** From Neil Postman, *Crazy Talk, Stupid Talk,* 1976. Used by permission. **63:** © Gahan Wilson. Used with permission. **65:** © The New Yorker Collection. 1983 Dana Fradon from cartoonbank.com. All rights reserved. **66:** CATHY © Cathy Guisewite. Reprinted with permission of Universal Press Syndicate. All rights reserved. **69:** "Complicated" by Lauren Christy, Scott Spock, Graham Edwards, Avril LaVigne. Copyright © 2002 Warner-Tamerlane Publishing Corp. (BMI), Mr. Spock Music (BMI), Hollylodge Music (BMI), Rainbow Fish Publishing (BMI), WB Music Corp. (ASCAP), Tix Music (ASCAP), Ferry Hill Songs (ASCAP) and Almo Music Corp. (ASCAP). All rights o/b/o Mr. Spock Music, Hollylodge Music and Rainbow Fish Publishing administered by Warner-Tamerlane Publishing Corp. All rights o/b/o Tix Music and Ferry Hill Songs administered by WB Music Corp. All rights reserved. Used by permission. **71:** From Mark Snyder, "The Many Me's of the Self-Monitor," *Psychology Today* (March 1983): 34. Reprinted with permission from *Psychology Today Magazine,* Copyright © 1983 Sussex Publishers, Inc. **72:** © The New Yorker Collection 1973 William Hamilton from cartoonbank.com. All rights reserved. **73:** From *Person to Person* by Barry Stevens. Copyright © 1967

King Features Syndicate. **261:** From "They Learn to Aid Their Customers by Becoming Good Listeners" by Beth Mohr. From *The San Diego Union* © 1976. Reprinted with permission.

Chapter 8 271: © The New Yorker Collection 1993 J.B. Handelsman from cartoonbank.com. All rights reserved. **272:** From Mark L. Knapp & Anita L. Vengelisti, *Interpersonal Communication and Human Relationships*, 2nd ed. Published by Allyn and Bacon, Boston, MA. Copyright © 1992 by Pearson Education. Adapted by permission of the publisher. **277:** © The New Yorker Collection 1993 Mick Stevens from cartoonbank.com. All rights reserved. **280:** © The New Yorker Collection 1997 Tom Cheney from cartoonbank.com. All rights reserved. **282:** © Zits Partnership. Reprinted with special permission of King Features Syndicate. **284:** From "Technology and Indian Marriage in India: A Match Made in Heaven," *Economist*, Oct. 22, 2005, p. 70. Reprinted by permission. **287:** © The New Yorker Collection 2005 Mick Stevens from cartoonbank.com. All rights reserved. **289:** Drawing by Mike Ewers. Reprinted by permission. **292:** From *The Accidental Tourist* by Anne Tyler. Copyright © 1995 by Anne Tyler Modarressi. Used by permission of Alfred A. Knopf, a division of Random House, Inc. Used in Canada by permission of Penguin Group (Canada), a division of Pearson Penguin Canada Inc.

Chapter 9 300: © The New Yorker Collection 1997 Bruce Eric Kaplan from cartoonbank.com. All rights reserved. **303:** "Lonely Gay Teen Seeking Same" by Jennifer Egan, *New York Times Magazine*, Dec. 10, 2000. Copyright © 2000 by the New York Times Co. Reprinted by permission. **309:** © The New Yorker Collection 1984 Jack Ziegler from cartoonbank.com. All rights reserved. **310:** Poem "Looking Out/Looking In" from *Stark Naked* by Ric Masten. Reprinted by permission of the publisher, Sunflower Ink, Palo Colorado Road, Carmel, CA 93923. **313:** © The New Yorker Collection 1995 Bruce Eric Kaplan from cartoonbank.com. All rights reserved. **318:** © The New Yorker Collection 2000 Leo Cullum from cartoonbank.com. All rights reserved. **319:** Table from "White Lies and Interpersonal Communication: A Taxonomy and Preliminary Investigation of Social Motivations" *Western Journal of Speech Communication* 48 (1984). Used by permission. **320:** From "Is Misleading Your Spouse Fraud or Tact" by Maria Cone, *Los Angeles Times*, April 11, 1993. Reprinted by permission of

Tribune Media Services. **321:** Figure from "Dimensions of Truthfulness and Equivocation" adapted from *Equivocal Communication* by J.B. Bavelas, A. Black, N. Chovil and J. Mullett. © 1990 by Sage Publications, Inc. Used by permission of the publisher. **322:** Dilbert © Scott Adams/Dist. by United Feature Syndicate, Inc.

Chapter 10 332: From "CEOs Vouch for Waiter Rule: Watch How People Treat Staff," *USA Today*, April 14, 2006. Reprinted by permission. **333:** "Fire and Ice" from *The Poetry of Robert Frost* edited by Edward Connery Lathem. Copyright © 1923, 1969 by Henry Holt and Company, copyright © 1951 by Robert Frost. Reprinted by permission of Henry Holt and Company, LLC. **334:** © The New Yorker Collection 2006 Bruce Eric Kaplan from cartoonbank.com. All rights reserved. **335:** From *Competence and Interpersonal Conflict* by W. Cupach and D. Canary, p. 51–52. Copyright © 1997. Reprinted by permission of The McGraw-Hill Companies. **336:** © 2006 Michael Crawford from cartoonbank.com. All rights reserved. **338:** © The New Yorker Collection 1986 Richard Cline from cartoonbank.com. All rights reserved. **341:** © The New Yorker Collection 2001 P.C. Vey from cartoonbank.com. All rights reserved. **344:** From "How to Argue Effectively" by Dave Barry. Dave Barry is a syndicated humor columnist with *The Miami Herald*. Used with permission. **345:** © The New Yorker Collection 1993 Bruce Eric Kaplan from cartoonbank.com. All rights reserved. **352:** CATHY © Cathy Guisewite. Reprinted with permission of Universal Press Syndicate. All rights reserved. **358:** © The New Yorker Collection 1997 Chon Day from cartoonbank.com. All rights reserved.

Chapter 11 374: © The New Yorker Collection 2000 David Sipress from cartoonbank.com. All rights reserved. **381:** © The New Yorker Collection 2001 David Sipress from cartoonbank.com. All rights reserved. **388:** © The New Yorker Collection 2002 David Sipress from cartoonbank.com. All rights reserved. **391:** Adapted from Rory Remer and Paul deMesquita, "Teaching and Learning Skills of Interpersonal Confrontation" in *Intimates in Conflict: A Communication Perspective* edited by Cahn, p. 227. Copyright © 1990. Used by permission of Lawrence Erlbaum Associates, Inc. **394:** © 2003 Bruce Kaplan from cartoonbank.com. All rights reserved.

Name Index

A

Abdullah (Crown Prince of Saudi Arabia), 212
Aboud, F. E., 415
Abrahams, D., 415
Acitelli, L. K., 420
Ackerman, N., 404
Ackerman, Peter, 357
Adamopoulos, J., 418
Adams, Morgan, 77
Adler, T., 402, 404, 405, 412
Agne, R., 419
Akkirman, A. D., 420
Alaimo, K., 404
Albada, K. F., 412, 415
Alberts, J. K., 404, 421
Alexander, E. R., 413
Allen, B., 404
Allen, M., 401, 404, 407, 415, 419, 422
Allen, M. W., 420, 422
Allport, G. W., 404
Almaney, A., 410
Alper, T., 412
Altman, Irwin, 305, 418, 419
Alwan, A., 410
Ambady, N., 406
Amodio, D. M., 415
Amos, J., 411
Andersen, J., 405
Andersen, P. A., 401, 405, 411, 412, 420
Anderson, Bruce C., 237
Anderson, C. M., 407, 422
Anderson, J., 405
Anderson, J. A., 403
Anderson, R., 414
Anderson, T. L., 416
Angelou, Maya, 27
Anthony, Ted, 22
Applegate, J., 405
Archer, R. L., 419
Argyle, M., 418
Aristotle, 136, 137
Arliss, L. P., 403
Arnold, C. C., 400
Aronson, E., 415, 419

Arr, T. D., 421
Arriaga, X. B., 404
Asante, M. K., 410
Asimov, Isaac, 21
Askew, Bonnette, 320
Askew, Ronald, 320
Athappilly, K., 417
Auden, W. H., 6, 226, 242
Aune, R. K., 408, 412
Avtgis, T. A., 416, 417
Axelrod, R., 422
Axtman, Kris, 164
Ayers, J., 408
Aylor, B., 400
Ayres, J., 401

B

Babyak, M. A., 422
Bach, George, 375
Bachman, G. F., 417
Backlund, P. M., 401
Baer, J., 411
Baesler, E., 412
Bagarozzi, D., 416
Bagby, J. W., 405
Bai, C., 419
Baker, M. T., 414
Bakker, A. B., 407
Bakwin, H., 412
Baldwin, J. R., 404
Baldwin, James, 369
Ball, Philip, 181
Ballard, D. I., 413
Ballard-Reisch, D. S., 417
Ball-Rokeach, S., 399
Balsam, Laura, 23
Balswick, J. O., 418
Bandura, A., 403
Banks, W. C., 405
Barbato, C. A., 399, 401, 420
Barefoot. J. C., 399
Bargh, J. A., 408
Barker, L., 215, 413, 415
Barnes, Brenda, 332
Barnes, S. B., 404
Baron, R. S., 404, 405
Barrett, L. F., 407

Barry, Dave, 280–281, 343, 344, 416
Basso, K., 410
Battaglia, D. M., 416
Battista, O. A., 355
Bauer, G. B., 409
Baumeister, R. F., 407
Bavelas, J. B., 321, 411, 419, 420
Baxter, J., 411
Baxter, L. A., 404, 416, 417, 418
Beatty, M. J., 401, 402, 407, 422
Beaupre, M. G., 411
Beavin, J. H., 400, 404, 417
Bechler, C., 413
Beck, A., 408
Beck, Lewis White, 324
Becker, J., 278, 416
Beers, Deborah, 4
Bejllovec, R. A., 416
Bell, R. A., 416, 417
Bellah, R., 418
Bello, R., 404
Bem, S. L., 405
Bemner, G., 413
Benchley, Robert, 145
Bennett, Milton, 112
Benoit, P. J., 421
Benoit, W. L., 421
Benvenuto, M., 407
Ben-Ze'ev, A., 418
Berger, C. R., 402, 413, 416
Berman, J., 57
Berntson, G. G., 399
Berscheid, E., 405, 415, 418
Bharti, A., 403
Bickman, L., 412
Bierce, Ambrose, 240
Biocca, F. A., 402
Bippus, A. M., 414
Birdwhistell, R., 411
Birk, T., 410
Black, A., 420
Black, G., 422
Blake, R. R., 412
Blake, William, 371

Subject Index